Junior Cycle Maths

Text & Tests

Higher Level Maths

2

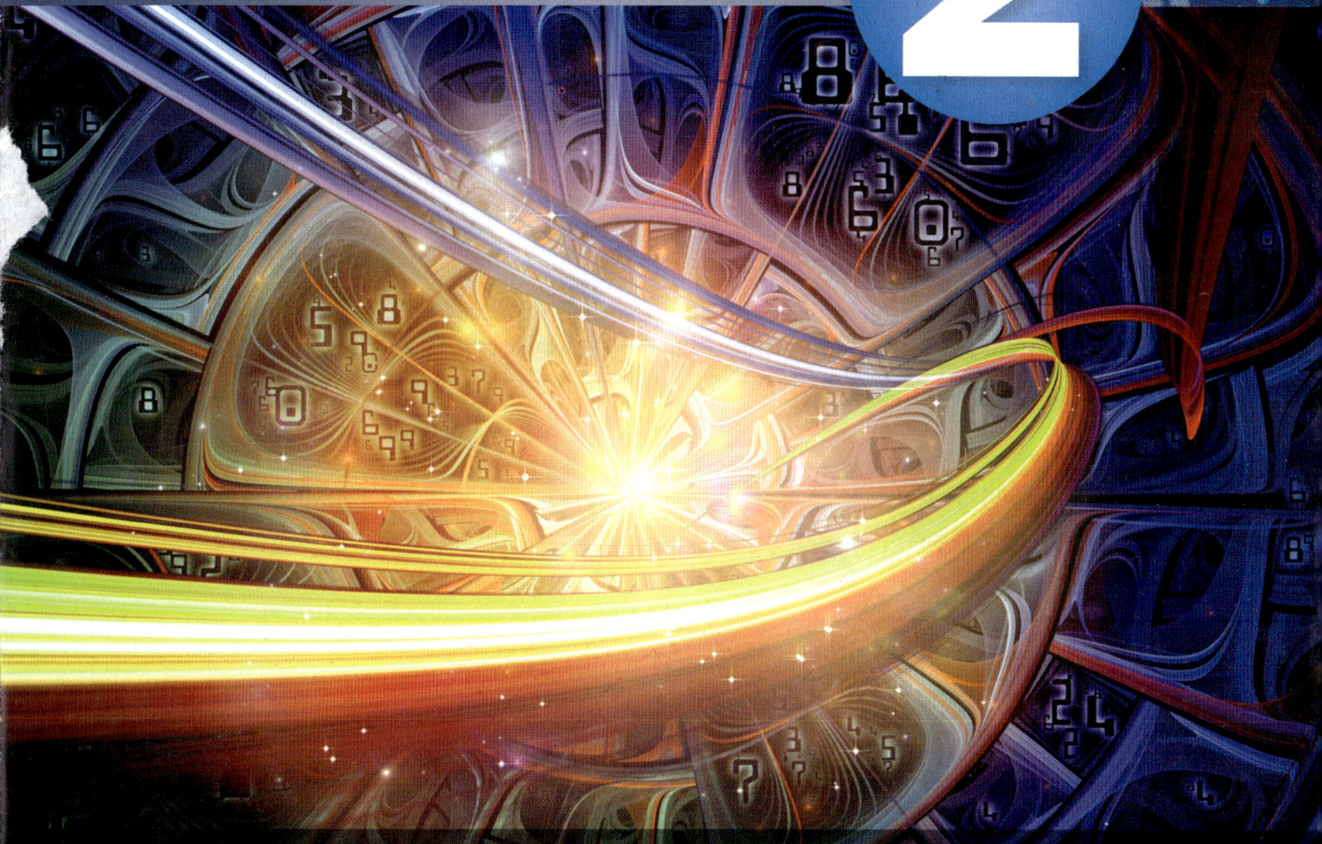

Paul Cooke • O.D. Morris • Deborah Crean

© Paul Cooke, O. D. Morris, Deborah Crean 2019

All rights reserved. No part of this publication may be reproduced, stored in a retrieval system or transmitted in any form or by any means, electronic, mechanical, photocopying, recording or otherwise, without the prior written consent of the copyright holders.

> The paper stock used in this publication comes from managed forests.
> This means that at least one tree is planted for every tree felled. The inks used for printing are environmentally friendly and vegetable based.

Acknowledgements
We would like to express our deep appreciation to Paul Behan for his contribution to the Geometry sections of this text.

First Published in May 2019 by
The Celtic Press
Ground Floor – Block B
Liffey Valley Office Campus
Dublin 22

This Reprint May 2023

ISBN: 978-0-7144-2752-2

Contents

1. **Algebra 1** 1
   - 1.1 Simplifying expressions 1
   - 1.2 Removing brackets 3
   - 1.3 Evaluating expressions 6
   - 1.4 Solving linear equations 8
   - 1.5 Solving problems using linear equations 10
   - 1.6 Algebraic division 13
   - 1.7 Plotting numbers on the number line 15
   - 1.8 Solving inequalities 19
   - Test Yourself 1 22
   - Assignment 24

2. **Factors** 25
   - 2.1 Factorising with common factors 25
   - 2.2 Factorising by grouping terms 27
   - 2.3 Difference of two squares 29
   - 2.4 Factorising quadratic expressions 32
   - 2.5 Using factors to simplify algebraic fractions 35
   - Test Yourself 2 36
   - Assignment 37

3. **Sets** 38
   - 3.1 Revision of sets terminology 38
   - 3.2 Set difference 43
   - 3.3 Venn diagrams involving three sets 46
   - 3.4 Solving problems using three sets 52
   - Test Yourself 3 58
   - Assignment 61

4. **Applied Arithmetic** 62
   - 4.1 VAT – profit and loss 62
   - 4.2 Household bills 67
   - 4.3 Income tax 70
   - 4.4 Currency exchange 77
   - 4.5 Compound interest 80
   - Test Yourself 4 87
   - Assignment 90

5. **Statistics 1 – Collecting Data** 91
   - 5.1 Statistical questions 91
   - 5.2 Sampling 100
   - Test Yourself 5 104
   - Assignment 106

6. Perimeter, Area, Volume 107
- 6.1 Review of perimeter and area 107
- 6.2 Area of parallelogram 111
- 6.3 Area and circumference of a circle 114
- 6.4 Rectangular solids 122
- 6.5 Prisms 129
- 6.6 Scale drawing 134
- Test Yourself 6 138
- Assignment 141

7. Statistics 2 – Averages and Variability 142
- 7.1 Summary statistics 142
- 7.2 The mean 146
- 7.3 Which average to use? 149
- 7.4 Frequency tables 152
- 7.5 Range and variability 159
- Test Yourself 7 162
- Assignment 164

8. Geometry 1 – Triangles, Quadrilaterals, Theorems 165
- 8.1 Revision of lines and angles 165
- 8.2 Angles of a triangle 168
- 8.3 Quadrilaterals 173
- 8.4 Congruent triangles 177
- 8.5 The theorem of Pythagoras 184
- 8.6 Understanding formal proofs of theorems 1, 2, 3, 5, 10, 13, 15 191
- Test Yourself 8 195
- Assignment 198

9. Probability 199
- 9.1 Revision of listing outcomes 199
- 9.2 Chance and the probability scale 203
- 9.3 Probability and equally likely outcomes 206
- 9.4 Two events – use of sample spaces: tree diagrams/two-way tables 212
- 9.5 Estimating probabilities from experiments 215
- 9.6 Probability using Venn diagrams 222
- 9.7 Tree diagrams – probability of multiple events 225
- Test Yourself 9 229
- Assignment 234

10. Simultaneous Equations 235
- 10.1 Solving simultaneous equations 235
- 10.2 Solving simultaneous equations graphically 238
- Test Yourself 10 244
- Assignment 246

11. Coordinate Geometry – the Line — 247
- 11.1 Distance and mid-point formulae — 247
- 11.2 The slope of a line — 251
- 11.3 The equation of a line — 257
- 11.4 The equation $y = mx + c$ — 260
- 11.5 Parallel and perpendicular lines — 264
- 11.6 Graphing lines — 266
- 11.7 Intersection of two lines — 270
- 11.8 Rates of change — 272
- Test Yourself 11 — 276
- Assignment — 280

12. Ratio, Time, Speed — 281
- 12.1 Ratio and proportion — 281
- 12.2 Times and timetables — 287
- 12.3 Speed, distance, time — 290
- Test Yourself 12 — 294
- Assignment — 296

13. Statistics 3 – Presenting Data — 297
- 13.1 Revision of line plots and bar charts — 297
- 13.2 Pie charts — 302
- 13.3 Histograms — 306
- 13.4 Stem and leaf plots — 310
- 13.5 Misleading graphs — 317
- Test Yourself 13 — 320
- Assignment — 324

14. Indices – Standard form – Surds — 325
- 14.1 The law of indices — 325
- 14.2 Fractional indices — 328
- 14.3 Equations involving indices — 330
- 14.4 Irrational numbers – surds — 333
- 14.5 Numbers in standard form — 337
- 14.6 Significant numbers – approximation — 341
- 14.7 Using a calculator — 344
- Test Yourself 14 — 347
- Assignment — 349

15. Quadratic Equations — 350
- 15.1 Solving quadratic equations using factors — 350
- 15.2 Using the quadratic formula — 354
- 15.3 Problems leading to quadratic equations — 356
- 15.4 Forming a quadratic equation given its roots — 359
- Test Yourself 15 — 361
- Assignment — 363

16.	**Geometry 2 – Similar Triangles, Circles, Theorems**		**364**
	16.1 Similar triangles		364
	16.2 Transversals and triangles		371
	16.3 Angles and circles		377
	16.4 Understanding proofs of theorems 4, 6, 9, 14, 19		386
	Test Yourself 16		390
	Assignment		394
17.	**Cylinder, Sphere**		**395**
	17.1 The cylinder		395
	17.2 The sphere and hemisphere		399
	17.3 Rates of flow		405
	Test Yourself 17		407
	Assignment		411
18.	**Patterns and Sequences**		**412**
	18.1 Sequences		412
	18.2 Repeating patterns		417
	18.3 Linear sequences		419
	18.4 Finding the nth term T_n, of a linear sequence		422
	18.5 Sequences (linear) formed from shapes		424
	18.6 Quadratic sequences		428
	18.7 Graphing sequences		431
	Test Yourself 18		438
	Assignment		441
19.	**Functions**		**442**
	19.1 Functions		442
	19.2 Mapping diagrams		444
	19.3 Notation for functions		449
	19.4 Finding coefficients of functions		452
	Test Yourself 19		458
	Assignment		460
20.	**Drawing and Interpreting Real-life Graphs**		**461**
	20.1 Distance-time graphs		461
	20.2 Directly proportional graphs		467
	20.3 Real-life graphs		472
	Assignment		477

21. Algebra 2 — **479**
- 21.1 Adding algebraic fractions — 479
- 21.2 Solving equations involving fractions — 482
- 21.3 Solving problems involving fractions — 484
- 21.4 Rearranging formulae — 487
- 21.5 Evaluating and writing formulae — 489
- Test Yourself 21 — 493
- Assignment — 496

22. Trigonometry — **497**
- 22.1 The theorem of Pythagoras — 497
- 22.2 Sine, cosine and tangent ratios — 501
- 22.3 Using a calculator to find ratios and angles — 504
- 22.4 Solving right-angled triangles — 507
- 22.5 Using trigonometry to solve problems — 512
- Test Yourself 22 — 518
- Assignment — 522

23. Graphing functions — **523**
- 23.1 Graphing linear functions — 523
- 23.2 Graphs of quadratic functions — 528
- 23.3 Using quadratic graphs — 532
- 23.4 Quadratic graphs and real-life problems — 541
- 23.5 Graphs of exponential functions — 544
- Test Yourself 23 — 548
- Assignment — 551

24. Geometry 3 – Transformations, Constructions — **553**
- 24.1 Transformation geometry — 553
- 24.2 Symmetries — 557
- 24.3 Rotation — 564
- 24.4 Constructions 1 — 568
- 24.5 Constructing triangles and rectangles — 575
- Test Yourself 24 — 581
- Assignment — 583

Answers — **584**

Preface

Text & Tests 2 (Higher Level) is written as a complete two-year course, comprehensively covering the new specification for Junior Cycle Higher Level students who are beginning their second year.

It revisits topics covered in ***Text & Tests 1*** (new edition) and encourages the further development of the student's mathematical knowledge and skills. Each chapter contains the following key features:

- Chapter outlines
- Clear explanations and examples
- A large number of well-structured, graded questions
- Detailed diagrams
- Test Yourself revision exercises

The book emphasises discussion, cooperation and communication in acquiring an understanding of the fundamental concepts in the mathematics specification by using:

- Investigations
- Assignments

Free-to-access associated online resources contain Reviews of each chapter.

While retaining many features of the bestselling previous ***Text & Tests*** series, this book is designed to help students prepare for final exams at the Higher Level and to complete the classroom-based assessments with a focus on being numerate; working with others; being creative; communicating; collecting and managing information.

Paul Cooke
Deborah Crean
O.D. Morris

Algebra 1

From first year, you will recall how to:

- use symbols for unknown quantities,
- identify terms and expressions,
- add and subtract like terms,
- multiply out expressions containing brackets,
- multiply different terms,
- substitute values for variables in an expression,
- find an expression for the area of a rectangle,
- form and solve equations,
- use algebra to solve word problems.

In this chapter, you will learn to:

- solve perimeter and area problems involving algebra,
- perform algebraic division,
- plot numbers from N, Z and R on the number line,
- plot inequalities on a number line,
- solve algebraic inequalities and graph the solution,
- recall that if an inequality is multiplied or divided by a negative number, the sign must be reversed.

Section 1.1 Simplifying expressions

$2x^2 + 3x - 4$ is called an **expression**.
It consists of 3 **terms**.
The terms are separated by a plus (+) or a minus (−) sign.
The letter x is called a **variable**.
A **coefficient** is a number before a variable.
In $2x^2$, the coefficient is 2; in $3x$, the coefficient is 3.
The term -4 is known as a **constant**; it does not change.

In the expression $2x^2 + 5x - 2 + 3x + 4x^2$,

$2x^2$ and $4x^2$ are called **like terms**;
$5x$ and $3x$ are also like terms.

Text & Tests 2 Higher Level

The expression $2x^2 + 5x - 2 + 3x + 4x^2$ may be simplified by combining the like terms as follows:

$2x^2 + 5x - 2 + 3x + 4x^2$
$= 2x^2 + 4x^2 + 5x + 3x - 2$
$= 6x^2 + 8x - 2$

> Like terms only may be added or subtracted.

Example 1

Simplify (i) $4a + 6b + 6 - 2a + b - 3$ (ii) $2x^2 - 3x - 7 - x^2 - 5x + 3$

(i) $4a + 6b + 6 - 2a + b - 3$
   $= 4a - 2a + 6b + b + 6 - 3$
   $= 2a + 7b + 3$

(ii) $2x^2 - 3x - 7 - x^2 - 5x + 3$
   $= 2x^2 - x^2 - 3x - 5x - 7 + 3$
   $= x^2 - 8x - 4$

Exercise 1.1

Simplify each of the following by adding like terms:

1. $3x + 4x - 2x$
2. $7a + 3 + 4a + 6$
3. $5x + y - 2x + 4y$
4. $5a + 2b - 2a - 4b$
5. $12a + b + 3a + 5b$
6. $3x + 2y + 3 + 4x + 3y + 1$
7. $5x - 4 + 2x + 8$
8. $7x - 4 - 3x + 7$
9. $6a + b + 3 + 2a + 2b - 1$
10. $3x + 4 + 2x - 6 + x + 3$
11. $3a - b + 4a + 5b - 2a$
12. $2ab + 4 + 3ab - 2$
13. $2p + 3q - r + p - 4q + 2r$
14. $5k + 3 - 4k + 6 + k - 4$
15. $2ab + c + 5ab - 4c$
16. $3xy + 2z + xy + 9z$
17. $6ab + 2cd - ab + 3cd$
18. $6x - xy + 5x - 7xy$
19. $x^2 - 3x + 4 - 2x^2 + 5x - 3$
20. $3x^2 - 3x + x^2 - 8x + 7$
21. $3a^2 - 2a - 6a + 4a^2 - 3$
22. $y^2 - 8y - 3y^2 + 2y - 3$
23. $3x^2 - 2 + 5x - 4 - 7x + 1$
24. $5a^2 + 2a - 3a^2 + 4 - 3a + 2$

25. $3x^2 - 2x + 4xy + 8$ is an expression.
    (i) How many terms are there in the expression?
    (ii) What is the coefficient of xy in the expression?
    (iii) How many variables are there in the expression?
    (iv) What is the constant in the expression?

Chapter 1 Algebra 1

26. Work out and simplify an expression for the perimeter of each of these.

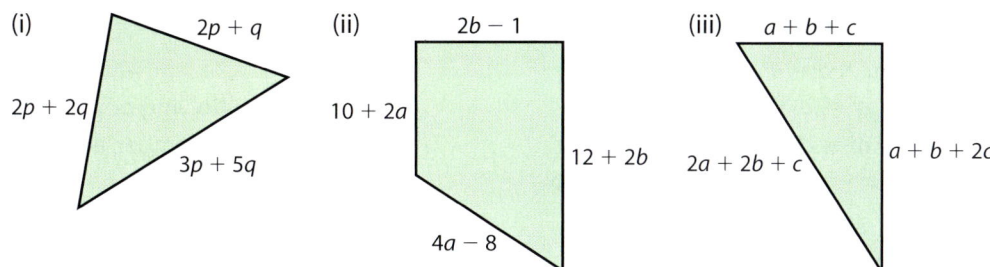

27. Work out an expression for each length marked **?**.

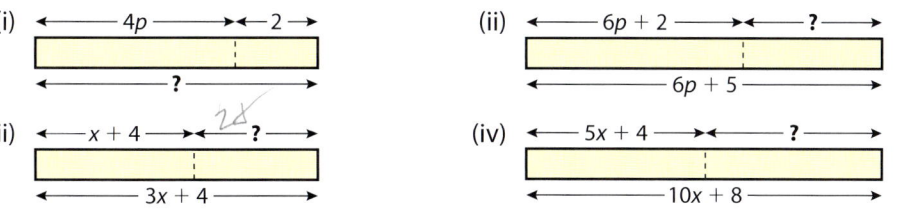

Section 1.2 Removing brackets

To write $3x \times 4y$ as a single term, we multiply the coefficients 3 and 4 and then multiply the variables x and y.

Thus, $3x \times 4y = 3 \times 4 \times x \times y = 12xy$.

Similarly, (i) $3a \times 6b = 18ab$ (ii) $-3p \times 4q = -12pq$

In your study of algebra so far, you will have learned how to remove brackets as follows:

$a(b + c) = ab + ac$ Here each term inside the bracket is multiplied by a.

Remember $3(a + 2) = (a + 2) + (a + 2) + (a + 2) = a + a + a + 2 + 2 + 2 = 3a + 6$

Similarly, (i) $5(2x + 6) = 10x + 30$
(ii) $-4(5a - 2) = -20a + 8$
(iii) $-(6x - 4) = -6x + 4$
(iv) $-(-9a + 6) = 9a - 6$

If there is a minus outside the brackets, the sign of each term inside the brackets is changed when the brackets are removed.

3

Text & Tests 2 Higher Level

Multiplication involving indices

As 5×5 can be written as 5^2, similarly $x \times x$ is written as x^2.
Also, $a \times a \times a = a^3$
and $a^2 \times a^2 = a \times a \times a \times a = a^4$
$a^2 \times a^3 = a \times a \times a \times a \times a = a^5$
$3x(2x^2 - x + 4) = 6x^3 - 3x^2 + 12x$

> When multiplying powers of the same number, add the indices.

Multiplying two expressions

Here is a reminder of how to multiply two expressions, each containing two terms:

$(2x + 3)(3x - 5) =$

	$2x$	$+3$
$3x$	$6x^2$	$+9x$
-5	$-10x$	-15

$= 6x^2 + 9x - 10x - 15$
$= 6x^2 - x - 15$

Example 1

Remove the brackets and simplify each of these:

(i) $(2x - 3)(3x + 4)$ (ii) $(2x - 4)(x^2 - 3x + 5)$

(i) $(2x - 3)(3x + 4) =$

	$2x$	-3
$3x$	$6x^2$	$-9x$
$+4$	$8x$	-12

$= 6x^2 - 9x + 8x - 12$
$= 6x^2 - x - 12$

(ii) $(2x - 4)(x^2 - 3x + 5) =$

	x^2	$-3x$	$+5$
$2x$	$2x^3$	$-6x^2$	$+10x$
-4	$-4x^2$	$+12x$	-20

$= 2x^3 - 6x^2 - 4x^2 + 10x + 12x - 20$
$= 2x^3 - 10x^2 + 22x - 20$

Note: $(2x - 3)(3x + 4) = 2x(3x + 4) - 3(3x + 4)$
$= 6x^2 + 8x - 9x - 12 = 6x^2 - x - 12$

Exercise 1.2

1. Express each of the following as a single term:

   (i) $3 \times 4a$ (ii) $3a \times 5a$ (iii) $2a \times b$ (iv) $3x \times 4y$
   (v) $-2a \times 3a$ (vi) $2ab \times 4b$ (vii) $2a^2b \times ab$ (viii) $4 \times a \times 6 \times a^2$

Remove the brackets and simplify each of these:

2. $3(2x - 1) + 5(x + 2)$
3. $2(x - 4) + 3(2x + 5)$
4. $5(3x - 2) - 2(x - 1)$
5. $3(3x + 2) - 4(2x + 1)$
6. $6(2x - 3) + 2(3x - 1)$
7. $5(x - 2) - (2x + 4)$
8. $3(2a - 7) - 5(a - 4)$
9. $2(3a - 4) - (5a - 3)$
10. $2(x^2 - 3x + 1) + 2(x^2 + x - 4)$
11. $5(x^2 - x - 4) - 2(2x^2 - 3x + 2)$

12. Complete the following grid to find the product of,

$(2x + 4)(x + 3) =$

×	2x	+4
x	2x²	
+3		

Find the product of each of these:

13. $(3x + 2)(2x + 4)$
14. $(3x + 1)(2x - 4)$
15. $(5x - 2)(2x + 3)$
16. $(2x - 3)(x - 5)$
17. $(5x + 1)(3x - 3)$
18. $(3x + 1)(x^2 + 2x + 1)$
19. $(2x + 4)(2x^2 - x - 3)$
20. $(5x - 2)(x^2 - x + 4)$
21. $(3x - 2)(2x^2 - 3x + 7)$
22. $(4x - 1)(x^2 - 4x + 6)$
23. $(4x - 3)(2x^2 - 3x + 2)$
24. $(3a - 4)(2a^2 - 3a + 2)$
25. $(2y - 7)(y^2 + 3y + 1)$

26. Find an expression for the area of each of these shapes.
    Simplify each expression fully.

(i) rectangle with sides $2x$, y, $2x$, y

(ii) 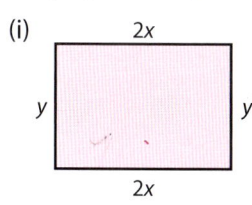 L-shape with $2m$, k, m, n, m, $n+k$

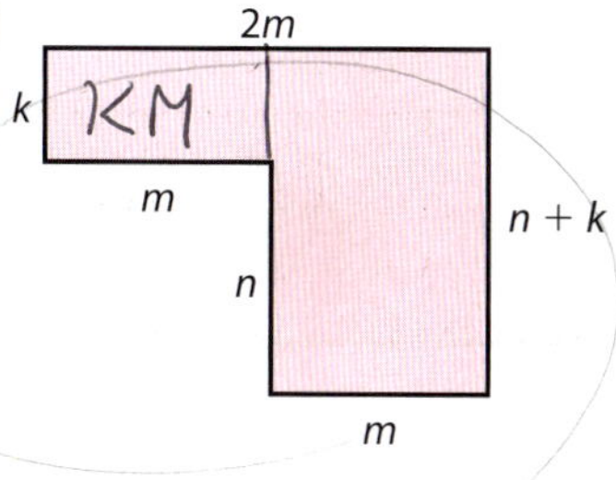

(iii) 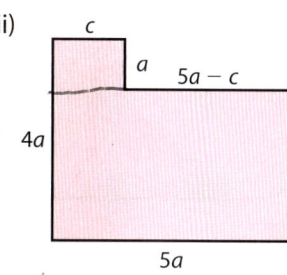 shape with c, a, $5a - c$, $4a$, $5a$

27. Find the missing expressions in these statements.
    (i) $d(\square) = d^2 + 5d$
    (ii) $2n(\square) = 2n^2 - 8n$
    (iii) $3p(\square) = 15p - 3p^2$
    (iv) $5k(\square) = 20k + 5k^2$

28. Find the missing term in each statement.
    (i) $5p \times \square = 10pq$
    (ii) $\square \times 7n = 21mn$
    (iii) $3a^2 \times \square = 9a^2b$
    (iv) $\square \times 2y^2 = 10x^2y^2$
    (v) $3cd^2 \times \square = 15c^3d^2$
    (vi) $\square \times 7vw^3 = 28v^3w^4$

Text & Tests 2 Higher Level

Section 1.3 Evaluating expressions

When $x = 3$, the value of $2x + 5$ is $2(3) + 5 = 6 + 5 = 11$
When $x = 2$, the value of $3x^2 - 6x$ is $3(2)^2 - 6(2) = 3(4) - 12 = 12 - 12 = 0$

Example 1

If $a = 2$, $b = 3$ and $c = -4$, find the value of

(i) $a + b$ (ii) $2a - b$ (iii) $3a^2 - 2c$ (iv) $2c^2 - 4ab$

(i) $a + b = 2 + 3 = 5$

(ii) $2a - b = 2(2) - 3$
$= 4 - 3 = 1$

(iii) $3a^2 - 2c = 3(2)^2 - 2(-4)$
$= 3(4) + 8$
$= 12 + 8 = 20$

(iv) $2c^2 - 4ab = 2(-4)^2 - 4(2)(3)$
$= 2(16) - 4(6)$
$= 32 - 24 = 8$

Remember

When evaluating an expression,
(i) multiply and divide before you add or subtract
(ii) any number multiplied by zero is zero, e.g. $6 \times 0 = 0$

Example 2

If $x = 3$ and $y = -2$, find the value of $3x^2 - 4xy - 2y^2$.

$3x^2 - 4xy - 2y^2 = 3(3)^2 - 4(3)(-2) - 2(-2)^2$
$= 3(9) - 4(-6) - 2(4)$ ... square before you multiply
$= 27 + 24 - 8$
$= 51 - 8$
$= 43$

Exercise 1.3

1. If $x = 4$, find the value of each of these:

   (i) $3x$ (ii) $2x + 6$ (iii) $7 - x$ (iv) $x^2 + 3$ (v) $3x^2 - 2x - 7$

2. If $a = 3$ and $b = -2$, find the value of each of these:

   (i) $2a + b$ (ii) $a^2 + ab$ (iii) $2a^2 + b^2$ (iv) $3ab + 2b^2$

Chapter 1 Algebra 1

3. If $a = 1, b = 2$ and $c = 3$, find the value of:
  (i) $2a + b$
  (ii) $3ab - c$
  (iii) $4abc + 3c$
  (iv) $3bc - 4ab$
  (v) $3abc - 2ac$
  (vi) $5bc - 2ab$
  (vii) $\dfrac{3a + 6b}{c}$
  (viii) $\dfrac{4b - 2a}{c}$
  (ix) $\dfrac{6c - ab}{4b}$

4. If $x = 1\tfrac{1}{2}$ and $y = \tfrac{1}{2}$, find the value of:
  (i) $4x + 2y$
  (ii) $3x + y$
  (iii) $2x - 4y$
  (iv) $8xy$

5. If $a = 4$ and $b = 3$, find the value of:
  (i) $a^2 + b$
  (ii) $b^2 - 2a$
  (iii) $3a^2 - 2b^2$
  (iv) $a^2b - 2ab$

6. If $x = 2$, find the value of $2x^2 - 3x + 5$.

7. If $a = 5, b = 2$ and $c = 8$, evaluate each of these:
  (i) $a - bc$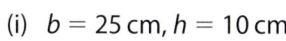
  (ii) $2a^2 - bc$
  (iii) $a(b - c)^2$

8. Calculate the value of each of the following expressions when $p = 2, q = 3$ and $r = 6$:
  (i) $r(p + q)$
  (ii) $rp + q$
  (iii) $\dfrac{r}{pq}$
  (iv) $\dfrac{q + r}{p}$
  (v) $5r^2$

9. If $x = 2, y = -3$ and $z = 1$, evaluate
  (i) $x^2 - 3xy + 2z$
  (ii) $2y^2 - 3xy$
  (iii) $z^2 - 3x^2y + 4y$

10. The area of a triangle is given by the formula $A = \dfrac{bh}{2}$.
Work out the areas of triangles where
  (i) $b = 25$ cm, $h = 10$ cm
  (ii) $b = 16$ cm, $h = 12$ cm

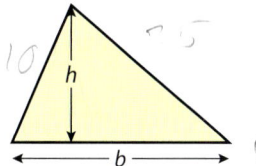

11. The area, A square units, of a trapezium is given by the formula $A = \tfrac{1}{2}(a + b)h$.
(a, b and h are shown on the diagram.)
Use the formula to calculate the areas of trapeziums for which
  (i) $a = 9$ cm, $b = 16$ cm, $h = 10$ cm
  (ii) $a = 14$ cm, $b = 30$ cm, $h = 11$ cm

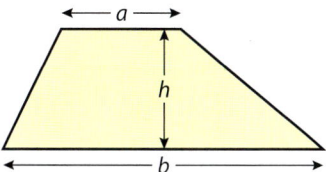

12. When $m = -1, n = -2$ and $p = 8$, there are four matching pairs here.
Can you find them?

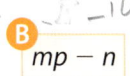 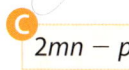 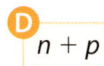 | D $n + p$ | E $\dfrac{p}{n}$ |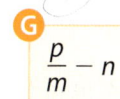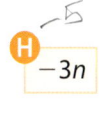

13. Evaluate $\dfrac{3}{x + 3} + \dfrac{4}{2x + 6}$, when $x = \tfrac{1}{3}$.

7

Text & Tests 2 Higher Level

Section 1.4 Solving linear equations

An **expression** $3x + 2$ can have many values depending on the value of the **variable** x.

If $x = 1$, then $3x + 2 = 3(1) + 2 = 5$
If $x = 6$, then $3x + 2 = 3(6) + 2 = 20$

If $3x + 2 = 14$, to find the value of x that resulted in 14 we must **solve the equation** $3x + 2 = 14$ **for x**.

The three scales below will help you recall the steps involved in solving an equation.
To solve the equation $3x + 2 = 14$.

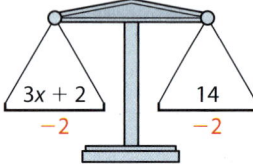 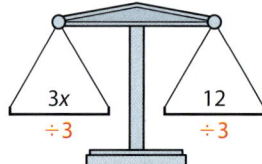 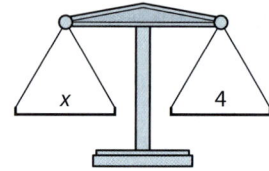

Take 2 from both sides   Divide both sides by 3 $x = 4$ is the solution

The scales above illustrate that solving an equation requires us to change the equation into a simpler one. This is done by adding, subtracting, multiplying or dividing both sides of the equation by the **same number**.

Example 1

Solve the equation $3x - 5 = 16$

$3x - 5 = 16$
$3x - 5 + 5 = 16 + 5$ ... add 5 to both sides
$3x = 21$
$x = 7$ ... divide both sides by 3

Example 2

Solve the equation $3(2x - 6) = 2(2x + 1)$

$3(2x - 6) = 2(2x + 1)$
$6x - 18 = 4x + 2$ ... remove the brackets
$6x - \mathbf{4x} - 18 = 4x + 2 - \mathbf{4x}$ ... take $4x$ from each side
$2x - 18 = 2$
$2x - 18 + \mathbf{18} = 2 + \mathbf{18}$ ... add 18 to each side
$2x = 20$
$x = 10$ ... divide each side by 2

Chapter 1 Algebra 1

Exercise 1.4

1. Write down the missing numbers to make these equations true:

(i) ☐ + 8 = 15 (ii) 12 − ☐ = 8 (iii) ☐ × 3 = 30

(iv) ☐ × 6 + 2 = 26 (v) 27 ÷ ☐ + 1 = 10 (vi) $7 + 5 + \frac{☐}{2} = 15$

2. Solve each of these equations:

(i) $2x = 8$ (ii) $3x = 27$ (iii) $5x = 35$ (iv) $6x = 42$ (v) $9x = 63$

Solve each of these equations:

3. $4x + 2 = 14$ **4.** $2x − 9 = 3$ **5.** $2x − 7 = 5$

6. $3 + 2x = 11$ **7.** $6 + 3x = 9$ **8.** $2 + 7x = 30$

9. $6x − 2 = 4x + 10$ **10.** $7x − 9 = 3x + 11$ **11.** $9x − 15 = 3x + 3$

12. $x + 7 = 2x − 1$ **13.** $2x + 6 = 4x − 6$ **14.** $3x + 1 = 5x − 13$

15. $5x − 2 = 40 − x$ **16.** $3x + 7 = 32 − 2x$ **17.** $6 + 2x = 33 − x$

Remove the brackets and solve the following equations:

18. $3(2x + 1) = 2x + 11$ **19.** $2(2x + 5) = 5x + 5$

20. $4(2x − 3) = 2(3x − 5)$ **21.** $4(3x + 6) = 3(5x − 2)$

22. $5(2x − 4) + 1 = 3(2x − 1)$ **23.** $6(2x + 1) + 4 = 5(3x − 1)$

24. $5(x − 2) − 3x = 3(x − 5)$ **25.** $5(2x + 3) = 4(2x + 1) + 15$

26. $5(m + 3) − 25 = 6(2 − m)$ **27.** $10(x + 4) − 1 = 3(2x + 5)$

28. $4(x − 2) − 9 = 3 − (x + 5)$ **29.** $3(y − 1) = 18 − 5(y + 1)$

30. $3(5k + 7) + 2(3k − 5) = 5(2k + 11)$ **31.** $5(3x − 2) = 3(2x + 1) + 2x + 1$

32. Work out what x stands for in each of these.

(i) 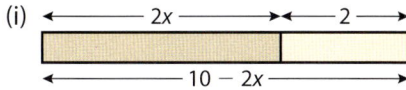   (ii)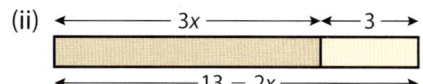

33. Find the values of x and f in these figures.
The perimeter is given in each case.

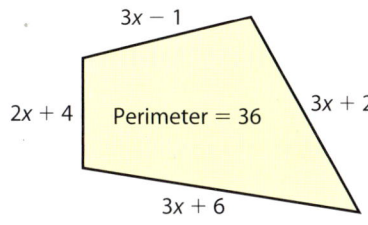 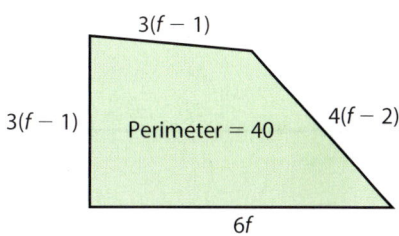

Section 1.5 Solving problems using linear equations

The ability to change a problem expressed in words into a mathematical equation and then solve it is very important in mathematics.

The following examples will show how equations can be formed from word problems.

Example 1

When five times a certain number is reduced by 4, the result is the same as adding 7 to four times the number.
Find the number.

Let x be the required number.

Equation: $5x - 4 = 4x + 7$
$5x - 4 - \mathbf{4x} = 4x + 7 - \mathbf{4x}$ … take $4x$ from each side
$x - 4 = 7$
$x - 4 + \mathbf{4} = 7 + \mathbf{4}$ … add 4 to each side
$x = 11$

The required number is 11.

Example 2

(i) Find an expression, in terms of x, for the perimeter of this rectangle.
Give your answer in its simplest form.

(ii) The perimeter of the rectangle is 44 cm.
Write down an equation and solve it to find the value of x.

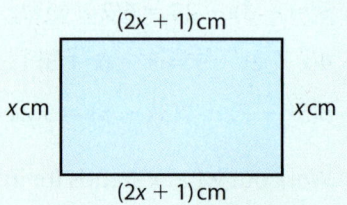

(i) Perimeter $= (2x + 1) + x + (2x + 1) + x$
$= (6x + 2)$ cm

(ii) Perimeter $= 44 \Rightarrow 6x + 2 = 44$
$6x + 2 - \mathbf{2} = 44 - \mathbf{2}$
$6x = 42$
$x = 7$

Exercise 1.5

1. If I multiply a number by 4 and then add 3, the result is the same as adding 8 to three times the number.
   Form an equation in x and solve it to find the number.

2. I think of a number, multiply it by 8 and then subtract 2.
   I get the same result as when I multiply this number by 2 and add 10. What is this number?

3. One number is 5 greater than another number.
   If the smaller number is added to twice the larger number, the answer is 28.
   Find the two numbers.

4. Ann is 3 years older than Helen.
   If twice the sum of their ages is 50 years, how old is Ann?

5. (i) Find an expression for the perimeter of this triangle.
   (ii) What value of x gives a perimeter of 55?

   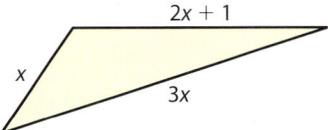

6. If we subtract 4 from a number and then multiply the result by 5, the answer is 15.
   Find the number.

7. I think of a number, increase it by 4 and double the answer.
   The result is 20 more than the number. Find this number.

8. Use your knowledge of angles to form an equation and solve it to find the value of a.

   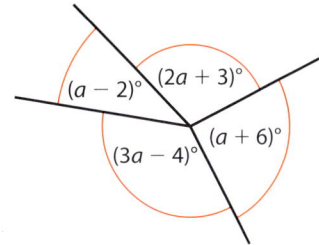

9. A triangle and rectangle are shown below:

   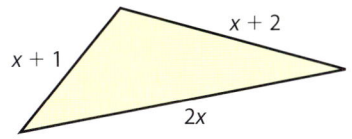 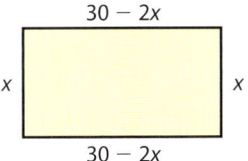

   Find the value of x which
   (i) gives a triangle with a perimeter of 63
   (ii) gives a triangle and rectangle with equal perimeters
   (iii) makes the rectangle into a square.

Text & Tests 2 Higher Level

10. Here is a fraction: $\frac{x}{\Box}$.

    The denominator of the fraction is 5 more than the numerator.
    If 1 is added to the numerator and 2 is subtracted from the denominator, the fraction will become $\frac{4}{5}$. Find the fraction.

11. The number in each brick is found by adding the two numbers above it.
    Find the missing expressions in each of the diagrams below.
    Write equations to find the value of *x* in each case.

    (i)
18	x	23
□	□	
	57	

    (ii)
3x + 2	□	x − 3
	4x + 5	□
	35	

12. In an arithmagon, the number in a square is the sum of the numbers in the two circles either side of it.

    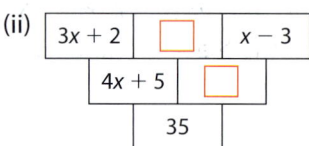

    (i) Explain why the number in circle **B** is $20 - x$.
    (ii) What is the number in circle **C** in terms of *x*?
    (iii) Form an equation across the base of the triangle and solve it to find the value of *x*.

13. Find an expression in *x* for the area of the shaded portion of this figure.

    If the area of this shaded portion is 38 cm², find the value of *x*.

    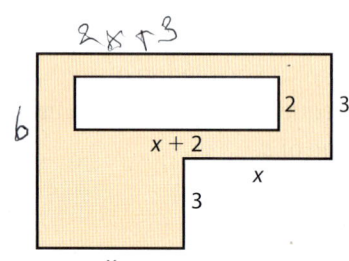

14. Ruth is *x* years old. Write, in terms of *x*,
    (i) her age 6 years ago
    (ii) her age in 12 years time.

    In 12 years time, Ruth will be three times as old as she was 6 years ago.
    Find Ruth's age now.

15. 166 people live in an apartment block and of these, *x* are women.
    There are 8 fewer men than women and there are 30 more children than women.
    How many women live in the block?

Chapter 1 Algebra 1

16. In a race between two cities, one person travels by air, another by sea and the third by train.

    The sea voyage takes 120 minutes longer than the train journey, and the air route takes 80 minutes less than the train journey.

    If the total travelling time is 10 hours and 40 minutes, use algebra to find the time taken by each of the race participants.

    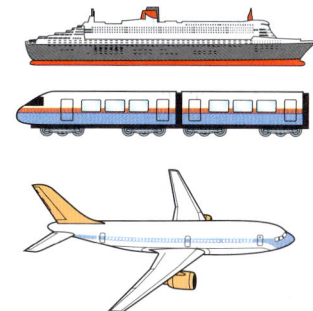

17. The sum of three consecutive numbers is 168. By letting x be the first number, form an equation and hence find the three numbers.

18. Find x in each triangle.

    (i) 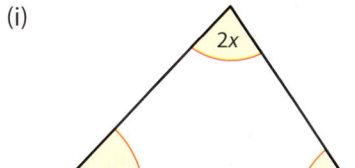   (ii)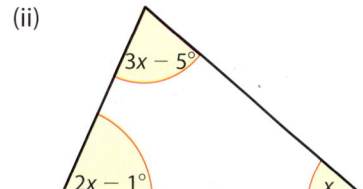

19. Petra has €12 and Patrick has nothing. They both receive the same money for doing a delivery job. Now Petra has three time as much as Patrick. How much did they get for doing the job?

20. A premium ticket for a football match was one and a half times the price of a standard ticket. If the total cost for 4 standard and 2 premium tickets was €322, write an equation to show this information. Solve the equation to find the cost of a standard ticket.

21. Aaron and Paul have the same number of golf balls. Aaron has two full boxes and 18 loose balls. Paul has three full boxes and 6 loose balls. Find the number of balls in each box if each box holds the same number of balls.

Section 1.6 Algebraic division

We have already learned how to multiply two algebraic expressions such as $(x + 4)(x - 3)$.

In this section, we will learn how to divide an expression such as $x^2 + x - 12$ by $(x + 4)$ by using the array method in reverse.

    Place x^2 in box 1.

Divide x^2 by x and place result (x) above box 1.

Multiply the result, x, by $+4$ and place result ($4x$) in box 2.

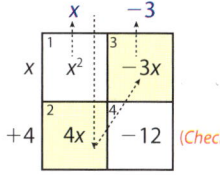

Calculate the term needed for box 3 so that the total for box 2 and 3 is the middle term x.

i.e. $-3x$.

Divide $-3x$ by x and place the result (-3) above box 3.

Check that $(+4) \times (-3)$ gives the constant term -12.

Example 1

Divide $2x^3 + x^2 - 13x + 6$ by $x + 3$.

Divide $2x^3$ by x and place result ($2x^2$) above box 1.

Multiply the result ($2x^2$) by $+3$ and place answer ($6x^2$) in box 2.

Calculate the term needed for box 3 ($-5x^2$) so that the total for box 2 and 3 is the second term x^2.

Divide $-5x^2$ by x and place result ($-5x$) above box 3.

Multiply the result ($-5x$) by $+3$ and place result ($-15x$) in box 4.

Calculate the term needed for box 5 ($+2x$) so that the total for box 4 and 5 is the third term $-13x$.

Divide $2x$ by x and place result ($+2$) above box 5

Check that $(+3) \times (+2) =$ the constant term $= 6$

The answer is $2x^2 - 5x + 2$.

		$2x^2$	$-5x$	$+2$
x	1	$2x^3$	3 $-5x^2$	5 $+2x$
$+3$	2	$6x^2$	4 $-15x$	6 $+6$

Take the expression $x^3 + 11x - 30$. Here there is no term in x^2.

If we are asked to divide $x^3 + 11x - 30$ by $(x - 2)$, we rewrite the first expression as $x^3 + 0x^2 + 11x - 30$, and then divide by $(x - 2)$.

Example 2

Divide $4x^3 - 13x - 6$ by $x - 2$.

Rewrite $4x^3 - 13x - 6$ as $4x^3 + 0x^2 - 13x - 6$.

Box 2 + 3 must cancel (since there are $0x^2$).

Box 4 + 5 must add to $-13x$

$\therefore$ $4x^3 - 13x - 6 \div x - 2$ is $4x^2 + 8x + 3$.

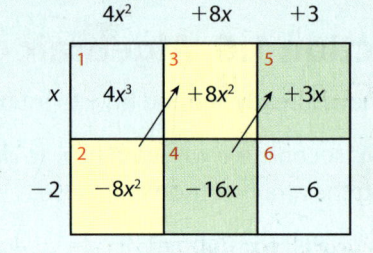

		$4x^2$	$+8x$	$+3$
x	1	$4x^3$	3 $+8x^2$	5 $+3x$
-2	2	$-8x^2$	4 $-16x$	6 -6

Chapter 1 Algebra 1

Exercise 1.6

Divide each of the following:

1. $x^2 + 5x + 6 \div x + 3$
2. $x^2 + 8x + 15 \div x + 5$
3. $x^2 + 9x + 14 \div x + 2$
4. $2x^2 + 9x + 4 \div x + 4$
5. $6x^2 + 5x + 1 \div 2x + 1$
6. $2x^2 + x - 10 \div 2x + 5$
7. $\dfrac{6x^2 - 10x - 4}{3x + 1}$
8. $\dfrac{2x^2 - 7x - 4}{x - 4}$
9. $3x^2 - 22x + 7 \div 3x - 1$
10. $6x^2 + 11x - 35 \div 2x + 7$
11. $10x^2 - 7x - 12 \div 2x - 3$
12. $15x^2 - 26x + 8 \div 5x - 2$
13. $x^3 + 3x^2 + 5x + 3 \div x + 1$
14. $x^3 + 5x^2 + 11x + 10 \div x + 2$
15. $x^3 + 3x^2 - 10x - 24 \div x - 3$
16. $3x^3 - 2x^2 - 19x - 6 \div 3x + 1$
17. $\dfrac{2x^3 - x^2 - 7x + 6}{2x - 3}$
18. $\dfrac{2x^3 - 3x^2 - 12x + 20}{2x + 5}$
19. $2x^3 + 9x^2 - 55x + 50 \div 2x - 5$
20. $2x^3 + 3x^2 - 8x - 12 \div 2x + 3$
21. $x^3 - 19x - 30 \div x - 5$
22. $4x^3 - 11x + 3 \div 2x - 3$
23. $6x^3 - 13x^2 + 4 \div 2x + 1$
24. $3x^3 + 9x^2 + 48 \div x + 4$

25. If the area of a rectangle is found by multiplying the length by the breadth, find the missing side in each of these rectangles.

    (i) Area = $6x^2 - x - 12$, ?, $3x + 4$

    (ii) Area = $10x^2 + x - 2$, $2x + 1$, ?

Section 1.7 Plotting numbers on the number line

In your study of numbers so far, you will have dealt with **natural numbers** and **integers**. These numbers are described again below and illustrated on the number line.

1. **Natural numbers** are the counting numbers starting at 1.
   They are denoted by the capital letter **N**.
   $N = 1, 2, 3, 4, 5, \ldots$

   The arrow indicates that the dots continue indefinitely.

2. **Integers** are whole numbers which may be positive or negative.
   They are denoted by the capital letter **Z**.
   The integers are illustrated here on the
   number line.
   Z = ... , −3, −2, −1, 0, 1, 2, 3, ...

   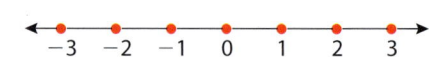

3. **Real numbers** describe all the numbers on the number line.
   These numbers include natural numbers, integers, fractions, decimals and numbers such as $\sqrt{5}, \sqrt{7}, \pi, \ldots$

   Since every number on the number line is a real number, we say that real numbers 'fill' the number line. For this reason, real numbers are represented on the number line by a heavy or 'bold' line as shown below.
   The capital letter **R** is used to denote the set of real numbers.

Inequalities

The speed limit for cars driving in a city is
generally 60 km/hr.
This could be written as speed ⩽ 60 or S ⩽ 60.
This means that S could be 60, 58, 56, 40, ...
The statement S ⩽ 60 is an example of an **inequality**.

$x + 3 = 7$ is an example of an **equation** since one side is *equal* to the other.
However, $x + 3 > 7$ is an example of an **inequality** since one side is **not equal** to the other side.

Here are the four inequality signs we will use.

>	<	⩾	⩽
is greater than	is less than	is greater than or equal to	is less than or equal to

We will now use these inequality signs to show how different numbers can be shown on the number line.

1. Natural numbers

The inequality $x \geqslant 4, x \in N$ means that x may be any whole number greater than or equal to 4, i.e., 4, 5, 6, 7, ...
These are represented on the number line below:

2. Integers

The inequality $x > -2, x \in Z$ represents all the integers greater than -2,
i.e., $-1, 0, 1, 2, 3, \ldots$
These are represented on the number line below:

3. Real numbers

The inequality $x \geq 3, x \in R$ is the set of all real numbers greater than or equal to 3.
The inequality $x \geq 3$ is represented on the number line as follows:

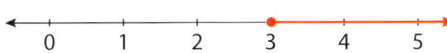

The 'bold' line indicates that all the points on the line are included and the closed circle at 3 shows that the number 3 is **included**.

The inequality $x < -2, x \in R$ is shown below.
The 'empty' circle at -2 is used to show that -2 is not included.

4. Real line intervals

If $x \geq -3$ and $x < 2$ and $x \in R$, an interval of values is obtained starting at $x = -3$ and finishing at $x = 2$ but not including 2. On a number line this is represented as follows:

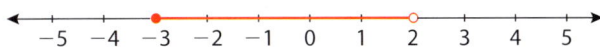

Since $x \geq -3$ can be written as $-3 \leq x$ ($5 > 3$ is the same as saying $3 < 5$),

the two inequalities can be put together as one combined inequality $-3 \leq x < 2$.

Exercise 1.7

1. State whether each of the following is true or false:
   (i) $3 \in N$ (ii) $4 \in Z$ (iii) $-5 \in N$ (iv) $2.5 \in R$
   (v) $-3\frac{1}{2} \in N$ (vi) $0.5 \in N$ (vii) $2\frac{3}{8} \in R$ (viii) $\sqrt{17} \in R$

2. Insert $>$ or $<$ in each of the boxes below:
   (i) $6 \square 4$ (ii) $-5 \square 2$ (iii) $6 \square -2$ (iv) $-4 \square 3$

3. Write a mathematical sentence for each of these:
   (i) x is less than 4
   (ii) 2 is greater than -3
   (iii) the speed limit (S) is 40 km/hr
   (iv) b is less than or equal to -5
   (v) the minimum age (A) is 18
   (vi) the maximum age (A) is 60.

Text & Tests 2 Higher Level

4. If $x \in N$, state the values x may have in each of the following inequalities:
   (i) $x < 4$
   (ii) $x \leq 5$
   (iii) $x < 6\frac{1}{2}$
   (iv) $x > 2$ and $x < 7$
   (v) $x \geq 1$ and $x \leq 4$
   (vi) $x \geq 2$ and $x < 8$

5. If $x \in Z$, state the values x may have in each of the following inequalities:
   (i) $x \geq -2$ and $x \leq 1$
   (ii) $x \geq 0$ and $x \leq 4$
   (iii) $x \geq -3$ and $x \leq 0$
   (iv) $x \geq -4$ and $x < 1$
   (v) $x > -5$ and $x < 2$
   (vi) $x > -2\frac{1}{2}$ and $x < 3\frac{1}{4}$

6. Graph each of the following inequalities on the number line:
   (i) $x \geq 3, x \in N$
   (ii) $x \leq 4, x \in N$
   (iii) $x > 3, x \in N$
   (iv) $x \leq 2, x \in Z$
   (v) $x \geq -3, x \in Z$
   (vi) $x > -2, x \in Z$

7. Choose one of $x = 3, x \leq 3, x < 3, x > 3$ or $x \geq 3$ to describe each graph below:
   (i)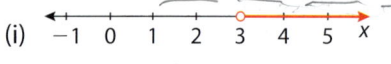
   (ii)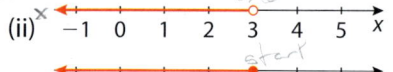
   (iii)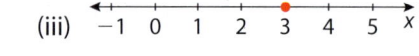
   (iv)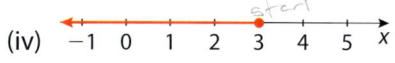

8. Write the inequality represented by each of these number lines:
   (i)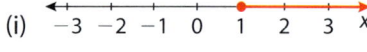
   (ii)
   (iii)  (iv)
   (v)  (vi)

9. Graph each of the following on the number line:
   (i) $x \geq 1, x \in R$
   (ii) $x \geq -3, x \in R$
   (iii) $x \leq 4, x \in R$
   (iv) $x > 3, x \in R$
   (v) $x < -1, x \in R$
   (vi) $x < 4, x \in R$

10. Write an inequality for each of the following diagrams:
    (i)
    (ii)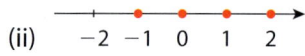
    (iii)
    (iv)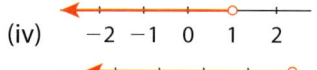
    (v) 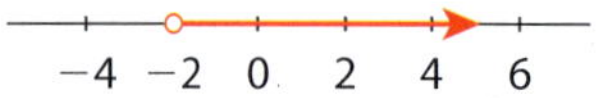 (vi)

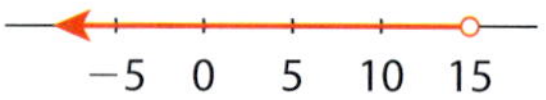

11. Which of the numbers in the given panel are in the set of values given by $0 < x \leq 5, x \in R$?

    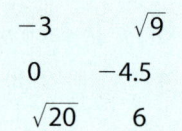

12. m is a multiple of 4.
    Find all the values of m so that $10 \leq m \leq 24$.

13. Which of the numbers below satisfy the inequality $x^2 < 100$?
    9   15   10   −4   −11   0   10.5

18

$3(y-1) = 18 - 5(y+1)$
$3y - 3 = 15y + 15$
$3y - 15y = 3 + 15$
$-12y = 18$
18

$3(y-1) = 18 - 5(y+1)$
$3y - 3 = 18y + 1, -5y + 5$
$3y + 5y = 3 + 1$
$26y = $

$x = 2$

$3(y-1) = 18 - 5(y+1)$
$3y - 3 = 18y + 18, -5y * 5$
$3y - 18y + 5 = 3 \quad 18 \quad 5$
$-10y \qquad\qquad 26$

14. Write each of the following sentences as a mathematical statement.
Let *n* stand for the number in each case.

(i) I have at least 6 shirts in my wardrobe.
(ii) The temperature in a fridge must be 5°C or less.
(iii) Hand baggage must not exceed 10 kg.
(iv) Gillian has more than 5 DVDs.
(v) There are at least 20 pupils in my class but definitely not more than 30.
(vi) I think of a number *n*, multiply it by 5 and then subtract 12.
The result is greater than -7.

15. Graph each of the following intervals on the number line.
(i) $-5 \leq x < 3, x \in R$ (ii) $-3 < x \leq 3, x \in R$ (iii) $-2 < x < 6, x \in R$

16. Write an inequality for each of the following intervals

(i) 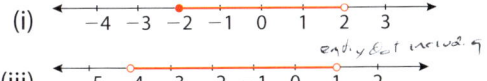 (ii)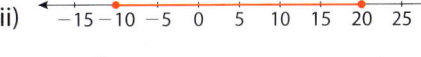

(iii) 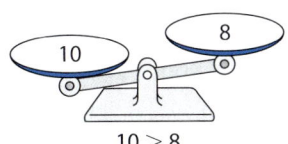 (iv)

Section 1.8 Solving inequalities

Here are scales that show $10 > 8$.

Would the scales stay as they are if

› the same amount is added to both sides
› the same amount is subtracted from both sides
› the mass on each side is doubled
› the mass on each side is halved?

The answer to each question is 'yes'.
The answers to the four questions above illustrate two very important results for inequalities:

Rules for inequalities
1. An inequality remains true when the same number is added to or subtracted from both sides.
2. An inequality remains true when both sides are multiplied or divided by the same **positive** number.

Here are some numerical examples:

We know that the inequality	$6 > 4$
Add 4 to both sides:	$10 > 8$ … true
Subtract 7 from both sides:	$3 > 1$ … true
Multiply both sides by 3:	$18 > 12$ … true
Divide both sides by 2:	$3 > 2$ … true

Multiplication by a negative number

Consider again the inequality $6 > 4$.
Multiply both sides by -2: $\quad -12 > -8$ … false … as $-12 < -8$.

This illustrates that the inequality sign must be changed or reversed when both sides of an inequality are multiplied or divided by the same **negative** number.

(i) $2 < 5$, but $2 \times (-2) > 5 \times (-2)$
   i.e. $-4 > -10$

(ii) $8 > 6$, but $\dfrac{8}{-2} < \dfrac{6}{-2}$
   i.e. $-4 < -3$

> If an inequality is multiplied or divided by the same negative number, the inequality sign must be reversed.

Example 1

Solve the inequality $5x - 3 \geqslant 12, x \in N$ and graph the solution on the number line.

$5x - 3 \geqslant 12$
$\quad 5x \geqslant 12 + 3 \quad$ …add 3 to both sides
$\quad 5x \geqslant 15$
$\quad\quad x \geqslant 3 \quad$ …divide both sides by 5

The solution is graphed on the number line below.

Example 2

Solve the inequality $4 - 3x > -5, x \in Z$ and graph the solution on the number line.

$4 - 3x > -5$
$\quad -3x > -5 - 4 \quad$ …take 4 from each side
$\quad -3x > -9$
$\quad\quad 3x < 9 \quad$ …multiply both sides by -1 and reverse the inequality sign
$\quad\quad\; x < 3 \quad$ …divide both sides by 3
$\therefore\; x = 2, 1, 0, -1, …$

The solution is graphed on the number line below.

Exercise 1.8

1. Which of the following inequalities are equivalent to $a \geq 10$?
   - **A** $a - 5 \geq 5$
   - **B** $2a \geq 20$
   - **C** $a + 5 \geq 5$
   - **D** $\frac{1}{2}a \geq 5$
   - **E** $a + \frac{1}{2} \geq 10\frac{1}{2}$

2. Which of the following inequalities are equivalent to $m < 3$?
   - **A** $m + 2 < 5$
   - **B** $2m < 4$
   - **C** $3 > m$
   - **D** $8 > m + 5$
   - **E** $6 > 2m$

Solve the following inequalities and graph the solution on the number line in each case:

3. $x - 1 \leq 4, x \in N$
4. $3x - 2 \leq 10, x \in N$
5. $4x - 5 \leq 11, x \in N$
6. $3x + 5 \leq 14, x \in N$
7. $2x + 5 \leq 1, x \in Z$
8. $3x - 5 \leq 7, x \in Z$
9. $3x - 1 < -10, x \in Z$
10. $5x - 2 \leq 8, x \in Z$
11. $3x - 5 \leq 7, x \in R$
12. $2x + 2 \leq 8, x \in R$
13. $5x + 7 < 17, x \in R$
14. $3 - x \leq 4, x \in R$
15. $5 - 2x \geq -7, x \in R$
16. $1 - 5x > -14, x \in R$

17. If $A = \{x \mid 2x - 4 \leq 6\}$ and $B = \{x \mid 4 - 2x < 0\}$ where $x \in N$ in each set, list the elements of $A \cap B$.

18. If $a > b$, which *one* of the following is not true for all $a, b \in R$?
    - (i) $2a > 2b$
    - (ii) $-a < -b$
    - (iii) $a - 3 < b - 3$
    - (iv) $\frac{a}{5} > \frac{b}{5}$

19. List all the integers, x, for which $x^2 < 24$.

20. A new toll-road is built and c represents the number of cars entering the city per hour.
    - (i) Write an inequality for c, if the number of cars is known to be between 350 and 500 during peak hour.
    - (ii) Show the inequality on a number line.
    - (iii) Write a new inequality for c, if the number of cars is known to be between 120 and 200 inclusive during the middle of the day.
    - (iv) Show the inequality for c on a number line.
    - (v) Write a new inequality for c, if the traffic flow at night is thought to be about one-tenth of the traffic during the middle of the day.

Text & Tests 2 Higher Level

Test yourself 1

1. (i) Remove the brackets and simplify this expression:
   $2x(3x - 4) - 3(1 - 3x)$
   (ii) Solve the equation $2(x + 2) - 3(x - 3) = x + 7$

2. Solve the inequality $4 \leqslant 5x - 6, x \in R$, and illustrate your solution on the number line.

3. Write an expression for the perimeter of the given rectangle.
   If the perimeter of the rectangle is 36 cm, find the value of x.

   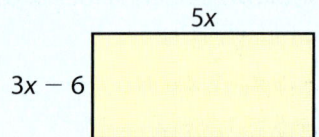

4. (i) Which of the expressions in the boxes has the highest value when $x = 5$?
   (ii) Which of the expressions has the lowest value when $x = 5$?

   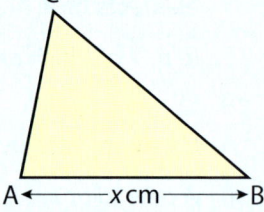

5. The side [AB] of this triangle is x cm long. [BC] is 3 cm longer than [AB], and [CA] is 1 cm shorter.
   (i) Write down an expression for the length of [BC].
   (ii) Write down an expression for the length of [CA].
   (iii) Write down and simplify an expression for the perimeter of triangle ABC.
   (iv) The perimeter of the triangle is 44 cm.
   Form an equation in x and solve it to find the lengths of the three side.

6. (i) By forming an equation, work out what x stands for.
   (ii) What is the length of the plank?

   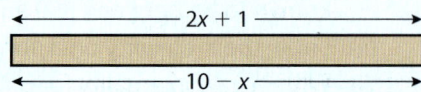

7. Show on the number line the range of values of x for which
   $2x - 1 < 7, x \in R$.

8. The given figure consists of a square and a rectangle.
   (i) If the perimeter of the figure is p cm, express p in terms of x, y and z.
   (ii) If $x = 2y, y = 2z$ and $p = 55$, find the value of x.

   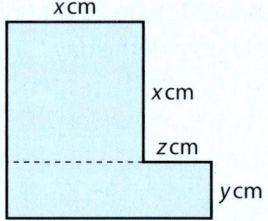

22

9. Solve the equation $5(x - 2) + 11 = 6x - 10$.

10. (i) Expand and simplify $(3x - 2)(2x^2 + x + 3)$.
    (ii) Evaluate $\dfrac{ab}{a - b}$ when $a = \tfrac{1}{2}$ and $b = \tfrac{1}{3}$.

11. One number is 4 greater than another number. When three times the smaller number is added to twice the larger one, the result is 43. Find the numbers.

12. Find the perimeter of each triangle below when $x = 3$.

    (i) 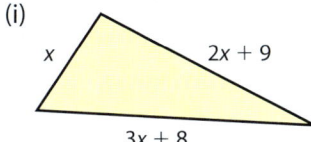   (ii)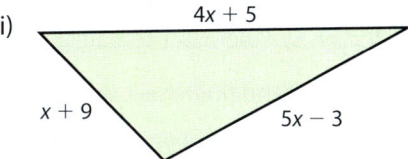

13. (i) Find an expression for the perimeter of the yellow triangle above.
    (ii) What value of x gives a yellow triangle with a perimeter of 143?

14. (i) Find an expression for the perimeter of the green triangle above.
    (ii) What value of x gives a green triangle with a perimeter of 50?
    (iii) What value of x gives both triangles above the same perimeter?

15. Divide each of the following:
    (i) $\dfrac{x^2 + 4x - 21}{x - 3}$ (ii) $\dfrac{2x^3 + 9x^2 + 3x - 4}{x + 4}$

16.
    A 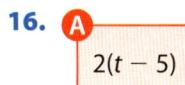 **B** $2(t^2 - 7)$ **C** $\dfrac{4t + 3}{-5}$ **D** $5 - t^2$ **E** $3t^2 - 11$ **F** $\dfrac{3t - 17}{2}$

    (i) When $t = 3$, three of the above expressions have a value of -4. Find these expressions.
    (ii) When $t = -2$, three of the above expressions have the same value. Find these expressions.

17. The given rectangle consists of a shaded part and an unshaded part. The shaded part is $3x$ by $2x$.

    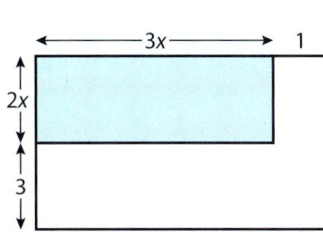

    (i) Find, in terms of x, the area of the whole rectangle.
    (ii) Find, in terms of x, the area of the unshaded part.
    (iii) If the area of the unshaded part is 58 sq. units, find the value of x.

Assignment:

Using forensic science, the height of a skeleton can be estimated from the length of various bones.

If a *humerus* is discovered, then the formula for the height(H) of the skeleton is,

$H = 3.08\, l_h + 70.45$ cm (for males)

Or $H = 3.36\, l_h + 57.97$ cm (for females)

where l_h is the length of the *humerus* bone.

Identify the *humerus*, *ulna* and *tibia* on the skeleton.

In groups, test the accuracy of the formula for each of the following bones by measuring the approximate length of each bone for one student.

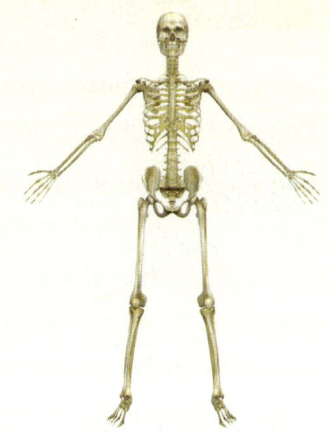

Male	Formula	$H_{formula}$	H_{true}	%Difference
Ulna	$3.7\, l_u + 70.45$ cm			
Humerus	$3.08\, l_h + 70.45$ cm			
Tibia	$2.52\, l_t + 75.79$ cm			

Female	Formula	$H_{formula}$	H_{true}	%Difference
Ulna	$4.27\, l_u + 57.76$ cm			
Humerus	$3.36\, l_h + 57.97$ cm			
Tibia	$2.90\, l_t + 59.24$ cm			

Using the length of a tibia or ulna or humerus of a student from a different group, predict the height of the student.

Factors

chapter 2

From first year, you will recall how to:

- identify terms and expressions,
- find factors,
- find the Higher Common Factor (HCF) of a group of numbers.

In this chapter, you will learn to:

- find the HCF of an algebraic expression,
- factorise by grouping terms,
- factorise the difference of two squares (DOTS),
- factorise a quadratic expression,
- use factors to simplify algebraic fractions.

Section 2.1 Factorising with common factors

Since $9 \times 5 = 45$, we say that 9 and 5 are **factors** of 45.
15 and 3 are also factors of 45.

The factors of 24 are 1, 2, 3, 4, 6, ⑫, 24.
The factors of 36 are 1, 2, 3, 4, 6, 9, ⑫, 18, 36.
The highest common factor is 12.

Here are two algebraic terms: $6xy$ and $12x$.
The highest common factor of the numbers is 6.
The highest common factor of the variables is x.
So the highest common factor of the two terms is $6 \times x$, i.e. $6x$.

Similarly, the highest common factors of:

(i) $3a$ and $6a^2 = 3a$ (ii) $6x^2 - 12xy = 6x$
(iii) $5a^2b - 15ab = 5ab$ (iv) $4x^2 + 16xy^2 = 4x$

Take the expression $5x + 10$.
$\quad 5x + 10 = 5(x + 2)$
$\quad$ 5 and $(x + 2)$ are called the **factors** of $5x + 10$.

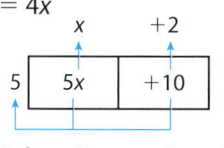

(Highest Common Factor)

Text & Tests 2 Higher Level

To factorise an algebraic expression:
> Find the highest common factor and write it outside the brackets or outside the array.
> Divide each term by this factor and write the results inside the brackets or on top of the array.
> Check your result by expanding the brackets.

Here are some expressions that have been factorised:

Using the array method.

(i) $x^2 + 7x = x(x + 7)$

	x	$+7$
x	x^2	$+7x$

(ii) $3x^2 - 9x = 3x(x - 3)$

	x	-3
$3x$	$3x^2$	$-9x$

(iii) $3xy - 12y = 3y(x - 4)$

	x	-4
$3y$	$3xy$	$-12y$

Exercise 2.1

1. Write down the highest common factor of each of these:
   (i) 9 and 12 (ii) 12 and 18 (iii) 14 and 21 (iv) 21 and 35

2. Write down the highest common factor of each of these:
   (i) $4x$ and $12x$ (ii) $3n$ and $9n$ (iii) $10x$ and $15x$
   (iv) $3a^2$ and $6a$ (v) $3xy$ and $12x^2$ (vi) $2a^2b$ and $6ab$

3. Copy and complete each of these:
   (i) $7x + 14y = 7($) (ii) $16a + 24b = 8($)
   (iii) $ab + bc = b($) (iv) $3a^2 + 6a = 3a($)
   (v) $5x^2 - 15xy = 5x($) (vi) $12xy - 18yz = 6y($)
   (vii) $15x^3 + 10x^2y = 5x^2($) (viii) $6a^2b - 8ab^2 + 4ab = 2ab($)

Factorise each of the following:

4. $6x + 18y$
5. $3ab + 3bc$
6. $6ax - 12ay$
7. $6a^2 - 12a$
8. $7x^2 - 28x$
9. $15x^2 + 25xy$

10. $3x^2 - 6x^2y$ **11.** $3ab^2 - 6ab$ **12.** $3p^2 - 6pq$

13. $4x^2 - 6xy + 8xz$ **14.** $5xy^2 - 20x^2y$ **15.** $4x^2y^2 - 8xy$

16. $2a^2b - 4ab^2 + 12abc$

Investigation:

(i) $3a^2 - 15ab$ $2a^3 - a^2b$ $7ab - 35b^2$

(ii) $4a^2 - 2ab$ $2a^2b + 2a$ $2ab - 10b^2$

(iii) $7ab + 7b^2$ $5a - 25b$ $2ab^2 + 2b$

(iv) $4ab - 2b^2$ $3b^2a + 3b^3$ $a^3 - 5a^2b$ $2a^2b + 3ab^2$

Fully factorise each expression above.
Use the code below to find a letter for *each* factor.

Code	E	H	P	S	O	A	I	L	G	R	T	U	N
	5	$2a$	$3a$	$2b$	$7b$	a^2	ab	$3b^2$	$a+b$	$a-5b$	$2a-b$	$ab+1$	$2a+3b$

Rearrange each set of letters to spell a bird.

(i) _ _ _ _ _ _   (ii) _ _ _ _ _ _   (iii) _ _ _ _ _ _   (iv) _ _ _ _ _ _ _ _

Note: $3b^2a + 3b^3 = 3b^2(a+b)$

Section 2.2 Factorising by grouping terms

Some four-termed expressions do not have an overall common factor but can be factorised using pairs of brackets or by using the array method.

Factorise $\underbrace{ab + ac}_{} + \underbrace{bd + dc}_{}$

$= a(b+c) + d(b+c)$ ... factorising each pair separately

$= (b+c)(a+d)$ ... factorising the common factor

Or $ab + ac + bd + dc$ (Array – method)

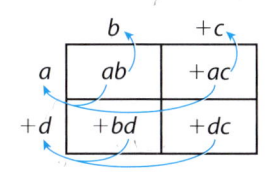

	b	+c
a	ab	+ac
+d	+bd	+dc

27

Example 1

Find the factors of   (i) $2ab + 2ac + 3bx + 3cx$
                           (ii) $3ax - bx - 3ay + by$

(i) $2ab + 2ac + 3bx + 3cx$

	b	$+c$
$2a$	$2ab$	$+2ac$
$+3x$	$+3bx$	$+3cx$

$= (b + c)(2a + 3x)$

(ii) $3ax - bx - 3ay + by$

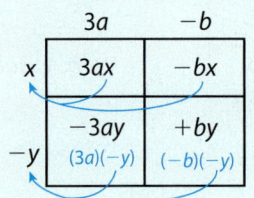

	$3a$	$-b$
x	$3ax$	$-bx$
$-y$	$-3ay$ $(3a)(-y)$	$+by$ $(-b)(-y)$

Note:
(i) $-3ay$ is factored as $3a(-y)$
(ii) $+by$ is factored as $(-b)(-y)$

$= (3a - b)(x - y)$

Note: Sometimes it may be necessary to reorder terms before the method shown above can be used.

Example 2

Factorise $6x^2 + 2a - 3ax - 4x$

Regroup: $6x^2 - 3ax + 2a - 4x$

$3x(2x - a) + 2(a - 2x)$ ...

$= 3x(2x - a) - 2(2x - a)$

$= (2x - a)(3x - 2)$

or

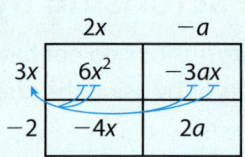

	$2x$	$-a$
$3x$	$6x^2$	$-3ax$
-2	$-4x$	$2a$

Note: Rearrange the terms so that an x can be factored horizontally and vertically.
Note: $-4x$ is factored as $2x(-2)$ and $+2a$ is factored as $-a(-2)$

∴ $6x^2 + 2a - 3ax - 4x = (2x - a)(3x - 2)$

Note: Be careful when dealing with negative terms.

For example,   (i) $-3ax - 6ay = -3a(x + 2y)$
                     (ii) $-5x^2 + 10xy = -5x(x - 2y)$

Chapter 2 Factors

Exercise 2.2

Factorise fully each of the following using the array or brackets method:

1. $2a(x + y) + 3(x + y)$
2. $3x(2a - b) - 4(2a - b)$
3. $3a(2b - c) - 4(2b - c)$
4. $2x(5y - z) + b(5y - z)$
5. $2a(x - 2y) - (x - 2y)$
6. $a^2 + ab + ac + bc$
7. $x^2 - ax + 3x - 3a$
8. $ab + ac - 5b - 5c$
9. $ab + 5b + 3a + 15$
10. $3x^2 - 3xz + 4xy - 4yz$
11. $2c^2 - 4cd + c - 2d$
12. $2ax - 6ay - 3x + 9y$
13. $2ac - 4ad + bc - 2bd$
14. $3xy - 3xyz + 2z - 2z^2$
15. $8ax + 4ay - 6bx - 3by$
16. $6ax^2 + 9a - 8x^2 - 12$
17. $x(2y - z) - 2y + z$
18. $an - 5a - 5b + bn$
19. $2x^2y - 2xz - 3xy + 3z$
20. $7y^2 - 21by + 2ay - 6ab$
21. $4a^2b - 3b - 6a + 2ab^2$
22. $12a^2 - 8ab + 9ac - 6bc$
23. $3abx^2 - 5axy - 3bxy + 5y^2$
24. $6a^2c - 6ab - 4bc + 9a^3$
25. $x^2 - x(2a - b) - 2ab$
26. $6x^2 - 3y(3x - 2a) - 4ax$

Section 2.3 Difference of two squares

Numbers such as 1, 4, 9, 16, 25, ... are called **perfect squares** as they are obtained by multiplying some whole number by itself, e.g., $4 = 2^2, 9 = 3^2, ...$

Similarly, in algebra, $4x^2 = (2x)^2$ and $9y^2 = (3y)^2$.

Expressions such as $10^2 - 4^2, x^2 - y^2$ and $4x^2 - 9$ are known as the **difference of two squares**.

When you multiply $(x + y)(x - y)$, you get $x^2 - y^2$.
Thus, the factors of $x^2 - y^2$ are $(x + y)(x - y)$.

	x	$+y$
x	x^2	$+xy$
$-y$	$-xy$	$-y^2$

$$x^2 - y^2 = (x + y)(x - y)$$

In words: $(\text{first})^2 - (\text{second})^2 = (\text{first} + \text{second})(\text{first} - \text{second})$

Investigation:

Consider a large square of area x^2 with a smaller square of area y^2 cut from it.

A: Copy and complete the following:

In terms of A, B, C and D:

(i) the area of the large square, $x^2 =$
(ii) the area of the smaller square, $y^2 =$
(iii) ∴ the area of $x^2 - y^2 =$

In terms of x and y:

(i) the area of A =   (ii) the area of B =

∴ (iii) the area of A + B =   , which factorises as =

Conclusion ∴ $x^2 - y^2 =$

B: If C is the image of B by reflection in the line l, the area of C = the area of B.
In terms of x and y write down the length of (i) $a =$ (ii) $b =$
∴ the area of (A + B) = the area of (A + C) = (length) × (width) =

Conclusion ∴ $x^2 - y^2 =$

Example 1

Factorise

(i) $9x^2 - 4$ (ii) $25a^2 - 81b^2$ (iii) $x^2y^2 - 4a^2b^2$

(i) $9x^2 - 4 = (3x)^2 - (2)^2 = (3x + 2)(3x - 2)$

(ii) $25a^2 - 81b^2 = (5a)^2 - (9b)^2 = (5a + 9b)(5a - 9b)$

(iii) $x^2y^2 - 4a^2b^2 = (xy)^2 - (2ab)^2 = (xy + 2ab)(xy - 2ab)$

Example 2

Factorise $12x^2 - 75y^2$

Here it is not immediately obvious that $12x^2 - 75y^2$ involves the difference of two squares.

However, if we take out the common factor 3 we get $3(4x^2 - 25y^2)$.

$$12x^2 - 75y^2 = 3(4x^2 - 25y^2)$$
$$= 3[(2x)^2 - (5y)^2]$$
$$= 3(2x + 5y)(2x - 5y)$$

Chapter 2 Factors

Exercise 2.3

Factorise each of the following:

1. $x^2 - y^2$
2. $a^2 - b^2$
3. $x^2 - 4y^2$
4. $x^2 - 16y^2$
5. $4x^2 - y^2$
6. $9x^2 - 16y^2$
7. $4a^2 - 25b^2$
8. $36x^2 - 49y^2$
9. $64x^2 - 9y^2$
10. $36 - 121y^2$
11. $49a^2 - 4b^2$
12. $(xy)^2 - 4$
13. $(ab)^2 - 25$
14. $x^2y^2 - 16$
15. $a^2b^2 - 49$
16. $(5xy)^2 - 36$
17. $16a^2b^2 - 25$
18. $9x^2y^2 - 1$
19. $4a^2b^2 - 49c^2d^2$
20. $121a^2 - 64b^2c^2$
21. $81h^2k^2 - 25p^2q^2$

22. First take out the highest common factor and then factorise each of the following:
    (i) $3x^2 - 27y^2$
    (ii) $12x^2 - 3y^2$
    (iii) $27x^2 - 3y^2$
    (iv) $45 - 5x^2$
    (v) $45k^2 - 20$
    (vi) $4a^2x^2 - 36y^2$

23. Simplify $(3x + b)(6x - 2b) - (2y + b)(4y - 2b)$.
    Now factorise fully the simplified expression.

24. Simplify and hence factorise $(3x - 2y)^2 - y(5y - 12x)$.

Investigation:

A: A practical application of the "difference of two squares" is to be able to calculate some sums quickly without using a calculator.
Remember: $a^2 - b^2 = (a - b)(a + b)$
Make a large poster evaluating each of the following. (The first one is done for you)

$51^2 - 49^2$	$(51 - 49)(51 + 49)$	$(2)(100)$	200
$96^2 - 4^2$			
$23^2 - 17^2$			
$(7.9)^2 - (2.1)^2$			
$(9.4)^2 - (0.6)^2$			

Using the last line of the chart above make up your own "difference sum" [Examine the previous sums carefully]

B: Given that a^4 can be written as $(a^2)^2$ investigate how $a^4 - b^4$ can be written as the product of three factors.

$a^4 - b^4 = ((\quad)^2 - (\quad)^2) = (\quad)(\quad) = (\quad)(\quad)(\quad)$

Text & Tests 2 Higher Level

Section 2.4 Factorising quadratic expressions

An expression of the form $ax^2 + bx + c$, where a, b and c are numbers is called a **quadratic expression** since the highest power of x is 2.

Since $(x + 5)(x + 2) = x^2 + 7x + 10$, we say that $(x + 5)$ and $(x + 2)$ are the factors of $x^2 + 7x + 10$.

To find the factors of a quadratic expression, we use the array method in reverse, e.g. to find the factors of $x^2 + 7x + 10$.

1.
	x	( )
x	x^2	?
( )	?	10

2.
	x	+5
x	x^2	5x
+2	2x	10

$1 \times 10 = 10$

	1	10
*	2	5	→ 7

> An expression in the form $ax^2 + bx + c$ is generally called a quadratic trinomial as it contains 3 terms.

$x^2 + 2x + 5x + 10 = x^2 + 7x + 10$
$\therefore x^2 + 7x + 10 = (x + 5)(x + 2)$

Notes:
(i) The grid on the right helps to find the factors of the constant term which add up to the coefficient of the middle term.
(ii) If the coefficient of x^2 is greater than 1, the same grid is used to find the factors of the product of the constant term and the coefficient of x^2 which add to the middle term.

> **Example 1**
>
> Factorise $3x^2 + 10x + 8$.
>
> The factors of $3x^2 + 10x + 8$ will take the form $(3x + ?)(x + ?)$
>
> 1.
> | | x | |
> |---|---|---|
> | 3x | $3x^2$ | ? |
> | | ? | 8 |
>
> 2.
> | | x | +2 |
> |---|---|---|
> | 3x | $3x^2$ | 6x |
> | +4 | 4x | 8 |
>
> $3 \times 8 = 24$
>
> | | 1 | 24 |
> |---|---|---|
> | | 2 | 12 |
> | | 3 | 8 |
> | * | 4 | 6 | → 10
>
> $3x^2 + 4x + 6x + 8 = 3x^2 + 10x + 8$
> $\therefore 3x^2 + 10x + 8 = (3x + 4)(x + 2)$

Chapter 2 Factors

Final term positive

If the third term of a quadratic expression is positive and the middle term is negative, e.g. $x^2 - 8x + 15$, the factors will take the form shown on the right.

$(x - ?)(x - ?)$

Example 2

Find the factors of $2x^2 - 11x + 12$.

The factors will take the form $(2x - ?)(x - ?)$

1.

	$2x$	
x	$2x^2$	?
	?	$+12$

2.

	$2x$	-3
x	$2x^2$	$-3x$
-4	$-8x$	$+12$

$2 \times 12 = 24$

-1	-24
-2	-12
* -3	-8	→ -11
-4	-6

$2x^2 - 8x - 3x + 12 = 2x^2 - 11x + 12$

$\therefore 2x^2 - 11x + 12 = (2x - 3)(x - 4)$

Final term negative

If the final term is negative, the factors will take either of the forms shown on the right.

$(x + ?)(x - ?)$
or
$(x - ?)(x + ?)$

Example 3

Factorise (i) $8x^2 + 10x - 3$ (ii) $7x^2 - 19x - 6$

(i) $8x^2 = (4x)(2x)$

1.

	$2x$	
$4x$	$8x^2$	
		-3

2.

	$2x$	$+3$
$4x$	$8x^2$	$+12x$
-1	$-2x$	-3

$8 \times -3 = -24$

-1	$+24$
* -2	$+12$	→ $+10$
-3	$+8$
-4	$+6$
-6	$+4$
-8	$+3$
-12	$+2$

$8x^2 + 12x - 2x - 3 = 8x^2 + 10x - 3$

$\therefore 8x^2 + 10x - 3 = (4x - 1)(2x + 3)$

Text & Tests 2 Higher Level

(ii) $7x^2 = (7x)(x)$

1.

	x	
$7x$	$7x^2$	?
	?	-6

2.

	x	-3
$7x$	$7x^2$	$-21x$
$+2$	$2x$	-6

$7 \times -6 = -42$

-1	42
-2	21
-3	14
-6	7
-7	6
-14	3
*-21	2	$\rightarrow -19$

$7x^2 - 21x + 2x - 6 = 7x^2 - 19x - 6$

$\therefore 7x^2 - 19x - 6 = (x - 3)(7x + 2)$

Exercise 2.4

Factorise each of the following:

1. $x^2 + 5x + 6$
2. $x^2 + 8x + 12$
3. $x^2 + 9x + 14$
4. $x^2 + 11x + 24$
5. $x^2 + 12x + 20$
6. $x^2 + 12x + 27$
7. $x^2 + 11x + 30$
8. $x^2 + 15x + 44$
9. $x^2 + 20x + 36$
10. $2x^2 + 5x + 2$
11. $2x^2 + 11x + 14$
12. $5x^2 + 21x + 4$
13. $x^2 - 7x + 12$
14. $x^2 - 9x + 18$
15. $x^2 - 9x + 20$
16. $x^2 - 14x + 24$
17. $x^2 - 12x + 27$
18. $x^2 - 13x + 36$
19. $2x^2 - 7x + 3$
20. $3x^2 - 17x + 10$
21. $5x^2 - 17x + 6$
22. $3x^2 - 17x + 20$
23. $5x^2 + 27x - 18$
24. $3x^2 - 14x + 15$
25. $x^2 - 4x - 12$
26. $x^2 - 3x - 10$
27. $x^2 + 7x - 18$
28. $x^2 + 7x - 30$
29. $x^2 - 13x - 30$
30. $x^2 - 18x - 40$
31. $12x^2 - 11x - 5$
32. $6x^2 + x - 15$
33. $8x^2 - 14x + 3$
34. $3x^2 + 13x - 10$
35. $9x^2 + 24x + 16$
36. $5x^2 - 31x + 6$
37. $3x^2 - x - 14$
38. $6x^2 - 11x + 3$
39. $12x^2 - 23x + 10$
40. $9x^2 + 25x - 6$
41. $6x^2 + x - 22$
42. $9x^2 - x - 10$
43. $4x^2 - 11x + 6$
44. $10x^2 - 17x - 20$
45. $36x^2 - 7x - 4$
46. $12x^2 - 17x + 6$
47. $15x^2 - 14x - 8$
48. $24x^2 + 2x - 15$

Chapter 2 Factors

Section 2.5 Using factors to simplify algebraic fractions

The fraction $\frac{10}{15}$ can be simplified by dividing above and below by the common factor 5.

$$\frac{^2 10}{_3 15} = \frac{2}{3}$$

Similarly, $\frac{x^2 - 4}{x + 2}$ can be simplified by dividing above and below by a common factor.

$$\frac{x^2 - 4}{x + 2} = \frac{(x + 2)(x - 2)}{(x + 2)} = x - 2$$

> **Example 1**
>
> Simplify (i) $\frac{3n - 12}{n - 4}$ (ii) $\frac{3x^2 - 5x - 2}{x - 2}$
>
> (i) $\frac{3n - 12}{n - 4} = \frac{3(n - 4)}{(n - 4)}$
> $= 3$
>
> (ii) $\frac{3x^2 - 5x - 2}{x - 2} = \frac{(3x + 1)(x - 2)}{(x - 2)}$
> $= 3x + 1$

Exercise 2.5

1. Simplify each of the following:

(i) $\frac{14}{35}$ (ii) $\frac{7x}{14}$ (iii) $\frac{9x^2}{3x}$ (iv) $\frac{8p^2}{2p}$ (v) $\frac{9x^2 y}{3xy}$

2. Simplify each of the following:

(i) $\frac{4x + 4y}{4}$ (ii) $\frac{12(a + b)}{3(a + b)}$ (iii) $\frac{3x + 12}{x(x + 4)}$ (iv) $\frac{4a - 8b}{3(a - 2b)}$

Simplify each of the following, using factors where necessary:

3. $\frac{(x - 1)(x + 3)}{x + 3}$ **4.** $\frac{2(y - 1)(y + 3)}{y - 1}$ **5.** $\frac{x^2 + 8x + 7}{x + 1}$

6. $\frac{x - 4}{x^2 - 6x + 8}$ **7.** $\frac{x - 2}{x^2 + 5x - 14}$ **8.** $\frac{3x - 3}{x^2 - 2x + 1}$

9. $\frac{2x - 6}{x^2 + x - 12}$ **10.** $\frac{x^2 + x - 30}{x - 5}$ **11.** $\frac{a^2 + 2ab}{3a + 6b}$

12. $\frac{x^2 - 9}{x - 3}$ **13.** $\frac{a^2 - 16}{3a - 12}$ **14.** $\frac{n + 9}{n^2 + 18n + 81}$

15. $\frac{4x - 8}{x^2 - 4}$ **16.** $\frac{2x^2 + 5x - 3}{2x - 1}$ **17.** $\frac{2x^2 + 11x + 15}{2x + 5}$

18. $\frac{ab - ac}{b - c}$ **19.** $\frac{5 - x}{x - 5}$ **20.** $\frac{3a + 9}{a^2 - 1} \div \frac{a + 3}{a - 1}$

Text & Tests 2 Higher Level

Test yourself 2

Note: When the phrase "factorise fully" is used, you must include all the constant and algebraic factors in your answer.

1. (i) Complete the following: $6x^2 - 18xy = 6x(\qquad)$
   (ii) Factorise $x^2 - 10x + 24$

2. Factorise each of these:
   (i) $7a + 7b + xa + xb$
   (ii) $25a^2 - 81$

3. Factorise and hence simplify $\dfrac{4x^2 - 7x - 2}{4x^2 - 8x}$

4. Factorise each of these:
   (i) $6x^2 - x - 2$
   (ii) $6a^2 + 2ab + 3ac + bc$

5. Factorise each of these:
   (i) $6a^2x + 3ax^2 - 9ax$
   (ii) $3x^2 - 48$

6. Factorise fully and simplify $\dfrac{6x^2 - 11x - 10}{4x^2 - 25}$

7. Factorise each of these:
   (i) $8a^2b + 2ab^2$
   (ii) $3x^2 - 16x + 21$

8. Factorise fully each of these:
   (i) $2x^2 - 8y^2$
   (ii) $2xy - xz - 2y + z$

9. Simplify $(2x - z)(6x + 3z) - (6a - 3z)(2a + z)$ and factorise fully the simplified expression.

10. Factorise each of the following:
    (i) $15bc - 3c^2$
    (ii) $24x^2 + x - 3$

11. Factorise fully each of these:
    (i) $8x^2 - 2y^2$
    (ii) $ax - 2ay + 2by - bx$

12. Factorise fully and simplify $\dfrac{10x^2 - 29x + 10}{4x^2 - 25}$

13. Factorise each of the following:
    (i) $3x^2 + 2x - 8$
    (ii) $a^2 + ab - 2a - 2b$

14. Factorise fully each of these:
    (i) $5a^2 - 125b^2$
    (ii) $2x^3 + 3x^2 - 2xy^2 - 3y^2$

15. Factorise and simplify $\dfrac{2x^2 - 15x + 18}{x^3 - 36x}$

Chapter 2 Factors

Assignment:

An expression containing a term with x^3 in it is called a CUBIC expression and has three factors.

If we know one of the factors of a cubic expression, we can work out the other factors.

Study each of the following boxes. Copy and complete the grid by deducing the values of A, B, C, D, E and F.

1. Find the factors of $x^3 - x^2 - 5x - 3$, if one factor is $x - 3$.

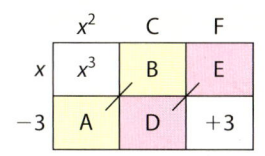

	x^2	C	F
x	x^3	B	E
-3	A	D	$+3$

The factors of $x^3 - x^2 - 5x - 3$ are $(x - 3)(x^2 \qquad)$

Now factorise the quadratic factor to give;

$$x^3 - x^2 - 5x - 3 = (x - 3)(x \quad)(x \quad)$$

2. Find the factors of $2x^3 - x^2 - 13x - 6$, if one factor is $x + 2$.

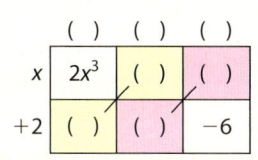

	( )	( )	( )
x	$2x^3$	( )	( )
$+2$	( )	( )	-6

$\therefore 2x^3 - x^2 - 13x - 6 = (x + 2)(2x^2 \qquad)$

$\therefore 2x^3 - x^2 - 13x - 6 = (x + 2)(2x \quad)(x \quad)$

3. Design a poster to show how to find **all** the factors of $x^3 + 4x^2 - 17x - 60$ if we know that one of the factors is $(x - 4)$.

chapter 3 Sets

From first year, you will recall how to:

- define a set and an element,
- identify a null set,
- identify the universal set,
- use the symbols, ∈, ∉, ∪, ∩,
- identify equal sets,
- find subsets of a given set,
- draw and interpret 2 – set Venn diagrams,
- find the cardinal number, #, of a set,
- find the complement of a set.

In this chapter, you will learn to:

- generate rules to define a given set,
- find the set difference, using the symbol /,
- place the number sets, *N, Q, Z* and *R* into a Venn Diagram,
- investigate whether the operations of intersection, union and difference are commutative,
- investigate whether the operations of intersection, union and difference are associative,
- draw and interpret Venn Diagrams involving 3 sets,
- use Venn Diagrams to solve word problems.

Section 3.1 Revision of sets terminology

In this section we will revise the sets operations that you will have met in first-year.

1. Equal sets

Two sets are **equal** if they contain exactly the same elements.
If $A = \{2, 4, 6, 8\}$ and $B = \{4, 6, 8, 2\}$, then **A = B**.

2. Union of two sets (*A* ∪ *B*)

The **union** of two sets *A* and *B* is the set of elements that are in *A* or *B*.

It is found by putting together all the elements of *A* and *B* into a new set without repeating any element. The new set is written as **A ∪ B**.

If $A = \{1, 2, 3, 4\}$ and $B = \{3, 4, 5, 6\}$,
then $A \cup B = \{1, 2, 3, 4, 5, 6\}$.

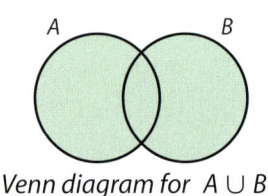

Venn diagram for A ∪ B

Chapter 3 Sets

3. Intersection of two sets (A ∩ B)

The **intersection** of two sets A and B is the set of elements that are in both A **and** B.

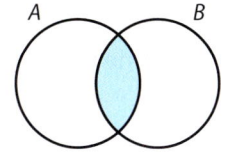

It is found by putting all the elements *common* to both A and B into a new set.

The new set is written as **A ∩ B**.

If A = {1, 2, 3, 4} and B = {3, 4, 5, 6}
then A ∩ B = {3, 4}

In the given Venn diagram, A ∩ B is shaded.

4. Subsets (B ⊂ A)

Set B is a **subset** of set A if all the elements of B are contained in A.

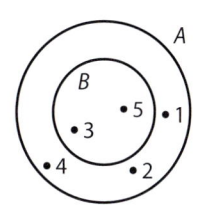

It is written **B ⊂ A**.

If A = {1, 2, 3, 4, 5} and B = {3, 5}, then B ⊂ A.

5. The universal set (U)

The set from which all other sets being considered are taken is called the **universal set**.

It is denoted by the capital letter **U** and is represented by a rectangle.

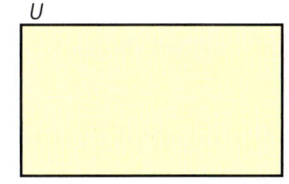

6. The complement of a set (A′)

The complement of a set A is the set of elements in the universal set U which are not in A.

It is written as **A′** and is illustrated by the shaded area in the given Venn diagram.

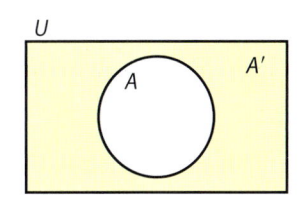

If U = {1, 2, 3, 4, 5, 6, 7, 8, 9, 10}
and A = {2, 3, 5, 7}, the set of *prime* numbers between 1 and 10.
then A′ = {1, 4, 6, 8, 9, 10}, the set of *non-prime* numbers in U.

7. The cardinal number of a set (#)

The number of elements in a set is called the **cardinal number** of the set.

The symbol **#** is used to denote the cardinal number.

From the given Venn diagram,

#A = 6   #B = 6
#(A ∩ B) = 2   #(A ∪ B) = 10.

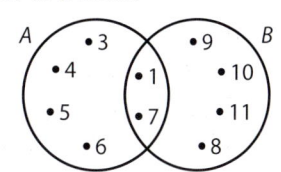

39

Text & Tests 2 Higher Level

8. Rules for generating sets

When the number of elements in a set is small we usually list the elements.

A rule is needed to generate the elements of a large set.

e.g. $A = \{x \mid -8 \leq x \leq 8, x \in Z\} \therefore A = \{-8, -7, -6, -5, \ldots \ldots 5, 6, 7, 8\}$
$B = \{x \mid 1 \leq x \leq 25, x \in Z\} \therefore B = \{1, 2, 3, 4, \ldots \ldots, 22, 23, 24, 25\}$

Note; $A \cap B = \{1, 2, 3, 4, 5, 6, 7, 8\}$

e.g. $C = \{2x + 1 \mid -3 < x < 2, x \in Z\} \therefore C = \{-3, -1, 1, 3\}$

Remember

The set of natural numbers is $N = \{1, 2, 3, 4, 5, \ldots\}$
The set of integer numbers is $Z = \{\ldots -3, -2, -1, 0, 1, 2, 3, \ldots\}$
The sets of rational numbers (fractions) is $Q = \left\{\dfrac{a}{b}, \text{ where } a, b \in Z \text{ and } b \neq 0\right\}$
The set of real numbers is R.

Example 1

In a class of 30 pupils, 17 study German, 16 study Spanish and 5 study both German and Spanish.

Represent this information on a Venn diagram.

Use the Venn diagram to write down the number of pupils who study

(i) German only (ii) Spanish only (iii) neither German nor Spanish.

We use the given information to fill in the Venn diagram.

First place 5 in the set $G \cap S$.

(i) German only $= 17 - 5 = 12$
(ii) Spanish only $= 16 - 5 = 11$
(iii) Neither $= 30 - 12 - 5 - 11$
$= 2$

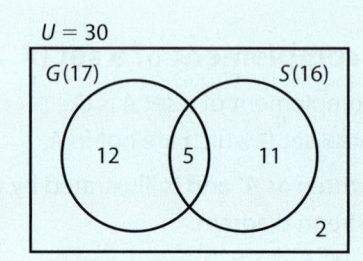

$U = 30$
$G(17)$ $S(16)$
12 5 11
2

Example 2

Find the set $A \cap B \cap C$ given that:

(i) $A = \{x \mid -3 < x \leq 12, x \in Z\}$
(ii) $B = \{x \mid 2 < x < 9, x \in N\}$
(iii) $C = \{2x \mid -4 \leq x \leq 10, x \in Z\}$

$A = \{-2, -1, \ldots \ldots, 11, 12\}$
$B = \{3, 4, \ldots \ldots, 7, 8\}$
$C = \{-8, -6, -4, \ldots \ldots \ldots 16, 18, 20\}$
$\therefore A \cap B \cap C = \{4, 6, 8\}$

Chapter 3 Sets

Exercise 3.1

1. From the given Venn diagram, list the elements of each of these sets:
   (i) A
   (ii) B
   (iii) A ∩ B
   (iv) A ∪ B

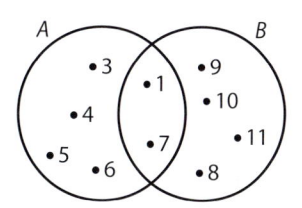

2. Using the Venn diagram on the right, list the elements of the following sets:
   (i) A
   (ii) A ∩ B
   (iii) A'
   (iv) B'
   (v) (A ∪ B)'
   (vi) A' ∩ B

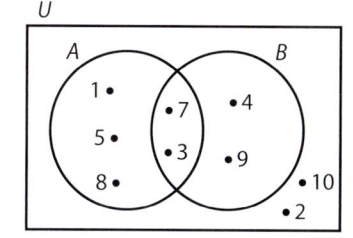

3. In the given Venn diagram, each dot represents an element.
   Write down
   (i) #A
   (ii) #B
   (iii) #U
   (iv) #(A ∪ B)
   (v) #(A ∩ B)
   (vi) #(A ∪ B)'

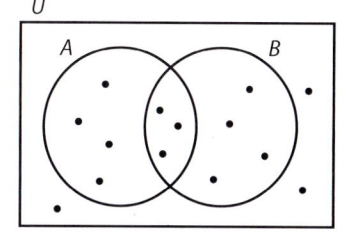

4. Draw a Venn diagram to illustrate this information:
   #(A) = 15, #(B) = 14 and #(A ∩ B) = 7
   Find #(A ∪ B).

5. Given U = {1, 2, 3, ..., 12}
   A = {1, 2, 3, 4, 5, 6}
   B = {3, 5, 7, 9, 11}

   Make a copy of the given Venn diagram and fill in the given information.

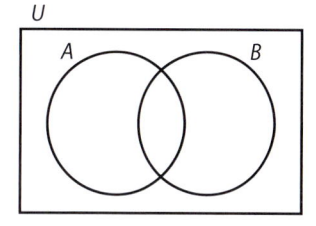

6. Copy the given Venn diagram and fill in the four regions, given that
   #U = 42, #A = 21, #B = 18 and #(A ∩ B) = 6
   Now write down
   (i) #(A ∪ B)
   (ii) #B'
   (iii) #(A ∪ B)'

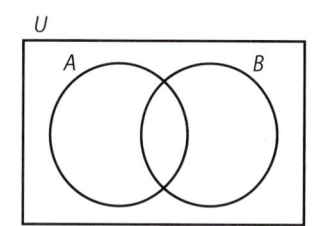

41

Text & Tests 2 Higher Level

7. Copy this Venn diagram and shade in the region that represents $A' \cap B$.

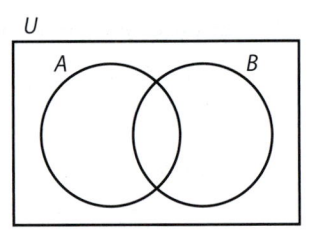

8. In the given Venn diagram,
   U is the set of pupils in the class
   B is the set of pupils who play basketball
   F is the set of pupils who play football.
   (i) How many pupils play both games?
   (ii) How many pupils are there in the class?
   (iii) How many pupils play football only?
   (iv) How many pupils play neither of the two games?

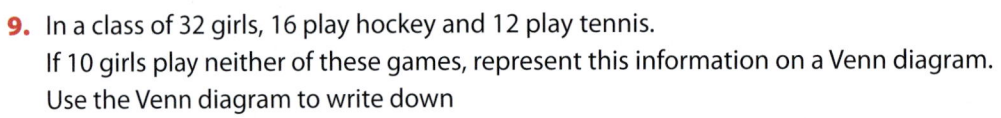

9. In a class of 32 girls, 16 play hockey and 12 play tennis.
   If 10 girls play neither of these games, represent this information on a Venn diagram.
   Use the Venn diagram to write down
   (i) the number of girls who play both games
   (ii) the number of girls who play hockey but not tennis.

10. In a survey of 40 households, 22 had a dog and 16 had a cat.
    If 8 households had both a cat and a dog, represent this information on a Venn diagram and write down how many households had neither.

11. (a) In words describe the following sets:
    (i) N   (ii) Z   (iii) Q

    (b) What set is equal to each of the following sets:
    (i) $N \cap Z$ (ii) $N \cup Z$ (iii) $Q \cup Z \cup N$ (iv) $Q \cap (N \cup Z)$

12. 30 students in Laura's class filled in their subject choices for fifth year.
    3 students wanted to study both French (A) and Spanish (B)
    6 students wanted to study neither.
    Twice as many wanted to study French as Spanish.
    Copy and complete the Venn diagram for the subject choices in her class.
    [Hint: let x be the number of students in B only]

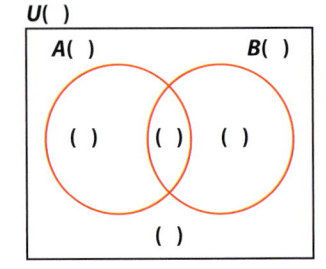

13. List the elements in each of the following sets:
   (i) $A = \{x \mid -2 < x \leq 8, x \in Z\}$
   (ii) $B = \{2x \mid -4 \leq x \leq 2, x \in N\}$
   (iii) $C = \{3x + 2 \mid -1 < x \leq 4, x \in Z\}$
   (iv) $D = \{4x - 1 \mid -2 < x < 2, x \in Z\}$

14. Find the elements in (i) $A \cap B$ (ii) $A \cup B$
given that $A = \{x \mid -5 < x \leq 3, x \in Z\}$ and $B = \{2x \mid -3 < x < 4, x \in Z\}$

15. All 32 pupils in a class study French (F) or German (G) or both.
24 study French and 18 study German.
If $\#(F \cap G) = x$, write an equation in x and solve it to find its value.

16. Given that $\#(U) = 18$, $\#(A) = 11$ and $\#(B) = 13$, find
   (i) the minimum value of $\#(A \cap B)$
   (ii) the maximum value of $\#(A \cup B)$
   (iii) the maximum value of $\#(A \cap B)$.

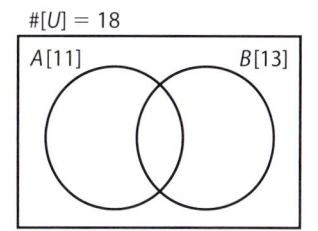

17. In the given Venn diagram,
$\#(A) = 24$, $\#(B) = 16$ and $\#(A \cup B)' = 6$.
Use this diagram to find
   (i) the maximum value of $\#(A \cap B)$
   (ii) the maximum value of $\#(U)$
   (iii) the minimum value of $\#(U)$.

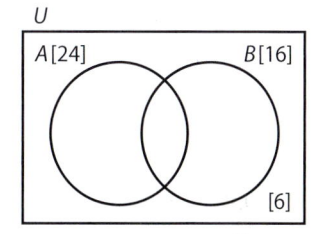

Section 3.2 Set difference

In this section we introduce a new term called **set difference**.

To illustrate set difference, we take two sets A and B, where

$A = \{1, 2, 3, 4, 5, 6\}$ and $B = \{4, 6, 8, 10\}$.

If we remove from set A all the elements which are in set B, we have **A less B**.

A less B is denoted by **A\B**.

$\therefore \ A \backslash B = \{1, 2, 3, 5\}$

Set difference $A \backslash B$ is the set of elements of A which are not in B.

Set difference can be illustrated by Venn diagrams as follows:

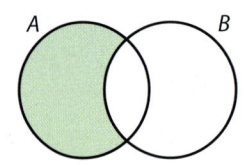

The shaded area is **A\B**.
The set of elements that are in *A* but **not** in *B*.

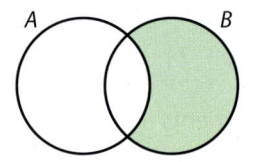

The shaded area is **B\A**.
The set of elements that are in *B* but **not** in *A*.

Example 1

If $A = \{a, b, c, d, e, f, g\}$, and $B = \{e, f, g, h, i\}$, find

(i) $A \backslash B$ (ii) $B \backslash A$ (iii) $(A \cup B) \backslash (A \cap B)$

(i) $A \backslash B$ is the set of elements of *A* which are not in *B*.
∴ $A \backslash B = \{a, b, c, d\}$

(ii) $B \backslash A = \{h, i\}$

(iii) $A \cup B = \{a, b, c, d, e, f, g, h, i\}$ and $A \cap B = \{e, f, g\}$
∴ $(A \cup B) \backslash (A \cap B) = \{a, b, c, d, h, i\}$

Investigation:

A: Copy and complete the following table by describing in words and where possible in symbols, each set of numbers below.

Set	Words	Symbols
$Z \backslash N$	The set of integers less the set of natural numbers i.e. the set of negative numbers including 0.	
$Z \cup N$		
$Z \cap N$		
$Q \backslash Z$		
$Q \cup Z$		
$Q \cap Z$		
$R \backslash Q$		
$R \cup Q$		
$R \cap Q$		

B: Fill in the missing sets: Generally; if $A \subset B$ then (i) $A \cup B =$
(ii) $A \cap B =$

The commutative property

It is obvious that $3 + 4 = 4 + 3$ and that $3 \times 4 = 4 \times 3$.

This illustrates that addition and multiplication are **commutative**.

By this we mean that we can change the order in which two numbers are added (or multiplied) without changing the result.

However, since $6 - 2 \neq 2 - 6$, we can say that subtraction is **not commutative**.

Again, if $A = \{2, 3, 4, 5\}$ and $B = \{4, 5, 6, 7\}$,
then $A \cup B = B \cup A = \{2, 3, 4, 5, 6, 7\}$.
Also, $A \cap B = B \cap A = \{4, 5\}$.

The union of sets and the intersection of sets are commutative.

Taking the sets A and B above, we have
(i) $A \backslash B = \{2, 3\}$ (ii) $B \backslash A = \{6, 7\}$

This illustrates that $A \backslash B \neq B \backslash A$ and so set difference is not commutative.

Remember Set difference is not commutative.

Exercise 3.2

1. $A = \{1, 2, 3, 4, 5, 6, 7, 8\}, B = \{3, 6, 9, 10\}$ and $C = \{2, 4, 6, 8\}$.
   List the elements of the following sets.
   (i) $A \backslash B$ (ii) $B \backslash C$ (iii) $A \backslash C$ (iv) $C \backslash A$

2. From the given Venn diagram, list the elements of
   (i) $A \backslash B$
   (ii) $B \backslash A$
   (iii) $U \backslash A$
   (iv) $U \backslash (A \cap B)$

3. Based on the given Venn diagram, say if each of the following is true or false:
   (i) $3 \in A \backslash B$ (ii) $7 \in B \backslash A$
   (iii) $\#(B \backslash A) = 3$ (iv) $\#U = 12$
   (v) $\#(A \cap B) = 2$ (vi) $6 \in U \backslash A$
   (vii) $\#(U \backslash A) = 6$ (viii) $\#(U \backslash B) = 8$

4. Given $X = \{2, 4, 6, 8, 10, 12\}$ and $Y = \{3, 6, 9, 12, 15\}$.
   Find (i) $X \backslash Y$ (ii) $Y \backslash X$
   Is $X \backslash Y = Y \backslash X$? What has your result shown?

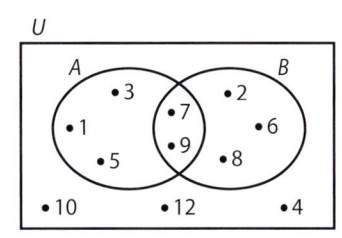

Text & Tests 2 Higher Level

5. $U = \{a, b, c, d, e, f, g, h, i\}, A = \{d, f, g, e, i\}, B = \{b, e, h, i\}$.
   Draw a Venn diagram to illustrate these sets.
   Use the Venn diagram to write down
   (i) #(A\B) (ii) #(U\A) (iii) #[U\(A ∪ B)] (iv) #[U\(A ∩ B)]

6. Make three copies of the Venn diagram on the right and shade in
   (i) A\B
   (ii) U\A
   (iii) U\(A ∩ B)

7. If U = {All the people who live in Newtown}
   A = {Car owners who live in Newtown}
   B = {Retired people who live in Newtown},
   describe in words each of the following sets:
   (i) U\A (ii) U\B (iii) A\B (iv) B\A (v) A ∩ B

8. Sandra drew the Venn diagram below for her project on Sets of Numbers.
   (i) What sets do the letters R, Q, Z and N represent?
   (ii) Describe in words the following sets:
      (a) Z\N (b) R\Q
   (iii) Copy the diagram and write one element into each of the following regions:
      (a) N (b) Z\N
      (c) Q\Z (d) R\Q.
   (iv) Where should Sandra place the number, 0, in her diagram?

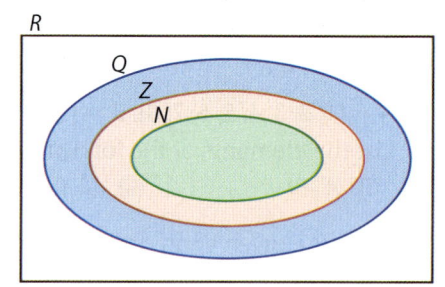

Section 3.3 Venn diagrams involving three sets

A Venn diagram for three sets in the universal set U is shown on the right.

The eight regions shown are described below.

Region 1 represents $A \cap B \cap C$ Region 2 represents $(A \cap C) \backslash B$
Region 3 represents $C \backslash (A \cup B)$ Region 4 represents $(A \cap B) \backslash C$
Region 5 represents $A \backslash (B \cup C)$ Region 6 represents $(B \cap C) \backslash A$
Region 7 represents $B \backslash (A \cup C)$ Region 8 represents $(A \cup B \cup C)'$

Chapter 3 Sets

In words:

Region 1 is the set of elements in *A* **and** *B* **and** *C*.

Region 2 is the set of elements in *A* **and** *B* but **not in** *C*.

Region 3 is the set of elements in *C* **but not in** *A* **or** *B*.

Region 3 could also be described as the set of elements in *C* **only**.

> **Example 1**
>
> $U = \{1, 2, 3, 4, 5, 6, 7, 8, 9, 10, 11, 12\}$ $A = \{2, 4, 6, 8, 10\}$
> $B = \{3, 4, 5, 6\}$ $C = \{5, 6, 7, 8\}$
>
> Illustrate these sets on a Venn diagram and list the elements of
> (i) $A \cap B \cap C$ (ii) $B \cap C$ (iii) $(A \cap B) \setminus C$ (iv) $B \setminus (A \cap B \cap C)$.
>
> The Venn diagram is shown on the right. 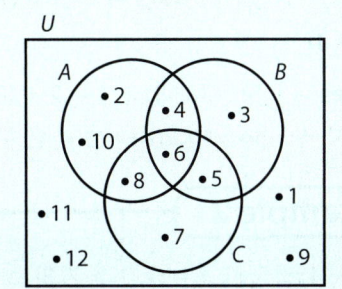
> (i) $A \cap B \cap C = \{6\}$
> (ii) $B \cap C = \{5, 6\}$
> (iii) $A \cap B = \{4, 6\}$
> $\therefore (A \cap B) \setminus C = \{4, 6\} \setminus \{5, 6, 7, 8\} = \{4\}$
> (iv) $B \setminus (A \cap B \cap C) = \{3, 4, 5, 6\} \setminus \{6\}$
> $= \{3, 4, 5\}$

Investigation:

Three more difficult regions are shaded here.

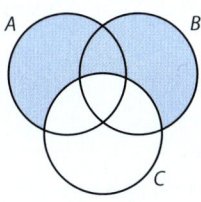

$(A \cup B) \setminus C$ 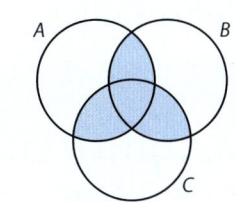 $(A \cap B) \cup (B \cap C) \cup (A \cap C)$ 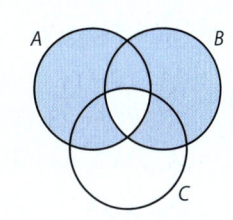 $(A \cup B) \setminus (A \cap B \cap C)$

By studying the first set of Venn diagrams above, find a link between the words "and", "or", "not in" and the mathematical symbols $\cap$, $\setminus$, $\cup$. Hence copy and complete the following chart for the diagram above.

Symbol	Words
$\cap$	
$\setminus$	
$\cup$	

	Words
$(A \cup B) \setminus C$	
$(A \cap B) \cup (B \cap C) \cup (A \cap C)$	
$(A \cup B) \setminus (A \cap B \cap C)$	

47

Text & Tests 2 Higher Level

The associative property

Earlier in this chapter it was stated that addition is **commutative**, since $3 + 4 = 4 + 3$ or $a + b = b + a$.

We will now consider any three numbers a, b and c and examine what happens under the operations of addition, subtraction, multiplication and division.

Take the addition of the numbers 3, 4 and 5.

If we combine them using different pairs, it can be seen that

$(3 + 4) + 5 = 3 + (4 + 5)$, since both add up to 12.

Notice that the numbers can be combined using different pairs without changing the result.

Definition
> An operation (∗) is said to be **associative** if
> $(a * b) * c = a * (b * c)$.

Examples (i) $(2 + 3) + 4 = 2 + (3 + 4)$ illustrates that addition is associative.

(ii) $(12 \div 6) \div 2 \neq 12 \div (6 \div 2)$ illustrates that division is not associative.

Example 2

$A = \{1, 3, 5, 6\}$, $B = \{2, 3, 5, 7, 8\}$ and $C = \{3, 4, 6, 8\}$ are three sets.

Investigate whether (i) $(A \cap B) \cap C = A \cap (B \cap C)$

(ii) $(A \setminus B) \setminus C = A \setminus (B \setminus C)$

(i) $A \cap B = \{3, 5\}$
$(A \cap B) \cap C = \{3, 5\} \cap \{3, 4, 6, 8\} = \{3\}$
$(B \cap C) = \{3, 8\}$
$A \cap (B \cap C) = \{1, 3, 5, 6\} \cap \{3, 8\} = \{3\}$
Since $(A \cap B) \cap C = A \cap (B \cap C) = \{3\}$, this illustrates that the intersection of sets is associative.

(ii) $A \setminus B = \{1, 3, 5, 6\} \setminus \{2, 3, 5, 7, 8\} = \{1, 6\}$
$(A \setminus B) \setminus C = \{1, 6\} \setminus \{3, 4, 6, 8\} = \{1\}$
$A \setminus (B \setminus C) = \{1, 3, 5, 6\} \setminus \{2, 5, 7\} = \{1, 3, 6\}$
This shows that $(A \setminus B) \setminus C \neq A \setminus (B \setminus C)$.

Remember
> Union and intersection of sets are associative but set difference is not.

Example 3

By shading the Venn diagram state whether each of the following sentences is true or false.

(i) $A \cup (B \cap C) = (A \cup B) \cap (A \cup C)$

(ii) $A \setminus (B \cup C) = (A \setminus B) \cup (A \setminus C)$

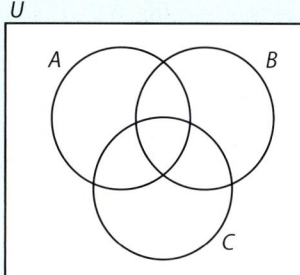

(i)

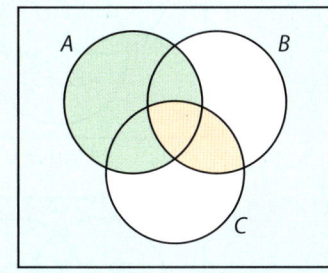

$A \cup (B \cap C)$

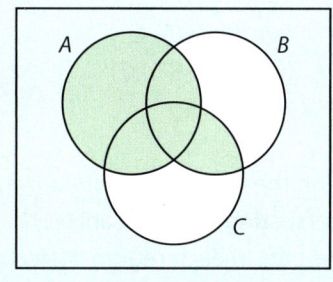

$(A \cup B) \cap (A \cup C)$

∴ $A \cup (B \cap C) = (A \cup B) \cap (A \cup C)$ is true.

(ii)

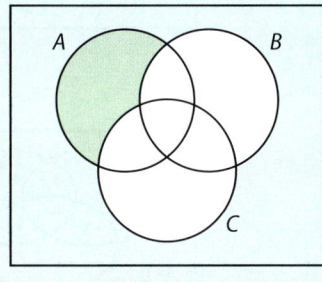

$A \setminus (B \cup C)$

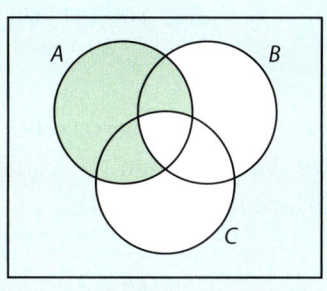

$(A \setminus B) \cup (A \setminus C)$

∴ $A \setminus (B \cup C) = (A \setminus B) \cup (A \setminus C)$ is false.

Exercise 3.3

1. The given Venn diagram shows three sets A, B and C.
   List the elements of these sets:

   (i) A
   (ii) B
   (iii) A ∩ B
   (iv) A ∩ B ∩ C
   (v) A\B
   (vi) B\(A ∪ C)

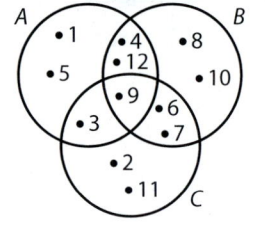

2. The given Venn diagram shows three sets A, B and C in the universal set U.
   List the elements of the following sets:

   (i) A ∩ B ∩ C
   (ii) A ∩ B
   (iii) A\(B ∪ C)
   (iv) (A ∩ B)\C
   (v) C\(A ∪ B)
   (vi) (A ∪ B ∪ C)'

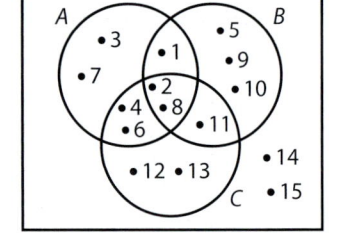

3. The Venn diagram on the right shows the universal set U and three intersecting sets A, B and C. The number of elements in each region is given in brackets.

   Use the Venn diagram to find

   (i) #(A)
   (ii) #[(A ∪ B)\C]
   (iii) #(A ∪ B ∪ C)'
   (iv) #[A\(B ∪ C)]
   (v) #[(A ∩ C)\B].

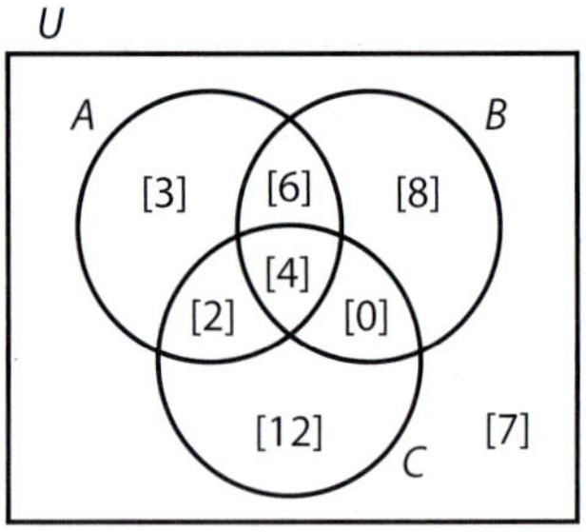

4. A, B and C are three sets in the universal set U, as shown in the given Venn diagram.
   Say if each of the following statements is true or false:

   (i) A\B = {x, y}
   (ii) #B = 5
   (iii) C\A = {o, t, l}
   (iv) #(A ∪ C) = 6
   (v) B ∩ C = {l, o, t}
   (vi) #(A ∪ B) = 9
   (vii) A ∩ B ∩ C = {l}
   (viii) (A ∩ C)\B = {y, l}

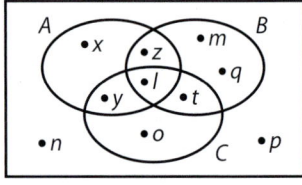

5. Draw a Venn diagram showing three intersecting sets A, B and C in the universal set U.
   Enter the correct cardinal number in each region based on the following information:

   #(A ∩ B ∩ C) = 2   #(A ∩ B) = 7   #(B ∩ C) = 6   #(A ∩ C) = 8
   #(A) = 16   #(B) = 20   #(C) = 19   #(U) = 50.

   Use your diagram to find

   (i) #(A ∪ B)'
   (ii) #[A\(B ∪ C)]
   (iii) #[(A ∪ B)\C].

6. Describe the set indicated by the shaded area in each of the following Venn Diagrams:

   (i) A ∪ C

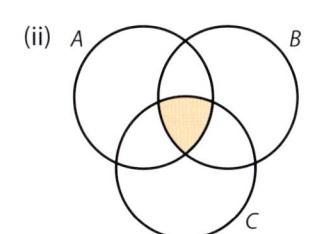

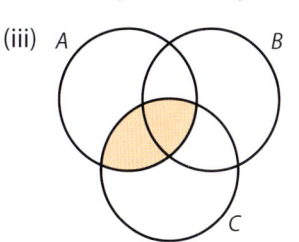

   (ii) A ∩ B ∩ C

   (iii) (A ∩ B) \ C

7. Using separate Venn diagrams similar to that shown on the right, shade in the region that represents each of the following sets:

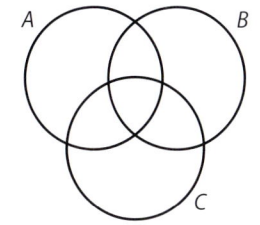

   (i) A ∩ B
   (ii) (A ∩ B)\C
   (iii) A\(B ∪ C)
   (iv) (B ∩ C)\A.

8. State whether each of the following statements is always true for $a, b, c \in R$. If the statement is not true, give an example to show why.

   (i) $a + b = b + a$
   (ii) $(a + b) + c = a + (b + c)$
   (iii) $a \div b = b \div a$
   (iv) $a - b = b - a$
   (v) $(a - b) - c = a - (b - c)$
   (vi) $a \div (b \div c) = (a \div b) \div c$

9. Name the property of real numbers illustrated by each of these examples:

   (i) $6 + 7 = 7 + 6$
   (ii) $(3 \times 4) \times 5 = 3 \times (4 \times 5)$
   (iii) $6 - 4 \neq 4 - 6$
   (iv) $(8 - 4) - 2 \neq 8 - (4 - 2)$
   (v) $(24 \div 6) \div 2 \neq 24 \div (6 \div 2)$

10. $A = \{0, 2, 4, 6, 8, 10\}$, $B = \{1, 2, 3, 4, 5\}$ and $C = \{3, 4, 5, 6, 7\}$.
    Use these three sets to show that
    $$A \cup (B \cap C) = (A \cup B) \cap (A \cup C).$$

11. Use the sets in Question 10 above to show that
    $$(A \setminus B) \setminus C \neq A \setminus (B \setminus C)$$
    What property of sets does this statement illustrate?

12. Which property of sets is illustrated by each of the following?

    (i) $A \cup B = B \cup A$
    (ii) $A \cap (B \cap C) = (A \cap B) \cap C$
    (iii) $(A \cup B) \cup C = A \cup (B \cup C)$
    (iv) $A \setminus (B \setminus C) \neq (A \setminus B) \setminus C$

13. Use the symbols ∪, ∩, ′ and \, describe each of the following shaded areas.

(i)

(ii)

14. Copy the Venn diagram given and shade in the region given by the set of elements in (A or B) but not in (A and B and C).

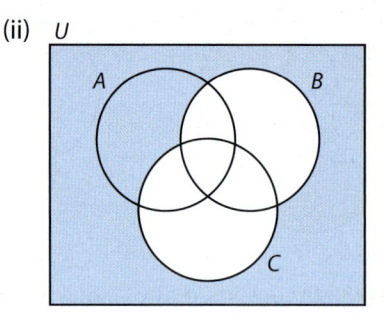

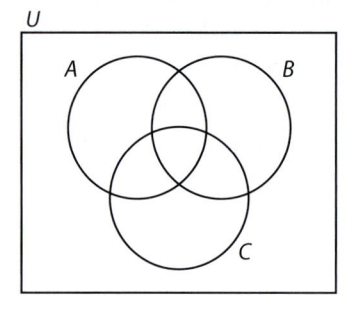

Section 3.4 Solving problems using three sets

In this section we will deal with problems that involve the use of three sets.

With this type of problem, it is always advisable to fill in the number of elements in the region that represents the intersection of the three sets.

If the number of elements in this region is not given directly, we let x represent this number.

> ### Example 1
>
> 100 students were asked which of the three items – sweets (S), soft drinks (D) or crisps (C) – they had bought during a school outing.
>
>   6 students bought all three   31 students bought crisps
> 41 students bought sweets   23 students bought a soft drink only
> 14 students bought crisps and a soft drink   15 students bought crisps and sweets
> 12 students bought sweets and a soft drink
>
> Illustrate this information on a Venn diagram and write down the number of students who bought
>   (i)   none of these items   (ii) sweets only
> (iii) two items only   (iv) one item only.

We draw three intersecting circles S, D and C to represent sweets, soft drinks and crisps, respectively.

$S \cap D \cap C = 6$
$C \cap D = 14$; so $\#(C \cap D) \setminus S = 14 - 6 = 8$
$C \cap S = 15$; so $\#(C \cap S) \setminus D = 15 - 6 = 9$
$S \cap D = 12$; so $\#(S \cap D) \setminus C = 12 - 6 = 6$

We can now complete the Venn diagram from the given information and write down the required answers.

(i) Number that bought none of these is:
$$100 - (20 + 6 + 6 + 9 + 23 + 8 + 8)$$
$$= 100 - 80 = 20$$

(ii) Number that bought sweets only $= 20$

(iii) Number that bought two items only $= 9 + 6 + 8 = 23$

(iv) Number that bought one item only $= 20 + 23 + 8 = 51$

Example 2

There are 86 students taking languages in a school and all take at least one of the languages – French, German and Spanish.

57 take French, 42 take German and 31 take Spanish.

If 25 take French and German, 17 take French and Spanish and 5 take German and Spanish, find how many students take all three languages.

(In this type of problem, where we are asked for the cardinal number of the intersection of the three sets, we denote the number in this region by x. We then express the cardinal numbers of the other regions in terms of x, as shown opposite.)

The number of students taking French only is obtained as follows:

$$57 - [25 - x + x + 17 - x]$$
$$= 15 + x$$

Similarly, $(12 + x)$ take German only and $(9 + x)$ take Spanish only.

The sum of the cardinal numbers of all the regions is 86.

∴ $(15 + x) + (25 - x) + x + (17 - x) + (9 + x) + (5 - x) + (12 + x) = 86$
∴ $83 + x = 86$
∴ $x = 3$

Therefore 3 students take all three languages.

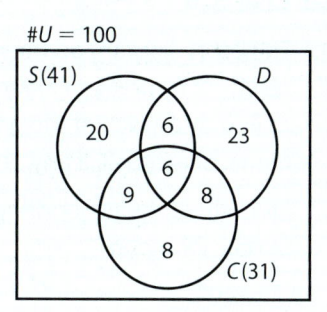

Text & Tests 2 Higher Level

Exercise 3.4

1. The Venn diagram on the right shows the results of a survey of a number of adults to find out which of the games golf, tennis or football, if any, they play.

   From the diagram, find the number of people who play
   - (i) golf
   - (ii) both golf and tennis
   - (iii) all three games
   - (iv) football only
   - (v) none of these games
   - (vi) both football and tennis
   - (vii) both tennis and football but not golf.

   What was the total number of people surveyed?

   U
   Golf: 12, 5, 4, 7, 14, 10
   Tennis: 26
   Football: 22

2. In a language school, all students attending study one or more of the three languages French, English and German.

   85 students study French, 60 study English and 25 study German.

   If 18 study both French and English, 10 study both French and German, 8 study both English and German and 5 study all three languages, illustrate this information by a Venn diagram and use it to find
   - (i) how many students attend the school
   - (ii) how many students study one language only
   - (iii) how many students study both English and French but not German.

3. At a road checkpoint, 100 cars were examined for defective tyres, brakes and lights. It was found that 12 had defective tyres, 9 had defective brakes, 13 had defective lights, 6 had defective lights and brakes, 7 had defective lights and tyres, 6 had defective tyres and brakes, while 4 cars had all three defects.
   Represent this information by a Venn diagram and find
   - (i) the number of cars which had defective brakes only
   - (ii) the number of cars which had two defects only
   - (iii) the number of cars which had defective tyres and brakes but not defective lights
   - (iv) the number of cars with no defect.

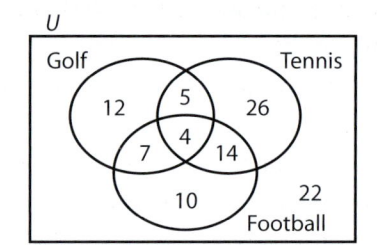

4. At the end of a touring holiday, 90 US tourists were asked which of the three cities – Dublin, Cork or Galway – they had visited.
60 had visited Dublin, 18 had visited Cork and 50 had visited Galway.
30 visited both Dublin and Galway; 10 visited both Dublin and Cork; 6 visited both Cork and Galway.
If 4 had visited all three cities, find how many tourists
   (i) visited Cork only
   (ii) visited both Dublin and Galway but not Cork
   (iii) visited none of the three cities.

5. 100 people were asked which of the papers – *Times*, *Mail* or *Independent* – they had bought on the previous Sunday.
The results showed that 32 people had bought the *Times*, 48 had bought the *Independent* and 35 had bought the *Mail*.
It was found also that 12 people bought both the *Independent* and the *Times*, 11 bought both the *Times* and the *Mail*, 13 bought both the *Independent* and the *Mail*, while 5 people bought all three papers.
Illustrate this information on a Venn diagram and then answer these questions:
   (i) How many people bought none of these 3 papers?
   (ii) How many people bought the *Times* only?
   (iii) How many people bought the *Independent* and the *Mail* but not the *Times*?
   (iv) How many people bought two papers only?

6. A survey was taken of 54 students, each of whom was studying one or more of the 3 subjects *A*, *B* and *C*.
6 students studied *B* and *C*.
5 students studied *A* and *C*.
3 times as many students studied *A* and *B* as studied all 3 subjects.
20 students altogether studied *B*.
17 students studied *C* only and 14 students studied *A* only.
Using x to represent those students who studied all 3 subjects, illustrate the above information on a Venn diagram.
Hence find the value of x.

7. In a survey, 100 people were asked which of three magazines – A, B and C – they had read on the previous day.
   It was found that 29 people read A, 40 people read B and 38 people read C.
   Also, 10 people read A and B but not C
   12 people read B and C but not A
   7 people read A and C but not B
   and 30 people did not read any of the three magazines.
   Find (i) the number of people who read all three magazines
   (ii) the number of people who read one magazine only.

8. 120 Junior Certificate Students took examinations in Maths, Science and French and all students passed in at least one subject. M represents those who passed in Maths, S those who passed in Science and F those who passed in French.
   The following are the results of the examination:
   $\#M = 80$, $\#S = 90$, $\#(M \cap S \cap F) = 45$, $\#(M \cap S) = 58$,
   $\#(M \cap F) = 55$ and $\#[S \setminus (M \cup F)] = 15$.
   (i) How many students passed in Science only?
   (ii) How many students passed in Science and French but failed Maths?
   (iii) How many students passed in two subjects only?

9. A survey was taken of a group of 44 students, each of whom was studying one or more of the three subjects – History, Geography and Art.

   28 studied History.
   30 students studied Geography.
   22 students studied Art.
   6 students studied History only.
   15 students studied both History and Geography.
   3 students studied all three subjects.

   (i) Use a Venn diagram to find the number of students who studied History and Geography but not Art.
   (ii) How many students studied History and Art but not Geography?
   (iii) Find the number of students who studied Geography only.

   (**Hint:** Let x represent the number of students who studied Geography and Art but not History.)

Chapter 3 Sets

Investigation:

Draw a large poster of a 3 set Venn diagram based on data collected from your class.

E.g. Which of these three countries have you visited?

	Countries visited:	
A	Spain	
B	France	
C	Greece	
	None of the above	

E.g. Languages that you would like to be able speak well.

	Language	
A	French	
B	Spanish	
C	Irish	
	None of the above	

Using your Venn diagram draw a chart (as below) describing in words each region of your diagram and the number of students in that region.

Region	In words	#Number
$(A \cap B \cap C)$		
$(A \cup B \cup C)$		
$(A \cup B \cup C)'$		
$(A \cap B)$		
$(A \cap B) \setminus C$		
$(A \cap C)$		
$(A \cap C) \setminus B$		
$(B \cap C)$		
$(B \cap C) \setminus A$		
$A \setminus (C \cup B)$		
$B \setminus (A \cup C)$		
$C \setminus (A \cup B)$		

Text & Tests 2 Higher Level

Test yourself 3

1. $U = \{1, 2, 3, ..., 10\}, A = \{1, 3, 5, 7\}$ and $B = \{5, 7, 8, 9\}$.
   List the elements of these sets:
   (i) $A \cap B$ (ii) $(A \cup B)'$.

2. Copy this Venn diagram and shade in the region that represents $A' \cap B$.

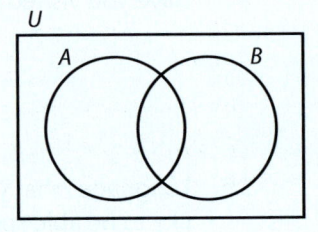

3. X and Y are sets in the universal set U.
   If $\#U = 50, \#X = 28, \#Y = 34$ and $\#(X \cup Y) = 43$, draw a Venn diagram to illustrate this information.
   Now find (i) $\#(X \cap Y)$ (ii) $\#(X \setminus Y)$ (iii) $\#(X \cup Y)'$ (iv) $\#X'$

4. Based on the given Venn diagram, write down the elements of these sets:
   (i) A (ii) $A \setminus B$
   (iii) A' (iv) $(A \cup B)'$

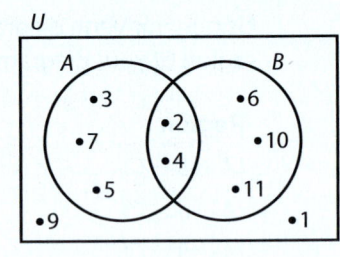

5. 50 soccer fans were asked which of three soccer matches – A, B and C – they had seen over a given weekend.
   5 said they had seen all three matches;
   16 had seen both A and B;
   15 had seen both B and C;
   8 had seen match B only;
   a total of 23 had seen match C and a total of 25 had seen match A;
   2 people did not see any of the matches.
   Draw a Venn diagram to illustrate this information and then answer these questions:
   (i) How many people had seen match B?
   (ii) How many people had seen both match A and match C but not B?
   (iii) How many people had seen match A only?

6. The given Venn diagram shows the number of elements in each of the sets A, B and C.
   Use the Venn diagram to write down
   (i) $\#(A \cup B)$ (ii) $\#[(A \cup B) \setminus C]$
   (iii) $\#[(B \cap C) \setminus A]$ (iv) $\#[A \cup B \cup C]$

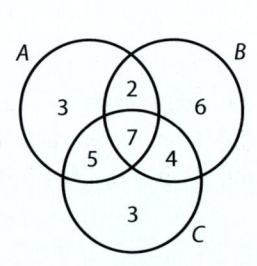

Chapter 3 Sets

7. The number of elements in P or Q is 22.
   The number of elements in P and Q is 2.
   If the number of elements in Q but not in P is four times the number of elements in P but not in Q, find
   (i) #P   (ii) #Q

8. In the given Venn diagram, #X = 30, #Y = 18 and #(X ∪ Y)' = 8.
   (i) What is the greatest possible value of #U?
   (ii) What is the least possible value of #U?
   (iii) If #U = 44, find #(X ∩ Y).

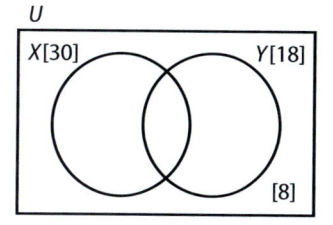

9. A = {1, 2, 3, 6, 8, 10, 12}, B = {3, 4, 5, 6} and C = {3, 5, 8, 10}.
   Investigate if A ∩ (B ∪ C) = (A ∩ B) ∪ (A ∩ C).

10. In a survey, 100 people were asked if they had been on a sun holiday or a skiing holiday the previous year.
    60 had been on a sun holiday, 15 had been on a skiing holiday and 30 had been on neither.
    Copy the given Venn diagram and insert the appropriate numbers in the brackets.

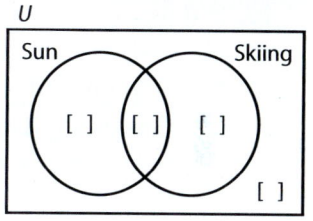

11. In the given Venn diagram,
    #U = 80, #A = 40, #B = 50,
    #(A ∩ B) = x and #(A ∪ B)' = y.
    (i) What is the maximum value of x?
    (ii) What is the minimum value of x?
    (iii) What is the maximum value of y?
    (iv) What is the value of x when y = 4?

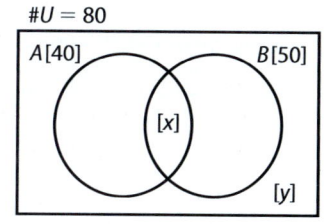

12. In the given Venn diagram,
    #(U) = u, #(A) = a, #(B) = b,
    #(A ∩ B) = c and #(A ∪ B)' = d.
    (i) Express u in terms of a, b, c and d.
    (ii) Express d in terms of u, a, b, and c.
    (iii) If c = b, what can you say about the sets A and B?
    (iv) If b > a, what is the maximum value of c?

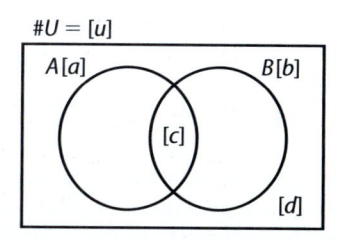

13. A number of people were asked which of the three papers – *The Journal* (J), *The News* (N) and *The Tribune* (T) – they had bought the previous week.

Some of the results are shown in the Venn diagram on the right.

Copy and complete the Venn diagram given that
  (i) 20 people bought *The News*
  (ii) 23 people bought *The Journal*
  (iii) 10 people bought *The Journal* and *The Tribune*
  (iv) 8 people bought *The Tribune* only.

Given that there were 40 people in the survey who bought *The Tribune* or *The Journal* or both, find the value of *x*.

14. In the Venn diagram on the right, which **one** of the following statements is true?
  (i) $6 \in (A \setminus B)$
  (ii) $\#A = 2$
  (iii) $\#(A \cup B) = 2$
  (iv) $\#(A \cup B)' = 2$

15. In the given Venn diagram,
$\#U = 50$, $\#A = 24$, $\#B = b$,
$\#(A \cap B) = 8$ and $\#(A \cup B)' = g$.
  (i) What is the value of *g* when $b = 30$?
  (ii) What is the maximum value of *g*?
  (iii) What is the minimum value of *b*?
  (iv) What is the maximum value of *b*?

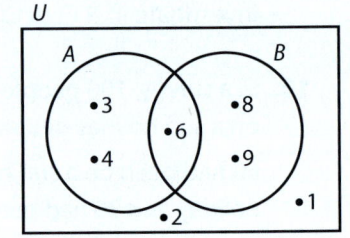

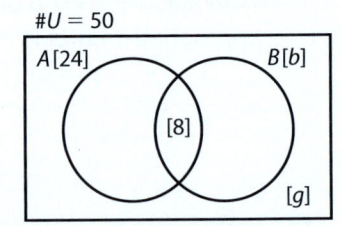

16. In Alice's class of 25 students, 6 students never came to school by car or bus. 28% of the students used car and bus. She found that the ratio of students who used bus only to car only was 2:1.

Draw a Venn diagram of this data.

How many students came to school by bus only?

17. Of the 30 students in Peter's class, 2 did not play hurling or football. 5 students played both hurling and football and twice as many played football, as played hurling.

Find out how many in Peter's class students played hurling.

Chapter 3 Sets

Assignment:

A: Make a poster of the following chart, marking a "Yes" or a "No" into each section.

	N	Z	Q	R\Q	R
$\sqrt{7}$					
6					
−3					
$\frac{\pi}{2}$					
1.2					
2.3					
30%					
$\sqrt{16}$					
5^{-1}					
0					

B: Design a Venn diagram to illustrate the chart above.

Chapter 4 Applied Arithmetic

From first year, you will recall how to:

- find the percentage of a quantity,
- increase or decrease a quantity by a percentage,
- calculate VAT,
- calculate percentage profit or loss.

In this chapter, you will learn to:

- calculate profit margin and markup,
- calculate household bill charges,
- apply standard rate and higher rate income tax charges,
- calculate USC and PRSI deductions,
- evaluate net pay after all deductions,
- convert between different currencies,
- apply compound interest to investments and loans,
- use the compound interest formula,
- find the rate or principal of an investment or loan,
- calculate deprecation.

Section 4.1 VAT – Profit and loss

When dealing with problems involving percentages, it is very important to be able to convert a percentage to a decimal.

> To find 4%, multiply by 0.04.   To find 104%, multiply by 1.04.

1. Value-added tax (VAT)

Value-added tax or **VAT** is a government tax which is added to many of the things that we buy. In most shops the marked price of an item includes VAT and so we do not have to calculate it.

Sometimes the prices of more expensive items such as television sets and furniture are given without VAT. In these cases the shopkeeper calculates the VAT amount and adds it to the price of the item.

Chapter 4 Applied Arithmetic

If an article is priced at €280 plus VAT at 23%, the full price can be worked out as follows:

100% + 23% = 123%

using a calculator: €280 × 123 **SHIFT** **(** = €344.4

Example 1

The rate of VAT on electrical goods is 23%.

(i) Find the selling price of a washing machine priced at €650 + VAT.
(ii) If the selling price of an *ipad* is €738, find its price before VAT is added on.

(i) 23% of €650 = €650 × 0.23 = €149.50
∴ the selling price of the washing machine = €650 + €149.50
OR = €799.50
Adding 23% gives 123%.
123% of €650 = €650 × 1.23 = €799.50 ... as above.

(ii) €738 represents 123% of the price before VAT is added.

$$123\% = €738$$
$$1\% = \frac{738}{123}$$
$$100\% = \frac{738}{123} \times \frac{100}{1} = €600$$

> You may also divide by 1.23 to get your answer.

Example 2

A rail fare goes up by 6% to €42.40.
What was the old fare?

The old fare is multiplied by 1.06 to get the new fare.
So the new fare has to be divided by 1.06 to get the old fare.
Old fare = €42.40 ÷ 1.06 = €40.

? → × 1.06 → €42.40

€40 ← ÷ 1.06 ← €42.40

2. Percentage profit and loss

When dealing with percentage profit or loss, we base this percentage on the **cost price** unless otherwise stated.

$$\text{Percentage profit} = \frac{\text{Profit}}{\text{Cost price}} \times \frac{100}{1}; \quad \text{Percentage loss} = \frac{\text{Loss}}{\text{Cost price}} \times \frac{100}{1}$$

Text & Tests 2 Higher Level

> ### Example 3
>
> By selling a car for €14 400, a dealer would lose 4% on the purchase price.
> (i) What did the dealer pay for the car?
> (ii) Find his percentage profit if he had sold the car for €17 250.
>
> (i) €14 400 represents 96% of the purchase price.
>
> $\quad\quad$ 96% = €14 400
> $\quad\quad$ 1% = €150
> $\quad\quad$ 100% = €15 000, i.e., the purchase price = €15 000.
>
> (ii) Profit = €17 250 − €15 000 = €2250
>
> $\quad$ Percentage profit $= \dfrac{2250}{15\,000} \times \dfrac{100}{1} = 15\%$

Investigation:

Company A increased its profit by 5% in 2017 and by a further 5% in 2018.
Company B increased its profit by 10% over the same two years. (2017/2018)

Investigate if there is a difference between the profits of the two companies for the two years 2017/2018.
Show all the work done in support of your answer.

Exercise 4.1

1. Express each of these percentages as decimals:
   (i) 7%   (ii) $3\frac{1}{2}$%   (iii) 12%   (iv) 15%   (v) $16\frac{1}{2}$%
   (vi) 104%   (vii) 110%   (viii) 114%   (ix) 125%   (x) $87\frac{1}{2}$%

2. (i) Increase 120 by 10%   (ii) Increase 150 by 6%
   (iii) Decrease 600 by 5%   (iv) Decrease 820 by $12\frac{1}{2}$%

3. Train fares are increased by 4%.
   (i) Find the new fare if the old fare was €28.
   (ii) If the new fare is €36.40, find the old fare.

4. The price of a theatre ticket goes up 7% to €26.75.
   What was the price before the increase?

5. The price of a bicycle is €520 plus VAT at 23%.
   Find the price of the bicycle after VAT is added.

6. The price of a television set is €984.
   If this includes VAT at 23%, find the price before VAT is added.

7. An electricity bill amounts to €204.30 after VAT at $13\frac{1}{2}$% is added.
   Find the amount of the bill before VAT is added.

8. In a sale, the price of a piece of furniture was reduced by 15%.
   If the sale price was €1360, what was the price before the sale?

9. In a sale, the marked prices are reduced by 30%.
   (i) Calculate the sale price of a jacket if the marked price is €350.
   (ii) Find the marked price of a dress if the sale price is €168.

10. By selling a jacket for €416, a store makes a profit of 30%.
    (i) Find the cost price of the jacket.
    (ii) If the jacket is reduced by 10% in a sale, calculate the percentage profit the store now has on the cost price.

Investigation:

In the retail trade, the terms **Mark-up** and **Margin** are used regularly.
Using the definitions below, copy and complete the table to investigate how these percentages change as the profit changes.

$$(\text{Mark-up})\% = \frac{\text{Profit}}{\text{Cost price}} \times 100\% \qquad (\text{Margin})\% = \frac{\text{Profit}}{\text{Selling price}} \times 100\%$$

Cost price	Profit	Selling price	% Mark–up	% Margin
€100	€10			
€100	€20			
€100	€30			
€100	€40			
€100	€50			
€100	€60			
€100	€70			
€100	€80			
€100	€90			
€100	€100			

Note: The '% mark-up' is another name for the 'percentage profit'.

11. A jacket selling at €250 has a margin of 50%, find:
   (i) the profit   (ii) the cost price of the jacket   (iii) the mark-up on the jacket.

12. A washing machine costing €500 is sold with a mark-up of 25%, find
   (i) the profit   (ii) the selling price of the machine   (iii) the margin on the machine

13. By selling a laptop for €1150 a store makes a profit of 25%.
   (i) Copy and complete the data table for this item.

Cost price	Selling price	Profit	% Mark-up	% Margin

   (ii) At what price should the laptop be sold to make a profit of 20%

14. When an item is sold for €176, the profit is 10% on the cost price. When the selling price is increased to €192, calculate the percentage profit on the cost price.

15. A greengrocer buys 30 boxes of strawberries at €5.25 each and sells 28 of them at a profit of 30%. If the remaining two boxes are unsaleable, find his percentage profit on the deal.

16. The price of a games console is €615 which includes VAT at 23%.

   Store A offers a discount of 24% on the selling price.
   Store B says it will not charge VAT.
   Store C says it will reduce the price before VAT is added by 25% and then charge VAT at 23% on the reduced price.

   In which store is the selling price the cheapest and by how much?

17. *Kelly Og's* Corn Flakes are sold in standard packs of 500 g for €2.40.
   During a promotion, the quantity in a pack is increased by 20%, but the price stays the same.
   Calculate the percentage reduction in the price per kilogram during the promotion.

18. A shop advertised "Everything half price in our sale", but also now advertises that there is "An additional 15% off sale prices".
   To what percentage reduction on the original price is the new offer equivalent?

19. Let x be the cost price and y be the selling price, then in table form;

Cost price	Selling price	Profit	% Mark-up	% Margin
x	y	$y - x$	$\dfrac{y-x}{x} \times \dfrac{100}{1}$ %	$\dfrac{y-x}{y} \times \dfrac{100}{1}$ %

   (i) If $\dfrac{y-x}{x} \times \dfrac{100}{1}\% = a\%$ show that $\dfrac{y-x}{y} = \dfrac{a}{100+a}$.

   (ii) Hence if 5% is the % mark-up find the % margin.

Chapter 4 Applied Arithmetic

5. The price of a bicycle is €520 plus VAT at 23%.
   Find the price of the bicycle after VAT is added.

6. The price of a television set is €984.
   If this includes VAT at 23%, find the price before VAT is added.

7. An electricity bill amounts to €204.30 after VAT at $13\frac{1}{2}$% is added.
   Find the amount of the bill before VAT is added.

8. In a sale, the price of a piece of furniture was reduced by 15%.
   If the sale price was €1360, what was the price before the sale?

9. In a sale, the marked prices are reduced by 30%.
   (i) Calculate the sale price of a jacket if the marked price is €350.
   (ii) Find the marked price of a dress if the sale price is €168.

10. By selling a jacket for €416, a store makes a profit of 30%.
    (i) Find the cost price of the jacket.
    (ii) If the jacket is reduced by 10% in a sale, calculate the percentage profit the store now has on the cost price.

Investigation:

In the retail trade, the terms **Mark-up** and **Margin** are used regularly.
Using the definitions below, copy and complete the table to investigate how these percentages change as the profit changes.

$$(\text{Mark-up})\% = \frac{\text{Profit}}{\text{Cost price}} \times 100\% \qquad (\text{Margin})\% = \frac{\text{Profit}}{\text{Selling price}} \times 100\%$$

Cost price	Profit	Selling price	% Mark–up	% Margin
€100	€10			
€100	€20			
€100	€30			
€100	€40			
€100	€50			
€100	€60			
€100	€70			
€100	€80			
€100	€90			
€100	€100			

Note: The '% mark-up' is another name for the 'percentage profit'.

11. A jacket selling at €250 has a margin of 50%, find:
   (i) the profit   (ii) the cost price of the jacket   (iii) the mark-up on the jacket.

12. A washing machine costing €500 is sold with a mark-up of 25%, find
   (i) the profit   (ii) the selling price of the machine   (iii) the margin on the machine

13. By selling a laptop for €1150 a store makes a profit of 25%.
   (i) Copy and complete the data table for this item.

Cost price	Selling price	Profit	% Mark-up	% Margin

   (ii) At what price should the laptop be sold to make a profit of 20%

14. When an item is sold for €176, the profit is 10% on the cost price. When the selling price is increased to €192, calculate the percentage profit on the cost price.

15. A greengrocer buys 30 boxes of strawberries at €5.25 each and sells 28 of them at a profit of 30%. If the remaining two boxes are unsaleable, find his percentage profit on the deal.

16. The price of a games console is €615 which includes VAT at 23%.

   Store A offers a discount of 24% on the selling price.
   Store B says it will not charge VAT.
   Store C says it will reduce the price before VAT is added by 25% and then charge VAT at 23% on the reduced price.

   In which store is the selling price the cheapest and by how much?

17. *Kelly Og's* Corn Flakes are sold in standard packs of 500 g for €2.40.
   During a promotion, the quantity in a pack is increased by 20%, but the price stays the same. Calculate the percentage reduction in the price per kilogram during the promotion.

18. A shop advertised "Everything half price in our sale", but also now advertises that there is "An additional 15% off sale prices".
   To what percentage reduction on the original price is the new offer equivalent?

19. Let x be the cost price and y be the selling price, then in table form;

Cost price	Selling price	Profit	% Mark-up	% Margin
x	y	$y - x$	$\dfrac{y-x}{x} \times \dfrac{100}{1}$ %	$\dfrac{y-x}{y} \times \dfrac{100}{1}$ %

   (i) If $\dfrac{y-x}{x} \times \dfrac{100}{1}\% = a\%$ show that $\dfrac{y-x}{y} = \dfrac{a}{100+a}$.

   (ii) Hence if 5% is the % mark-up find the % margin.

Chapter 4 Applied Arithmetic

Section 4.2 Household bills

The questions in this section deal with various household bills such as electricity, gas, phone, postage and insurance.

Each utility bill shows:

> how many units of energy were used
> the cost of each unit (unit price)
> extra charges e.g. standing charges, levies
> VAT

When dealing with bills that involve meter readings, the number of units used is found as follows:

> Number of units used = Present Reading − Previous Reading

Example 1

Calculate the electricity bill from the information given below:

    Standing charge: €18.60
    Present meter reading: 38423   Previous meter reading: 37483
    Cost per unit: 23 cent
    VAT on total bill: 13%

Number of units used = 38423 − 37483 = 940
Cost of electricity used = 940 × 23 cent = 940 × €0.23
                                            = €216.20
Amount of bill before VAT = €18.60 + €216.20 = €234.80
VAT = €234.80 × 0.13 = €30.52 | Or
Total bill = €234.80 + €30.52   Cost + VAT = 113% = 1.13
        = €265.32   ∴ Bill = €216.20 × 1.13 = €265.32

Exercise 4.2

1. A householder's electricity bill is charged in the following way:
    (i) A standing charge of €26.80
    (ii) 1256 units at 23c per unit
    (iii) VAT at 13% on the total bill.
    Find the total amount of the electricity bill.

Text & Tests 2 Higher Level

2. A supplier charges for electricity supplied in the following way:

   Day rate: 24c per unit   *Night rate:* 10.5c per unit.

   Calculate the electricity bill for each of the following users based on the unit rates given above. VAT at $12\frac{1}{2}$% is added to each bill.

Name	No. of units used at *day rate*	No. of units used at *night rate*	Standing Charge
D. Maher	420	130	€28.90
G. O'Gorman	560	370	€25.60

3. Mrs Heaton received a bill of €130.80 for electricity used in a two-month period. The bill included a standing charge of €25.20.
   If each unit of electricity cost 22 cent, find how many units were used.

4. Rachel's gas meter was read on 1 March.
   The reading was 1 7 4 2
   92 days later the meter was read again.
   The reading was 1 9 5 6
   Calculate the total gas bill that Rachel will have to pay for the 92 days from 1 March if VAT at 13% is added.

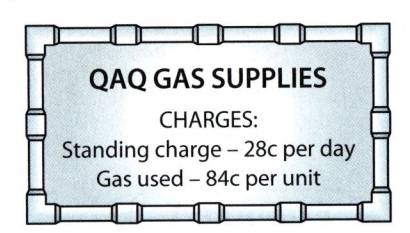

   QAQ GAS SUPPLIES
   CHARGES:
   Standing charge – 28c per day
   Gas used – 84c per unit

5. A householder is charged for the gas that he uses in the following way:
   Standing charge €26.30.
   Reducing rate for therms used:

   0–20 therms: €1.40 per therm
   21–40 therms: €1.26 per therm
   over 40 therms: €1.06 per therm.

   Calculate the householder's bill for a period in which he uses 54 therms and VAT at $12\frac{1}{2}$% is added.

6. John hired the car for 8 days and drove 850 kilometres.
   (i) How much did the hire of the car cost him?
   (ii) Elaine hired a similar car for 10 days. If her bill for hiring the car amounted to €1610, how many kilometres did she travel?

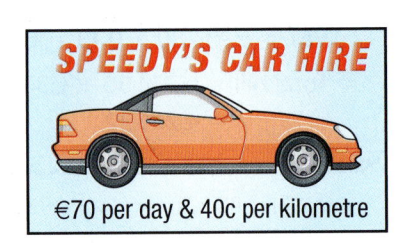

   SPEEDY'S CAR HIRE
   €70 per day & 40c per kilometre

Chapter 4 Applied Arithmetic

7. Alan earns €12.80 per hour for working a basic week of 38 hours.
   Overtime is paid at 'time and a half'.
   The table below shows the hours Alan worked last week.

Day	Monday	Tuesday	Wednesday	Thursday	Friday
Hours	10	8	7	9	12

   (i) How many hours overtime did he work last week?
   (ii) Calculate his total pay for last week.
   (iii) If Alan earned €582.40 in a particular week, how many hours overtime did he work?

8. *Eircom* charges 15c for each metered unit used. If each local call uses 1 unit every 3 minutes (or part thereof) during peak time, calculate the cost of each of these local calls made at peak time:

	Starting time	Finishing time
(i)	9.07 a.m.	9.12 a.m.
(ii)	12.49 p.m.	1.04 p.m.
(iii)	11.54 a.m.	12.16 p.m.

9. The charges for Olivia's 'bill-pay' phone per month are as follows.

   Fixed charge: €15
   Call charges: First 50 minutes free.
                   Additional minutes, 18 cent per minute.
   Text messages: First 100 text messages free.
                   Additional text messages, 14 cent each.

   During June, Olivia used 120 minutes call-time and sent 128 text messages.
   (i) Calculate the charge for all her phone calls.
   (ii) Find the total amount of her bill for the month.

   During July, Olivia used 143 minutes call-time and sent x text messages.
   (iii) If her bill amounted to €39.02, find the value of x.

10. When Anna uses her car on a business trip, she is allowed to claim 68 cent per km for the first 80 km and 42 cent per kilometre for the rest of the journey.
    (i) How much can she claim for a 135 km journey?
    (ii) On one occasion she claimed €119.08. How far did she travel?

Text & Tests 2 Higher Level

11. Kate wants a smartphone.
These are the tariffs offered.

If Kate wants to use her phone for at least 120 minutes per month (but always less than 143), which tariff should she choose for the cheapest deal?

Tariff	Cost/month	Call cost/min
1	€15	40c
2	€24	26c
3	€30	15c
4	€40	8c

Section 4.3 Income tax

In this country, wage and salary earners pay income tax on all their incomes at one of two rates.
These rates are called the **Standard Rate** and the **Higher Rate**.
In 2019, the **Standard Rate** was 20% and the **Higher Rate** was 40%.
However these rates can change from year to year.

At the beginning of the year, each employed person is given a **tax credit** and a **standard rate cut-off point**. If the standard rate cut-off point is €35 300, this means that the person pays income tax at the standard rate (say 20%) on the first €35 300 of income. Any income above €35 300 is taxed at the higher rate (say 40%). When this income tax has been calculated, it is called the **gross tax**. The person's tax credit is then deducted from the gross tax to give the **tax payable**.
Tax credits reduce the amount of tax you have to pay, they depend on your personal circumstances, e.g. single/married, number of children etc.

> Tax payable = Gross tax − tax credit

Example 1

A printer has a weekly wage of €800. He pays income tax on all his wages at the standard rate of 20%. If he has a tax credit of €48 a week, find how much income tax he pays.

Gross tax = 20% of €800
= €800 × 0.2 = €160
Tax payable = Gross tax − tax credits
= €160 − €48
= €112

∴ he pays €112 income tax each week.

Chapter 4 Applied Arithmetic

The Higher Rate

The diagram below illustrates the amount of income tax a person with a gross weekly wage of €700 would pay if the standard rate cut-off point is €500 and the tax credit is €80 per week.

Standard Rate (20%)	Higher Rate (40%)
€500 @ 20% = €100	€200 @ 40% = €80

↑ Standard rate cut-off point (€500)

Gross tax = €500 @ 20% + €200 @ 40%
       = €100   + €80   = €180

Tax payable = Gross tax − tax credits = €180 − €80 = €100

Example 2

A woman's income for the year is €45 000. The standard rate cut off is €35 300 and she has a tax credit of €4000. If the standard rate of tax is 20% and the higher rate is 40%, how much income tax does she pay for the year?

Gross tax = 20% of €35 300 + 40% of (€45 000 − €35 300)
       = 0.2 × €35 300 + 0.4 × €9700
       = €7600 + €3880 = 11 480

Tax payable = Gross tax − tax credit = €11 480 − €4000

∴ Tax payable = €7480

Example 3

A man pays €4500 income tax for the year and he has a tax credit of €2400. If he pays tax at the standard rate of 20% on all his income, calculate his gross income for the year.

Tax payable = Gross tax − tax credit
⇒   €4500 = Gross tax − €2400
⇒ Gross tax = €4500 + €2400 = €6900

Gross tax = 20% of gross income
⇒ 20% of gross income = €6900

$$1\% \text{ of gross income} = €\frac{6900}{20}$$

$$100\% \text{ of gross income} = €\frac{6900}{20} \times \frac{100}{1}$$

∴ gross income = €34 500

Text & Tests 2 Higher Level

Universal Social Charge (USC)

The Universal Social Charge (USC) came into effect on 1st January 2011.
It replaced other levies which were abolished from that date.

The rates of USC per year and per week are given below (2019):

Income thresholds (2019)		
Per year	**Per week**	**Rate of USC**
€0 − €12 012	Up to €231	0.5%
€12 012 − €19 874	From €231 to €382	2.0%
€19 874 − €70 044	From €382 to €1347	4.5%
€70 044 +	€1347 +	8.0%

PRSI (Pay-Related Social Insurance)

PRSI is another deduction from a person's wage or income.

It is used by the state to pay unemployment benefits and old-age pensions.

The most widely-used rate is 4% of total salary.

Example 4

Conor has a weekly wage of €840.
He pays USC at the usual rate and PRSI at 4%.
He has a tax credit of €65 per week and pays income tax at the standard rate of 20%.
Calculate his take home pay after all deductions.

USC: €231 @ 0.5% + (€382 − €231) @ 2.0% + (€840 − €382) @ 4.5%
= €231 × 0.005 + €151 × 0.02 + €458 × 0.045
= €24.79

PRSI: €840 @ 4% = €840 × 0.04 = €33.60

Income tax: Tax payable = Gross tax − tax credit
= €840 @ 20% − €65
= €103

Total deductions: = €24.79 + €33.60 + €103
= €161.39

Take-home pay: = €840 − €161.39 = €678.61

Exercise 4.3

1. Tom's weekly wage is €800.
   His tax credit is €90 a week.
   He pays income tax at the rate of 20%.
   Copy and complete the table on the right to find Tom's take-home pay.

Gross pay	€800
Tax @ 20%	……
Tax credit	€90
Tax due	……
Take-home pay	……

2. Helen's gross pay for the year is €34 800.
   Her tax credit is €2585.
   She pays income tax at the rate of 22%.
   Copy and complete the table on the right.

Gross pay	
Tax @ 22%	
Tax credit	
Tax due	
Take-home pay	

3. Leah has a weekly wage of €750.
   Her weekly tax credit is €72 and the standard rate of tax is 25%.
   How much income tax does she pay each week?

4. Conor has a monthly wage of €3200.
   His monthly tax credit is €280 and the standard rate of tax is 22%.
   Find how much income tax he pays each month.

5. Jill has an annual salary of €42 000.
   Her annual tax credit is €3600 and the standard rate of tax is 22%.
   How much income tax does she pay for the year?

6. A carpenter has a weekly wage of €1050.
   His weekly tax credit is €78 and the standard rate of income tax is 24%.
   (i) Find how much income tax he pays each week.
   (ii) What is his net pay for the week?

7. Angela has an annual salary of €46 000.
   Her standard rate cut-off point is €35 300 and her tax credit is €3200.
   If the standard rate of income tax is 20% and the higher rate is 40%, find
   (i) the gross income tax for the year
   (ii) the amount of income tax paid for the year.

Text & Tests 2 Higher Level

8. A journalist has a weekly wage of €980.
   His standard rate cut-off point is €679 and his tax credits amount to €44. The standard rate of income tax is 20% and the higher rate is 40%.
   Find (i) his gross tax for the week
   (ii) the amount of tax he pays each week.

9. Niamh has an annual salary of €48 000.
   She has a standard rate cut-off point of €34 000 and a tax credit of €4600.
   If the standard rate of income tax is 20% and the higher rate is 40%, find how much income tax she pays.

Investigation:

Given that the standard rate of tax is 20% and the higher rate is 40% with a standard rate cut-off of €35 000, copy and complete the table and graph below.

Salary €	Tax @20%	Tax @40%	Total
10000	€2000	€0	€2000
20000		€0	
30000		€0	
35000	€7000	€0	€7000
40000			
50000		€6000	
60000			
70000			

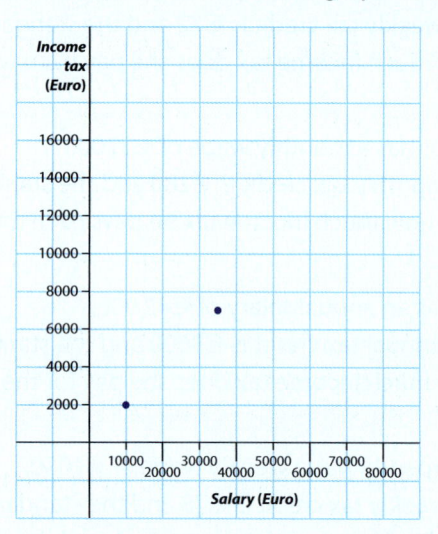

If a tax credit of € 3000 is assumed for each of the above salary levels, investigate the effect of this deduction on the graph by drawing a new graph on the same set of axes. Make a poster of your results.

Chapter 4 Applied Arithmetic

10. The Universal Social Charge (USC) rates are given in the table below:

Income thresholds (2019)		
Per year	**Per week**	**Rate of USC**
€0 – €12 012	Up to €231	0.5%
€12 012 – €19 874	From €231 to €382	2.0%
€19 874 – €70 044	From €382 to €1347	4.5%
€70 044 +	€1347 +	8.0%

  (i) Aidan has an annual salary of €57 000.
      Calculate his USC for the year.
 (ii) Paula has a weekly wage of €950.
      Calculate her USC for the week.
(iii) A salesperson has an annual salary of €63 000.
      Calculate her USC for the year.
(iv) A plumber has a weekly wage of €1200.
      Calculate his USC for the week.

11. A manager has an annual salary of €43 000. Her tax credits amount to €3500 and she pays income tax on all her income at the standard rate of r%.
If she pays €5960 in income tax for the year, find r.

12. A bus driver has a tax credit of €60 a week and pays income tax on all his wages at the standard rate of 20%.
If he pays €140 in income tax for the week, find his gross weekly wage.

13. Linda has a gross annual salary of €48 000 and her standard rate cut-off point is €31 000. The standard rate of income tax is 20% and the higher rate is 35%.
If she pays €7200 in income tax for the year, calculate her tax credit.

14. Helen paid €4400 in income tax for the year. Her tax credits amounted to €2600 and she paid income tax on all her salary at the standard rate of 20%.
Find her gross salary for the year.

15. Finian has a weekly wage of €900.
His tax credit is €68 and his standard rate cut-off point is €620.
The standard rate of tax is 20% and the higher rate is 40%.
He pays USC at the rates given in Question 10 above.
He also pays PRSI at the rate of 4% on all his wage.
  (i) How much income tax does he pay for the week?
 (ii) How much does he pay in USC?
(iii) Calculate how much he pays in PRSI.
(iv) What is his net pay for the week?

> Net pay is the same as take-home pay.

75

Text & Tests 2 Higher Level

16. John White is a factory manager and earns €54 000 a year.
    His yearly tax credit is €4300 and his standard rate cut-off point is €36 000.
    The standard rate of tax is 20% and the higher rate is 40%.
    He pays USC as in Question 10 above and PRSI on all his salary at the rate of 4%.
    (i) How much income tax does he pay in the year?
    (ii) How much does he pay in USC?
    (iii) How much in PRSI does he pay?
    (iv) Calculate his take-home pay for the year.
    (v) Express his take-home pay as a percentage of his gross salary.
        Give your answer to the nearest whole number.

17. Emma is paid €10.40 per hour for a 35 hour working week.
    For each hour over 35 hours, she is paid $1\frac{1}{2}$ times the normal hourly rate.
    Her tax credit for the week is €68 and the standard rate of tax is 26%.
    She pays USC as in Question 10 above and PRSI at the rate of 5%.

    If in a particular week she worked 45 hours, find
    (i) her gross wage for the week
    (ii) the amount of income tax she paid
    (iii) the amount of USC she paid
    (iv) the amount of PRSI she paid
    (v) her net pay for the week.

18. A woman paid €6600 in income tax for the year.
    She had a tax credit of €4600 and her standard rate cut-off point was €28 000.
    The standard rate of income tax was 20% and the higher rate was 40%.
    (i) Calculate her gross tax for the year.
    (ii) How much income tax did she pay at the standard rate?
    (iii) How much income tax did she pay at the higher rate?
    (iv) How much income did she earn in excess of €28 000?
    (v) What was the woman's gross income for the year?

19. Patricia has a gross income of €38 500 for the year
    She has an annual tax credit of €3300
    The standard rate cut-off point is €33 800
    The standard rate of income tax is 20% and the higher rate is 40%.
    (a) Find Patricia's **net income** for the year.
    Patricia receives a pay rise. As a result her **net income** for the year increases to €34 780.
    (b) Find Patricia's new **gross income** for the year.

Chapter 4 Applied Arithmetic

Section 4.4 Currency exchange

If we travel to a country not in the euro currency zone, we generally change our euro to the currency of that country.

If you see €1 = $1.35 displayed in a bank, how do you convert $100 to euro?

If we require euro in our answer, we put euro on the right-hand side of the 'equation'.

If €1 = $1.35, then

$1.35 = €1   ... Reverse the order

$1 = €$\frac{1}{1.35}$

$100 = €$\frac{1}{1.35} \times \frac{100}{1}$ = €74.07

∴ $100 = €74.07

> Put the currency required on the right-hand side of the 'equation'.

Example 1

If €1 = 120 yen, find
(i) how many yen you would get for €1200
(ii) how many euro would you get for 8000 yen.

(i) €1 = 120 yen
€1200 = (120 × 1200) yen
= 144 000 yen

(ii) €1 = 120 yen
120 yen = €1
1 yen = €$\frac{1}{120}$
8000 yen = €$\frac{1}{120} \times \frac{8000}{1}$
= €66.666
= €66.67

Note: Answers involving money are always rounded to 2 decimal places.

Example 2

A US visitor exchanged $2000 for euro when the exchange rate was €1 = $1.36. A charge was made for this service. If the person received €1444.20, calculate the charge in euro.

Text & Tests 2 Higher Level

We require euro in our answer, so we put euro on the right-hand side of the equation.

$$€1 = \$1.36$$
$$\Rightarrow \$1.36 = €1$$
$$\$1 = €\frac{1}{1.36}$$
$$\$2000 = €\frac{1}{1.36} \times \frac{2000}{1}$$
$$\$2000 = €1470.59$$

The person received €1444.20.
$\Rightarrow$ the charge = €1470.59 − €1444.20 = €26.39
The charge is €26.39.

Exercise 4.4

1. If €1 = 1.3 US dollars, find
    (i) how many dollars you would get for €450
    (ii) how many euro you would get for 800 dollars.

2. If €1 = 120 yen, find
    (i) how many yen you would get for €900
    (ii) how many euro you would get for 9000 yen.

3. Given that €1 = £0.80 sterling, find
    (i) how many pounds sterling you would get for €1200
    (ii) how many euro you would get for £600.

4. On a visit to Switzerland, a person bought a leather jacket for 560 Swiss francs.
    If €1 = 1.4 Swiss francs, find the cost of the jacket in euro.

5. If €1 = 1.4 Canadian dollars,
    (i) how many Canadian dollars would you get for €3500?
    (ii) how many euro would you get for 5600 Canadian dollars?

6. A Swiss visitor exchanged 4200 Swiss francs for euro at an exchange bureau.
    The rate of exchange was €1 = 1.4 Swiss francs.
    Find, in euro, what the visitor received if the bureau charged 1% commission.

Chapter 4 Applied Arithmetic

7. A Thai tourist paid 140 000 Thai baht to a travel agent for a holiday in Ireland.
   The cost to the travel agent of organising the holiday was €2460.
   Calculate, in baht, the profit made by the travel agent if €1 = 40 baht.

8. A bank displays the following sign above the foreign currency desk.
   Tom changed €800 for his trip to Japan.
   How many yen did he receive?
   He changed 2080 yen back into euro when he returned.
   How many euro did he receive?

	We buy	We sell
Yen	130	127

9. When the exchange rate was €1 = 9.8 South African Rand, a woman exchanged 12 000 South African Rand for euro at a bank. The bank charged a fee for this transaction. If the woman received €1166.60, find, in euro, the fee charged by the bank.

10. On a trip to Sweden, a tourist exchanged €4500 for Swedish krona when the exchange rate was €1 = 8.75 krona. He spent 25 400 krona and then on his return, exchanged what he had left back into euro when the exchange rate was now €1 = 8.60 krona. How much did he receive in euro?

11. An Australian tourist exchanged A$2500 for euro at an Irish bank.
    The bank charged a percentage commission for the transaction.
    If the exchange rate was €1 = A$1.36 and the tourist received €1801.47, find the percentage commission charged by the bank.

12. A dealer bought Swiss francs when the exchange rate was €1 = 1.45 francs.
    If he received 43 400 francs, find how many euro he exchanged.
    Give your answer to the nearest euro.

    He sold the Swiss francs when the exchange rate was €1 = 1.28 francs.
    Find, correct to the nearest euro, how much the dealer lost or gained in the transaction.

13. On a trip from the USA to Mexico, Michelle and Martha stopped at a town in the US where Michelle bought a sweater for $61.56.

    In Mexico, Martha bought the same sweater for 828.75 pesos.

    Given the exchange rates in the two countries, in which country was the sweater cheaper and by how much?

    Exchange rates
    €1 = $1.15
    €1 = 22.6 pesos

Text & Tests 2 Higher Level

Section 4.5 Compound interest

If we invest €100 in a bank for one year at 6% per annum (per year), we will earn €6 interest.

€100 is called the **principal (P)**.
6% is the **rate** per annum (***i***).
€106 is called the **final amount (F)**.

> Final amount is principal + interest.

If €400 is invested for 1 year at a rate of interest of 5%,
the interest earned is €400 × 5% = €400 × 0.05 = €20

The rate *i* is always expressed as a **decimal**.

If €800 is invested for 1 year at 6% per annum, then;

(i) to find the interest we multiply €800 by 0.06
    i.e. Interest = €800 × 0.06 = €48
(ii) to find the final amount we multiply €800 by 1.06
    i.e. Final amount = €800 × 1.06 = €848

> i = rate of interest
> P = principal invested
> Interest earned = $P \times i$

> €800 + €800 × 0.06
> = €800 × (1 + 0.06)
> = €800 × 1.06

Compound interest

Jack invested €800 in a credit union at 6% per annum.
His interest for the first year was €800 × 0.06 = €48.
At the end of the first year he had €848 in his account.
For the second year, €848 earned interest at 6%, that is, the interest earned in the first year was now itself earning further interest in the second year.
This kind of interest is called **compound interest**.

The basic method for calculating compound interest is illustrated in the following example.

> **Example 1**
>
> €1200 is invested for 3 years at 4% per annum compound interest.
> What will the investment amount to?
>
> | | |
> |---|---|
> | Principal for the first year | = €1200 |
> | Interest for the first year | = 4% of €1200 |
> | | = 1200 × 0.04 = €48 |
> | Principal for the second year | = €1200 + €48 = €1248 |
> | Interest for the second year | = 4% of €1248 |
> | | = 1248 × 0.04 = €49.92 |

Principal for the third year = €1248 + €49.92 = €1297.92
Interest for the third year = 4% of €1297.92
 = 1297.92 × 0.04
 = 51.9168 = €51.92

Final amount at end of third year = €1297.92 + €51.92
 = €1349.84

	P(principal)	R(rate)	I(interest)	FA(final amount)
Year 1	€1200	4%	€48	€1248
Year 2	€1248	4%	€49.92	€1297.92
Year 3	€1297.92	4%	€51.92	€1349.84

Investigation:

Copy and complete the table below to calculate the compound interest earned on €1200 invested at a rate of 3% over four years.

	Principal (start of year)	Final amount (F) (end of year)
Year 1	€1200	€1200 × 1.03 = €1200 × (1.03)$^{(\ )}$
Year 2	€1200 × (1.03)$^{(\ )}$	€1200 × ( )$^{(\ )}$ × ( ) = €1200 × (1.03)$^{(\ )}$
Year 3	€1200 × (1.03)$^{(\ )}$	€1200 × ( )$^{(\ )}$ × ( ) = €1200 × (1.03)$^{(\ )}$
Year 4	€1200 × (1.03)$^{(\ )}$	€1200 × ( )$^{(\ )}$ × ( ) = €1200 × (1.03)$^{(\ )}$

Complete the following line to calculate the final amount of €1200 invested for 't' years at 3% compound interest.

Year t		= €1200 × (1.03)$^{(\ )}$

Conclusion: If €P is invested for t years at i % then the final value F =

Text & Tests 2 Higher Level

$$F = P(1 + i)^t$$

F = final amount
P = principal
i = interest rate
t = number of years

Note: We can only use this formula for the period of time when *i*, the interest rate is constant and no withdrawals or lodgements are made.

Example 2

Use the compound interest formula to find the compound interest which accrues on €2800 invested for 3 years at 7.5% per annum.

$F = P(1 + i)^t$
$\quad = 2800(1 + 0.075)^3$
$\quad = 2800(1.075)^3$
$F = €3478.43$ ... by calculator

Compound interest = €3478.43 − €2800 = €678.43

Finding the rate and the principal

If €300 is invested for 1 year at 6% per annum, then the interest is €300 × 0.06 = €18.
However, if we are given that €300 earns €18 in one year, how do we find the interest?
We could reason that if €300 earns €18, then €100 would earn €6, that is, a rate of 6%.

Thus the rate is $\dfrac{18}{\cancel{300}_{3}} \times \dfrac{\cancel{100}^{1}}{1} = \dfrac{18}{3} = 6\%$

$$\text{Rate} = \dfrac{\text{Interest}}{\text{Principal}} \times \dfrac{100}{1} \%$$

Example 3

If €650 amounts to €702 in one year, find the rate.

Interest = €702 − €650 = €52

$\text{Rate} = \dfrac{\text{Interest}}{\text{Principal}} \times \dfrac{100}{1} = \dfrac{52}{650} \times \dfrac{100}{1} = 8$

∴ the rate = 8%

Chapter 4 Applied Arithmetic

Example 4

What sum of money, invested at 4% per annum compound interest, will amount to €3149.62 after 3 years?

$F = P(1 + i)^t$
$3149.62 = P(1.04)^3$
$P(1.04)^3 = 3149.62$ ... here we are looking for the principal, P.
$P = \dfrac{3149.62}{(1.04)^3} = \dfrac{3149.62}{1.1249} = €2800$

The amount invested was €2800.

Depreciation

If a car depreciates in value by 20% a year, then its value at the end of the first year will be 80% of its value at the beginning of the year.
To find 80% of a sum of money, multiply by 0.8 as 80% = 0.8.

If a car cost €25 000 and depreciates in value by 15% each year, then its value

(i) at the end of the first year = €25 000 × 0.85
(ii) at the end of the second year = €25 000 × 0.85 × 0.85 = €25 000 × (0.85)²
(iii) at the end of the third year = €25 000 × 0.85 × 0.85 × 0.85
  = €25 000 × (0.85)³
....

At the end of 8 years, its value is €25 000 × (0.85)⁸.

Example 5

A machine depreciates in value by 10% per annum.
If the machine is worth €58 320 at the end of 3 years, find its value when new.

Let P be the value of the machine when new.
Value of P at the end of 3 years = $P(0.9)^3$

∴ $P(0.9)^3 = 58\,320$
$P(0.729) = 58\,320$
$P = \dfrac{58\,320}{0.729} = 80\,000$

The value of the machine when new is €80 000.

Exercise 4.5

Find the compound interest earned on the investments in Questions 1–10, without using the compound interest formula. (Q1. and Q2. are partially completed).

1. €400 for 2 years at 6%

	P(principal)	R(rate)	I(interest)	FA(final amount)
Year 1	€400	6%		€424
Year 2		6%		

   Total compound interest =

2. €800 for 2 years at 8%

	P(principal)	R(rate)	I(interest)	FA(final amount)
Year 1	€800	8%	€64	
Year 2		8%		

   Total compound interest =

3. €900 for 2 years at 5%
4. €1000 for 2 years at 9%
5. €700 for 2 years at 4%
6. €850 for 2 years at 10%

7. Use the compound interest formula to find the final amount, correct to the nearest cent, of each of the following investments:

   (i) €600 for 2 years at 5%
   (ii) €1800 for 2 years at 9%

8. €4600 was invested for 2 years at compound interest.
   If the rate for the first year was 4% and for the second year was 5%, find the total interest for the two years.

9. €1500 was invested for 2 years at compound interest.
   The rate for the first year was 3% and the rate for the second year was 4%.
   Find the final amount at the end of the two years.

10. A company borrowed €12 000 from a bank at 11% per annum compound interest.
    The company repaid €5 000 at the end of the first year. Use the table format below to find out how much the company owed at the end of the second year.

	P(principal)	R(rate)	I(interest)	FA(final amount)	Repayment
Year 1	€12 000	11%			− €5000
Year 2		11%			

Chapter 4 Applied Arithmetic

11. €700 will amount to €756 after one year if invested at 8% per annum.
   (i) By what number is €700 multiplied to get €756?
   (ii) By what number is €756 divided to get €700?

12. A sum of money is invested at 7% per annum.
If it amounts to €6848 after one year, find the sum invested.

13. €2500 was invested in a building society.
If it amounted to €2612.50 after one year, calculate the rate of interest.

14. What sum of money invested for 3 years at 8% per annum compound interest would amount to €1007.77?

15. What sum of money invested at 5% per annum compound interest would amount to €10 988.78 in 6 years?

16. €8000 is invested for 3 years at compound interest.
The rate for the first year is 5% and for the second year is 6%.
Find the amount of the investment at the end of two years.
At the end of the third year, the money invested amounted to €9260.16.
Calculate the rate of interest for the third year.

17. A person borrows €15 000 for two years.
Interest for the first year is charged at 12% per annum.
The person repays €6000 at the end of the first year.
If the amount owed at the end of the second year is €12 042, find the rate of interest for the second year.

18. A sum of money was invested for 2 years.
The rate of interest for the first year was 4% and for the second year was 5%.
The amount at the end of the second year was €9282.
   (i) By what number is €9282 divided to get the amount at the end of the first year?
   (ii) By what number is the amount at the end of the first year divided to get the sum invested?
   What is the sum of money invested?

19. A person invested €10 000 in a building society.
The rate of interest for the first year was $2\frac{1}{2}$%.
At the end of the first year, the person invested a further €1000.
The rate of interest for the second year was 2%.
Calculate the value of the investment at the end of the second year.

At the end of the second year, a further €2000 was invested.
At the end of the third year, the total investment amounted to €14 014.
Calculate the rate of interest for the third year.

20. A machine cost €15 000.
If it depreciated in value by 15% per annum, find its value at the end of two years.

21. Vans depreciate in value by 20% per annum.
  (i) If a van is bought for €23 000, find its value at the end of three years.
 (ii) If the value of a van is €11 520 after two years, find its value when new.

22. A new car was bought for €24 000. It decreased in value by 20% in the first year.
If its value at the end of the second year was €16 128, by what percentage did its value decrease during the second year?

23. Aidan invests €5000 in a special savings account for two years.
The rate is 3% for the first year with a higher rate for the second year.
Tax at 40% will be deducted each year from the interest earned.
  (a) How much will Aidan's investment be worth at the end of the first year, after tax is paid?
  (b) Aidan calculates that, after tax has been deducted, his investment will be worth €5196.89 at the end of the second year. Calculate the rate of interest for the second year.

Chapter 4 Applied Arithmetic

Test yourself 4

1. In a two-month period, the McCabes used 980 units of electricity.
   Each unit of electricity cost 21c and the standing charge was €21.30.
   Find the total amount of their bill when VAT at $12\frac{1}{2}$% was added on.

2. Sylvia has an annual salary of €42 800.
   Her tax credit is €3350 and her standard rate cut-off point is €31 000.
   If the standard rate of income tax is 20% and the higher rate is 40%, calculate how much income tax she pays for the year.

3. A man borrowed €8000 from a bank at 12% per annum compound interest.
   He repaid €3000 at the end of the first year.
   How much did he owe the bank at the end of the second year?

4. €4500 was invested for 2 years at compound interest.
   The rate for the first year was 8% and for the second year 6%.
   Find the total interest earned.

5. When the exchange rate is €1 = US$1.28, a person changes US$1920 to euro.
   A charge is made for this service.
   What is the percentage charge if the person receives €1462.50?

6. During a sale, all items of mens' clothing are reduced by 20% of the marked price.
   (i) If the sale price of an overcoat was €336, what was the marked price?
   (ii) If the store made a profit of 5% on the cost price of the overcoat during the sale, what percentage profit did it make on the marked price before the sale?

7. Lizzy bought 0.8 kg of pears at €1.90 per kilogram and 1.4 kg of apples. The total cost was €4.46.
   What was the price per kilogram of the apples?

8. A jar with 8 chocolates in it weighs 160 g.
   The same jar with 20 chocolates in it weighs 304 g.
   How much does the jar weigh on its own?

9. A sum of money invested at compound interest amounted to €5342.40 at the end of two years.
   (i) If the interest rate for the second year was 6%, how much was the investment worth at the end of the first year?
   (ii) If the original sum invested was €4800, find the rate for the first year.

10. Mark often travels to Dublin by train.
An ordinary return ticket costs €34.50.
A *leap card* costs €70. If he has one, the return ticket is only €23.
If he buys one of these integrated travel cards, what is the least number of return trips to Dublin he must make for the total cost to be less than for ordinary tickets?

11. Joan Buckley has an annual salary of €39 000.
Her tax credits amount to €4750 and her standard rate cut-off point is €31 000.
If the standard rate of income tax is 20% and the higher rate is 40%, find how much income tax she pays for the year.

12. A sum of money was invested for two years at compound interest.
The rate for the first year was 6% and for the second year $5\frac{1}{2}$%.
If the value of the investment at the end of the two years was €6709.80, find the sum invested.

13. Ruth's electricity bill is based on the following details:

Previous meter reading	46523
Present meter reading	48249
Charge per unit	21.5 cent
Standing charge	€21.40
VAT on total bill	$13\frac{1}{2}$%

Work out the total bill, including VAT.

14. An Australian visitor to Ireland exchanged 2000 dollars for euro when the exchange rate was €1 = 1.6 Australian dollars.
What was the percentage charge for the transaction if she received €1225?

15. During the first year, a new car depreciates in value by 20% and during the second year, the car depreciates in value by 15% of its value at the beginning of that year.
What is the cost of a new car if its value at the end of the second year is €15 640?

16. Jonathan is offered a choice of the following pay deals:

Ⓐ: 6% increase this year followed by a 6% increase next year

Ⓑ: $5\frac{1}{2}$% increase this year followed by a $6\frac{1}{2}$% increase next year

Which offer should Jonathan accept? Explain your answer.

17. A woman invested €12 000 in a building society at 7% per annum.
At the end of the first year, she withdrew €B. If the value of her investment at the end of the second year was €8923.80, find the value of B.

Chapter 4 Applied Arithmetic

18. Cecil has a tax credit of €3600 a year and his standard rate cut-off point is €30 000. The standard rate of income tax is 20% and the higher rate is 35%. If Cecil pays €7650 income tax for the year, find his gross salary.

19. Desmond and his 3 friends need to book their summer holiday.
    They plan to share two twin rooms at the Pacific hotel.
    The cost of the rooms is as per brochure below:

	6th - 3rd June July	4th - 7th July August	8th - 12th August September	13th September	- 15th October
	7 nights	14 nights	7 nights	14 nights	7 nights	14 nights	7 nights	14 nights
Single room	€525	€675	€595	€765	€625	€780	€575	€720
Double room	€605	€775	€675	€865	€705	€880	€645	€800
Twin room	€605	€785	€685	€880	€715	€895	€645	€810
Special Offer; 2% discount for every month in advance that full payment is made up to a maximum of six months.							

    Each price shown is the price per person.
    The friends wish to go on the 24th of August for 14 nights.
    Desmond has €245 and borrows the remaining cost of the holiday from his parents.
    He pays for the holiday on the 22rd March.
    He repays his parents all the money he owed over 5 months in equal monthly amounts.
    How much is each monthly amount?

20. Cyril invested €5000 in a special bank account which offered 3% interest for the first year and a higher rate for the second year if the money is left on deposit.
    At the end of each year DIRT tax of 40% was paid. If the final amount in his account at the end of the second year, having paid all his taxes, was €5212.16, find:
    (i) the final amount in his account at the end of the first year.
    (ii) the rate of interest paid for the second year.

21. Fergus's salary for the year was €38 500 with a tax credit of €3300 and a standard cut-off of €33 800.
    (i) Given that the standard rate of tax is 20% and the higher rate is 40%, find his net income for the year.
    (ii) As a result of a pay rise Fergus's net income increased to €34 780. Find his gross income for the year.

Text & Tests 2 Higher Level

Assignment:

This assignment asks you to estimate the cost of painting (a) a classroom (b) a school.

(a) In groups, work out the dimensions of the painted surfaces in your classroom.

By checking the 'coverage' of paint, calculate the number of litres of paint needed to paint the room. (Assume only 1 coat is needed)

Estimate the number of hours needed to prepare and paint the room.

Estimate the cost of the equipment needed, i.e. brushes, rollers, tape, protective coverings, etc.

Estimate how much a 'professional' painter would charge per hour considering overheads such as, insurance, transport (van), etc.

Copy and complete a chart, like the one below with the average values of your group.

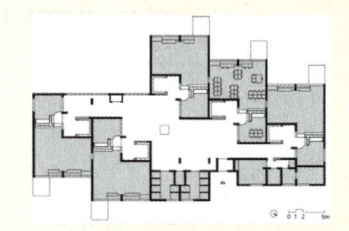

	Cost per unit	Total Cost	Total cost + VAT
Litres needed = ( )			
Hours needed = ( )			
Equipment			

Estimate for painting your classroom. 　€

(b) Since a school has many similar classrooms it is easy to multiply the cost of a single room to estimate the total cost of painting the classrooms.

Connecting spaces (corridors), special rooms (offices, hall, etc) are different.

Make a list of all the rooms in your school and use a multiplier to estimate the cost of painting the special rooms. (e.g. a porch might = 1 × classroom, a corridor might = 4 × classroom etc)

Design your own chart to include the spaces to be painted in your school.

Spaces	Multiplier	Cost (+VAT)
Classrooms		
Hall		
Corridor		

Estimate for painting your school. 　€

Compare your estimate with other groups.

Statistics 1 – Collecting data

Chapter 5

From first year, you will recall how to:

- plan a survey,
- collect data,
- identify numerical and categorical data,
- understand populations and bias,
- write questionnaires,
- get a simple random sample,
- get representative samples.

In this chapter, you will learn to:

- identify data collected through primary and secondary sources,
- use frequency tables to organise collected data,
- identify how social media can cause bias in data collection,
- identify the limitations of sample data.

Section 5.1 Statistical questions

The purpose of statistics is to answer questions and provide information on relevant topics.

In most countries, the government is the biggest collector of statistics.

Our government provides information about:

> The numbers out of work
> Inflation
> The number of visitors to Ireland.
> The number of students sitting examinations per year etc.

Other organisations are interested in statistical questions such as:

> The average rainfall per month, etc.
> The change in the value of shares.
> The most popular models of car, etc.

Companies do **market research** to find out what customers like/dislike about certain products or services.
Having statistics helps us plan.

Investigation:

Governments, planning for the future, will collect information in different ways to help them make policy decisions.
The words (i) Opinion Poll (ii) Census (iii) Referendum, are all used at different times.
Research the words and write a short definition of each, concentrating on the differences between them.

Investigation:

Carefully listen to / read news reports;

(i) on a radio or television
(ii) in a newspaper or magazine
(iii) on the internet.

Make a list of 3 sets of statistics that are mentioned.

Write down the statistical question that is being asked by each statistical report.

Types of data

All statistics start with a question.
e.g. How long did people spend watching the world cup?
To answer each question we need **data**.

Data is another name for the facts and pieces of information that we collect.
Data that is not in an organised form is called **raw data**.
Data can be divided into two broad categories, namely **categorical data** and **numerical data**.

Data which fits into a group or category is called **categorical data**.
It is generally described using terms such as 'colour', 'favourite sport' or 'country of birth'.

Chapter 5 Statistics 1 – Collecting data

Categorical data such as:
- types of car, e.g. diesel, electric, hybrid, petrol.
- male or female
- true/false
- favourite musicians.

Data which can be counted or measured is called **numerical data** because the answer is a number.

Here is a summary of data types:

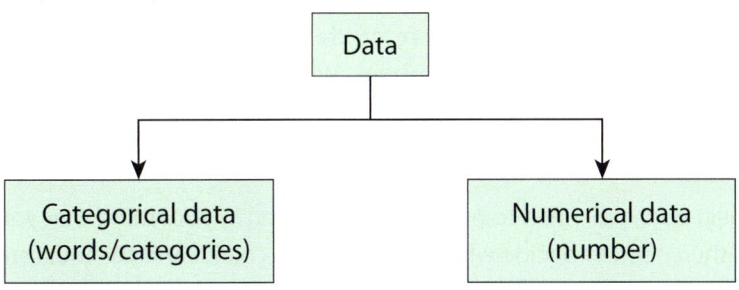

```
              Data
             /    \
   Categorical    Numerical data
   data           (number)
   (words/categories)
```

Example 1

For each of the following, write down whether it is numerical or categorical data:
  (i) the number of goals scored in a hockey match
  (ii) the temperature of an oven
  (iii) people's hair colours
  (iv) countries where cars were manufactured
  (v) star ratings of the quality of hotels
  (vi) time taken for athletes to run 400 metres.

(i) numerical   (ii) numerical   (iii) categorical
(iv) categorical   (v) categorical   (vi) numerical

Collecting data

Data is collected for a variety of reasons and from a variety of sources.
- Companies do **market research** to find out what customers like or dislike about their products and to see whether or not they would like new products.
- The government carries out a **census** of every person in the country every five years. The information gathered is used by other people and organisations for further planning.

Data can be collected by any of these methods:
- **Surveys**: doing a survey by means of a questionnaire and recording what people say.
- **Experiments**: carrying out an experiment that may involve the use of technology or data logger.
- **Research**: researching sources such as reference books, websites, data bases, newspapers, historical records.

When stating conclusions based on data collected it is important to note whether the data was
 (i) **primary data**, i.e. a survey or an experiment carried out by yourself or
 (ii) **secondary data**, i.e. data obtained by researching other sources, e.g. newspapers, magazines or internet sources e.g. Facebook, Wikipedia, etc.

The reliability of data, particularly secondary data, is essential when making conclusions based on that data.

Before you collect data, you need to have a clear question in your mind that you want answered. You then need to decide what sort of data to collect and the most suitable and efficient method of collecting it.

Surveys

Primary data is generally collected by means of a **survey**.
The main survey methods are:
- personal interviews in which people are asked questions; this is generally done by means of a **questionnaire**.
- **telephone surveys**: here the interview is conducted by phone
- **observation**: this involves monitoring behaviour

Experiments

These are particularly useful for collecting scientific data; drug companies carry out experiments to test the benefits and the side-effects of new drugs.

Questionnaires

A **questionnaire** is a set of questions designed to obtain data from individuals.

People who answer questionnaires are called **respondents**.

There are two ways in which the questions can be asked.
- An interviewer asks the questions and fills in the questionnaire.
- People are given a questionnaire and asked to fill in the responses themselves.

Chapter 5 Statistics 1 – Collecting data

When you are composing questions for a questionnaire,
› be clear what you want to find out and what data you need
› ask short, concise questions
› start with simple questions to encourage the person who is giving the responses
› provide response boxes where possible: Yes ☐   No ☐
› avoid leading questions such as
     'Don't you agree that there is too much sport on television?'
  or   'Do you think that professional footballers are overpaid?'
› avoid personal questions such as those which involve name, exact age or weight.

Avoiding bias

When you are collecting data, you need to make sure that your survey or experiment is **fair** and avoids **bias**. If bias exists, the data collected might be unrepresentative.

Social media sites are now being used to **source data** for research purposes.

Technology is used to analyse this information.

Benefits: hundreds of millions of users.

Dangers: selection bias can occur by excluding large sections of the population with little or no access to social media.

Here are some questions which should be avoided because they suggest a particular answer or they may cause embarrassment or shame.

Have you ever stolen money from your parents? Yes ☐ No ☐	Few students are likely to answer this question honestly if they have already stolen.
Do you agree that the Minister for Finance should resign because of the poor state of the economy? Yes ☐ No ☐	This wording of this question suggests that the right answer is 'yes'. It is a leading question and therefore likely to be **biased**.

Frequency tables

If conducting a survey, we often collect a lot of data.
We need to organise this **raw data** so that it makes sense.
A frequency table is useful for grouping and counting data scores in an efficient way.
The **frequency** of a score is the number of times that score appears in the set of data.

Text & Tests 2 Higher Level

> ### Example 1
>
> Twenty people were surveyed about the number of cars owned in their household. This is the data collected:
>
> | 2 | 2 | 1 | 2 | 0 | 3 | 2 | 1 | 1 | 4 |
> |---|---|---|---|---|---|---|---|---|---|
> | 1 | 1 | 1 | 2 | 2 | 0 | 3 | 2 | 1 | 2 |
>
> Use tally marks to construct a frequency table for the data.
>
> For each score in the data set, we draw a tally mark in the tally column. The first score is a 2, so we mark a '|' in the tally column beside 2. We continue until we have made a tally mark for each score.
>
> The completed frequency table is shown on the right.
>
> Always check that the total is equal to the total number of given data.
>
> | Score | Tally | Frequency |
> |---|---|---|
> | 0 | || | 2 |
> | 1 | |||| || | 7 |
> | 2 | |||| ||| | 8 |
> | 3 | || | 2 |
> | 4 | | | 1 |
> | Total | | 20 |

Exercise 5.1

1. State whether each of the following is numerical or categorical data:
    (i) The number of cars sold by a certain garage last month
    (ii) The favourite soccer teams of pupils in your class
    (iii) The continent of birth of people who came to Ireland in the past year
    (iv) The number of horses in a race
    (v) The time taken by the winning horse to complete the race
    (vi) The blood-types of the teachers in your school
    (vii) The types of trees in a wood
    (viii) The length of time taken to complete a sudoku puzzle.

2. State whether each of the following is an example of primary data or secondary data:
    (i) Conor tossed a coin 100 times and recorded the result to investigate if the coin was fair.
    (ii) Brenda counted the number of SUVs that passed the school gate between 9 a.m. and 10 a.m.

Chapter 5 Statistics 1 – Collecting data

(iii) Shane used the internet to check the number of medals Ireland won in boxing in the last four Olympic Games.
(iv) Emer checked the Central Statistics Office website to check the number of people on the Live Register for each of the last twenty four months.

3. A brewery wants to produce a new type of beer.
Suggest how they might use both primary and secondary data to do market research.

4. Niamh wants to find out how often adults go to the cinema.
She uses this question on a questionnaire.

'How many times do you go to the cinema?'
☐ ☐ ☐
Not very often   Sometimes   A lot

(i) Write down **two** things wrong with this question.
(ii) Design a better question for her questionnaire to find out how often adults go to the cinema.
You should include some response boxes.

5. Eamonn is trying to find out what people think of the *FFG Political Party*.
He is trying to decide between these two questions for his questionnaire.
Which question should he use? Explain your answer.
(i) How do you rate the *FFG Party's* economic policies?
Strongly   Don't   Strongly
agree ☐   Agree ☐   know ☐   Disagree ☐   disagree ☐
(ii) Do you agree that the *FFG Party* has the best economic policies?
Yes ☐   No ☐

6. The graphic on the right shows the midday temperatures for each day in July.
(i) Outline the categorical data contained in the graphic
(ii) Are the dates July 1, 2, 3, ... numerical or categorical?
Explain your conclusion.

July Midday Temperatures

JULY

SUN	MON	TUE	WED	THU	FRI	SAT
	1 17	2 16	3 18	4 18	5 18	6 17
7 19	8 20	9 22	10 22	11 21	12 21	13 22
14 22	15 23	16 24	17 23	18 23	19 23	20 24
21 24	22 23	23 23	24 24	25 25	26 23	27 23
28 25	29 25	30 24	31 25			

97

7. A Premier League team has 24 first-team players.
   Their average age is 26 years.
   They were born in Ireland, England, Croatia, Senegal, Italy, France and the Ivory Coast.

   Describe the data contained in each of the three statements above.

8. Explain what is wrong with each of the following survey questions.
   Suggest a better alternative for each question.
   (i) What age are you?
   (ii) Would you describe yourself as being well-educated?
   (iii) Normal people like animals.
   Do you like animals?
   (iv) Would you agree that top actors are paid too much?
   (v) Have you ever taken illegal drugs?
   (vi) Where exactly do you live?
   (vii) In view of the huge numbers of road accidents outside this school, do you think the speed limit should be reduced?

9. Aidan wants to find out what students think about the library service at his college.
   Part of the questionnaire he has written is shown.

   Q1. What is your full name? ....
   Q2. How many times a week do you go to the library?
   ☐ Often   ☐ Sometimes   ☐ Never

   (i) Why should Q1 not be asked?
   (ii) What is wrong with the choices offered in Q2?

10. This question was included in a questionnaire.

    How old are you?   Young ☐   Middle-aged ☐   Elderly ☐

    (i) What is wrong with the question and responses?
    (ii) Rewrite the question and responses in a better way.

11. Valerie is the manager of a supermarket.
    She wants to find out how often people shop at her supermarket.
    She will use a questionnaire.

    Design a suitable question for Valerie to use on her questionnaire.
    You must include some response boxes.

Chapter 5 Statistics 1 – Collecting data

12. Give a reason why questions A and B below should be re-worded before being included in a questionnaire.
Rewrite each one showing exactly how you would present it in a questionnaire.

Question A: Do you live in a working-class or middle-class area?
Question B: The new supermarket seems to be a great success. Do you agree?

13. For each of these questions or statements, what would be the best way to collect the data? Choose from the box.

> **A** questionnaire or data collection sheet
> **B** experiment **C** other source

   (i) What sport people in your class watch most often.
   (ii) How often people go to the theatre. On which days?
   (iii) The percentage of motor vehicle accidents in Ireland that occur between 6 p.m. and midnight.
   (iv) Eoin wants to find out if a dice is biased.

14. A mobile phone company wants to carry out a survey.
It wants to find out the distribution of the age and sex of its customers and the frequency with which they use their phones.
The company intends to use a questionnaire.
Write three questions and corresponding responses that will enable the company to efficiently carry out the survey.

15. The ages of the members of the school drama club are as follows:

12, 13, 12, 14, 15, 18, 13, 15, 16, 15, 15, 17, 13, 14, 15, 14, 16,
17, 15, 15, 16, 12, 13, 14, 14, 17, 16, 14, 15, 13, 16, 14, 15, 13

   (i) Create and complete a frequency table to display the data.
   (ii) What is the difference in age between the eldest and youngest student in the club?
   (iii) What is the most common age of students in the club?
   (iv) What is the least common age of students in the club? Can you suggest a reason for this?
   (v) What percentage of the club are seniors, i.e. 15 years and older, correct to the nearest whole number?

16. Angelina wants to find out what type of music the students in her year group like best. Design a data collection sheet that she could use to collect this information.

17. The final round scores in the Irish Open by the top 30 leading golfers were:

64, 70, 68, 72, 70, 70, 66, 67, 69, 70, 71, 70, 66, 68, 70,
68, 70, 74, 72, 71, 69, 69, 68, 70, 66, 69, 70, 70, 71, 70.

Using a tally chart, make a frequency table for this data.
   (i) What was the gap between the highest and lowest score?
   (ii) Which was the most common score?
   (iii) What percentage scored higher than the most common score?

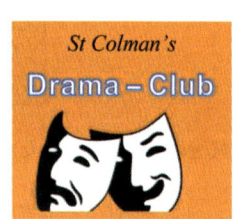

18. Susan is trying to find out opinions about the local soccer club. She posts a question to their Facebook page. Give a reason why the data collected might be biased.

19. Alex has decided to do a project on social media use in his class.
Write a question he might use that would give numerical data.

Section 5.2 Sampling

If you were asked to investigate the claim,

'Rugby players in Ireland are taller than Gaelic football players',

do you measure the heights of all rugby players and all Gaelic football players in the country? This would be an enormous task as there are thousands of players in these categories.

In this study, we use the word **population** to describe **all** the rugby and Gaelic footballers in the country.

When a population is too large for a study, we collect data from some members of the population only. In statistics, this group is called a **sample**. The purpose of a sample is to collect data from some of the population and use it to draw conclusions about the whole population.

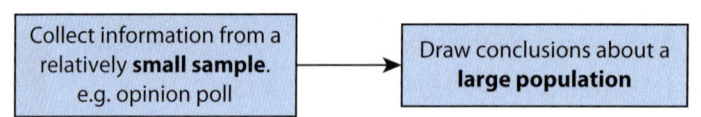

Collect information from a relatively **small sample**. e.g. opinion poll → Draw conclusions about a **large population**

Note: Raw data can be collected from a whole population in the case of a small village.

However a **sample** is needed to collect data from the population of a city.

Bias

The sample you select for your study is very important. If the sample is not properly selected, the results may be **biased**. If **bias** exists, the results will be distorted and so will not be properly representative of the population as a whole.

The **size** of a sample is also important. If the sample is too small, the results may not be very reliable. If the sample is too large, the data may take a long time to collect and analyse.

Random sample

One of the ways to avoid bias in a survey is to take a **random sample**.

In a random sample, every member of the population being considered has an equal chance of being selected. Random samples need to be carefully chosen.

Chapter 5 Statistics 1 – Collecting data

Methods for choosing a **random sample** could involve giving each member of the population a number and then selecting the numbers for the sample in one of these ways:
- putting the numbers into a hat and then selecting however many you need for the sample
- using a random number table
- using a random number generator on your calculator or computer.

Electronic calculators are very useful for generating random numbers.

If you want to generate 3-digit numbers, press $\boxed{\text{SHIFT}}$, and then press $\boxed{\text{Ran \#}}$.

Now press $\boxed{=}$ and disregard the decimal point.

If the number displayed is 0.107, write 107.

Press $\boxed{=}$ repeatedly to get more random numbers.

Limitations of statistics

It is almost certain that a large set of data will contains errors.
  (i)   Mistype: The correct value was obtained but it was written down incorrectly
        e.g. 1183 instead of 1138, 993 instead of 93.
 (ii)   Mistaken answer: A person earning €25 000 per year replies €25 000 when asked their monthly salary.
(iii)   Incorrect measurement: e.g. rounding masses, e.g. 20 g, 30 g, 40 g, etc. instead of
        20 g, 25 g, 30 g, 35 g, 40 g, etc.
(iv)   Biased sampling: as mentioned above.

It is important to check every data set for unusual values and to be very specific when asking questions for a questionnaire.

Investigation:

In the British Parliament, two MPs debated the need for road signs in Wales to be given in both English and Welsh as follows:

MP **A**: "Since less than 10% of the population of Wales speak Welsh, it is **unnecessary to include directions in Welsh**."

MP **B**: "Over 90% of the area of Wales is inhabited by a population whose principal language is Welsh, therefore **directions in Welsh are essential**."

At the time, both statements were true but led to opposite conclusions.

Explain how both statements could have been true.

Text & Tests 2 Higher Level

Exercise 5.2

1. A school has 820 students and an investigation concerning the school uniform is being conducted.
   40 students from the school are randomly selected to complete the survey on their school uniform. In this situation,
   (i) what is the population size?
   (ii) what is the size of the sample?

2. Jack wanted to find information on how much pocket money the 900 students in his school got each week. He planned to have a sample size of (i) 4 **or** (ii) 40 **or** (iii) 400.

   Which sample size should he pick? Explain why you did not choose the remaining two options.

3. Would you collect data from the whole population or just a sample in each of the following cases?

Population	Data required
(a) Students in your class	Birthdays
(b) Trees in school grounds	Circumference of trunk
(c) Trees in a forest	Circumference of trunk
(d) Shoppers in local supermarket	Daily spend
(e) Cars in local car dealership	Price of second hand cars

4. Melanie wants to find out how often people go to the cinema.
   She gives a questionnaire to all the women leaving a cinema.

   Her sample is biased.
   Give **two** possible reasons why.

5. Amy wants to find out how often people play sport.
   She went to a local sports shop and questioned the people she met.
   Explain why this sample is likely to be biased.

6. Dara wants to find out how people get to work each day.
   Which of the following is the most appropriate group to question?
   A: Every fourth person at a bus stop.
   B: A group of people at lunch break.
   C: People arriving late for work.

7. Jennifer wants to investigate if people want longer prison sentences for criminals.
   Which of the following is the most appropriate group to question?
   A: Members of the gardaí.
   B: People at a football match.
   C: People who have been in prison.
   Explain your answer.

8. Amanda wants to choose a sample of 500 adults from the town where she lives.
   She considers these methods of choosing her sample:

   Method 1:   Choose people shopping in the town centre on Saturday mornings.
   Method 2:   Choose names at random from the electoral register.
   Method 3:   Choose people living in the streets near her house.

   Which method is most likely to produce an unbiased sample?
   Give a reason for your answer.

9. Comment on any possible bias in the following situations:
   (i) Sixth-year students only are interviewed about changes to the school uniform.
   (ii) Motorists stopped in peak-hour are interviewed about traffic problems.
   (iii) Real estate agents are interviewed about the prices of houses.
   (iv) A 'who will you vote for?' survey at an expensive city restaurant.

10. A research company is canvassing peoples' opinions on whether smoking should be banned in all public places.

    They canvass people standing outside buildings in the city during office hours. Explain why the data collected is likely to be biased.

11. Use the ⎡Ran #⎤ key on your calculator to choose a sample of 8 pupils from a year-group of 100.

12. Which of the following samples are likely to be representative samples?
    For those that are not representative, give a reason why they are not.

    Ⓐ Survey task: To test the effectiveness of a new drug for migraines.
        Sample: Chosen by giving the drug to all patients, of just one doctor, who suffer from migraines.

    Ⓑ Survey task: To survey opinion about fresh bread baked in a local supermarket.
        Sample: Chosen by interviewing every 20th shopper at the supermarket checkout on a Saturday

    Ⓒ Survey task: To survey the voting intentions of residents of a particular constituency in the coming election.
        Sample: A random sample of people at the local train station between 7 a.m. and 9 a.m. are surveyed.

Text & Tests 2 Higher Level

Test yourself 5

1. State whether each of the following sets of data is numerical or categorical:
    (i) Favourite type of apple.
    (ii) The number of bicycles in a household.
    (iii) The weights of three-year-old children.
    (iv) The brands of dog-food on sale in a supermarket.
    (v) County of birth.
    (vi) The amount of rainfall in each month of the year.

2. State whether each of the following is primary data or secondary data:
    (i) Counting the number of hatchback cars passing the school gate.
    (ii) Looking at records to see how many people passed through Shannon Airport each day in June one year.
    (iii) Examing tourist brochures to find the average weekly snowfall at a skiing resort.
    (iv) Checking *Wikipedia* to see how many gold medals each country won at the London Olympics.

3. The manager of an Aqua Park asks the following two questions on a questionnaire.

    'Do you go to the Aqua Park?'   Sometimes ☐   Often ☐
    'How old are you?'   0 to 10 years ☐   10 to 20 years ☐   over 20 years ☐

    (i) What is wrong with each of these questions?
    (ii) For both questions above, write a better version that the manager can use.

4. Which of the two questions and responses below are the more suitable for inclusion in a questionnaire?
    Give a reason for your selection.
    (i)
    Do you agree that having a lovely, warm, relaxing bath at night helps you go to sleep?
    Yes ☐   No ☐

    (ii)
    Does a warm bath at night help you go to sleep?
    Yes ☐   No ☐   Not sure ☐

Chapter 5 Statistics 1 – Collecting data

5. Explain what is wrong with each of the following survey questions and suggest better alternatives.
   (i) How many phones are there in your home?
   (ii) What type of car do you own?
   (iii) What is your email address?

6. The pupils in a third-year class carried out a survey to find the average amount of time spent in the computer room per person each week.
   The pupils decided to give the questionnaire to one of the following groups.
   Which of these is a good sample?
   Give a reason why each of the others is not a good sample.

   Sample 1 the pupils who used the computer room during one lunch break
   Sample 2 all the pupils in the library during one lunch break
   Sample 3 the first 50 pupils to arrive at school on a particular morning
   Sample 4 every 8th pupil on the school roll

7. The management of a theme park have made some changes to the amusements. They want to use a questionnaire to find out what people think about the changes.
   The following questions are suggested.
   Write down what is wrong with each of them and design a new question and responses for each that is more suitable.
   (i) What do you think of the new amusements?
      Very good ☐   Good ☐   Satisfactory ☐
   (ii) How much money would you normally expect to pay for each amusement?
      €6–€8 ☐   €8–€10 ☐   More than €10 ☐
   (iii) How often do you visit the park each year?
      Often ☐   Not very often ☐

8. Draw a frequency table for the following set of data.

   9 13 11 11 9 10 11 10
   11 12 10 10 12 10 9 8
   7 10 11 13 12 13 11 13

9. Elizabeth surveyed 30 students in her year to determine the number of children in each family.
   This resulted in the following data.

   2 3 1 3 4 2 1 3 2 5
   1 3 2 5 6 2 1 2 1 4
   4 2 2 3 1 1 2 3 1 2

   (i) Draw a frequency table for this data.
   (ii) In what % of homes were there 3 children?
   (iii) Why did the number 0 not appear in the data?

Assignment:

A: "Do the same percentages of boys and girls in your school have the same colour eyes?"

Design a questionnaire to collect data to answer the question above.

Choose a maximum of 4 categories of colour of eyes.
 (i) Decide how to pick a random sample of 30.
 (ii) Decide how to pick a random sample of 50.

Draw a frequency table of your results.

Convert your numbers in each category into percentages.

Draw a conclusion.

Did the sample size make a significant difference to your results? Explain.

B: Using a random sample of at least 30 from 1st year and 6th year group, carry out the following survey:

To compare the number of siblings, 1, 2, 3, 4, greater than 4 (including the responder) in the 1st year group, with the number of siblings in 6th year of your school.

Present your results in percentages in the form of a frequency table.

Write any conclusions about the changes, if any, in the size of families you can deduce from your data.

Perimeter – Area – Volume

chapter 6

From first year, you will recall how to:

- convert between different units of measurement,
- find the perimeter of straight edged shapes,
- find the area of rectangles, triangles and compound shapes,
- calculate the surface area and volume of rectangular solids.

In this chapter, you will learn to:

- find the area of a parallelogram,
- use the irrational number, π,
- find the area and circumference of a circle or sector,
- solve problems involving circular shapes,
- draw the net of a rectangular solid,
- calculate the surface area and volume of a given prism,
- draw and interpret scaled diagrams.

Section 6.1 Review of perimeter and area

In *Text & Tests 1*, you found the perimeter and area of squares, rectangles and triangles.

The box below summarises what you learned.

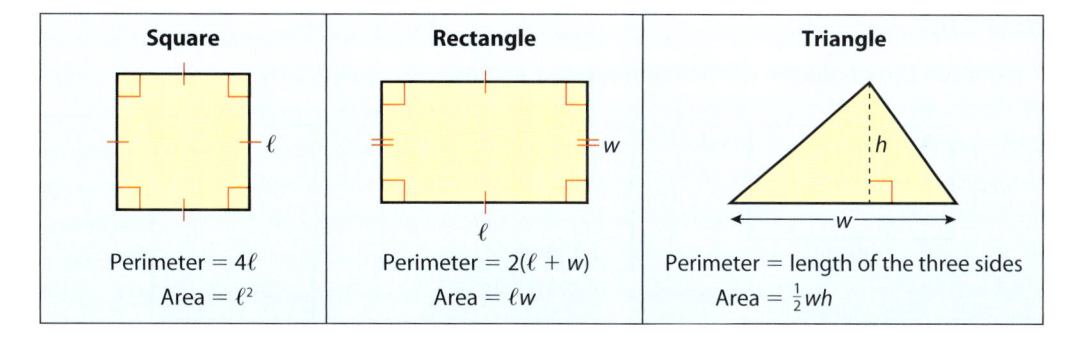

Square	Rectangle	Triangle
Perimeter = 4ℓ	Perimeter = $2(\ell + w)$	Perimeter = length of the three sides
Area = ℓ^2	Area = ℓw	Area = $\frac{1}{2}wh$

Text & Tests 2 Higher Level

Here are three triangles which all have different shapes.

In each triangle, the base (b) and perpendicular height (h) are shown.

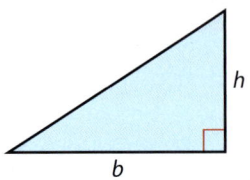

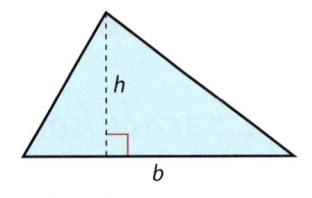

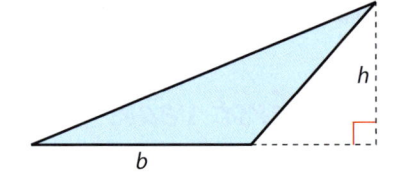

For each triangle, the area = $\frac{1}{2}bh$.

> **Example 1**
>
> Find the area of the shaded region of this figure.
>
> Shaded area = area of rectangle − area of triangle
> $= 20 \times 16 - \frac{1}{2} \times 12 \times 9$
> $= 320 - 54$
> $= 266 \text{ cm}^2$

> **Example 2**
>
> The area of the given triangle is 56 cm².
> Find the perpendicular height, h.
>
> Area $= \frac{1}{2} \times 14 \times h$
> $\therefore \frac{1}{2} \times 14 \times h = 56$
> $7h = 56$
> $h = 8 \text{ cm}$

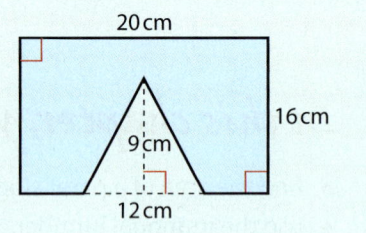

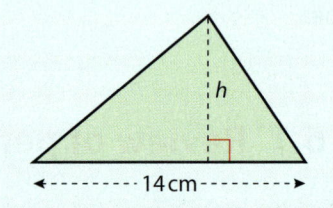

Exercise 6.1

1. Work out the perimeter of each of these rectangles:

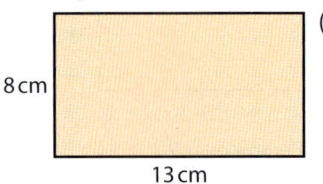

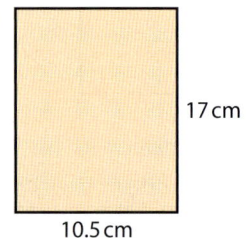

   (i) 9 cm by 14 cm

   (ii) 8 cm by 13 cm

   (iii) 17 cm by 10.5 cm

2. Find the area of each of the rectangles in Question **1.** above.

Chapter 6 Perimeter – Area – Volume

3. Find the length of the missing side in each of these rectangles:

(i) ? | 84 cm² | 12 cm

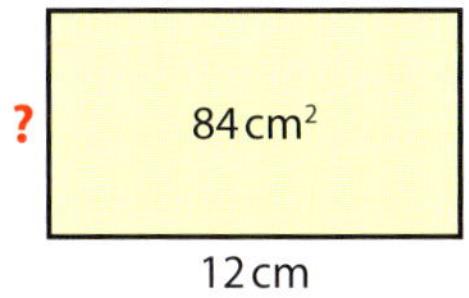

(ii) ? | 176 cm² | 11 cm

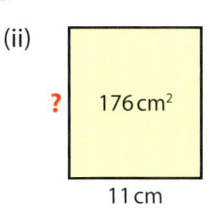

(iii) 198 cm² | 9 cm | ?

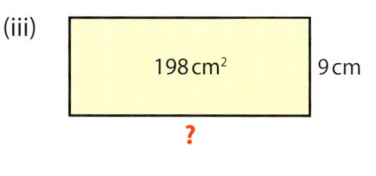

4. Work out the perimeter of each of these shapes, where all the angles are right angles:

(i) 9 cm, 8 cm, 6 cm, 15 cm

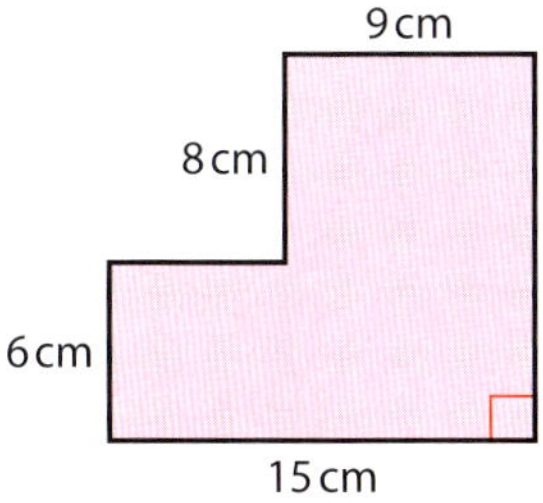

(ii) 12 cm, 15 cm

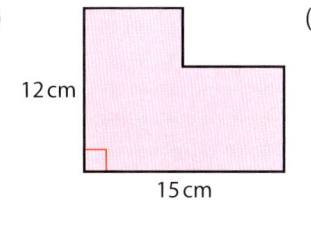

(iii) 12 cm, 3 cm, 14 cm

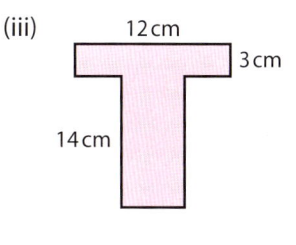

(You have sufficient dimensions to find these perimeters.)

5. Find the length of the side of each square shown below:

(i) Area = 25 cm²

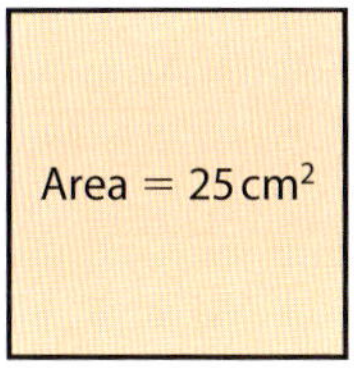

(ii) Area = 144 m²

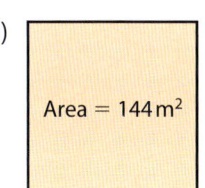

(iii) Area = 625 cm²

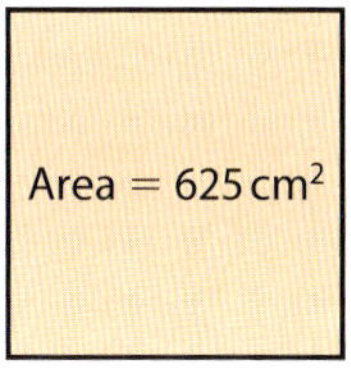

6. Find the area of each of these triangles:

(i) 8 cm, 14 cm

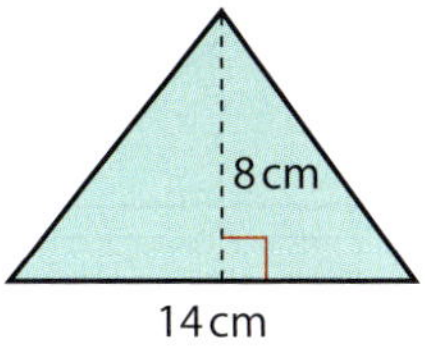

(ii) 12 cm, 20 cm

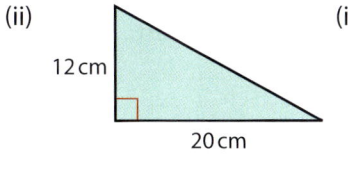

(iii) 24 cm, 10 cm

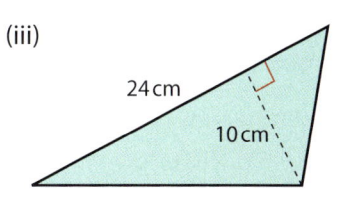

7. Work out the areas of these triangles:

(i) 7 cm, 9 cm

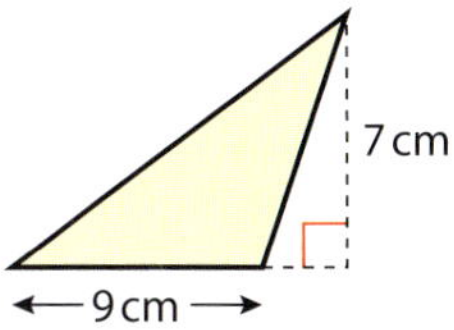

(ii) 8 cm, 15 cm

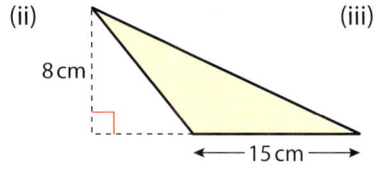

(iii) 20 cm, 12 cm, 24 cm

109

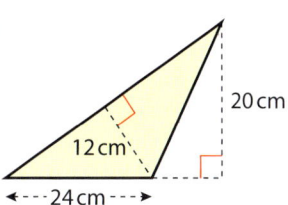

Text & Tests 2 Higher Level

8. Find the length of the line segment marked x in each of these triangles:

   (i) Area = 90 cm², base = 18 cm, height = x

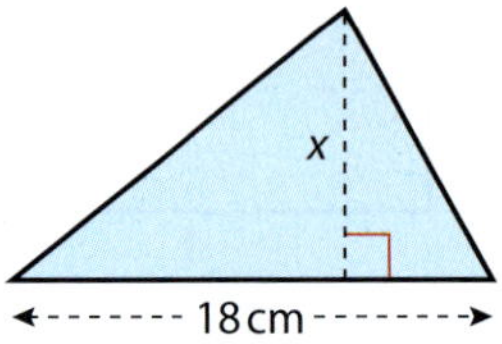

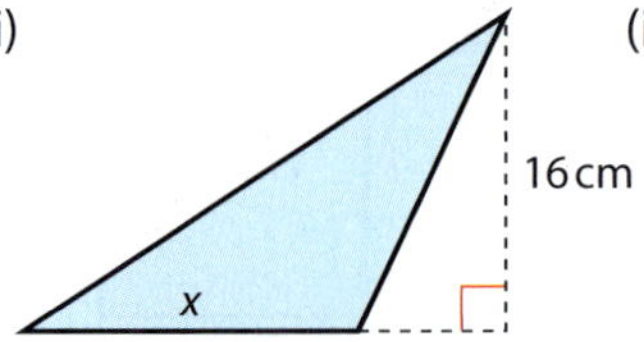

   (ii) Area = 112 cm², height = 16 cm, base = x

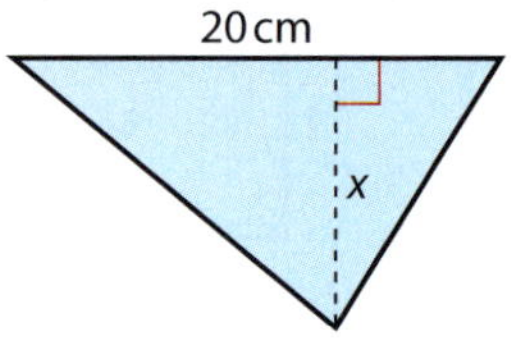

   (iii) Area = 120 cm², one side = 20 cm, x = other side

9. Find the areas of the following shapes which are composed of rectangles and triangles.

   (i) 11 cm, 6 cm, 8 cm

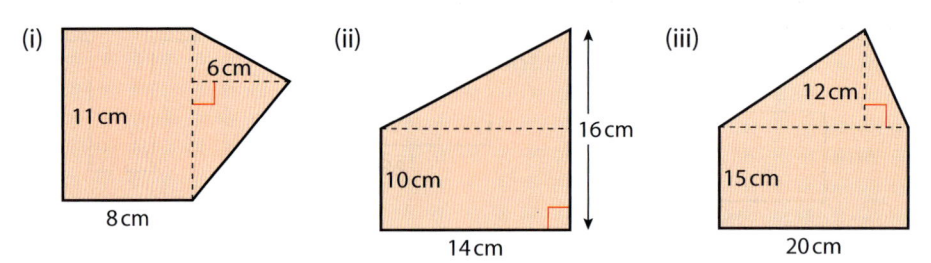

   (ii) 10 cm, 14 cm, 16 cm

   (iii) 12 cm, 15 cm, 20 cm

10. Triangle B is double the area of triangle A.
    The height of both triangles is 6 cm.

    (i) Find the area of triangle A.
    (ii) Find the area of triangle B.
    (iii) Work out the value of x.

    (A: base 4 cm, height 6 cm; B: base x)

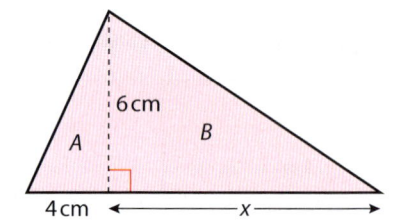

11. Find the area of the shaded portion of the diagram on the right.

    Hence find the area of the unshaded part.

    (3 m, 6 m, 5 m, 7 m)

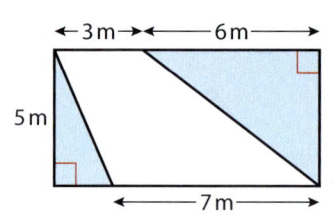

12. Find the area of the shaded figure in the given diagram.

    (17 cm, 17 cm, 20 cm, 10 cm, 12 cm, 12 cm)

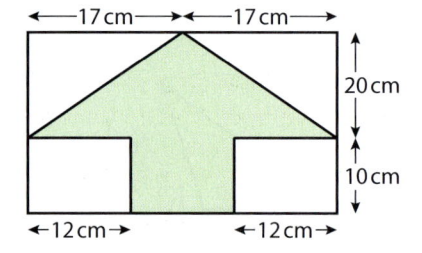

13. Under each figure below, the area is given.
Work out the values of *x*, *y* and *z*.

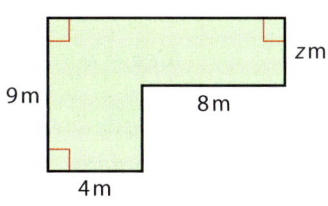

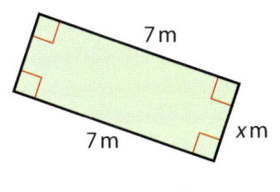

Area = 28 m² (rectangle: 7 m by x m)

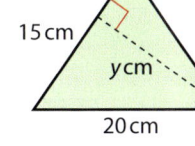

Area = 120 cm² (triangle: base 20 cm, side 15 cm, height y cm)

Area = 60 m² (L-shape: 9 m, 8 m, z m, 4 m)

14. The shape on the right has been drawn on centimetre dot paper.

Work out the area of this shaded shape.

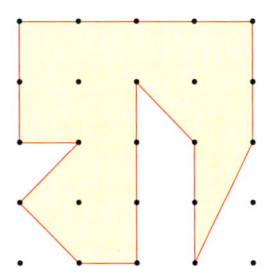

15. Garry has seven tiles.
Each tile is a square of side 10 cm.

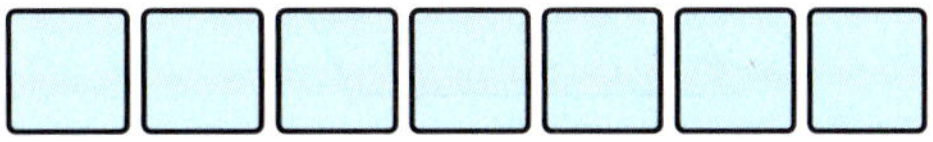

The tiles must be laid edge-to-edge, similar to that shown on the right.
   (i) How can Garry arrange the seven tiles so that the resulting shape has the greatest possible perimeter? 
   (ii) How can Garry arrange the seven tiles so that the resulting shape has the smallest possible perimeter?

Section 6.2 Area of a parallelogram

A parallelogram is a figure in which the opposite sides are both equal in length and parallel.

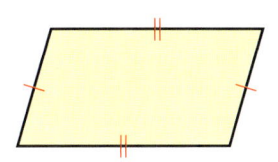

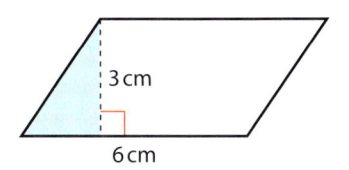

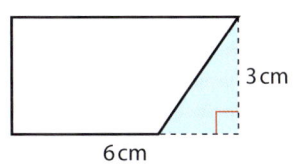

By cutting the parallelogram on the left above along the dotted line and then placing the blue triangle at the other end, a rectangle is formed.

Area of rectangle = 6 cm × 3 cm = 18 cm²

∴ area of parallelogram is also 18 cm², i.e., 6 cm by 3 cm

111

Text & Tests 2 Higher Level

Area of parallelogram is
    base × perpendicular height.

Area = $b \times h$

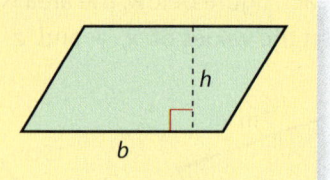

Area of this parallelogram
= base × perpendicular height
= 12 cm × 8 cm
= 96 cm²

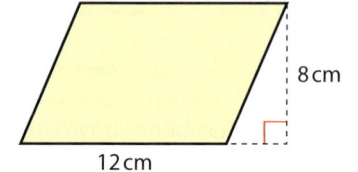

Exercise 6.2

1. Find the area of each of these parallelograms:

    (i) 12 cm, 20 cm
    (ii) 7 cm, 9 cm
    (iii) 11 cm, 15 cm

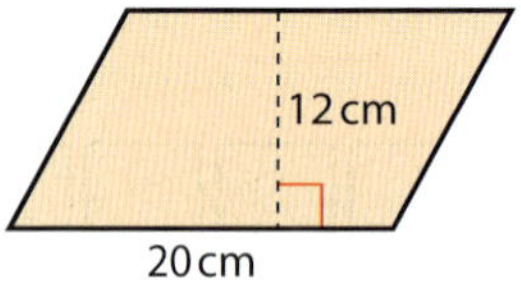

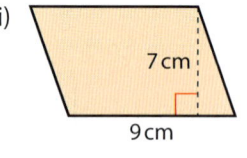

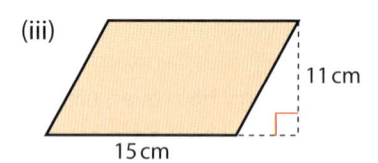

2. Work out the area of each of these parallelograms:

    (i) 6 cm, 10 cm
    (ii) 7 cm, 7.5 cm, 9 cm
    (iii) 6 cm, 5 cm, 7.5 cm

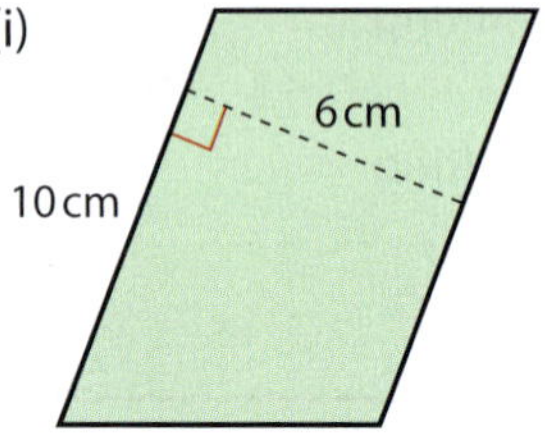

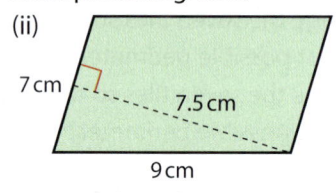

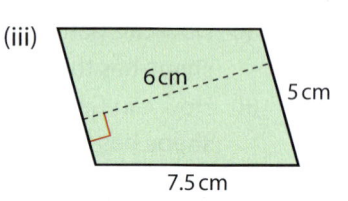

3. Write down the value of h in each of these parallelograms:

    (i) h, 5 cm, Area = 30 cm²
    (ii) h, 9 cm, Area = 63 cm²
    (iii) h, 6 cm, Area = 27 cm²

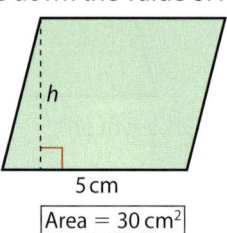

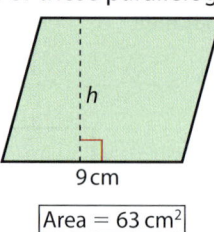

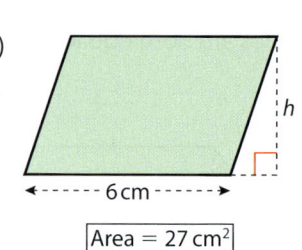

4. Find the area of the parallelogram shown.
   Now find the value of x.

   18 cm, 14 cm, x cm, 22 cm

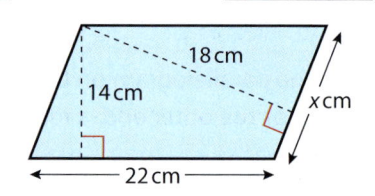

Chapter 6 Perimeter – Area – Volume

5. This design has been drawn on centimetre squared paper.
   Calculate:
   (i) the total blue area
   (ii) the total yellow area
   (iii) the ratio of the blue area to the yellow area

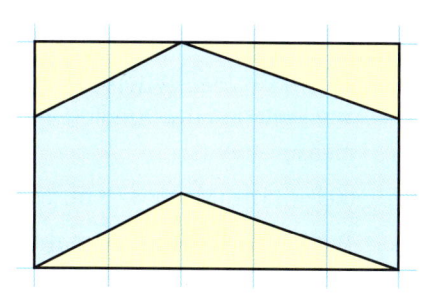

6. Calculate the missing length in each parallelogram:
   (i) 7 cm, ?, Area = 35 cm²
   (ii) ?, 12 cm, Area = 78 cm²
   (iii) ?, 9 cm, Area = 108 cm²

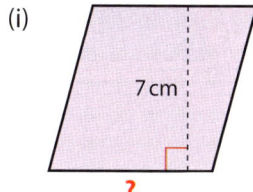

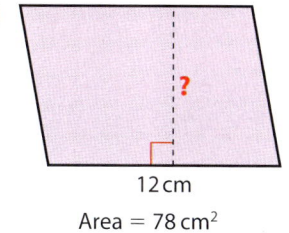

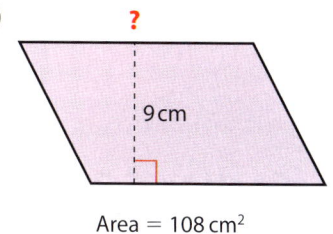

7. Work out the missing length in each parallelogram:
   (i) 2 cm, 4 cm, 3 cm, ?
   (ii) 3 cm, 2 cm, 2.4 cm, ?
   (iii) 3 cm, 2.4 cm, 1.8 cm, ?

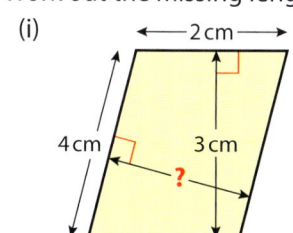

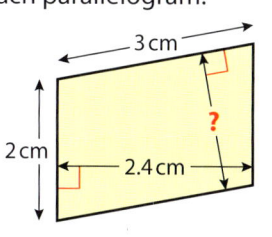

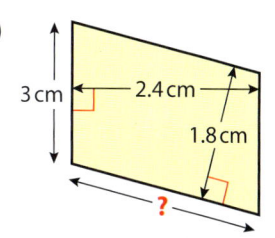

8. Work out the area of the given shaded parallelogram. Hence find the measure of the perpendicular height, h.
   2 cm, 12 cm, 10 cm

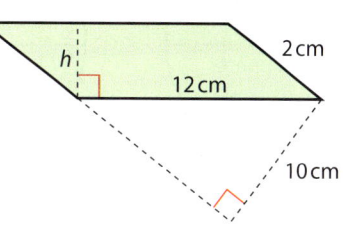

9. Find the areas of the shaded parts of these figures:
   (i) 32 m, 28 m, 60 m
   (ii) 22 m, 20 m, 8 m, 38 m

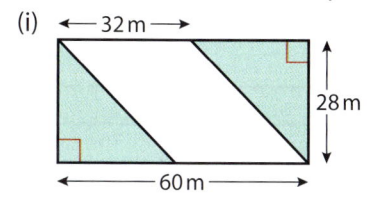

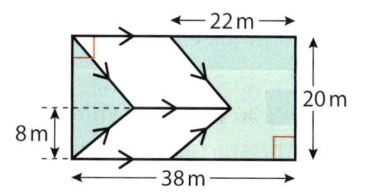

10. Work out the shaded area of the given rectangle where arrows indicate parallel lines.
    23 cm, 14 cm, 34 cm

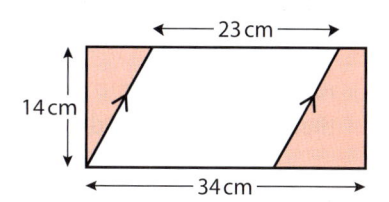

11. Anna estimated the amount of glass needed for one side of the building shown.
She sketched the building and took the following measurements:

|KL| = 35 m, |MN| = 32.5 m, |IJ| = 25 m.

The depth of the frame at the top and bottom was 1 m.

Find (i) the amount of glass needed

  (ii) the % of the side covered by glass.

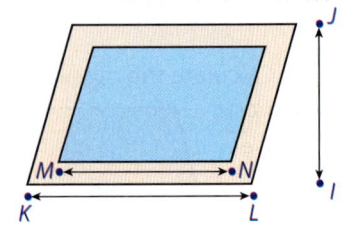

Section 6.3 Area and circumference of a circle

The circle on the right was drawn by placing the point of a compass at O.

The point O is called the **centre** of the circle.

The line that traces the circle is called the **circumference**.

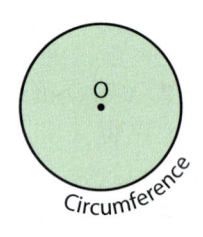

The terms that we will use when dealing with circles are given in the diagrams below:

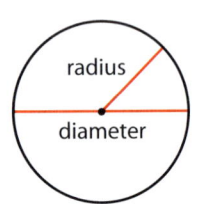

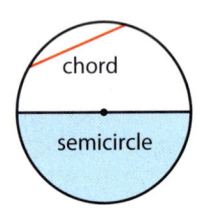

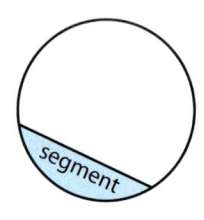

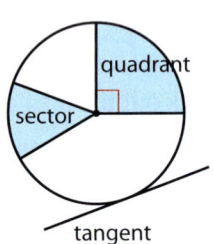

radius, diameter, chord, semicircle, segment, sector, quadrant, tangent

Length of circumference

› Mark a point on the circumference of a 20 cent coin.
› Place the coin on the ruler with the mark pointing to the start of the scale.
› Roll the coin along the ruler until the mark returns again to the start of the scale.
› Read the length of the circumference from the ruler and you will find that it is a little more than three times the diameter.

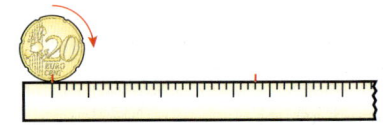

The circumference is more than 3 diameters.

Chapter 6 Perimeter – Area – Volume

The number by which we multiply the diameter is represented by the Greek letter π (pronounced 'pie').

π has no exact decimal or fraction value.

However, when using decimals, we generally use 3.14 as an approximate value.

When using fractions, we use $\frac{22}{7}$ as an approximate value.

Approximate values for π
$\pi = 3.14$ or $\pi = \frac{22}{7}$

Circumference of a circle

The length of the circumference of a circle is
$$2\pi r \quad \text{or} \quad \pi d$$
where r = radius and d = diameter

The π key on your calculator gives a more exact value than 3.14 or $\frac{22}{7}$.
When using your calculator, you should use this key unless told otherwise.

Perimeter of a sector

A sector is part of a circle that is bounded by two radii and an arc.

To find the arc length, ℓ, of a sector, we divide the angle in the sector by 360° to find a fraction.

Then we find this fraction of the circumference.

Length of arc:
$$\ell = \frac{\theta}{360°} \times 2\pi r$$

Example 1

Find the length of the circumference of this circle using 3.14 as an approximation for π.

12 cm

Circumference = $2\pi r$
= 2 × 3.14 × 12
= 75.36 cm
= 75.4 cm, correct to 1 decimal place

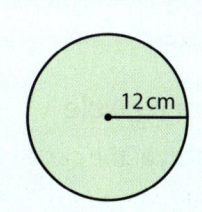

115

Example 2

The diagram on the right shows a sector of a circle of radius 21 cm.
Find the length of the perimeter of this figure.
Use $\frac{22}{7}$ as an approximation for π.

The perimeter consists of the arc AB and two radii.
$60° = \frac{1}{6}$ of $360°$, so arc AB is $\frac{1}{6}$ of circumference.

Length of arc AB $= \frac{1}{6} \times 2\pi r$

$= \frac{1}{6} \times \frac{2}{1} \times \frac{22}{7} \times \frac{21}{1}$

$= 22$ cm

Total perimeter $= 22 + 21 + 21 = 64$ cm

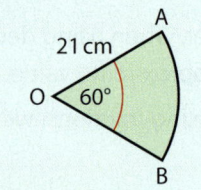

Example 3

The length of the circumference of a circle is 120 cm.
Find the length of the radius of the circle, correct to 1 decimal place.

Circumference $= 2\pi r$

$\therefore \; 2\pi r = 120$

$r = \dfrac{120}{2\pi} = \dfrac{120}{2 \times \pi}$

$r = 19.099$ cm ... use π key on calculator

radius $= 19.1$ cm

Calculator tip:
When using your calculator to find the value of e.g., $\dfrac{120}{2 \times \pi}$, make sure to check that calculator display matches the sum exactly before pressing '='.

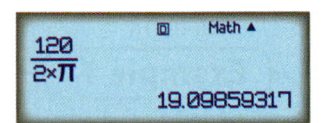

The area of a circle

If the 12 sectors of the circle below are cut neatly, they can be formed into a 'parallelogram', as shown.

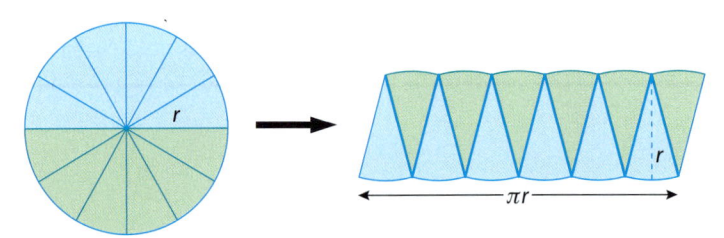

Chapter 6 Perimeter – Area – Volume

Explain why the length of the 'parallelogram' is πr and its height is r.

What is the area of the rectangle?

Explain why the area of the circle is πr^2.

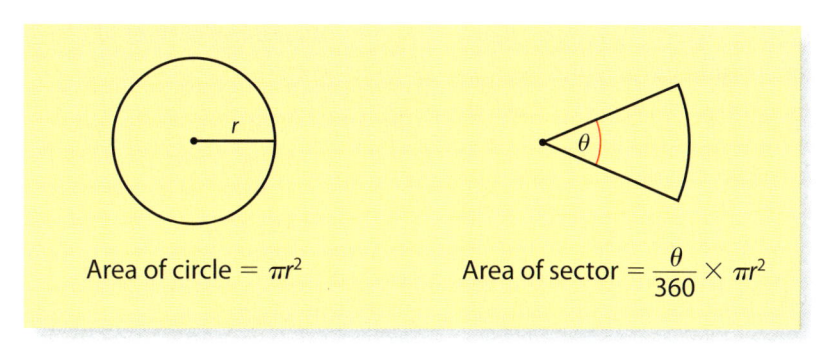

Area of circle = πr^2

Area of sector = $\dfrac{\theta}{360} \times \pi r^2$

Investigation:

The 'formulae and tables' booklet published by the State Examinations Commission contains formulae for the area and volume of different shapes and many useful formulae besides.

Investigate the page numbers where each of the following formulae might be found:

Formula	Page number	Formula	Page number
Circle: $\ell = 2\pi r$		Parallelogram: $A = ah$	
Sphere: $A = 4\pi r^2$		Geometry: $\|AB\|$	
Algebra: $x = \dfrac{-b \pm \sqrt{b^2 - 4ac}}{2a}$		Sets: $\cap, \cup, \emptyset$ etc.	
SI Units: time(t)		Prefixes: kilo	

Text & Tests 2 Higher Level

> **Example 4**
>
> (i) Find the area of a circle of radius 14 cm. (Take $\pi = \frac{22}{7}$)
>
> (ii) Find the radius of a circle of area 1386 cm².
> Use the π key on your calculator and give your answer correct to the nearest whole number.
>
> (i) Area = πr^2
> $= \frac{22}{7} \times 14^2$
> $= \frac{22}{{}_1\cancel{7}} \times \cancel{14}^2 \times 14$
> $= 616 \text{ cm}^2$
>
> (ii) $\pi r^2 = 1386$
> $r^2 = \frac{1386}{\pi}$
> $r^2 = 441.178$
> $r = \sqrt{441.178} = 21.004$
> $r = 21$ cm

Exercise 6.3

1. Name the feature shown, in red, on each circle.

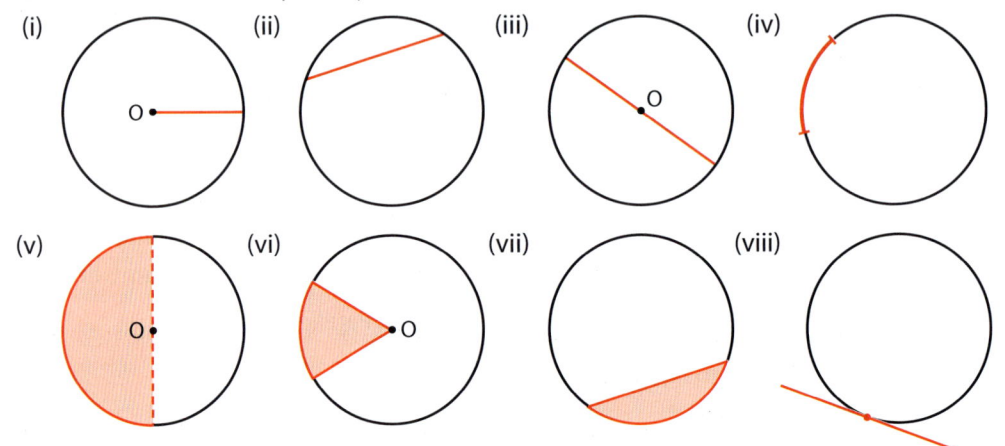

(i) (ii) (iii) (iv)

(v) (vi) (vii) (viii)

2. Calculate the circumference of each of these circles, using $\pi = 3.14$.

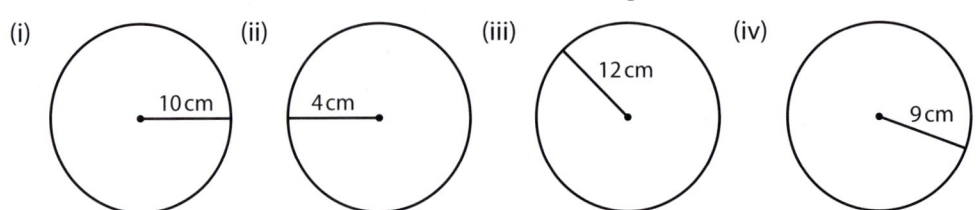

(i) 10 cm (ii) 4 cm (iii) 12 cm (iv) 9 cm

Chapter 6 Perimeter – Area – Volume

3. Use the π key on your calculator to find (a) the area and (b) the perimeter of each of these circles.
Give each answer correct to 1 decimal place.

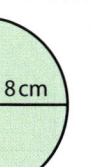

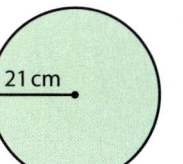

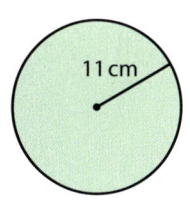

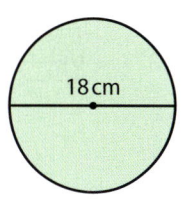

(i) 8 cm   (ii) 21 cm   (iii) 11 cm   (iv) 18 cm

4. Using 3.14 as an approximate value for π, calculate the lengths of the circumferences of these circles.
  (i) radius = 13 cm   (ii) diameter = 30 cm   (iii) radius = 40 cm

5. What fraction of the area of a complete circle is each of these sectors?
  (i)   (ii) 120°   (iii) 60°   (iv) 45°

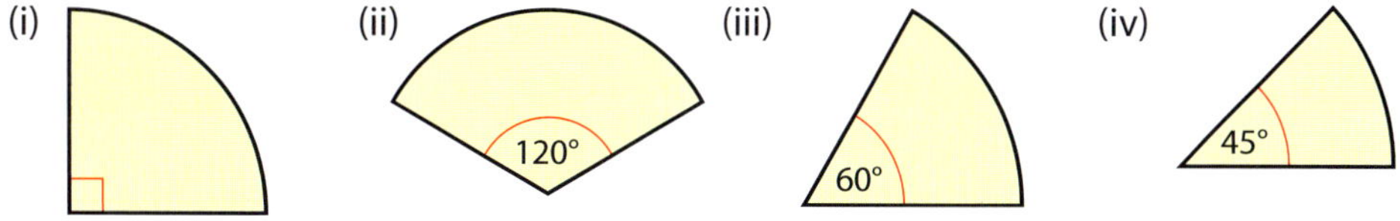

6. Find the length of the arc AB in each of these sectors, taking π = 3.14. Give your answer correct to 2 decimal places.
  (i) A, 21 cm, B
  (ii) A, 45°, 14 cm, B
  (iii) A, 120°, 28 cm, B

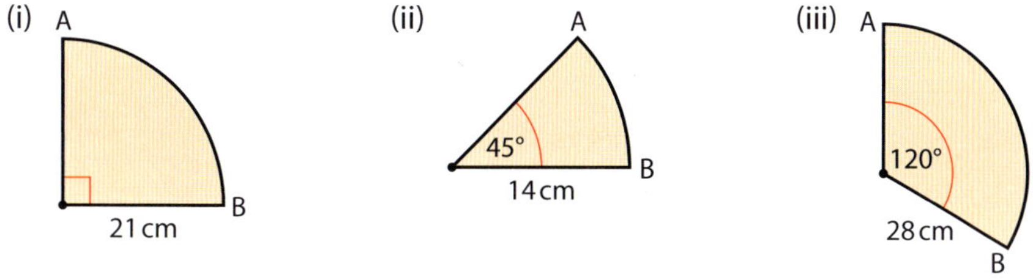

7. Using π = 3.14, find the area of each of the sectors in Question 8 above. Give your answer correct to 2 decimal places.

8. Find the perimeters of these shapes, taking π = 3.14. Give your answer correct to 2 decimal places.
  (i) 28 cm
  (ii) 60°, 14 cm
  (iii) 7 cm

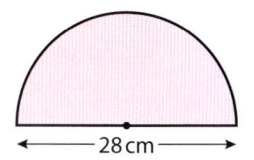

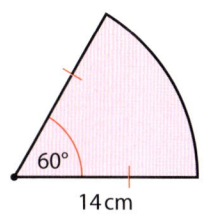

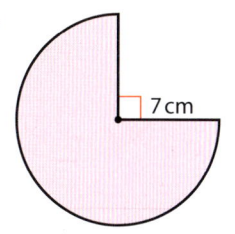

9. (i) Find the length of the perimeter of this pizza slice, taking π = 3.14.
  (ii) If this pizza fits exactly into a box, find the area of the unused surface in the box. Give your answer correct to 2 decimal places.
  45°, 14 cm

119

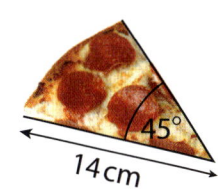

Text & Tests 2 Higher Level

10. Using $\pi = 3.14$, find the area of each of these shapes.

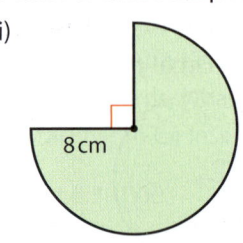

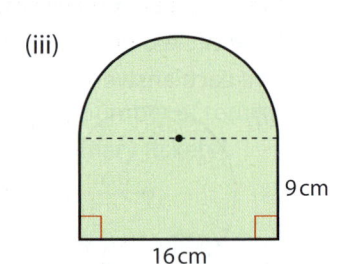

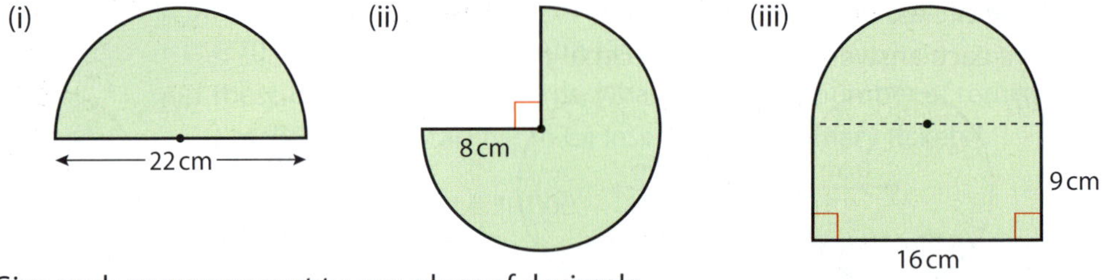

   (i) 22 cm

   (ii) 8 cm

   (iii) 9 cm, 16 cm

   Give each answer correct to one place of decimals.

11. A running track is in the shape of a rectangle with semi-circular ends.
    (i) Calculate the length of the inner lane of the track.
    (ii) If each lane 1 m wide, calculate the length of each lane (2, 3, 4, 5).
    (iii) Hence find the length of the 'stagger' so that after 1 lap each runner will have travelled the same distance.
    (iv) How many laps would an athlete have to complete in a 10 000 metre race?

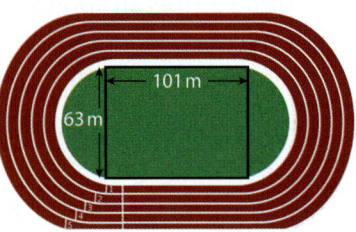

   (63 m measured to the centre of the first lane)

12. Taking $\pi = 3.14$, find
    (i) the perimeter
    (ii) the area of the given coloured figure.

    Give each answer correct to one decimal place.

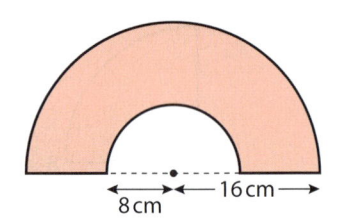

    8 cm, 16 cm

13. The area of each circle below is given in terms of π. Find the length of the radius of each circle.

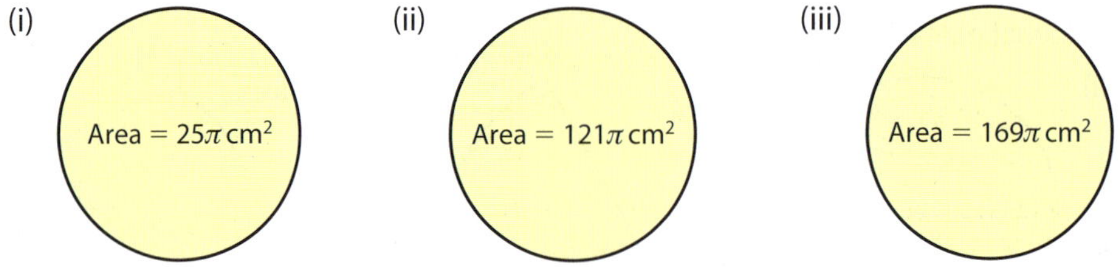

    (i) Area = 25π cm²

    (ii) Area = 121π cm²

    (iii) Area = 169π cm²

14. The area of a circle is 154 cm². Taking $\pi = \frac{22}{7}$, find
    (i) the length of the radius
    (ii) the length of the circumference.

Chapter 6 Perimeter – Area – Volume

15. Stephen has a counter device on his bike.
It counts the number of revolutions his wheel has made.
His wheels are 40 cm in diameter.

   (i) Stephen cycles to his grandmother's house.
The counter reads 1989.
How far away does his grandmother live?

   (ii) How many revolutions does his wheel have to make to travel 1 km?

Give each answer correct to the nearest whole number.

16. Which is the shorter path from A to B

   (i) along the 4 semicircles, or

   (ii) along the larger semicircle?

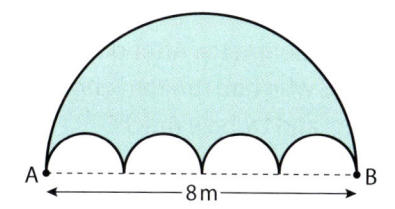

17. Taking $\pi = \frac{22}{7}$, find the area of the shaded portion of the given figure.

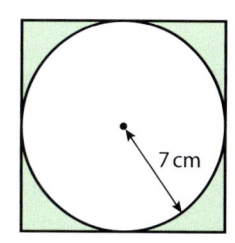

18. The quadrant shown is cut from a circle of centre O.

   (i) Find the area of △OAB.

   (ii) Find the area of the shaded region, taking $\pi = \frac{22}{7}$.

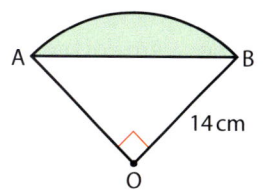

19. To water this rectangular field, a gardener uses eleven identical sprinklers, which cover the blue areas shown on the diagram.
The three sprinklers in the middle of the field cover circular areas; the four sprinklers on the sides cover semi-circular areas; and the four sprinklers at the corners cover quadrant areas.

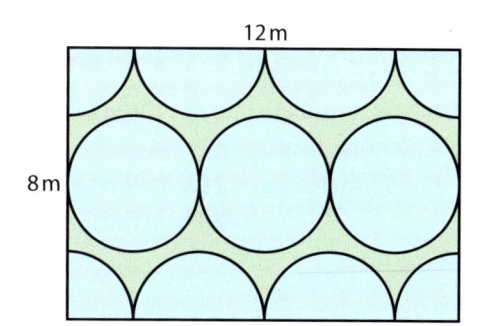

   (i) What is the radius of each circle?

   (ii) What is the total (blue) area watered by the sprinklers?

   (iii) Find, correct to the nearest whole number, the percentage of the lawn that is watered.

Text & Tests 2 Higher Level

20. A car with a rectangular rear windscreen (160 cm long and 80 cm wide) has one large wiper of length 75 cm. The wiper covers the shaded area in the diagram on the right. What percentage of the windscreen area is **not** cleaned by the wiper?
Give your answer to the nearest whole number.

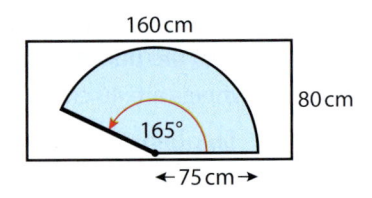

21. Alan and Billy raced each other around this athletics track. Alan ran along the outside perimeter while Billy ran along the inside perimeter. After one lap of the track, who had run the longer distance, and by how much?
Answer correct to the nearest metre.

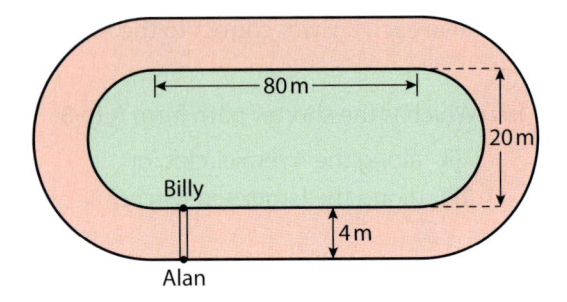

Section 6.4 Rectangular solids

The volume of any rectangular solid is given by;
  Volume = Length × Width × Height.
From the diagram it can be seen that
Length × Width = Area of the base.
  ∴ Volume = Area of base × Height 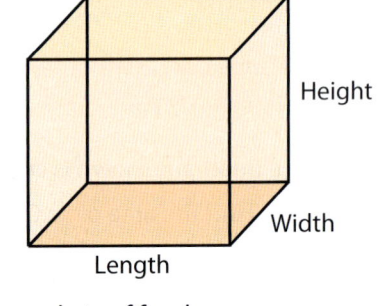
The units of volume are; $m × m × m = m^3$ (cubic metres)
e.g. used for containers on ships,
  or $cm × cm × cm = cm^3$ (cubic centimetres) e.g. used for packets of food,
  or $mm × mm × mm = mm^3$ (cubic millimetres) e.g. used for tablets, medicines.

Surface Area of rectangular solid

Each rectangular solid has three pairs of rectangular faces.
  ∴ Surface area = $2\ell w + 2hw + 2\ell h$
         = $2(\ell w + hw + \ell h)$

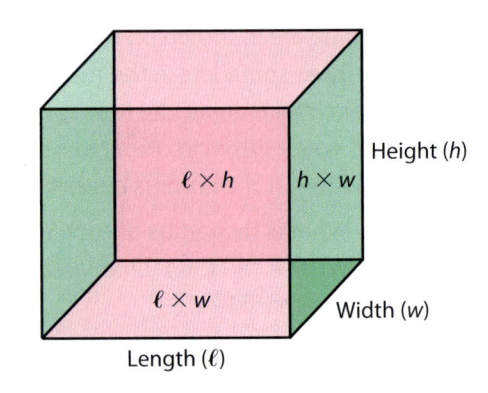

Chapter 6 Perimeter – Area – Volume

Volume of rectangular solid
$= \ell \times w \times h$

Surface area of rectangular solid
$= 2(\ell w + hw + \ell h)$

ℓ = length, w = width, h = height

Volume of cube
$= \ell \times \ell \times \ell = \ell^3$

Surface area of cube
$= 6(\ell \times \ell) = 6\ell^2$

for a cube; $\ell = w = h$

Example 1

An insulating panel has the dimensions
1.5 m × 1.2 m × 10 cm as shown.

Find the volume of this panel.

Volume of panel = Length × Width × Height
$= 1.5\text{ m} \times 1.2\text{ m} \times 0.1\text{ m}$
$= 0.18\text{ m}^3$

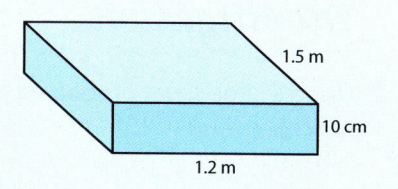

$10\text{ cm} = \dfrac{10}{100}\text{ m} = 0.1\text{ m}$

Example 2

A cube has a surface area of 73.5 cm².
Find its volume.

Surface area of cube = $6\ell^2$, ℓ is the length of an edge.
$\therefore 6\ell^2 = 73.5\text{ cm}^2$
$\therefore \ell^2 = \dfrac{73.5}{6}\text{ cm}^2 = 12.25\text{ cm}^2$
$\therefore \ell = \sqrt{12.25\text{ cm}^2} = 3.5\text{ cm}$

$\therefore$ volume $= \ell^3 = (3.5\text{ cm})^3 = 42.875\text{ cm}^3$

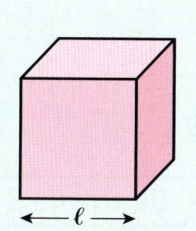

Nets of solids

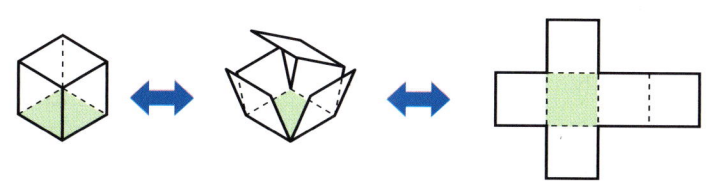

Nets of solids are used to study the surface area of a solid.
Above is shown the net of a cube. There are 11 possible different nets of a cube.

On the left below is the net of a closed rectangular box.
On the right is the net of an open rectangular box.

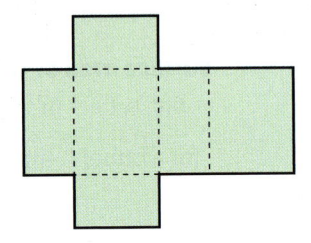

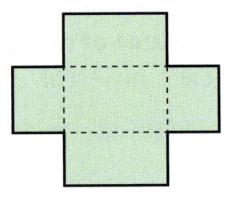

Investigation:

Using a large sheet of squared paper copy and complete the 11 possible **different** nets for a cube.

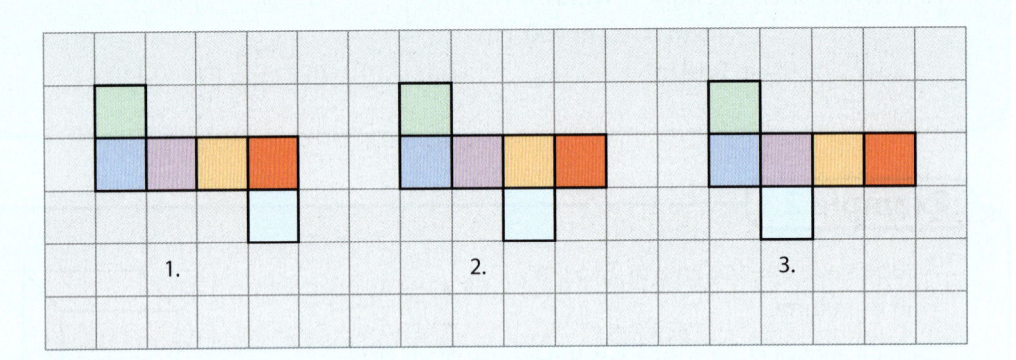

1.
2.
3.

Example 3

This is the net of an open box.
If this net is folded along the dotted lines to make a box, find
  (i) the volume of the box
  (ii) the surface area of the outside of the box.

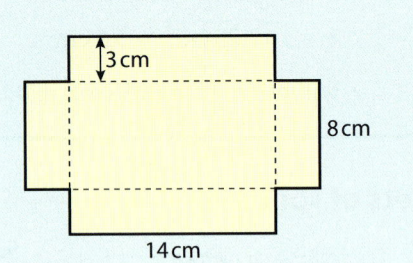

3 cm
8 cm
14 cm

(i) This is the box that is formed from the net.

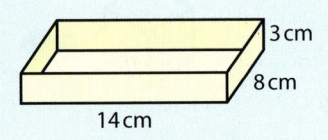

   Volume = 14 × 8 × 3
          = 336 cm³

3 cm
8 cm
14 cm

(ii) Surface area = 2(14 × 3) + 2(8 × 3) + (14 × 8) … no top on box
                  = 84 + 48 + 112 = 244 cm²

Chapter 6 Perimeter – Area – Volume

Capacity – the litre

The capacity of a container is the amount of liquid it can hold.
The most commonly-used metric measure of capacity is the **litre**.
A cube with edge of length 10 cm contains 1 litre.

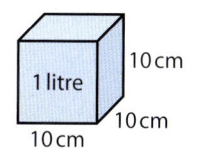

∴ 1000 cm³ = 1 litre

Remember To convert cubic centimetres (cm³) to litres, divide by 1000.

Exercise 6.4

1. Find the volume of each of the following rectangular solids.

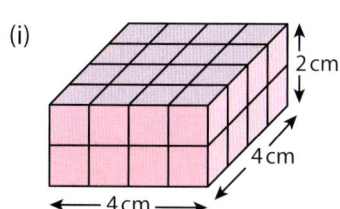

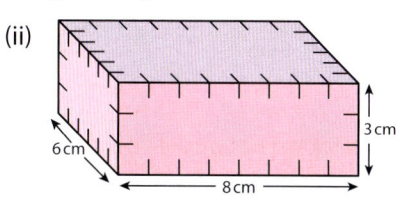

(i) 4 cm × 4 cm × 2 cm

(ii) 8 cm × 6 cm × 3 cm

2. Find the surface area of each of the solids in Question 1 above.

3. Find (a) the volume (b) the surface area of these solid cuboids.

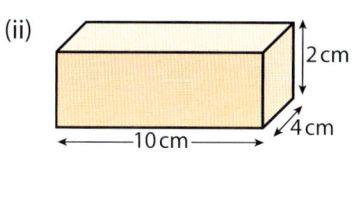

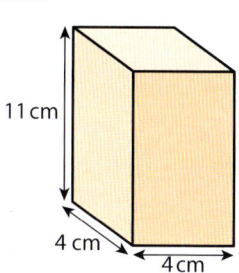

(i) 12 cm × 6 cm × 4 cm

(ii) 10 cm × 4 cm × 2 cm

(iii) 11 cm × 4 cm × 4 cm

4. The diagram shows a rectangular box partly filled with cubes of side 1 cm.
How many more of these cubes are required to fill the box?

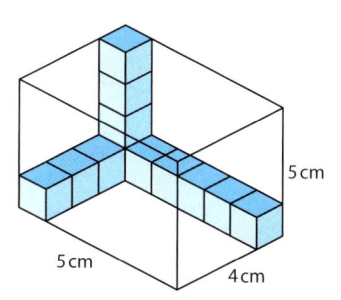

5 cm × 5 cm × 4 cm

125

Text & Tests 2 Higher Level

5. Seven cubes of side 3 cm are joined to make the solid shown. Find the surface area of the solid.

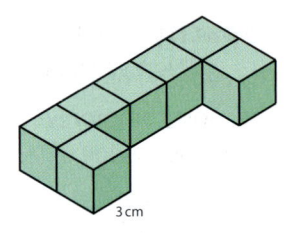

6. Each of the solid shapes below can be broken into two or more rectangular solids. The dotted lines indicate how the figures may be divided.
   Now find the total volume of each of these shapes:

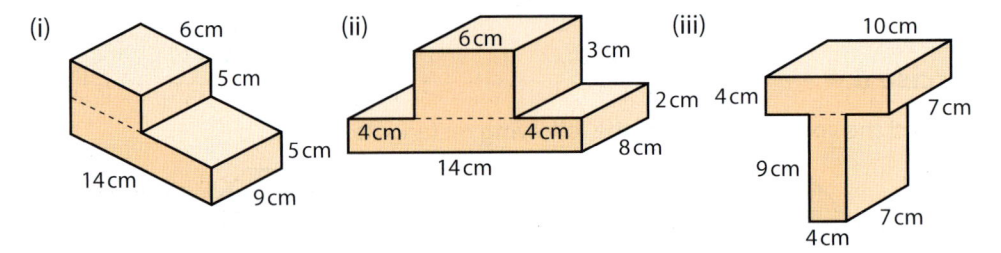

   (i) 6 cm, 5 cm, 14 cm, 5 cm, 9 cm

   (ii) 6 cm, 3 cm, 4 cm, 4 cm, 2 cm, 14 cm, 8 cm

   (iii) 10 cm, 4 cm, 7 cm, 9 cm, 4 cm, 7 cm

7. The framing of a toolshed consists of square, galvanised tubing which costs €12.80 a metre. Find the total cost of the tubing necessary to make the framing of the shed illustrated.

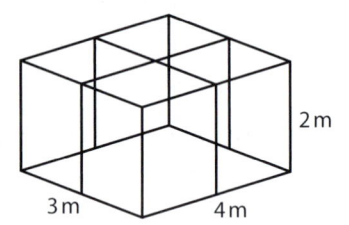

   2 m, 3 m, 4 m

8. The figure on the right shows a stack of cubes each of side 2 cm.
   Find (i) the volume of the stack in cm^3
         (ii) the surface area of the stack in cm^2.

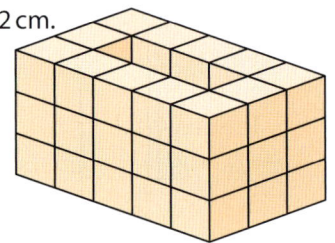

9. The volume of each of the following rectangular solids is given. Find the length of the side marked with a letter.

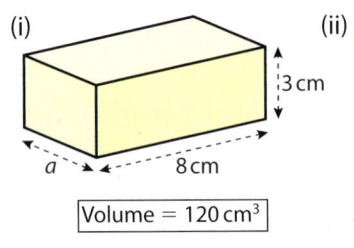

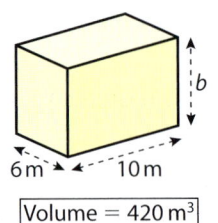

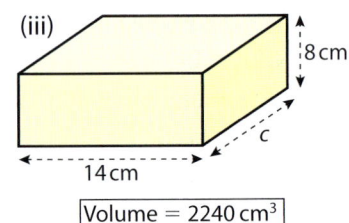

   (i) a, 3 cm, 8 cm   Volume = 120 cm^3

   (ii) 6 m, b, 10 m   Volume = 420 m^3

   (iii) 14 cm, 8 cm, c   Volume = 2240 cm^3

126

Chapter 6 Perimeter – Area – Volume

10. Given that the surface area of a cube is 216 cm², show that the volume of the cube is 216 cm³.

11. Mr Shannon decided to build a stand-alone garage beside his house. The garage was to be 6 m × 4 m × 2.5 m in height. The bricks he chose had dimensions 22 cm × 10 cm × 7cm in height and and he estimated that he would need 4 000 bricks. Is his estimate reasonable? Explain your answer. (Note: 3 walls needed)

12. The volume of a cube is 64 cm³.
    Find (i) the length of the side of the cube
    (ii) the surface area of the cube.

13. Having finished the repairs on the bottom of a hotel swimming pool on Monday at 5 o'clock, Patrick started to refill the pool at a rate of 1 m³ every 10 min.

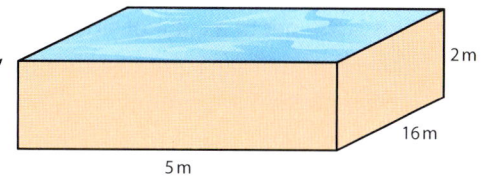

    If the pool is full 20 cm from the rim, when will the pool reopen?

14. How many small boxes measuring 20 cm × 10 cm × 5 cm will fit into a large box measuring 1 m × 1 m × 1 m?

15. The net on the right folds to make a rectangular box. The rectangle that is shaded blue is the base.
    (i) What is the height of the box?
    (ii) The volume of the box is 84 cm³. Find the value of x.
    (iii) Find the surface area of the box.

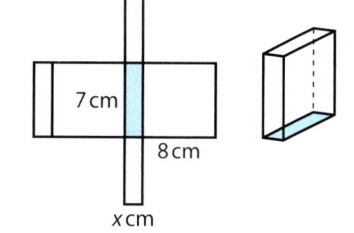

16. This net is folded to make a cube.
    (i) Which vertex will join to N?
    (ii) Which line will join to [CD]?
    (iii) Which line will join to [IH]?

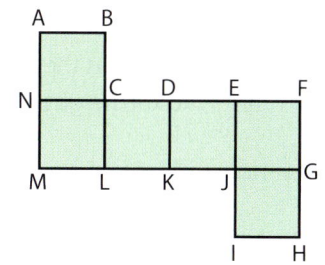

17. An open cereal box measures 4 cm × 15 cm × 20 cm.
    (i) Draw a net of the open box and hence find the external surface area of the box.
    (ii) If this box is 80% full of cereal, find the volume of the open space at the top of the box.

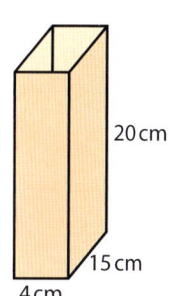

Text & Tests 2 Higher Level

18. Here are nets of a cube.

   A
	1		
2	3	4	
	5		
	6		

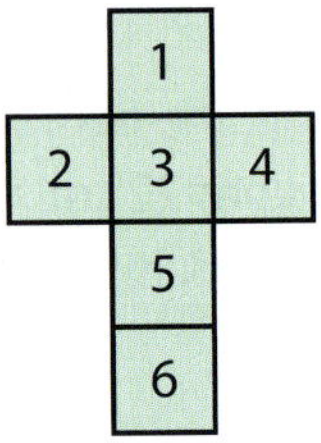

   B
	5		
4	1	2	3
	6		

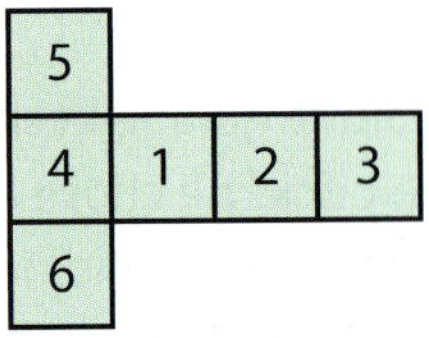

   C
1			
2	3	4	5
			6

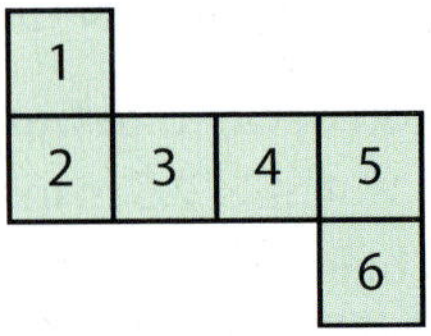

   Imagine that each of these nets is folded to make a cube.
   For each net, which face would be opposite face 1 when folded?

19. This is the net of a cube of side x cm.
    The volume of the cube is numerically equal to the surface area of the cube.
    Write an equation in x and solve it to find the length of the side of the cube.

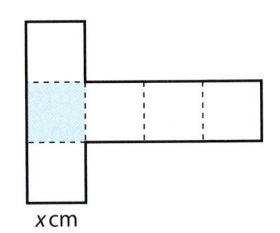

20. If 1 litre = 1000 cm³, find the capacity of these rectangular containers in litres.

    (i) 20 cm × 15 cm × 20 cm
    (ii) 8 cm × 10 cm × 20 cm
    (iii) 30 cm × 15 cm × 15 cm

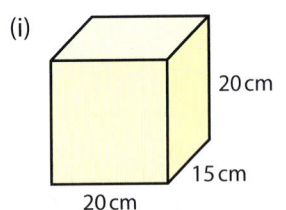

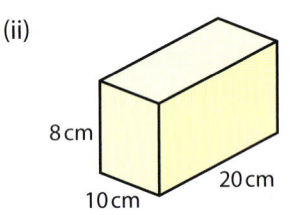

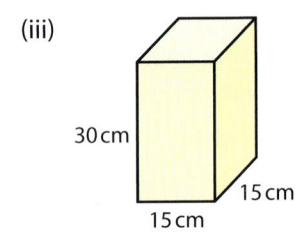

21. The rectangular container on the right has a capacity of 4.8 litres.
    (i) Write down the volume of the container in cm³.
    (ii) Find the height h of the container in centimetres.

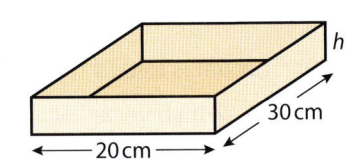

22. How many litres would a container measuring 1 m × 1 m × 1 m hold?

23. A large cardboard box is designed to hold 20 small boxes measuring 5 cm × 15 cm × 20 cm. What is the capacity of the large box in litres?
    Design two different boxes that could be used to hold the 20 smaller boxes, giving the dimensions in each case. (It is assumed that there is no wasted space in the large box.)

Chapter 6 Perimeter – Area – Volume

Investigation:

Investigate the relationship between the surface area and the volume of a cube by copying and completing the table below.
Examine how algebra (line 8) can be used to predict line 6.

Side	Surface Area	Vol
1 cm		
2 cm		
3 cm		
4 cm		
5 cm		
6 cm		
7 cm		
x cm		

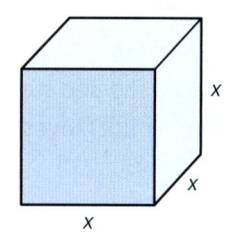

Section 6.5 Prisms

In the rectangular solid shown, vertical slices parallel to the front face will all be the same size and shape. We say that solids like this are solids of **uniform cross-section**. The cross-section in this case is a triangle.

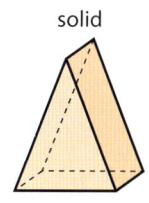

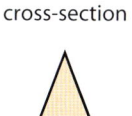

solid   cross-section

> A solid figure with the same cross-section along its length is called a **prism**.

The following solids are all prisms. The cross-sections are shaded.

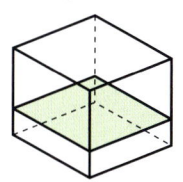

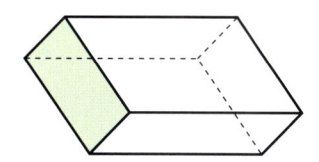

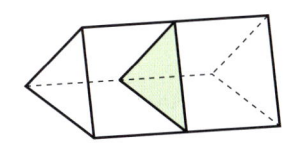

Text & Tests 2 Higher Level

The solid on the right is not a prism because the cross-sections are not uniform.

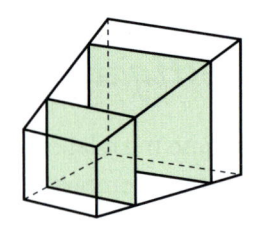

Investigation:

Having studied the diagram above, Alan drew this diagram of a solid and stated that this was a prism. Is he correct or not? Investigate! Give reasons for your answer.

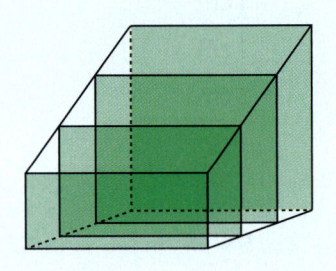

Volume of a prism

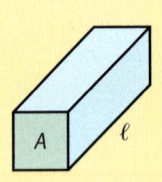

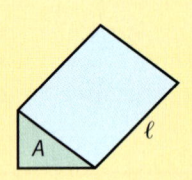

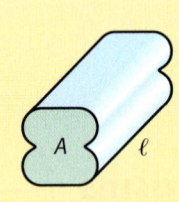

Volume of a prism = area of cross-section × length
$$= A \times \ell$$

Example 1

Find the area of the triangular cross-section of this prism.
Hence find the volume of the prism.

Area of cross-section $= \frac{1}{2}bh$
$= \frac{1}{2} \times 8 \times 6 = 24\,\text{cm}^2$

Volume = Area of cross-section × length
$= 24\,\text{cm}^2 \times 10\,\text{cm}$

Volume = $240\,\text{cm}^3$

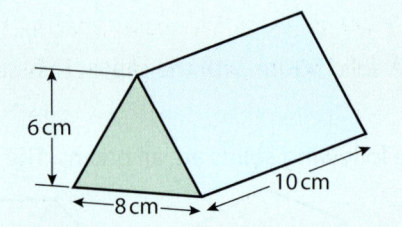

$A = \frac{1}{2}bh$

130

Chapter 6 Perimeter – Area – Volume

Surface area of a prism

The surface area of a prism is the sum of the areas of its faces.

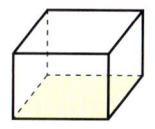

Example 2

Find the total surface area of this solid shape.

The net of this solid has 5 surfaces.

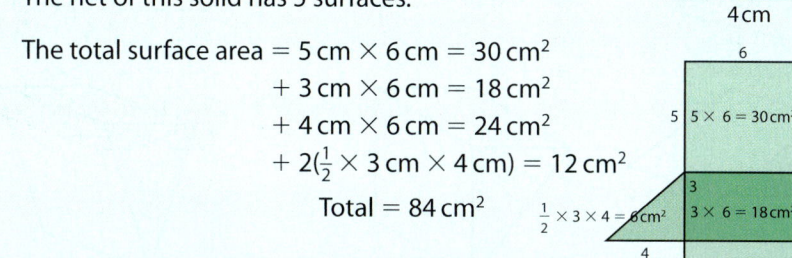

The total surface area = 5 cm × 6 cm = 30 cm²
+ 3 cm × 6 cm = 18 cm²
+ 4 cm × 6 cm = 24 cm²
+ 2($\frac{1}{2}$ × 3 cm × 4 cm) = 12 cm²

Total = 84 cm²

The net of the given triangular prism is shown on the right.

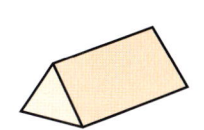

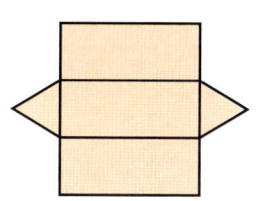

Exercise 6.5

1. The areas of the cross-sections of these prisms are given. Find the volume of each prism.

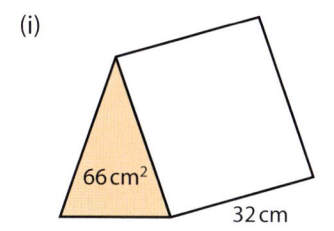

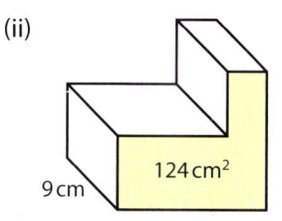

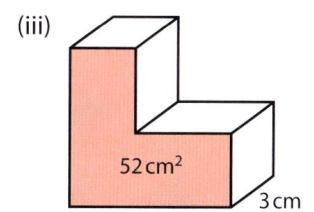

   (i) 66 cm², 32 cm

   (ii) 124 cm², 9 cm

   (iii) 52 cm², 3 cm

2. (i) What is the area of the shaded cross-section of this triangular prism?
   (ii) What is the volume of the prism?

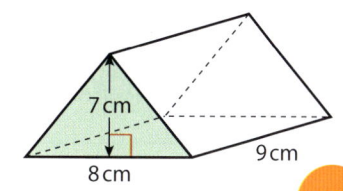

   7 cm, 8 cm, 9 cm

Text & Tests 2 Higher Level

3. The cross-section of this prism is a right-angled triangle. Work out the volume of this prism.

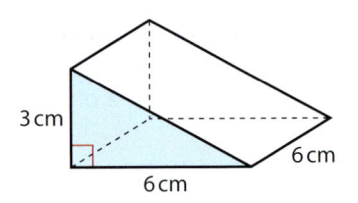

3 cm
6 cm
6 cm

4. Work out the volume of each of these prisms:

(i) 12 m, 5 m, 15 m

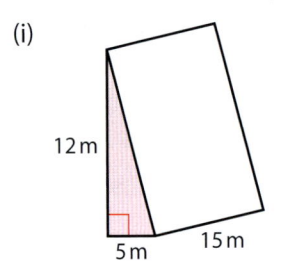

(ii) 8 cm, 12 cm, 30 cm

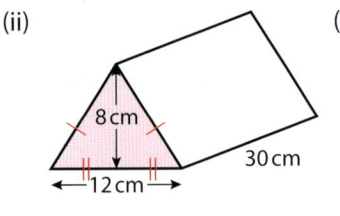

(iii) 3 cm, 4 cm, 8 cm

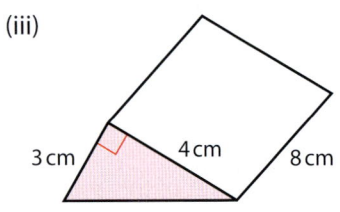

(iv) 2 cm, 8 cm, 6 cm

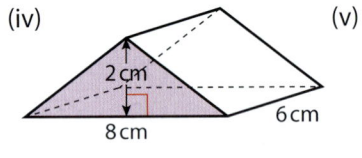

(v) 6 mm, 8 mm, 11 mm

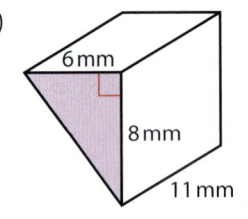

(vi) 12 m, 18 m, 14 m

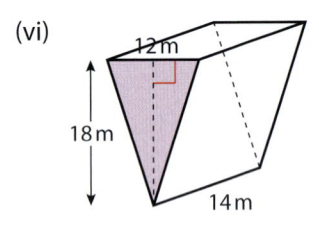

5. (i) How many faces has this prism?
   (ii) How many faces are triangular in shape?
   (iii) Work out the total surface area of the prism.

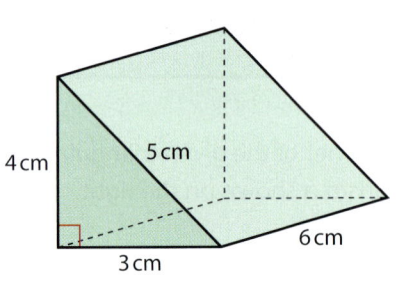

4 cm, 5 cm, 3 cm, 6 cm

6. Find the total surface area of each of these prisms.

(i) 4 cm, 5 cm, 6 cm, 8 cm

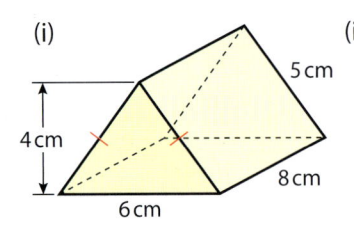

(ii) 5, 13, 8, 12

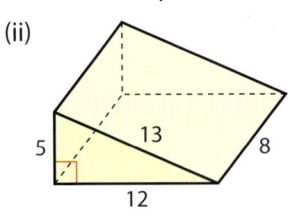

(iii) 8.5 cm, 6 cm, 6 cm, 10 cm

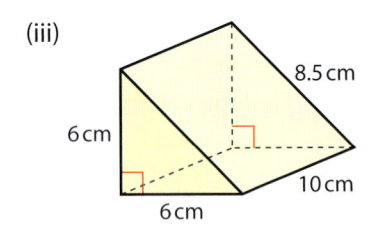

7. Find the total surface areas of these prisms:

(i) 20 cm, 25 cm, 15 cm, 8 cm

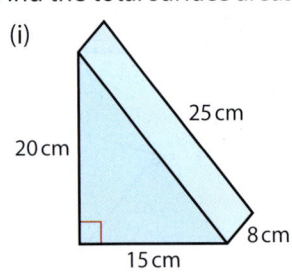

(ii) 13 mm, 5 mm, 2 mm, 12 mm

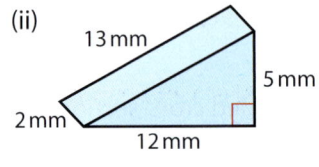

(iii) 2 cm, 8 cm, 17 cm, 15 cm

132

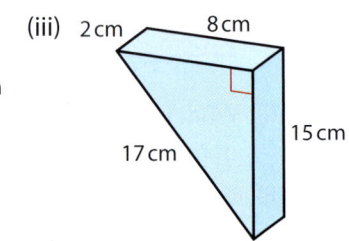

Chapter 6 Perimeter – Area – Volume

8. Find (a) the volume (b) the surface area of each of these prisms:

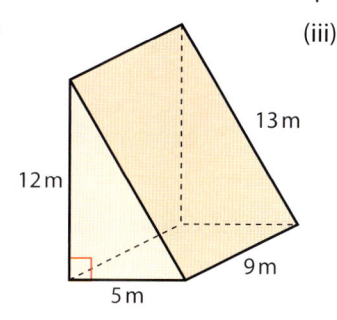

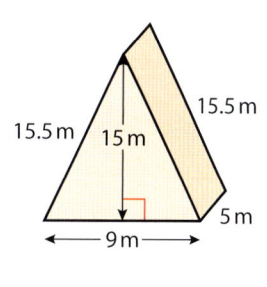

(i) 12 m, 20 m, 5 m, 16 m

(ii) 13 m, 12 m, 5 m, 9 m

(iii) 15.5 m, 15.5 m, 15 m, 9 m, 5 m

9. Calculate the surface area of each of the following prisms.

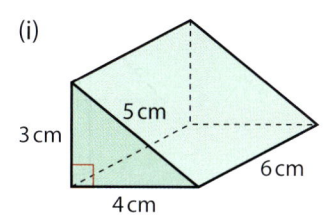

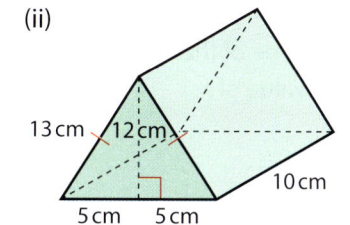

(i) 3 cm, 5 cm, 6 cm, 4 cm

(ii) 13 cm, 12 cm, 10 cm, 5 cm, 5 cm

10. Caroline manufactures tents, as shown on the right.
  (i) Find the surface area of the tent, including the floor.
  (ii) Caroline buys material at €20 per square metre. How much does it cost Caroline for the material to make a tent? Give your answer correct to the nearest €10.

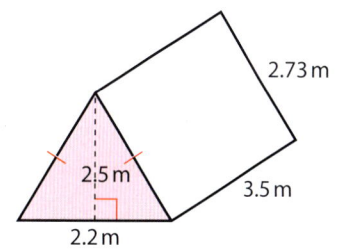

2.73 m, 2.5 m, 2.2 m, 3.5 m

11. This is the net of a triangular prism.
  Find (i) the volume of the prism
     (ii) the surface area of the prism.

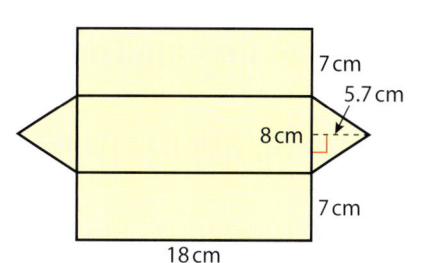

7 cm, 5.7 cm, 8 cm, 7 cm, 18 cm

12. This is a triangular prism.
  The ends of the prism are equilateral triangles.
  (i) Draw a rectangle 7 cm by 4 cm in the middle of a sheet of paper.
  (ii) Use this rectangle to complete an accurate net for this prism.

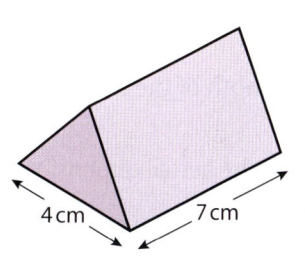

4 cm, 7 cm

133

13. Here are four pictures of the same cube.

Which shapes are opposite each other?

14. This is the net of a 3-D object.
   (i) When this net is folded, describe the figure it will make.
   (ii) If the volume of the figure is 378 cm³, find the value of x.

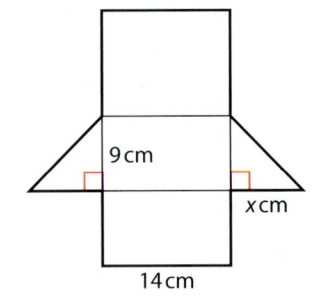

9 cm

x cm

14 cm

Section 6.6 Scale drawing

In everyday life, people such as architects and engineers make scale drawings of buildings and bridges. Builders must then be able to read and understand them so that the structures can be built properly.

> Scale drawings have the same shapes as the objects that they represent but they are of different sizes.

> The scale of a drawing is length of drawing : real length.
   A scale of 1 : 100 means that the real size is 100 times the size of the drawing.

> The scale determines the size of the drawing.
   A 1 : 10 scale drawing would be bigger than a 1 : 100 scale drawing of the same object.

Here is a scale drawing of a clock.

The scale is 1 : 6.

The drawing is 5 cm by 5 cm.

The actual length of the clock is 5 cm × 6
                                 = 30 cm

Accordingly, the actual dimensions of the clock are 30 cm by 30 cm.

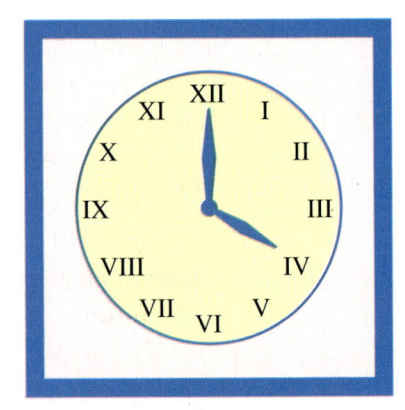

Scale 1 : 6

Chapter 6 Perimeter – Area – Volume

> **Example 1**
>
> Part of a house plan drawn to a scale of 1 : 100 is shown.
> Bedroom 1 is 5 cm by 5 cm on the plan.
>
> (i) Find the actual length of the bedroom in metres.
> (ii) The kitchen in the house is 6.5 metres by 4.8 metres. What are the dimensions of the kitchen in the drawing?
>
> 5 cm
>
> Bedroom 1
>
> 5 cm
>
> (i) On the plan, 1 cm = 100 cm   ... 1:100 scale
>   5 cm = 500 cm
>   = 5 metres.
>   The length of the bedroom is 5 metres.
>
> (ii) The kitchen is 6.5 m by 4.8 m or 650 cm by 480 cm.
>   Since the scale is 1 : 100, we divide 650 cm and 480 cm by 100 to find the dimensions in the plan.
>   Dimensions in the plan = $\frac{650}{100}$ cm by $\frac{480}{100}$ cm
>   = 6.5 cm by 4.8 cm

> **Example 2**
>
> The scale on a map is 1 : 100 000.
> (i) Find the distance in kilometres between two towns which are 7 cm apart on the map.
> (ii) Two train stations are 25 km apart.
>   How many centimetres are they apart on the map?
>
> (i) Scale = 1 : 100 000
>   ∴ 1 cm = 100 000 cm
>   7 cm = 700 000 cm
>   = $\frac{700\,000}{100}$ metres = 7000 m = 7 km
>   The towns are 7 km apart.
>
> (ii) 25 km = $\frac{25}{100\,000}$ km on the map
>   = $\frac{25 \times 1000}{100\,000}$ metres
>   = $\frac{25}{100}$ m = 0.25 m = 25 cm
>   The train stations are 25 cm apart on the map.

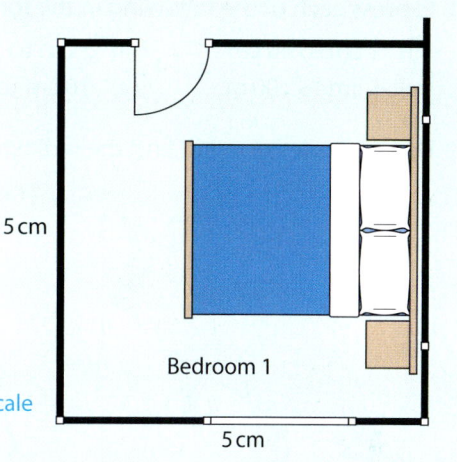

Text & Tests 2 Higher Level

Exercise 6.6

1. Express each of the following in the form $1:n$, where $n \in N$.
   - (i) 1 cm to 40 cm
   - (ii) 1 cm to 1 metre
   - (iii) 1 cm to 600 m
   - (iv) 5 cm to 100 m
   - (v) 10 cm to 1 km
   - (vi) 1 mm to 10 m

2. Use the scales given to find the indicated heights of the animals below:

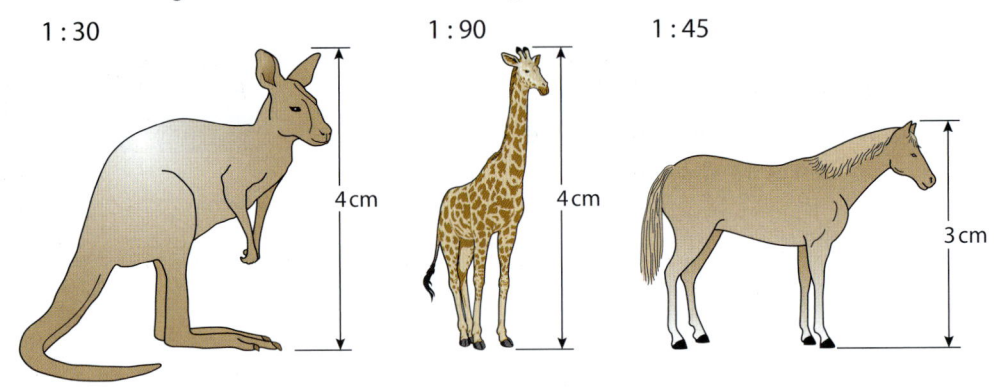

   1 : 30   1 : 90   1 : 45

   4 cm   4 cm   3 cm

3. The scale on a building plan is 1 : 100.
   Find the actual lengths in the building that are represented on the plan by:
   - (i) 5 cm
   - (ii) 11 cm
   - (iii) 8.5 cm
   - (iv) 14.8 cm

4. Find the actual lengths of the following lines on a building plan for which the scale is given:
   - (i) 2 cm, scale is 1 : 300
   - (ii) 8 cm, scale is 1 : 500
   - (iii) 3.6 cm, scale is 1 : 800
   - (iv) $5\frac{3}{4}$ cm, scale is 1 : 250

5. This is the scale drawing of a lorry.
   The scale is 1 : 100.
   Measure the length of this drawing and hence write down the actual length of the lorry.
   Find also the maximum height of the lorry.

   Scale 1:100

6. A walking map has a scale of 1 : 25 000.
   - (i) Find the actual distance for each of these scaled distances:
     - (a) 2 cm
     - (b) 5 cm
     - (c) 8.5 cm
     - (d) 6.75 cm
   - (ii) Find the distances on the map for these actual distances:
     - (a) 10 km
     - (b) 4 km
     - (c) 6.5 km
     - (d) 12.75 km

Chapter 6 Perimeter – Area – Volume

7. A map has a scale of 1 : 500 000.
   (i) The distance between two service stations on the map is 3.4 cm.
       What is the actual distance?
   (ii) The next emergency phone is 22 km away.
       How many centimetres would this be on the map?

8. A surveyor needs to draw an accurate plan of this awkwardly-shaped field.
   The scale he will use is 1 cm = 10 m.
   (i) What lengths will these lines have on the plan?
       (a) [AB]   (b) [BC]
   (ii) Construct an accurate scale drawing of this field using the given scale.

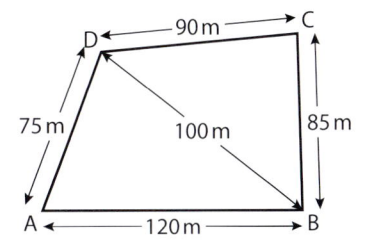

9. The scale on a map is 5 cm to 2 km. Express this in the form 1 : n.
   Find also the distance in cm on the map between two towns, A and B, which are in reality 30 km apart.

10. A girl made this scale drawing to calculate the height, |AB|, of a triangular wall.
    (i) Measure the distance |CB| on the scale drawing and calculate the scale of the drawing.
    (ii) By measurement and calculation, find the real height |AB|.
    (iii) Find the area of this triangular wall.

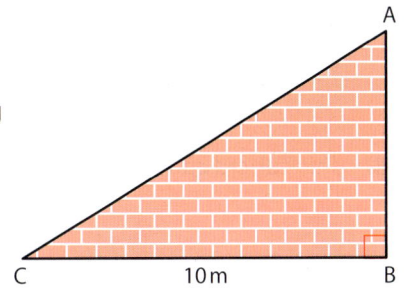

Text & Tests 2 Higher Level

Test yourself 6

1. Find (i) the volume
   (ii) the total surface area of the given triangular prism.

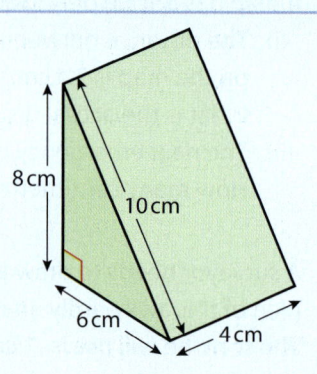

2. Taking $\pi = 3.14$, find the area of the sector shown.

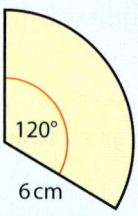

3. Find the area of the given parallelogram. Hence find the value of h.

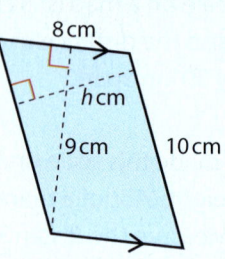

4. This cuboid can be made from a piece of card shaped like this.

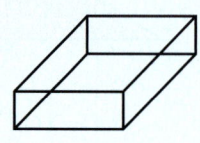

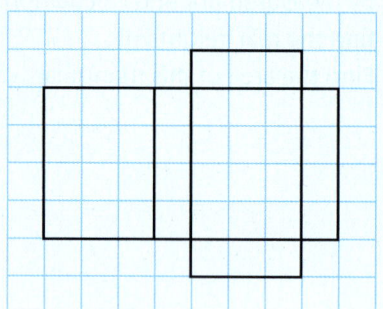

    If each square on the grid for the net is 3 cm in length, find
    (i) the volume of the cuboid
    (ii) the total surface area of the cuboid.

5. The given figure consists of a square and a semicircle. Taking $\pi = 3.14$, find correct to 1 decimal place,
    (i) the area of the figure
    (ii) the perimeter of the figure.

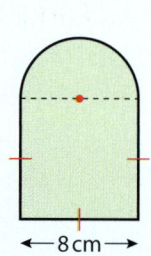

138

Chapter 6 Perimeter – Area – Volume

6. (i) A 1 : 50 scale model of a yacht is to be built.
   If the yacht is 25 m long, how long will the model yacht be?
   (ii) A scale drawing is to be made of a car.
   If the car is 6.25 m long and the model is to be 25 cm long, what should the scale be?

7. (i) Show that prisms Ⓐ and Ⓑ have the same volume.
   (ii) Find the surface area of each prism.
   Are the surface areas the same?
   (iii) Prism Ⓑ represents a large tent (with a floor) made of canvas.
   Find the cost of the canvas used if each square metre of canvas costs €24.50.

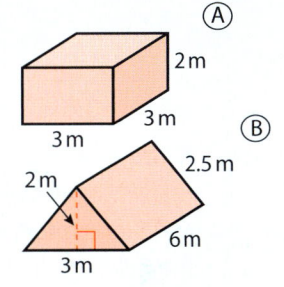

8. The diagram shows a quadrant, AOB, of a circle of radius 14 cm.
   Taking $\pi = \frac{22}{7}$, find the area of the shaded portion of the figure.

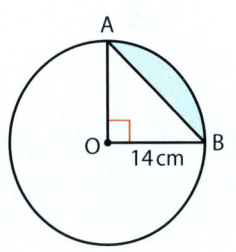

9. The figure shown is made from two identical overlapping rectangles which are 20 cm long and 15 cm wide.
   Calculate the area of the figure.

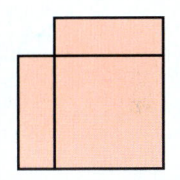

10. When the minute-hand of a clock moves through an angle of 75°, it covers an area of 88 cm². What is the length of the minute-hand?
    Give your answer correct to 2 decimal places and use the π key on your calculator.

11. (i) Find the surface area of the walls of this swimming pool.
    (ii) Find the cost of tiling the walls if the tiles cost €40 per m² (incl. VAT). Allow 2 m² extra for off-cuts and breakages.

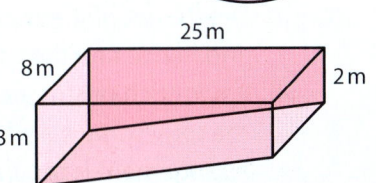

Text & Tests 2 Higher Level

12. A map has a scale of 1 : 25 000.
   (i) What is the actual distance if the scaled distance is 4 cm?
   (ii) What is the scaled distance if the actual distance is 3.5 km?

13. The volume of this prism is 245 cm^3.
Find the value of k.

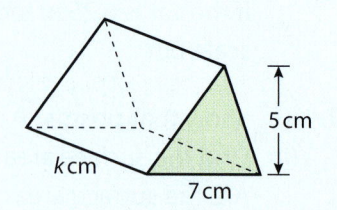

14. A farmer wants to sell his field. He wants more than €24 per square metre.
Mr Dunne offers him a total of €90 000 for the field.
Should the farmer accept this offer?
Give an explanation for your answer.

15. The net shown will fold to make a prism.
Describe fully the prism it will make.
Now find (i) the volume
(ii) the surface area of the prism.

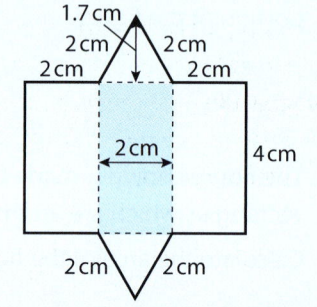

16. The large circle has an area of 129 cm^2.
What is the area of the shaded region?
Give your answer correct to one decimal place.

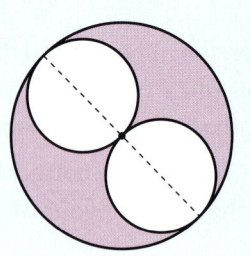

17. (i) Draw a net of the triangular prism shown and hence find the total surface area.
(ii) If two such prisms are glued together find the total surface area if the new arrangement is too have:
   (a) a minimum surface area,
   (b) a maximum surface area.

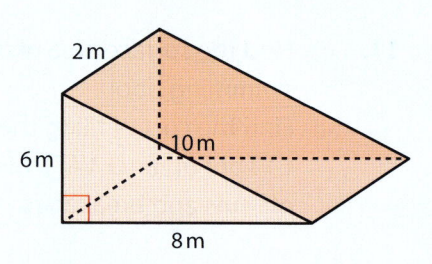

140

Chapter 6 Perimeter – Area – Volume

Assignment:

A:

Draw an outline plan of your PE hall.

Using a suitable scale, inscribe on the plan the markings for the different sports played in the hall.

Complete the table below showing the number of metres of tape needed to outline each court.

	Sport	Length of court
1		
2		
3		

B:

Using a dividers and a map of Ireland and Great Britain, compare the length of the coastlines of the two islands. Express your answer as a ratio corrected to the nearest whole number.

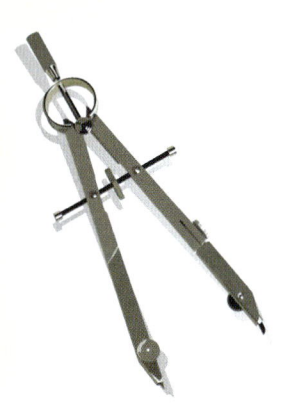

Chapter 7: Statistics 2 – Averages and Variability

In this chapter, you will learn to:

- find the mode of a data set,
- find the median of a data set,
- calculate the mean of a data set,
- identify an outlier,
- use the range to show how spread out a data set is,
- select the correct average to compare two sets of data,
- find a missing piece of data from a set if you know the mean,
- read data from a frequency table,
- calculate the mean and mode from a frequency table,
- calculate the mean from a grouped frequency table.

Section 7.1 Summary Statistics

Summary statistics is information that gives a quick and simple description of collected data.

Our course includes measures of **average** which give information about the centre of the data (often called measures of **central tendency**) and **range** which gives information about the spread (or **variability**) of the data.

Averages

When we look for an average, we are trying to find a **single or typical value** that will represent the many values we have collected. Averages also give a sense of the centre of the collected data.

The idea of an average is extremely useful because it enables us to compare one set of data with another by comparing just two values, namely their averages.

There are several ways of expressing an average, but the most commonly used averages are the **mode**, the **median** and the **mean**.

1. The Mode

The **mode** is the most common value in a set of data. The mode is very useful when one value appears much more often than any other. It is easy to find and can be used for non-numerical data such as the colours of cars sold by a garage.

Chapter 7 Statistics 2 – Averages and Variability

> **Example 1**
>
> The ages of students on a school bus are:
>
> 12, 15, 12, 13, 14, 16, 15, 11, 12
> 16, 15, 16, 14, 10, 13, 17, 15, 17
>
> Placing these in order we get:
>
> 10, 11, 12, 12, 12, 13, 13, 14, 14, 15, 15, 15, 15, 16, 16, 16, 17, 17
>
> The number in this list with the greatest frequency is 15.
>
> ∴ the mode = 15

2. The Median

To find the median of a list of numbers, put the numbers in order of size, starting with the smallest. The **median** is the middle number.

> **Example 2**
>
> (i) Find the median age of the Byrne family whose members' ages are:
>
> 19 31 21 3 6 14 19 24 11
>
> (ii) Find the median of the following scores:
>
> 62 64 81 68 95 57
>
> (i) Arrange the values in ascending order:
>
> 3 6 11 14 | 19 | 19 21 24 31
> 4 values   ↑   4 values
>
> Since there are nine values, the middle one is the fifth value.
> The median age is 19 years.
>
> (ii) Arrange the six scores in order:
>
> 57 62 64 | 68 81 95
> 3 values ↑ 3 values
>
> Now there are two middle scores, 64 and 68.
>
> Take the average of 64 and 68:
>
> $$\frac{64 + 68}{2} = \frac{132}{2} = 66$$
>
> The median is 66.
>
> There will always be two middle scores when there is an even number of scores.

Text & Tests 2 Higher Level

Note: › The median depends on the **number** of scores in the data set, but not the actual scores themselves.
› In a set with an **odd number** of scores, the median will always be one of the scores.
› In a set with an **even number** of scores, the median is the average of the two middle scores.

Exercise 7.1

1. Write down the mode of these sets of data:
   (i) 15, 12, 16, 19, 12, 14, 16, 12
   (ii) 67, 43, 89, 45, 54, 86, 45, 76, 53
   (iii) 5.6, 5.4, 5.7, 5.5, 5.7, 5.6, 5.7
   (iv) 3, 3, 7, 8, 7, 9, 8, 5, 7, 11, 12
   (v) bus, car, bus, walk, car, bus, cycle, car, bus, bus, walk, cycle, car, walk, bus
   (vi) $\frac{1}{2}, \frac{1}{4}, \frac{3}{4}, \frac{1}{4}, 1, \frac{1}{4}, \frac{3}{4}, 1, 0, \frac{1}{4}, 0, \frac{1}{4}, \frac{3}{4}, \frac{1}{2}, 1, \frac{1}{4}, \frac{1}{2}$

2. The mode of these numbers is 5. Find the value of *.

    2, 3, 7, 5, 2, 6, *, 5, 3

3. Rewrite the following array of numbers in order of size:

    3, 3, 7, 8, 7, 9, 8, 5, 7, 11, 12

    Now write down (i) the mode, (ii) the median.

4. Rearrange the following marks in order and then write down the median in each case.
   (i) 9, 5, 8, 3, 2, 7, 6
   (ii) 8, 12, 18, 9, 14, 7, 10, 6

5. A rugby team played 10 games.
   Here are the numbers of points the team scored.

    12, 22, 14, 11, 7, 18, 22, 14, 36, 14

   (i) Write down the mode.
   (ii) What is the median number of points scored?

6. Work out
   (i) the mode
   (ii) the median for this set of data:

    5, 7, 9, 9, 8, 7, 9, 10, 12, 11, 9, 9, 5

7. In this set of data, the mode is 9.

    7, 4, 3, 3, 12, 9, x, 10, 9

   (i) Find the value of x.
   (ii) What is the median of the set?

144

Chapter 7 Statistics 2 – Averages and Variability

8. Matthew's marks in eight tests are shown below.
   What mark did he score in the ninth test if his median mark was then 6?

   5   9   7   3   7   4   5   8

9. The hourly pay rates for 10 workers are as follows:

   €12.40, €14.80, €10, €9.20, €14.20, €12.30, €15, €11.80, €15.20, €13.20.

   Find the median hourly rate.

10. The following set of data has 2 modes.

    2, 3, 4, 4, 5, 6, 7, 8, $a + 1$, 4, 3, 5

    What are the possible values of a?

11. Joana did a survey to find the shoe sizes of pupils in her mixed class.
    The bar chart illustrates her data.

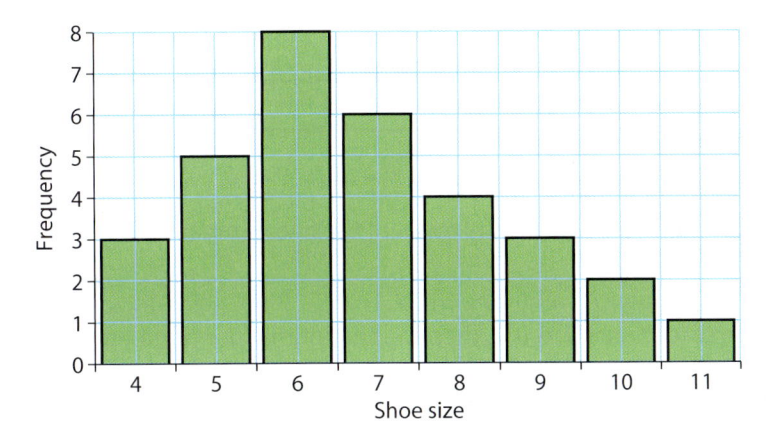

    (i) How many pupils are there in Joana's class?
    (ii) What is the modal shoe size?
    (iii) Can you tell from the bar chart which are the boys or which are the girls in her class?
    (iv) Joana then decided to draw a bar chart to show the shoe sizes of the boys and the girls separately. Do you think that the mode for the boys and the mode for the girls will be the same as the mode for the whole class? Explain your answer.

Text & Tests 2 Higher Level

Section 7.2 The Mean

The **mean** of the numbers

    4, 5, 7, 9, 10

$$\text{Mean} = \frac{\text{Sum of the numbers}}{\text{Number of numbers}}$$

is the sum of these numbers divided by the number of numbers.

$$\therefore \quad \text{Mean} = \frac{4 + 5 + 7 + 9 + 10}{5} = \frac{35}{5} = 7$$

In everyday language, the word 'average' is generally used instead of 'mean'.
The mean is a very important value in statistics as it takes into account all the values in the set of data.

Example 1

In five basketball matches, Joan scored 16 points, 10 points, 22 points, 18 points and 24 points. Calculate her mean score for the five matches.

$$\text{Mean} = \frac{16 + 10 + 22 + 18 + 24}{5} = \frac{90}{5} = 18$$

Example 2

The mean of four numbers is 7.
When a fifth number is added, the mean of the five numbers is 9.
Find the fifth number.

If the mean of four numbers is 7, then the sum of the four numbers is
4×7, i.e. 28.

The mean of five numbers $= 9 \Rightarrow$ sum of the five numbers $= 45$

$\therefore$ the fifth number $= 45 - 28$

                                 $= 17$

Extreme values

Here are the marks scored by six pupils in a maths test:

    26, 35, 34, 46, 52, 95

The mean mark is

$$\frac{26 + 35 + 34 + 46 + 52 + 95}{6} = \frac{288}{6} = 48$$

Notice that four out of the six pupils are below the mean mark.

This is caused by one mark, i.e. 95, which is much higher than all the other marks.

Chapter 7 Statistics 2 – Averages and Variability

Such a mark is generally known as an **outlier** or **extreme value**.
When an outlier exists, the mean may not fully or accurately represent the set of data given. This happens, in particular, when the number of data items is small.

Example 3

The mean of 10, 7, 3, 6, x is 8. Find the value of x.

There are 5 scores.

$$\therefore \frac{10 + 7 + 3 + 6 + x}{5} = 8$$

$$\frac{26 + x}{5} = 8$$

$$26 + x = 40$$

$$x = 40 - 26$$

$$x = 14$$

Exercise 7.2

1. Find the mean of each of these arrays of numbers:
    (i) 2, 4, 5, 6, 8
    (ii) 14, 17, 21, 13, 6, 13
    (iii) 1, 0, 5, 7, 17, 12
    (iv) 19, 12, 6, 18, 40, 18, 5, 40

2. Ava's marks in six subjects were 47, 68, 62, 76, 59 and 54.
   Find her mean mark.

3. A snooker player scored 208 points in 8 visits to the table.
   What was his average number of points per visit?

4. The mean of six numbers is 14. Find the sum of the six numbers.

5. The mean of four numbers is 9.
    (i) What is the sum of the four numbers?
    (ii) If three of the numbers are 6, 11 and 14, find the fourth.

6. The three sides of this triangle have a mean length of 10 cm.
   Find the length of the side [AC].

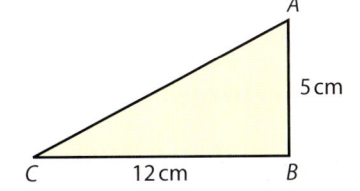

7. The mean of three numbers is 8. When a fourth number is added, the mean is 9. Find the fourth number.

Text & Tests 2 Higher Level

8. In the first three frames of a snooker match, a player got a mean score of 27.
   In the fourth frame he scored 19. Find his mean score for the four frames.

9. The mean of seven numbers is 12.
   One of the numbers is removed. Find its value if
   (i) the mean of the remaining numbers is reduced to 11.
   (ii) the mean of the remaining numbers is unchanged.
   (iii) the mean of the remaining numbers is increased to 14.

10. The mean price of five packets of biscuits is €1.80.
    The prices of two of the packets are €2.10 and €1.71.
    The other three packets are all the same price. Find this price.

11. Write down five numbers so that the mode
    is 4, the mean is 6 and the median is 5.

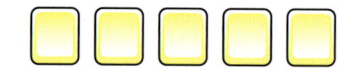

12. The mean height of a group of eight students is 165 cm.
    (i) What is the total height of all eight students?

    A ninth student joins the group. He is 168 cm tall.
    (ii) What is the mean height of all nine students?

13. The numbers 4, 8, 12, 17, x are arranged in order of size.
    If the mean of the numbers is equal to the median, find x.

14. (i) The mean of 3, 7, 8, 10 and x is 6. Find x.
    (ii) The mean of 1, k, 3, 6 and 8 is 7. Find k.

15. The mean of five numbers is 39.
    Two of the numbers are 103 and 35 and each of the other three numbers is equal to x.
    Find (i) the total of the five numbers
         (ii) the value of x.

16. Nicky's marks in four tests were:
       8, 4, 5, 3
    What mark did she get in her fifth and sixth tests if her modal mark was 4 and her mean mark was 5 after the six tests?

17. Here are two sets of data:

    (A) 19 31 21 3 6 14 19 24 11
    (B) 19 31 21 3 6 14 19 24 91

    (i) Calculate the mean (to one decimal place) of each set.
    (ii) What is the only difference between the two sets of data?
    (iii) What effect does the difference identified in part (ii) have on the mean?

18. A basketball team scored 43, 55, 41 and 37 points in their first four matches.
  (i) What is the mean number of points scored for the first four matches?
  (ii) What score will the team need to shoot in the next match so that they maintain the same mean score?
  (iii) The team shoots only 24 points in the fifth match. What is the mean number of points scored for the five matches?
  (iv) The team shoots 41 points in their sixth and final match. Will this increase or decrease their previous mean score?
  What is the mean score for all six matches?

19. Jane had seven spelling tests, each with twelve words, but could only find the results of five of them.
These were: 9, 5, 7, 9 and 10.
She asked her teacher for the other two results and the teacher said that the score which occurred most frequently was 9 and the mean was 8.
What are the two missing results, given that Jane knows that her worst result was a 5?

20. On four tests, each marked out of 100, my mean score was 85. What is the lowest mark I could have scored on any one test?

Section 7.3 Which average to use?

The three averages – the **mean**, the **mode** and the **median** – are all useful but depending on the data, one may be more suitable than the others.

We try to select the 'average' that is most representative of a set of data.

If you use the wrong average, your results may lead to an incorrect conclusion.

The mode   The **mode** is useful in situations where you want to know for example,
  › which dress size is the most common
  › which brand of dog food is most popular.

The mean   The **mean** is useful for finding a 'typical' value when most of the data is closely grouped. The mean may not give a typical value if the data is very spread out or if it includes a few values that are very different from the rest (outliers).

The median   Here are the monthly salaries of 8 people in a small company:
  Director: €14 000 per month
  5 people: €3500 per month
  2 people: €2400 per month

Text & Tests 2 Higher Level

The mean salary is $\dfrac{14\,000 + (3500 \times 5) + (2400 \times 2)}{8}$

$= €4537.50$

Here the mean monthly salary is €4537.50 which is not typical of most of the monthly salaries.

In situations like this, the **median** (€3500) is a more appropriate average.

Example 1

Here are the marks obtained by a group of ten students in a maths test.

  6, 7, 83, 84, 85, 86, 86, 87, 88, 89

Find (i) the mean   (ii) the median.

State which of these averages best represents the data.

(i) Mean $= \dfrac{6 + 7 + 83 + 84 + 85 + 86 + 86 + 87 + 88 + 89}{10}$

$= \dfrac{701}{10} = 70.1$

(ii) The median $= \dfrac{85 + 86}{2} = 85.5$

In the data, eight out of the ten marks are in the eighties.
Since the mean is only 70.1, the median is a more suitable average.

Investigation:

Consider the random set of numbers A = 2, 5, 5, 7, 9, 14

Calculate the mean, mode, and median of this data set.

Create a second set of numbers by adding 3 to each element of A.

Calculate the mean, mode and median of this new data set.

Create a third set of numbers by multiplying each element of A by 2.

Calculate the mean, mode, and median of this new data set.

What conclusions can you make about changes to the mean, mode and median when a number is added (or subtracted) and when a number is multiplied by a data set?

Chapter 7 Statistics 2 – Averages and Variability

Exercise 7.3

1. The numbers of computers in eight classrooms are:

   3, 15, 1, 2, 1, 30, 2, 1

   (i) What is the median number of computers?
   (ii) What is the modal number of computers?
   (iii) Why would the mean not be a sensible average for this data?

2. For the set of numbers below, find the mean and the median.

   1, 3, 3, 3, 4, 6, 99

   Which average best describes the set of numbers?

3. Find (i) the mean (ii) the median of these numbers:

   9, 11, 11, 15, 17, 18, 94

   Which of these two averages would you choose to best describe these numbers?

4. Jack and Daniel are backpacking in Australia and have recorded these midday temperatures for a week.

Day	1	2	3	4	5	6	7
Midday temperature (°C)	32	30	30	28	33	31	30

   (i) Find the mean midday temperature, correct to the nearest whole number.
   (ii) Give a reason why the mean is appropriate for this data.

5. (i) Find the mean of this set of numbers:

   37, 28, 37, 18, 18, 22, 26, 18, 37, 37, 19

   (ii) Why is the mode a bad choice of average in this case?

6. In March, Rachel and Dave sold five different types of jacket in their clothes shop in the amounts shown.

Jacket	Leather	Suede	Denim	PVC	Cotton
Amount sold	45	17	64	28	52

   (i) Find the modal type of jacket sold.
   (ii) Why is the mode appropriate for this data?

7. Decide which average you would use for each of the following.
   Give a reason for your choice.
   (i) The average mark in an examination.
   (ii) The average uniform size for all the pupils in a class.
   (iii) The average height of the players in a basketball team.
   (iv) The colours of the shirts sold by a department store.
   (v) The average salary of seven people who work for a small business.

8. There are 10 apartments in a block.
   On a particular day, the number of letters delivered to each of the apartments is
       2, 0, 5, 3, 4, 0, 1, 0, 3, 15
   Calculate the mean, mode and median number of letters.
   Which of these averages is the most suitable to represent this data?
   Give a reason for your answer.

9. A student wants to use an 'average' to show how he has performed in eight science tests.
   Here are his marks: 56   56   58   58   85   97   56   54
   Should he use the mean, mode or median to impress his parents?
   Give a reason for your answer.

10. A restaurant records the number of diners it has every day for a week. The numbers are as follows.
        28   40   28   38   110   170   33
    (i) Write down the mode.
    (ii) Work out the median number of diners.
    (iii) Work out the mean number of diners, correct to one decimal place.
    (iv) The manager wishes to sell the restaurant.
    What average is he likely to use when talking to prospective buyers?
    Give a reason for your answer.

Section 7.4 Frequency tables

The number of children in each of 50 families in a certain district was recorded in the following way:

    1, 3, 4, 3, 2, 2, 4, 2, 6, 7, 6, 2, 4, 5, 5, 4, 3, 4, 3, 2, 1, 6, 2, 5, 1,
    4, 4, 4, 3, 5, 3, 6, 2, 4, 5, 7, 2, 4, 3, 5, 5, 3, 3, 4, 1, 2, 5, 3, 4, 4.

This list could be much more useful and easier to read if it was presented in the form of a table, as shown below.

Number of children per family	1	2	3	4	5	6	7
Number of families	4	9	10	13	8	4	2

The table above is called a **frequency table** or **frequency distribution**.
This table shows the numbers of families (i.e. the frequency) with 1 child, 2 children and so on.
For example, there are 13 families with 4 children per family.

Chapter 7 Statistics 2 – Averages and Variability

Mean and mode of a frequency distribution

The frequency table below shows the numbers of children aged from 2 to 7 living on a certain road.

Age	2	3	4	5	6	7
Number of children	1	3	5	10	8	3

From the table it can be seen that the **mode** or **modal age** is 5 as it occurs more often than any other age.

To find the **mean** age of the children from the table, we perform these operations:

1. Find the sum of the ages of all the children.
2. Find the number of children.
3. Divide the sum of the ages by the number of children.

1. To find the sum of the ages, we multiply each age by the number of children of that age and add up the results.

   Sum of ages = $(1 \times 2) + (3 \times 3) + (5 \times 4) + (10 \times 5) + (8 \times 6) + (3 \times 7)$
   $= 2 + 9 + 20 + 50 + 48 + 21 = 150$

2. The number of children is $1 + 3 + 5 + 10 + 8 + 3 = 30$.

3. The mean age = $\dfrac{\text{Sum of all the ages}}{\text{Number of children}} = \dfrac{150}{30} = 5$

If x stands for the variable (e.g. age) and f stands for the frequency, then the data above can be extended as follows:

Age(x)	2	3	4	5	6	7	Totals
Number of children (f)	1	3	5	10	8	3	Total number of children = sum of f = Σf = 30
(fx)	2	9	20	50	48	21	Total age of children = sum of fx = Σfx = 150

The mean of the frequency table is given by;

$$\text{Mean} = \frac{\text{Total age of children}}{\text{Total number of children}} = \frac{\Sigma fx}{\Sigma f} = \frac{150}{30} = 5 \text{ years.}$$

$$\text{Mean} = \frac{\Sigma fx}{\Sigma f} = \frac{\text{sum of variables} \times \text{corresponding frequency}}{\text{sum of the frequencies}}$$

Text & Tests 2 Higher Level

> **Example 1**
>
> A road-check on 30 motor vehicles yielded the following record of the number of occupants each carried:
>
> 2, 1, 3, 4, 5, 3, 2, 1, 2, 3, 1, 1, 2, 4, 6, 5, 4, 2, 2, 1, 1, 2, 4, 6, 5, 2, 6, 2, 5, 3
>
> Make out a frequency table of the above data and find the mean and mode of the distribution.
>
> | Number of occupants per vehicle | 1 | 2 | 3 | 4 | 5 | 6 |
> |---|---|---|---|---|---|---|
> | Number of vehicles | 6 | 9 | 4 | 4 | 4 | 3 |
>
> $$\text{Mean} = \frac{(6 \times 1) + (9 \times 2) + (4 \times 3) + (4 \times 4) + (4 \times 5) + (3 \times 6)}{6 + 9 + 4 + 4 + 4 + 3}$$
>
> $$= \frac{90}{30} = 3$$
>
> Mode = 2, as 2 occurs with the greatest frequency.

Grouped frequency distributions

When dealing with a large number of variables, such as the ages of people in a certain district, it is often convenient to arrange the data in **groups** or **classes**.

Thus, when recording the ages of people, the results could be grouped (0–9) years, (10–19) years … etc.

The grouped frequency distribution table below shows the marks (out of 25) achieved by 50 students in a test.

Marks achieved	1–5	6–10	11–15	16–20	21–25
No. of students	11	12	15	9	3

While it is not possible to find the exact mean of a grouped frequency distribution, we can find an estimate of the mean by taking the **mid-interval value** of each class.

The mid-interval value in the (1–5) class is found by adding 1 and 5 and dividing by 2.

The mid-interval of the (1–5) class is $\frac{1+5}{2} = \frac{6}{2} = 3$.

The table given above is reproduced with the mid-interval values written in smaller size over each class interval.

	3	8	13	18	23
Marks achieved	1–5	6–10	11–15	16–20	21–25
No. of students	11	12	15	9	3

Chapter 7 Statistics 2 – Averages and Variability

$$\text{Mean} = \frac{\Sigma fx}{\Sigma f} = \frac{11(3) + 12(8) + 15(13) + 9(18) + 3(23)}{11 + 12 + 15 + 9 + 3} = \frac{555}{50} = 11.1$$

For the **grouped** table above, we cannot give the exact mode, but we can say that the **modal class** is the interval (11–15) because this interval contains the greatest frequency.

> ### Example 2
>
> Thirty people were given a test and each received a score out of 10.
>
> 5 6 2 5 7 7 8 5 4 7 6 8 10 6 4
> 7 6 8 7 6 4 7 5 6 7 5 9 7 6 6
>
> (i) Calculate the mean score.
> (ii) Complete the grouped-frequency table.
> (iii) Using the table **estimate** the mean value of the data.
>
> | Interval | 2–4 | 5–7 | 8–10 |
> |---|---|---|---|
> | Tally | | | |
> | Frequency | | | |
>
> (i) Mean $= \dfrac{186}{30} = 6.2$
>
> (ii)
>
> | Interval | 2–4 | 5–7 | 8–10 |
> |---|---|---|---|
> | Mid-interval value (x) | 3 | 6 | 9 |
> | Tally | \|\|\|\| | ₩₩ ₩₩ ₩₩ ₩₩ \| | ₩₩ |
> | Frequency (f) | 4 | 21 | 5 |
> | (fx) | 12 | 126 | 45 |
>
> (iii) Mean $= \dfrac{\Sigma fx}{\Sigma f} = \dfrac{12 + 126 + 45}{4 + 21 + 5} = \dfrac{183}{30} = 6.1$

Exercise 7.4

1. Thirty students in a class were given a test which was marked out of 10.
   The results of the test are shown below.
   4, 6, 7, 5, 9, 8, 6, 4, 3, 5, 6, 9, 8, 7, 6, 10, 1, 3, 6, 7, 9, 8, 5, 3, 2, 4, 7, 9, 10, 5
   Copy and complete the frequency table shown below:

Marks per student	1	2	3	4	5	6	7	8	9	10
Number of students			3							

   From the table, write down the number of students who got
   (i) 5 marks   (ii) 8 marks   (iii) 10 marks.
   What mark was got most frequently?

2. A factory produces 50 television sets per day.
   Tests at the end of one day gave rise to the following data:

Number of faults per set	0	1	2	3	4	5	6
Number of sets	1	8	12	11	9	5	4

   (i) How many sets had no fault?
   (ii) How many sets had 6 faults?
   (iii) What was the modal number of faults?
   (iv) What was the total number of faults recorded in all the sets?
   (v) Find the mean number of faults per set.

3. The table below shows the numbers of goals scored in a number of hockey matches on a Sunday morning.

Goals scored	1	2	3	4	5	6
Number of matches	14	16	8	8	6	8

   (i) In how many matches were 6 goals scored?
   (ii) What was the modal number of goals scored?
   (iii) What was the total number of goals scored?
   (iv) Find the mean number of goals scored.

4. The following frequency table shows the numbers of goals scored in 60 football matches.

Goals scored	1	2	3	4	5	6
Number of matches	15	14	9	6	10	6

   (i) Find the mean number of goals scored per match.
   (ii) What was the modal number of goals scored?
   (iii) In what percentage of the matches were 3 or 4 goals scored?
   (iv) Find the greatest number of matches which could have ended in a draw.

5. A die was thrown 30 times.
   The results are shown here.

Score	1	2	3	4	5	6
Frequency	3	4	6	8	7	2

   Find the mean score.

Chapter 7 Statistics 2 – Averages and Variability

6. Carol is trying to estimate how many words she has written in an essay.
   She records the number of words she wrote on each line of one page.
   Her results are given in the table below.

Words per line	10	11	12	13	14	15
No. of lines	1	3	6	9	7	4

   (i) How many lines in total were there on the page?
   (ii) How many lines contained 14 words?
   (iii) What was the modal number of words per line?
   (iv) Calculate the mean of the distribution.

7. The marks of 36 students in third-year are given below:

   31 49 52 79 40 29 66 71 73 19 51 47 81 67 40 52 20 84
   65 73 60 54 60 59 25 89 21 91 84 77 18 37 55 41 72 38

   Copy and complete the grouped frequency table below:

Marks	1–20	21–40	41–60	61–80	81–100
Number of students					

   (i) How many students scored between 21 and 60 inclusive?
   (ii) What is the modal class?
   (iii) Which class had the second largest number of students?
   (iv) Name one disadvantage of a grouped frequency table.

Investigation:

Copy the frequency distribution in Q 7, adding in a row for mid-interval values 10.5, 30.5, etc.

Using the data calculate the mean value of (i) the frequency distribution
(ii) the raw data.

What conclusion can you make from your results?

8. People attending a course were asked to choose one of the whole numbers from 1 to 12. The results were recorded as follows:

Number	1–3	4–6	7–9	10–12
No. of people	3	17	2	8

   (i) Write down the modal class of the distribution.
   (ii) Use the mid-interval value of each class to estimate the mean of the distribution.

9. The frequency table shows the numbers of books bought by 20 pupils in the past year.

Number of books	0–4	5–9	10–14	15–19
Frequency	2	4	6	8

Find an estimate for the mean number of books bought by each pupil.

10.

Class	14–16	16–18	18–20	20–22	22–24
Frequency	1	5	12	3	0

   (i) Give a reason why Carla said it was not possible to find the mean of this grouped frequency distribution as it was.
   (ii) Using mid-interval values of 15, 17, 19, etc, what estimate did she find for the mean?
   (iii) What assumption had Carla to make about the class intervals, e.g. 14–16, 16–18, etc?

11. One hundred people were asked to record the numbers of mobile phonecalls they received on a particular day. The results are shown in the table below.

No. of calls	0–4	5–9	10–14	15–19	20–24
Frequency	45	29	17	8	1

   (i) What is the modal group?
   (ii) What is the greatest number of people who could have received more than 18 calls?
   (iii) What is the least number of people who could have received less than 8 calls?
   (iv) Use the mid-interval values to find an estimate for the mean number of phonecalls received.
      Give your answer correct to the nearest whole number.

12. The table below shows the distances travelled by seven paper aeroplanes after they were thrown.

Aeroplane	A	B	C	D	E	F	G
Distance (cm)	188	200	250	30	380	330	302

   (i) Find the median of the data.
   (ii) Find the mean of the data.
   (iii) Aeroplane D is thrown again and the distance it travels is measured and recorded in place of the original measurement. The median of the data remains unchanged and the mean is now equal to the median. How far did aeroplane D travel the second time?
   (iv) What is the minimum distance that aeroplane D would need to have travelled in order for the median to have changed?

Chapter 7 Statistics 2 – Averages and Variability

Section 7.5 Range and variability

Range

The **range** for a set of data is the highest value of the set minus the lowest value.

For the data   3, 7, 9, 15, 21, 28
                Range = 28 − 3 = 25

> The range is largest value minus smallest value.

The range shows how **spread out** a set of data is. It is very useful when comparing two sets of data.

The marks, out of 20, scored by Ava and Sean in 6 maths tests are given below:

Ava   12, 10, 18, 14, 8, 10

Sean   12, 10, 16, 13, 11, 10

For **Ava**:   Mean = $\frac{72}{6}$ = 12   Range = 18 − 8 = 10

For **Sean**:   Mean = $\frac{72}{6}$ = 12   Range = 16 − 10 = 6

Notice that the mean mark for both is the same but Sean's marks have a smaller range. Since Sean's marks are less **spread out**, it shows that Sean's results are more **consistent** than Ava's.

This spread-out nature of Ava's marks compared to Sean's marks illustrates the variability of data and how important it can be.

The **range** is generally used as a measure of variability as it is easy to find and easy to understand.

Investigation:

What conclusions can be made about **changes to the range** of a set of numbers when a number is (i) added (or subtracted) (ii) multiplied by the set of numbers.

Comparing data

To compare two sets of data, we use the **range** and either the **mean**, the **mode** or the **median**.

In the example above comparing Ava's and Sean's marks, we used the range and the mean.

Text & Tests 2 Higher Level

Exercise 7.5

1. Find the range for each of the following sets of data:
   (i) 3, 7, 6, 8, 12, 6, 14
   (ii) 8, 2, 9, 6, 7, 10, 4, 18, 5, 23

2. Which of these two sets of data has the bigger range?
   (i) 23, 36, 42, 29, 34, 27
   (ii) 81, 74, 92, 77, 85, 89

3. Saskia's marks in six French tests were: 54, 82, 65, 72, 38, 66
   John's marks in the same six tests were: 58, 62, 51, 66, 71, 64
   (i) Find the range of marks for Saskia and for John.
       Use your results to find which of the two had the more consistent marks.
   (ii) Which of the two had the higher mean mark?

4. In a golf competition between two clubs, the captain had to choose between Emer and Anna to play in the first round. In the previous eight rounds, their scores were as follows:
   Emer: 80, 73, 72, 88, 86, 90, 75, 92
   Anna: 88, 84, 79, 85, 76, 85, 87, 80
   (i) Calculate the mean score for each golfer.
   (ii) Find the range of scores for each golfer.
   (iii) Which golfer would you choose to play for you in the competition?
         Explain your answer. (Lower scores are better.)

5. Sinead has five cards. The five cards have a mean of 7 and a range of 4.

   [7] [7] [7] [ ] [ ]

   What are the missing numbers?

6. Miss Moore gave her class a maths test. Here are the marks for the girls:
   7, 5, 8, 5, 2, 8, 7, 4, 7, 10, 3, 7, 4, 3, 6
   What is (i) the median mark   (ii) the range of marks?
   The median mark for the boys in her class was 7 and the range of marks for the boys was 4.
   By comparing the results, explain whether the boys or girls did better in the test.

7. A set of cards has these numbers on them.

   [3] [3] [4] [5] [6] [6] [7]

   (i) Find five cards from this set with median 6 and range 4.
   (ii) Find four cards with median 6 and range 3.

8. There are 9 children at a party. The mean age of the children was 15 and the range of their ages was 5.

Write each sentence below and state whether it is **True**, **Possible** or **Impossible**.
   (i) Every child at the party was currently 15 years of age.
   (ii) All the children were at least 13 years of age.
   (iii) The oldest child was 5 years older than the youngest.

9. Two greenhouses had the following temperatures measured (in °C) at midnight for a week.

Greenhouse A   1, −2, 4, 0, 5, 2, −1.
Greenhouse B   4 −3, 2, −1, 3, 0, −2

Compare the two sets of data using the range and the median temperature.

10. There are 5 children in a family. The youngest child is 8 years old and another child is 15 years old. The median child's age is 13. The range of the children's ages is 17. The mean age is 14. Find the ages of the 5 children.

11. A greengrocer sold boxes of apples from different countries.
A box contained 9 French apples.

The weight of each apple is given below, in grams.

   101, 107, 98, 109, 115, 103, 96, 112, 104

   (i) Calculate the mean weight of a French apple.
   (ii) Find the range of the weights of the French apples.

Another box contained 9 South African apples.
Their mean weight was 107 g and their range was 19 g.
   (iii) Make two comments on the weights of the apples in the two boxes.

Text & Tests 2 Higher Level

Test yourself 7

1. The mean of 3, 7, 8, 10, x is 8. Find x.

2. Find (i) the mean (ii) the median for the following set of data:

    3, 5, 4, 7, 29, 9, 2, 4, 10, 8

    Which of these two averages is the more suitable to represent the data? Give a reason for your answer.

3. Find the mean and median of the set of numbers 2, 2, 3, 3, 3, 5, 101. Which average best describes the set of numbers?

4. The mean height of six girls is 1.63 m.
   The mean height of five of the girls is 1.61 m.
   Find the height of the sixth girl.

5. A group of boys and girls took a Geography test. These are the marks which the boys got:

    13, 14, 14, 15, 14, 14, 15, 17, 16, 14, 16, 12
    (i) Find the range of the boys' marks.
    (ii) Calculate the mean mark of the boys.

    The mean mark for the girls in the class was 13.2 and the girls' marks had a range of 7.
    (iii) Make two statements about the differences between the boys' and girls' marks in the Geography test.

6. Find a set of three numbers for which the median is 15, the mean is 13 and the range is 12.

7. The results of 24 students in a test are given in a grouped frequency table as:

Mark (x)	40–54	55–69	70–84	85–99
Mid-interval value				
Frequency (f)	5	8	7	4
(fx)				

    (i) Copy and complete the table.
    (ii) Using the mid-interval values estimate the mean mark.

8. The table below shows the number of goals scored in a series of football matches.

Number of goals	1	2	3
Number of matches	7	7	x

    (i) If the modal number of goals is 3, find the smallest possible value of x.
    (ii) If the median number of goals is 2, find the largest possible value of x.

Chapter 7 Statistics 2 – Averages and Variability

9. There were six people living in a house. The median age of the people was 20 and the range of their ages was 3. Write each of the sentences below and add **T(True), P(Possible) or I(Impossible)** after each one.
   (i) Every person was either 19 or 20 years of age.
   (ii) The oldest person in the house was 23 years
   (iii) All six people in the house could speak Irish.

10. Find the mean, correct to one decimal place, and the mode(s) of this set of numbers:
    34, 28, 38, 19, 19, 21, 28, 19, 37, 36, 19.
    Why is the mode a bad choice of average in this case?

11. A sample of 10 measurements has a mean of 15.7 and a sample of the other 20 measurements has a mean of 14.3. Find the mean of all 30 measurements.
    Give your answer correct to one decimal place.

12. In a diving competition, the five judges gave scores of 8, 7.5, 8.5, 9 and 8.
    (i) Delete the highest and lowest scores and find the mean of the remaining three scores. Multiply this by the Degree of Difficulty of 2.8 to get the score for the dive.
    (ii) Repeat the process above to find the score for a dive with a Degree of Difficulty of 3.2, if the judges' scores are 6, 6.5, 6.5, 7, 7.5.
    Give each answer correct to two decimal places.

13. The weekly wages of the employees of a fast-food takeaway are listed below:
    €300, €250, €240, €220, €200, €1050.
    Find (i) the mean wage
         (ii) the median wage
    Why can't you find the mode?
    Which of the averages – mean or median – best represents the 'typical' wage?

14. The range for eight numbers is 40 and seven of these numbers are shown.
    Find two possible values for the missing number.

    27 5 33 42
    11 □ 13 19

15. The frequency table shows the numbers of postage stamps bought by 20 people in the past month.

Number of stamps	0–4	5–9	10–14	15–19
Frequency	2	4	6	8

    Use the mid-interval values to find an estimate of the mean number of stamps bought.

16. Over the complete assessment period, Jenny averaged 35 out of a possible 40 marks for her maths tests. However, when checking her files, she could only find 7 of the 8 tests. For these, she scored 29, 36, 32, 38, 35, 34 and 39. Determine how many marks out of 40 she scored for the eighth test.

17. Ten men travelled to watch a rugby match. The mean age of the men was 25 years and the range of their ages was 6.
Write each statement below and then write next to it whether it is

  (i) true   (ii) could be true   or   (iii) false.

  (a) The youngest man was 18 years old.
  (b) All the men were at least 20 years old.
  (c) The oldest person was 4 years older than the youngest.
  (d) Every man was between 20 and 26 years old.

Assignment:

Select three textbooks, e.g. English, Science and Maths.

Pick a random sample of pages from each book.

Count the number of words in each sentence of a page.

Copy and complete a table of results for each text as follows:

English				
Number of words per sentence	Mid-interval value (x)	Tally	Frequency (f)	fx
1–5	3			
6–10	8			
11–15				
16–20				
Etc.				

Using the data, calculate the **mode, median and mean** number of words per sentence for each textbook. Compare your results for the three texts.

Geometry 1 – Triangles
– Quadrilaterals
– Theorems

chapter 8

From first year, you will recall how to:

- recognise an acute, obtuse or reflex angle,
- identify vertically opposite, corresponding, alternate and interior angles,
- tell the difference between a line, line segment and ray,
- identify the interior and exterior angles in a triangle.

In this chapter, you will learn to:

- find missing angles on straight lines, triangles and compound shapes,
- identify the properties of a quadrilateral,
- decide if two triangles are congruent,
- understand and use the Theorem of Pythagoras,
- investigate shapes and make observations and deductions,
- understand specific terms related to Geometry such as axiom and theorem.
- understand theorems 1, 2, 3, 5, 10, 13.

Section 8.1 Revision of lines and angles

The diagrams below will help you recall some of the facts and terms you will have met in your study of geometry so far.

1. Lines

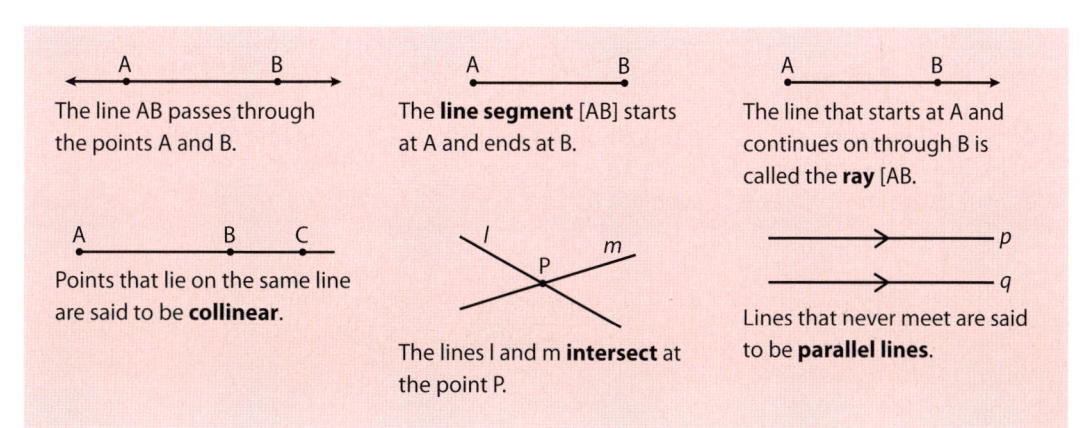

The line AB passes through the points A and B.

The **line segment** [AB] starts at A and ends at B.

The line that starts at A and continues on through B is called the **ray** [AB.

Points that lie on the same line are said to be **collinear**.

The lines l and m **intersect** at the point P.

Lines that never meet are said to be **parallel lines**.

165

2. Angles

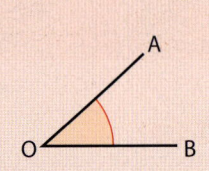

The angle above is written ∠AOB.

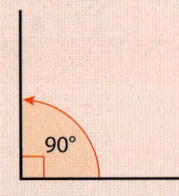

The angle above is called a **right angle**.
A right angle = 90°.

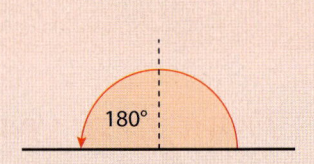

A half a revolution makes a **straight angle**.
A straight angle = 180°.

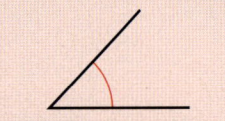

An angle that is less than 90° is called an **acute angle**.

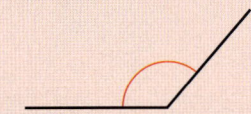

An angle between 90° and 180° is called an **obtuse angle**.

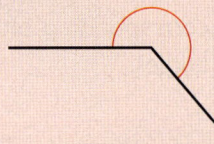

An angle between 180° and 360° is called a **reflex angle**.

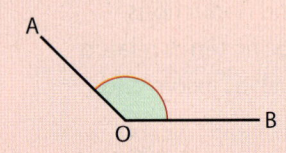

The shaded angle, which is less than 180°, is generally referred to as an **ordinary angle**.

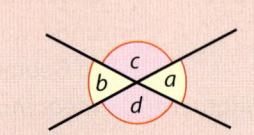

Vertically opposite angles are equal in measure.

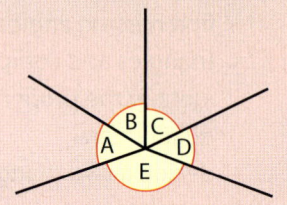

Angles at a point add up to **360°**.

3. Angles and parallel lines

Angles formed when a straight line crosses a pair of parallel lines have the following properties:

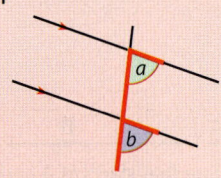

Corresponding angles are equal. So $a = b$. You can find them by looking for an F shape.

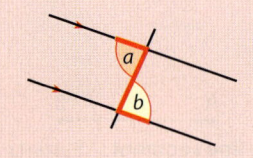

Alternate angles are equal. So $a = b$.
Look for a Z shape.

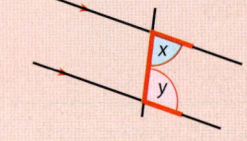

The **interior angles** x and y sum to 180°.
So $x + y = 180°$.

Chapter 8 Geometry 1 – Triangles – Quadrilaterals – Theorems

Exercise 8.1

1. Describe in words each of the following diagrams:
   (i)  A————B   (ii) A⟷B   (iii) A⟵——B

2. Find the measure of the angle marked with a letter in each of the following diagrams:

   [63°, A]   [67°, B, 28°]   [C, 45°]
   [150°, D, 70°]   [E, 70°, 80°, 140°]   [F, 84°, 145°, 108°]

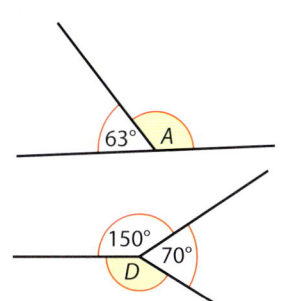

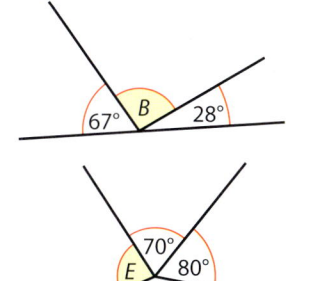

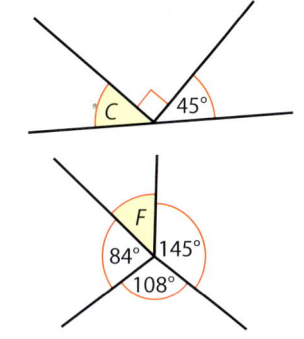

3. Work out the angles marked with a letter in each of the following diagrams:

   [A, B, 70°]   [30°, 150°, C, D]   [E, F, 140°]

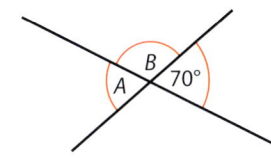

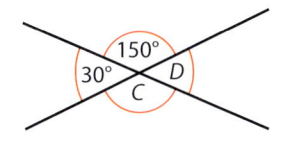

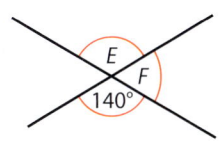

4. In each of the following diagrams, write down the number of the angle that **corresponds** to the shaded angle:

   (i) 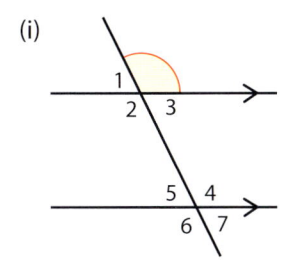   (ii) 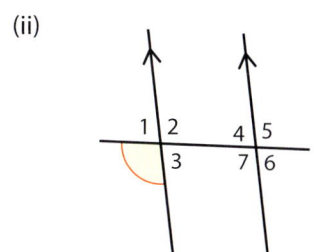   (iii)

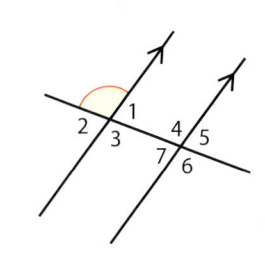

5. Write down the sizes of the angles marked with letters in each of the following diagrams, where arrows indicate parallel lines.

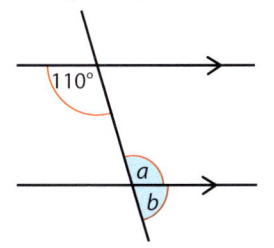

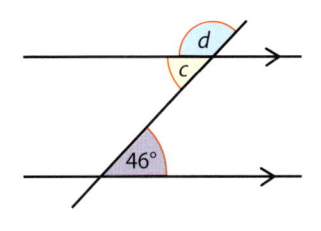

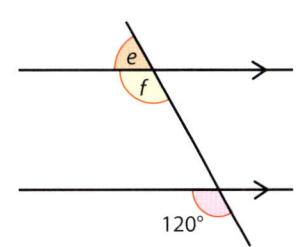

   [110°, a, b]   [c, d, 46°]   [e, f, 120°]

Text & Tests 2 Higher Level

6. Find the measures of the angles marked with letters in the given diagram, where the arrows indicate parallel lines.

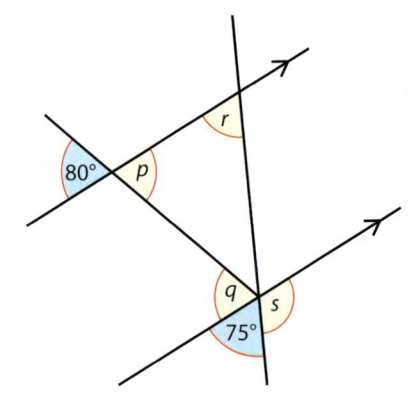

7. Find the sizes of the angles marked a, b, c, d, e, f and g in the given figure, where arrows indicate parallel lines.

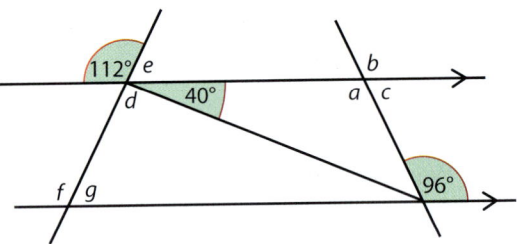

8. Find the value of n in each of the figures below:
   (i)   (ii)   (iii)

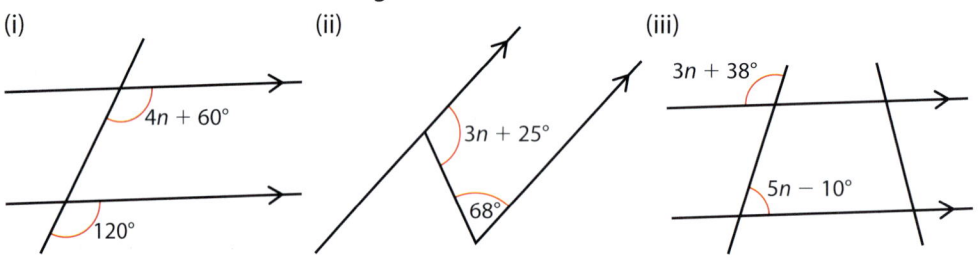

   Arrows indicate parallel lines.

Section 8.2 Angles of a triangle

The diagrams below will help you recall some important facts about the angles of a triangle.

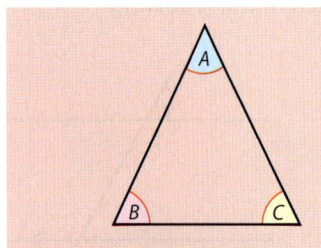

The angles of a triangle sum to 180°.
$|\angle A| + |\angle B| + |\angle C| = 180°$

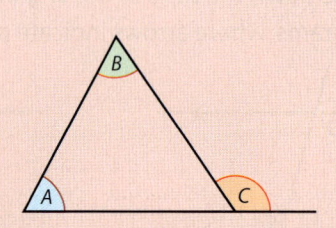

The **exterior angle** of a triangle is equal to the sum of the interior opposite angles.
$|\angle C| = |\angle A| + |\angle B|$

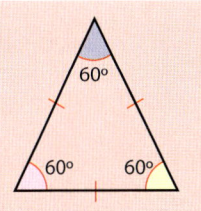

Chapter 8 Geometry 1 – Triangles – Quadrilaterals – Theorems

An **equilateral triangle** has
3 equal sides
3 equal angles
Each angle is 60°.

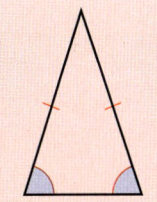

An **isosceles triangle** has
2 equal sides
base angles equal.

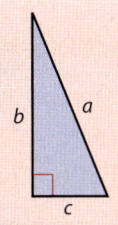

A **right-angled triangle** has an angle of 90°.
$a^2 = b^2 + c^2$

It is stated in the box above that in an isosceles triangle, the angles opposite the equal sides are also equal.

Conversely, it can be shown that if a triangle contains two equal angles, then that triangle is isosceles.

Investigation:

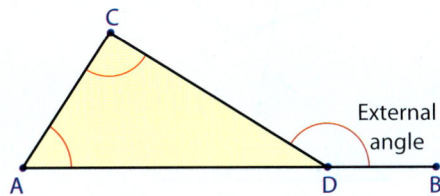

By copying and completing the following lines, investigate what conclusion can be made about the angles in the diagram above.

1. ∠CDB + ∠(   ) = 180° ... because AB is a _____ line.

2. ∠ACD + ∠CAD + ∠(   ) = 180°... because ACD is a _____.

∴ ∠CDB = ∠(   ) + ∠(   ).

In words; The external angle is _____.

Example 1

In the given figure, MN is parallel to PO.
If |∠NPO| = 29°, find
 (i) |∠MNP|
 (ii) |∠PMN|.

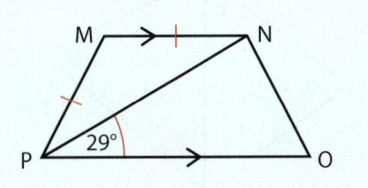

Text & Tests 2 Higher Level

(i) $|\angle MNP| = 29°$... alternate angles as PO∥MN

(ii) $|\angle MPN| = 29°$... isosceles triangle as $|PM| = |MN|$
$|\angle PMN| = 180° - 29° - 29°$
$|\angle PMN| = 122°$

Exercise 8.2

1. Find the size of the angle marked with a letter in each of the following triangles:

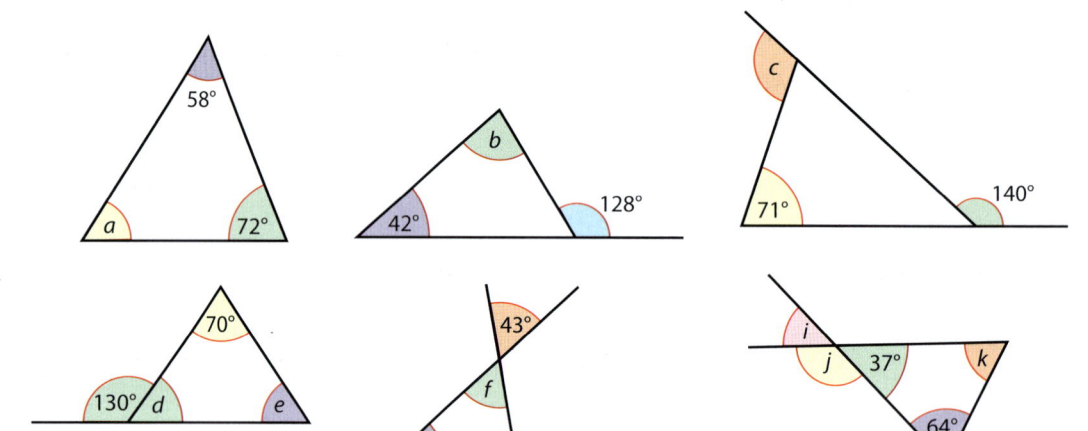

2. Work out the sizes of the missing angles in each of these isosceles triangles:

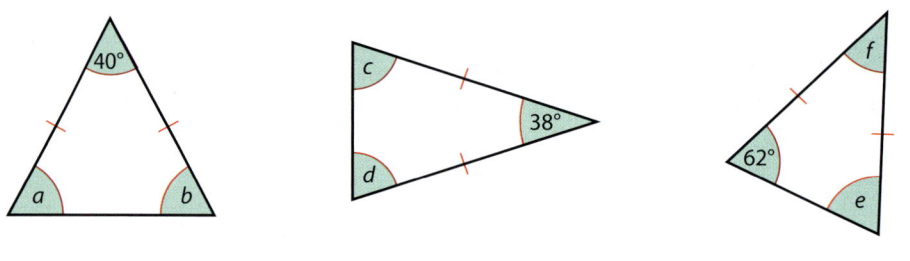

3. Find the size of the angle marked with a letter in the following figures:

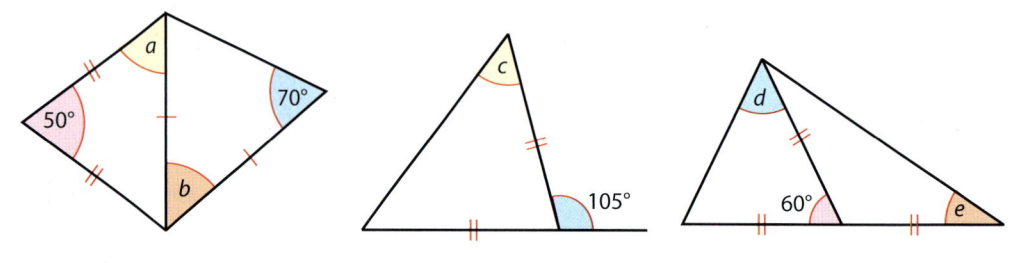

170

Chapter 8 Geometry 1 – Triangles – Quadrilaterals – Theorems

4. Calculate the size of each angle marked with a letter:

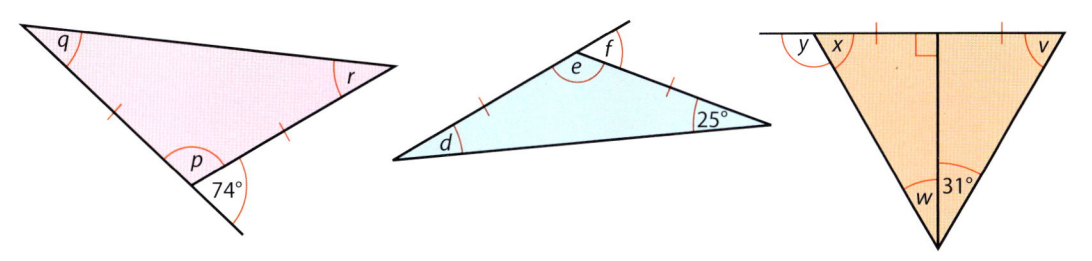

5. In the given figure, BD, AE and BE are straight lines.
   $|BC| = |CE|$,
   $|\angle ACD| = 130°$ and $|\angle BAC| = 72°$.
   Work out the sizes of the angles marked a, b and c.

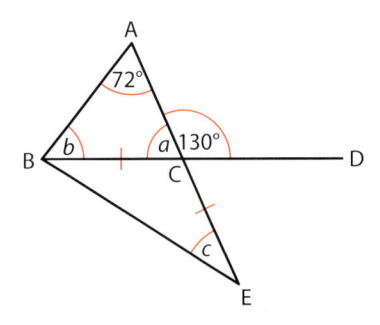

6. Find the values of a, b, c and d in the following triangles:

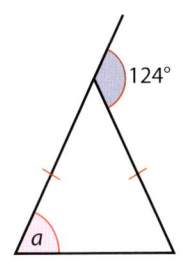

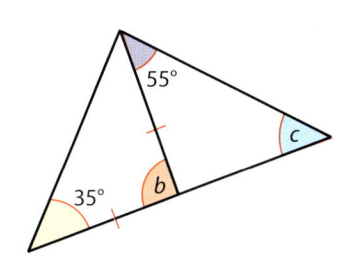

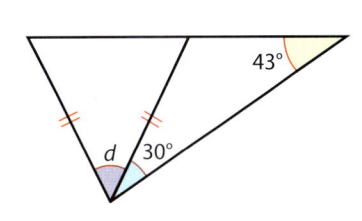

7. In the given diagram, AC is parallel to BE.
   If $|\angle BCA| = 80°$ and $|\angle CAB| = 55°$, find
   (i) x
   (ii) y.
   Give a reason for your answer in each case.

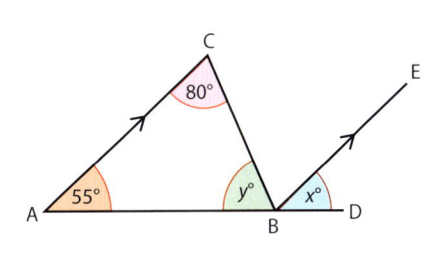

8. Find the sizes of the angles marked with letters in these diagrams:

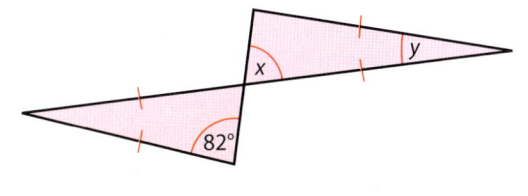

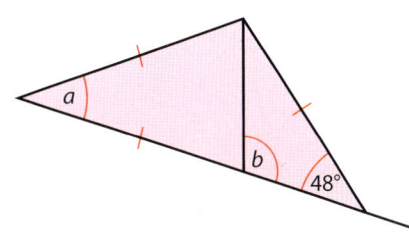

Text & Tests 2 Higher Level

9. In the given figure, two right angles are marked. Find the sizes of the angles marked with letters. Give reasons for your answers.

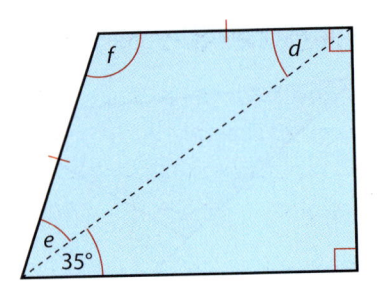

10. Find the measure of the angle marked with a letter in each of the following diagrams, where the arrows indicate parallel lines:

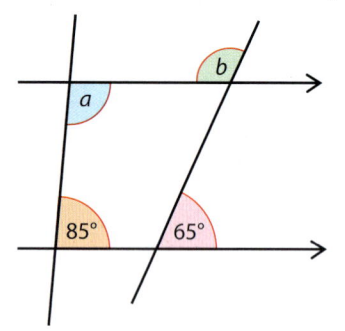

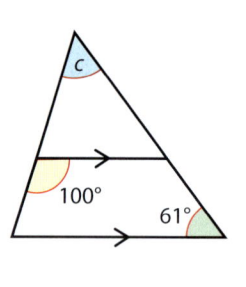

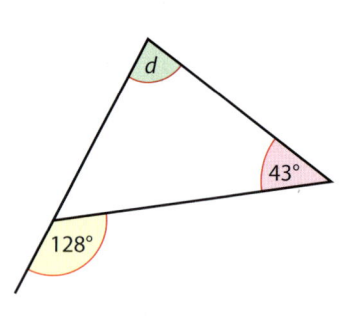

11. In the given figure, $|\angle AED| = |\angle DCB|$.
Explain why $|\angle ADE| = |\angle EBC|$.

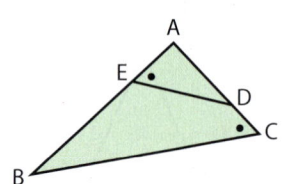

12. Explain why the given triangle is isosceles.

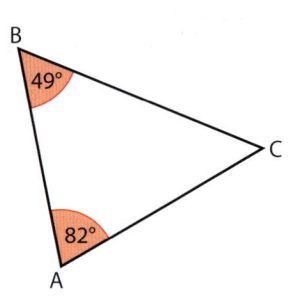

13. The diagram shows two equal squares joined to a triangle. Find the angle x.

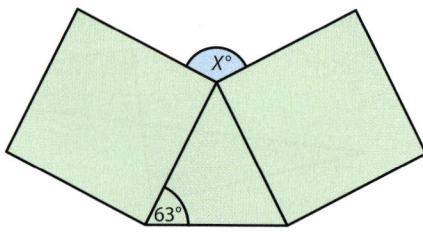

Chapter 8 Geometry 1 – Triangles – Quadrilaterals – Theorems

Section 8.3 Quadrilaterals

A figure which has four sides is called
a **quadrilateral**.
In the quadrilateral shown, the sides have different
lengths and the angles have different sizes.

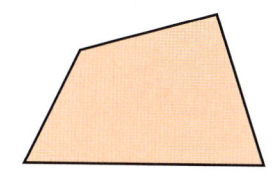

However, there are quadrilaterals with special properties which you should recognise. Some of these special quadrilaterals are shown below.

A parallelogram
A parallelogram is a quadrilateral which has opposite sides that are parallel.
> the opposite sides are parallel
> the opposite sides are equal in length
> the opposite angles are equal.

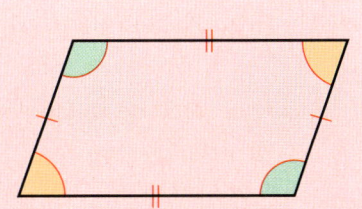

A rectangle
A rectangle is a parallelogram with four equal angles of 90°.
> each pair of opposite sides are parallel and equal in length
> all four angles are right angles.

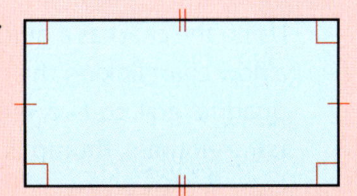

A rhombus
A rhombus is a quadrilateral in which all the sides have equal length.
> there are 4 equal sides
> opposite sides are parallel
> opposite angles are equal.

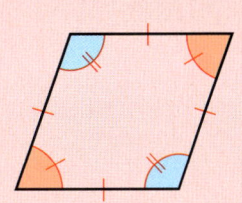

A square
A square is a rhombus with four equal angles of 90°.
> all four sides are the same length
> opposite sides are parallel
> all four angles are right angles.

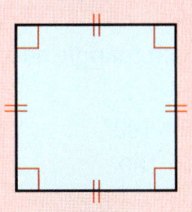

Text & Tests 2 Higher Level

Investigation:

Having studied the properties of quadrilaterals, squares, rectangles, parallelograms and rhombuses, copy and complete the following chart.

	True or False		True or False
All quadrilaterals are rectangles		All rectangles are parallelograms	
All rhombuses are squares		All parallelograms are rhombuses	
All squares are rectangles		All squares are rhombuses	
All rectangles are quadrilaterals		All rectangles are squares	
All parallelograms are quadrilaterals		All rhombuses are parallelograms	

Using the chart as a guide, create a flow chart linking the terms, quadrilateral, square, rectangle, parallelogram, rhombus.

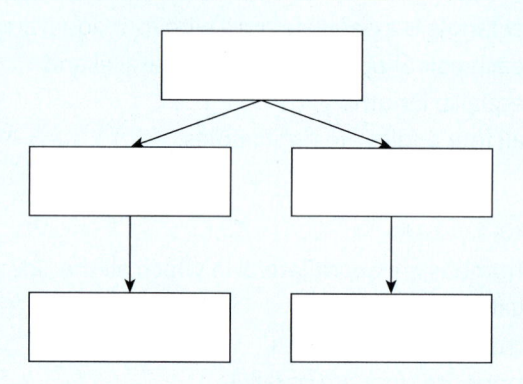

The angles of a quadrilateral

The quadrilateral shown is divided into two triangles.
The angles in each triangle add up to 180°.
$\angle a + \angle b + \angle c = 180°$
$\angle d + \angle e + \angle f = 180°$
$\therefore \angle a + \angle b + \angle c + \angle d + \angle e + \angle f = 360°$
So the angles in a quadrilateral add up to 360°.

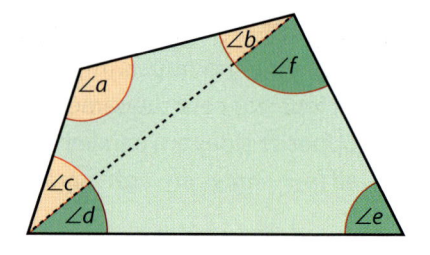

The interior angles in a quadrilateral add up to 360°.

Chapter 8 Geometry 1 – Triangles – Quadrilaterals – Theorems

Diagonals

In the special quadrilaterals shown below, the diagonals bisect each other.

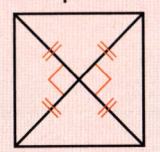

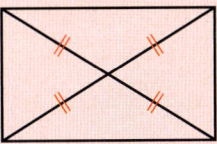

Square — Diagonals are equal and bisect each other at right angles.

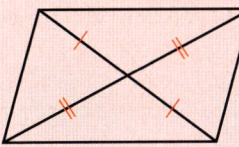

Rectangle — Diagonals are equal and bisect each other.

Parallelogram — Diagonals bisect each other.

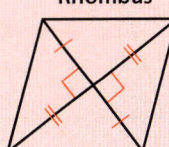

Rhombus — Diagonals bisect each other at right angles.

Theorem The diagonals of a parallelogram bisect each other.

Example 1

In the given parallelogram ABCD,
$|\angle BAD| = 115°$ and $|\angle BDC| = 28°$.
Find (i) $|\angle BCD|$ (ii) $|\angle ABD|$
(iii) $|\angle ADC|$ (iv) $|\angle DBC|$
Give a reason for each answer.

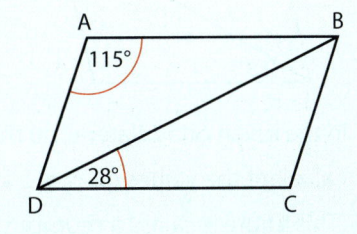

(i) $|\angle BCD| = 115°$... opposite angles are equal
(ii) $|\angle ABD| = 28°$... alternate angles
(iii) $|\angle ADC| = 180° - 115°$... interior angles sum to 180°
    $= 65°$
(iv) $|\angle DBC| = 180° - 115° - 28°$... $|\angle BCD| = 115°$ from (i) above
    $= 37°$

Note: In the example above, we have also proven the corollary that; 'a diagonal BD divides a parallelogram into two congruent triangles'.

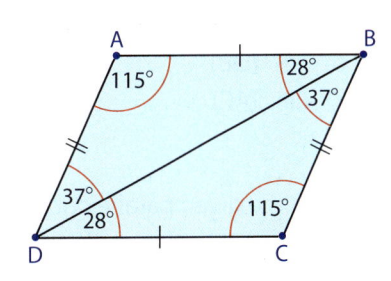

Text & Tests 2 Higher Level

Exercise 8.3

1. Find the measure of the angle marked with a letter in each of these parallelograms.

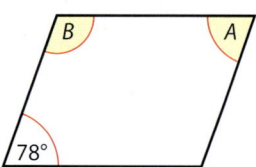

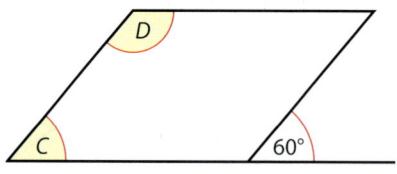

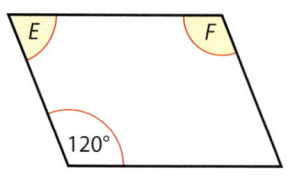

2. Find the size of the angle marked with a letter in each of these parallelograms:

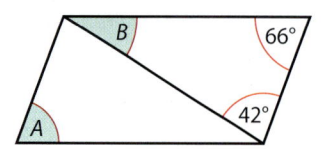

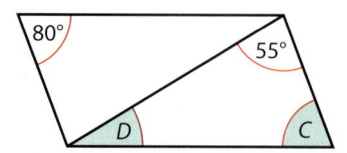

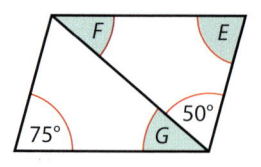

3. Find the size of the angle marked with a letter in each of these parallelograms:

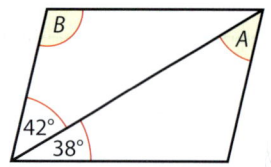

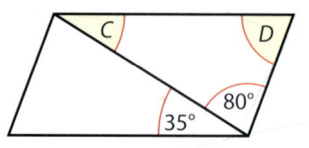

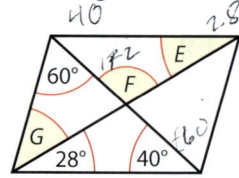

4. In the given quadrilateral, all the sides are equal, as marked.
   Calculate the values of x, y, z and r.
   (This figure is called a rhombus.)

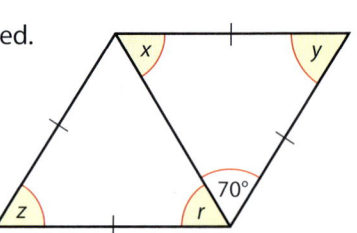

5. ABCD is a parallelogram with the diagonals intersecting at the point O.
   Write down the length of
   (i) [OB] (ii) [AB]
   (iii) [AC] (iv) [BC]

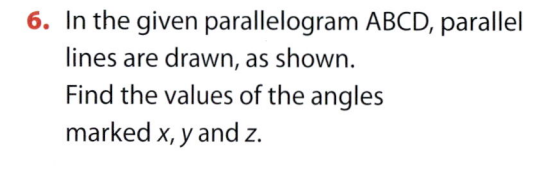

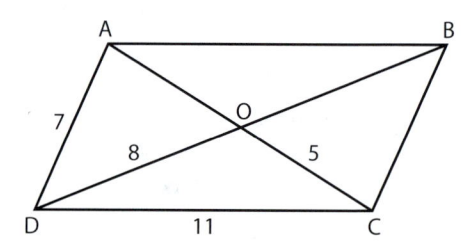

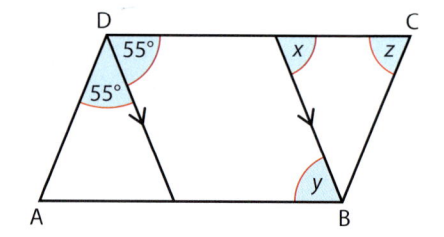

6. In the given parallelogram ABCD, parallel lines are drawn, as shown.
   Find the values of the angles marked x, y and z.

Chapter 8 Geometry 1 – Triangles – Quadrilaterals – Theorems

7. In the given parallelogram, all the sides are equal in length.
   AB and CD are straight lines.
   Find the sizes of the angles marked g and h.

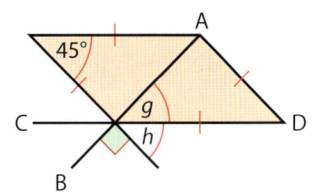

8. Find the size of the angle marked with a letter in each of these figures.

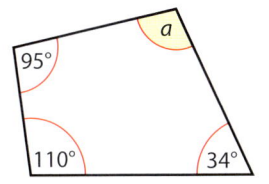

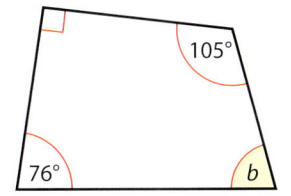

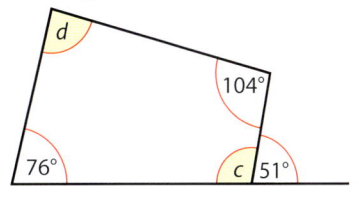

9. Find the value of x in each of the diagrams below:

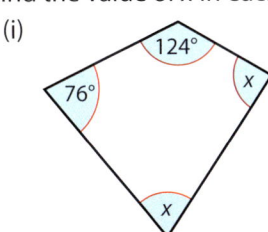

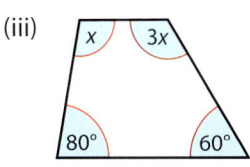

10. Find the value of y in each of the diagrams below:

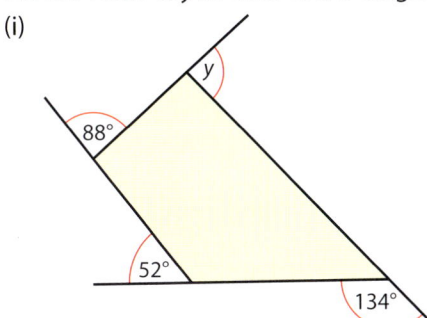

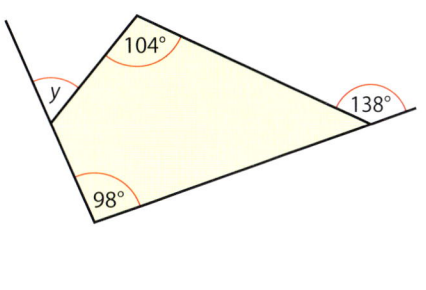

Section 8.4 Congruent triangles

Figures which are exactly the **same size and shape** are said to be **congruent**.
The following diagrams illustrate some congruent shapes, even though some of these shapes are turned over or upside down.

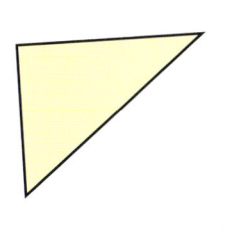

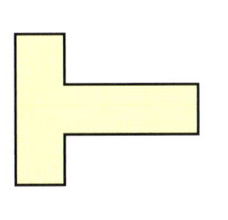

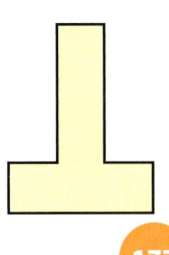

Text & Tests 2 Higher Level

The two triangles below are congruent because all the angles and sides of one triangle are exactly the same as the angles and sides of the other triangle.

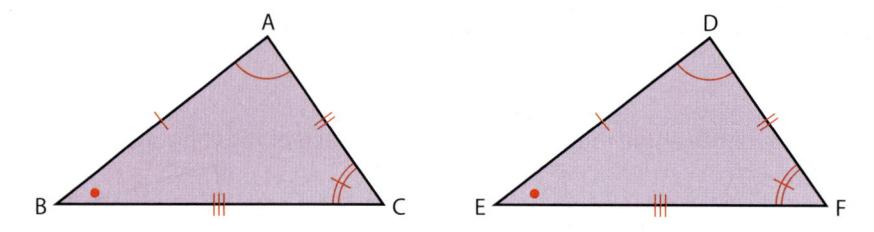

These two triangles are in fact congruent but it is not as immediately obvious.

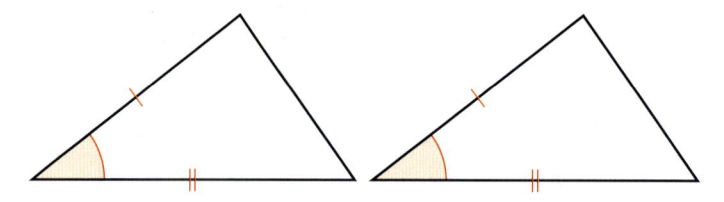

To help us identify congruent triangles, at least one of the following conditions must exist:

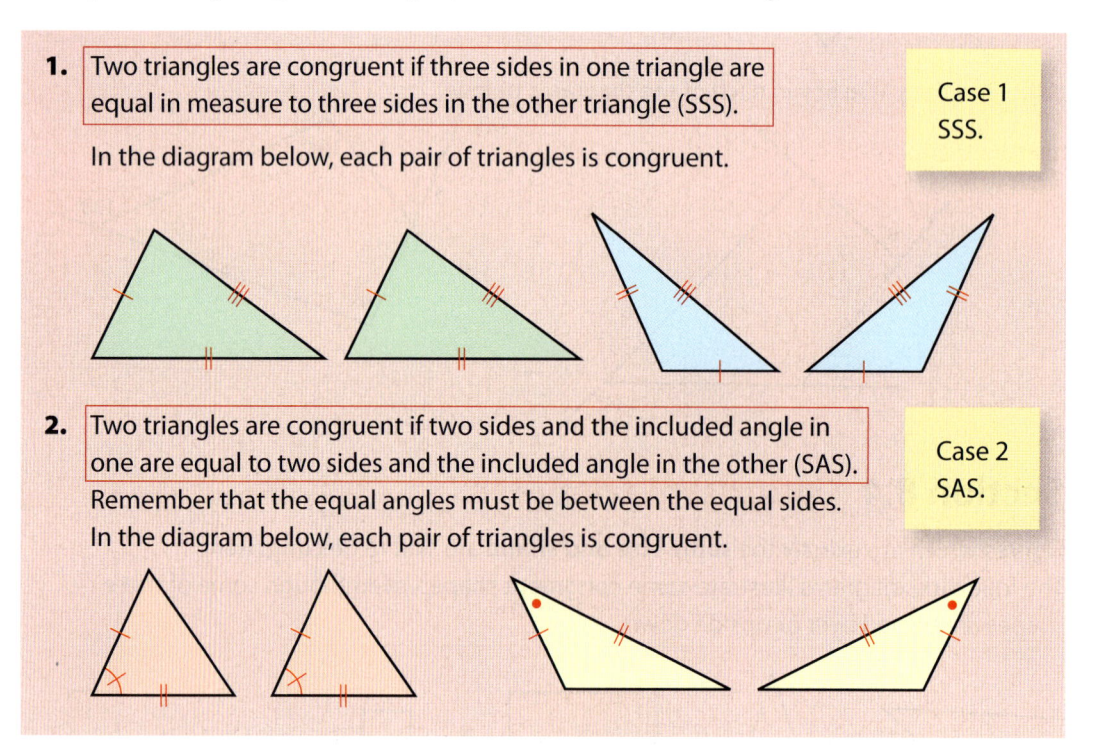

1. Two triangles are congruent if three sides in one triangle are equal in measure to three sides in the other triangle (SSS).

   In the diagram below, each pair of triangles is congruent.

   Case 1
   SSS.

2. Two triangles are congruent if two sides and the included angle in one are equal to two sides and the included angle in the other (SAS). Remember that the equal angles must be between the equal sides.
   In the diagram below, each pair of triangles is congruent.

   Case 2
   SAS.

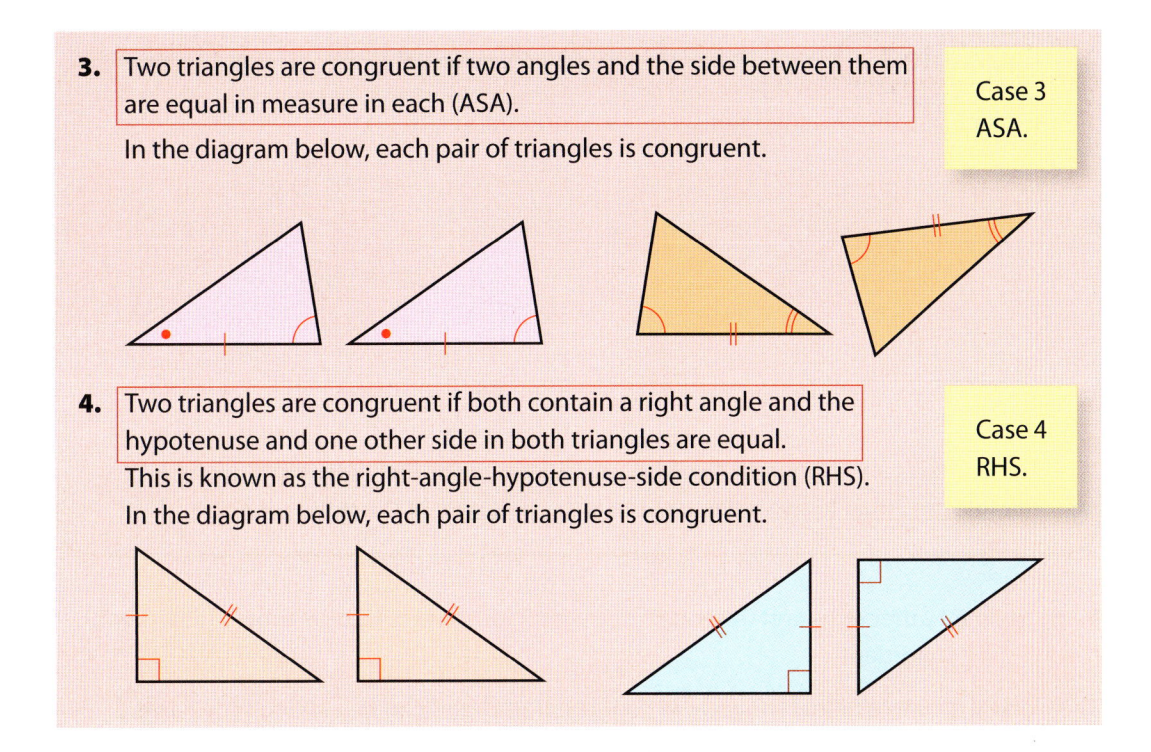

Chapter 8 Geometry 1 – Triangles – Quadrilaterals – Theorems

3. Two triangles are congruent if two angles and the side between them are equal in measure in each (ASA).

Case 3 ASA.

In the diagram below, each pair of triangles is congruent.

4. Two triangles are congruent if both contain a right angle and the hypotenuse and one other side in both triangles are equal.
This is known as the right-angle-hypotenuse-side condition (RHS).

Case 4 RHS.

In the diagram below, each pair of triangles is congruent.

Corresponding sides and angles

The two triangles ABC and DEF are congruent (ASA).

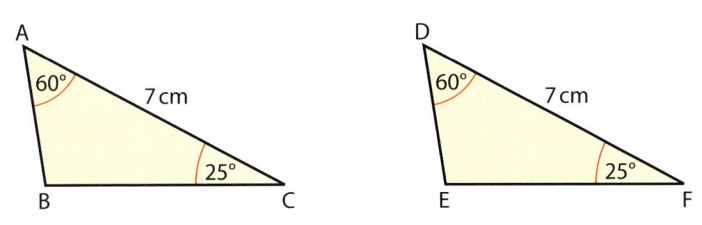

The side [DE] corresponds to the side [AB] as they are both opposite the 25° angle.
Similarly, [EF] corresponds to [BC] as they are both opposite the 60° angle.
The angle ABC corresponds to the angle DEF as they are both opposite the side of length 7 cm.
Since the triangles are congruent, it also implies that [BC] and [EF] are equal in length.

> In mathematics, the word **implies** means that when one statement is made, another statement follows on logically from the first statement.

Note: If the triangles ABC and DEF are congruent, it can be written as △ABC ≡ △DEF.

Text & Tests 2 Higher Level

Example 1

Explain why the two triangles shown are congruent.

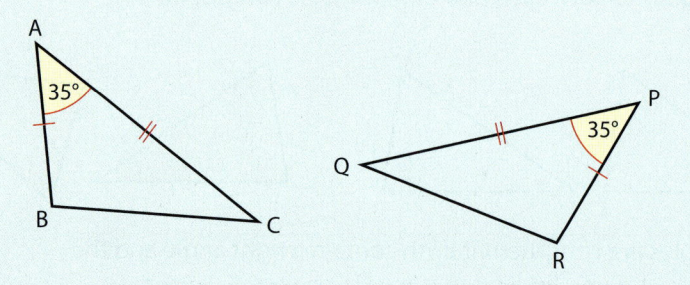

The triangles are congruent because two sides and the included angle in one triangle are equal to two sides and the included angle in the other triangle.

Many geometry theorems and other geometric problems are solved by showing that two triangles are congruent.

The worked example below shows how congruent triangles can be used to prove a very important property of isosceles triangles.

Example 2

Given an isosceles triangle with $|AB| = |AC|$.
Prove that the base angles are equal i.e. $\angle ABC = \angle ACB$.
Given

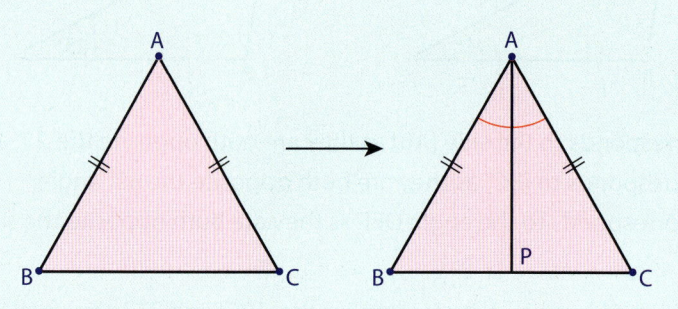

Bisect the angle at A.
In the triangles, ABP and APC.   (i) $|AC| = |AB|$ … given
(ii) $|AD| = |AD|$ … common side
(iii) $\angle BAP = \angle CAP$ … AP is the bisector of $\angle CAB$

∴ △ABP ≡ △ACP … SAS, the triangles are congruent.
∴ $\angle ABC = \angle ACB$

Chapter 8 Geometry 1 – Triangles – Quadrilaterals – Theorems

Exercise 8.4

1. Explain why the two triangles shown are congruent.

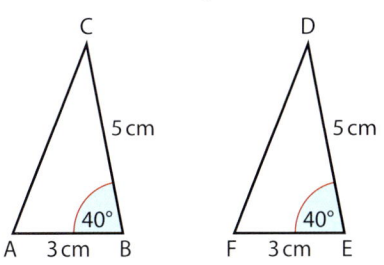

2. State why each of the following pairs of triangles are congruent, using SSS, SAS, ASA or RHS as reasons for your answers:

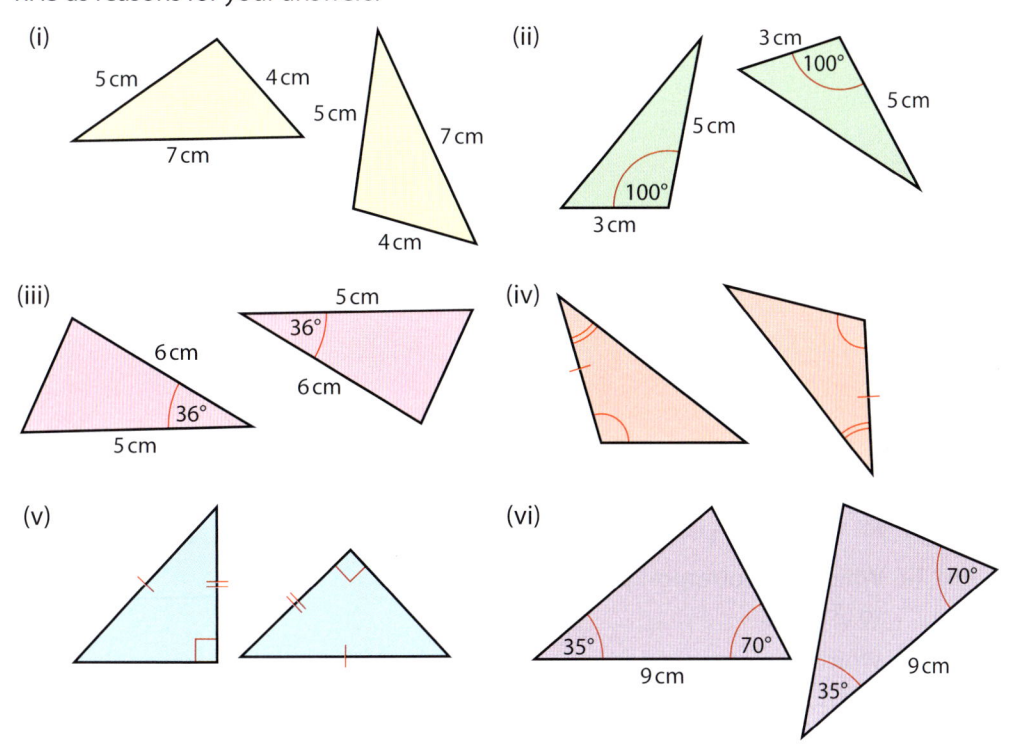

(i)

(ii)

(iii)

(iv)

(v)

(vi)

3. Which two of these triangles are congruent to each other?
Give a reason for your answer.

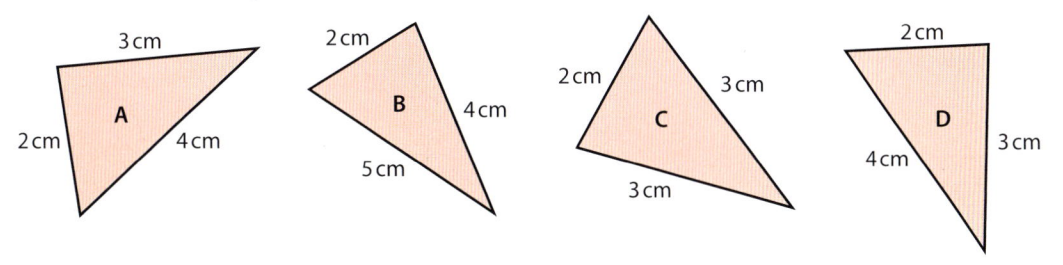

181

Text & Tests 2 Higher Level

4. State whether the following pairs of triangles are congruent. Give reasons for your answers.

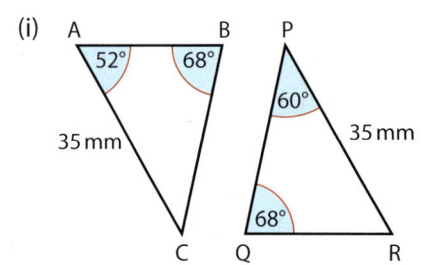

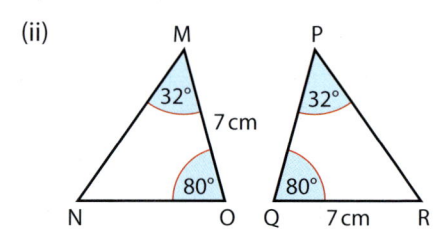

   (i) [Triangle ABC with angle A = 52°, angle B = 68°, AC = 35 mm; Triangle PQR with angle P = 60°, angle Q = 68°, PR = 35 mm]

   (ii) [Triangle MNO with angle M = 32°, angle O = 80°, MO = 7 cm; Triangle PQR with angle P = 32°, angle Q = 80°, QR = 7 cm]

5. Are the triangles ABD and BCD on the right congruent? Give a reason for your answer.

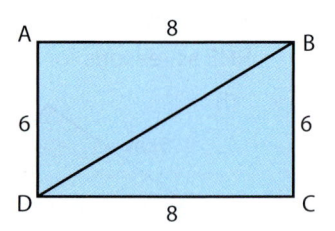

   [Rectangle ABCD with diagonal BD, AB = 8, AD = 6, BC = 6, DC = 8]

6. Explain why the triangles AOB and COD are congruent.

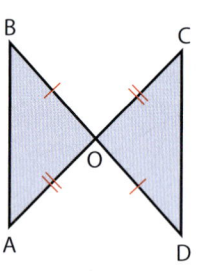

   [Two triangles meeting at point O, with tick marks showing OA = OD and OB = OC]

7. Explain why the two triangles shown below are congruent.

   (i) Which side corresponds to [BC]?
   (ii) Which side corresponds to [DE]?
   (iii) Find |∠DEF|.

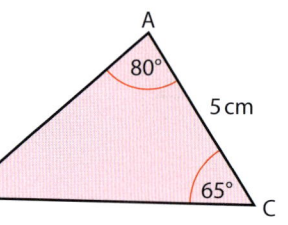

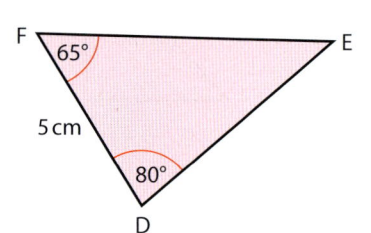

   [Triangle ABC with angle A = 80°, AC = 5 cm, angle C = 65°; Triangle DEF with angle F = 65°, FD = 5 cm, angle D = 80°]

8. These triangles are congruent.
   Write down the values of x and y.

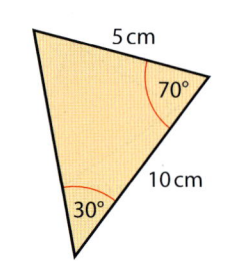

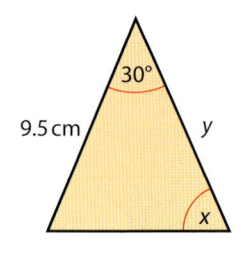

   [Triangle with side 5 cm, angle 70°, side 10 cm, angle 30°; Triangle with angle 30°, side 9.5 cm, angle y, angle x]

182

Chapter 8 Geometry 1 – Triangles – Quadrilaterals – Theorems

9. ABCD is a parallelogram.

   Show that the triangles ABC and ACD are congruent.

   Hence explain why the angles ABC and ADC are equal in size.

10. The straight lines [AB] and [CD] are equal in length and parallel.

    Prove that triangles AEB and DEC are congruent.

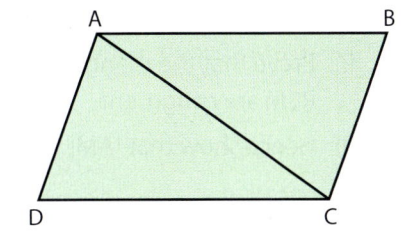

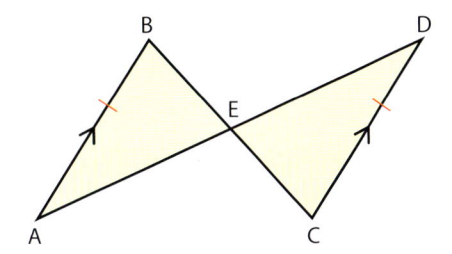

11. PQR is an isosceles triangle with $|PQ| = |PR|$.

    M is the midpoint of [PQ].

    N is the midpoint of [PR].

    Prove that triangle PQN is congruent to triangle PRM.

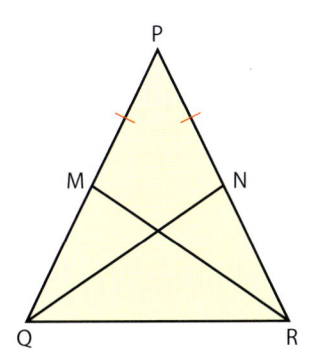

12. ABCD is a quadrilateral with $|AD| = |AB|$.

    Angle ADC = angle ABC = 90°.

    Prove that triangles ADC and ABC are congruent.

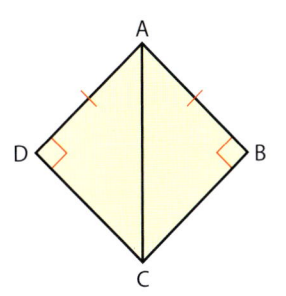

13. ABC is an isosceles triangle with $|AB| = |AC|$.

    Prove that triangles ACD and ABE are congruent.

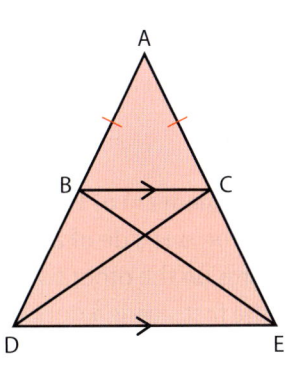

14. ABCD is a parallelogram and M is the midpoint of [CD].
    (i) Prove that the triangles ADM and PCM are congruent.
    (ii) Hence show that $|AM| = |MP|$.

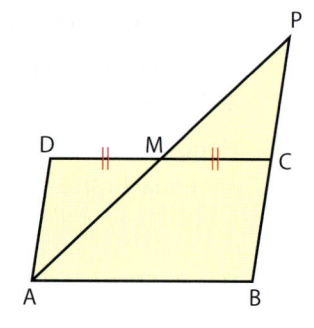

Section 8.5 The Theorem of Pythagoras

The diagram on the right shows a right-angled triangle of sides 3, 4 and 5 cm.

Squares are drawn on each of the three sides.

By counting the number of cm² in each of these squares, you will notice that the area of the square on the hypotenuse is 25 cm², while the other two squares have areas 16 cm² and 9 cm².

This diagram illustrates that the square on the hypotenuse is equal to the sum of the squares on the other two sides.

This important theorem is called the **Theorem of Pythagoras**.

Pythagoras was a Greek philosopher and mathematician who died about 500 BC.

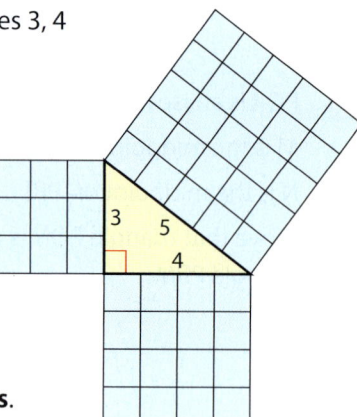

> **Theorem of Pythagoras**
> In a right-angled triangle, the square on the hypotenuse is equal to the sum of the squares on the other two sides.

The Theorem of Pythagoras can be expressed very neatly through algebra, as shown.

$$a^2 = b^2 + c^2$$

The converse of the Theorem of Pythagoras is also true and is stated below.

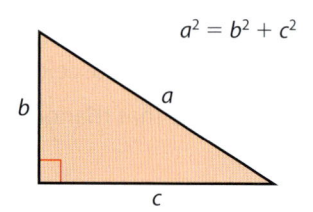

> **Converse of Theorem of Pythagoras**
> If the square on one side of a triangle is equal to the sum of the squares on the other two sides, then the angle opposite the first side is a right angle.

Chapter 8 Geometry 1 – Triangles – Quadrilaterals – Theorems

The triangle shown is right-angled since
$$10^2 = 8^2 + 6^2$$
i.e. $100 = 100$.

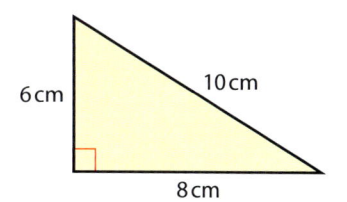

Example 1

Find the lengths of the sides marked x in the following right-angled triangles.

(i)

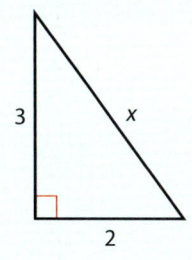

(ii)

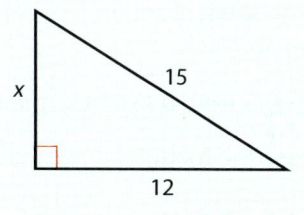

By the Theorem of Pythagoras:

(i) $\quad x^2 = 3^2 + 2^2$
$\quad\quad x^2 = 9 + 4$
$\therefore \quad x^2 = 13$
$\therefore \quad x = \sqrt{13}$
$\therefore \quad x = 3.6$

(ii) $\quad\quad 15^2 = 12^2 + x^2$
$\quad\quad\quad 225 = 144 + x^2$
$225 - \mathbf{144} = 144 + x^2 - \mathbf{144}$
$\quad\quad\quad\quad x^2 = 81$
$\therefore \quad x = \sqrt{81}$
$\therefore \quad x = 9$

Example 2

Calculate the lengths marked x and y.

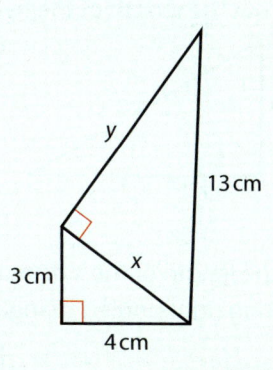

First $\quad x^2 = 3^2 + 4^2$
$\quad\quad\quad x^2 = 9 + 16 = 25$
$\quad\quad\quad\ x = \sqrt{25}$
$\quad\quad\quad\ x = 5\,\text{cm}$

Then $\quad y^2 + x^2 = 13^2$
$\quad\quad\quad y^2 + 5^2 = 13^2$
$\quad\quad\quad y^2 + 25 = 169$
$\quad\quad\quad\quad y^2 = 169 - 25 = 144$
$\quad\quad\quad\quad\ y = \sqrt{144}$
$\quad\quad\quad\quad\ y = 12\,\text{cm}$

Text & Tests 2 Higher Level

Investigation:

A Pythagorean triad is a set of three numbers that obey Pythagoras' theorem.

e.g. {3, 4, 5} is a Pythagorean triad because $5^2 = 3^2 + 4^2$.

To find other Pythagorean triads, we use the formula $\left\{x, \frac{1}{2}(x^2 - 1), \frac{1}{2}(x^2 + 1)\right\}$.

A: Copy and complete the table below to find the first 5 sets of Pythagorean triads.

B: On a large sheet of squared paper, draw the sides AB and BC on a grid as below. Join AC.

Scale the y-axis from 0 to 6 (AB), the x-axis from 0 to 19 (BC).

Superimpose the triangles. Investigate any patterns formed.

AB	BC	AC
x	$\frac{1}{2}(x^2 - 1)$	$\frac{1}{2}(x^2 + 1)$
2	1.5	2.5
3		
4		
5		
6		

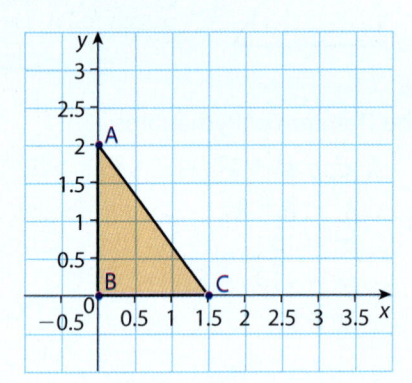

Exercise 8.5

1. Work out the length of the hypotenuse in each of these triangles:

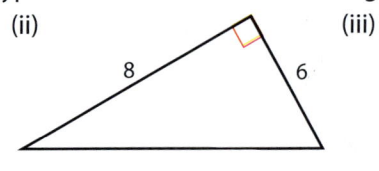

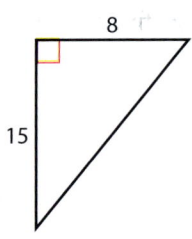

   (i) sides 3 and 4

   (ii) sides 8 and 6

   (iii) sides 8 and 15

2. Find the length of the side marked with a letter in each of the following right-angled triangles.

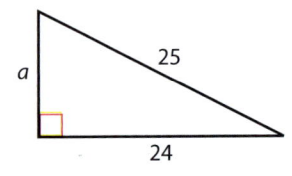

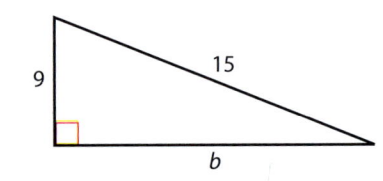

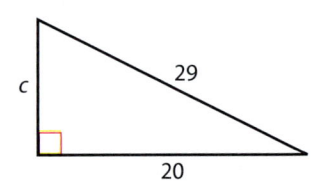

   a, 25, 24

   9, 15, b

   c, 29, 20

Chapter 8 Geometry 1 – Triangles – Quadrilaterals – Theorems

3. Remembering that $(\sqrt{2})^2 = 2$, find the value of x in each of these triangles:

   (i) Right triangle with legs 2 and $\sqrt{5}$, hypotenuse x.

   (ii) Right triangle with legs $\sqrt{11}$ and x, hypotenuse 6.

   (iii) Right triangle with legs 5 and x, hypotenuse $\sqrt{39}$.

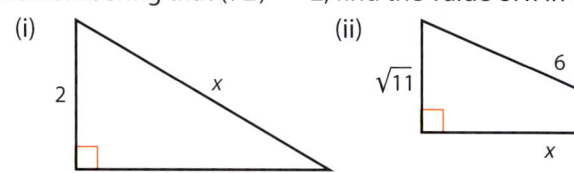

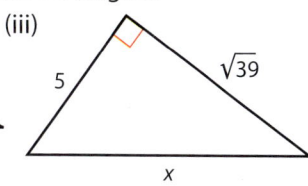

4. Use the **Theorem of Pythagoras** to find the area of the square marked with a letter in each of these figures:

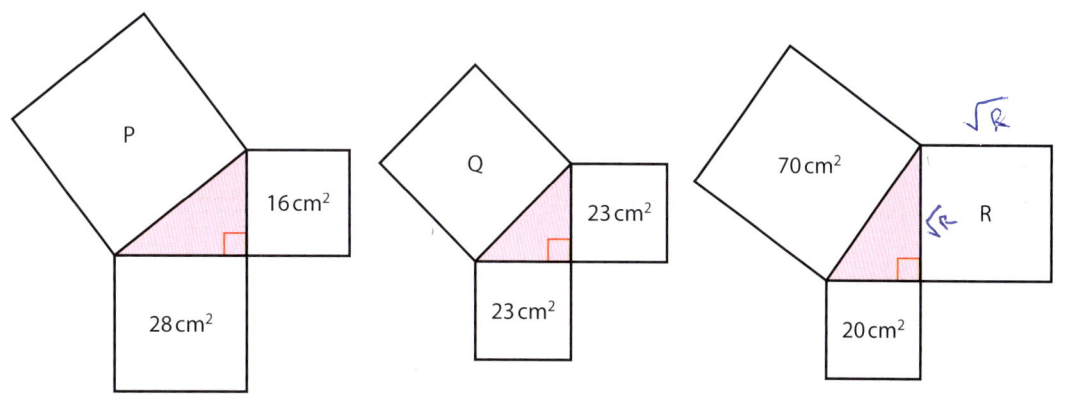

   Figure 1: Square P on hypotenuse; other squares 16 cm² and 28 cm².

   Figure 2: Square Q on hypotenuse; other squares 23 cm² and 23 cm².

   Figure 3: Square 70 cm² on hypotenuse; other squares 20 cm² and R. ($\sqrt{R}$)

5. Find the length of the side marked x in each of the following right-angled triangles:

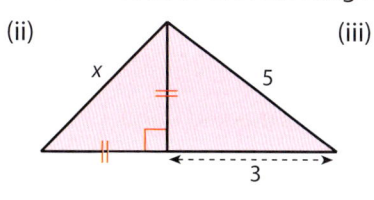

   (i) Triangle with sides 3, 3, 7 and x.

   (ii) Triangle with x, 5 and base segment 3.

   (iii) Triangle with x, 8 and base segments 4 and 2.

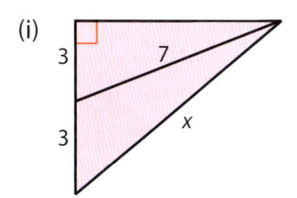

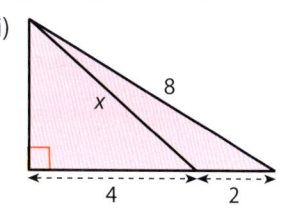

6. Find $|AB|$ in the given right-angled triangle.

   Now find the area of the triangle ABC.

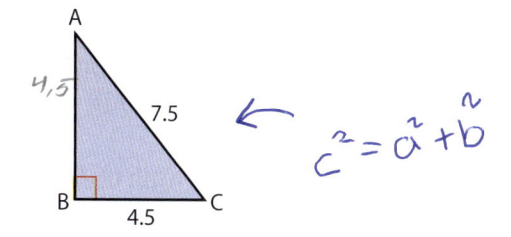

   Triangle ABC with $|AC| = 7.5$, $|BC| = 4.5$, right angle at B. $|AC| = 4.5$ (labelled 4,5)

   $c^2 = a^2 + b^2$

   $(7.5)^2 = (a)^2 + (4.5)^2$

   $56.25 = a^2 + 20.25$

   $56.25 - 20.25 = a^2$

   $36 = a^2$

   $\sqrt{36} = a$

Text & Tests 2 Higher Level

7. Find the value of x and y in each of the figures.
   Where necessary, give your answer correct to the nearest whole number.

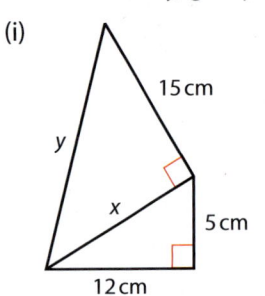

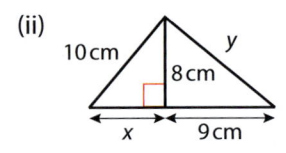

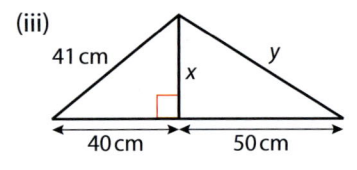

   (i) [triangle with sides 15 cm, 12 cm, 5 cm, and segments x, y with right angles]

   (ii) [triangle with sides 10 cm, 8 cm, 9 cm, segment x, y with right angle]

   (iii) [triangle with sides 41 cm, 40 cm, 50 cm, segments x, y with right angle]

8. Find the values of x and y in the given diagram.
   [triangle with 13, $\sqrt{29}$, x, y, 2]

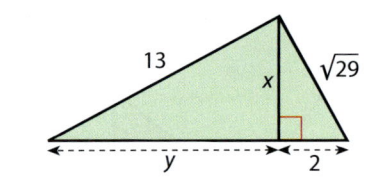

9. The diagram shows the side-view of a car ramp.
   The ramp is 110 cm long and 25 cm high.
   The top part of the ramp is 40 cm long.
   Calculate the length of the sloping part of
   the ramp, correct to the nearest cm.
   [diagram: 40 cm top, 25 cm high, 110 cm base]

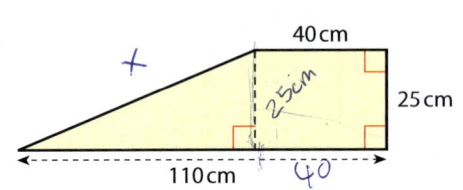

10. In the given figure, $|\angle ACB| = |\angle CDB| = 90°$.
    Find the lengths of the sides marked x and y.
    [figure with C, D, 6, $\sqrt{44}$, A, B, 12, x, y]

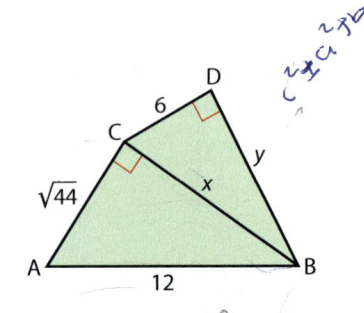

11. ABCD represents one end of a garden shed.
    $|AB| = 2.30$ m, $|AD| = 2.25$ m and $|BC| = 3.15$ m.
    Calculate
    (i) the length of [CD]
    (ii) the perimeter of ABCD
    (iii) the area of ABCD.
    Give each answer correct to 2 decimal places.

12. A suitcase is 80 cm long and 60 cm wide.
    Jane has an umbrella of length 1.05 m.
    Will it fit in the bottom of her suitcase? Explain.

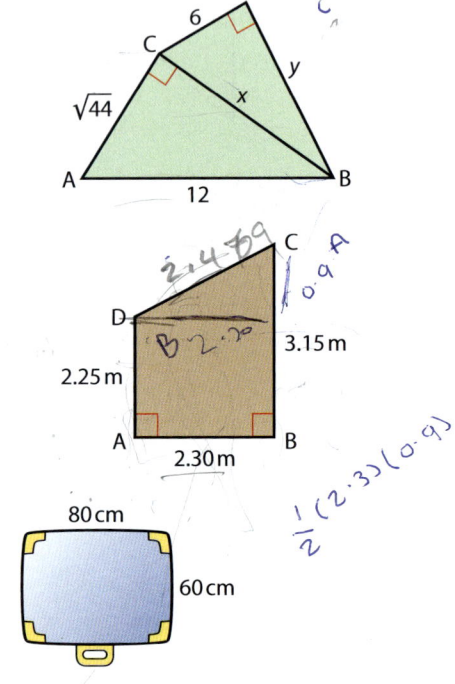

Chapter 8 Geometry 1 – Triangles – Quadrilaterals – Theorems

13. Use Pythagoras' theorem to decide whether or not these triangles have a right angle.

(i) 11 cm, 7 cm, 15 cm

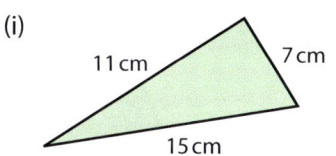

(ii) 12 cm, 9 cm, 15 cm

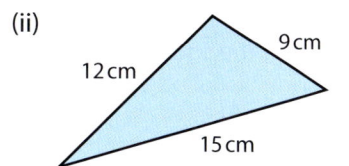

14. Two right-angled triangles are joined together to make a larger triangle ACD.
  (i) Show that the perimeter of triangle ACD is 78 cm.
  (ii) Show that triangle ACD is also a right-angled triangle. Explain why.

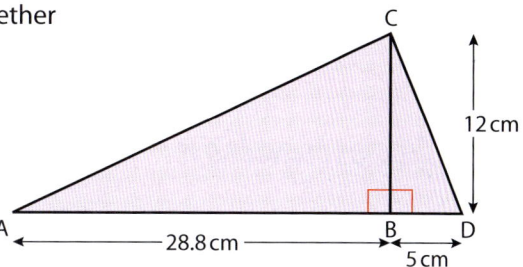

(AC = 28.8 cm, CB = 12 cm, BD = 5 cm)

15. This glass tank is a cuboid. It has length 12 cm, width 5 cm and height 8 cm.

  (i) Work out the length of the diagonal [HF].
  (ii) Hence work out the length of the diagonal [BH], in cm, correct to 1 decimal place.

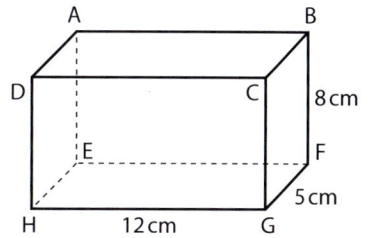

16. Semicircles are drawn on the sides of the given right-angled triangle. Investigate if the area of the semicircle on the hypotenuse is equal to the sum of the areas of the semicircles on the other two sides.

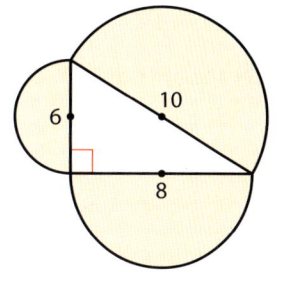

(sides 6, 8, 10)

Area of circle = πr^2

17. ABCD is a quadrilateral in which AC ⊥ BD.
Explain why $|AB|^2 = |AM|^2 + |BM|^2$.
Hence show that
$|AB|^2 + |CD|^2 = |AD|^2 + |BC|^2$.

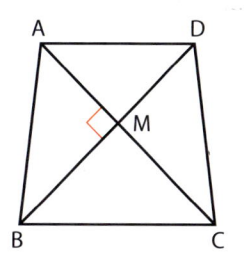

189

Text & Tests 2 Higher Level

18. The area of the right-angled triangle ABC is 24 cm², |AB| = 6 cm.
Find the area of the square ACED.

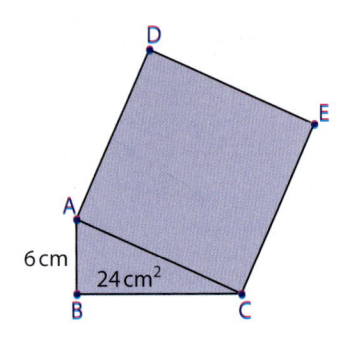

Investigation:

Studying Question 18 Ex 9.5, to find the area of ACED,

Sophie drew vertical and horizontal lines as shown.

She said:

1. that by congruence: △ABC =

   △ALC = △CKE = △DJE = △DMA = 24 cm²

   ∴ the area of △ALC + △CKE + △DJE + △DMA

   = 4 × 24 cm² = 96 cm².

2. |ML| = |LK| = |KJ| = |JM| = 2 cm.

   ∴ the area of MLKJ = 4 cm².

3. ∴ the area of the square ACED = (96 + 4) cm²

   = 100 cm²

Draw a large diagram of the triangle and square to scale.

Draw the parallel and perpendicular lines as shown.

Prove that the triangles △ABC, △ALC, △CKE, △DJE, △DMA are congruent.

Prove that |ML| = |LK| = |KJ| = |JM| = 2 cm.

State which method algebraic (Q 18) or Sophie's geometrical method you prefer and why.

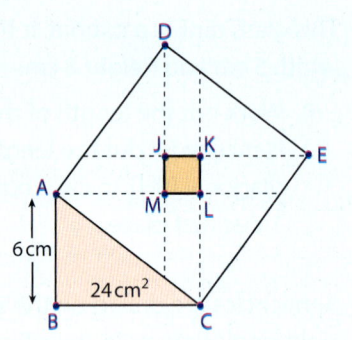

Chapter 8 Geometry 1 – Triangles – Quadrilaterals – Theorems

Section 8.6 Understanding formal proofs of theorems 1, 2, 3, 5, 10, 13, 15

Geometry results or theorems are proved in a formal or structured way by using previously established results and axioms to explain the statements we make.

This method of proving geometric results was first used by a Greek mathematician named Euclid about 300 BC.

The proofs of numerous theorems are contained in his famous book on geometry called *Elements*. Today over 2000 years later, we still use Euclid's approach to solve many problems in geometry.

In this section, the formal proofs of several theorems are given.

The full formal proofs will **not** be examined but '**an understanding**' of the proofs and corollaries will be tested, more than likely in the context of a geometric problem.

A clear understanding of the terms used in geometry, e.g. axiom, corollary, etc. will also be examined.

Axiom: A statement that is taken to be true or self-evident.
e.g. The angles in a straight line add up to 180°

Theorem: A major result that has been proved to be true and that can be used when solving problems or proving other theorems.
e.g. The angles in a triangle add up to 180°

Proof: A list of statements/axioms that are used to prove a theorem.

Corollary: Is a statement attached to a theorem that follows on from another theorem.

Implies: Means a second statement follows logically from a first statement.
e.g. If A > B and B > C this **implies** that A > C

Converse: Is the result of reversing a conditional statement (theorem).
e.g. If the base angles of a triangle are equal then the triangle is an isosceles triangle.
Note; converses may or may not be true.

Congruent: Two figures are congruent if they have the same shape and size.

Theorem 1	Vertically opposite angles are equal in measure.

Given: Line CD intersecting line AB at E.

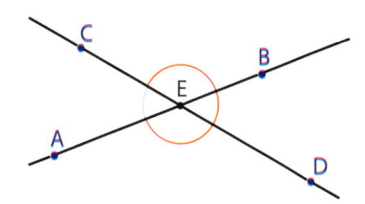

To Prove: $\angle CEB = \angle AED$

Proof: $\angle CEB + \angle CEA = 180°$ … angles on a straight line add to 180°
$\angle AED + \angle CEA = 180°$ … angles on a straight line add to 180°
$\angle CEB - \angle AED = 0°$ … subtracting
$\therefore \angle CEB = \angle AED$

Text & Tests 2 Higher Level

| **Theorem 2** | In an isosceles triangle, the angles opposite the equal sides are equal. Converse: If two sides are equal then the triangle is isosceles. |

Given: △ABC with $|AB| = |AC|$

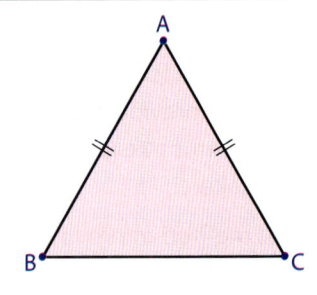

To Prove: $\angle ABC = \angle ACB$

Proof: △ABC is congruent to △ACB ... $|AB| = |AC|$,

$|AC| = |AB|$ and BC is common

∴ $\angle ABC = \angle ACB$

Converse:

Given: $\angle ACB = \angle ABC$

To prove: $|AB| = |AC|$

Proof: △ABC is congruent to △ACB ... $\angle ABC = \angle ACB$, $\angle ACB = \angle ABC$, $|BC| = |BC|$

∴ $|AB| = |AC|$

| **Theorem 3** | If a transversal makes equal alternate angles on two lines, then the lines are parallel. |

Given: Lines *l* and *m* and a transversal *t*.

Given: $\angle G = \angle C$

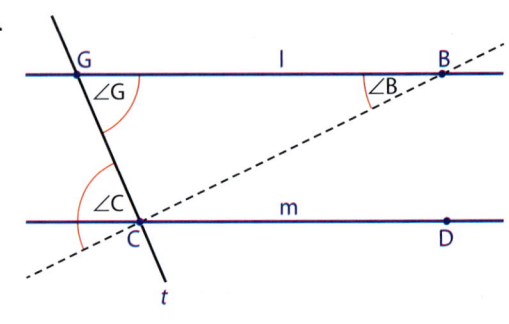

To Prove: *l* is parallel to *m*

Construction: Let *m* intersect *l* at B.

Chapter 8 Geometry 1 – Triangles – Quadrilaterals – Theorems

Proof   If GB and CD do not intersect, then *l* is parallel to *m*.

Otherwise:

let GB and CD intersect at a point B.

∠C = ∠G + ∠B   … exterior angle equal to the opposite and interior angles.

But ∠C = ∠G

∴ ∠B = 0 ⇒ *l* = *m* or *l* is parallel to *m*.

Theorem 5	Two lines are parallel if and only if, for any transversal, the corresponding angles are equal.

Given: Two lines *l* and *m* and a transversal *t*.

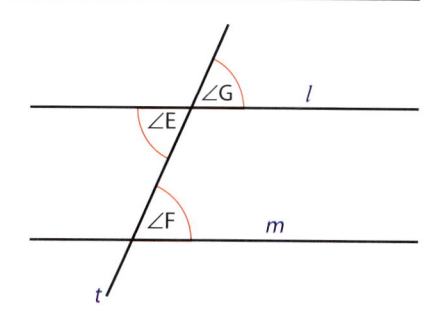

Given: ∠G = ∠F

To Prove: *l* is parallel to *m*

Proof   ∠G = ∠E … vertically opposite angles

∴ ∠F = ∠E … **∠G = ∠F**

∴ ∠F and ∠G are corresponding angles.

∴ *l* is parallel to *m*

Theorem 10	The diagonals of a parallelogram bisect each other.

Given: A parallelogram ABCD

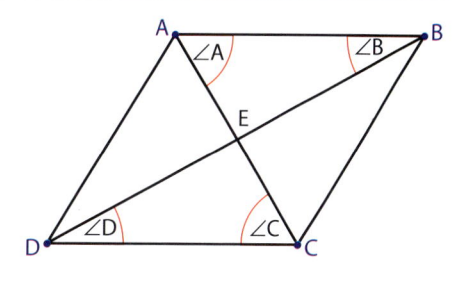

To Prove: |AE| = |EC|

Proof   ∠A = ∠C … alternate angles

∠B = ∠D … alternate angles

|AB| = |DC| … ABCD is a parallelogram

∴ △AED ≡ △ECD

∴ |AE| = |EC| and |BE| = |ED|

Text & Tests 2 Higher Level

Theorem 13	If two triangles are similar, then their sides are proportional, in order.

Given: Similar triangles △ABC and △DEF

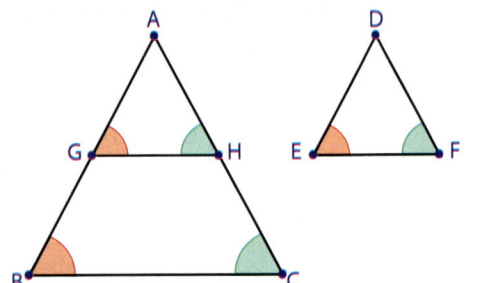

To Prove: $\dfrac{|DE|}{|AB|} = \dfrac{|DF|}{|AC|} = \dfrac{|EF|}{|BC|}$

Construction: Mark $|AG| = |DE|$ and $|AH| = |DF|$

Proof △AGH and △DEF are congruent   ... SAS

∴ ∠AGH = ∠DEF = ∠ABC

∴ GH is parallel to BC   ... corresponding angles ∠AGH, ∠ABC

∴ $\dfrac{|AG|}{|AB|} = \dfrac{|AH|}{|AC|}$ ... theorem 12

∴ $\dfrac{|DE|}{|AB|} = \dfrac{|DF|}{|AC|} = \dfrac{|EF|}{|BC|}$

Theorem 15 (Converse of Theorem 14)	If the square of one side of a triangle is the sum of the squares on the other two sides, then the angle opposite the first side is a right angle.

Given: $|AB|^2 = |AC|^2 + |CB|^2$

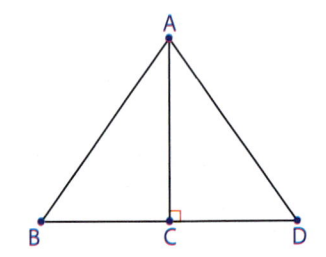

To Prove: ∠ACB = 90°

Construction: Draw DC ⊥ AC, and $|CD| = |CB|$

Proof $|AD|^2 = |AC|^2 + |CD|^2$ ... ∠ACD = 90° and Pythagoras

$|AD|^2 = |AC|^2 + |CB|^2$ ... $|CD| = |CB|$

$|AD|^2 = |AB|^2$ ... $|AB|^2 = |AC|^2 + |CB|^2$

$|AD| = |AB|$

∴ △ABC is congruent to △ACD ... SSS

∴ ∠ACB = ∠ACD = 90°

Chapter 8 Geometry 1 – Triangles – Quadrilaterals – Theorems

Test yourself 8

1. Find the size of each angle marked with a letter in the figures below, where the arrows indicate parallel lines:

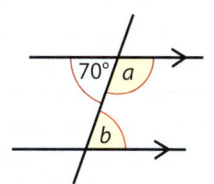

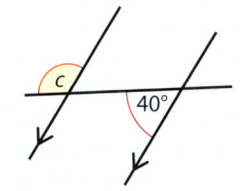

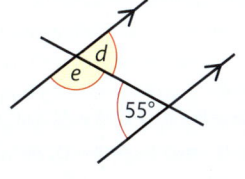

2. Find the size of the angle marked with a letter in each of these triangles:

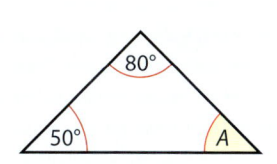

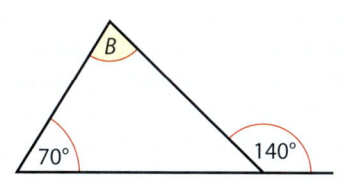

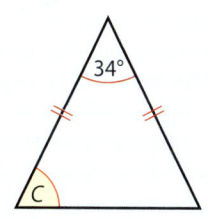

3. Find the measures of the angles marked *a* and *b* in the triangles below, where equal sides are marked.

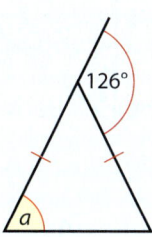

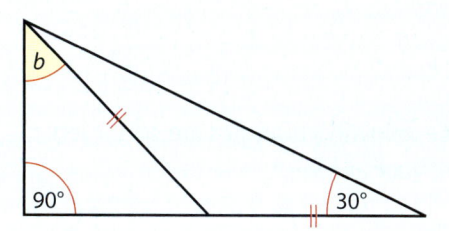

4. Find the measure of each angle marked with a letter in the following parallelograms:

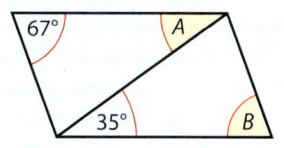

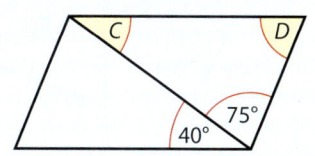

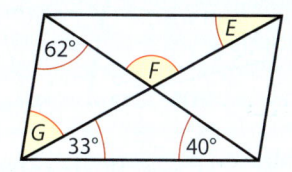

5. Find the measure of each angle marked with a letter in each of the following figures, where the arrows indicate parallel lines.

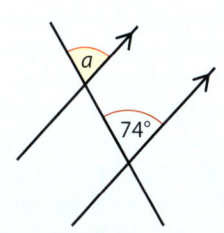

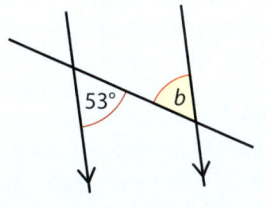

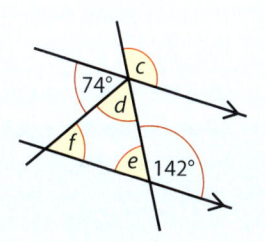

195

6. Find the value of *x* in the given triangle.
   What can be deduced about the triangle?

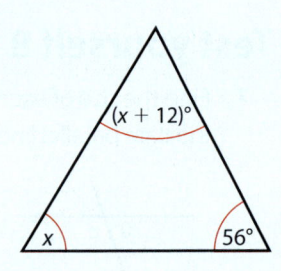

7. If *l*∥*m*, find the sizes of the angles *a*, *b*, and *c* in the given figure.

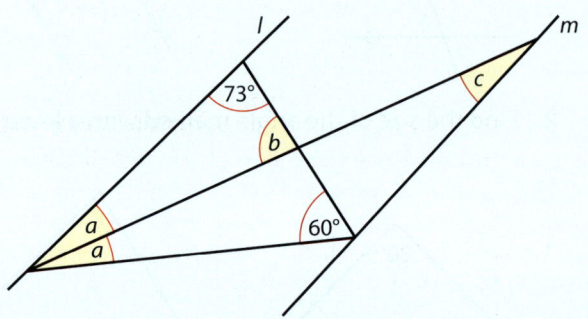

8. In the given figure, equal sides are indicated. Find the sizes of the angles marked *a* and *b*.

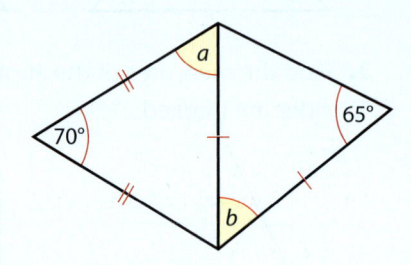

9. Which two of the following triangles are congruent? Give a reason for your answer.

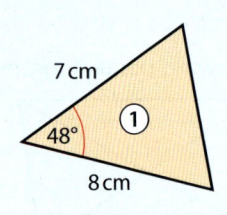

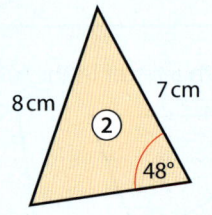

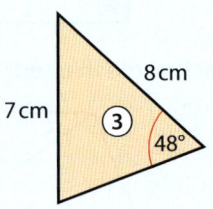

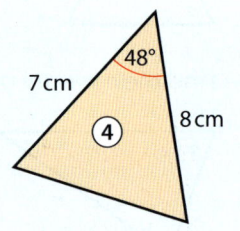

10. ABC is an isosceles triangle with |AB| = |AC|.
    AE is parallel to BC.
    [BA] is produced to D.
    (i) Prove that AE bisects ∠DAC.
    (ii) Would the result in part (i) still apply if |AB| and |AC| were not equal?
        Give a reason for your answer.

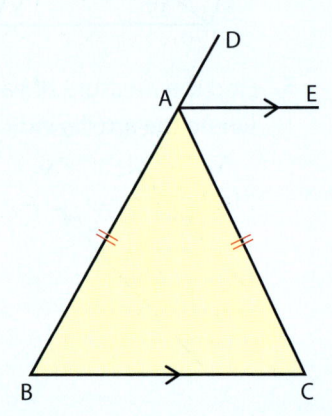

Chapter 8 Geometry 1 – Triangles – Quadrilaterals – Theorems

11. Find the value of the angle marked *x* in each of the following diagrams, where the arrows indicate parallel lines.

(i) 56°, *x*

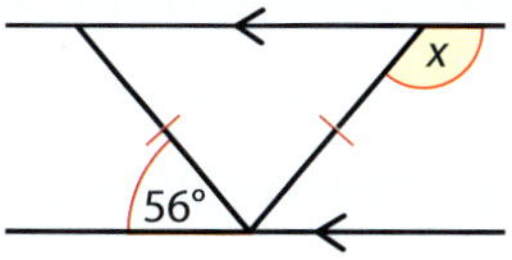

(ii) 141°, 78°, *x*

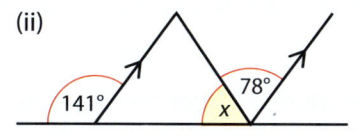

(iii) 24°, 68°, *x*

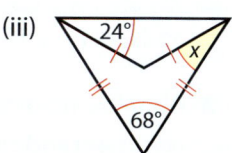

12. A 4.5 m long pipe rests on a 2 m high fence. One end of the pipe is on the ground, 3 m from the base of the fence.
How much of the pipe overhangs the fence?
Give your answer in metres, correct to one decimal place.

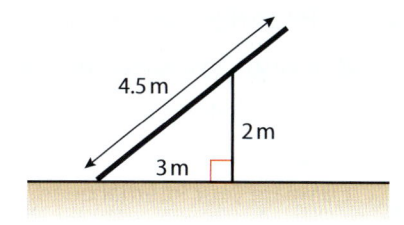

13. LMNP is a trapezium.
$|LP| = |MN|$ and $|\angle PLM| = |\angle NML|$.
Prove that the triangle PLM is congruent to the triangle NML.

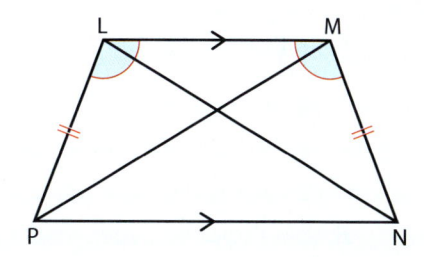

14. Find the values of *x* and *y* in each of the following triangles.

(i) *y*, *x*, 20°

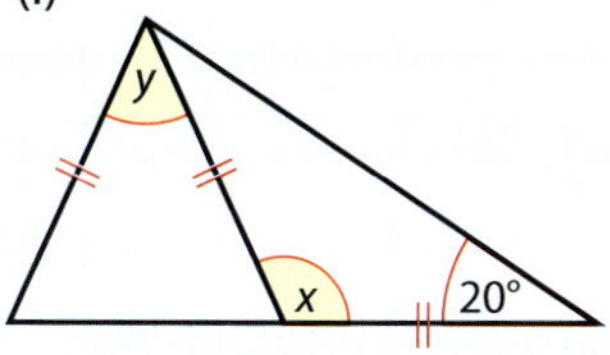

(ii) 3*x*, 4*x*, 2*x*, *y*

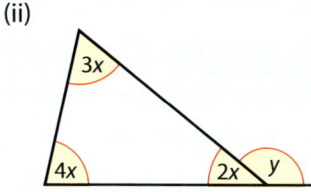

(iii) *x*, 2*y*, *y*, 69°

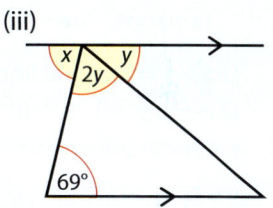

15. A room has floor dimensions 5 m by 4 m, as shown. The height of the room is 3 m.
  (i) Find $|BD|$ in metres, correct to 1 decimal place.
  (ii) Find the distance from the corner-point D on the floor to the opposite corner-point A on the ceiling, correct to the nearest metre.

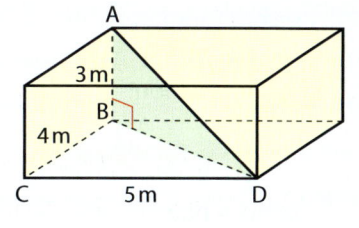

16. In the given diagram, $|AX| = |XC| = |BX|$.
By marking equal angles, explain why $|\angle ABC| = 90°$.

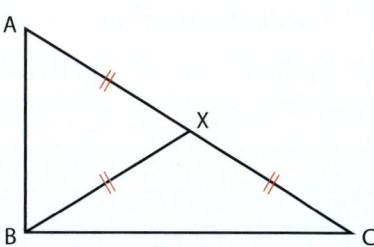

197

Text & Tests 2 Higher Level

Assignment:

A: Using squared paper, mark any four points **at random** and join them to form a quadrilateral.

By measuring the lengths of each side, find the midpoints and join them to form another quadrilateral.

Compare your internal quadrilateral with other groups in your class.

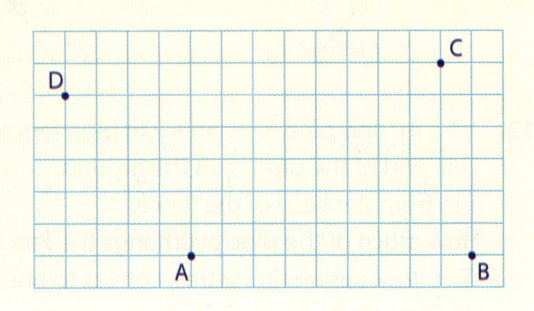

What observation can you make about the internal quadrilateral?

Observation:

B: Using squared paper, mark three points to form a triangle (for ease of drawing, mark two of the points [AB] on the same horizontal line).

Draw a horizontal line (**parallel to** AB) through the midpoint of a side of the triangle and continue until it intersects the second side.

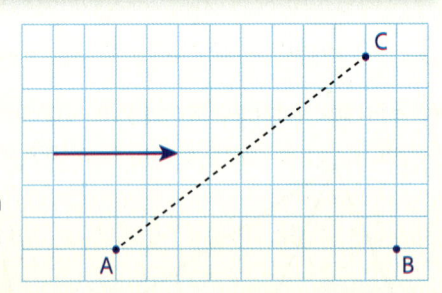

What observation can you make about the position of the intersection with the second side?

Observation:

Deduce how this may be linked to your observation about the (internal) quadrilateral above.

Write a report on your findings from this assignment.

Chapter 9

Probability

From first year, you will recall how to:

- list the outcomes of events,
- use the fundamental principle of counting,
- use two-way tables,
- link events and outcomes,
- link chance with probability,
- check for equally likely outcomes,
- use fractions to measure probability,
- identify favourable outcomes,
- make a probability scale,
- understand fair / biased events,
- apply probability to the tossing of coins, the rolling of dice, spinning of spinners, picking of cards from a deck of cards etc.

In this chapter, you will learn to:

- draw and interpret tree diagrams,
- estimate probability from experiments,
- calculate the expected frequency of an event,
- work with outcomes that are not equally likely to occur,
- answer probability questions based on Venn Diagrams,
- find the probability of one event <u>and</u> another event happening,
- find the probability of one event <u>or</u> another event happening.

Section 9.1 Revision of listing outcomes

Here is a spinner with 8 sectors.
It has 8 different numbers and 3 different colours.
If the spinner is spun, you may get any of the numbers
1, 2, 3, 4, 5, 6, 7 or 8.
These are called **outcomes**.
If we are interested in colours only, then the possible outcomes are green, blue and yellow.

For the spinner above, we **listed** all the **possible outcomes** for numbers and for colours.

We will now consider the outcomes when this spinner is spun and a coin is tossed.

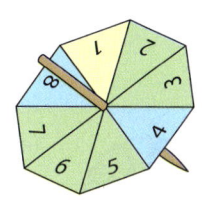

Text & Tests 2 Higher Level

Here is the list of the possible outcomes:

1H, 2H, 3H, 4H, 5H, 6H, 7H, 8H, 1T, 2T, 3T, 4T, 5T, 6T, 7T, 8T.

where H stands for head and T stands for tail.
Notice that there are **16** outcomes.

The number of outcomes can be found much more easily by multiplying **8** (number of outcomes for the spinner) and **2** (number of outcomes for the coin), i.e. 8 × 2 = 16.

The preceding example illustrates the **Fundamental Principle of Counting** which is given on the right.

> If one event has **m** possible outcomes and a second event has **n** possible outcomes, the two events have **m × n** possible outcomes.

Investigation:

Draw a chart of events / experiments, listing the number of outcomes for each event.

Some suggestions are given below.

	Event / Experiment	Number of outcomes
	(a) Tossing a coin (b) Tossing two coins (c) Tossing three coins	(a) (b) (c)
	(a) Rolling a die (b) Rolling a die and tossing a coin (c) Rolling two dice	(a) (b) (c)
	(a) Picking a suit of cards (b) Picking a spade from a deck (c) Picking a king (d) Picking a red card (e) Picking a card with a value lower than 5	(a) (b) (c) (d) (e)
	(a) Picking a red colour (b) Picking a number (c) Picking a number > 200 (d) Picking a red number > 300	(a) (b) (c) (d)
	(a) Selecting a student from your class (b) Selecting a girl from your class	(a) (b)

200

Two-way tables

When the two spinners on the right are spun, the possible outcomes can be shown in an organised way by means of a **two-way table**, as shown below.

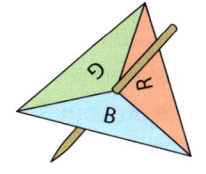

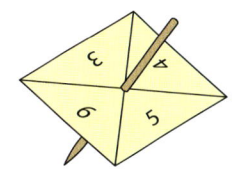

Numbers

Colours	3	4	5	6
R	3R	4R	5R	6R
B	3B	4B	5B	6B
G	3G	4G	5G	6G

Number of possible outcomes is
$4 \times 3 = 12$

The **Fundamental Principle of Counting** can be extended to any number of events.

If a boy has to choose a shirt, a tie and a jacket from 5 shirts, 3 ties and 4 jackets he has,

$5 \times 3 \times 4$ choices

Tree diagrams

Tree diagrams can also be used to work out the number of outcomes when two or more events occur. Each possibility is written at the end of a branch.

For example, a school offers senior cycle students the choice of; 3 modern languages L_1, L_2, L_3, 2 science subjects S_1, S_2 and 2 business subjects B_1, B_2.

Picking one subject from each set, a tree diagram gives the following choices (outcomes) for students.

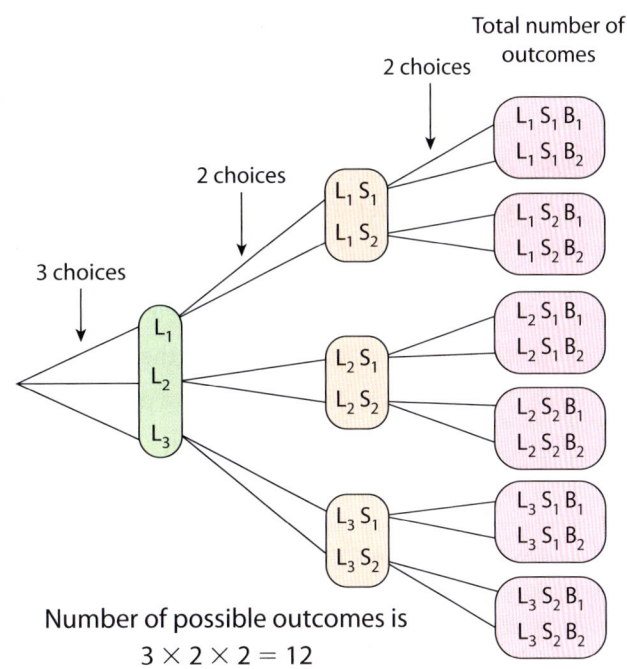

Number of possible outcomes is
$3 \times 2 \times 2 = 12$

Exercise 9.1

1. An 'early-bird' menu consists of 3 starters and 4 main courses. How many different 2-course meals can you have?

2. Two coins are tossed.
   List all the possible outcomes using H for head and T for tail.

Text & Tests 2 Higher Level

3. This spinner is spun and the die is thrown.
    (i) How many different outcomes of colour and number can you have?
    (ii) How many of these outcomes will have the colour yellow?
    (iii) How many of the outcomes will have the number 3?

4. A code consists of one of the letters A, B, C or D followed by a digit from 1 to 9. How many different codes are possible?

5. A lunch menu consists of 3 starters, 4 main courses and 2 desserts. How many different 3-course meals can a person have?

6. A car manufacturer produces different types of cars as follows:
    › the model can be Saloon, Estate or Hatchback
    › the colours can be silver, black or red
    › the style can be Standard, Deluxe or Premium.
   How many different choices of car does a buyer have?

7. A game consists of spinning the given spinner and throwing a die.
    (i) If the outcome of the game is a letter and a number, how many different outcomes are possible?
    (ii) If the game consists of a colour and a number, how many different outcomes are possible?

8. Gary suggests a game of chance, rolling a die and tossing a coin.
    (i) Draw a tree diagram showing the different outcomes that are possible.
    (ii) How many outcomes result in a prime number and a head?
   Gary then decides to roll a die and toss two coins.
    (iii) How many outcomes result in an odd number and two heads?

9. A restaurant advertises its lunch menu using the sign shown on the right.
    (i) The menu has a choice of five starters and nine main courses.
       How many items must appear on the dessert menu to justify the claim of 180 different lunches?
    (ii) On a particular day, one of the starters and one of the main course are not available.
       How many different three-course lunches is it possible to have on that day?

> **Lunch Menu**
> 3 courses for €18
> Choose from our range of starters, main courses and desserts.
> 180 different lunches to choose from.

10. The 5 class prefects Eimear(E), Samantha(S), Mia(M), Paul(P) and Neil(N) had to supervise in the morning or afternoon.
    The year-head in charge insisted that two students, a boy and a girl, must supervise at the same time.
    Using a tree diagram, list out all the combinations possible.

11.

	Swimming	Tennis	Football	Totals
Boys	12			
Girls	16		11	40
Totals		22	36	

The two-way table above shows the sport preference of 2nd year students in a school.
   (i) Copy the table and fill in the missing numbers
   (ii) How many students are in second year?
   (iii) Which is the least popular sport?
   (iv) Which is the most popular sport among girls?
   (v) What fraction of the students prefer tennis?
   (vi) What percentage of girls preferred swimming?

Section 9.2 Chance and the probability scale

You will already be familiar with words such as

   Impossible   Unlikely   Even chance   Likely   Certain

to describe the **chance** or **probability** of something happening.

If we want to be more specific, we use numbers to describe how likely something is to happen.

An event which is **certain to happen** has a **probability of 1**.

An event which **cannot happen** has a **probability of 0**.

All other probabilities will be a number greater than 0 and less than 1.

The more likely an event is to happen, the closer the probability is to 1.

The line shown below is called a **probability scale**.

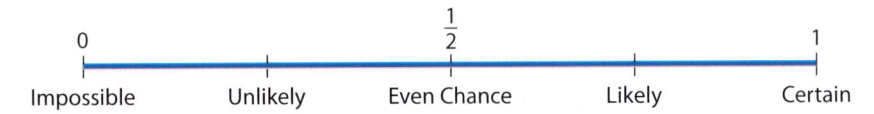

```
        0              1/2             1
        |---------------|---------------|
    Impossible  Unlikely  Even Chance  Likely  Certain
```

There is an **even chance** that the next person you meet on the street will be a male.

It is **certain** that the sun will rise tomorrow.

It is **impossible** to get 7 when a normal die is rolled.

Text & Tests 2 Higher Level

Exercise 9.2

1. Which of these labels best describes the likelihood of each of the events below occurring?

   | Impossible | Unlikely | Even Chance | Likely | Certain |

   (i) A coin will show 'tails' when you toss it.
   (ii) You are more than ten years old.
   (iii) The sun will not rise in Ireland tomorrow.
   (iv) You will win an Olympic medal.
   (v) The next person you meet on the street will be Irish.
   (vi) You will get an even number when an ordinary dice is thrown.
   (vii) You will get less than 5 winning numbers when playing the *Euromillions* some Friday.
   (viii) It will snow later today.
   (ix) I draw a red card from a standard pack of cards.
   (x) You will get homework tonight.

2. For each of the events given below, choose one of these words:

   impossible   unlikely   even chance   likely   certain

   (i) A die is to be thrown.
   Event 1:   A 6 will be thrown.
   Event 2:   A number less than 4 will be thrown.
   Event 3:   A number greater than 3 will be thrown.
   Event 4:   A zero will be thrown.
   Event 5:   A number less than 7 will be thrown.

   (ii) One card is to be chosen at random from these five.
   Event 1:   The card will be a *heart*.
   Event 2:   The card will be less than 8.
   Event 3:   The card will be a *diamond*.
   Event 4:   The card will be a 2.
   Event 5:   The card will not be a 3.

3. Here are four spinners with different colours:

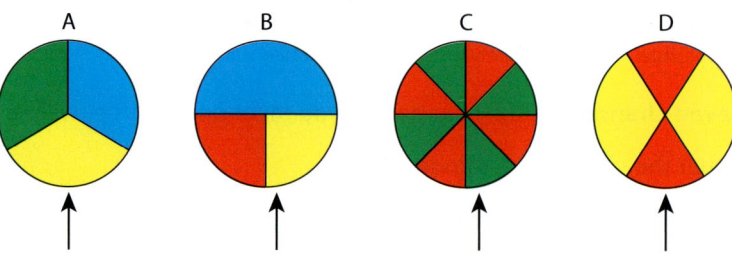

   A   B   C   D

If the spinners are spun,
  (i) Which spinner has an even chance of showing blue?
  (ii) Which spinner has an even chance of showing red?
  (iii) Which spinner has the least chance of showing yellow?
  (iv) Which spinner has one chance in three of showing yellow?
  (v) Which spinner has one chance in four of showing red?
  (vi) Which spinner has the greatest chance of showing red?

4. Order each of the events below from least likely to most likely:
  (i) A die is to be thrown.
     (a) The number showing will be even.
     (b) The number showing will be larger than 4.
     (c) The number showing will be less than 6.
  (ii) One card is to be chosen at random from these six.
     (a) The card will be a 2.
     (b) The card will be a 7.
     (c) The card will be greater than a 3.

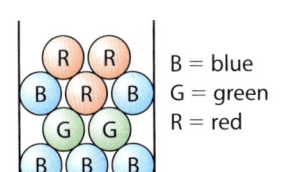

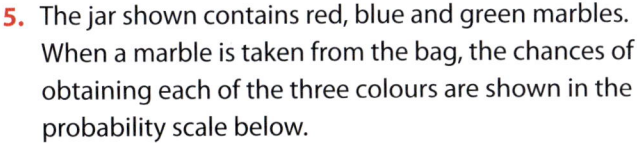

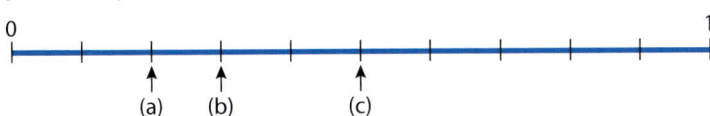

5. The jar shown contains red, blue and green marbles. When a marble is taken from the bag, the chances of obtaining each of the three colours are shown in the probability scale below.

   Link each colour to either (a), (b) or (c):

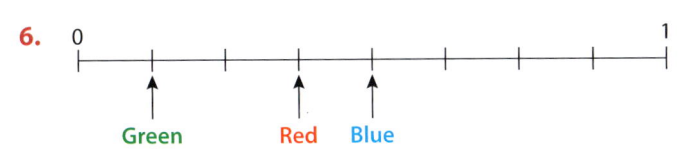

6. In a game, Todd spins an arrow.
   The arrow stops in one of sixteen equal sectors of a circle.
   Each sector of the circle is coloured.
   The probability scale shows how likely it is for the arrow to stop on any one colour.
   How many sectors are
     (i) coloured red
     (ii) coloured blue
     (iii) coloured green?

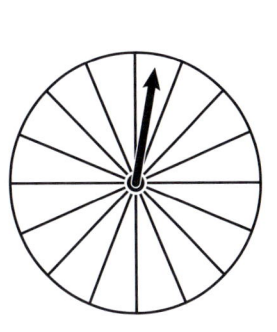

Section 9.3 Probability and equally likely outcomes

Before you can start a certain game, you must throw a die and get a six.

The act of throwing a die is called a **trial**.

The numbers 1, 2, 3, 4, 5 and 6 are all the possible **outcomes** of the trial.

The list of all possible outcomes is called a **sample space**.

The desired result is called an **event**.

If you require an even number when throwing a die, then the **events** or **favourable outcomes** are the numbers 2, 4 and 6.

> The result we want is called an **event** or **favourable outcome**

Equally likely outcomes

Two events are **equally likely** if they have the same chance of happening.

The chance of getting a red with this spinner is the same as the chance of getting a blue. Getting a red and getting a blue are **equally likely**.

The chances of getting a red or getting a blue with this spinner are **not** equally likely. The probability of getting a red when this spinner is spun is one chance in four.

We write this as Probability (red) $= \frac{1}{4}$.
This is shortened to P(red) $= \frac{1}{4}$.

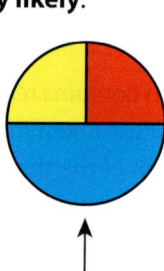

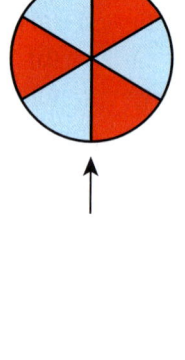

> For **equally likely outcomes**, the probability of event E occurring is given as
>
> $$P(E) = \frac{\text{Number of favourable outcomes}}{\text{Number of possible outcomes}}$$

For the spinner on the right,

P(green) $= \frac{1}{5}$, because 1 of the 5 sections is green

P(yellow) $= \frac{2}{5}$, because 2 of the 5 sections are yellow.

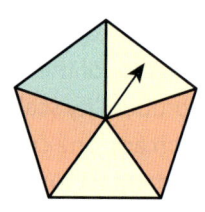

Chapter 9 Probability

Example 1

Below is a number of lettered tiles.

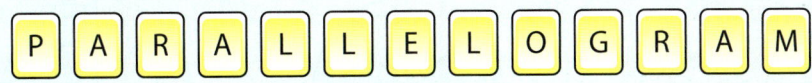

P A R A L L E L O G R A M

One of these tiles is selected at random.
Work out the probability of getting:

(i) an A (ii) an L (iii) an O
(iv) an A or an L (v) an A or an O (vi) an L or an O

(i) There are 3 tiles lettered A out of the 13 tiles.
$$P(A) = \frac{\text{number of As}}{\text{total number}} = \frac{3}{13}$$

(ii) $P(L) = \dfrac{\text{number of Ls}}{\text{total number}} = \dfrac{3}{13}$

(iii) $P(O) = \dfrac{1}{13}$

(iv) $P(A \text{ or } L) = \dfrac{\text{number of As + Ls}}{\text{total number}} = \dfrac{6}{13}$

(v) $P(A \text{ or } O) = \dfrac{4}{13}$

(vi) $P(L \text{ or } O) = \dfrac{4}{13}$

Investigation:

Probabilities that are written in fraction form can easily be converted to percentage / decimal form and vice versa.

Make a poster of events A, B, C, D, E, F and G, completing the chart below, showing the probability of these events in fraction / percentage / decimal form. Plot each of the events on a probability scale as shown below.

Event	Fraction	Probability Percentage	Decimal
A	$\frac{1}{4}$		0.25
B		50%	
C			0.6
D		75%	
E	$\frac{3}{10}$		
F			0.01
G		23%	

0 0.1 0.2 0.3 0.4 0.5 0.6 0.7 0.8 0.9 1

Text & Tests 2 Higher Level

Exercise 9.3

1. (i) State the sample space for each of these spinners:

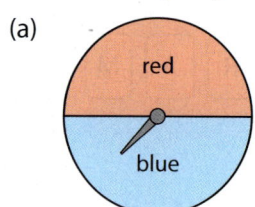

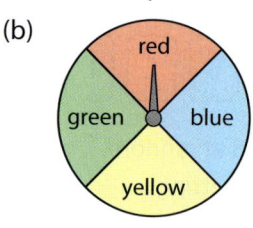

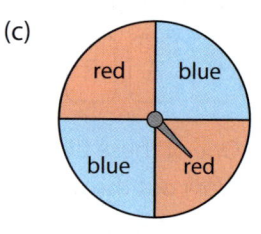

    (a) red, blue
    (b) red, green, blue, yellow
    (c) red, blue, blue, red

    (ii) For each of the spinners, write down the probability that the spinner ends on red.

2. What is the probability of getting a 6 on each of these spinners?

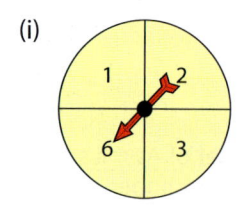

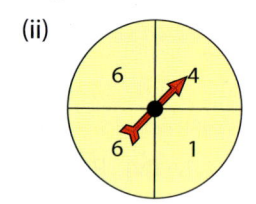

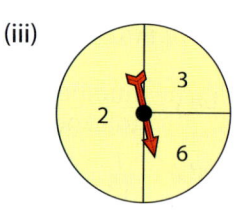

    (i) 1, 2, 6, 3
    (ii) 6, 4, 6, 1
    (iii) 3, 2, 6, (blank)

    What is the probability of getting a 2 or a 6 on spinner (iii)?

3. A fair die is rolled.
   What is the probability of getting

    (i) a 5
    (ii) a 1 or a 2
    (iii) 4 or more
    (iv) an odd number
    (v) less than 3
    (vi) a prime number?

4. Here is a selection of shapes.

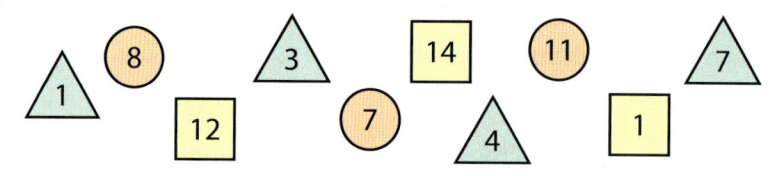

    (Shapes: triangle 1, circle 8, triangle 3, square 14, circle 11, triangle 7, square 12, circle 7, triangle 4, square 1)

    One of these shapes is chosen at random. Work out the probability that the shape will be:

    (i) a square
    (ii) a triangle
    (iii) a square or a triangle
    (iv) an odd number
    (v) a 2-digit number
    (vi) a green odd number.

5. A letter is chosen at random from the word PROBABILITY.
   Write down the probability that it will be

    (i) A
    (ii) B
    (iii) I
    (iv) a vowel
    (v) a B or an I.

6. A dart board has 36 sectors, labelled 1 to 36. Determine the probability that a dart thrown at the board hits:
- (i) a multiple of 4
- (ii) a number between 6 and 9 inclusive
- (iii) a number greater than 20
- (iv) 9
- (v) a multiple of 13
- (vi) an odd number that is a multiple of 3.

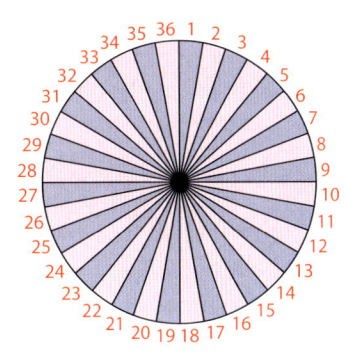

7. A standard pack of cards has 4 suits; hearts (♥), diamonds (♦), clubs (♣) and spades (♠). There are 13 cards in each suit and 52 cards altogether.

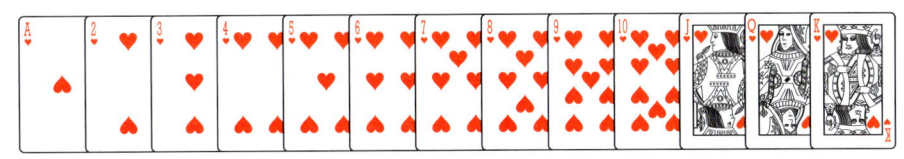

The first of these cards is called an **Ace**. The last three cards are the *picture* or *court* cards: the **Jack**, the **Queen** and the **King**.

From the 13 cards shown above, one card is to be chosen at random. What is the probability that the card chosen will be:
- (i) the 7
- (ii) the Ace
- (iii) a picture card
- (iv) a heart
- (v) a spade
- (vi) either a 9 or a 10?

8. From a standard pack of 52 cards, a card is chosen at random. What is the probability that the card will be:
- (i) a diamond
- (ii) a red card
- (iii) a black card
- (iv) a 3
- (v) a picture card
- (vi) either an Ace or a King?

9. A box contains twelve green marbles, six blue marbles and eight white marbles. A marble is selected at random.
What is the probability that the marble selected is:
- (i) green or white
- (ii) blue or white
- (iii) not green
- (iv) orange?

10. A square dart board is divided into sixteen smaller squares. Fourteen of the squares are painted as shown.
- (i) What colour(s) should the remaining squares be painted so that the probability of landing on red is $\frac{3}{8}$ and it is impossible to land on black?
- (ii) What colour(s) should the remaining squares be painted so that the probability of landing on red is twice the probability of landing on blue?

red	yellow	red	blue
white	red	white	blue
red	blue	white	red
white	yellow	?	?

Text & Tests 2 Higher Level

11. What is the probability that the pointer of these spinners lands in the blue section?
    (i) (ii) (iii) (iv)

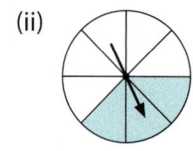

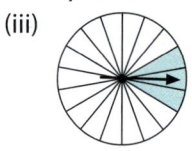

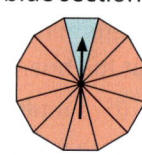

12. Design a spinner for which the probability of the pointer landing in the blue section is:
    (i) half
    (ii) less than half
    (iii) three times as likely as on red

13. Assuming that a person is equally likely to be born on any day of the week or in any month of the year, what is the probability that a randomly chosen person has his/her birthday
    (i) on a Tuesday
    (ii) on a Saturday or Sunday
    (iii) in January or February?

14. A bag contains five red discs with the numbers 1 to 5 painted on them and seven blue discs painted with the numbers 1 to 7. If a disc is chosen at random, what is the probability of choosing
    (i) a red disc
    (ii) a disc numbered 3
    (iii) a disc numbered 6
    (iv) the blue disc numbered 1
    (v) an even numbered disc
    (vi) an odd numbered disc?

    Explain why the probabilities in (v) and (vi) sum to 1.

15. In a pre-election poll of 400 people, 120 supported the A party, 140 supported the B party and the rest were undecided. If a person is selected at random from this group, what is the probability that they:
    (i) support the A party
    (ii) support the B party
    (iii) support a party
    (iv) are undecided?

16. At the end of a Summer Camp, 50 boys and girls were asked to name their favourite game at the camp. The results are given in the table below:

	Tennis	Basketball	Volleyball
Girls	15	10	5
Boys	6	12	2

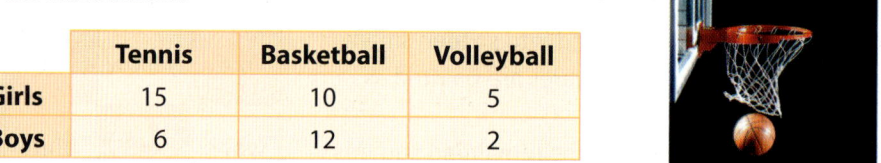

    If a person was selected at random from the group of 50, find the probability that the person
    (i) was a boy
    (ii) was a girl who named tennis as her favourite game

(iii) named basketball as her/his favourite game.

If a girl was selected, find the probability that she had named volleyball as her favourite game.

17. Of 100 tickets sold in a raffle, Luke bought 10, Heather bought 5 and Alan bought 1.
A ticket was chosen at random to determine who won the prize.
What is the probability that the prize was won by:
  (i) Alan
  (ii) Luke
  (iii) Heather
  (iv) none of these three people?

How many of the 100 tickets would I need to buy for the probability of my winning to be:
  (v) $\frac{3}{10}$
  (vi) 0.2
  (vii) 25%
  (viii) 100%?

18. There are 8 counters in a box.
The probability of taking a green counter out of the box is $\frac{1}{2}$.
A green counter is taken out of the box and put to one side.
Gerry now takes a counter at random from the box.
What is the probability it is green?

19. A game is played by picking a card at random from a pack of 52 playing cards.
The table shows the results of picking various cards.

Card	Result
Ace	Win €2
K, Q or J	Win 50c
6, 7, 8, 9, 10	No result
2, 3, 4, 5	Lose 50c

If Eileen picks a card, what is the probability that she will
  (i) lose money
  (ii) win money
  (iii) neither win nor lose
  (iv) not lose money?

20. This table shows information about a group of children.

	Boys	Girls
Blue eyes	3	6
Brown eyes	12	9

  (i) How many children are in the group altogether?
  (ii) If a child is chosen from the group at random, what is the probability of that child
    (a) having blue eyes
    (b) being a boy?
  (iii) If a boy is chosen from the group, what is the probability that he has blue eyes?

21. Mark did a project on language choices in 5th year in his school.

He collected the following information:
The 125 students in 5th year studied either French, German or Spanish.
22 girls studied French. There were 70 girls in total.
25 boys did German. There were 42 students in the Spanish class of which 12 were boys.
He then used a two-way table to present his results.

	French	German	Spanish	Total
Boys		25	12	
Girls	22			70
Totals			42	125

(a) Fill in the missing numbers to complete the table
(b) How many students studied French in 5th year?
(c) How many boys were in 5th year?
(d) What fraction of the students studied German.
(e) If a student was selected at random from 5th year what is the probability that the student;
  (i) studied French,
  (ii) was a girl who studied Spanish,
  (iii) was a boy who studied German?

Section 9.4 Two events – Use of sample spaces – Tree diagrams / Two-way tables

When a die is thrown and a coin is tossed, the set of possible outcomes is as follows:

{H1, H2, H3, H4, H5, H6, T1, T2, T3, T4, T5, T6}.

This set of possible outcomes is called a **sample space**.

Sample spaces can be created using tree diagrams or two-way tables as we have seen in the last section.

Using the sample space above, we can write down the probability of getting a head and a 6, for example.

i.e. $P(H, 6) = \frac{1}{12}$

The probability of a head and an even number can be found by counting the required outcomes.
These are H2, H4 and H6.

∴ $P(H \text{ and even number}) = \frac{3}{12} = \frac{1}{4}$

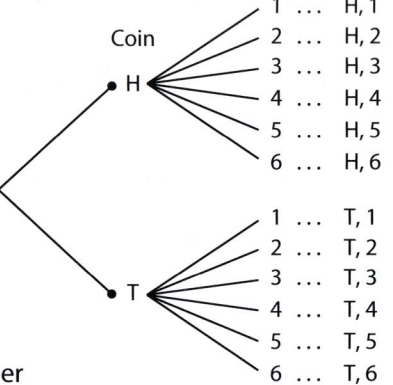

An experiment such as throwing two dice has a large number of possible outcomes, so we need to set out the sample space in an organised way, as shown in the following example.

Chapter 9 Probability

> **Example 1**
>
> If two dice are thrown and the scores are added, set out a sample space giving all the possible outcomes. Now find the probability that
> - (i) the total is exactly 7
> - (ii) the total is 4 or less
> - (iii) the total is 11 or more
> - (iv) the total is a multiple of 5.
>
> The sample space is set out on the right.
> There are 36 outcomes.
>
> (i) There are 6 totals of 7.
> $$\Rightarrow P(7) = \tfrac{6}{36} = \tfrac{1}{6}$$
>
> (ii) There are 6 totals of 4 or less.
> $$\Rightarrow P(4 \text{ or less}) = \tfrac{6}{36} = \tfrac{1}{6}$$
>
> (iii) There are 3 totals of 11 or more.
> $$\Rightarrow P(11 \text{ or more}) = \tfrac{3}{36} = \tfrac{1}{12}$$
>
> (iv) The multiples of 5 are 5 and 10.
> There are 7 totals of 5 or 10.
> $$\Rightarrow P(\text{multiple of } 5) = \tfrac{7}{36}$$
>
> Total = 4 or less
>
> | | 1 | 2 | 3 | 4 | 5 | 6 |
> |---|---|---|---|---|---|---|
> | 1 | 2 | 3 | 4 | 5 | 6 | 7 |
> | 2 | 3 | 4 | 5 | 6 | 7 | 8 |
> | 3 | 4 | 5 | 6 | 7 | 8 | 9 |
> | 4 | 5 | 6 | 7 | 8 | 9 | 10 |
> | 5 | 6 | 7 | 8 | 9 | 10 | 11 |
> | 6 | 7 | 8 | 9 | 10 | 11 | 12 |
>
> Total = 7

Exercise 9.4

1. These are the possible outcomes when two coins are tossed:

    HH, HT, TH, TT

    Write down the probability of getting
    - (i) 2 tails
    - (ii) 2 heads
    - (iii) a head and a tail.

2. When these two spinners are spun and the scores are added, you get the results shown on the right.

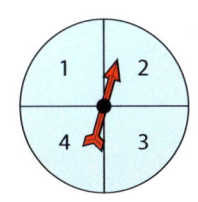

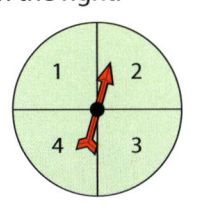

    Number on 1st spinner

	1	2	3	4
1	2	3	4	5
2	3	4	5	6
3	4	5	6	7
4	5	6	7	8

    Number on 2nd spinner

    Use the table to write down the following probabilities:
    - (i) The total score is 6
    - (ii) the total score is an odd number
    - (iii) the total score is 7 or more
    - (iv) the total score is 2 or 3.

3. A fair three-sided spinner has sections labelled 2, 4 and 6. The spinner is spun once and a fair six-sided die is thrown once.

The number that the spinner lands on is added to the number that the dice shows. This gives the score.

Copy and complete the table to show all possible scores.

Use the table to write down the probability that the score is
- (i) 4
- (ii) 5
- (iii) 7
- (iv) 9 or more
- (v) 5 or less
- (vi) a multiple of 4

	Dice					
+	1	2	3	4	5	6
2	3					
4						
6						12

Spinner

4. Karl has two fair spinners, numbered as shown. He spins them and finds the **product** of the two scores.
- (i) Copy and complete the grid, to show all possible outcomes of the two spins.
- (ii) What is the probability that the product is
  - (a) 12
  - (b) greater than 10
  - (c) a multiple of 3?

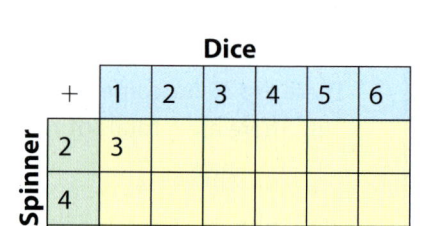

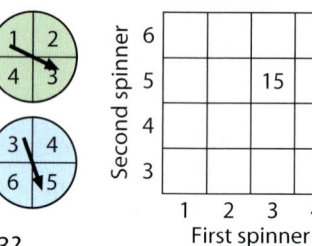

5. The ace, king, queen and jack of clubs and the ace, king, queen and jack of diamonds are put into two piles. The sample space diagram shows all the possible outcomes when a card is taken from each pile.

```
      J | AJ  KJ  QJ  JJ
      Q | AQ  KQ  QQ  JQ
Clubs K | AK  KK  QK  JK
      A | AA  KA  QA  JA
          A   K   Q   J
              Diamonds
```

Write down the probability that
- (i) both cards will be kings
- (ii) one card will be a club
- (iii) only one of the cards will be a queen
- (iv) the cards will make a matching pair
- (v) at least one of the cards will be a queen
- (vi) neither card will be a jack.

6. Three fair coins are tossed.
Using a tree diagram make out a sample space for all the possible outcomes.

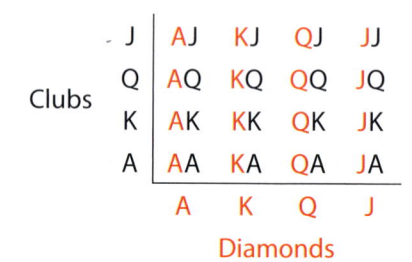

Now write down the probability that the outcome will be
- (i) three heads
- (ii) two heads and one tail
- (iii) no heads
- (iv) at least one head.

7. Two dice are thrown and the scores obtained are added. The resulting outcomes are shown in the given sample space.
   Find the probability that the sum of the two numbers is
   (i) 9
   (ii) 10
   (iii) 3 or less
   (iv) 10 or 11.

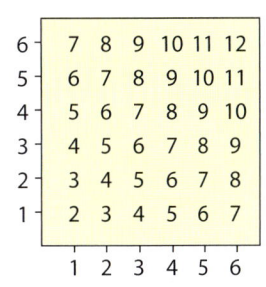

8. Chloe is playing a word game and chooses a vowel and a consonant at random from her letters.
   (i)   Show all the possible choices she can make using a tree diagram.
   (ii) What is the probability of choosing A and R?
   (iii) What is the probability of choosing I and L?
   (iv) What is the probability of choosing I and not choosing L?

9. Bag A contains 2 red beds and 1 white bead.
   Bag B contains 1 red bead and 2 white beads.
   A bead is drawn at random from each bag.
   Draw a tree diagram showing the outcomes of this experiment and hence write out the sample space for this experiment.
   Find the probability that (i) both beads are red (ii) two beads are the same colour.
   (iii) the pair of beads will be different in colour.

Section 9.5 Estimating probabilities from experiments

So far we have calculated probabilities on the basis that all outcomes are equally likely to happen. However, in real-life situations, events are not always equally likely and some other way must be found to make an estimate of the probability.

In such cases we carry out an **experiment** or **survey** to estimate the probability of an event happening.

Experiment

John suspected that a coin was biased.
In an experiment, he tosses the coin 1000 times with the help of his friends.
He counted the number of heads obtained after 10, 20, 100 … and 1000 times.
The results are shown in the table on the right:

As the number of tosses increases, the values of the number of heads divided by the number of tosses gets closer to 0.5, i.e. $\frac{1}{2}$.

The value of the number of heads divided by the number of tosses is called the **experimental probability** or **relative frequency**.

Number of tosses	Number of heads	Heads ÷ tosses
10	6	0.6
20	11	0.55
100	53	0.53
200	108	0.54
400	194	0.485
500	242	0.484
1000	490	0.49

Text & Tests 2 Higher Level

It gives an **estimate** of the true probability.

As the number of trials or experiments increases, the value of the experimental probability gets closer to the true or theoretical probability.

Since the probability of getting a head after tossing the coin 1000 times is very close to the true probability of $\frac{1}{2}$, John concludes that the coin is not biased.

Thus an estimate of the probability that an event will occur by carrying out a survey or experiment is given by

$$\text{Relative frequency} = \frac{\text{Number of successful trials}}{\text{Total number of trials}}$$

Example 1

Derek collects data on the colours of cars passing the school gate. His results are shown in the table.

Colour	Tally	Frequency
White	IIII IIII IIII IIII IIII	24
Red	IIII IIII IIII IIII IIII IIII II	32
Black	IIII IIII IIII	14
Blue	IIII IIII IIII I	16
Green	IIII IIII	10
Other	IIII	4

(i) How many cars did Derek survey?
(ii) What was the relative frequency of blue cars?
(iii) What was the relative frequency of red cars? Give your answer as a decimal.
(iv) Write down an estimate of the probability that the next car passing the school gate will be green.
(v) How can the estimate for the probability of green cars be made more reliable?

(i) The number of cars in the survey is the sum of the frequencies. This is 100 cars.

(ii) Relative frequency of blue cars $= \frac{16}{100} = \frac{4}{25}$

(iii) Relative frequency of red cars $= \frac{32}{100} = 0.32$

(iv) Probability of next car green = relative frequency of green cars
$$= \frac{10}{100} = \frac{1}{10}$$

(v) The estimate for the probability of green cars can be made more reliable by increasing the number of cars observed. Five hundred cars would give a very accurate estimate of the true probability.

Chapter 9 Probability

Investigation:

Compare *experimental probability* and *true (or theoretical) probability*.

If a fair die is rolled, we know that each face is equally likely to occur.

The probability of each face occurring is $\frac{1}{6} \approx 0.167$.
This is the true (or theoretical) probability.

Copy the chart below and with the help of a group of students, roll a die and record your results in the form of a tally chart.

Every 30 throws find the experimental probability of each number occurring on the die. Add the sets of 30 throws together until the die is rolled 120 times.

Number of rolls	1	2	3	4	5	6
30						
Probability	$=\frac{(\ )}{30}$	$=\frac{(\ )}{30}$	$=\frac{(\ )}{30}$	$=\frac{(\ )}{30}$	$=\frac{(\ )}{30}$	$=\frac{(\ )}{30}$
30 (60)						
Probability	$=\frac{(\ )}{60}$	$=\frac{(\ )}{60}$	$=\frac{(\ )}{60}$	$=\frac{(\ )}{60}$	$=\frac{(\ )}{60}$	$=\frac{(\ )}{60}$
30 (90)						
Probability	$=\frac{(\ )}{90}$	$=\frac{(\ )}{90}$	$=\frac{(\ )}{90}$	$=\frac{(\ )}{90}$	$=\frac{(\ )}{90}$	$=\frac{(\ )}{90}$
30 (120)						
Probability	$=\frac{(\ )}{120}$	$=\frac{(\ )}{120}$	$=\frac{(\ )}{120}$	$=\frac{(\ )}{120}$	$=\frac{(\ )}{120}$	$=\frac{(\ )}{120}$

Compare the experimental probability to the true (theoretical) probability as the number of times the die is rolled is increased.

Write a conclusion:

Text & Tests 2 Higher Level

Expected frequency

This bag contains 5 red discs and 3 blue discs.

A disc is chosen at random from the bag and then replaced.

The probability of getting a blue disc is $\frac{3}{8}$.

This means that, on average, you expect 3 blue discs in every 8 chosen or 30 blue discs in every 80 chosen.

To find the expected number of blue discs when you choose a disc 400 times,
   (i) Work out the probability that the event happens once.
   (ii) Multiply this probability by the number of times the experiment is carried out.
   Thus the expected number of blue discs is

$$\frac{3}{8} \times \frac{400}{1} = 150.$$

> Expected frequency is:
>
> probability × number of trials.

Example 2

This spinner is biased.
The probability that the spinner will land on each of the numbers 1 to 4 is given in the table below.

Number	1	2	3	4	5
Probability	0.35	0.1	0.25	0.15	

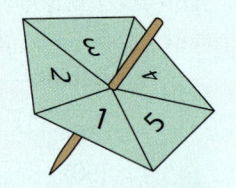

The spinner is spun once.
   (i) Work out the probability that the spinner will land on 5.
   (ii) Write down the number on which the spinner is most likely to land.
   (iii) If the spinner is spun 200 times, how many times would you expect it to land on 3?

(i) The sum of all the probabilities is 1.
   Let x be the probability of the spinner landing on 5.
   $\therefore \quad x + 0.35 + 0.1 + 0.25 + 0.15 = 1$
   $\qquad\qquad\qquad x + 0.85 = 1 \Rightarrow x = 0.15$
   $\therefore \quad$ P(spinner lands on 5) = 0.15
(ii) This spinner is most likely to land on 1 as it has the highest probability.
(iii) P(landing on 3) = 0.25 = $\frac{1}{4}$

In 200 spins, the number of times you would expect the spinner to land on 3 is $\frac{1}{4} \times 200 = 50$.

Exercise 9.5

1. A fair coin is tossed 100 times.
   How many heads would you expect to get?

2. A fair six-sided die is thrown 60 times.
   (i) How many sixes would you expect to get?
   (ii) How many twos would you expect to get?
   (iii) How many even numbers would you expect to get?

3. One ball is selected at random from the bag shown and then replaced. This procedure is done 400 times.
   How many times would you expect to select:
   (i) a blue ball,
   (ii) a red ball?

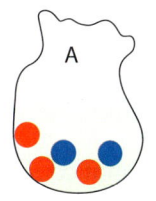

4. 50 cars are observed passing the school gate. 15 of these cars are red.
   Use these results to estimate the probability that the next car to pass the school gate will be red.

5. Jane and Nicky both did the 'dropping a drawing pin' experiment.
   Here are their results.

   Jane

Trials	20
'Point up'	10

   Nicky

Trials	100
'Point up'	75

   Another drawing pin is dropped.
   (i) For Jane, what is the probability of getting 'point up'?
   (ii) For Nicky, what is the probability of getting 'point up'?
   (iii) Whose result is likely to be more reliable? Explain your answer.

6. Ciara surveyed the colours of vehicles passing her home. Here are her results.

Colour	Red	Black	Silver	Green	White	Other
Frequency	6	10	24	4	12	8

   Calculate an estimate of the probability that the next vehicle to pass will be
   (i) silver
   (ii) not black.

7. Eoin is carrying out an experiment – 'dropping a spoon'.
   He records whether the spoon lands up or down.
   (i) Copy and complete this table of Eoin's results.

Number of drops	5	10	20	25	50	100
Number of times landed up	3	7	11	15	32	63
Probability	0.6	0.7				

(ii) What do you think could be a reasonable estimate for the true probability of a spoon landing up? Give your answer as a decimal, correct to 1 decimal place.
(iii) If Eoin dropped the spoon 300 times, how many times is it likely to land up? (i.e., the expected frequency.)

8. A bag contained coloured beads. Darren randomly selects a bead and then replaces it. He does this 60 times. Here are the results.

Colour	White	Green	Blue
Frequency	10	30	20

Estimate the probability that on his next draw he will select:
(i) a white bead   (ii) a green bead   (iii) a white bead or a blue bead

9. A bag contains eight counters. Each counter is blue or red or yellow.
Helena takes a counter at random from the bag. She records the colour of the counter and then puts the counter back in the bag.
She performs this experiment 400 times. The table shows her results.

Colour of counter	Blue	Red	Yellow
Frequency	210	98	92

(i) Estimate how many of the eight counters are blue.
Give an explanation for your answer.
(ii) Estimate how many of the eight counters are yellow.
Give an explanation for your answer.

10. Olivia, Ben and Joe each rolled a different die 360 times.

Only one of the dice was fair. Whose was it?
Explain your answer.
Whose die is the most biased?
Explain your answer.

Number	Olivia	Ben	Joe
1	27	58	141
2	69	62	52
3	78	63	56
4	43	57	53
5	76	56	53
6	67	64	5

11. A fair six-sided die has its faces painted red, white or blue.
The die is thrown 36 times.
Here are the results:

Colour	Frequency
Red	7
White	11
Blue	18

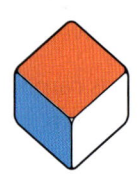

Based on the results, how many faces do you think are painted each colour?

12. Lyra made a spinner with three colours – yellow, blue and red.
She tested it by spinning it 500 times.

Her results were: yellow 240
 blue 160
 red 100

(i) Estimate the probability of the spinner landing on yellow.

(ii) She then spun the spinner 100 times.
About how many times would you expect the spinner to land on yellow?

13. Carol spins a red and a green spinner 50 times each. She records whether or not each spinner lands on a 1. The tables show her results.

Red spinner

Lands on a 1	Does not land on a 1
7	43

Green spinner

Lands on a 1	Does not land on a 1
24	26

(i) Work out the relative frequency of getting a 1 on each spinner.

(ii) Both spinners are fair six-sectored spinners.

How many sides of each spinner do you think will have a 1 on them?
Give an explanation for your answers.

14. The probability of having to wait for more than 5 minutes at a post office is $\frac{2}{7}$.
350 people use the post office in one day.
Work out an estimate for the number of people who have to wait for more than 5 minutes.

15. David and Rory are keen golfers
Out of their last 20 rounds, Rory has won 14.

(i) Based on these results, give and estimate of the probability that David will win the next round.

(ii) Given that David wins the next five rounds, give an estimate of the probability that Rory wins the next round after that.

Text & Tests 2 Higher Level

Section 9.6 Probability using Venn diagrams

If information is presented in the form of a Venn diagram, it is easy to write down the probability of different events occurring.

The diagrams below illustrate the main regions when two Venn diagrams intersect.

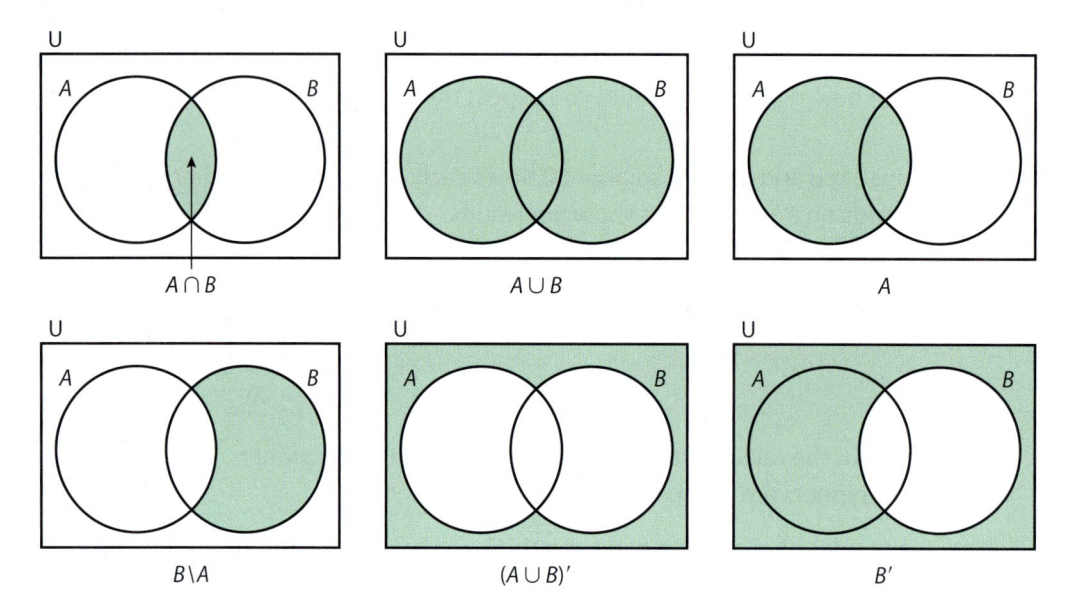

$A \cap B$

$A \cup B$

A

$B \setminus A$

$(A \cup B)'$

B'

Example 1

The Venn diagram shows the sports played by members of a club.
How many members played
(i) both football and tennis
(ii) tennis but not football
(iii) neither of these two games
(iv) football or tennis?
Now write down the probability of each of the above.

(i) Both football and tennis = 10
(ii) Tennis but not football = 35
(iii) Neither of these two games = 45
(iv) Football or tennis = 40 + 10 + 35 = 85

$$P(i) = \frac{10}{\text{total membership}} = \frac{10}{130} = \frac{1}{13} \qquad P(ii) = \frac{35}{130} = \frac{7}{26}$$

$$P(iii) = \frac{45}{130} = \frac{9}{26} \qquad P(iv) = \frac{85}{130} = \frac{17}{26}$$

Chapter 9 Probability

Three sets

The diagram on the right shows the sports played by a group of second-year students.

The probabilities of various events are given below. Verify these probabilities by examining the diagram.

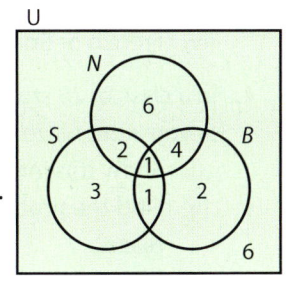

Note: 6 + 2 + 1 + 4 + 3 + 1 + 2 + 6 = 25 = Total number of students.

(i) P(student plays all three games) = $\frac{1}{25}$

(ii) P(student plays netball) = $\frac{6+2+1+4}{25} = \frac{13}{25}$

(iii) P(student doesn't play soccer) = $\frac{6+4+2+6}{25} = \frac{18}{25}$

(iv) P(student plays two games only) = $\frac{2+4+1}{25} = \frac{7}{25}$

N = netball
B = basketball
S = soccer

Exercise 9.6

1. In the given Venn diagram,

    U represents the houses in a given street,
    C represents those which have a cat and
    D represents those which have a dog.

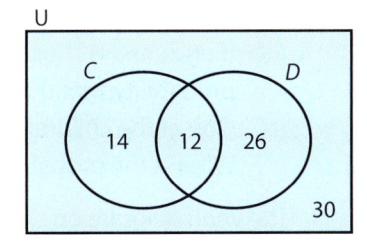

    If a household is selected at random, what is the probability that it has

    (i) a cat (ii) a cat and a dog (iii) a dog but not a cat
    (iv) a cat or a dog (v) neither a cat nor a dog?

2. In the given Venn diagram,

    U = the students in class 1K
    F = the students in the class who play football
    B = the students in the class who play badminton.

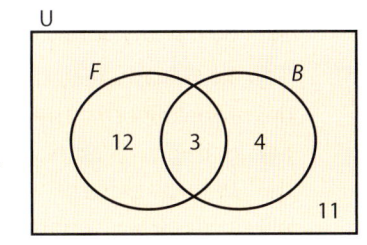

    (i) How many students are there in the class?
    (ii) How many students play badminton?

    If a student is selected at random from the class, find the probability that the student
    (iii) plays both games (iv) plays neither game
    (v) plays badminton but not football (vi) plays one game only.

3. The given Venn diagram shows the modern languages, if any, taken by a group of 50 students.

    (i) Find the value of x.

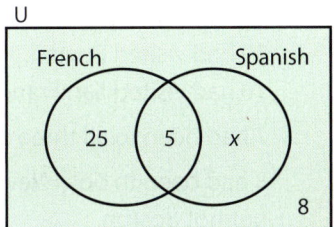

223

If a student is selected at random, find the probability that the student takes
  (ii) French
  (iii) both French and Spanish
  (iv) French or Spanish
  (v) one of these languages only.

4. In a class of 28 students, 25 were wearing blazers or ties or both. Seven wore blazers with no tie and eight wore blazers and ties.
   (i) Show this information on a Venn diagram.
   (ii) Find the probability that a student selected at random was wearing a tie but not a blazer.
   (iii) Find the probability that a student selected at random was wearing neither a tie nor a blazer.

5. In a class of 40 children, a survey was carried out to find out how many children liked chocolate and how many liked ice-cream. The Venn diagram shows the results but the region marked A is not filled in. 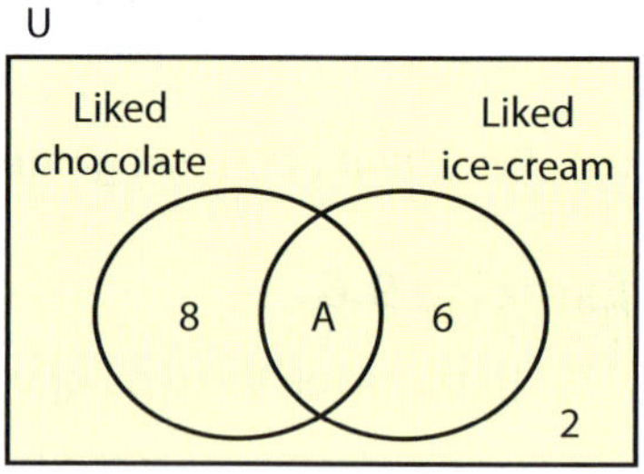
   (i) What is the number in region A?
   (ii) What can you say about the children in region A?
   (iii) If one child is chosen at random, what is the probability that the child liked ice-cream but not chocolate?
   (iv) One of the children who liked chocolate is chosen at random. What is the probability that the child also liked ice-cream?

6. The Venn diagram on the right shows the results of a survey of a number of adults to find out which of the games golf, tennis or football, if any, they play. 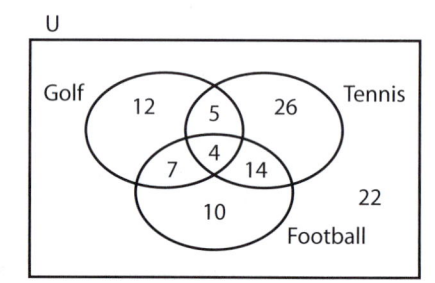
   (i) How many adults were surveyed?

   If an adult was selected at random, find the probability that the person plays
   (ii) golf
   (iii) both golf and tennis
   (iv) all three games
   (v) football only
   (vi) football and tennis
   (vii) football and tennis but not golf.

7. 35 people coming back from America were asked if they had visited New York, Boston or San Francisco. The results were as follows:

   20 had visited New York.
   13 had visited Boston.
   16 had visited San Francisco.

   7 had been to all three cities.

   3 had been to both New York and San Francisco, but not Boston.

1 had been to both New York and Boston, but not San Francisco.
8 had been to Boston and San Francisco.

(i) Display this information in a Venn diagram.
(ii) If one person is chosen at random from the group, what is the probability that the person had not visited any of the three cities?
(iii) If one person is chosen at random, what is the probability that the person had visited New York only?
(iv) If one person is chosen at random, what is the probability that the person had visited Boston or New York?
(v) A person who visited New York is chosen at random. What is the probability that the person also visited Boston?

Section 9.7 Tree diagrams – probability of multiple events

The possible outcomes of two or more events can be shown in a particular type of diagram called a **probability tree diagram**.

The branches of the tree represent all possible outcomes for each event.

The tree diagram below represents all possible outcomes in a three-child family.

From the tree diagram, it can be seen that there are 8 possible outcomes.

Placing the probability of each event along the branches produces a probability tree-diagram. The probability of each extended branch is obtained by multiplying the separate probabilities.

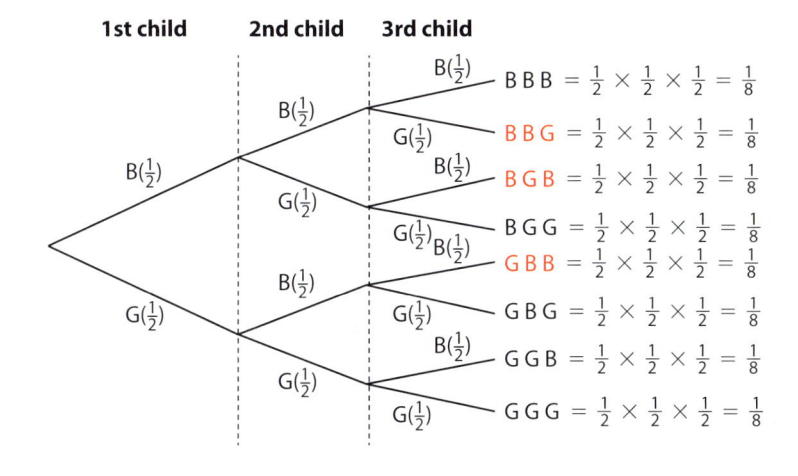

1st child   **2nd child**   **3rd child**

$B(\tfrac{1}{2})$ — B B B $= \tfrac{1}{2} \times \tfrac{1}{2} \times \tfrac{1}{2} = \tfrac{1}{8}$
$B(\tfrac{1}{2})$
$G(\tfrac{1}{2})$ — B B G $= \tfrac{1}{2} \times \tfrac{1}{2} \times \tfrac{1}{2} = \tfrac{1}{8}$
$B(\tfrac{1}{2})$
$B(\tfrac{1}{2})$ — B G B $= \tfrac{1}{2} \times \tfrac{1}{2} \times \tfrac{1}{2} = \tfrac{1}{8}$
$G(\tfrac{1}{2})$
$G(\tfrac{1}{2})$ — B G G $= \tfrac{1}{2} \times \tfrac{1}{2} \times \tfrac{1}{2} = \tfrac{1}{8}$
$B(\tfrac{1}{2})$ — G B B $= \tfrac{1}{2} \times \tfrac{1}{2} \times \tfrac{1}{2} = \tfrac{1}{8}$
$B(\tfrac{1}{2})$
$G(\tfrac{1}{2})$ — G B G $= \tfrac{1}{2} \times \tfrac{1}{2} \times \tfrac{1}{2} = \tfrac{1}{8}$
$G(\tfrac{1}{2})$
$B(\tfrac{1}{2})$ — G G B $= \tfrac{1}{2} \times \tfrac{1}{2} \times \tfrac{1}{2} = \tfrac{1}{8}$
$G(\tfrac{1}{2})$
$G(\tfrac{1}{2})$ — G G G $= \tfrac{1}{2} \times \tfrac{1}{2} \times \tfrac{1}{2} = \tfrac{1}{8}$

Text & Tests 2 Higher Level

Note:
(i) P(3 boys) = P(B **and** B **and** B) = P(B, B, B) = $\frac{1}{2} \times \frac{1}{2} \times \frac{1}{2} = \frac{1}{8}$

(ii) The three highlighted results above represent the families that have one girl.
∴ P(one girl) = P(B and B and G **or** B and G and B **or** G and B and B)
= P(B, B, G **or** G, B, G **or** G, B, B) = $\frac{1}{8} + \frac{1}{8} + \frac{1}{8} = \frac{3}{8}$

Tree diagrams are especially useful for events that do not have an equal chance of happening as the next example indicates.

Example 1

Each of the spinners shown on the right is spun once.
Draw a tree diagram to represent these spins.
Use the tree diagram to write down these probabilities:

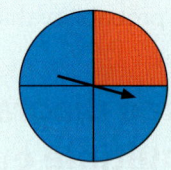

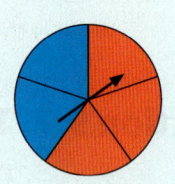

Spinner A   Spinner B

(i) P(A red, B red)   (ii) P(both the same colour).

The tree diagram and the probabilities along each branch are shown below.

Spinner A   Spinner B

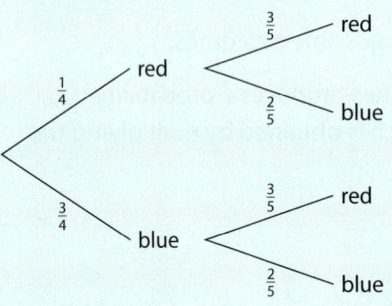

$\frac{3}{5}$ red   probability of (A red, B red) = $\frac{1}{4} \times \frac{3}{5} = \frac{3}{20}$

$\frac{1}{4}$ red

$\frac{2}{5}$ blue   probability of (A red, B blue) = $\frac{1}{4} \times \frac{2}{5} = \frac{2}{20}$

$\frac{3}{5}$ red   probability of (A blue, B red) = $\frac{3}{4} \times \frac{3}{5} = \frac{9}{20}$

$\frac{3}{4}$ blue

$\frac{2}{5}$ blue   probability of (A blue, B blue) = $\frac{3}{4} \times \frac{2}{5} = \frac{6}{20}$

(i) P(red, red) = $\frac{3}{20}$

(ii) P(both the same colour) = probability of (A red, B red) + probability of (A blue, B blue)
= $\frac{3}{20} + \frac{6}{20} = \frac{9}{20}$

(Notice that the sum of the probabilities at the end of the four branches adds up to 1.)

Chapter 9 Probability

Exercise 9.7

1. When a motorist approaches any traffic lights, there is an even chance that they will be red or green.
   If a motorist has to go through two sets of lights, copy and complete the tree diagram on the right.
   Write down the probability of each of these:
   (i) P(both green)
   (ii) P(one red, one green).

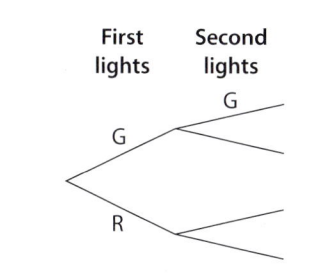

   First lights   Second lights

2. Copy and complete the tree diagram for these two spinners.

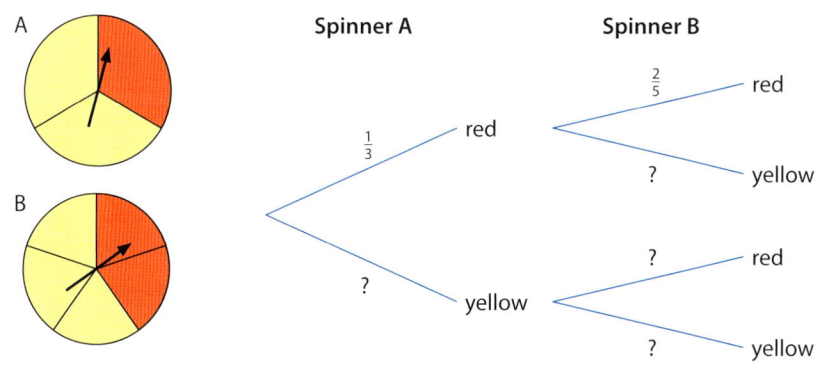

   Spinner A   Spinner B

   What is the probability that A and B show
   (i) the same colour
   (ii) different colours?

3. Paula has a die with 5 red faces and 1 green face.
   She rolls the die twice.
   (i) Copy and complete the tree diagram.
   (ii) Find the probability that the die shows the same colour each time.
   (iii) Find the probability that the die shows green and red in that order.

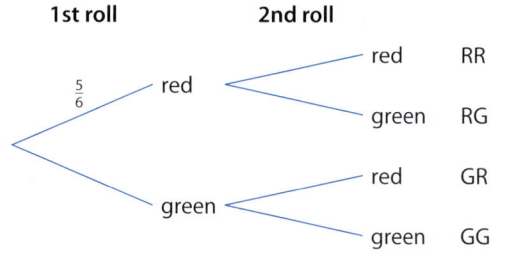

   1st roll   2nd roll
              red   RR
        red
              green   RG
              red   GR
        green
              green   GG

4. A bag contains 4 **red** beads and 2 **blue** beads.
   A second bag contains 2 **red** beads and 4 **blue** beads.
   Jack takes one bead at random from each bag.
   (i) Complete the probability tree diagram.
   (ii) Find the probability that Jack takes
       (a) 2 red beads
       (b) red and blue in that order
       (c) red and blue in any order.

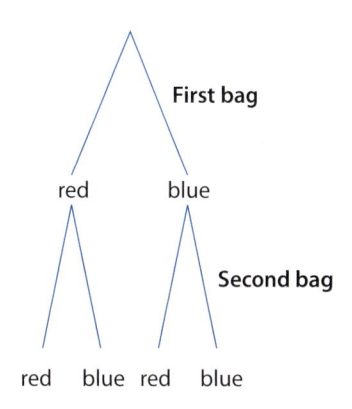

   First bag: red, blue
   Second bag: red, blue, red, blue

227

5. Gerry has a coin which is weighted so that the probability that it lands 'head' is $\frac{3}{5}$ and 'tail' $\frac{2}{5}$.
   (i) Copy and complete the tree diagram for two tosses of the coin, writing the probabilities on the branches.
   (ii) Find the probability of getting one 'head' and one 'tail'.

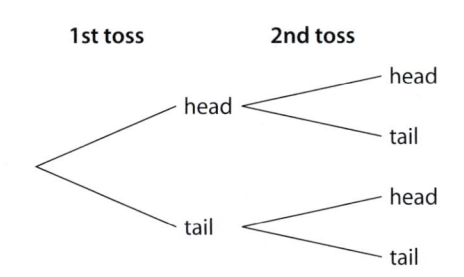

6. A bag contains 10 coins.
   There are 6 gold coins and the rest are silver.
   A coin is taken at random from the bag.
   The type of coin is recorded and the coin is then returned to the bag.
   A second coin is then taken at random from the bag.
   (i) The tree diagram shows all the ways in which two coins can be taken from the bag. Copy the diagram and write the probabilities on it.
   (ii) Use your tree diagram to calculate the probability that one coin is gold and one coin is silver.

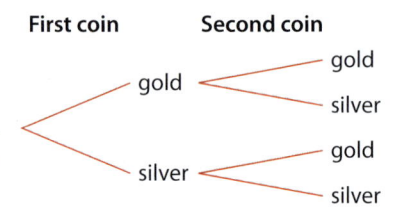

7. Silvia throws an ordinary die twice.
   (i) Copy and complete this tree diagram.
   (ii) Use the tree diagram to write down the probability that Silvia gets
      (a) two sixes
      (b) one six only.

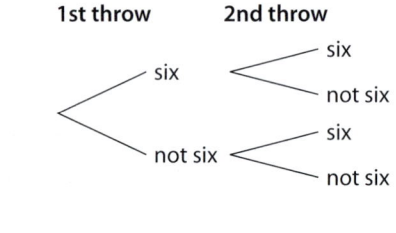

8. Helen tosses a fair coin three times.
   Draw a tree diagram for the three tosses.
   Find the probability that
   (i) all three tosses give the same result
   (ii) two tosses give 'head' and the other 'tail'.

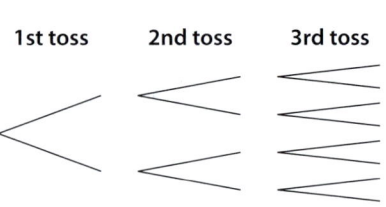

9. Two fair dice, each having faces numbered 1, 1, 2, 2, 2, 2, are thrown.
   Draw up a probability tree and use the tree to find the probabilities of these events:
   (i) the total score is 4
   (ii) the total score is 3
   (iii) at least one dice shows a 2.

Test yourself 9

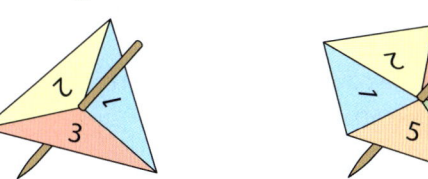

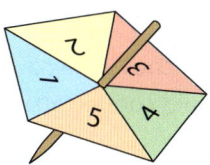

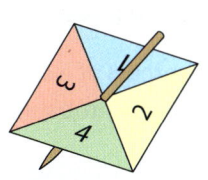

1. A   B   C

For which of these spinners is the probability of spinning a 3 equal to:
  (i) 20%   (ii) 25%   (iii) $\frac{1}{3}$?

2. The first 100 vehicles to pass a checkpoint gave the results in the table. If these figures truly represent the traffic at any time past this checkpoint, determine the experimental probability that the next vehicle will be:
  (i) a car   (ii) a motor cycle
  (iii) a bus   (iv) *not* a car
  (v) *not* a car or truck

Type of vehicle	Frequency
Cars	70
Trucks	15
Motor cycles	10
Buses	5

3. A bag contains 50 marbles: 20 are red, 12 are green and 18 are black. What is the probability that a marble selected at random is:
  (i) red   (ii) green   (iii) not black?

4. Ken has two spinners, each numbered 1 to 4. Only one of them is a fair spinner. These tables show the results of spinning each spinner 80 times.
Which spinner do you think is fair, spinner **A** or spinner **B**? Explain your decision.

A Score	Frequency
1	19
2	22
3	21
4	18

B Score	Frequency
1	15
2	18
3	15
4	32

5. These are two sets of cards.

  SET P   3 6 8   SET Q   2 4 7

A card is taken at random from set P and another from set Q.
  (i) List all the possible outcomes.
  (ii) What is the probability of getting two even numbers?
  (iii) What is the probability of getting two consecutive numbers?

Text & Tests 2 Higher Level

6. The contents of 20 matchboxes were examined and the results recorded.

Number of matches	48	49	50	51	52	53
Number of boxes	1	5	8	3	2	1

If the contents of a similar box of matches were counted, what would be the experimental probability that it would contain 50 matches or more?

7. There are 5 green beads and x golden beads in a bag.
What is the value of x if the probability of drawing a golden bead is $\frac{2}{3}$?

8. The Venn diagram on the right shows the numbers of students who take Maths (M), English (E) and History (H).

   If a student is selected at random, find the probability that the student takes
   (i) English (ii) both Maths and History
   (iii) Maths or English (iv) Maths only
   (v) all three subjects (vi) English or History.

9. Explain what is meant by a probability of
   (i) 0 (ii) 0.5 (iii) 75% (iv) 1.

10. A biased die is rolled.
    This table gives the probability that it will land on each of the numbers 1, 2, 4, 5 and 6.

	1	2	3	4	5	6
Probability	0.1	0.1		0.2	0.3	0.1

   (i) Work out the probability that the die will land on 3.
   (ii) Work out the probability that the die will land on an even number.

11. An ordinary pack of playing cards is shuffled well and a card is drawn out. Determine the probability that it is:
    (i) a red card (ii) the ace of spades
    (iii) a number less than ten and greater than four
    (iv) a black picture card (v) an ace
    (vi) a number between four and ten inclusive.

12. Jenny tossed four coins 30 times and the number of heads was recorded each time. The bar chart shows the results. 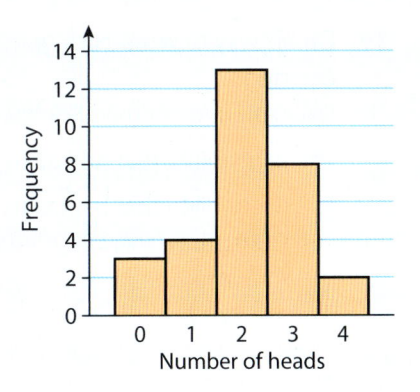
    (i) From this experiment, what is the probability that when four coins are thrown there will be:
       (a) no heads
       (b) two heads
       (c) at least three heads?
    (ii) If this experiment were to be repeated, would you expect the same results? Explain your answer.

13. In a group of 25 students, 18 study Maths, 12 study Science and 5 study neither Maths nor Science.
    Illustrate this information on a Venn diagram.
    If a student is selected at random, what is the probability that the student studies
    (i) Mathematics only   (ii) Science only
    (iii) Mathematics or Science or both   (iv) both Mathematics and Science?

14. The probability that a biased die will land 3 up is 0.4.
    Mark rolls the biased die 200 times.
    Work out an estimate for the number of times that the die will land 3 up.

15. A drawing pin can land 'point up' or 'point down'.
    Nelson dropped it first 10, then 20, then 30, … times.
    Which of these graphs of relative frequency of landing 'point up' versus number of trials is most likely to show Nelson's results?

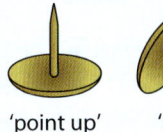

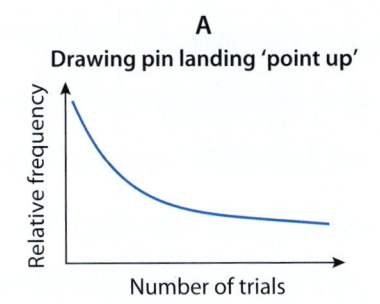

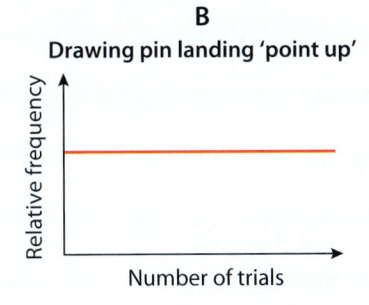

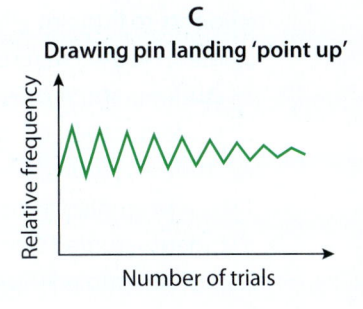

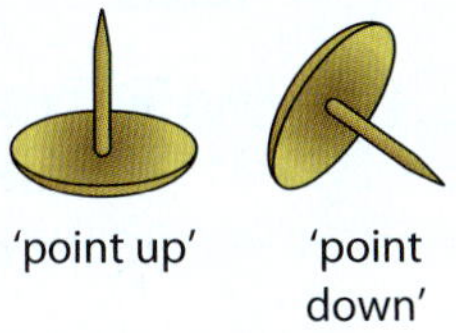

16. On his way to work, Nick goes through a set of traffic lights and then passes over a level crossing.

Over a period of time, Nick has estimated the probability of stopping at each of these.

The probability that he has to stop at the traffic lights is $\frac{2}{3}$.

The probability that he has to stop at the level crossing is $\frac{1}{5}$.
  (i) Construct a tree diagram to show this information.
  (ii) Calculate the probability that Nick will not have to stop at either the lights or the level crossing on his way to work.

17. 100 students go on a school trip.

On the trip, they each have a drink of water, orange juice or milk. 24 out of the 57 boys drank milk.
27 girls drank water.

A total of 24 students drank orange juice, $\frac{1}{3}$ of these are girls.

Copy and complete the two-way table.

	Milk	Water	Orange juice	Totals
Boys	24			57
Girls		27		
Totals			24	100

Find (a) the probability that a student chosen at random from the group is drinking water.
  (b) the probability that a boy chosen at random from the group is drinking water.

18. Dave sent out a questionnaire to 5th year students to find out what languages they studied. He discovered:
13 students studied German.
20 students studied Spanish.
25 students studied French.
1 student studied all three.
3 students studied German and Spanish.
3 students studied German and French.
3 students studied Spanish and French.
10 students did not study any of these.

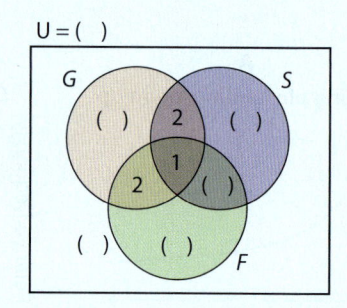

(a) Copy and complete the Venn diagram he drew of his results.
(b) How many students answered the questionnaire?
If one of the students is chosen at random, what is the probability that the student:
(c) studied French only
(d) studied French or Spanish
(e) studied French and Spanish
(f) did not study French or German or Spanish?

19. (i) Explain why $\frac{2}{7}$ and $\frac{4}{14}$ are called equivalent fractions.

Write down another fraction equivalent to $\frac{2}{7}$.

(ii) A box contains red and blue pencils.
The probability of picking a red pencil is $\frac{2}{7}$.
What is the probability of picking a blue pencil?

(iii) Write down three possible combinations of red and blue pencils in the box.

(iv) Some green pencils are added to the box.
The green pencils make up 25% of the pencils in the box.
Find the probability of picking a blue pencil from the box.

Assignment:

Three identical discs are placed on a table. The letter P(Prize) is written on the back of one of the discs.
Working in pairs, your partner looks away and the discs are shuffled and placed in a straight line.
(You must keep track of the P disc.)
Your partner is asked to pick a disc at random to find the prize.
You turn over one of the two remaining discs which you are **certain has no P** behind it.
You ask your partner "Do you wish to change your mind and pick the other disc?"

Make a note of whether they would have won the prize if they had changed their mind.
Repeat the experiment 20 times.
Change partners and repeat the experiment twice.
Find the probability, using the table above, of winning the Prize (given that they had changed their mind).

Number of trials	Number of times they would have won if they had changed their mind
20	
20	
20	
Total (60)	

Show that if they had changed their mind (and swapped) they would have had a better chance of winning the prize.

Note: For accuracy sake, it is important that no identifying marks are on the discs, so that the choice is strictly random. (Small plates, saucers, inverted cups, etc. can be used, once they are identical.)
Write a report on the experiment. Include in your report how the **probability of success** changes as a clear disc is turned up.

Simultaneous equations

Chapter 10

From first year, you will recall how to:
- add and subtract like terms,
- multiply algebraic terms by a constant,
- form and solve equations,
- use algebra to solve word problems.

In this chapter, you will learn to:
- multiply equations by a constant,
- add and subtract equations,
- remove fractions from an equation,
- solve a pair of equations with two variables,
- interpret the point of intersection of two lines,
- create two equations with two unknowns from a word problem.

Section 10.1 Solving simultaneous equations

Consider the equation
$$3x + y = 9.$$
The values $x = 2$ and $y = 3$ satisfy this equation.
The values $x = 1$ and $y = 6$ also satisfy the equation.
In fact, there are many pairs of values for x and y which satisfy the equation.

Now we take a second equation
$$2x - y = 1.$$
The values $x = 2$ and $y = 3$ satisfy this equation also.
Thus, the values $x = 2$ and $y = 3$ satisfy both equations
$$3x + y = 9 \text{ and } 2x - y = 1.$$

> When two equations are both satisfied by the same values for x and y, they are said to be simultaneous equations.

Only **one** set of values for x and y will satisfy a pair of simultaneous equations.
There are many ways of solving simultaneous equations.
One method is called the **elimination method**.
In this method, we 'eliminate' one of the variables.
This method is discussed in the following investigation.

Text & Tests 2 Higher Level

Investigation:

$5x + 3y = 23$ and $2x - 3y = 5$ are two equations.

We can illustrate them using scales.

On the red scales $5x + 3y$ balances 23

On the green scales $2x - 3y$ balances 5

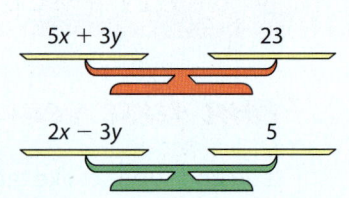

Investigate what would happen if we add the left-hand sides and the right-hand sides to a new blue scales.

(i) Would the blue scales balance?
(ii) What are the totals on each side of the blue scales?
(iii) How can you use these totals to find a value for x?
(iv) How can you use the value of x to find a value for y?

From the 'investigation' above, it can be seen that it is easy to solve simultaneous equations if one of the variables can be eliminated by **adding or subtracting** the two equations.

If a variable cannot be eliminated by adding or subtracting, then we have to multiply one or more of the equations by a number to make the elimination possible.

Example 1

Solve the simultaneous equations
$x + 2y = 10$
$2x - y = 5$

(To solve these equations, we must make the number of x's or the number of y's equal. We then add or subtract as necessary.
For convenience, we call the first equation ① and the second equation ②.)

Equation ①:	$x + 2y = 10$	Equation 2:	$2(4) - 3 = 5$
Equation ② × 2:	$4x - 2y = 10$		$8 - 3 = 5$
Adding:	$5x = 20$		$5 = 5$
	$\therefore\ x = 4$		

Substituting $x = 4$ in ① we get: $4 + 2y = 10$
$2y = 6$
$\therefore\ y = 3$

The solution is $x = 4$ and $y = 3$.

(Note: It is important to check that $x = 4$ and $y = 3$ satisfy both equations.)

Chapter 10 Simultaneous equations

> **Example 2**
>
> Solve the simultaneous equations $\quad 2x - 5y = 9$
> $\qquad\qquad\qquad\qquad\qquad\qquad\quad 3x + 2y = 4$
>
> We number the equations $\quad 2x - 5y = 9 \quad$ ①
> ① and ② for convenience. $\quad 3x + 2y = 4 \quad$ ②
>
> We now multiply equation ① by 3 and equation ② by 2 to equate the number of x's.
>
> ① × 3: $\quad 6x - 15y = 27 \qquad\qquad$ Checking values in equation 2;
> ② × 2: $\quad \underline{6x + 4y = 8} \qquad\qquad\qquad\quad 3(2) + 2(-1) = 4$
> Subtract: $\quad\quad -19y = 19 \qquad\qquad\qquad\qquad 6 - 2 = 4$
> $\qquad\qquad\quad\; 19y = -19 \qquad\qquad\qquad\qquad\quad 4 = 4$
> $\qquad\qquad\qquad y = -1$
>
> We now substitute -1 for y in equation ①
> $\qquad\qquad\qquad 2x - 5y = 9$
> $y = -1 \;\Rightarrow\; 2x + 5 = 9$
> $\qquad\quad\;\Rightarrow\; 2x = 4 \;\Rightarrow\; x = 2$
> $\therefore \; x = 2$ and $y = -1$ are the solutions.

Equations containing fractions

Here are two simultaneous equations:

$\quad 3x - 2y = 19 \;\ldots\;$ ①

$\quad \dfrac{x}{3} + \dfrac{y}{2} = 5 \;\ldots\;$ ②

To solve these equations, we 'get rid of the fractions' in equation ② by multiplying each term by 6 (the LCM of 3 and 2).

Thus, equation ② becomes: $\quad 6\left(\dfrac{x}{3}\right) + 6\left(\dfrac{y}{2}\right) = 6 \times 5$

$\qquad\qquad\qquad\quad$ i.e. $\qquad 2x + 3y = 30$

The simultaneous equations can now be solved as in Example 2, on the previous page.

Exercise 10.1

1. $2x + y = 8$
   $3x - y = 2$

2. $3x + y = 14$
   $2x - y = 6$

3. $3x + y = 7$
   $x + y = 5$

4. $4x + y = 17$
   $2x + y = 11$

5. $8x - 2y = 10$
   $5x - 2y = 4$

6. $3x - 2y = 8$
   $x + y = 6$

7. $3x + y = 13$
   $x - 2y = -5$

8. $x + 2y = 12$
   $3x - 5y = 3$

9. $3x - y = 3$
   $x + 3y = 11$

237

10. $2x - 3y = 14$
$2x - y = 10$

11. $3x + y = 5$
$5x - 4y = -3$

12. $2x - y = 12$
$3x + 2y = 11$

13. $x + 2y = 12$
$3x - 5y = 3$

14. $x - 3y = 1$
$4x + y = 30$

15. $3x + 7y = 20$
$x - 2y = -2$

16. $2x - 3y = 24$
$\dfrac{5x}{3} - \dfrac{y}{2} = 12$

17. $2x - y = 18$
$\dfrac{x}{3} - \dfrac{y}{4} = 2$

18. $x + y = 5$
$\dfrac{4x}{3} - \dfrac{y}{2} = -8$

19. $3x - 2y = 19$
$\dfrac{x}{3} + \dfrac{y}{2} = 5$

20. $9 = 2x - 3y$
$3y + x = 9$

21. $3x = y - 4$
$3y = 34 - 2x$

22. $\dfrac{x}{2} + \dfrac{y}{5} = 4$
$\dfrac{x}{4} + \dfrac{y}{2} = 6$

23. $4x + y = 17$
$\dfrac{x-3}{4} + \dfrac{y}{2} = \dfrac{5}{2}$

24. $3x + y = 19\dfrac{1}{2}$
$x - 2y = 3$

Section 10.2 Solving simultaneous equations graphically

Investigation:

Investigate the two lines: $2x - y = -4$ ... (A)
and $x + y = 1$ ... (B)

By finding two points on each line, draw a graph of each line.

For (A) let $x = 0$ and find the value of y.
Let $y = 0$ and find the value of x.

$\therefore$ (0, ?) and (?, 0) are two points on line A.

For (B) let $x = 0$ and find the value of y.
Let $y = 0$ and find the value of x.

$\therefore$ (0, ?) and (?, 0) are two points on line B.

Copy and scale the x-axis from -3 to $+3$ and the y-axis from -1 to $+5$ as above.

Plot the points belonging to line A and line B.

Draw the two lines and mark the only point common to both lines, **the point of intersection of the two lines**. Write down the coordinates of the point of intersection.

Now investigate the solution of the simultaneous equations

$x + y = 1$ and $2x - y = -4$ using the **elimination method**.

What conclusion can you make about the graphical method?

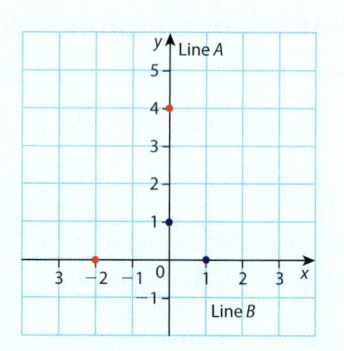

Chapter 10 Simultaneous equations

From the 'investigation' on the previous page, you will have discovered that two simultaneous equations may be solved by drawing graphs of the two equations (lines) and then reading the x-value and y-value of their point of intersection. Graphical methods are repeated in more detail in chapter 11.

Using simultaneous equations to solve problems

Simultaneous equations are particularly useful for solving problems which have two unknowns. Generally, two different pieces of information enable us to write down two equations.
The following examples illustrate this procedure.

> **Example 1**
>
> The sum of two numbers is 19.
> When twice the second number is taken from three times the first number, the result is 22.
> Find the two numbers.
>
> Let x be the first number and y be the second number.
>
> Equation ①: $\quad x + y = 19$
> Equation ②: $\quad 3x - 2y = 22$
>
> Equation ① × 2: $\quad 2x + 2y = 38$
> Equation ②: $\quad \underline{3x - 2y = 22}$
> Add: $\quad\quad\quad\quad\; 5x \quad\quad = 60$
> $\quad\quad\quad\quad\quad\;\; x \quad\quad = 12$
>
> Substituting 12 for x in equation ①, we get: $\quad 12 + y = 19$
> $\quad\quad\quad\quad\quad\quad\quad\quad\quad\quad\quad\quad\quad\quad\quad\quad\quad\quad y = 19 - 12$
> $\quad\quad\quad\quad\quad\quad\quad\quad\quad\quad\quad\quad\quad\quad\quad\quad\quad\quad y = 7$
>
> The two numbers are 12 and 7.

> **Example 2**
>
> Tickets to a movie cost €8 or €10.
> If 300 tickets were sold and the total amount of money collected was €2640, how many of each type of ticket were sold?
>
> Let x = number of €8 tickets sold, and
> $\quad\;\; y$ = number of €10 tickets sold.
>
> ① Total number of tickets: $\quad\quad x + y = 300$
> ② Total amount of money: $\quad 8x + 10y = 2640$
>
> ① × 8: $\quad\quad\quad\quad\quad\quad\quad\quad\;\, 8x + 8y = 2400$
> ②: $\quad\quad\quad\quad\quad\quad\quad\quad\quad\; 8x + 10y = 2640$
> Subtract: $\quad\quad\quad\quad\quad\quad\quad\quad\;\; -2y = -240$
> $\quad\quad\quad\quad\quad\quad \Rightarrow \quad\quad\quad\quad 2y = 240$
> $\quad\quad\quad\quad\quad\quad \Rightarrow \quad\quad\quad\quad\; y = 120$

239

Text & Tests 2 Higher Level

> Substituting 120 for *y* in equation ①, we get:
>
> $$x + y = 300$$
> $$y = 120: \quad x + 120 = 300$$
> $$x = 180$$
>
> ∴ $x = 180$ and $y = 120$
>
> ∴ 180 €8 tickets and 120 €10 tickets were sold.

Exercise 10.2

1. The given diagram shows the graphs of the lines $x - y = 1$ and $x + 2y = 4$.

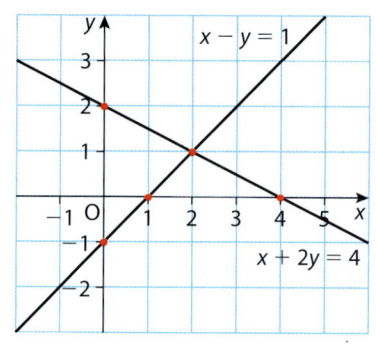

   (i) Write down the point of intersection of the two lines.
   (ii) Solve the simultaneous equations $x - y = 1$ and $x + 2y = 4$.
   (iii) Explain the connection between your answers in (ii) to the answer you found in (i) above.

2. Graph the lines $2x - y = 1$ and $x - y = -1$.
   Hence write down the point of intersection of the two lines.

3. Solve these simultaneous equations by drawing graphs:
   (i) $2x - y = -1$
       $x - y = 1$
   (ii) $2x - y = 1$
       $x - y = -2$

4. Use graphs to solve each pair of simultaneous equations.
   (i) $x + y = 6$
       $x - y = 2$
       Draw axes for *x* and *y* from −3 to 7.
   (ii) $y + 2x = 5$
       $x - y = 1$
       Draw axes for *x* and *y* from −2 to 6.

   Check each solution by substituting into the equations.

Chapter 10 Simultaneous equations

5. Use the given graphs to solve each pair of simultaneous equations.
   (i) $x + y = 10$
       $y - 2x = 1$
   (ii) $2x + 5y = 17$
        $y - 2x = 1$
   (iii) $x + y = 10$
         $2x + 5y = 17$

   Check each solution by substituting into the equations.

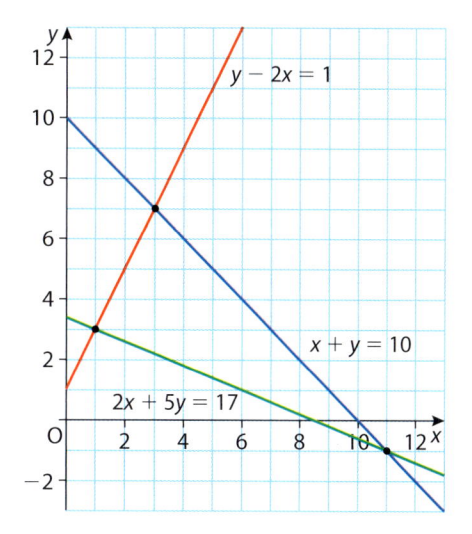

6. (i) Use the graphs to solve each pair of simultaneous equations.
   (a) $2x - y = -4$ (b) $2x - y = -1$
       $x + y = 4$ $x + y = 4$

   Check each solution by substituting into the equations.

   (ii) How do you know there is no solution to the following pair of simultaneous equations?
        $2x - y = -4$
        $2x - y = -1$

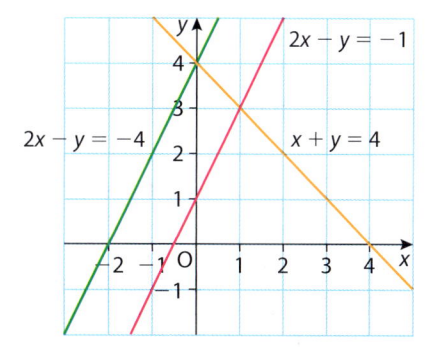

7. The sum of two numbers is 9. If twice the first number is added to three times the second, the answer is 15. Find the two numbers.

8. The difference of two numbers is 7. When three times the smaller number is taken from twice the larger, the result is 11. Find the two numbers.

9. Examine the rectangle shown and write down two equations in x and y.

   Now solve these equations to find the value of x and the value of y.

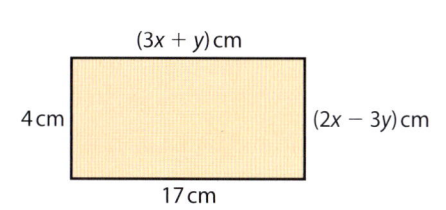

   (Rectangle: $(3x + y)$ cm by 4 cm; other sides 17 cm and $(2x - 3y)$ cm)

10. Three nuts and six bolts have a combined weight of 72 g. Four nuts and five bolts have a combined weight of 66 g. Find the combined weight of one nut and one bolt.

Text & Tests 2 Higher Level

11. Three chocolate bars and four chocolate eggs weigh 465 grams.
Three chocolate bars and two chocolate eggs weigh 315 grams.

  (i) Which of these pairs of equations is correct for the chocolate bars and eggs?

  A
  $3b + 2e = 465$
  $3b + 4e = 315$

  B
  $b + 4e = 465$
  $b + 2e = 315$

  C
  $3b + 4e = 465$
  $3b + 2e = 315$

  (ii) Solve the pair of simultaneous equations that is correct to find the values of b and e.

12. A bag contains 34 coins, all of them either 5c or 10c coins. If the value of the money in the bag is €2.40, find how many of each coin the bag contains.
[Hint: Convert €2.40 to cents.]

13. Two small mugs and one large mug weigh 758 grams.
Four small mugs and three large mugs weigh 1882 grams.

The weight of a small mug is s grams and the weight of a large mug is l grams.

Write down two equations connecting s and l.
Solve these simultaneous equations to find the weight of each size of mug.

14. In the Venn diagram on the right, the numbers in the brackets represent the number of elements in each region.
If $\#(U) = 50$ and $\#(B) = 16$, find the value of x and the value of y.

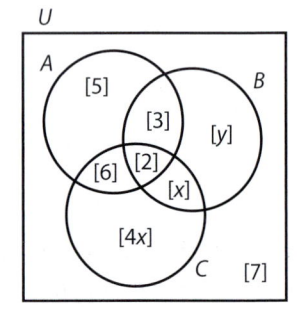

15. The diagram shows a rectangle.
All sides are measured in centimetres.

  (i) Write down a pair of simultaneous equations in a and b.

  (ii) Solve your pair of simultaneous equations to find a and b.

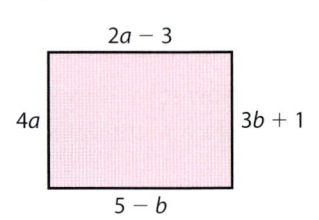

Chapter 10 Simultaneous equations

16. A car-hire company charges €x per day to hire a car and then adds a charge of €y for each kilometre travelled.

John hires a car for 2 days and travels 250 km. He is charged €200.

Emer hires a car for 5 days and travels 620 km. She is charged €498.

Write two equations in x and y and solve them to find the charge per day and the charge for each kilometre.

17. The sum of the ages of a father and a son is 52 years.

Eight years ago, the father was eight times as old as his son.

If the father is now x years and the son y years of age, write two equations and solve them to find the values of x and y.

18. A person has €60 made up of €1 and 50 cent coins.

He has 78 coins altogether.

If the number of €1 coins is x and the number of 50 cent coins is y, write down two equations in x and y to represent this information.

Solve the equations to find the values of x and y.

19. In this puzzle, each different symbol stands for a number.
What does each symbol stand for?

■ + ♥ + ■ + ♥ + ♥ = 68
♥ + ■ + ♦ + ♦ = 28
♥ + ■ + ■ = 28

20. In the Venn Diagram on the right,

    U = {students in a third-level college}
    F = {students who study French}
    G = {students who study Geography}
    H = {students who study History}.

The numbers of students in the various subsets are shown.

For example, 7 students study French and Geography but not History, and y students study none of these subjects.

Given that #(U) = 75 and #(F) = 46, calculate the value of x and the value of y.

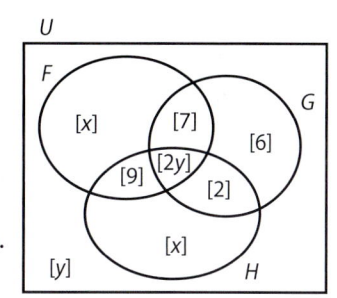

Text & Tests 2 Higher Level

Test yourself 10

1. Solve these simultaneous equations:
   $x + 2y = 13$
   $3x - 5y = 6$

2. The weight of a blue brick is b grams.
   The weight of a red brick is r grams.

   4 blue bricks and 3 red bricks weigh 58 grams.
   5 blue bricks and 6 red bricks weigh 86 grams.

   (i) Write two equations to represent these diagrams.
   (ii) Solve the equations to find the weight of a blue brick and the weight of a red brick.
   (iii) Find the total weight of 3 blue bricks and 6 red bricks.

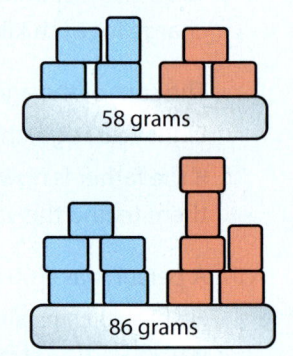

3. Solve the simultaneous equations:
   $3x = 5y + 13$
   $2x + 5y = -8$

4. ABC is an equilateral triangle.
   All lengths are in centimetres.
   (i) Form two simultaneous equations and solve them to find the value of x and the value of y.
   (ii) Now find the length of the side of the triangle.

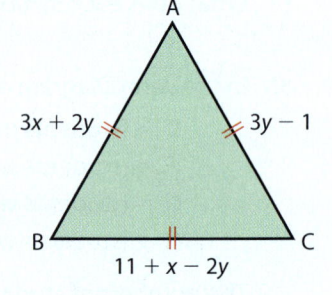

   Sides: $3x + 2y$, $3y - 1$, $11 + x - 2y$

5. Solve these simultaneous equations:
   $2x + 3y = 17$
   $3x - 2y = 6$

6. The graphs of three lines are shown opposite:
   (i) Use the graph to find the solution of the simultaneous equations $x + 2y = 12$ and $x + y = 5$.
   (ii) Use the graph to write down two simultaneous equations which have the solution $x = 3, y = 2$.

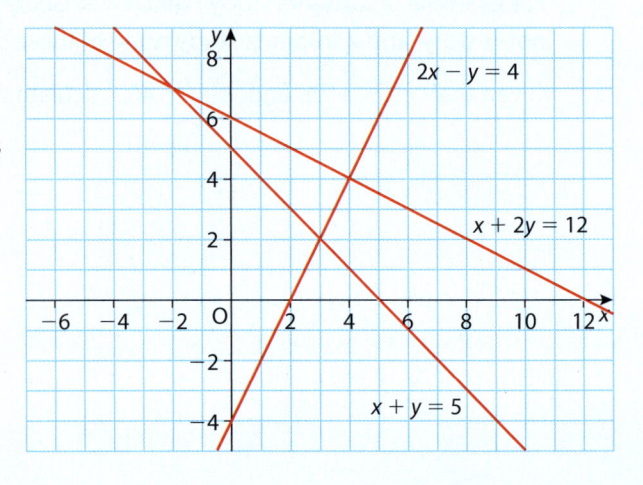

   Lines shown: $2x - y = 4$, $x + 2y = 12$, $x + y = 5$

Chapter 10 Simultaneous equations

7. A woman is paid €x per hour for a 30-hour week and is paid €y for each hour overtime worked. In a particular week, she worked 35 hours and received €660. The following week, she worked 42 hours and received €828.
   Write two equations in x and y and solve them to find their values.

8. Solve the simultaneous equations:
   $$2x - y = 18$$
   $$\frac{x}{3} - \frac{y}{4} = 2$$

9. The cost €C of hiring a car for n days is given by the formula $C = a + bn$, where $a, b \in N$. It costs €420 for 5 days and €870 for 11 days to hire a car.
   Write two equations in a and b and solve them to find their values.
   Hence find the cost of hiring a car for 15 days.

10. At what point do the lines $2x + 3y = 1$ and $5x - 2y = 12$ intersect?

11. Solve the simultaneous equations:
    $$3x = 22 + 2y$$
    $$5y = 2x$$

12. The shape ABCD is a parallelogram. Write two equations in x and y and solve them to find their values.

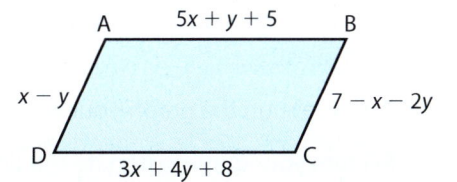

    Sides: A to B: $5x + y + 5$; B to C: $7 - x - 2y$; D to C: $3x + 4y + 8$; A to D: $x - y$

13. A mother is x years old, her son is y years old and the sum of their ages is 58 years. Five years ago, the mother was five times as old as the son.
    Write two equations in x and y and solve them to find the age of the mother and the age of the son.

14. When the numerator of a certain fraction is increased by 3 and the denominator increased by 1, its value changes to 1¼, but when the numerator is increased by 4 and the denominator is decreased by 1½, its value is equal to 4.
    Find the original fraction.

15. A rectangular piece of paper has a perimeter of 92 cm. When it is folded in half, along the shorter line of symmetry, it now has a perimeter of 62 cm.
    What are the dimensions of the paper?
    Compare your method to solve this problem with the methods used by different students in your class.

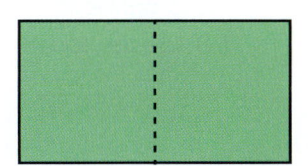

245

Assignment:

The rate at which cylindrical candles burn depends on the diameter of the candle.
Thinner candles burn more quickly than fatter ones.

Consider the two candles shown.

The first candle is 400 mm long and burns at a rate of 5 mm per hour.

The second candle is 490 mm long and burns at a rate of 8 mm per hour.

A: Explain why; $h_1 = 400 - 5t$, is the height, in millimetres, of the first candle after t hours.

B: Write down an equation for the height, in millimetres, of the second candle after t hours.

C: Use both equations to find out how long it will take each candle to 'burn out'.

D: Graph both equations on the same set of axes.

E: Indicate on the graph your answers to C.

F: From your graph, estimate the time at which both candles have the same height.

G: Using simultaneous equations, verify your answer to F.

H: If you want both candles to 'go out' together:
 (i) Which candle should you light first?
 (ii) How long after the first would you light the second one?
 (iii) From your graph, estimate the height of the first candle when the second candle is lit.
 (iv) Use the equation in A to verify your answer to (iii).

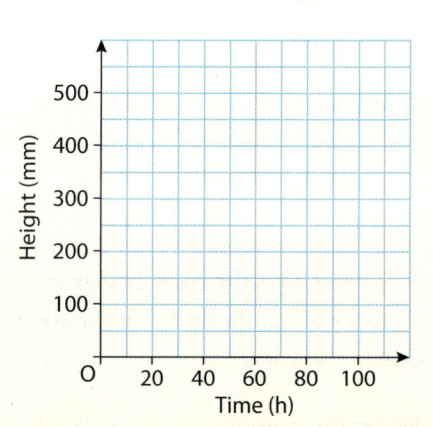

Coordinate Geometry – The Line

chapter 11

From first year, you will recall how to:

- use a coordinated plane,
- locate the midpoint of a line segment,
- find the slope of a line segment,
- identify a positive or negative slope.

In this chapter, you will learn to:

- calculate the distance between two points,
- identify parallel and perpendicular lines using their slopes,
- create the equation of a line,
- find the slope of a line from its equation,
- name the y-intercept of a line from its equation,
- draw the graph of a line segment,
- locate the point of intersection between two lines,
- verify that a point in on a line,
- interpret real life graphs including their rates of change.

Section 11.1 Distance and mid-point formulae

When two points are plotted in the coordinated plane, we use formulae to find (i) the distance between the points and (ii) the mid-point between them.

1. Distance between two points

To find the distance between the points $A(x_1, y_1)$ and $B(x_2, y_2)$ a right-angled triangle is drawn as shown in the diagram.
From the diagram, $|BC| = y_2 - y_1$ and $|AC| = x_2 - x_1$.

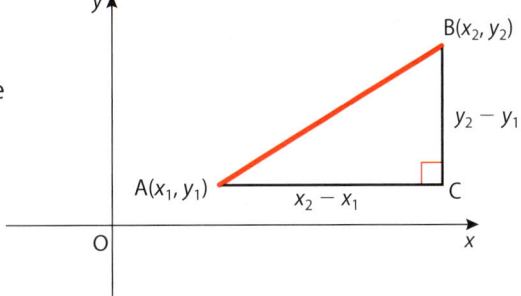

Using the Theorem of Pythagoras:
$$|AB|^2 = |AC|^2 + |BC|^2$$
$$= (x_2 - x_1)^2 + (y_2 - y_1)^2$$
$$\therefore \quad |AB| = \sqrt{(x_2 - x_1)^2 + (y_2 - y_1)^2}$$

The distance between $A(x_1, y_1)$ and $B(x_2, y_2)$ is
$$|AB| = \sqrt{(x_2 - x_1)^2 + (y_2 - y_1)^2}$$

2. The midpoint of a line segment

In *Test & Tests 1*, we learned that the mid-point of any line segment is half-way between the *x*-coordinates and half-way between the *y*-coordinates of the end-points of the line segment.

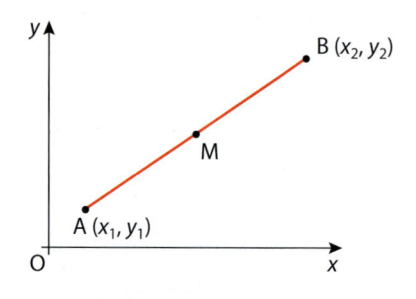

> The midpoint, M, of the line segment joining $A(x_1, y_1)$ and $B(x_2, y_2)$ is
> $$\left(\frac{x_1 + x_2}{2}, \frac{y_1 + y_2}{2}\right)$$

Example 1

If $A(-1, 3)$ and $B(5, 7)$ are two points in the plane, find

(i) $|AB|$ (ii) the midpoint of $[AB]$.

(i) $|AB| = \sqrt{(x_2 - x_1)^2 + (y_2 - y_1)^2}$
$= \sqrt{(5 - (-1))^2 + (7 - 3)^2}$
$= \sqrt{36 + 16}$
$= \sqrt{52}$

$A(-1, 3) \quad\quad B(5, 7)$
$\downarrow \quad\quad\quad\quad \downarrow$
$(x_1, y_1) \quad\quad (x_2, y_2)$

(ii) Midpoint of $[AB] = \left(\dfrac{x_1 + x_2}{2}, \dfrac{y_1 + y_2}{2}\right)$
$= \left(\dfrac{-1 + 5}{2}, \dfrac{3 + 7}{2}\right)$
$= (2, 5)$

Exercise 11.1

1. Write down the coordinates of each of the points marked in the coordinated plane on the right:

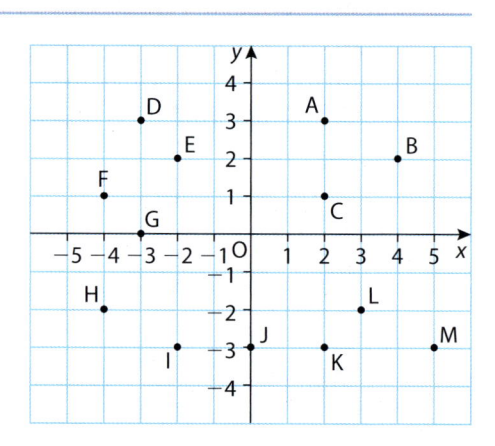

Chapter 11 Coordinate Geometry – The Line

2. Draw a coordinated plane from -5 to 5 on the *x*-axis and from -4 to 4 on the *y*-axis. Now plot each of the following points:
   (i) A(3, 4)   (ii) B(−1, 3)   (iii) C(4, −3)   (iv) D(−4, −3)   (v) E(1, −3)

3. The four quadrants are shown on the right. In which quadrant does each of the following points lie?
   (i) (3, 5)
   (ii) (−2, −3)
   (iii) (1, −4)
   (iv) (−3, 1)
   (v) (3, −3)
   (vi) (−1, −3).

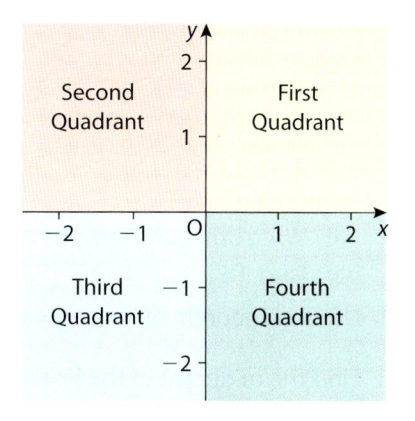

4. On which axis does each of the following points lie?
   (i) (4, 0)   (ii) (−3, 0)   (iii) (0, 4)   (iv) (0, −3)   (v) (0, 0).

5. The points A, B, C and D are shown.
   Find (i) |AB|
   (ii) |AC|
   (iii) |AD|.
   Is |DC| = |BC|?

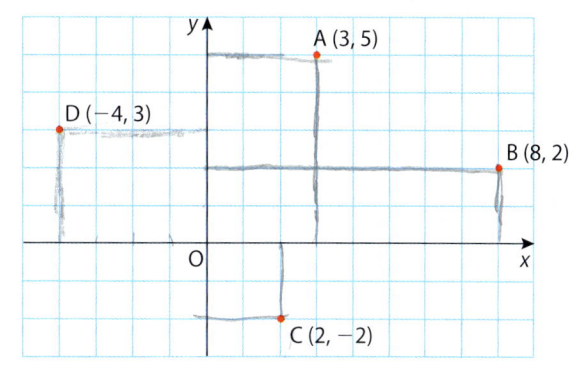

6. Find the distance between each of the following pairs of points:
   (i) (2, 1) and (3, 4)
   (ii) (1, 5) and (2, 3)
   (iii) (−1, 4) and (2, 6)
   (iv) (3, −2) and (−5, 3)
   (v) (−6, −1) and (1, −3)
   (vi) (4, −2) and (0, −5)

7. A(1, 1), B(3, 6) and C(5, 1) are the vertices of a triangle. Show that |AB| = |BC|.

8. The centre of a circle is (−3, 1) and (4, 3) is a point on the circle. Find the length of the radius of the circle.

9. The points A(2, 1), B(6, 1), C(5, −2) and D(1, −2) are the vertices of a parallelogram. Plot the parallelogram on a coordinated plane.
   Find   (i) |AC| (ii) |BD|.
   Are the diagonals equal in length?

Text & Tests 2 Higher Level

10. The given diagram shows the points D, E and F.

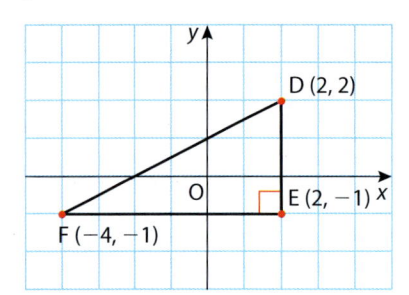

(i) Write down the lengths of [FE] and [ED].
(ii) Find |DF|.
Use the Theorem of Pythagoras to show that the triangle DEF is right-angled.

11. Find the midpoint of the line segment joining these points:
    (i) (2, 4) and (6, 2) (ii) (2, 4) and (0, 2) (iii) (2, −1) and (4, 3)
    (iv) (−2, 4) and (4, −2) (v) (2, −3) and (0, −1) (vi) (−3, 4) and (−1, −4).

12. Find the midpoint of the line segment joining (−3, 4) and (3, 7).
    On which axis does the midpoint lie?

13. The points (−2, 3) and (6, 5) are the end points of the diameter of a circle.
    Find the coordinates of the centre of the circle.

14. A(4, 3), B(1, −3), C(−2, −2) and D(1, 4) are the vertices of a parallelogram.
    Draw a sketch of this parallelogram.
    Find the midpoint of [AC].
    Verify that the midpoint of [AC] is also the midpoint of [BD].

15. Find M, the midpoint of the line segment joining A(−3, 4) and B(1, −6).
    Now show that |AM| = |MB|.

16. The given diagram shows the points
    A(1, 2), M(3, 5) and B.
    If M is the midpoint of [AB], find by inspection
    the coordinates of the point B.

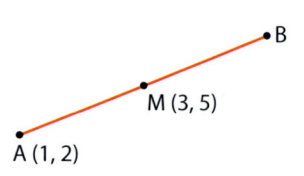

17. A(5, 2), and B(x_1, y_1) are two points.
    If M(2, 4) is the midpoint of [AB], find the coordinates of B.

Chapter 11 Coordinate Geometry – The Line

Section 11.2 The slope of a line

The slope of the line AB is defined as

$$\frac{\text{vertical change}}{\text{horizontal change}} \quad \text{or} \quad \frac{\text{rise}}{\text{run}}$$

The slope of AB $= \frac{3}{6} = \frac{1}{2}$.

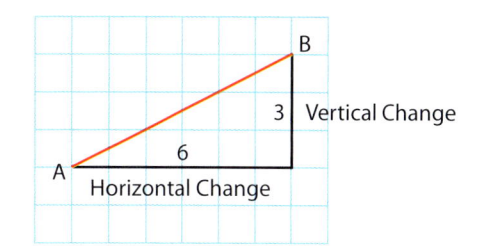

In the diagram on the right, the slope of AB is found by getting the

$$\frac{\text{vertical change}}{\text{horizontal change}} = \frac{y_2 - y_1}{x_2 - x_1}$$

Thus the slope, m, of AB is $= \frac{y_2 - y_1}{x_2 - x_1}$.

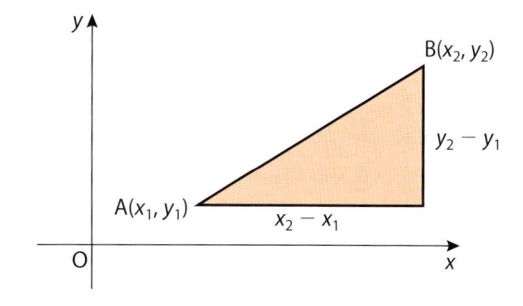

> The slope, m, of the line passing through (x_1, y_1) and (x_2, y_2) is
> $$m = \frac{y_2 - y_1}{x_2 - x_1}$$

Example 1

If $A = (3, -1)$ and $B = (5, 2)$, find the slope of the line AB.

$$m = \frac{y_2 - y_1}{x_2 - x_1}$$

$(3, -1) \quad (5, 2)$
$\downarrow \quad \quad \downarrow$
$(x_1, y_1) \quad (x_2, y_2)$

$$= \frac{2 + 1}{5 - 3} = \frac{3}{2}$$

The slope of AB $= \frac{3}{2}$.

Investigation:

A: Investigate any slope in the school grounds or on a driveway at home.

Use a long measuring tape (or string) and a small level.

Measure the distance 'ℓ' which is the **Run**, then measure 'h', the **Rise**.

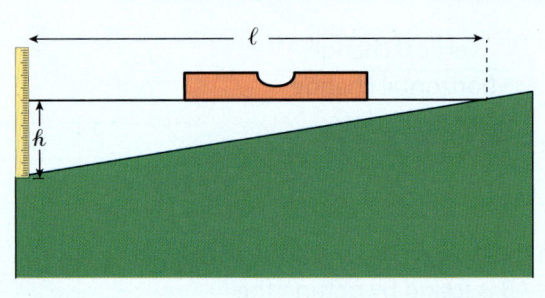

Make sure that the string or tape is kept horizontal using the level and that the metre-stick is vertical.

The slope is calculated from, $m = \dfrac{Rise}{Run}$.

Compare your answers with other groups.

Investigate why a hill on a road may have a negative and positive slope at the same time.

Note: the slope of a line (road) is often called the *gradient* of the line (road).

B: Using a map with contour lines, investigate how the spacing of the lines gives a measure of the slope (gradient) of the map at that point.

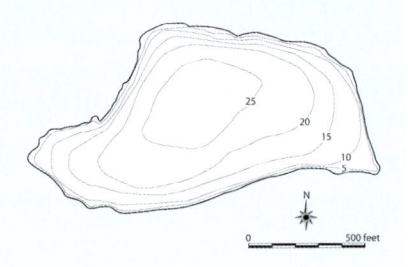

Positive and negative slopes

As we go from left to right, the slope is positive if the line is rising and the slope is negative if the line is falling.

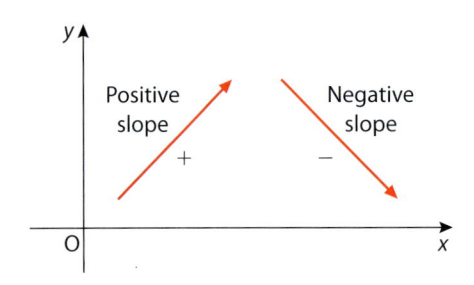

Chapter 11 Coordinate Geometry – The Line

Parallel lines

The lines a and b in the given diagram both have the slope $\frac{3}{2}$.

These lines are **parallel**.

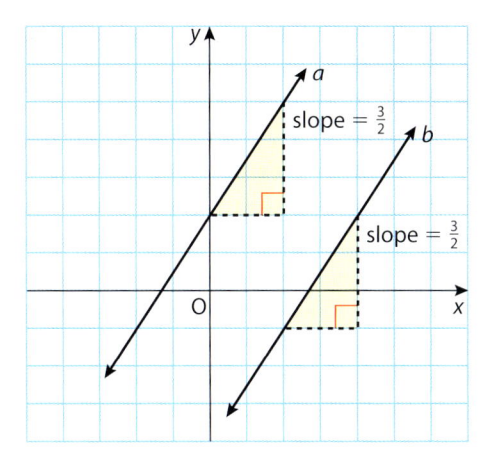

Parallel lines have equal slopes.

Perpendicular lines

The given lines a and b are perpendicular.

The slope of $a = \frac{3}{2}$.

The slope of $b = -\frac{2}{3}$.

Notice that one slope is minus the reciprocal of the other.

Notice also that the product of the two slopes is -1, i.e.,

$$-\frac{2}{3} \times \frac{3}{2} = -1$$

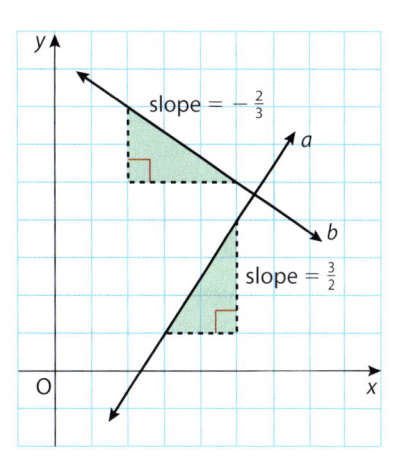

If two lines are perpendicular, the product of their slopes is -1, i.e.,
$$m_1 \times m_2 = -1$$

253

Text & Tests 2 Higher Level

Example 2

A(−1, 0), B(3, 2), C(−1, 4) and D(2, −2) are four points in the plane.
Show that AB is perpendicular to CD.

Let m_1 be the slope of AB and m_2 be the slope of CD.

$$A(-1, 0) \quad B(3, 2) \qquad\qquad C(-1, 4) \quad D(2, -2)$$
$$\downarrow \qquad\qquad \downarrow \qquad\qquad\qquad \downarrow \qquad\qquad \downarrow$$
$$(x_1, y_1) \quad (x_2, y_2) \qquad\qquad (x_1, y_1) \quad (x_2, y_2)$$

$$m_1 = \frac{y_2 - y_1}{x_2 - x_1} \qquad\qquad m_2 = \frac{y_2 - y_1}{x_2 - x_1}$$

$$= \frac{2 - 0}{3 + 1} \qquad\qquad\qquad = \frac{-2 - 4}{2 + 1}$$

$$= \frac{2}{4} = \frac{1}{2} \qquad\qquad\qquad = \frac{-6}{3} = -2$$

$$m_1 \times m_2 = \frac{1}{2} \times (-2)$$
$$= -1$$

AB is perpendicular to CD as the product of the slopes is −1.

Exercise 11.2

1. The diagram shows four lines a, b, c and d.

   (i) Which lines have positive slopes?
   (ii) Which lines have negative slopes?

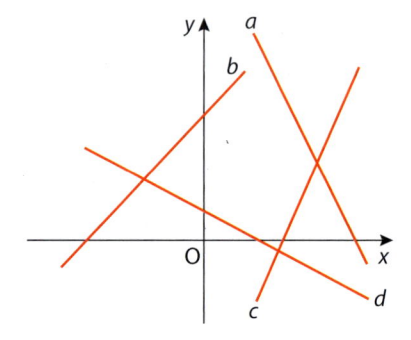

2. Write down the slope of each of the lines shown on the grid below:

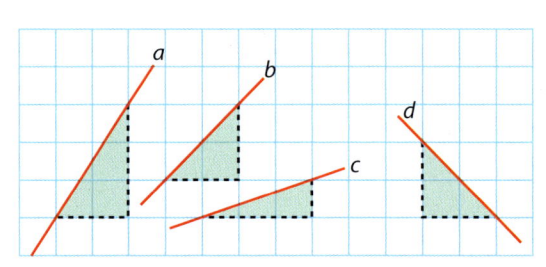

Chapter 11 Coordinate Geometry – The Line

3. Three lines *a*, *b* and *c* are drawn on the grids below:

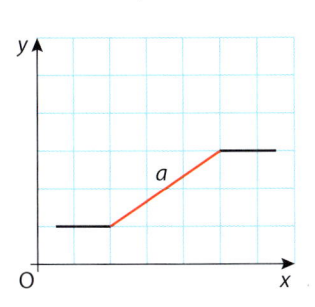

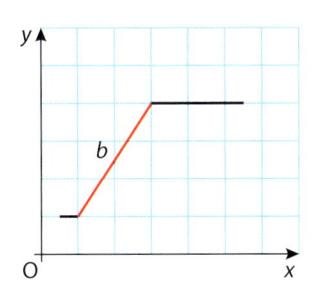

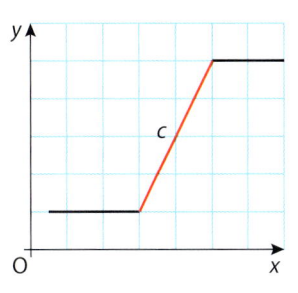

   (i) Which line has a slope of $\frac{3}{2}$?
   (ii) What is the slope of line *a*?
   (iii) What is the slope of line *c*?

4. Why is the slope of the given line negative?
Use the grid to work out the slope of the line.

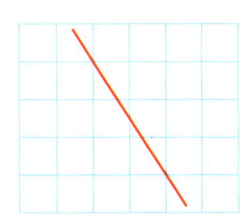

5. Find the slope of the line AB in each of the following:
   (i) A(3, 1) and B(5, 3)
   (ii) A(−1, 2) and B(3, −4)
   (iii) A(−1, −3) and B(0, 5)
   (iv) A(3, 0) and B(−1, −4)

6. Show that the line passing through A(−1, −2) and B(3, 0) has the same slope as the line passing through C(2, 3) and D(−2, 1).
What can you say about the lines AB and CD?

7. The line ℓ contains the points (1, 1) and (2, 4).
The line *m* contains the points (4, 1) and (3, −2).
Investigate if ℓ is parallel to *m*.

8. A(−2, −4), B(5, −1), C(6, 4) and D(−1, 1) are the vertices of a quadrilateral.
Draw a rough sketch of the figure.
Now verify that AB∥CD and AD∥BC.

9. The given diagram shows three lines *a*, *b*, and *c*.
Match the lines with these slopes:
    2, $\frac{1}{2}$,   1.

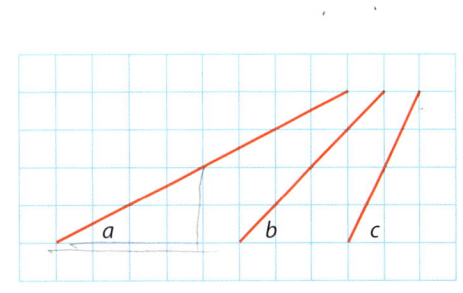

255

Text & Tests 2 Higher Level

10. The slope of a line ℓ is $\frac{3}{4}$.
    (i) Write down the slope of a line m if m is parallel to ℓ.
    (ii) Write down the slope of a line n if n is perpendicular to ℓ.

11. The slopes of five lines are given below.
    Write down the slope of any line that is perpendicular to each of these lines:
    (i) $\frac{2}{3}$ (ii) $\frac{4}{5}$ (iii) $-\frac{3}{4}$ (iv) $-\frac{2}{5}$ (v) $-\frac{1}{2}$

12. The line m contains the points $(3, -1)$ and $(4, -2)$.
    (i) Find the slope of any line parallel to m.
    (ii) Find the slope of any line perpendicular to m.

13. $A(-1, 1)$, $B(1, 3)$, $C(6, 2)$ and $D(4, 4)$ are four points in the plane.
    Find the slope of (i) AB (ii) CD. Verify that AB $\perp$ CD.

14. If the slope of the line through the points $(3, 2)$ and $(8, k)$ is $\frac{3}{5}$, find the value of k.

15. The slope of the line through $(3, -2)$ and $(1, k)$ is $\frac{1}{3}$. Find the value of k.

16. The line ℓ contains the points $(-2, 0)$ and $(4, 3)$.
    The line m contains the points $(1, -1)$ and $(k, 1)$.
    (i) Find the slope of ℓ.
    (ii) Find, in terms of k, the slope of m.
    (iii) If $\ell \| m$, find the value of k.

17. A county council uses the rule that the gradient of a wheelchair ramp must not be above 0.08.
    Which of these ramps would be suitable for wheelchairs?

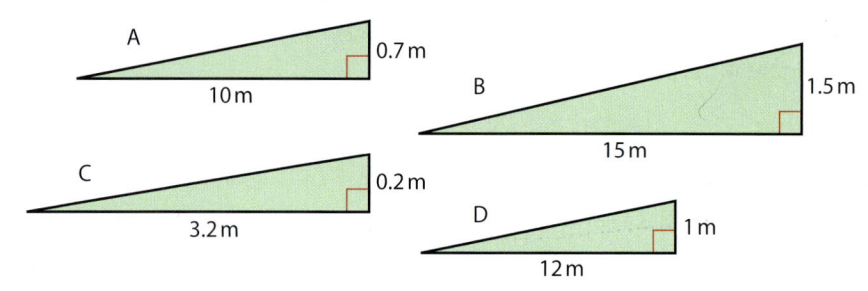

Chapter 11 Coordinate Geometry – The Line

Investigation:

Question: Is the slope of a curve constant or does it change?
Investigate the slope of a curve by using the triangles given.

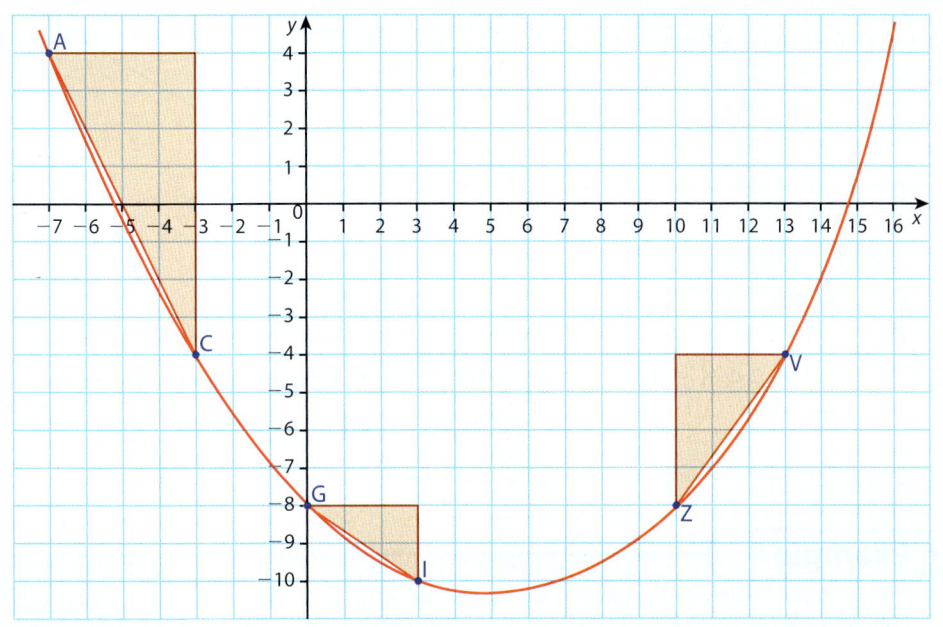

Slope$_{AC}$ =
Slope$_{GI}$ =
Slope$_{ZV}$ =

Where on this curve is the slope 0?

Sean said that since -3 was less than 3, so a slope of -3 was less than a slope of 3.
Jessica said that he was wrong.
Who was correct and why?

Section 11.3 The equation of a line

In the given line ℓ, the sum of the x and y values of each point is 5, e.g. $2 + 3 = 5$.

For any point (x, y) on this line;

$x + y = 5$.

$x + y = 5$ is called the **equation of a line**, or a **linear equation**.

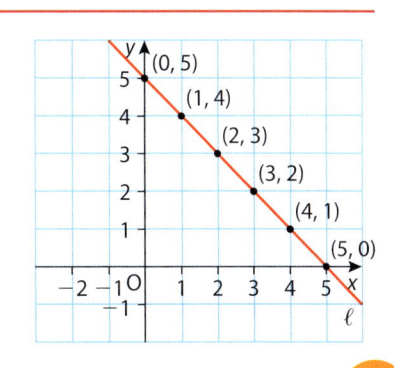

257

The equation was found by observing the relationship between the *x* and *y* values of each point and discovering that for all the points, $x + y = 5$.

We will now consider the figure on the right.

The line ℓ contains the fixed point (x_1, y_1) and has slope *m*.

Let (x, y) be **any** other point on ℓ.

From the diagram, the slope of ℓ is $\dfrac{y - y_1}{x - x_1} = m$.

If we multiply both sides by $(x - x_1)$ we get,

$y - y_1 = m(x - x_1)$

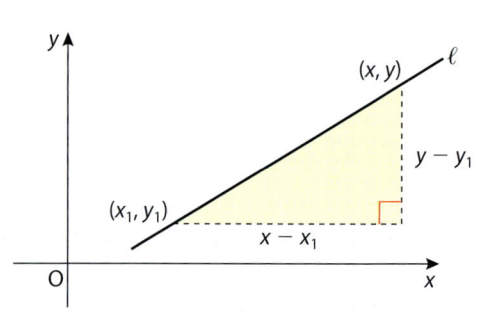

> The equation of the line through (x_1, y_1), with slope *m*, is found by using
> $$y - y_1 = m(x - x_1)$$

Example 1

Find the equation of the line containing the point $(-3, 2)$ and whose slope is $\tfrac{2}{3}$.

Equation of the line is: $\quad y - y_1 = m(x - x_1) \qquad\qquad m = \tfrac{2}{3}$

$\qquad\qquad\qquad\qquad y - 2 = \tfrac{2}{3}(x + 3) \qquad\qquad (x_1, y_1) = (-3, 2)$

Multiply each term by 3: $\quad 3y - 6 = 2(x + 3)$

$\qquad\qquad\qquad\qquad\qquad 3y - 6 = 2x + 6$

$\qquad\qquad\qquad\qquad\qquad 2x - 3y + 12 = 0$

∴ the equation of the line is: $\quad 2x - 3y + 12 = 0$

Equation of a line when given two points on the line

To find the equation of a line containing two points, we first find the slope of the line using the formula $\dfrac{y_2 - y_1}{x_2 - x_1}$.

We then use the formula $y - y_1 = m(x - x_1)$ to find the equation of the line.

You may then use either of the two points as (x_1, y_1).

Chapter 11 Coordinate Geometry – The Line

> **Example 2**
>
> Find the equation of the line containing the points $(-2, 3)$ and $(3, 1)$.
>
> Slope of line: $m = \dfrac{y_2 - y_1}{x_2 - x_1}$
>
> $\qquad\qquad\quad = \dfrac{1 - 3}{3 + 2} = \dfrac{-2}{5}$
>
> $\qquad\qquad(-2, 3) \qquad (3, 1)$
> $\qquad\qquad\;\downarrow \qquad\qquad \downarrow$
> $\qquad\qquad(x_1, y_1) \quad\; (x_2, y_2)$
>
> We now use the slope $-\dfrac{2}{5}$ and the point $(-2, 3)$ …you may use either of the 2 points
>
> Equation of line: $\quad y - y_1 = m(x - x_1)$
>
> $\qquad\qquad\qquad\quad y - 3 = -\dfrac{2}{5}(x + 2)$
>
> $\qquad\qquad\qquad 5y - 15 = -2(x + 2) \qquad$ …multiply each term by 5
>
> $\qquad\qquad\qquad 5y - 15 = -2x - 4$
>
> $\Rightarrow \quad 2x + 5y - 11 = 0\;$ is the equation of the line.

Exercise 11.3

1. Find the equations of the following lines, given the slope and a point on the line in each case:
   (i) slope $= 2$; point $= (3, 4)$
   (ii) slope $= 4$; point $= (1, 5)$
   (iii) slope $= -5$; point $= (-3, -2)$
   (iv) slope $= \frac{2}{3}$; point $= (3, -1)$.

2. Find the equations of the following lines, given the slope and a point on the line in each case:
   (i) slope $= \frac{3}{4}$; point $= (1, -4)$
   (ii) slope $= \frac{3}{5}$; point $= (-4, 2)$.

3. Find the equation of the line through $(-2, 3)$ with slope
   (i) 4
   (ii) -2
   (iii) $\frac{3}{4}$
   (iv) $-\frac{2}{3}$

4. Find the equation of the line through $(0, 0)$ and whose slope is -3.

5. Find the equation of the line through $(0, 0)$ and whose slope is
   (i) 3
   (ii) -5
   (iii) $\frac{1}{3}$
   (iv) $-\frac{3}{2}$
   What do you notice about the equation of each of these lines?

6. Find the slope of the line through $A(3, -4)$ and $B(1, 2)$.
   Hence find the equation of the line AB.

7. Find the equations of the lines through the following pairs of points:
   (i) $(2, 3)$ and $(4, 6)$
   (ii) $(-1, 2)$ and $(2, -4)$
   (iii) $(-5, 1)$ and $(1, 0)$
   (iv) $(-2, 3)$ and $(3, -1)$

Text & Tests 2 Higher Level

8. Find the equation of the line through $(-2, 3)$ and the midpoint of the line segment joining $(1, -3)$ and $(3, -1)$.

9. Using any two points on each line, find the slopes of the lines shown below. Hence find the equation of each line.

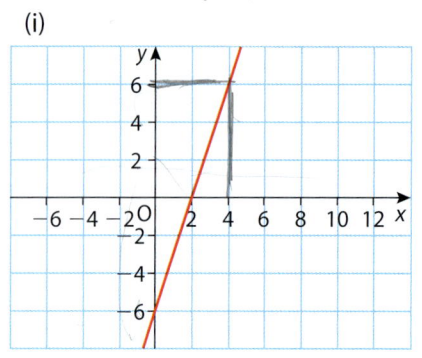

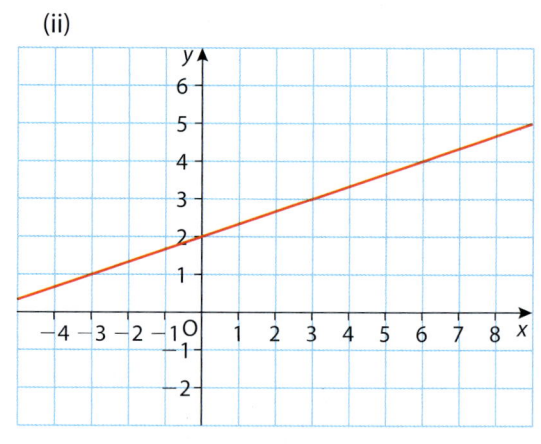

(i)

(ii)

Section 11.4 The equation $y = mx + c$

Consider the two parallel lines shown on the right.
The slope of each line is 2.
Notice that **2** is the coefficient of x in each line.
Each line is in the form $y = mx + c$.
m represents the slope of the line.

The line $y = 2x + 4$ intersects the y-axis at $(0, 4)$
The line $y = 2x - 3$ intersects the y-axis at $(0, -3)$

From these two examples we can see that if the equation of a line is in the form

$y = mx + c$, then

(i) the slope of the line is m
(ii) the line intersects the y-axis at $(0, c)$.

The point $(0, c)$ is called the **y-intercept**.

If a line is in the form $ax + by + c = 0$, changing the equation to the form $y = mx + c$, we can find the slope, m and the y-intercept $(0, c)$ easily.

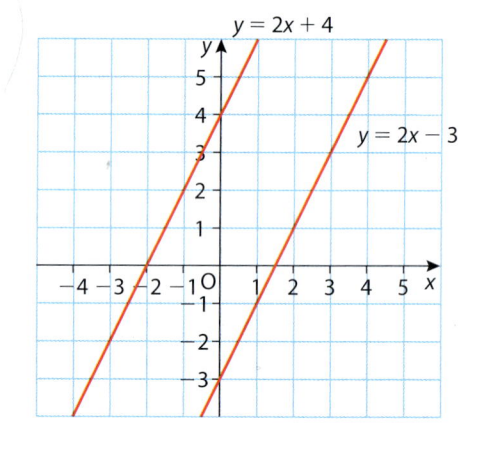

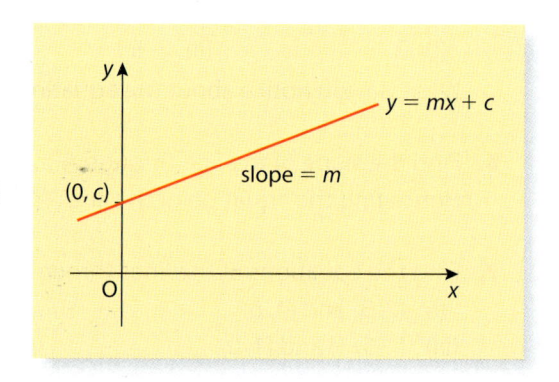

Chapter 11 Coordinate Geometry – The Line

Example 1

Find the slope of the line $3x - 2y - 9 = 0$.

We write the equation in the form $y = mx + c$.

$$3x - 2y - 9 = 0$$
$$\Rightarrow -2y = -3x + 9 \quad \text{…leave the } y \text{ term only on left-hand side}$$
$$\Rightarrow 2y = 3x - 9 \quad \text{…multiply each term by } -1$$
$$\Rightarrow y = \frac{3}{2}x - \frac{9}{2} \quad \text{…divide each term by 2}$$

$\therefore$ the slope of the line is $\frac{3}{2}$ and the line cuts the y axis at $-\frac{9}{2}$.

Example 2

ℓ is the line $2x - 3y + 6 = 0$ and k is the line $3x + 2y - 4 = 0$.
Show that ℓ is perpendicular to m.

Slope of ℓ:
$$2x - 3y + 6 = 0$$
$$\Rightarrow -3y = -2x - 6$$
$$\Rightarrow 3y = 2x + 6$$
$$\Rightarrow y = \frac{2}{3}x + 2$$
$$\Rightarrow \text{slope of } \ell = \frac{2}{3}$$

Slope of k:
$$3x + 2y - 4 = 0$$
$$\Rightarrow 2y = -3x + 4$$
$$\Rightarrow y = -\frac{3}{2}x + 2$$
$$\Rightarrow \text{slope of } k = -\frac{3}{2}$$

Slope of $\ell \times$ slope of $k = \frac{2}{3} \times \left(-\frac{3}{2}\right)$
$$= \frac{-6}{6} = -1$$

Since the product of the two slopes $= -1$, the lines are perpendicular.

Exercise 11.4

1. Write down the slope of each of these lines:
   (i) $y = 3x + 5$
   (ii) $y = 2x - 3$
   (iii) $y = \frac{1}{2}x + 4$

2. Write down the coordinates of the point where each of the lines in Question 1 above intersects the y-axis.

3. Express each of the following lines in the form $y = mx + c$ and hence write down the slope of the line:

(i) $x + y - 4 = 0$
(ii) $3x + y - 5 = 0$
(iii) $2x + 3y - 7 = 0$
(iv) $5x - 2y + 3 = 0$
(v) $3x + 4y - 2 = 0$
(vi) $3x - 4y + 6 = 0$.

4. Express the line $\ell: 2x + 3y - 7 = 0$ in the form $y = mx + c$.
  (i) Write down the slope of ℓ.
  (ii) What is the slope of any line parallel to ℓ?
  (iii) What is the slope of any line perpendicular to ℓ?

5. Show that the lines $x - 2y + 1 = 0$ and $3x - 6y - 7 = 0$ are parallel.
What is the slope of any line perpendicular to these lines?

6. Show that the lines $2x + 3y - 4 = 0$ and $3x - 2y + 1 = 0$ are perpendicular to each other.

7. If the equation of the line ℓ is $y = 3x - 4$, write down the equation of any line, in the form $y = mx + c$, that is
  (i) parallel to ℓ
  (ii) perpendicular to ℓ.

8. Investigate if the lines $y = \frac{2}{3}x + 4$ and $2x - 3y - 5 = 0$ are parallel.

9. (i) Match the equations below to give four pairs of parallel lines:

A $y = \frac{1}{2}x + 1$
B $y = \frac{1}{3}x + 5$
C $y = -\frac{3}{4}x + 3$
D $y = \frac{x}{5} - 1$
E $y = 9 + \frac{1}{2}x$
F $y = \frac{x}{3} - 2$
G $y = \frac{1}{5}x + 3$
H $y = \frac{4}{3}x + 2$
I $y = 1 - \frac{3}{4}x$

  (ii) Which equation is the odd one out?

10. (i) Write down the slope of the given line k.
  (ii) Write the equation of k in the form $y = mx + c$.

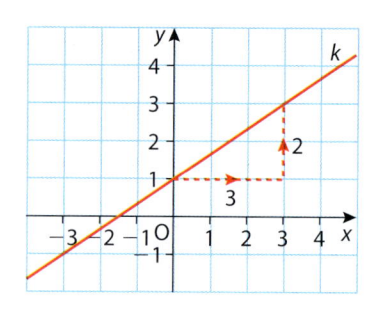

Chapter 11 Coordinate Geometry – The Line

11. The lines labelled *p*, *q*, and *r* match these equations:

$y = 2x + 5$

$y = x + 5$

$y = x - 2$

Match each line to its correct equation.

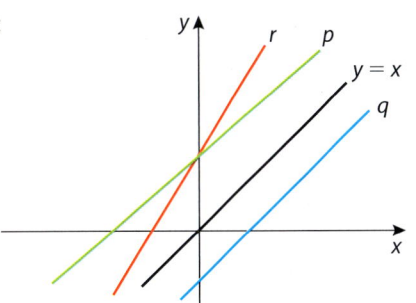

12. By finding the slope and *y*-intercept, write down the equation of the given line.

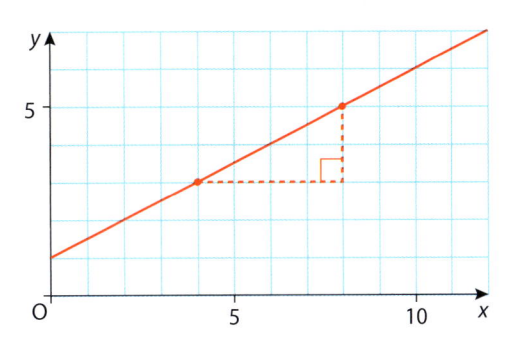

13. The equations of six lines are given below:
   a: $y = 2x - 3$
   b: $y = \frac{1}{2}x + 5$
   c: $y = x + 3$
   d: $y = -2x - 4$
   e: $y = -\frac{1}{2}x + 4$
   f: $y = 2x - 2$

   (i) Name a pair of parallel lines.
   (ii) Name a pair of perpendicular lines.
   (iii) Which line crosses the *y*-axis at (0, 4)?
   (iv) Which line crosses the *y*-axis at (0, −3)?

14. If the line $x + 2y - 6 = 0$ is parallel to the line $2x + ky - 5 = 0$, find the value of *k*.

15. If the line $2x - 3y + 7 = 0$ is perpendicular to the line $3x + ky - 4 = 0$, find the value of *k*.

16. Find the equation of each line sketched below:
   (i) passes through (2, 7) and y-intercept 3
   (ii) passes through (4, 6), x-intercept −2, y-intercept 2
   (iii) passes through (2, 3) and y-intercept −3

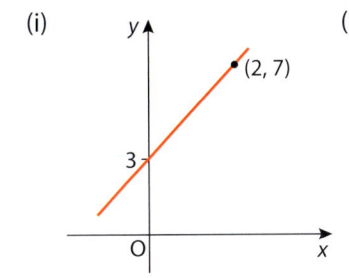

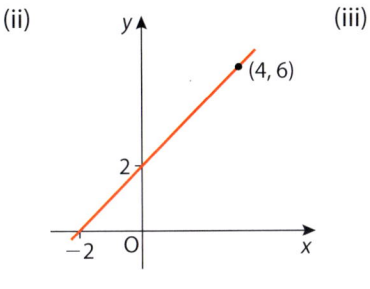

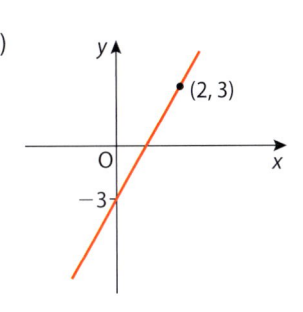

17. Which two of these lines are parallel to $y = \frac{1}{2}x - 3$?

   A $2y = x + 2$
   B $2x = y + 10$
   C $2y + 8 = x$
   D $y - 2x = 9$

263

Text & Tests 2 Higher Level

Section 11.5 Parallel and perpendicular lines

If we are given the equation of a line ℓ, such as $2x + 3y - 4 = 0$, we can find the slope of the line by expressing the equation in the form $y = mx + c$.

If we are also given a point (x_1, y_1), we can then find the equation of a line through (x_1, y_1) and which is parallel to or perpendicular to ℓ.

> **Example 1**
>
> Find the equation of the line through the point $(-2, 3)$ which is perpendicular to the line $2x - y + 5 = 0$.
>
> To find the slope of $2x - y + 5 = 0$, we express it in the form $y = mx + c$.
>
> $2x - y + 5 = 0$
> $\Rightarrow -y = -2x - 5$
> $\Rightarrow y = 2x + 5$ ...multiply each term by -1
> $\Rightarrow$ the slope is 2
>
> The slope of the line perpendicular to this line is $-\dfrac{1}{2}$
>
> Equation of line through $(-2, 3)$ with slope $-\dfrac{1}{2}$ is:
>
> $y - y_1 = m(x - x_1)$ $\qquad (x_1, y_1) = (-2, 3)$
>
> $y - 3 = -\dfrac{1}{2}(x + 2)$ $\qquad m = -\dfrac{1}{2}$
>
> $2y - 6 = -1(x + 2)$ ...multiply each term by 2
>
> $\Rightarrow 2y - 6 = -x - 2$
>
> $\Rightarrow x + 2y - 4 = 0$ is the required equation.

Exercise 11.5

1. Find the slope of the line $2x + y - 4 = 0$.
   Now find the equation of the line through the point $(2, 4)$ and which is parallel to the line $2x + y - 4 = 0$.

2. Find the equation of the line through the point $(1, -6)$ and which is parallel to the line $3x - y + 4 = 0$.

3. Find the slope of the line $2x - 3y + 1 = 0$.
   What is the slope of any line perpendicular to $2x - 3y + 1 = 0$?
   Now find the equation of the line through the point $(4, -1)$ and which is perpendicular to the line $2x - 3y + 1 = 0$.

Chapter 11 Coordinate Geometry – The Line

4. Find the equation of the line through $(-2, 1)$ and which is perpendicular to the line $3x + 2y - 4 = 0$.

5. Find the equation of the line through $(-4, 0)$ and which is parallel to the line $y = 3x - 5$.

6. The given diagram shows the lines a and b intersecting at the point $(5, 2)$.

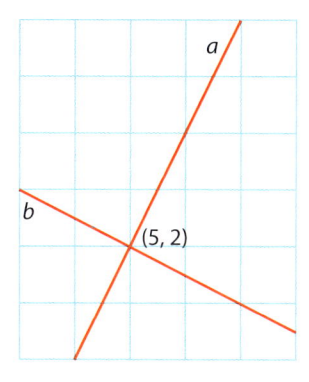

    (i) Use the grid to find the slopes of a and b.
    (ii) Investigate if a and b are perpendicular to each other.
    (iii) Find the equation of the line a.

7. The given diagram shows the points $A(-1, 5)$, $B(2, -1)$ and $C(0, 5)$.
   The line ℓ is parallel to AB and contains the point C.
   Find the equation of ℓ.

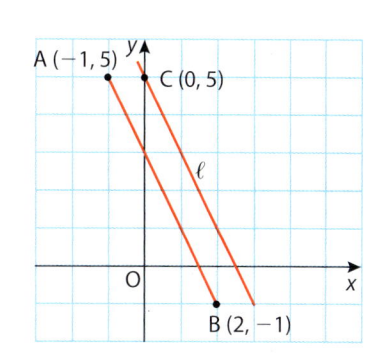

8. Which one of the following lines is parallel to $3x + y - 4 = 0$?

    A: $y = 3x - 2$ B: $y = \frac{1}{3}x + 4$ C: $6x + 2y + 7 = 0$ D: $x + 3y + 2 = 0$

9. The point A has coordinates $(1, 7)$ and the point B has coordinates $(3, 1)$.
   The midpoint of [AB] is P.
   Find the coordinates of P.
   Now find the equation of the line which passes through P and which is perpendicular to the line $x + 5y - 7 = 0$.

10. The line $y = 2x + 5$ intersects the y-axis at the point P.
    (i) Write down the slope of the line and the coordinates of P.
    (ii) Find the equation of the line through P and which is perpendicular to $y = 2x + 5$.

11. Use the grid in the given diagram to write down the slope of the line *a*.
Now write down the equation of *a* in the form $y = mx + c$.

Write down the coordinates of the point P and hence find the equation of the line through P which is perpendicular to *a*.

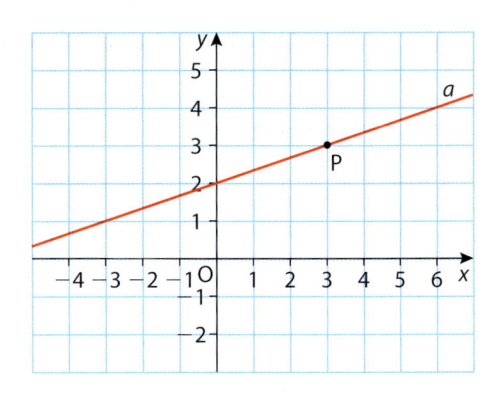

Section 11.6 Graphing lines

To draw a line such as $2x + 3y = 6$, we need to know at least two points on the line.

The easiest points to find are those at which the line crosses the *x*-axis and *y*-axis.

On the *x*-axis, $y = 0$; on the *y*-axis, $x = 0$.

Take the line $2x + 3y = 6$

When $x = 0$, then $2(0) + 3y = 6$
$$3y = 6$$
$$\Rightarrow y = 2$$

∴ (0, 2) is one point on the line

When $y = 0$, then $2x + 3(0) = 6$
$$2x = 6$$
$$x = 3$$

∴ (3, 0) is a second point on the line

A sketch of the line is shown on the right.

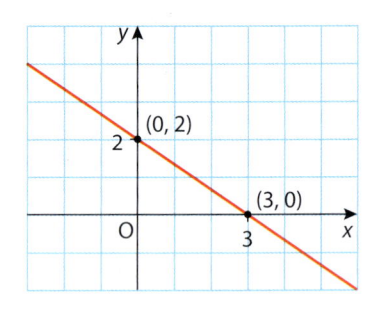

Sketch of line $2x + 3y = 6$

Lines parallel to the axes

The lines $x = 2$ and $x = 4$ are shown.

Notice that the *x*-value of each point on the line $x = 4$ is 4.

Similarly, the *x*-value of each point on the line $x = 2$ is 2.

All lines with equations of the form $x = a$ will be parallel to the *y*-axis.

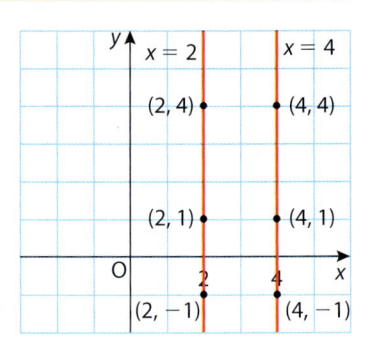

The diagram on the right shows the line $y = 2$.

Again, notice that the y-value of each of the points on this line is 2.

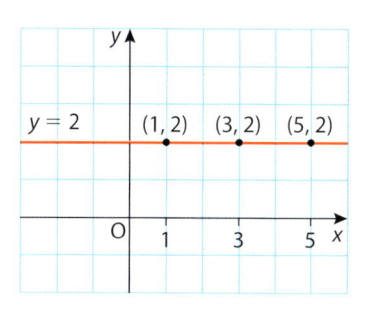

Lines containing the origin

A line such as $x + 2y = 0$, with no independent term, always contains the origin (0, 0).

To plot the line $x + 2y = 0$, we know that it contains the origin.

To find a second point, we select a value for x and then find the corresponding y-value.

Let $x = 2$: $\quad 2 + 2y = 0$
$\qquad\qquad\quad 2y = -2$
$\qquad\qquad\quad y = -1$

∴ $(2, -1)$ is a second point on the line.

A sketch of the line containing (0, 0) and $(2, -1)$ is shown.

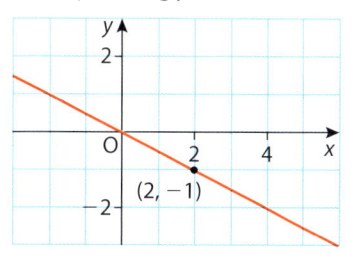

To verify that a point is on a given line

To investigate if the point $(3, -2)$ is on the line $x + 2y + 1 = 0$, we substitute 3 for x and -2 for y in the equation.

$\quad x + 2y + 1 = 0$
$\quad x = 3$ and $y = -2$
Test: $3 + 2(-2) + 1$
$\quad\quad 3 - 4 + 1$
$\quad\quad = 0$

> If a point is on a line, then the coordinates of the point will satisfy the equation of the line.

Since $(3, -2)$ **satisfies** the equation $x + 2y + 1 = 0$, it shows that the point is on the line.

However, $(-3, 4)$ is not on the line $x - 3y + 7 = 0$, since $-3 - 12 + 7 \neq 0$, i.e. it does not satisfy the equation.

Text & Tests 2 Higher Level

> **Example 1**
>
> If the point (k, 3) is on the line $4x - 3y + 1 = 0$, find the value of k.
>
> We substitute k for x and 3 for y in the equation $4x - 3y + 1 = 0$.
>
> $\Rightarrow$ $4k - 3(3) + 1 = 0$
> $\Rightarrow$ $4k - 9 + 1 = 0$
> $\Rightarrow$ $4k - 8 = 0$
> $\Rightarrow$ $4k = 8 \Rightarrow k = 2$

Exercise 11.6

1. Write down the equations of the lines a, b, c and d shown on the right.

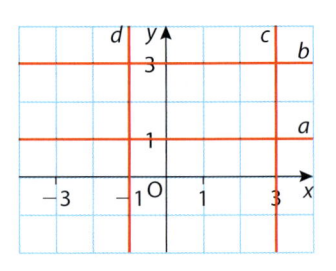

2. Draw a pair of axes and sketch these four lines:
    (i) $x = 4$ (ii) $y = 2$ (iii) $x = -2$ (iv) $y = -3$

3. Use the graph of the line $2x + y = 6$ to write down
    (i) the value of x when $y = 0$
    (ii) the coordinates of the point where the line crosses the y-axis
    (iii) the value of y when $x = 1$
    (iv) the value of x when $y = 2$
    (v) the area of the triangle formed by the line, the x-axis and the y-axis.

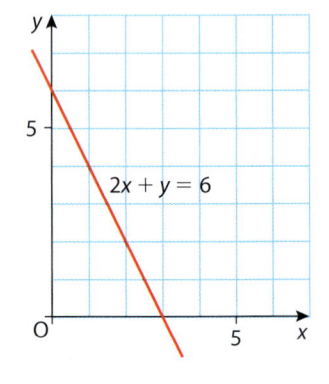

4. A straight line has equation $x + y = 5$.
    (i) By substituting $x = 0$, find the coordinates of the point where the line crosses the y-axis.
    (ii) By substituting $y = 0$, find the coordinates of the point where the line crosses the x-axis.
    (iii) Draw a graph of the line $x + y = 5$.

268

Chapter 11 Coordinate Geometry – The Line

5. Find the coordinates of the points at which the line $x - 2y - 6 = 0$ intersects the x-axis and y-axis.
   Now use these points to draw a sketch of the line.

6. Find the coordinates of the points where the line $x - 2y = 5$ intersects the x-axis and y-axis. Hence draw a sketch of the line.

7. Draw these graphs on the same diagram.
   (i) $x + y = 2$ (ii) $x + y = 3$ (iii) $x + y = 5$
   What do they all have in common?

8. Draw a sketch of the line $2x - y + 6 = 0$.
   Hence write down the area of the triangle formed by the x-axis, the y-axis and the line.

9. The equations of the lines a and b are:
       a: $y = \frac{2}{3}x + 2$
       b: $3x + 5y - 15 = 0$
   (i) Which line intersects the y-axis at (0, 2)?
   (ii) Which line intersects the x-axis at (5, 0)?
   (iii) Use the slopes of the two lines to investigate whether the lines are perpendicular to each other.
   (iv) Write down the area of the triangle formed by the line $3x + 5y - 15 = 0$, the x-axis and the y-axis.

10. The diagram shows a sketch of the line $2y = x + 4$
    (i) Find the coordinates of points A and B.
    (ii) What is the gradient of the line?

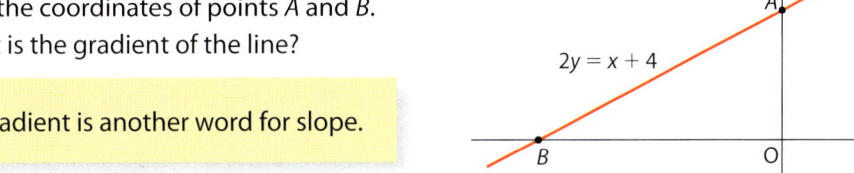

    > Gradient is another word for slope.

11. Each of the following lines contains the origin (0, 0).
    By taking a value for x and then finding the corresponding y-value, sketch each of the lines on separate diagrams:
    (i) $x - 2y = 0$ (ii) $x + 3y = 0$ (iii) $3x - y = 0$ (iv) $x - 4y = 0$.

12. The lines a, b, c and d are graphed in the given diagram.
    Match each line with one of these equations:
    (i) $x = -2$
    (ii) $x - y = 0$
    (iii) $2x + 5y = 10$
    (iv) $y = 4$

13. (i) Verify that (2, −5) is on the line $2x + y + 1 = 0$.
    (ii) Verify that (2, −3) is on the line $y = x - 5$.

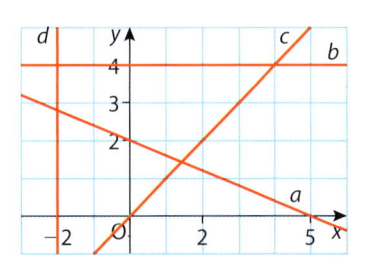

Text & Tests 2 Higher Level

(iii) Show that $(-3, 1)$ is not on the line $x - 3y + 1 = 0$.
(iv) Investigate if $(2, 0)$ is on the line $2x - y + 3 = 0$.

14. If $(1, 4)$ is on the line $2x + y + k = 0$, find the value of k.

15. If $(2, -3)$ is on the line $x + ky + 7 = 0$, find the value of k.

16. (i) Find the value of k if the line $2x + ky - 8 = 0$ contains the point $(3, 1)$.
(ii) If $(1, t)$ lies on the line $y = 2x + 3$, find the value of t.

Section 11.7 Intersection of two lines

A sketch of the lines $x + y = 4$ and $x + 3y = 6$ is shown below.

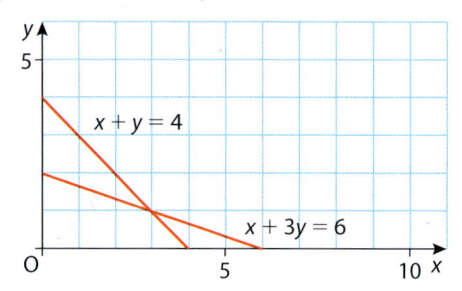

The point of intersection of the two lines can be read from the diagram.

This point is $(3, 1)$.

The point of intersection of any two lines can be found by sketching the lines on a grid and then reading their point of intersection from this grid.

However, the point of intersection of two lines may be found more easily by using simultaneous equations, as shown in the following example.

> Simultaneous equations (Chapter 10) can be used to find the point of intersection of two lines.

Example 1

Use simultaneous equations to find the point of intersection of the lines
$x + y = 5$ and $2x - y = 4$.

$x + y = 5 \ldots ①$
$2x - y = 4 \ldots ②$

Adding: $3x = 9 \Rightarrow x = 3$
From ①: $3 + y = 5 \Rightarrow y = 2$
$\therefore$ the point of intersection is $(3, 2)$.

Chapter 11 Coordinate Geometry – The Line

Exercise 11.7

1. Using the one diagram, sketch the lines
   $x + y = 5$ and $x + 4y = 8$.
   Use your sketch to write down the point of intersection of the two lines.

2. Use the diagram to solve these simultaneous equations:
   $x + y = 4$
   $2x - y = -1$

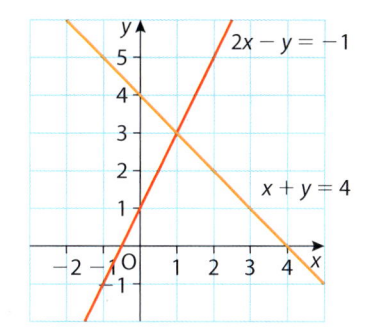

3. A sketch of the lines $2x + y = 6$ and $x + y = 5$ is shown.
   Use the sketch to write down the point of intersection of the two lines.
   Now use simultaneous equations to verify your answer.

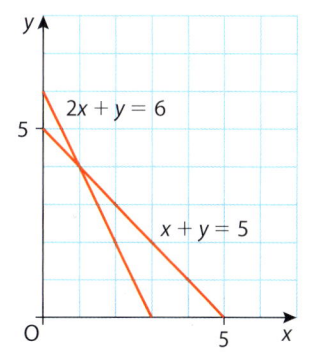

Use simultaneous equations to find the point of intersection of the following pairs of lines:

4. $x + y = 5$
   $2x - y = 1$

5. $x - y = 2$
   $2x + y = 7$

6. $2x + 5y = 1$
   $x - 3y = -5$

7. $2x - 3y = 4$
   $2x + 3y = -8$

8. $3x - 2y = 17$
   $4x + 3y = 0$

9. $x + 3y = 13$
   $2x + 5y = 21$

10. Use simultaneous equations to verify that the lines
    $2x + 3y = 12$ and $3x - 4y = 1$
    intersect at the point (3, 2).

11. In the diagram, the lines AB and CD are perpendicular to each other and intersect at the point (1, 4). The line AB crosses the x-axis at (3, 0).
    Calculate the coordinates of the points P and Q.

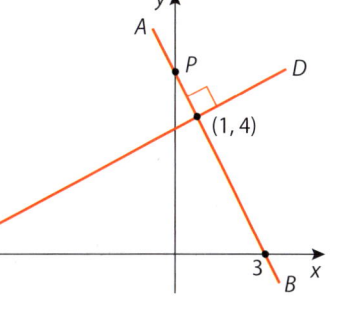

Text & Tests 2 Higher Level

Section 11.8 Rates of change

In the previous sections of this chapter, we learned how to find the slope of a line. In this section, we will show how to interpret what the slope means in different real-life situations.

Water is poured into a container at a steady rate over a period of 8 minutes. The graph on the right shows the volume of water in the container during these 8 minutes.

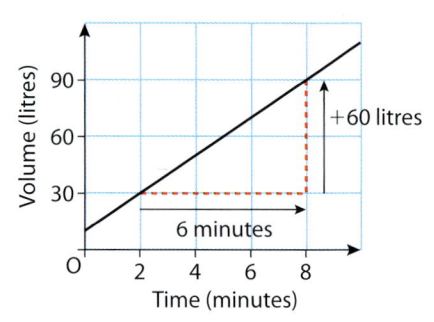

For a horizontal **increase** of 6 mins, there is a vertical **increase** of 60 litres.

The **slope** is $\frac{60}{6} = 10$.

60 litres in **6 minutes**, so **10 litres per minute**.

So the rate of flow of the water is **10 litres per minute**.
Since the slope is also 10, we can see that the slope in this example represents **the rate of flow**.

In the next graph, the rate of change of temperature is examined.
The two, line segments, OA and OB, show that as time increases, the temperature also increases.

After 3 minutes, A will be hotter than B.

The rate at which the temperature changes in A is greater than the rate at which the temperature of B changes.

The **slope** of a line segment is a measure of the **rate of change** of the variables.

The rate of change of the **temperature** A is 10 °C **per minute**.

The rate of change of the **temperature** B is $\frac{5}{3}$ °C **per minute**.

The slope of line OA is 10.
The slope of line OB is $\frac{5}{3}$.

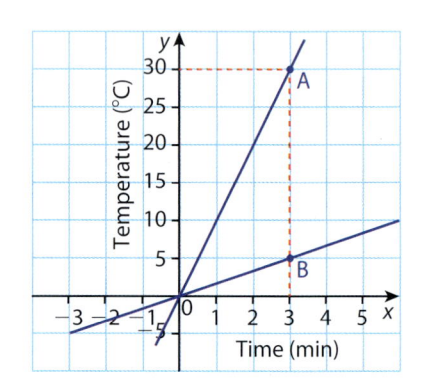

Chapter 11 Coordinate Geometry – The Line

Time–distance graphs

The distance–time graph given shows Emer's 3-hour journey.

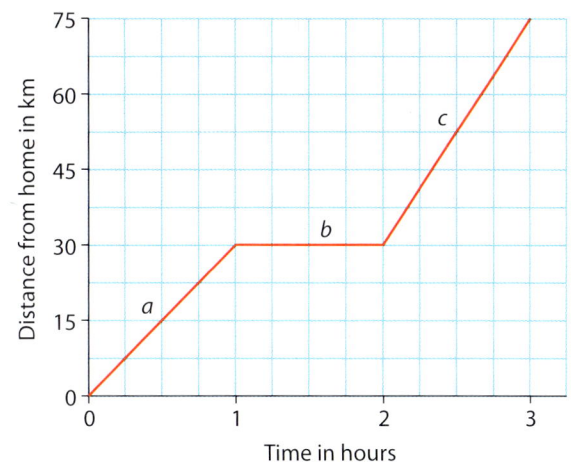

The slope of the line segment marked *a* has slope $\frac{30}{1} = 30$.

The line segment *a* shows that Emer travelled 30 km in 1 hour.
Thus her speed is 30 km/hr.
From these two results, we can see that the **slope** of the line represents the **speed**.
The line segment marked *b* shows that Emer has stopped travelling.
Here the speed is zero and the slope is zero.

Now verify that the slope of the line segment marked *c* represents the speed for that part of Emer's journey.

> In a distance–time graph, the slope of the line represents speed.

Exercise 11.8

1. What rates of flow, in litres per minute, are shown by the following graphs?
    (i) (a)   (b)

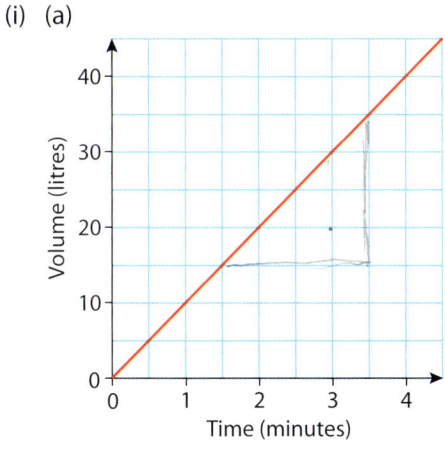

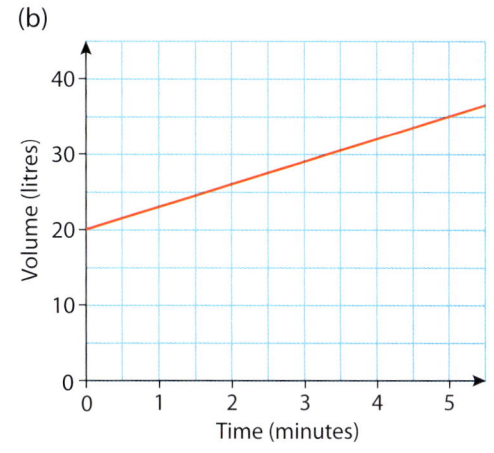

    (ii) Write down the slope of the line in each graph.
    (iii) What is the meaning of the slope in each case?

273

2. (i) Write down the rate of flow, in litres per second, in each of the diagrams below.

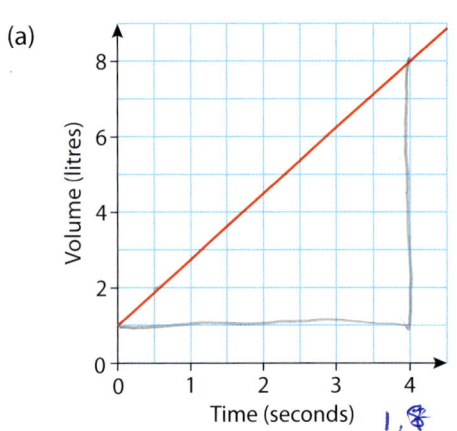

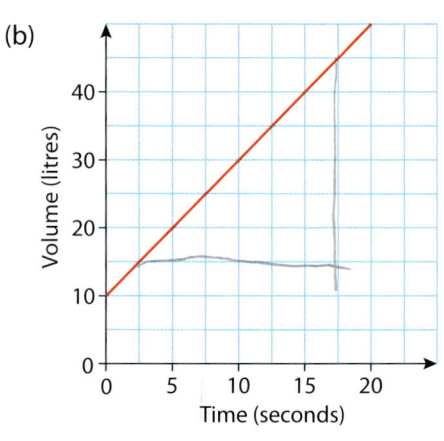

(a) [graph: Volume (litres) vs Time (seconds), line from (0,0) to (4,8)]

(b) [graph: Volume (litres) vs Time (seconds), line from (0,0) to (20,45)]

(ii) Find the slope of each of the lines drawn above.
(iii) Show that the slope of each line corresponds to the rate of flow in the diagram.

3. The graph opposite shows the distance Stephen travelled in the first 24 minutes of his journey.

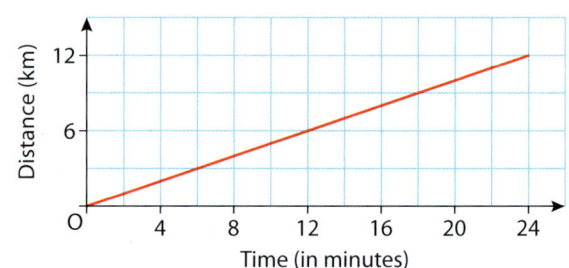

(i) Work out the slope of the line.
(ii) Which of the following statements is true?
  A: The slope represents the speed in km per hour.
  B: The slope represents the speed in metres per minute.
  C: The slope represents the speed in km per minute.

4. This graph shows the volume of oil in a tank.

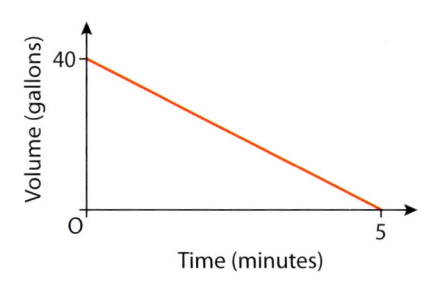

(i) Calculate the slope of the line.
(ii) What happens to the oil in the tank during these 5 minutes?
(iii) What is the rate of flow of oil from the tank?
(iv) Explain what the slope of the line means in this diagram.

Chapter 11 Coordinate Geometry – The Line

5. The following is a conversion graph between kilograms (kg) and pounds (lb).

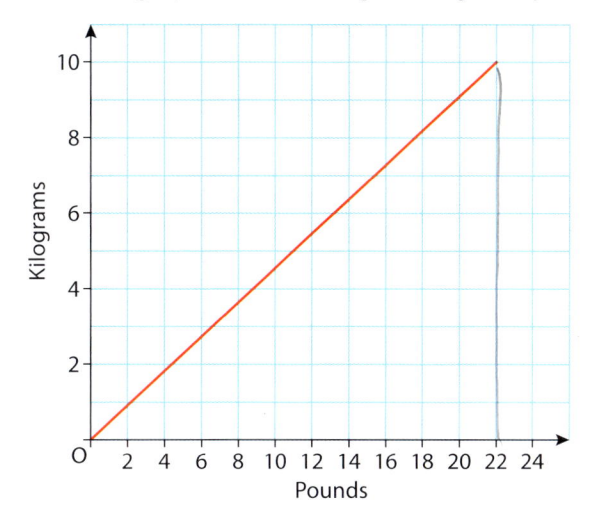

(i) Use the graph to convert
    (a) 20 lb to kg   (b) 4 kg to pounds
(ii) Use the grid to work out the slope of the line.
(iii) Explain what the slope means in the context of the question.
(iv) Work out the equation of the given line.
(v) Use the equation to estimate the number of pounds in 20 kilograms.

6. A hire firm hires out industrial blow heaters.
The following graph is used to find the approximate charge for the hiring of one of these heaters.

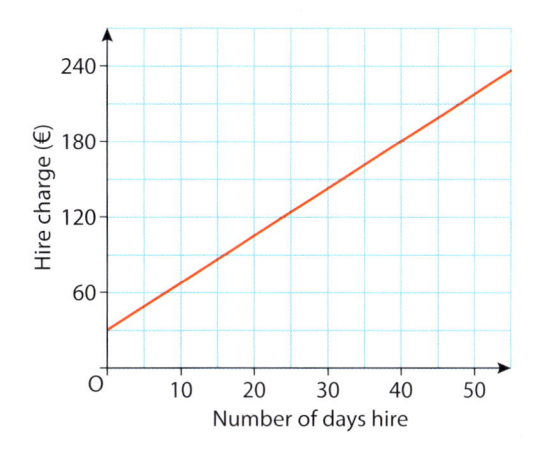

(i) Use the graph to find the approximate charge for hiring a heater for
    (a) 40 days   (b) 25 days.
(ii) Use the graph to find the number of days hire you would get for a cost of
    (a) €120   (b) €210.

(iii) Use the grid to work out the slope of the line.
(iv) Explain the meaning of the slope in the context of the graph.
(v) Use the graph to write down the fixed charge you are required to pay as well as the daily hire charge.

7. The graph below show the relationship between distances travelled and fuel consumption for John's car. The segments l_1 and l_2 represent the fuel consumption at steady speeds of 60 km/h and 100 km/h respectively.

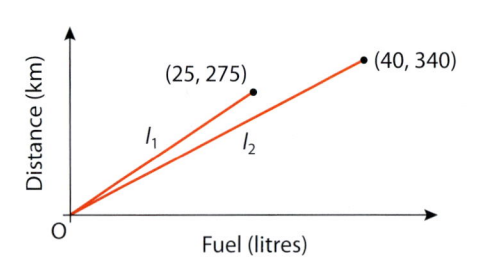

(i) Find the slopes of l_1 and l_2.
(ii) What do these slopes tell you about the fuel consumption of the car at these speeds?
(iii) Fuel costs €1.45 per litre.
John drives a distance of 200 km at a steady speed.
How much cheaper is the journey at 60 km/h than at 100 km/h?

Test yourself 11

1. The equation of a line is $y = 2x - 4$.
    (i) Write down the slope of this line.
    (ii) At what point does the line intersect the y-axis?
    (iii) At what point does the line intersect the x-axis?
    (iv) What is the slope of any line that is perpendicular to $y = 2x - 4$?

2. (i) Use the grid on the right to write down the slope of the line p.
   Now write down the equation of p in the form $y = mx + c$.

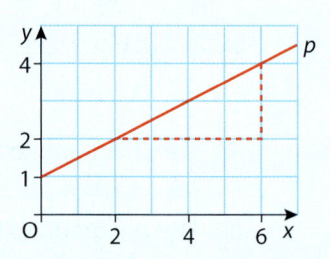

Chapter 11 Coordinate Geometry – The Line

3. Which of these lines is parallel to $2y - x = 3$?

- **A** $2y + x = 5$
- **B** $4y - 1 = 2x$
- **C** $y = 2x + 3$
- **D** $x = \frac{1}{2}y + 1$

4. $A(-3, 1)$ and $B(3, 9)$ are two points in the plane.
   (i) Find M, the midpoint of [AB]. On which axis does M lie?
   (ii) Find the slope of AB.
   (iii) Write down the slope of any line perpendicular to AB.
   (iv) Now find the equation of the line through the origin and which is perpendicular to AB.

5. This diagram shows three parallel lines.
   (a) Write down equations for lines A and B.
   (b) Write down an equation of any other line that is parallel to these three.

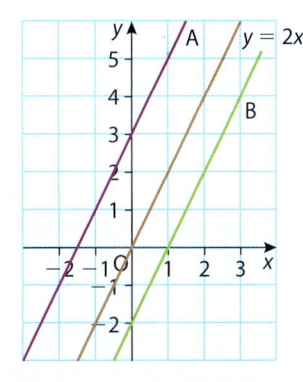

6. ℓ is the line $x - 2y + 2 = 0$.
   m is the line $3x + y - 8 = 0$.
   Use simultaneous equations to find the coordinates of P, the point of intersection of ℓ and m.

7. If the line $2x + y - 7 = 0$ is parallel to the line $4x + ky - 3 = 0$, find the value of k.

8. The line $2x + 3y - 6 = 0$ intersects the x-axis at A and the y-axis at B.
   Find the coordinates of A and B and hence find the area of the triangle OAB, where O is the origin.

9. A graph of the line $y = ax + b$ is shown.
   Find the values of a and b.

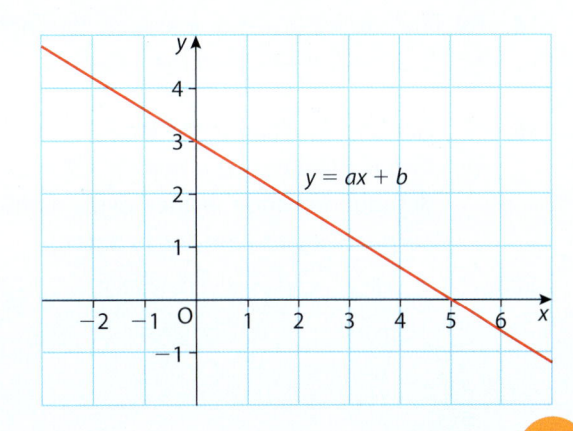

10. The given graph shows three lines *a*, *b* and *c*.

  (i) Which line(s) have negative slopes?
  (ii) Use the grid to find the slope of the line *a*.
  (iii) Associate each of the lines with one of these equations:
   D: $y = 2x + 1$
   E: $x + y = 10$
   F: $2x + 5y = 17$.

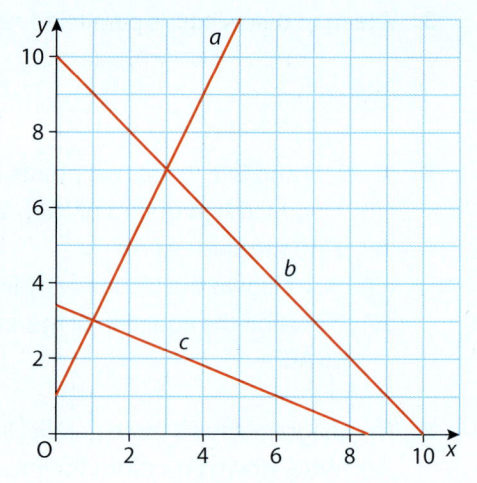

11. What is the equation of the line parallel to $y = 3x + 2$ that crosses the *y*-axis at $(0, -1)$?

12. This is a sketch of a child's slide.
  (a) Find the gradient of the sloping part of the slide.
  (b) For safety reasons, the gradient of the slide should be no greater than 0.7.
   Is this a safe slide?
   Explain your answer.

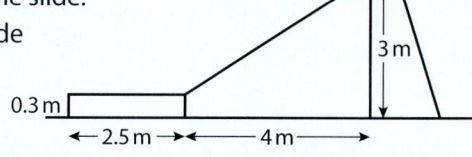

13. Copy the given diagram and using the same scale on the *x*-axis and *y*-axis, draw lines through A with slope
  (a) $\frac{1}{2}$ (b) -2.

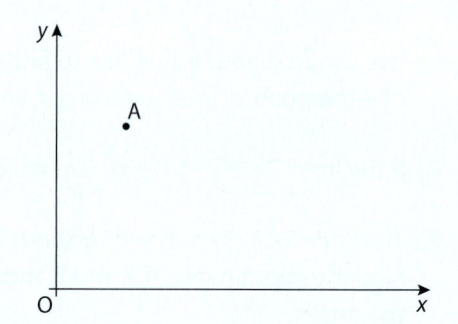

14. The line $ax + y + 1 = 0$ passes through the point of intersection of the lines $x = 2$ and the *x*-axis. Find the value of *a*.

15. (i) Find the equation of the straight line through $(0, 1)$ and $(3, 7)$.
  (ii) Another line has equation $y = 7 - 2x$.
   Without drawing the lines, explain how you can tell whether or not this line is perpendicular to the line in part (i).

Chapter 11 Coordinate Geometry – The Line

16. The map below shows part of a town containing a park and some streets. Distances are measured (in kilometres) horizontally and vertically from the Town Hall and shown in coordinate form.

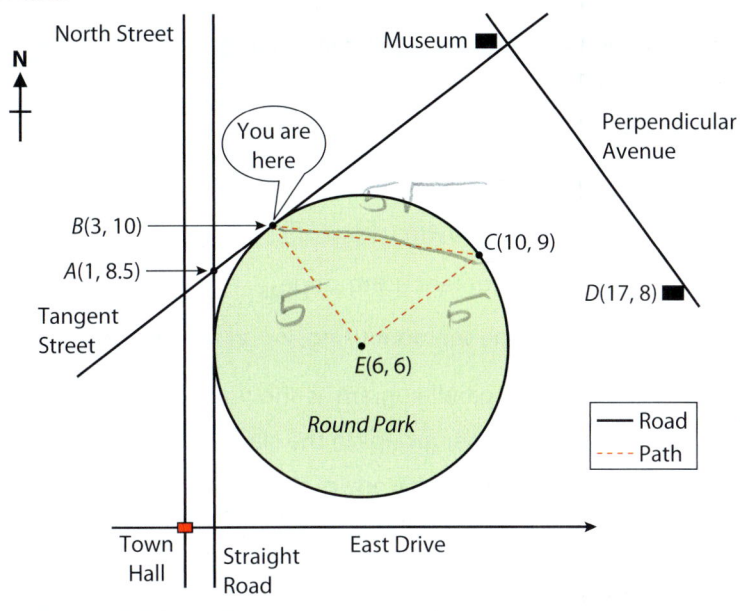

(i) How long is the path from B(3, 10) to C(10, 9)?
Give your answer correct to three significant figures.

(ii) E(6, 6) is the centre of *Round Park*.
How much shorter is it to walk directly from B to C rather than take the path to E and then on to C?
Give your answer correct to the nearest km.

(iii) The points A(1, 8.5) and B(3, 10) are on Tangent Street.
Find the equation of Tangent Street.

(iv) Perpendicular Avenue in perpendicular to Tangent Street and passes through D(17, 8).
Find its equation.

(v) The Museum is located at the intersection of Tangent Street and Perpendicular Avenue.
Find the coordinates of the museum.

(vi) John is at the Town Hall and wants to get to the Museum.
Give one possible route he might take and calculate the total distance he must travel if he takes that route.

Text & Tests 2 Higher Level

Assignment:

1. On a large sheet of squared paper, make a grid and select 4 points to form a parallelogram.
2. On the poster, label the points you have chosen.

On a separate sheet of paper, find:

(i) the length of each line segment using $|AB| = \sqrt{(x_2 - x_1)^2 + (y_2 - y_1)^2}$

(ii) the slope of each line segment using $\text{slope}_{AB} = m = \dfrac{y_2 - y_1}{x_2 - x_1}$

(iii) the equation of each line segment using, $y - y_1 = m(x - x_1)$

Write all your results on the parallelogram as shown.

Compare your results with other groups in the class.

(iv) By using, $m_1 \times m_2 = -1$, check if any of the parallelograms drawn is a rectangle.

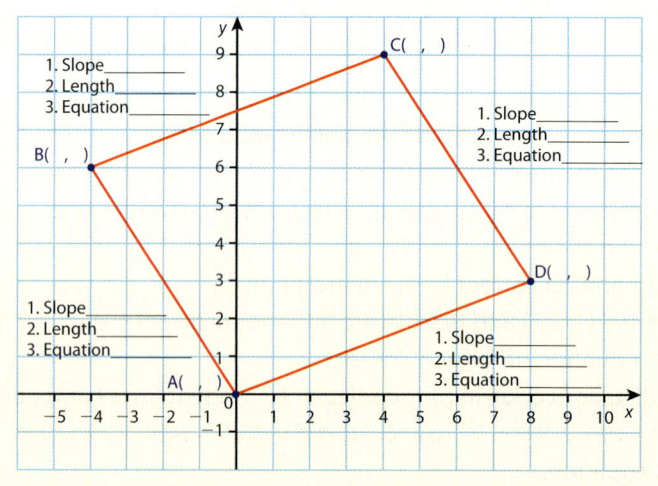

Ratio – Time – Speed

chapter 12

From first year, you will recall how to:
- change between fractions, decimals and percentages,
- divide numbers into a given ratio,
- use direct and inverse proportion.

In this chapter, you will learn to:
- understand the 24-hour clock,
- add and subtract time,
- convert between seconds, minutes and hours,
- read and interpret timetables,
- calculate speed, distance or time when given the other two variables,
- solve problems involving time, distance and speed.

Section 12.1 Ratio and proportion

1. Ratio

We use ratios to compare two quantities.
The ratio of blue discs to yellow discs is 5 : 3.
The ratio 12 : 8 can be simplified by dividing each term by 4.
Thus, 12 : 8 = 3 : 2.
3 : 2 is called the **simplest form** of the ratio.

A ratio is normally expressed as whole numbers.

The ratio $\frac{1}{3} : \frac{5}{6}$ can be expressed as whole numbers by getting a common denominator.

$\therefore \frac{1}{3} : \frac{5}{6} = \frac{2}{6} : \frac{5}{6} = 2 : 5$ ... multiplying both sides of the ratio by the common denominator.

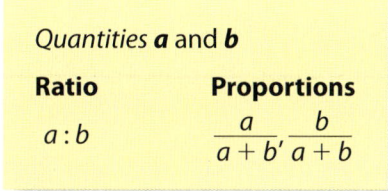

Quantities **a** and **b**	
Ratio	**Proportions**
$a : b$	$\dfrac{a}{a+b}, \dfrac{b}{a+b}$

281

Text & Tests 2 Higher Level

> ### Example 1
>
> A sum of money is divided in the ratio 1 : 3 : 5.
> If the smallest part is €250, find the sum of money.
>
> If a sum of money is divided in the ratio 1 : 3 : 5, we divide the total into 9 parts.
>
> $\frac{1}{9}, \frac{3}{9}, \frac{5}{9}$ ... nine parts in total
>
> $\Rightarrow \frac{1}{9} =$ €250
>
> $\Rightarrow \frac{9}{9} =$ €250 × 9 = €2250
>
> ∴ the sum of money is €2250

2. Proportion

While ratios compare one part to another part, proportion compares a part to the total.
The proportion of the given circle that is shaded red is $\frac{2}{6}$ or $\frac{1}{3}$.
Proportion is generally expressed as a fraction, decimal or percentage.

If 1 litre of petrol costs €1.60, 2 litres cost €3.20 and 3 litres cost €4.80.
Here the costs of 1 litre, 2 litres and 3 litres are in **direct proportion**.

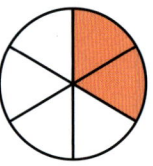

> ### Example 2
>
> A car travels 78 km on 9 litres of petrol.
>   (i) How far is it likely to travel on 21 litres of petrol?
>   (ii) How many litres would be required for a journey of 390 km?
>
>   (i) Here we are looking for **distance**, so we keep distance last.
>
>   9 litres do 78 km
>
>   1 litre does $\frac{78}{9}$ km
>
>   21 litres do $\left(\frac{78}{9} \times \frac{21}{1}\right)$ km = 182 km.
>
>   (ii) Here we are looking for litres, so we keep litres last.
>
>   78 km require 9 litres
>
>   1 km requires $\frac{9}{78}$ litres
>
>   390 km require $\left(\frac{9}{78} \times \frac{390}{1}\right)$ litres = 45 litres
>
>   ∴ 390 km would require 45 litres.

Chapter 12 Ratio – Time – Speed

3. Inverse proportion

When a dog eats 200 g of dogfood each day, a container lasts him 10 days.
If he eats 400 g each day, the container will last him only 5 days.

Notice that as the quantity of food eaten **increases**, the time that the food lasts **decreases**.
This is an example of of **inverse proportion**.

Example 3

Five painters can paint an office block in 12 days.
  (i) How long would it take three painters to paint the block?
 (ii) If the office block had to be painted in 3 days, how many painters would be needed?

 (i) 5 painters take 12 days

   1 painter takes $12 \times 5 = 60$ days   … 5 times as long

   3 painters take $\frac{60}{3} = 20$ days   … $\frac{1}{3}$ as long as 1 painter

(ii) To be painted in 12 days requires 5 painters.

   To be painted in 1 day requires 60 painters   … 12 times quicker so multiply 5 by 12

   To be painted in 3 days requires $\frac{60}{3} = 20$ painters

   ∴ 20 painters would be required to paint the office block in 3 days.

Exercise 12.1

1. Express each of these ratios in its simplest form:

  (i) 6 : 18   (ii) 25 : 45   (iii) 28 : 98   (iv) 50c : €2
  (v) 80c : €2.40   (vi) 50 cm : 4 m   (vii) 3 days : 3 weeks   (viii) 40 min : 3 hours

2. Express each of these ratios in its simplest form:

  (i) $\frac{1}{2} : \frac{1}{4}$ (ii) $\frac{3}{4} : \frac{1}{4}$ (iii) $\frac{1}{3} : \frac{1}{2}$ (iv) $\frac{1}{3} : \frac{1}{4}$
  (v) $\frac{2}{5} : \frac{1}{2}$ (vi) $\frac{3}{5} : \frac{7}{10}$ (vii) $3\frac{1}{2} : 1\frac{1}{2}$ (viii) $1\frac{3}{4} : 5\frac{1}{4}$

3. Divide €288 between Ann and David in the ratio 5 : 3.

4. Divide €2800 between three people in the ratio 4 : 2 : 1.

5. Divide €1300 in the ratio $\frac{3}{4} : 1\frac{3}{4}$.

Text & Tests 2 Higher Level

6. €1575 was shared among three people in the ratio $1:2:\frac{1}{2}$.
   Calculate the smallest share.

7. (i) Find two pairs of matching statements here.
   (ii) Write your own statement that matches the odd one out.

   A 20% of the class are girls.

   B The ratio of girls to boys is 1:5.

   C One sixth of the class are girls.

   D 25% of the class are girls.

   E The number of boys is 4 times the number of girls.

8. In a school, the ratio of girls to boys is 7:2.
   If there are 735 girls in the school, how many boys are there?

9. A prize fund is divided between A, B and C in the ratio 4:3:2 respectively.
   If C's share is €1224, find the total fund.

10. Brass is made from copper and zinc in the ratio 5:3 by weight.
    (i) If there are 6 kg of zinc, work out the weight of copper.
    (ii) If there are 25 kg of copper, work out the weight of zinc.

11. In a school, the ratio of the number of students to the number of computers is $1:\frac{2}{5}$.
    If there are 100 computers in the school, work out the number of students in the school.

12. Susan has 375 g of butter and adapts her apple pie recipe so that she can use all the butter.
    (i) What quantities of the other ingredients would she need?
    (ii) How many people would this serve?

    Apple Pie (for 4)
    3 large apples
    25 g brown sugar
    200 g flour
    75 g butter (or margarine)
    50 g caster sugar
    1 tablespoon water to mix

13. A glass contains alcohol and water in the ratio 1:4. A second glass has the same quantity of liquid but this time the ratio of alcohol to water is 2:3.
    Each glass is emptied into a third glass.
    What is the ratio of alcohol to water for the final mixture?

14. When a car is moving at 108 km/hr, it travels 18 km on a litre of petrol.
    If petrol costs €1.62 a litre, work out the cost of petrol per minute when driving the car at 108 km/hr.

Chapter 12 Ratio – Time – Speed

15. Alice builds a model of a house. She uses a scale of 1 : 20.

The height of the real house is 10 metres.
  (i) Work out the height of the model.

The width of the model is 80 cm.
  (ii) Work out the width of the real house.

16. A pastry mix is made from 2 parts butter mixed with 3 parts flour.
  (i) How much of each ingredient is needed to make one kilogram of pastry mix?
  (ii) Rachel has 200 g of butter and 400 g of flour. What is the most pastry mix she can make?
  (iii) Gina has 1.5 kg of butter and 1125 g of flour. What is the most pastry mix she can make?

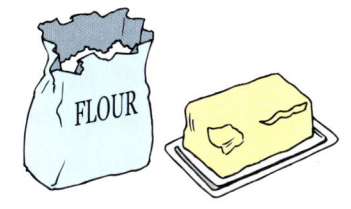

17. A motorist driving 90 km per day has enough diesel to last her 8 days. If she reduces her driving to 72 km per day, how long should the diesel last?

18. 12 blocklayers can build a wall in 15 days.
  (i) How long would it take 20 blocklayers working at the same rate to do so?
  (ii) How many blocklayers would be needed to build the wall in 10 days?

19. What is the ratio of the shaded area to the area of the largest square?

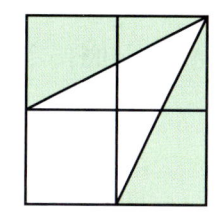

20. One full glass contains vinegar and water in the ratio of 1 : 3. Another full glass of twice the capacity of the first has vinegar and water in the ratio 1 : 4. If the contents of both glasses were mixed together, what then is the ratio of vinegar to water?

21. A male punky fish has 9 stripes and a female punky fish has 8 stripes. I count 86 stripes on the fish in my tank.
What is the ratio of male fish to female fish?

Text & Tests 2 Higher Level

22. In the diagram, $\frac{5}{6}$ of the circle is shaded and $\frac{2}{3}$ of the triangle is shaded.
What is the ratio of the area of the circle to the area of the triangle?

23. Two rectangles are drawn on squared cm paper as shown.
Find the following ratios:

(a) (i) $\dfrac{|FG|}{|AD|}$ (ii) $\dfrac{|FE|}{|AB|}$ (iii) $\dfrac{|FH|}{|AC|}$

(b) (i) $\dfrac{\text{Perimeter EFGH}}{\text{Perimeter ABCD}}$ (ii) $\dfrac{\text{Area EFGH}}{\text{Area ABCD}}$

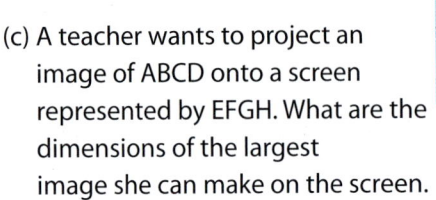

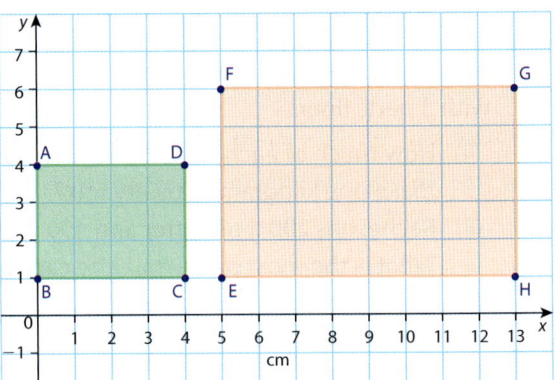

(c) A teacher wants to project an image of ABCD onto a screen represented by EFGH. What are the dimensions of the largest image she can make on the screen.

24. An extension [KLMN] to a square room of side 4 m is planned so that the ratio of sides of the extension will be the same as the ratio of sides of the overall building.

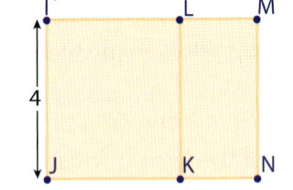

i.e. $\dfrac{|KL|}{|KN|} = \dfrac{|IM|}{|IJ|}$

(i) Write |KN| in terms of x.

(ii) Find the value of x, correct to two places of decimal.

Investigation:

Investigate a definition for the **golden** ratio.

Based on your answer for question 24, draw as accurately as you can a rectangle whose sides are in the golden ratio.

Chapter 12 Ratio – Time – Speed

Section 12.2 Time and timetables

The clock on the right shows the time to be 9.20.
This could be 9.20 a.m. or 9.20 p.m..

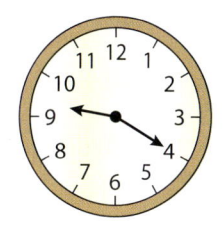

When we give a time containing a.m. or p.m. we are expressing it in **12-hour clock time**.

The letters **a.m.** are used to indicate times between midnight and noon.

Times between noon and midnight are indicated by **p.m.**.

The **24-hour clock** is another way of telling the time. This method uses 4 digits, e.g. 10.24.

> a.m. means *ante meridiem*
> – before noon
> p.m. means *post meridiem*
> – after noon

The first two digits give the hour after midnight and the second two digits give the number of minutes after the hour.

The table below shows times expressed in 12-hour and 24-hour clock times.

12-hour clock	10 a.m.	4.30 p.m.	4.20 a.m.	9.16 p.m.	12.10 a.m.
24-hour clock	10.00	16.30	04.20	21.16	00.10

In most bus and train timetables, for example, the decimal point in the 24-hour time is omitted and 21.16 is written as 2116.

> **Example 1**
>
> A film begins at 20.45 and ends at 22.14. How long does it last?
>
> We subtract 20.45 from 22.14 as follows:
> $$\begin{array}{r} 22.14 \\ -20.45 \end{array}$$
>
> When subtracting a larger number of minutes from a smaller number, change the top line by adding 60 to the minutes and taking away one hour as follows:
>
> $$\begin{array}{r} 22.14 \\ -20.45 \end{array} = \begin{array}{r} 21.74 \\ -20.45 \\ \hline 1.29 \end{array}$$ ... 14 minutes after 10 = 74 minutes after 9
>
> The film lasts 1 hour 29 minutes.

287

Text & Tests 2 Higher Level

Investigation:

By copying and completing the following table, investigate parts of an hour in fraction and decimal forms.

Minutes	Parts of an hour	
	Fraction	Decimal
6 minutes	$\frac{6}{60} = \frac{1}{10}$	0.1
		0.8
	$\frac{1}{5}$	
15 minutes		
	$\frac{3}{10}$	
		0.33

Minutes	Parts of an hour	
	Fraction	Decimal
	$\frac{2}{5}$	
30 minutes		
		0.6
	$\frac{2}{3}$	
		0.75
50 minutes		

Exercise 12.2

1. Perform the following additions and subtractions:

(i) hr min
     4   38
   + 3   46

(ii) hr min
      4   53
    − 2   17

(iii) hr min
       3   12
     + 1   46

(iv) hr min
      5   35
    − 3   54

2. Express each of these in minutes:

(i) 3 hours 24 min   (ii) 5 hours 36 min   (iii) 7 hours 54 min

3. Express each of these in 12-hour clock time:

(i) a.m.   (ii) p.m.   (iii) a.m.   (iv) p.m.

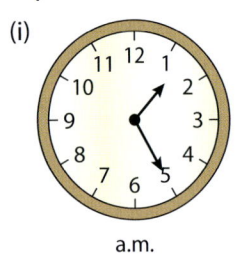

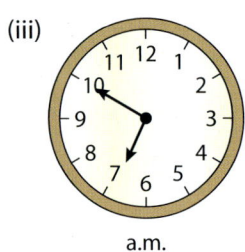

4. Write the following using a.m. or p.m.:

(i) 11.40   (ii) 15.35   (iii) 12.20   (iv) 00.30   (v) 22.15

Chapter 12 Ratio – Time – Speed

5. Write in 24-hour clock time:
   (i) 6 a.m.   (ii) 10.45 a.m.   (iii) 4 p.m.   (iv) 10.12 p.m.   (v) 12 noon

6. How many hours and minutes from
   (i) 9.45 a.m. to 2.15 p.m.
   (ii) 8.45 p.m. to 3.50 a.m.
   (iii) 08.30 to 16.45
   (iv) 06.42 to 15.10 ?

7. How many hours and minutes from
   (i) 10.35 to 14.45   (ii) 12.48 to 16.20   (iii) 10.36 to 18.45 ?

8. The times shown below give hours, minutes and seconds.
   Match the times on the clocks to the digital times in the blue boxes.

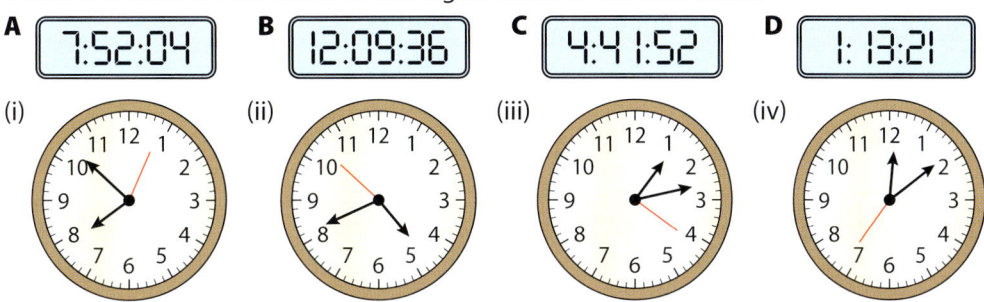

   A 7:52:04   B 12:09:36   C 4:41:52   D 1:13:21

   (i)   (ii)   (iii)   (iv)

9. A woman works from 08.45 to 12.30 and from 13.45 to 17.15 for 5 days each week. Calculate how many hours she works in the week.

10. A play started at 8.20 p.m. and lasted 2hr 35 min. At what time did it finish?

11. A train leaves Tralee at 10.52 and arrives in Dublin at 14.40.
    How long does the journey take?

12. A turkey needs to be cooked for dinner at 18.30.
    The cooking time is 28 minutes per kg, plus an extra 20 minutes.
    If the turkey weighs 8 kg, at what time should it be put in the oven?

13. The following is an extract from the Dublin to Westport train timetable:

		Train 1	Train 2
Dublin Heuston	dep.	08.30	17.10
Athlone	arr.	10.08	18.43
Athlone	dep.	10.10	18.45
Claremorris	arr.	11.25	20.08
Claremorris	dep.	11.44	20.11
Westport	arr.	12.05	20.38

    (i) How long does it take Train 1 to go from Dublin to Westport?
    (ii) For how long does Train 1 stop in Claremorris?

289

(iii) How long does it take Train 2 to go from Athlone to Westport?
(iv) Which is the faster train from Dublin to Athlone?
(v) How long does it take Train 1 to go from Dublin to Claremorris?
(vi) For how long does Train 2 stop in Athlone?
(vii) If I arrive at Heuston Station in Dublin at 07.52, how long do I have to wait for Train 1 to Westport?
(viii) Which is the faster train from Dublin to Westport?

Section 12.3 Speed – Distance – Time

If a car travels 100 km in 2 hours, then we say that the average speed of the car for the journey is 50 kilometres per hour (written as **50 km/hr**).

Again, if a train does 300 km in 3 hours, its average speed is 100 km/hr.

In each of these examples, the average speed $= \dfrac{\text{distance travelled}}{\text{time taken}}$.

The examples above could also be used to show that

(i) Time $= \dfrac{\text{Distance}}{\text{Speed}}$ (ii) Distance $=$ Speed $\times$ Time

The triangle on the right could help you to remember the formulae given.

Speed $= \dfrac{\text{Distance}}{\text{Time}}$

Time $= \dfrac{\text{Distance}}{\text{Speed}}$

Distance $=$ Speed $\times$ Time

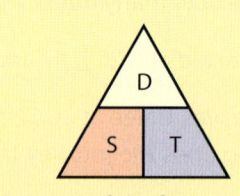

Use your thumb to cover the value you wish to find; for example to find speed, cover S.

speed $= \dfrac{\text{distance}}{\text{time}}$

Example 1

A train travels a journey of 210 km in $2\tfrac{1}{2}$ hours. Find its average speed.

Average speed $= \dfrac{\text{Distance}}{\text{Time}} = \dfrac{210}{2\tfrac{1}{2}} = \dfrac{210}{2.5} = 84$

∴ the average speed $= 84$ km/hr.

Chapter 12 Ratio – Time – Speed

Example 2

A motorist travelled 500 kilometres in six hours.
Her average speed for the first two hours was 100 km/hr.
Find her average speed in kilometres per hour for the last four hours.

Distance travelled in the first 2 hours is $100 \text{ km} \times 2 = 200 \text{ km}$.

Therefore she travelled 300 km in the last 4 hours.

Average speed $= \dfrac{\text{Distance}}{\text{Time}}$

$= \dfrac{300}{4}$ ... $500 \text{ km} - 200 \text{ km} = 300 \text{ km}$ and $6 \text{ hr} - 2 \text{ hr} = 4 \text{ hr}$.

$= 75$

∴ average speed for the last 4 hours = 75 km/hr.

Investigation:

Copy and complete both tables:

1 km = _____ m
1 hr = _____ s

18 **km**/hr =	18 × ( )**m**/hr =	$\dfrac{(\quad)}{(\quad)} = ($) **m/s**
10 **m/s** =	10 × ( )m/**hr** =	$\dfrac{(\quad)}{(\quad)} = ($) **km**/hr

Exercise 12.3

1. How far will a car travel
   (i) in 3 hours at an average speed of 75 km/hr
   (ii) in $2\frac{1}{4}$ hours at an average speed of 88 km/hr?

2. Find the time taken to travel
   (i) 200 km at an average speed of 80 km/hr
   (ii) 48 km at an average speed of 64 km/hr.

Text & Tests 2 Higher Level

3. Find the average speed, in km/hr, of a car if it does
   - (i) 120 km in 2 hours
   - (ii) 90 km in $1\frac{1}{2}$ hours
   - (iii) 25 km in 30 minutes
   - (iv) 90 km in 40 minutes.

4. A racing car completes a 15 km lap of a track in 5 minutes.
   Express this speed in km/hr.

5. A speedboat travels at 60 km/hr for two hours and then at 90 km/hr for one hour.
   Find its average speed over the three hours.

6. A journey takes 3 hours at an average speed of 120 km/hr.
   How long, in hours, will the journey take if the average speed is reduced to 80 km/hr?

7. A journey of 276 km began at 1040 hrs and ended on the same day at 1430 hrs.
   Find the average speed in km/hr.

8. It takes 4 hours and 20 minutes to travel a journey at an average speed of 120 km/hr.
   How many hours and minutes will it take to travel the same journey if the average speed is reduced to 100 km/hr?

9. A motorist travelled 320 km in five hours.
   Her average speed for the first 160 km was 80 km/hr.
   What was her average speed for the second 160 km?

10. A car journey of 559 kilometres took 6 hours and 30 minutes.
    - (i) Calculate the average speed, in km/hr, for the journey.
    - (ii) If the average petrol consumption for the journey was 8.3 km per litre, calculate the number of litres used, correct to the nearest litre.

11. A runner sets out at midday to run to the next village, a distance of 12 km.
    She wants to arrive at this village at 1330 hours.
    At what average speed should she run?

12. A cheetah can run 100 m in 5.4 seconds.
    A train takes 12 minutes to travel 7.7 km between two stations.
    Which has the faster average speed, the train or the cheetah?
    Express the difference in metres per minute.

13. Anne walks a distance of 1.7 km to school from home.
    She walks at an average speed of 5.1 km/hr.
    What is the latest she can leave home to be in school at 8.55 a.m.?

Chapter 12 Ratio – Time – Speed

14. The table on the right shows the times taken by some very fast animals to travel the distances given.
Arrange the animals in order, starting with the fastest.

Animal	Time taken	Distance in metres
Cheetah	18 seconds	500 m
Racehorse	16 seconds	300 m
Antelope	$4\frac{1}{2}$ min	6 000 m
Deer	42 min	32 000 m

15. A train is scheduled to make a journey of 300 km at an average speed of 120 km/hr.
It leaves six minutes late and its average speed is increased so that it arrives on time.
Find the new average speed.

16. Barbara's rule for mountain walkers is:

Allow 1 hour for every 5 km you must walk.
Add $\frac{1}{2}$ hour for every 300 metres you must climb.

Jasmine started a 4 km walk at 0800 hours.
The path climbed 1800 m from start to finish.
Jasmine wanted to work out at about what time she would finish the walk.
If she allows $2\frac{1}{2}$ hours for stops along the way, at about what time should she arrive?

Test yourself 12

1. Simplify these ratios as far as possible:
   (i) $28 : 35$
   (ii) $20\,cm : 1\,m$
   (iii) $250\,g : 3\,kg$
   (iv) $40c : €2$

2. A train left Dublin at 0945 and reached Limerick at 1215.
   (i) How long did the journey take?
   (ii) If the length of the journey is 220 km, find the average speed of the train in km/hr.

3. A rectangle is divided into four triangles, as shown.
   Find the ratio of
   Area of smallest triangle : Area of largest triangle

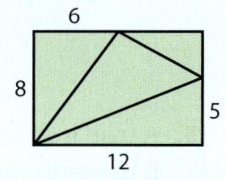

4. The ratio of sailing dinghies to motor cruisers moored in a harbour is $4 : 1$.
   If there are 24 dinghies in the harbour, how many motor cruisers are there?

5. A motorist travels at an average speed of 60 km/hr for $2\frac{1}{4}$ hours.
   If his car has an average fuel consumption of 1 litre of petrol per 15 km, find how many litres of petrol are used.

6. A large ball of wool is used to knit a scarf.
   The scarf is 40 stitches wide and 120 cm long.
   If the same size ball of wool is used to knit a scarf 25 stitches wide, work out the length of the new scarf.

7. (i) For this almond cake recipe, write the ratio of butter to sugar to flour to ground almonds in its simplest form.
   (ii) In another recipe, the ratio of flour to sugar is $3 : 2$. How much sugar is needed to mix with 1.2 kg of flour?

   Rich Almond Cake
   0.25 kg butter
   350 g sugar
   0.5 kg flour
   150 g ground almonds

8. A school's lessons begin at 9.00 a.m. and end at 3.40 p.m. with an hour's break at lunchtime and 20 minutes break mid-morning.
   If there are 8 lessons of equal length, how long is a lesson?

9. A T.G.V. travels 567 km from Bordeaux to Paris at an average speed of 252 km/hr.
   Find the arrival time in Paris, if it leaves Bordeaux at 1410.

Chapter 12 Ratio – Time – Speed

10. A bus travels for 2 hours at an average speed of 90 km/hr and then for a further hour at a speed of 60 km/hr.
   Find (i) the total distance travelled (ii) the total time taken
   (iii) the average speed of the bus for the whole journey in km/hr.

11. An alloy consists of copper, zinc and tin in the ratio 1 : 3 : 5.
   If there are 45 kg of tin in the alloy, find its total mass.

12. An aeroplane was due to take off from Shannon airport at 18:42 but it was 35 min late. During the flight, thanks to a tail wind, the plane made up the time and in fact landed 16 min before its scheduled arrival time of 00:05. (Assume that the plane did not cross any time zones on its journey.)
   (i) What time did the aeroplane take off?
   (ii) What time did it land?

13. A prize fund was divided between A, B and C in the ratio 5 : 2 : 1.
   If B received €520, find the total prize fund.

14. The Grand Old Duke of York, he had ten thousand men, he marched them up to the top of the hill, ...
   By 2 p.m. they were one third of the way up.
   By 4 p.m. they were three quarters of the way up.
   When did they set out?

15. A 500 ml jug is filled with orange squash and lemonade in the ratio 1 : 4.
   Another 1 litre jug is filled with orange squash and lemonade in the ratio 1 : 3.
   Both jugs are poured into one large jug.
   What is the ratio of orange squash to lemonade in the large jug?

16. The largest square is divided into 4 squares, as shown.
   What proportion of this diagram is shaded?
   Give your answer as a fraction.

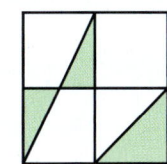

17. A contractor estimated that he could do a certain job in 1 year with 280 men.
   If he was asked to do the work in 10 months, how many more men would he need to employ?

18. A man walks 15 kilometres at an average speed of 6 km/hr.
   He then runs 9 kilometres at an average speed of 18 km/hr.
   Find (i) the total time taken for the two journeys
   (ii) his average speed for the two journeys.

19. In a grand prix, the winning car passed the chequered flag 0.3 seconds ahead of the next car.
   Both cars were travelling at 84 m/s.
   What was the distance between the two cars?

Assignment:

In groups, plan a school trip with your class.

The trip must include the use of at least one mode of transport: plane – train – bus.

You must research:

1. Places of interest to visit.

2. Best and most efficient ways to travel to your destination.

3. Timetables/calendars to decide dates and start / finish times.

4. Costs involved in travelling to and visiting your destination.

5. Possible discounts for groups.

Present your plan as a series of bullet points on a large poster, or as a digital presentation, to your class.

Compare plans and decide as a class which trip you would like to go on.

Statistics 3 – Presenting Data

chapter 13

From first year, you will recall how to:
- draw and interpret line plots,
- draw and interpret bar charts,
- draw and interpret stem and leaf plots,
- understand the key of a stem and leaf plot,
- use bar charts to measure frequency.

In this chapter, you will learn to:
- draw and interpret pie charts,
- draw and interpret histograms,
- understand the differences between bar charts and histograms,
- draw and interpret back-to-back stem and leaf plots,
- select the most appropriate graph or chart for a given set of data,
- evaluate the effectiveness of a graph or chart,
- identify misleading graphs or charts.

Section 13.1 Revision of line plots and bar charts

1. Line plots

The following data shows the daily maximum temperatures (in °C) in Barcelona during the month of June.

```
27  28  26  25  26  27  22  30  28  29
28  26  24  22  28  24  27  29  28  27
19  25  26  29  29  26  28  28  31  25
```

These temperatures are shown in the line plot below:

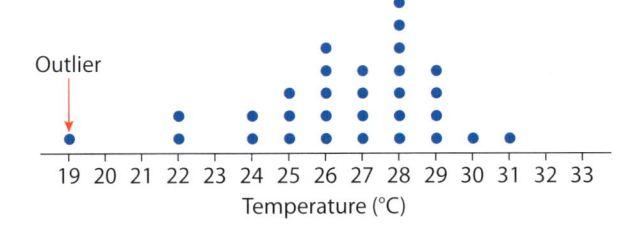

Each temperature is represented by a dot

Text & Tests 2 Higher Level

The **range** is 19°C to 31°C, i.e., 12°C.
The **mode** is 28°C as it occurs most frequently.
19°C is referred to as an **outlier** as it is significantly different from the rest of the scores.
The temperatures are bunched or **clustered** between 25°C and 29°C.

2. Bar charts

Bar charts are a simple but effective way of displaying data.

A bar chart consists of a series of bars of the same width, drawn either vertically or horizontally from an axis.

The heights (or lengths) of the bars always represent the frequencies.

The bars are generally separated by narrow gaps of equal width.

The bar chart below shows the numbers of text messages received by a group of students on a particular Saturday.

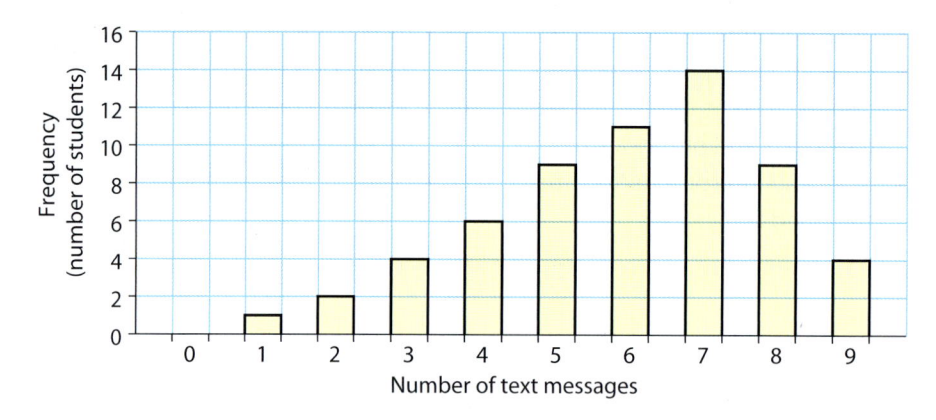

The total number of students =
$$1 + 2 + 4 + 6 + 9 + 11 + 14 + 9 + 4 = 60.$$

The total number of text messages received was =

$(1 \times 1) + (2 \times 2) + (4 \times 3) + (6 \times 4) + (9 \times 5) + (11 \times 6) + (14 \times 7) + (9 \times 8) + (4 \times 9) = 358$

The modal number of texts is 7 and the range is 1 to 9, i.e. 8 texts

The mean number of texts per student = $\frac{358}{60}$ = 6 (corrected to the nearest whole number)

Exercise 13.1

1. The line plot below illustrates the number of goals scored per match by a hockey team.

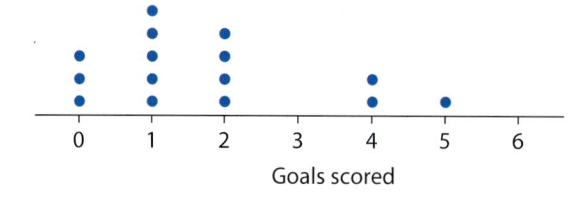

Chapter 13 Statistics 3 – Presenting Data

    (i) How many matches have the team played?
    (ii) Which number of goals scored is the mode?
    (iii) What is the range of the number of goals scored?
    (iv) What percentage of their matches were scoreless?

2. The daily maximum temperatures (in °C) at the Eiffel Tower during April are shown in this line plot: 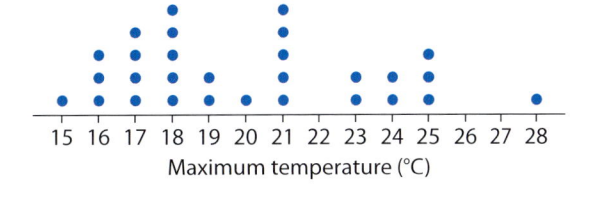
    (i) What is the mode?
    (ii) What is the outlier?
    (iii) On how many days was the maximum temperature 25°C?
    (iv) On what percentage of days did the maximum temperature drop below 20°C?
    (v) If a day is selected at random, what is the probability that the maximum temperature is less than 18°C?

3. This line plot shows the scores (out of 50) of a group of students in a maths exam:

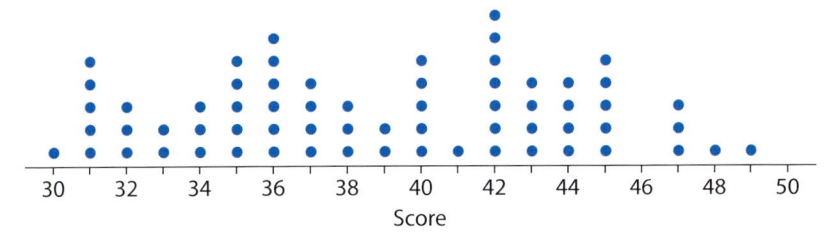

    (i) Which score was the most common?
    (ii) How many students scored 34?
    (iii) How many students scored 45 or more?
    (iv) What percentage of students scored 35 or less?
    (v) If a student was selected at random, what is the probability that he scored 40?

4. This bar chart shows the number of pictures remembered by each student in a memory experiment. 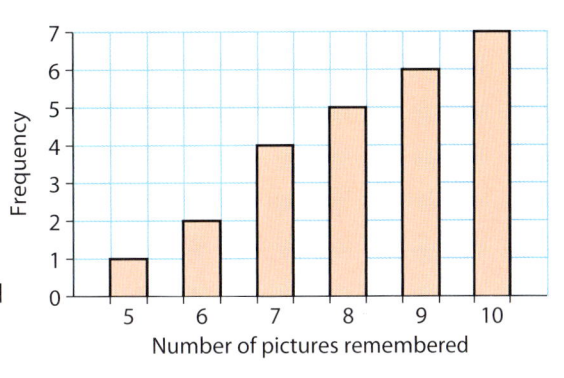
    (i) How many students took part in the experiment?
    (ii) What is the modal number of pictures remembered?
    (iii) How many students remembered less than 7 pictures?
    (iv) What is the range of the number of pictures remembered?

(v) What is the median number of pictures remembered?
(vi) What was the total number of pictures remembered by all the students?
(vii) What was the mean number of pictures remembered?

5. The bar chart shows the numbers of hours spent on homework each week by a group of second-year students.

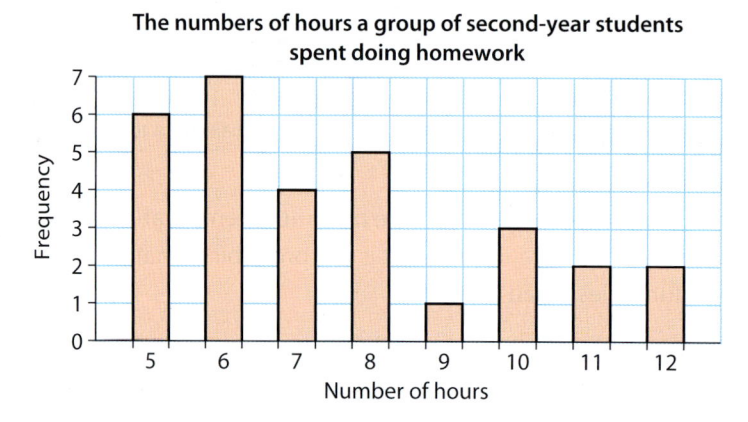

The numbers of hours a group of second-year students spent doing homework

(i) How many students spent 6 hours doing homework?
(ii) What was the greatest number of hours a student spent doing homework?
(iii) How many students spent less than 7 hours doing homework?
(iv) How many students spent more than 10 hours doing homework?
(v) How many students were surveyed?
(vi) What percentage of students spent 8 hours doing homework?
(vii) If a student is selected at random, what is the probability that the student spent 10 hours doing homework?

6. The numbers of goals scored in a series of football matches is represented in the bar chart shown on the right.
   (i) How many matches were played?
   (ii) Calculate the total number of goals scored.
   (iii) Calculate the mean number of goals scored per match, correct to one decimal place.

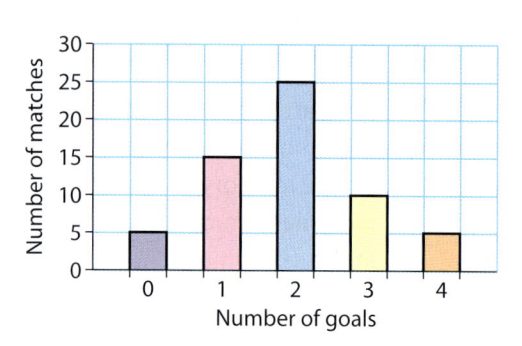

Chapter 13 Statistics 3 – Presenting Data

7. A group of 20 male and 20 female teenagers were asked their opinion on whether physical education should be compulsory. The results are displayed in this double-column bar chart.

(i) How many females strongly agree with compulsory physical education?

(ii) How many males strongly agree with compulsory physical education?

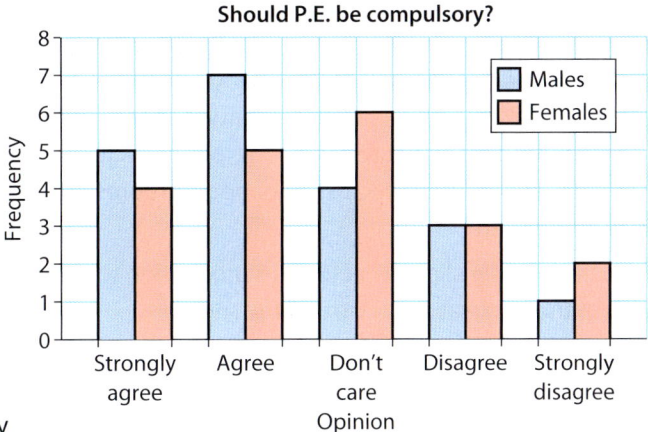

(iii) What is the total number of students who strongly disagree with compulsory physical education?

(iv) If a student was selected at random, what is the probability that the student strongly agreed that physical education should be compulsory? Give your answer as a decimal.

Investigation: Question 7 extension

Design a questionnaire to collect class opinion on the following questions:

(i) Should P.E. be compulsory?

and

(ii) Should a school uniform be compulsory?

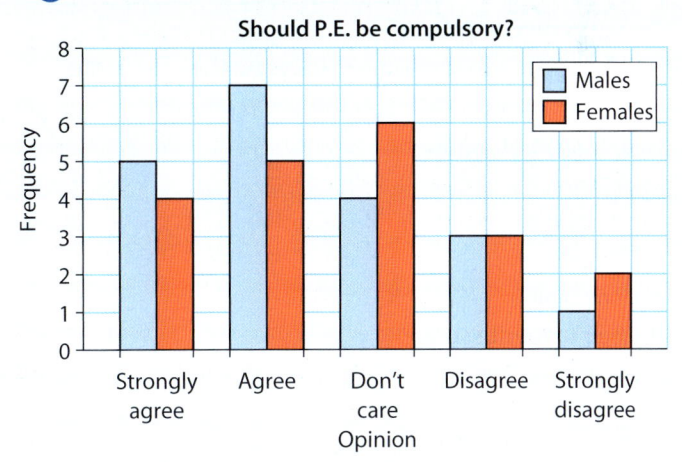

Use the categories:

  Strongly agree – Agree – Don't care – Disagree – Strongly disagree

Present your findings as a comparative bar chart (male v female or Junior v Senior). Describe how your findings differ from the chart in Question 7.

Text & Tests 2 Higher Level

Section 13.2 Pie charts

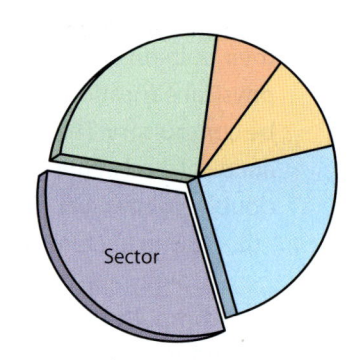

A **pie chart** is a good way of displaying information when we want to show how a given quantity is shared out or divided into different categories. The 'pie' or circle represents the total quantity and each 'slice' or **sector** represents the size of the share.

The size of each 'slice' or sector is in proportion to the size of the angle at the centre of the sector.

The angle at the centre of a circle or pie is 360°.
A half share will have an angle $\frac{1}{2} \times 360° = 180°$.

The diagram on the right shows how different shares are represented by sectors in a pie chart.

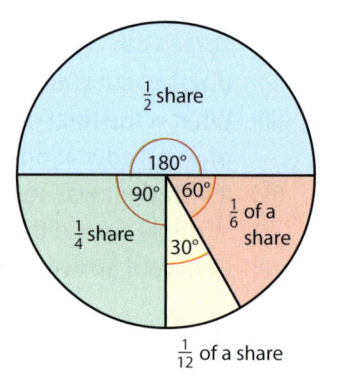

If the fraction of a share is $\frac{1}{6}$, the angle at the centre is found by getting $\frac{1}{6}$ of 360°.

$\frac{1}{6}$ of $360° = 360° \div 6 = 60°$.

Similarly, if the fraction is $\frac{1}{10}$, the angle at the centre is $\frac{1}{10}$ of $360° = 36°$.

> **Example 1**
>
> 120 first-year girls were asked to name their favourite sport. The result is shown in the given pie chart.
>
> How many girls named
> (i) tennis
> (ii) athletics
> (iii) hockey
> (iv) netball
> as their favourite sport? 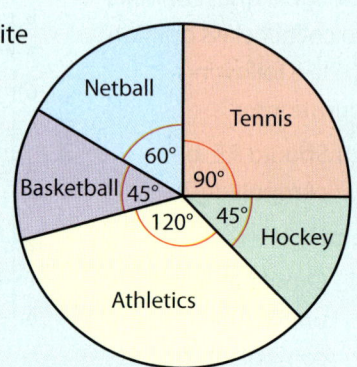
>
> Here we express each of the angles in the sectors required as a fraction of 360°.
>
> (i) **Tennis:** 90°; $\frac{90°}{360°} = \frac{1}{4}$ and $\frac{1}{4}$ of $120 = 30$
>
> ∴ 30 girls named tennis

Chapter 13 Statistics 3 – Presenting Data

(ii) **Athletics:** 120°; $\quad \frac{120°}{360°} = \frac{1}{3}$ and $\frac{1}{3}$ of 120 = 40

$\therefore \quad$ 40 girls named athletics

(iii) **Hockey:** 45°; $\quad \frac{45°}{360°} = \frac{9}{72} = \frac{1}{8}$ and $\frac{1}{8}$ of 120 = 15

$\therefore \quad$ 15 girls named hockey

(iv) **Netball:** 60°; $\quad \frac{60°}{360°} = \frac{1}{6}$ and $\frac{1}{6}$ of 120 = 20

$\therefore \quad$ 20 girls named netball

Example 2

In a survey, 72 people were asked what type of heating they had in their homes. The results are given in the table below:

Type of heating	Oil	Gas	Electricity	Solid fuel
Number of households	30	24	12	6

Draw a pie chart to illustrate this information.

The angle in each sector is found as follows:

Oil: $\quad \frac{30}{72} = \frac{5}{12}$ and $\frac{5}{12}$ of 360° $= \frac{5}{12} \times \frac{360}{1} = 150°$

Gas: $\quad \frac{24}{72} = \frac{1}{3}$ and $\frac{1}{3}$ of 360° = 120°

Electricity: $\quad \frac{12}{72} = \frac{1}{6}$ and $\frac{1}{6}$ of 360° = 60°

Solid fuel: $\quad \frac{6}{72} = \frac{1}{12}$ and $\frac{1}{12}$ of 360° = 30°

The results are represented by the pie chart on the right.

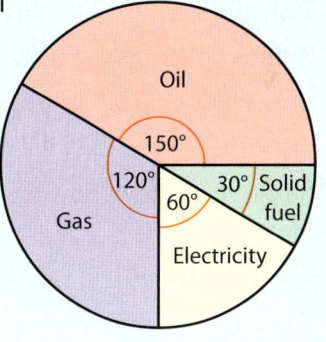

Exercise 13.2

1. Find the value of x in each pie chart shown.

(i) 45°, 90°, 120°, $x°$

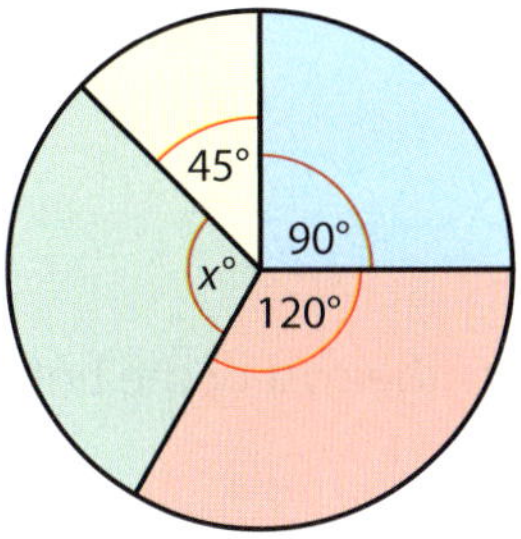

(ii) 30°, 150°, 60°, $x°$

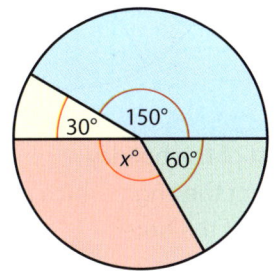

(iii) 45°, 60°, 130°, $x°$

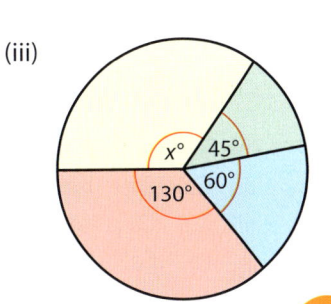

Text & Tests 2 Higher Level

2. On returning to Dublin, 240 holiday makers were asked to name countries they had visited.
   The results are shown in the pie chart on the right.
   (i) What is the size of the angle marked $x°$?
   (ii) How many people visited Portugal?
   (iii) Which country was visited by the most people?
   (iv) Which country was visited by $\frac{1}{4}$ of the people questioned?
   (v) Which two countries combined accounted for one half of the holiday makers questioned?

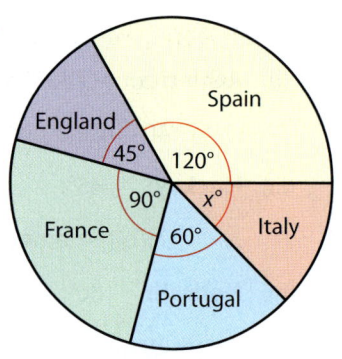

3. A packet of breakfast cereal weighing 600 g contains 4 ingredients as follows:

Oats	Barley	Wheat	Rye
150 g	100 g	75 g	275 g

   In the pie chart on the right, find the angle in the sector representing
   (i) oats   (ii) wheat   (iii) rye.

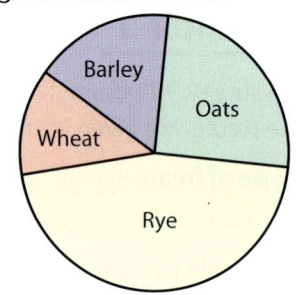

4. Sixty people were asked how they generally travel to work and the results are given in the following table:

Transport	Bus	Car	Train	Walk	Bicycle
Number of people	20	15	12	8	5

   (i) Calculate the angle in each of the sectors.
   (ii) Draw a pie chart to illustrate the data.

5. The pie chart shows how the cost of a holiday was shared between various items.

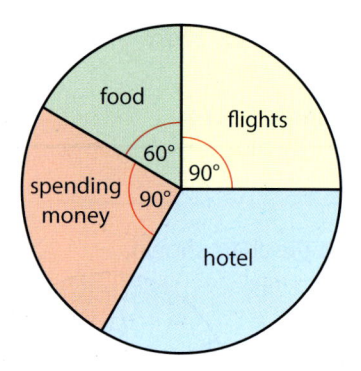

   The flights cost €450.
   (i) Calculate the total cost of the holiday.
   (ii) (a) Calculate the size of the angle which represents the cost of the hotel.
        (b) Calculate the cost of the hotel.

Chapter 13 Statistics 3 – Presenting Data

6. 100 people were asked to spell 'hypotenuse'.

   40 spelt it correctly, 35 would not try and 25 spelt it incorrectly.

   Select the pie chart below that correctly matches the information given.

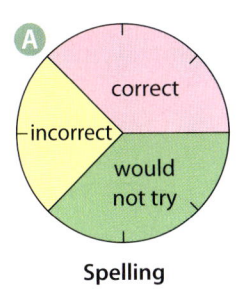

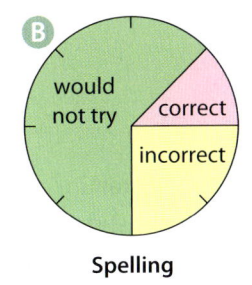

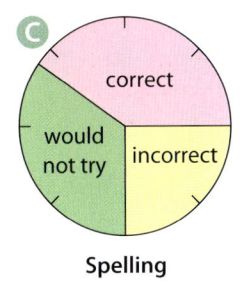

7. In a survey, some small children were asked to name their favourite pet.

   The following table shows the information about their answers.

Cat	Rabbit	Dog	Fish	Hamster
30	20	35	5	10

   Draw a pie chart to show the results of this survey.

8. These pie charts show what sorts of cards were in two stationery shops.

   Cardworld — 200 Cards

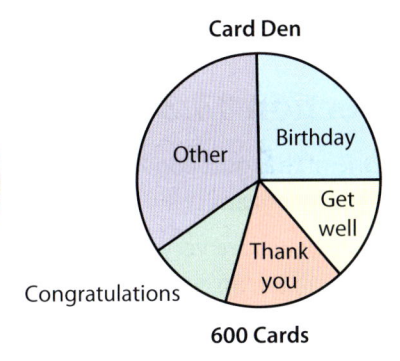

   Card Den — 600 Cards

   Cardworld had 200 cards and *Card Den* had 600 cards.
   (i) Approximately how many birthday cards were at *Card Den*?
   (ii) Jenny thought the pie charts above showed there were more *Congratulations* cards at *Cardworld* than at *Card Den*.
   Explain why the pie charts show that this is not so.

9. An ice cream stall sells vanilla, strawberry and chocolate ice creams. The pie chart illustrates the sales of ice cream for last Saturday. The number of vanilla and the number of chocolate ice creams sold were the same. The stall sold 60 strawberry ice creams. How many chocolate ice creams were sold?

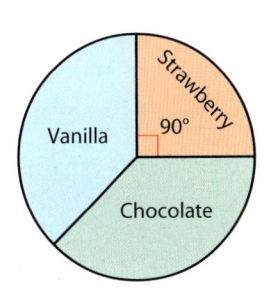

305

10. The pie chart illustrates the sales of four brands of crisps.
   (i) What percentage of total sales does *Tayto* have?
   (ii) If *Walkers* accounts for 35% of total sales, calculate the angles *x* and *y*.

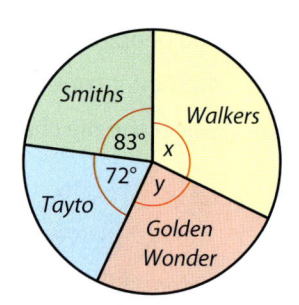

11. The pie-chart shows the proportion of the staff in Company A who work in sales / office / support / workshop when the workfoce totalled 260 employees on 1st June 2017.
   (i) Using a protractor, find the size of the angles in
       (a) workshop (b) office (c) support.
   (ii) Find the number of people who worked in
       (a) workshop (b) office (c) support (d) sales.

On 1st June 2016, the number of support staff was exactly half the number of sales staff.
The support staff then was 12% of the workforce. The sales staff increased by 30% from 1st June, 2016 to 1st June 2017. Calculate the size of the worforce on the 1st June 2016.

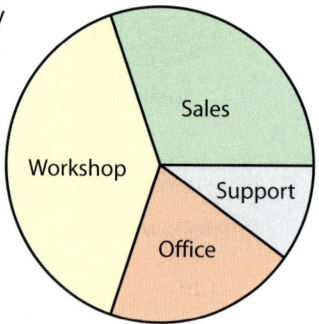

Section 13.3 Histograms

One of the most common ways of representing a frequency distribution is by means of a **histogram**.

Histograms are very similar to bar charts but there are some important differences:
› there are no gaps between the bars in a histogram
› histograms are used to show **continuous data**
   e.g. a continuous time interval from 0 to 25 minutes
   where the time is broken into **classes**,
   $0 \leq t < 5$ min, $5 \leq t < 10$ min, etc.
› the **area** of each bar or rectangle represents the frequency.

Histograms may have equal or unequal class intervals.
For our course, we will confine our study to histograms with **equal class intervals**.
When the class intervals are equal, drawing a histogram is very similar to drawing a bar chart.

Chapter 13 Statistics 3 – Presenting Data

Example 1

Fifty children were asked to solve a puzzle.
The table below records the time, in minutes, taken by the children.

Time (in mins)	0–5	5–10	10–15	15–20	20–25
Number of children	6	10	16	12	6

Note: 0–5 means all the values from 0 up to but not including 5, i.e. **0 ≤ t < 5 min**

All the groups have the same interval of 5 minutes.
To draw the histogram, you start by drawing the two axes.

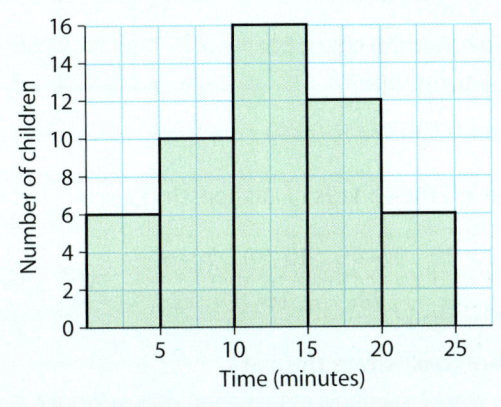

The horizontal axis shows the time. Each group or class is 5 minutes.
The vertical axis is labelled 'Number of children'.
We now draw the rectangles or bars for each class.
Notice that the heights of the bars represent the frequencies.
The **modal class** is (10–15) minutes because there are more children in this class than any other class.

Exercise 13.3

1. The histogram on the right shows the distances, in kilometres, travelled to work by people in an office block.
    (i) How many people travelled between 6 km and 9 km to work?
    (ii) How many people had to travel more than 9 km?
    (iii) What is the modal class?
    (iv) What is the total number of people included in the survey?

   Note: 0–3 means 0 km ≤ D < 3 km

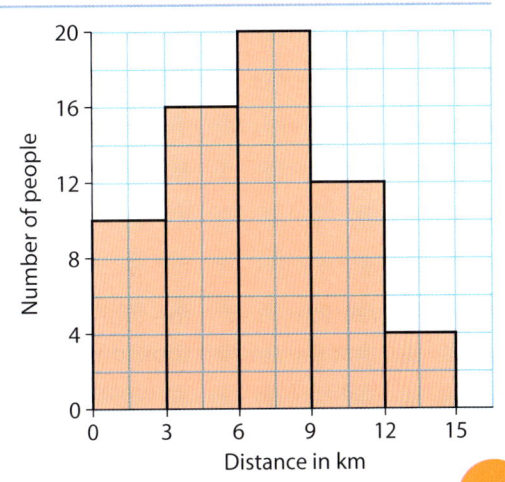

Text & Tests 2 Higher Level

2. The histogram shows the number of people who used a snack bar before lunch one weekday.

   (i) At what time do you think the snack bar opened?
   (ii) How many people used the snack bar during the first hour?
   (iii) Why do you think that the people used the snack bar at this time?

   The snack bar had another busy hour.

   (iv) When was it busy again?
   (v) Why do you think that the snack bar was busy for a second time?

   Note: 7:30–8:30 means $07{:}30 \leq t < 08{:}30$

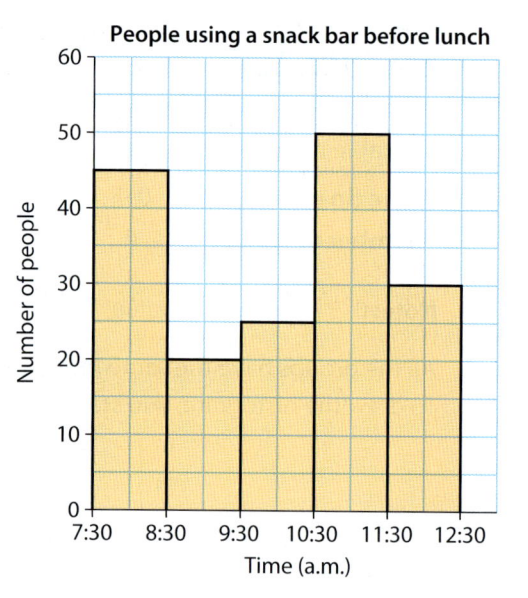

3. A Garda officer recorded the speeds of cars passing a school as follows:

Speed (in km)	20–30	30–40	40–50	50–60
Number of cars	8	20	16	12

   $20 \leq \text{speed} < 30$

   (i) Draw a histogram to illustrate this data.
   (ii) How many cars were travelling at less than 40 km/hour?
   (iii) If the speed limit was 55 km/hr, what is the maximum number of cars that could have exceeded this limit?

4. The histogram below shows the times taken by a group of students to solve a problem.

   (i) How many students were in the group?
   (ii) Write down the modal class.
   (iii) What percentage of students took between 20 seconds and 30 seconds to solve the problem?
   (iv) What is the greatest number of students who could have solved the problem in less than 35 seconds?
   (v) If a student is selected at random, what is the probability that the student took longer than 40 seconds to solve the problem?

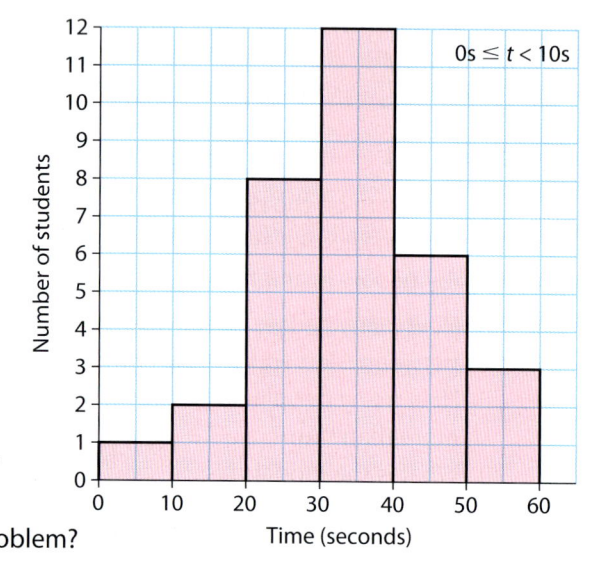

   $0s \leq t < 10s$

Chapter 13 Statistics 3 – Presenting Data

5. At the end of their journeys, 30 motorists were asked how many kilometres they had travelled. Their responses are shown in the table below:

Distance (in km)	0–20	20–40	40–60	60–80	80–100
Frequency	6	12	7	4	1

[0–20 means ⩾0 and <20]

(i) Draw a histogram to illustrate this data.
(ii) How many motorists had travelled 40 km or more?
(iii) What is the modal class?
(iv) If the median is the value that is halfway into the distribution, in which interval does the median lie?
(v) Use the mid-interval values to estimate the mean of the distribution.

6. The histogram opposite shows the annual salaries of a group of graduates in their first year of employment.

(i) How many graduates earned more than €40 000?
(ii) What is the modal class for the salaries?
(iii) What is the greatest number of graduates who could have earned more than €35 000?
(iv) How many graduates were surveyed?
(v) If a graduate was selected at random from the group, what is the probability that he/she earned between €10 000 and €20 000?

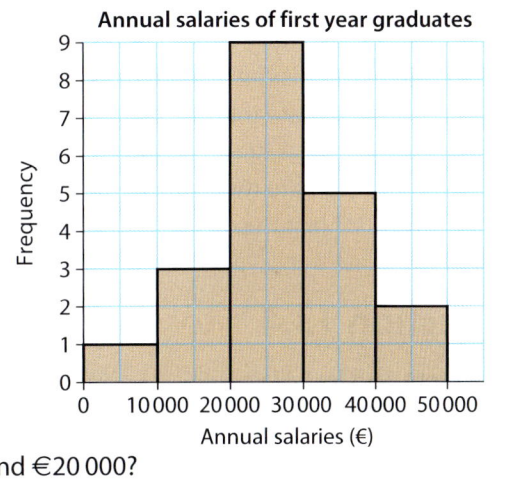

7. The histogram below shows the ages of people living in a village.

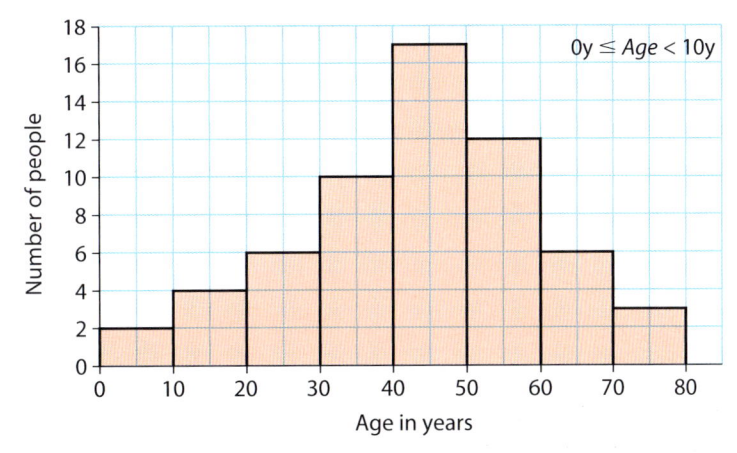

(i) How many people are aged under 30 years?
(ii) How many people live in the village?

(iii) Which interval contains 20% of the people?
(iv) If a person is selected at random, what is the probability that he/she is aged between 60 and 70 years?
(v) What is the greatest number of people who could be older than 55 years?
(vi) Use the mid-interval values to find an estimate of the mean age.

8. A frequency distribution of the heights of a group of students is shown.

Height (h cm)	$130 \leq h < 140$	$140 \leq h < 150$	$150 \leq h < 160$	$160 \leq h < 170$	$170 \leq h < 180$
Frequency	1	7	12	9	3

(i) Draw a histogram to illustrate this data.
(ii) What is the modal class of heights?
(iii) How many students were measured?
(iv) What is the median height of the students?
(v) Estimate the sum of all the heights of the students using mid-interval values.
   i.e. $130 \leq h < 140$ cm = 135 cm
(vi) Estimate the mean height of the students.
(vii) What is the greatest % of students whose height might be between 145 and 165 cm?

Section 13.4 Stem and leaf plots

A **stem and leaf diagram** is a very useful way of presenting data. It is useful because it shows all the original data and also gives you the overall picture or shape of the distribution.

It is similar to a horizontal bar chart, with the numbers themselves forming the bars.

Stem and leaf diagrams are suitable only for small amounts of data.

If data consists of 2 digits, the first digit is used as the stem and the second digit as the leaf.

The number 42 is written as 4|2.

A typical stem and leaf diagram is shown below.

```
0 | 6 9
1 | 2 5 (7)  ←──────── This represents 17.
2 | 3 3 6 8
3 | 0 2 7
4 | 1 2 6
5 | 3           Key: 3|2 = 32
```

> You must always add a key to show how the stem and leaf combine.

The data represented above is:

6, 9, 12, 15, 17, 23, 23, 26, 28, 30, 32, 37, 41, 42, 46, 53

Chapter 13 Statistics 3 – Presenting Data

Notice that all the numbers are in order of size, starting with the smallest and finishing with the largest.

This is called an **ordered** stem and leaf plot.

> **Example 1**
>
> Use a stem and leaf plot to show the following ages of the 21 musicians in an orchestra:
>
>   25   35   28   47   52   33   50   28   33   35   48
>   55   29   50   39   41   32   29   56   26   35
>
> (i) What is the mode of the data?
>
> (ii) What is the median age?
>
> The ages range from 25 to 56.
>
> We write 2, 3, 4 and 5 down the first column to make the stem.
>
> The leaves are the single digits written next to the stem: 25 is shown by writing a 5 next to the 2 stem.
>
> | Stem | Leaf |
> |---|---|
> | 2 | 5 8 8 9 9 6 |
> | 3 | 5 3 3 5 9 2 5 |
> | 4 | 7 8 1 |
> | 5 | 2 0 5 0 6 |
>
> This is an unordered stem and leaf plot.
>
> *In a stem and leaf plot, the numbers must align beneath one another.*
>
> It is more useful to rearrange the scores so they are in order, from smallest to largest. This results in an **ordered** stem and leaf plot.
>
> | Stem | Leaf |
> |---|---|
> | 2 | 5 6 8 8 9 9 |
> | 3 | 2 3 3 5 5 5 9 |
> | 4 | 1 7 8 |
> | 5 | 0 0 2 5 6 |
>
> Key: 3|2 = 32
>
> (i) The mode is 35 as it occurs most frequently.
>
> (ii) The median is the value that is halfway through the distribution.
> There are 21 values altogether.
> The median value is the 11th value.
> This value is 35, i.e. the median is 35.

Text & Tests 2 Higher Level

Back-to-back stem and leaf plots

Two stem and leaf diagrams can be drawn using the same stem.

These are known as back-to-back stem and leaf diagrams.

The leaves of one set of data are put to the right of the stem.

The leaves of the other set of data are put on the left.

A back-to-back stem and leaf diagram is very useful to compare two sets of data.

This is illustrated in the following example.

> **Example 2**
>
> The Science teacher decided to give her class a test on a particular topic. The class performed poorly. One week later she gave the class a similar test after a thorough revision of the topic.
> The results are shown in the back-to-back stem and leaf plot below.
>
> | | | | | | Leaf | Stem | Leaf | | | | |
> |---|---|---|---|---|---|---|---|---|---|---|---|
> | | | 9 | 8 | 6 | 6 0 | 3 | | | | | |
> | | 9 7 | 7 | 3 | 1 | 1 1 | 4 | 3 | 6 | 6 | 8 | |
> | | 9 8 | 8 | 5 | 3 | 3 0 | 5 | 1 | 7 | 9 | 9 | |
> | | | 9 | 8 | 7 | 5 3 | 6 | 3 | 8 | 9 | | |
> | | | | | | | 7 | 0 | 5 | 5 | 5 8 9 | |
> | | | | | | | 8 | 2 | 6 | 7 | 7 | |
> | | | | | | 0 | 9 | 0 | 0 | 1 | 3 | |
>
> Key: 3|6 = 63   Key: 8|2 = 82
>
> (i) What does the diagram show about the performance of the class in the two tests?
> (ii) Find the median mark in each test.
> (iii) Write down the range of the marks in each test.
> (iv) Do the median marks and the ranges support your conclusion in (i) above?
> (v) Identify any outliers in the test results.
>
> (i) The diagram shows that the class scored far better in the second test.
> 14 students scored 70 marks or higher in the second test while there was only one student with a mark higher than 70 in the first test.
> (ii) There are 25 students in the class.
> The median mark in each test is the 13th mark.
> The median mark in the first test is 50.
> The median mark in the second test is 75.
> (iii) The range in the first test is 90–30, i.e. 60.
> The range in the second test is 93–43, i.e. 50.

(iv) Since the median mark in the second test is 75 and only 50 in the first test, it confirms the conclusion that the students did better in the second test. Also the range is higher in the first test and this shows that the marks were more spread out (i.e. less consistent) in the first test.

(v) In the first test, the score 90 is an outlier.
In the second test, there are no outliers.

Exercise 13.4

1. The stem and leaf diagram below shows the ages, in years, of 25 people who wished to enter a 10 km walking competition.

stem	leaf
1	4 4 6 9
2	1 3 7 7 7 8
3	3 6 6 7 9
4	0 2 3 3 8 8
5	1 3 4 7

Key: 1|6 means 16 years old

(i) How many people were less than 20 years old?
(ii) Write down the modal age.
(iii) How many people were between 35 and 45 years old?
(iv) What was the median age?

2. The stem and leaf diagram on the right shows the marks obtained by a group of students in a Spanish test.

stem	leaf
5	1 4 6
6	2 3 3 6
7	2 3 5 7 8
8	0 0 2 4 6 6
9	3 4

Key: 7|3 means 73 marks

(i) How many students took this test?
(ii) How many students got between 70 and 79 marks?
(iii) What is the range of the marks obtained?
(iv) Find the median mark.

Text & Tests 2 Higher Level

3. The number of points scored per match by the Dragons basketball team are shown below:

85	67	56	69	99	97	59	65	84	97
49	72	89	78	66	81	92	88	53	73

Copy and complete the stem and leaf plot on the right.
  (i) Write down the range of the scores.
  (ii) Find the median score.
  (iii) In what percentage of matches was the number of points scored greater than 80?

stem	leaf
4	9
5	3 6
6	
7	
8	
9	

4. Twenty four pupils were asked how many CDs they had in their collection. The results are shown below:

23	2	18	14	7	4	25	21	32	26	31	6
17	6	18	19	31	21	12	1	0	8	14	15

  (i) Draw a stem and leaf diagram to represent this information.
  (ii) How many pupils had more than 20 CDs?
  (iii) What is the median number of CDs in the collections?
  (iv) What is the mean number of CDs in the collections?
     Give your answer to the nearest whole number.

5. The stem and leaf plot below shows the marks achieved by 19 students in a test.

stem	leaf
2	2
3	4 6
4	2 7 9
5	3 4 5 8 9
6	0 2 6 7
7	2 6
8	1 4

Key: 4|2 = 42 marks

  (i) Using class intervals of 20–29, 30–39, 40–49, 50–59, 60–69, 70–79, 80–89, draw a histogram of the data in the stem and leaf diagram.
  (ii) Name one advantage the stem and leaf diagram has as a representation of this data.

6. These are the speeds, in km/hr, of vehicles crossing a city-centre bridge one afternoon:

15	17	12	16	24	29	36	25	38	42	17
53	44	49	53	29	21	11	38	14	29	

  (i) Draw a stem and leaf diagram to show these speeds.
  (ii) Find the mean, median and mode of this data.

Chapter 13 Statistics 3 – Presenting Data

7. The back-to-back stem and leaf plot below shows the pulse rates of a class at the beginning and end of a PE lesson.

```
                Pulse rates (beats per minute)
                Before PE            After PE
                        8 7 | 4 |
                7 4 2 1 0 0 | 5 | 3 5
              8 8 6 5 5 3 1 | 6 | 0 3 6 8 9
                  7 5 5 1 0 | 7 | 1 4 4 7 9 9
                      6 2 1 | 8 | 3 3 6 6 7 8 9 9
                        5 0 | 9 | 0 3 5 8
```

Key: 1|8 = 81 bpm   Key: 8|3 = 83 bpm

  (i) Write down the range of the pulse rates before and after the PE lesson.
  (ii) Find the median of the pulse rates before and after the PE lesson.
  (iii) Use your answers to (i) and (ii) to write a brief statement about the pulse rates of the class before and after the PE lesson.

8. Two different brands of batteries were tested in the same toy to determine which lasted longer.
The following data was collected.

Dynamo										
42	36	28	52	43	28	11	26	47	53	44	42
50	45	37	14	23	34	35	36	34	38	52	

Energy Plus										
24	40	18	29	26	13	39	34	17	37	13	41
32	17	18	28	36	29	19	29	38	37	38	

  (i) Draw a back-to-back stem and leaf plot for this data.
  (ii) Find the median length for each brand.
  (iii) By comparing the medians and ranges for the two brands, which brand do you think is better? Explain your answer.

9. The data below shows the average male life expectancy (in years) of the main countries in Africa in the year 2000.

Algeria	68	Madagascar	57	South Africa	62
Angola	45	Mauritius	68	Sudan	54
Ethiopia	48	Nigeria	51	Tunisia	68
Ghana	56	Rwanda	41	Uganda	40
Kenya	52	Sierra Leone	36		

(i) Put this data into a stem and leaf plot with the data in order.

The data for the female life expectancy in the same African countries is given on the right.

Female life expectancy (years)

3	9		
4	2	3	8
5	2	4	6	6
6	0	0	8
7	0	1	5

Key: 5|2 = 52

(ii) Compare the life expectancies of males and females in these African countries using the median and range for each set of data.

10. Martina and Jack took part in several tests and their results are shown below.

Martina			Jack			
	2	1	1	x		
6	5	z	2	3	7	8
6	2	1	3	2	y	7
	7	4	4	0	1	3

Key: 1|3 = 31   Key: 4|0 = 40

(i) In how many tests did they each participate?
(ii) In how many tests did Martina obtain marks below 30?
(iii) If the range of Jack's marks is 31, find the value of x.
(iv) If the median mark for Jack is 34, find the value of y.

11. The stem and leaf diagram below shows the number of copies of a local paper sold each week in the local newsagent over a period of 17 weeks.

stem	leaf					
0	8					
1	6	6	7	9	9	9
2	0	1	5	6	8	
3	2	4				
4	1	3	p			

Where $p \in N, 1 \leq p < 10$.   Key: 3|2 = 32 copies of the paper.

(i) The range of this data is 39. Find the value of p.
(ii) Find the value of (a) the mode and (b) the median of this data.
(iii) The sum of this data is 431. Find the mean number of papers sold per week.
(iv) There was a greater number of copies sold in the 18th week. Find:
   (a) the modal number of copies sold per week over the whole 18 weeks.
   (b) the median number of copies sold per week over the 18 weeks.
(v) The mean number of copies sold per week over the 18 weeks was 28.5. Work out the number of copies sold in the 18th week.

12. The results for examinations in History and Geography for a group of students are shown. The marks are given in percentages.

History: 91 27 55 69 83 25 45 53 67 71

30 52 45 59 86 73 65 47 54 38

Chapter 13 Statistics 3 – Presenting Data

Geography: 45 40 48 65 75 55 36 85 76 69
                64 58 47 64 67 72 83 74 62 51

(i) Construct a stem and leaf diagram for this data.

(ii) Compare and comment on the results in History and Geography.

Section 13.5 Misleading graphs

Because graphs and tables are based on information gathered and presented, people tend to believe the impressions they give. However, graphs can be used by unscrupulous people to give a false or misleading impression.

The following three graphs were used by *Munchies* dog food to compare its sales figures to those of *Doggo's* dog food.

We will use these graphs to highlight some of the more common ways of drawing graphs that may be used to give a false impression.

1. This graph does not have a scale on the vertical axis. You cannot tell how big the difference is between *Munchies* sales and *Doggo's* sales.

> The vertical axis must be labelled.

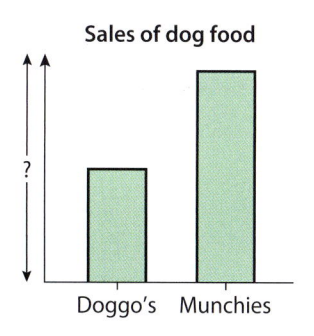

2. This graph shows only **part** of a scale. The scale does not start at 0. This makes the difference between *Munchies* sales and *Doggo's* sales look much bigger than it actually is.

> If an axis does not start from zero, or the zero is put in the wrong place, it can mislead people.

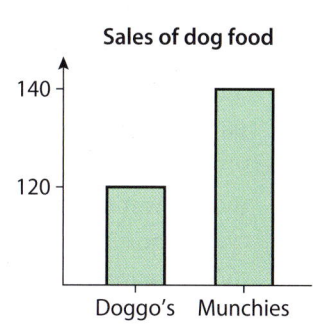

3. This graph uses pictures instead of columns. The *Munchies* dog is twice as tall as the *Doggo's* dog, but it is also twice as wide, making it seem much bigger (four times bigger).

Sales of dog food

> Using area or volume will mislead when only height is needed.

4. This graph shows the information correctly. The scale is regular and begins at 0. Notice that the difference in sales figures is not as large as it seemed in the three previous misleading graphs.

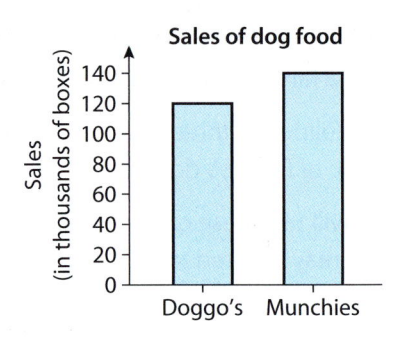

Sales of dog food

Exercise 13.5

1. **Boxit's Production of boxes 2001–2003**

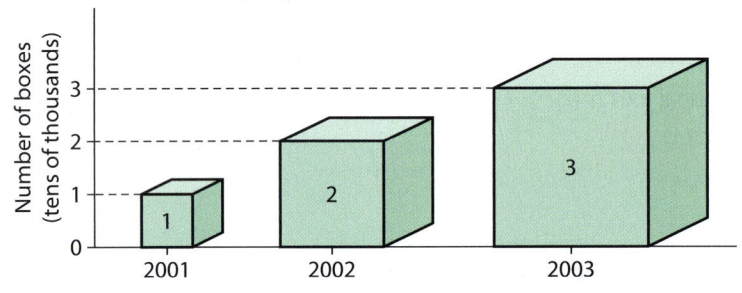

   (i) How many times greater is the height of box 2 than the height of box 1?
   (ii) How many times greater is the area of box 2 than the area of box 1?
   (iii) How many times greater is the volume of box 2 than the volume of box 1?
   (iv) How many times greater is the height of box 3 than the height of box 1?
   (v) How many times greater is the area of box 3 than the area of box 1?
   (vi) How many times greater is the volume of box 3 than the volume of box 1?
   (vii) Draw a vertical bar chart to represent the information shown here.

   > • Box 2 is meant to represent twice what box 1 represents, but it appears to be 8 times as big.
   > • Box 3 is meant to represent 3 times what box 1 represents, but it appears to be 27 times as big.

Chapter 13 Statistics 3 – Presenting Data

2. Give one reason why the graph on the right is misleading.

3. Describe the misleading or poor features of each of the following graphs:

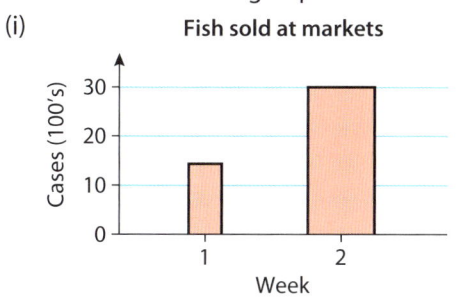

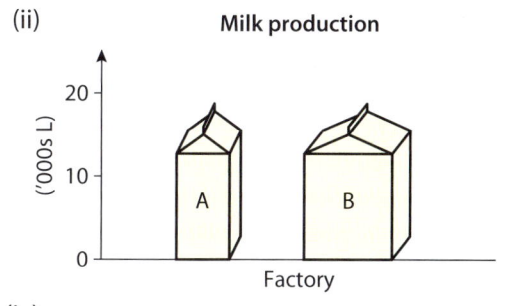

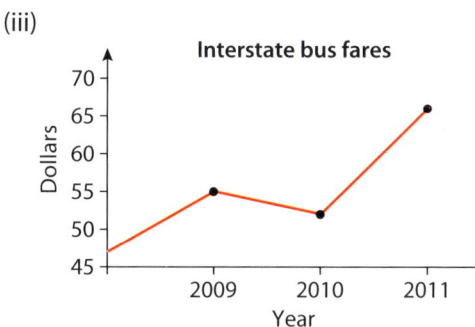

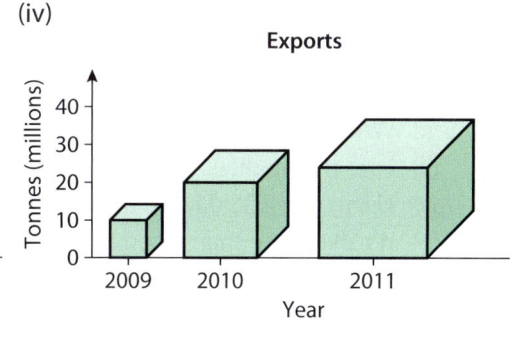

(i) Fish sold at markets

(ii) Milk production

(iii) Interstate bus fares

(iv) Exports

4. The Government releases the following graph showing the increase in employment in the tourism industry over recent years.

  (i) Explain why the graph is misleading.
  (ii) Redraw the graph in a way that more accurately indicates the increase in employment.

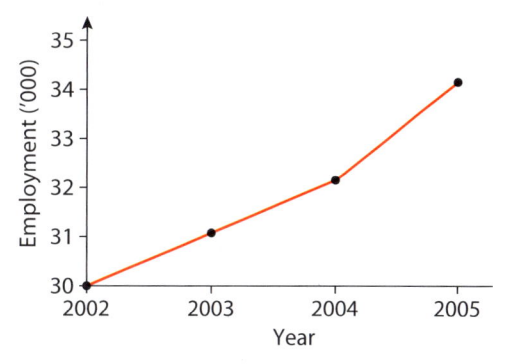

5. Draw a graph that gives a misleading impression for the data in the table below. Then draw another graph that illustrates the data correctly and accurately.

School sport	Hockey	Netball	Soccer
Number of players	14	12	10

319

Text & Tests 2 Higher Level

Test yourself 13

1. The pie chart shows how 180 boys at *Superfit Academy* chose five sports options.

    (i) Find the angle in the sector representing swimming.
    (ii) How many boys chose soccer?
    (iii) What percentage chose golf?

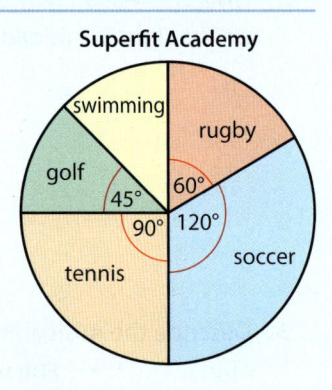

    Superfit Academy
    (pie chart: swimming, rugby 60°, soccer 120°, tennis 90°, golf 45°)

2. Neil records the number of emails he receives every day for 35 days. The data he collects is shown in the stem and leaf diagram.

stem	leaf
0	6 7 9 9
1	4 7 7 8 8 9 9
2	2 3 5 5 6 7 8 9 9 9
3	1 5 6 6 6 6 7
4	3 6 8 9
5	2 3 3

    Key: 3|1 = 31

    (i) Write down the mode of the data.
    (ii) Find the median.
    (iii) Using these 35 days as a sample, what is the probability that on the next day Neil receive more than 40 emails?

3. The histogram below shows information about the training times taken by some 100 m runners before the Olympic Games.

    (i) Write down the reason why there are no gaps between bars.
    (ii) Write down the number of runners that took between 10 and 12 seconds.
    (iii) Work out the number of runners that took 12 seconds or more.
    (iv) Work out how many runners there were altogether.
    (v) Using mid-interval values, find the mean time for the 100 m correct to one decimal place.

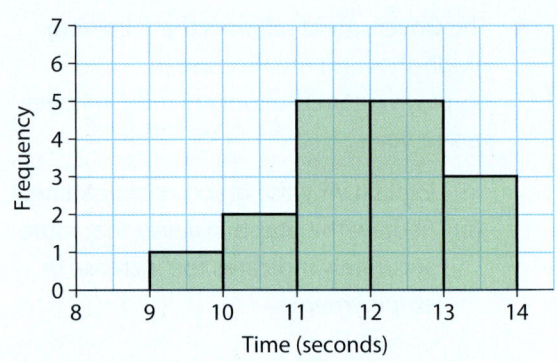

    Note: 9–10 means $9s \leq t < 10s$

Chapter 13 Statistics 3 – Presenting Data

4. These are the weights (in kg) of 24 babies born in a hospital.

   4.1 3.7 2.8 4.3 4.7 4.6 2.8 5.2 3.9 3.7 3.7 4.8
   3.8 3.4 4.9 4.6 4.7 4.2 3.0 3.1 2.5 5.0 4.5 4.5

   (i) Draw a stem and leaf plot for this data.
   (ii) Work out the mode and the median of the data.

5. These pie charts show the numbers of members in two tennis clubs.
   Greendale Club had 250 members altogether.
   Nevin Club had 100 members altogether.
   Lee thought the charts showed that Nevin Club had more senior female members than Greendale Club.
   Is this correct?
   Give a reason for your answer.

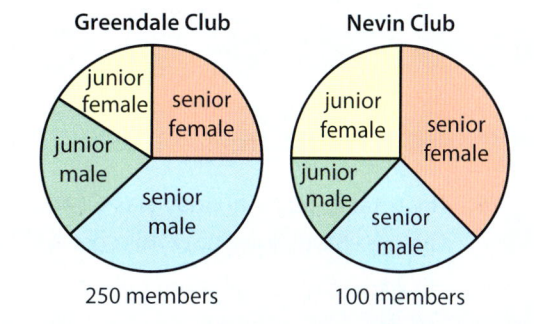

   Greendale Club — 250 members (sectors: junior female, senior female, junior male, senior male)
   Nevin Club — 100 members (sectors: junior female, senior female, junior male, senior male)

6. The numbers of drinks dispensed by a vending machine in one day are shown in the table.

Type of drink	Tea	Black coffee	Hot chocolate	Orange	Coke	Latte
Number of drinks	54	42	18	30	12	24

   (i) Find the angle in the sector representing orange.
   (ii) Find the angle in the sector representing black coffee.
   (iii) Draw a pie chart to represent this data.

7. Explain what is misleading about each of these diagrams.

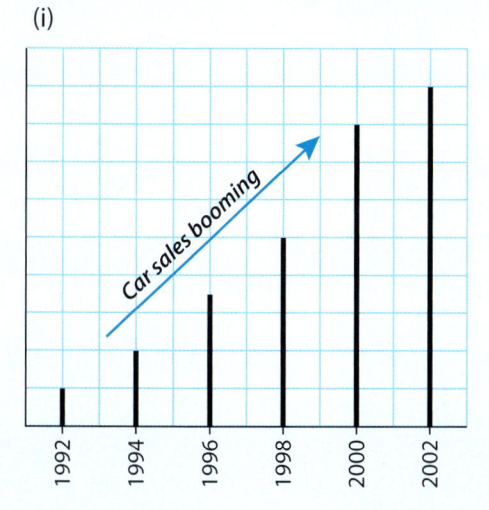

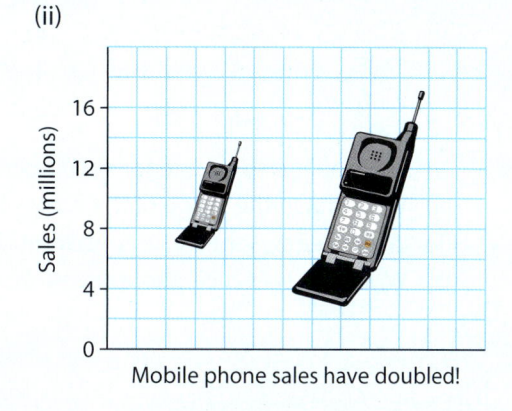

   (i) Car sales booming (bar chart, years 1992–2002)

   (ii) Mobile phone sales have doubled! (Sales in millions, 0–16)

8. Here are the maximum bench presses (in kg) of the members of an under-age rugby team.

| 54 | 42 | 61 | 47 | 24 | 43 | 55 | 62 | 30 | 27 |
| 28 | 43 | 54 | 46 | 25 | 32 | 49 | 73 | 50 | |

(i) Construct a stem and leaf diagram to show these results.
(ii) Write down the range of the weights.
(iii) Patrick was missing the day the team did the bench press exercise. How many presses must Patrick do so that the mean number of bench presses per member is 46?

9. The total cost of a holiday was €2400. The pie chart shows how this cost was made up.

(i) How much was spent on food?
(ii) How much was spent on travel?
(iii) How much was spent on the hotel?
(iv) How much was spent on other items?

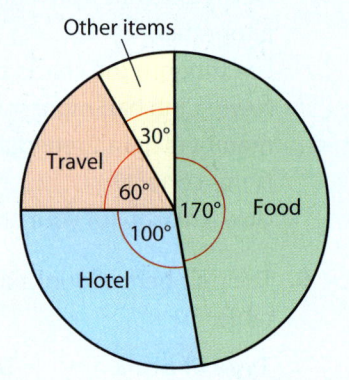

10. The following back-to-back stem and leaf plot show the points scored by *Sparks* and *Dynamos* in a series of matches.

Sparks		Dynamos
4 3	7	
8 7	8	9
5 0	9	5 7 8 9
4	10	0 2 6
9 3	11	0 2
2	12	

Key: 4|10 = 104   Key: 9|8 = 98

(i) Find the median score for each team.
(ii) Write down the range of the scores for each team.
(iii) Which team is the more consistent? Explain your answer.
(iv) Write one sentence about the scoring pattern of the *Sparks*.

Chapter 13 Statistics 3 – Presenting Data

11. John's third-year Physical Education class did a fitness test. The number of sit-ups that each student did in one minute is recorded below.

    59 48 27 53 36 29 52 46 45 37 49 51
    33 45 38 52 40 51 37 44 47 45 60 41

The students practised this exercise for the next three weeks and then repeated the test in the same order. The data for the second test is as follows:

    61 52 33 51 39 40 50 49 46 37 59 49
    38 48 39 58 44 52 38 44 49 51 62 44

  (i) Represent the data from the two tests in a back-to-back stem and leaf diagram.
  (ii) How many students are there in the class?
  (iii) What is the range of sit-ups for each test?
  (iv) Based on the data and the diagram, do you think that practice improves the ability to do sit-ups? Give a reason for your answer.
  (v) John did 41 sit-ups in Test 1 and 44 in Test 2.
      How did his performance compare with that of the rest of the class?

12. A survey was conducted to determine the numbers of hours students spent on the Internet per week. The results were as follows:

17	14	9	28	8	27	23	16	10	18
15	23	5	38	27	19	6	25	24	36
16	5	7	17	8	9	3	4	27	28
16	7	8	18	9	4	9	8	6	35

  (i) Arrange this information in a frequency distribution table using class intervals (1–10), (11–20), (21–30) and (31–40).
  (ii) Draw a bar chart to represent this information.
  (iii) How many students used the Internet for more than 30 hours per week?
  (iv) What percentage of students used the Internet for 25 hours or more per week?
  (v) What percentage of students used the Internet for fewer than 21 hours per week?

Text & Tests 2 Higher Level

Assignment:

A coin is tossed 4 times and the results noted as e.g. HHTH.
H for heads, T for tails.

Draw a large Chart A, listing all 16 possible outcomes.

Chart A

Chart B

Number of heads	0	1	2	3	4
Number of combinations					

Using Chart A, draw a Chart B showing the number of combinations of outcomes that have 0, 1, 2, etc, heads.

Chart C

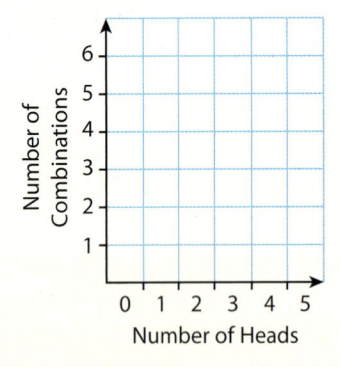

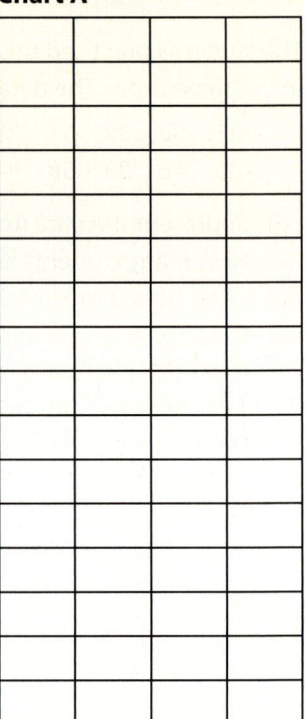

Draw a bar Chart C of the frequency distribution in Chart B

Using Chart B or Chart C, draw a Chart D of the probabilities of getting 0 *heads*, 1 *head*, 2 *heads*, 3 *heads*, 4 *heads* when tossing a coin 4 times.

Chart D

Number of heads	0	1	2	3	4
Probability					

What conclusion can you make about the sum of the probabilities?

324

Indices – Standard form – Surds

chapter 14

From first year, you will recall how to:

- round a number to a give number of decimal places,
- round a number to a given number of significant figures.

In this chapter, you will learn to:

- evaluate expressions written in index form using the Laws of Indices,
- solve equations involving indices,
- classify numbers as rational or irrational,
- simplify expressions involving surds,
- write a number in standard form,
- convert a number in standard form into decimal form,
- perform operations on numbers in standard form,
- correctly use a calculator to carry out multiple procedures at once.

Section 14.1 The laws of indices

$2^3 = 2 \times 2 \times 2 = 8$
2^3 is called '2 cubed' or '2 to the power of 3'.
3 is the **power** or **index** which tells us how many times the number 2 is multiplied by itself.

> **Power** is another word for **index**.

1. Multiplication

$4^2 \times 4^3 = (4 \times 4) \times (4 \times 4 \times 4)$
$ = 4^5$

Similarly, $x^2 \times x^3 = (x \times x) \times (x \times x \times x) = x^5$

So, $\quad x^2 \times x^3 = x^{2+3} = x^5$

> To **multiply** powers of the same number, **add** the indices.

2. Division

$\dfrac{3^5}{3^2} = \dfrac{3 \times 3 \times 3 \times 3 \times 3}{3 \times 3} = 3^3$

Similarly, $\dfrac{x^5}{x^2} = \dfrac{x \times x \times x \times x \times x}{x \times x} = x^3$

Thus, $\quad \dfrac{x^5}{x^2} = x^{5-2} = x^3$

> To **divide** powers of the same number, **subtract** the indices.

325

Text & Tests 2 Higher Level

3. A power to a power

$(x^2)^3$ means $(x^2) \times (x^2) \times (x^2) = x^6$
$\Rightarrow (x^2)^3 = x^{2+2+2} = x^6$
$\qquad \qquad = x^{2 \times 3}$

Similarly, $(x^4)^3 = x^{4 \times 3} = x^{12}$

> To **raise** a power to a further power, **multiply** the indices.

4. The power of zero

$\dfrac{2^3}{2^3} = \dfrac{8}{8} = 1$ and $\dfrac{2^3}{2^3} = 2^{3-3} = 2^0$

This shows that $2^0 = 1$.

> Any number to the power of zero is 1, i.e., $a^0 = 1$.

5. Negative indices

$\dfrac{4^3}{4^5}$ can be written as

$\dfrac{\cancel{4} \times \cancel{4} \times \cancel{4}}{\cancel{4} \times \cancel{4} \times \cancel{4} \times 4 \times 4} = \dfrac{1}{4^2}$

Also, $\dfrac{4^3}{4^5} = 4^{3-5} = 4^{-2} \Rightarrow \dfrac{1}{4^2} = 4^{-2}$

This shows that $\dfrac{1}{4^2} = 4^{-2}$.

> $a^{-n} = \dfrac{1}{a^n}$ e.g. $3^{-2} = \dfrac{1}{3^2}$

6. A product or quotient to a power

$(2 \times 3)^2 = 6^2 = 36$
Also, $(2 \times 3)^2 = 2^2 \times 3^2 = 4 \times 9 = 36$.
This illustrates that $(ab)^n = a^n b^n$.
Similarly, it can be shown that
$\left(\dfrac{a}{b}\right)^n = \dfrac{a^n}{b^n}$

> $(ab)^n = a^n b^n$
> $\left(\dfrac{a}{b}\right)^n = \dfrac{a^n}{b^n}$

Example 1

Express each of these as a single number without a power:

(i) $2^3 \times 2^2$ (ii) $\dfrac{3^5}{3^2}$ (iii) $(2^2)^3$ (iv) $\dfrac{1}{3^{-2}}$ (v) $(3 \times 4)^2$ (vi) 8^0

(i) $2^3 \times 2^2 = 2^{3+2} = 2^5 = 32$ (ii) $\dfrac{3^5}{3^2} = 3^{5-2} = 3^3 = 27$

(iii) $(2^2)^3 = 2^{2 \times 3} = 2^6 = 64$ (iv) $\dfrac{1}{3^{-2}} = 3^2 = 9$

(v) $(3 \times 4)^2 = 3^2 \times 4^2$ (vi) $8^0 = 1$
$\qquad \qquad = 9 \times 16 = 144$

326

Chapter 14 Indices – Standard form – Surds

Exercise 14.1

1. Write each of these as a single number without an index:
   (i) 7^2
   (ii) 4^3
   (iii) 2×2^3
   (iv) $\dfrac{5^4}{5^2}$
   (v) $\dfrac{6^5}{6^3}$

2. Write each of the following as a single number to a power:
   (i) $2 \times 2 \times 2$
   (ii) 2×2^3
   (iii) $4^2 \times 4^3$
   (iv) $5 \times 5^2 \times 5^3$
   (v) $a \times a^5$
   (vi) $2x^2 \times 3x$
   (vii) $2x^2 \times 4x^3$
   (viii) $\dfrac{a^5}{a^2}$

3. Express as a single number to a power:
   (i) 9
   (ii) 25
   (iii) 27
   (iv) 32
   (v) 1000
   (vi) 400

4. Express as a single number in index form:
   (i) $\dfrac{5^4}{5^2}$
   (ii) $\dfrac{3^5}{3}$
   (iii) $\dfrac{7^5}{7^3}$
   (iv) $\dfrac{3^8}{3^4}$
   (v) $\dfrac{5^8}{5}$
   (vi) $\dfrac{4^3 \times 4^2}{4}$

5. State whether each of the following statements is true or false:
   (i) $5^2 = 5 \times 2$
   (ii) $3^2 > 2^3$
   (iii) $2^6 < 5^2$
   (iv) $3^4 < 6^2$

6. Simplify each of these and express your answer as a whole number:
   (i) $\dfrac{2^4 \times 2^2}{2^3}$
   (ii) $\dfrac{4^3 \times 4}{4^2}$
   (iii) $\dfrac{3^7 \times 3}{3^6}$
   (iv) $\dfrac{7^6 \times 7^2}{7^5}$
   (v) $\dfrac{3^7 \times 3^4}{3^8 \times 3}$

7. Express each of the following as a whole number or as a fraction:
   (i) 3^{-2}
   (ii) $\dfrac{1}{2^{-3}}$
   (iii) $\dfrac{3}{2^{-2}}$
   (iv) $\dfrac{2^{-2}}{3}$
   (v) $\dfrac{2^{-4}}{4^{-2}}$

8. Write down the numbers missing from these calculations:
   (i) $8 \times 8^7 = 8^\square$
   (ii) $7^5 \times 7^\square = 7^8$
   (iii) $\dfrac{9^7}{9^\square} = 9^3$
   (iv) $\dfrac{3^9}{3^\square} = 3$

9. What does the question mark (?) stand for in each of the following?

   A $3^5 \times 3^{-2} = ?$

   B $\dfrac{3^3}{3^5} = ?$

   C $(2^3)^{-2} = ?$

   D $6^{-1} \times 6^{-2} = ?$

   E $\dfrac{7^2}{7^2} = ?$

   F $2^{-5} \times 2^3 = ?$

   G $(3^{-1})^{-2} = ?$

   H $\dfrac{5^3}{5^{-2}} = ?$

10. Simplify each of these:
    (i) $(2 \times 3)^2$
    (ii) $\left(\dfrac{1}{2}\right)^3$
    (iii) $\left(\dfrac{2}{3}\right)^2$
    (iv) $(ab)^3$
    (v) $\left(\dfrac{2a}{3b}\right)^2$

11. Copy and complete these:
    (i) $3^2 \times 5^3 \times 5^4 \times 3^6 = 3^\square \times 5^\square$
    (ii) $2 \times 9^2 \times 2^5 \times 9^3 = 2^\square \times 9^\square$
    (iii) $4^7 \times 3^\square \times 4 \times 3^2 = 3^{10} \times 4^\square$
    (iv) $3^4 \times 11^\square \times 3^\square \times 11^5 = 3^5 \times 11^8$

327

Text & Tests 2 Higher Level

12. Which of these statements is false?

  A $2^5 \times 3^4 \times 2^2 = 2^7 \times 3^4$ **B** $5^2 \times 6^3 \times 5^4 \times 6 = 5^6 \times 6^4$ **C** $2^2 \times 3^5 = 6^7$

13. Copy and complete these:

  (i) $(4^2)^3 = 4^\square$ (ii) $(2^4)^\square = 2^{12}$ (iii) $(2^4)^n = 2^\square$ (iv) $(5^x)^\square = 5^{4x}$

14. Write each of these numbers as a power of 3:

  (i) 9   (ii) 9^2 (iii) 27^3 (iv) 81^2 (v) 9^n

15. Find four matching pairs.

  A 3^{-2} **B** 2^{-3} **C** 4^{-2} **D** 6^{-1} **E** -6 **F** $\frac{1}{6}$ **G** $\frac{1}{16}$ **H** $\frac{1}{8}$ **I** $\frac{1}{9}$

16. Simplify each of these:

  (i) $a^4 \times a^{-5}$ (ii) $a^3 \times a^{-3}$ (iii) $3a^7 \times 2a^{-5}$ (iv) $\dfrac{a^{-2}}{a^{-6}}$

17. Copy and complete the following:

  (i) $3^\square \times 3^{-2} = 3^6$ (ii) $\dfrac{4^{-1}}{4^\square} = 4^{-5}$ (iii) $a^2 \times a^\square \times a^{-4} = a^{-3}$

Section 14.2 Fractional indices

Fractional indices

We use the laws of indices to show that $2^{\frac{1}{2}} = \sqrt{2}$.
$2^{\frac{1}{2}} \times 2^{\frac{1}{2}} = 2^{\frac{1}{2}+\frac{1}{2}} = 2^1 = 2$.
Also, $\sqrt{2} \times \sqrt{2} = 2$.
This shows that $2^{\frac{1}{2}} = \sqrt{2}$.
Similarly, $2^{\frac{1}{3}} = \sqrt[3]{2}$.

$2^{\frac{1}{2}} = \sqrt{2}$
$2^{\frac{1}{3}} = \sqrt[3]{2}$
....
$2^{\frac{1}{n}} = \sqrt[n]{2}$

One of the laws of indices is $(a^m)^n = a^{mn}$.
From this rule it follows that

  $27^{\frac{2}{3}} = (27^{\frac{1}{3}})^2 = (\sqrt[3]{27})^2 = 3^2 = 9$.

Similarly, $16^{\frac{3}{4}} = (16^{\frac{1}{4}})^3 = (\sqrt[4]{16})^3 = (2)^3 = 8$.

$8^{\frac{2}{3}} = (\sqrt[3]{8})^2$
$16^{\frac{3}{4}} = (\sqrt[4]{16})^3$
....
$x^{\frac{m}{n}} = (\sqrt[n]{x})^m$

Note: $16^{\frac{3}{4}}$ may also be expressed as $\sqrt[4]{16^3}$.

However, it is generally easier to get $\sqrt[4]{16}$ first and then raise your answer to the power of 3.

328

Chapter 14 Indices – Standard form – Surds

> **Example 1**
>
> Write as rational numbers:
>   (i) $16^{\frac{1}{4}}$
>   (ii) $25^{\frac{3}{2}}$
>   (iii) $81^{-\frac{3}{4}}$
>   (iv) $\dfrac{1}{27^{\frac{2}{3}}}$
>
> (i) $16^{\frac{1}{4}} = \sqrt[4]{16} = 2$
>
> (ii) $25^{\frac{3}{2}} = (\sqrt{25})^3 = 5^3 = 125$
>
> (iii) $81^{-\frac{3}{4}} = \dfrac{1}{81^{\frac{3}{4}}} = \dfrac{1}{(\sqrt[4]{81})^3} = \dfrac{1}{3^3} = \dfrac{1}{27}$
>
> (iv) $\dfrac{1}{27^{\frac{2}{3}}} = \dfrac{1}{(\sqrt[3]{27})^2} = \dfrac{1}{3^2} = \dfrac{1}{9}$

When using a calculator to find $27^{\frac{2}{3}}$, key in

$$27 \to \boxed{x^\blacksquare} \to \boxed{\tfrac{[\,]}{[\,]}} \to 2 \downarrow 3 \to = 9$$

Note: $\boxed{x^y}$ may appear as $\boxed{x^\blacksquare}$ or $\boxed{y^x}$, depending on the calculator model.

Note: It is important to be able to simplify fractional indices without using a calculator, e.g. to solve equations involving indices (Section 14.3).

Exercise 14.2

1. Write down the value of each of these:
   (i) $\sqrt{25}$
   (ii) $\sqrt{144}$
   (iii) $\sqrt[3]{27}$
   (iv) $\sqrt[3]{64}$
   (v) $16^{\frac{1}{2}}$
   (vi) $125^{\frac{1}{3}}$

2. Express each of these as a rational number:
   (i) $25^{\frac{1}{2}}$
   (ii) $64^{\frac{1}{3}}$
   (iii) $216^{\frac{1}{3}}$
   (iv) $\left(\dfrac{8}{27}\right)^{\frac{1}{3}}$
   (v) $\left(\dfrac{16}{25}\right)^{\frac{1}{2}}$
   (vi) $\left(\dfrac{16}{81}\right)^{\frac{1}{4}}$

3. Write each of the following without using the $\sqrt{}$ sign:
   (i) $\sqrt{x}$
   (ii) $\sqrt[3]{x}$
   (iii) $\sqrt[4]{a}$
   (iv) $\sqrt[3]{a^2}$
   (v) $\sqrt{a^3}$
   (vi) $\sqrt[4]{a^3}$

4. Find the value of each of these:
   (i) $\left(\dfrac{1}{4}\right)^{\frac{1}{2}}$
   (ii) $\left(\dfrac{1}{27}\right)^{\frac{1}{3}}$
   (iii) $16^{-\frac{1}{2}}$
   (iv) $\left(\dfrac{1}{9}\right)^{-\frac{1}{2}}$
   (v) $(100)^{-\frac{1}{2}}$
   (vi) $(0.01)^{\frac{1}{2}}$

5. Rewrite the following using the $\sqrt{}$ sign:
   (i) $a^{\frac{1}{2}}$
   (ii) $a^{\frac{1}{4}}$
   (iii) $a^{\frac{2}{3}}$
   (iv) $a^{\frac{5}{2}}$
   (v) $a^{\frac{3}{4}}$
   (vi) $\left(\dfrac{a}{x}\right)^{\frac{1}{2}}$

6. Find the value of each of the following:
   (i) $81^{\frac{1}{2}}$
   (ii) $8^{\frac{2}{3}}$
   (iii) $16^{\frac{3}{4}}$
   (iv) $4^{\frac{3}{2}}$
   (v) $27^{\frac{2}{3}}$
   (vi) $16^{\frac{3}{2}}$
   (vii) $64^{\frac{2}{3}}$
   (viii) $100^{\frac{3}{2}}$
   (ix) $81^{\frac{3}{4}}$
   (x) $125^{\frac{2}{3}}$

329

Text & Tests 2 Higher Level

7. Evaluate each of these:

   (i) 3^{-1} (ii) 4^{-2} (iii) $8^{-\frac{1}{3}}$ (iv) $\dfrac{1}{16^{-\frac{1}{4}}}$ (v) $64^{-\frac{1}{3}}$

8. Find the value of each of the following:

   (i) $16^{-\frac{1}{2}}$ (ii) $\dfrac{1}{8^{-\frac{2}{3}}}$ (iii) $16^{-\frac{3}{4}}$ (iv) $100^{-\frac{3}{2}}$ (v) $32^{-\frac{3}{5}}$

9. Noting that $\left(\dfrac{2}{3}\right)^{-3} = \dfrac{2^{-3}}{3^{-3}} = \dfrac{3^3}{2^3} = \dfrac{27}{8}$, evaluate each of these:

   (i) $\left(\dfrac{2}{3}\right)^{-2}$ (ii) $\left(\dfrac{1}{4}\right)^{-2}$ (iii) $\left(\dfrac{3}{5}\right)^{-2}$ (iv) $\left(\dfrac{4}{9}\right)^{-\frac{1}{2}}$ (v) $\left(\dfrac{9}{25}\right)^{-\frac{1}{2}}$

10. Simplify each of these:

    (i) $49^{-\frac{3}{2}}$ (ii) $\left(\dfrac{9}{25}\right)^{-\frac{3}{2}}$ (iii) $\left(\dfrac{9}{4}\right)^{\frac{3}{2}}$ (iv) $\left(\dfrac{27}{125}\right)^{-\frac{2}{3}}$ (v) $\left(\dfrac{8}{1000}\right)^{-\frac{1}{3}}$

11. If $a = 64^{\frac{2}{3}}$ and $b = 3^{-2}$, write a and b as rational numbers.

    Hence find the value of $\sqrt{\dfrac{a}{b}}$.

12. Express as rational numbers: (i) $\left(\dfrac{8}{27}\right)^{\frac{2}{3}}$ (ii) $\dfrac{1}{(25)^{\frac{3}{2}}}$

13. If $K = 2a^{\frac{1}{2}}b^{-\frac{1}{3}}$, find the value of K when $a = 100$ and $b = 64$.

14. Simplify $\dfrac{4^2 \times 16^{\frac{1}{2}}}{64^{\frac{2}{3}} \times 4^3}$, giving your answer in the form 4^n, where $n \in \mathbb{Z}$.

15. (i) Show that $8^{\frac{2}{3}} \cdot 16^{\frac{3}{4}} = 32$.

    (ii) Show that $\left(3\frac{3}{8}\right)^{\frac{1}{3}} + \left(11\frac{1}{9}\right)^{-\frac{1}{2}} = 1\frac{4}{5}$.

16. Express $\dfrac{81^{\frac{1}{2}} \times 9^{-1}}{27^{\frac{2}{3}}}$ in the form 3^x, where $x \in \mathbb{Z}$.

17. Using the rules of indices show that $\dfrac{27^{\frac{2}{3}} \times 9^{-\frac{1}{2}}}{\sqrt[4]{81}} = 1$.

18. $\dfrac{625^{\frac{3}{4}}}{125^{\frac{1}{3}}} + \dfrac{25^{\frac{5}{2}}}{5^3} = a \times 5^b$, find the values of a and b.

Section 14.3 Equations involving indices

If $5^x = 5^2$, then $x = 2$.

Similarly, if $7^x = 7^{\frac{1}{2}}$, then $x = \frac{1}{2}$.

In general, if $a^x = a^y$, then $x = y$.

Chapter 14 Indices – Standard form – Surds

If we are given the equation $25^x = 125$, we express each side as a power of the same base number. In this case, the base number is 5.

Thus, if $25^x = 125$, then $(5^2)^x = 5^3$
$$5^{2x} = 5^3$$
$$2x = 3$$
$$x = 1\tfrac{1}{2}$$

Example 1

Write each of these as whole numbers or fractions:

(i) $4^x = 16$ (ii) $16^x = 64$ (iii) $3^x = \dfrac{1}{27}$ (iv) $25^x = \dfrac{1}{125}$

(i) $4^x = 16$
$4^x = 4^2$
$x = 2$

(ii) $16^x = 64$
$(4^2)^x = 4^3$
$4^{2x} = 4^3$
$2x = 3 \Rightarrow x = 1\tfrac{1}{2}$

(iii) $3^x = \dfrac{1}{27}$
$3^x = \dfrac{1}{3^3}$
$3^x = 3^{-3}$
$x = -3$

(iv) $25^x = \dfrac{1}{125}$
$(5^2)^x = \dfrac{1}{5^3}$
$5^{2x} = 5^{-3}$
$2x = -3$
$x = -1\tfrac{1}{2}$

Example 2

Express (i) 9^{2x-3} (ii) $\dfrac{1}{27}$ as powers of 3.

Hence solve the equation $9^{2x-3} = \dfrac{1}{27}$

(i) $9^{2x-3} = (3^2)^{2x-3} = 3^{4x-6}$

(ii) $\dfrac{1}{27} = \dfrac{1}{3^3} = 3^{-3}$

$9^{2x-3} = \dfrac{1}{27} \Rightarrow 3^{4x-6} = 3^{-3}$
$\Rightarrow 4x - 6 = -3$
$4x = 3$
$x = \tfrac{3}{4}$

Text & Tests 2 Higher Level

Exercise 14.3

1. Express each of the following in the form 2^k, where k is an integer:
   - (i) 8
   - (ii) 16
   - (iii) $\frac{1}{4}$
   - (iv) $\frac{1}{8}$
   - (v) $\frac{1}{32}$

2. Express each of the following in the form 3^k, where k is an integer:
   - (i) 9
   - (ii) 27
   - (iii) 81
   - (iv) $\frac{1}{27}$
   - (v) $\frac{1}{81}$

3. Write each of the following as a power of 2:
   - (i) $2\sqrt{2}$
   - (ii) $8\sqrt{2}$
   - (iii) $\frac{4}{\sqrt{2}}$
   - (iv) $\frac{16}{\sqrt{2}}$
   - (v) $\frac{\sqrt{2}}{8}$

4. Solve these equations:
   - (i) $2^x = 8$
   - (ii) $3^x = 27$
   - (iii) $9^x = 27$
   - (iv) $8^x = 32$
   - (v) $4^x = 32$
   - (vi) $16^x = 64$
   - (vii) $25^x = 125$
   - (viii) $16^x = 32$

5. Solve each of these equations:
   - (i) $2^x = \frac{1}{4}$
   - (ii) $3^x = \frac{1}{27}$
   - (iii) $4^x = \frac{1}{8}$
   - (iv) $5^x = 125$

6. Solve each of these equations:
   - (i) $27^x = 81$
   - (ii) $\frac{1}{5^x} = 125$
   - (iii) $4^x = \frac{1}{32}$
   - (iv) $2^{x+1} = 16$

7. Find the value of x in each of the following:
   - (i) $3^{x-2} = 81$
   - (ii) $4^{x-1} = 2^{x+1}$
   - (iii) $4^{x-1} = \frac{1}{32}$
   - (iv) $25^{x-1} = \frac{1}{125}$

8. Express each of the following in the form 5^k, where k is a rational number:
   - (i) $\sqrt{5}$
   - (ii) $5\sqrt{5}$
   - (iii) $\frac{25}{\sqrt{5}}$
   - (iv) $125\sqrt{5}$
   - (v) $\frac{1}{25\sqrt{5}}$

9. Work out the value of x in each of these:
   - (i) $2^x = \frac{\sqrt{2}}{2}$
   - (ii) $3^x = \frac{1}{\sqrt{3}}$
   - (iii) $5^x = \frac{125}{\sqrt{5}}$
   - (iv) $2^{x+4} = \frac{8}{\sqrt{2}}$

10. Write $\frac{81}{\sqrt{3}}$ as a power of 3, and hence solve the equation $9^{x+1} = \frac{81}{\sqrt{3}}$.

11. Express $\frac{27}{\sqrt{3}}$ as a power of 3, and hence solve the equation $3^{2x+1} = \left(\frac{27}{\sqrt{3}}\right)^3$.

12. Express $\frac{16}{\sqrt{8}}$ as a power of 2, and hence solve the equation $2^{2x-2} = \frac{16}{\sqrt{8}}$.

13. Express $\frac{\sqrt{27}}{81}$ as a power of 3, and hence solve the equation $9^{3-x} = \frac{\sqrt{27}}{81}$.

14. Express (i) 16 (ii) $2\sqrt{2}$ as a power of 2.

    Hence solve the equation $2^{2x-1} = \left(\frac{16}{2\sqrt{2}}\right)^3$.

332

Chapter 14 Indices – Standard form – Surds

Section 14.4 Irrational numbers – Surds

1. Rational numbers

Rational numbers are numbers that can be written in the form $\frac{a}{b}$, where a and b are integers.
The decimal equivalent of a rational number either **terminates** or **recurs**.
Rational numbers are denoted by the letter **Q**.
Here are some examples:

(i) $\frac{7}{8} = 0.875$ (ii) $\frac{1}{3} = 0.333$
                                    $= 0.\dot{3}$

(iii) $\frac{3}{11} = 0.272727...$ (iv) $\frac{7}{12} = 0.58333...$
      $= 0.\dot{2}\dot{7}$ $= 0.58\dot{3}$

> When using the dot notation in a recurring decimal, a dot is written above the first and last digit of a recurring group.
> Example: $0.454545... = 0.\dot{4}\dot{5}$

From the examples above and below it can be seen that rational numbers include whole numbers, fractions, and decimals which terminate (end) or recur (repeat).

Examples of rational numbers are

(i) $4 = \frac{4}{1}$ (ii) $\frac{2}{3}$ (iii) $-\frac{7}{8}$ (iv) $0.45 = \frac{45}{100}$ (v) $0.666... = \frac{2}{3}$

2. Irrational numbers

If you use your calculator to find $\sqrt{2}$, you will get $1.414213562...$
This number is never-ending and non-repeating.
Such numbers are called **irrational numbers**.
They are called irrational because they cannot be expressed as rational numbers, that is, in the form of a fraction.

The square root of any number that does not have an exact square root is an irrational number.
Thus $\sqrt{5}, \sqrt{11}, \sqrt{15}, ...$ are irrational numbers.
However $\sqrt{9}, \sqrt{16}, \sqrt{25}$ are rational numbers as they have exact square roots.
A well-known irrational number is π, since $\pi = 3.14159265...$, a non-repeating and non-terminating decimal.

Remember
> Any number which can be expressed as a fraction is called a **rational number**.
> Numbers such as $\sqrt{2}, \sqrt{5}, \pi, ...$ which cannot be expressed as fractions, are called **irrational numbers**.

333

Text & Tests 2 Higher Level

When rational and irrational numbers are combined, they form the set of **real numbers**. The set of real numbers is denoted by the letter **R**.
The set of irrational numbers is denoted by **R\Q**, that is, the set of real numbers less the set of rational numbers.

3. Surds

Irrational numbers such as as $\sqrt{3}, \sqrt{8}, \sqrt{13}, \ldots$ are said to be expressed in **surd** form.

We will now consider $\sqrt{100}$ in two ways:

$\sqrt{100} = 10$. Also, $\sqrt{100} = \sqrt{25 \times 4} = \sqrt{25} \times \sqrt{4} = 5 \times 2 = 10$.

This illustrates a very important property of surds, as stated in the highlighted box.

We will now use these properties to show how a surd can be simplified if one of its factors is a **perfect square** such as 4, 9, 16, 25, …

$$\sqrt{ab} = \sqrt{a} \times \sqrt{b}$$

$$\sqrt{\frac{a}{b}} = \frac{\sqrt{a}}{\sqrt{b}}$$

(i) $\sqrt{8} = \sqrt{4} \cdot \sqrt{2}$
    $= 2\sqrt{2}$

(ii) $\sqrt{27} = \sqrt{9} \cdot \sqrt{3}$
     $= 3\sqrt{3}$

(iii) $\sqrt{48} = \sqrt{16} \cdot \sqrt{3}$
      $= 4\sqrt{3}$

(iv) $2\sqrt{45} = 2 \times \sqrt{9} \times \sqrt{5}$
     $= 2 \times 3 \times \sqrt{5}$
     $= 6\sqrt{5}$

$2\sqrt{2}$ is said to be the **simplest form** of $\sqrt{8}$.

4. Adding and subtracting surds

Surds may be added or subtracted only when they have the same irrational parts. If the irrational parts are not the same, we reduce each surd to its simplest form, where possible.

> **Example 1**
>
> Simplify $\sqrt{5} + \sqrt{45} - \sqrt{20}$.
>
> We first express each surd in its simplest form:
> $\sqrt{5} + \sqrt{45} - \sqrt{20} = \sqrt{5} + \sqrt{9}\sqrt{5} - \sqrt{4}\sqrt{5}$
> $= \sqrt{5} + 3\sqrt{5} - 2\sqrt{5}$
> $= 4\sqrt{5} - 2\sqrt{5} = 2\sqrt{5}$

5. Multiplying surds

When multiplying surds, multiply separately the rational factors and the irrational factors.

Chapter 14 Indices – Standard form – Surds

Examples (i) $\sqrt{6} \times \sqrt{2} = \sqrt{12} = \sqrt{4}\,.\sqrt{3} = 2\sqrt{3}$
(ii) $2\sqrt{3} \times 3\sqrt{5} = 2 \times 3 \times \sqrt{3} \times \sqrt{5} = 6\sqrt{15}$
(iii) $\sqrt{32} \times \sqrt{48} = \sqrt{16}\,.\sqrt{2} \times \sqrt{16}\,.\sqrt{3}$
$= 4\sqrt{2} \times 4\sqrt{3} = 16\sqrt{6}$

Remember
$\sqrt{6} \times \sqrt{6} = 6$

Example 2

Simplify $(2\sqrt{5} - 3)(2\sqrt{5} + 3)$.

$(2\sqrt{5} - 3)(2\sqrt{5} + 3) = 2\sqrt{5}\,(2\sqrt{5} + 3) - 3(2\sqrt{5} + 3)$
$= (2\sqrt{5})(2\sqrt{5}) + (2\sqrt{5})3 - (3)(2\sqrt{5}) - (3)(3)$
$= 4(5) + 6\sqrt{5} - 6\sqrt{5} - 9$
$= 20 - 9 = 11$

Exercise 14.4

1. Which of these numbers are rational?
   (i) $\frac{4}{9}$ (ii) $2\frac{1}{2}$ (iii) $\sqrt{5}$ (iv) $\sqrt{9}$ (v) π (vi) $-1\frac{3}{4}$

2. Which of these numbers are irrational?
   (i) $\sqrt{7}$ (ii) $\sqrt{16}$ (iii) $4\sqrt{7}$ (iv) $0.\dot{4}$ (v) $\frac{\pi}{2}$ (vi) $\sqrt{3} + 2$

3. Write down the value of each of these:
   (i) $\sqrt{25}$ (ii) $\sqrt{400}$ (iii) $3\sqrt{16}$ (iv) $\frac{\sqrt{100}}{2}$ (v) $2 + 3\sqrt{81}$ (vi) $\sqrt{36} + 2\sqrt{4}$

4. Write down an irrational number between:
   (i) 3 and 4   (ii) 4 and 5   (iii) 10 and 11   (iv) 0 and 1

5. Write each of these in the form $\sqrt{n}$, where n is an integer:
   (i) $\sqrt{2} \times \sqrt{5}$ (ii) $\sqrt{3} \times \sqrt{7}$ (iii) $\sqrt{8} \times \sqrt{3}$ (iv) $\sqrt{5} \times \sqrt{11}$

6. Evaluate each of these:
   (i) $\sqrt{5} \times \sqrt{5}$ (ii) $(\sqrt{6})^2$ (iii) $(2\sqrt{3})^2$ (iv) $\sqrt{2} \times \sqrt{8}$ (v) $\left(\frac{\sqrt{8}}{\sqrt{2}}\right)^2$

7. Express each of these surds in its simplest form:
   (i) $\sqrt{8}$ (ii) $\sqrt{12}$ (iii) $\sqrt{18}$ (iv) $\sqrt{27}$ (v) $\sqrt{45}$

8. Express these surds in their simplest forms:
   (i) $\sqrt{75}$ (ii) $\sqrt{125}$ (iii) $2\sqrt{8}$ (iv) $4\sqrt{27}$ (v) $2\sqrt{48}$

Text & Tests 2 Higher Level

9. Sort these into matching pairs of equivalent numbers.
   Which is the odd one out?

   A $\sqrt{4} \times \sqrt{9}$ **B** $3\sqrt{2}$ **C** $\sqrt{4} \times \sqrt{6}$ **D** $\sqrt{8} + \sqrt{10}$ **E** $\sqrt{20}$

   F $\sqrt{2} \times \sqrt{5}$ **G** $\sqrt{10}$ **H** $\sqrt{18}$ **I** $\sqrt{24}$ **J** $2\sqrt{5}$ **K** $\sqrt{36}$

10. Express each of the following in its simplest form:
    - (i) $5\sqrt{3} + 4\sqrt{3} - \sqrt{3}$
    - (ii) $2\sqrt{2} + 6\sqrt{2} - 3\sqrt{2}$
    - (iii) $2\sqrt{2} + \sqrt{18}$
    - (iv) $\sqrt{18} + \sqrt{32}$
    - (v) $\sqrt{27} + \sqrt{48}$
    - (vi) $\sqrt{75} + \sqrt{12} - \sqrt{48}$

11. How many times greater than $\sqrt{2}$ is $\sqrt{32}$?

12. Express each of these products as a whole number:
    - (i) $2\sqrt{5} \cdot \sqrt{5}$
    - (ii) $2\sqrt{3} \times 3\sqrt{3}$
    - (iii) $3\sqrt{5} \times 4\sqrt{5}$
    - (iv) $3\sqrt{7} \times \sqrt{7}$

13. Simplify each of these:
    - (i) $\sqrt{5}(\sqrt{5} - 2)$
    - (ii) $2\sqrt{3}(\sqrt{3} - 2)$
    - (iii) $\sqrt{2}(3\sqrt{2} - \sqrt{3})$

14. Express the following products in their simplest forms:
    - (i) $2\sqrt{5}(\sqrt{2} - \sqrt{5})$
    - (ii) $(\sqrt{2} + 1)(\sqrt{2} - 1)$
    - (iii) $(5 + \sqrt{3})(5 - \sqrt{3})$
    - (iv) $(\sqrt{7} - 4)(\sqrt{7} + 4)$
    - (v) $(1 - 2\sqrt{3})(1 + 2\sqrt{3})$
    - (vi) $(\sqrt{2} + \sqrt{5})(\sqrt{2} - \sqrt{5})$

15. Simplify each of these:
    - (i) $(2 - \sqrt{3})(4 + 2\sqrt{3})$
    - (ii) $(1 - 3\sqrt{2})(5 + 2\sqrt{2})$
    - (iii) $(3 + 2\sqrt{2})(3 - 2\sqrt{2})$

16. Write $(2 - 2\sqrt{5})^2$ in the form $a + b\sqrt{5}$, where $a, b \in Z$.

17. Given that $p = \sqrt{5} + \sqrt{3}$ and $q = \sqrt{5} - \sqrt{3}$, simplify $p^2 - q^2$.

18. In the given right-angled triangle, find the value of k, $k \in Z$.

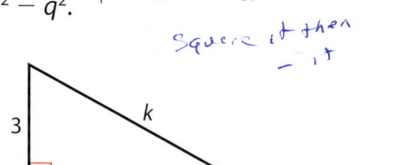

    (triangle with sides 3, k, and $\sqrt{12} + \sqrt{3}$)

19. $p = 2 + \sqrt{3}$ $q = 2 - \sqrt{3}$
    - (i) (a) Work out $p - q$.
      (b) State whether $p - q$ is rational or irrational.
    - (ii) (a) Work out pq.
      (b) State whether pq is rational or irrational.

Chapter 14 Indices – Standard form – Surds

Section 14.5 Numbers in standard form

If you use your calculator to perform the operation $60\,000 \times 4\,600\,000$, the screen will display the number 2.76×10^{11}.

This represents the number 2.76 multiplied by 10 eleven times.

The number 2.76×10^{11} is written in **scientific notation** or **standard form**.

Standard form is a convenient kind of shorthand for writing large and small numbers.

Definition   A number in the form $a \times 10^n$, where $1 \leq a < 10$, and n is an integer, is said to be expressed in scientific notation or standard form.

Example 6.8×10^4

This part is written as a number between 1 and 10.

This part is written as a power of 10.

Here are some numbers written in standard form:
(i) $5000 = 5 \times 1000 = 5 \times 10^3$
(ii) $64\,000 = 64 \times 1000 = 6.4 \times 10\,000 = 6.4 \times 10^4$
(iii) $380\,000 = 3.8 \times 10^5$

Notice that if you move the decimal point
(i)   1 place to the **left**, multiply by 10^1
(ii) 2 places to the **left**, multiply by 10^2
(iii) 3 places to the **left**, multiply by 10^3 ...

Numbers less than 1

To express a number such as 0.037 in standard form, move the decimal point 2 places to the right to get a number between 1 and 10, as shown below:

(i) $0.037 = \dfrac{3.7}{100} = \dfrac{3.7}{10^2} = 3.7 \times 10^{-2}$

(ii) $0.0045 = \dfrac{4.5}{1000} = \dfrac{4.5}{10^3} = 4.5 \times 10^{-3}$

In these examples, if you move the decimal point
(i) 2 places to the **right**, multiply by 10^{-2}
(ii) 3 places to the **right**, multiply by 10^{-3} ...

337

Text & Tests 2 Higher Level

On your calculator there is an $\boxed{\text{EXP}}$ or $\boxed{\times 10^x}$ key which stands for 'exponential' or 10 to any power.
To change the number 2.54×10^3 to decimal form, key in 2.54 $\boxed{\text{EXP}}$ 3 $\boxed{=}$.
The calculator will display 2540.

Adding and subtracting numbers in standard form

To add or subtract numbers expressed in standard form, convert each number to a decimal number and perform the addition or subtraction. You may also use a calculator as shown in the following example.

Example 1

Express in standard form: $1.84 \times 10^2 + 8.7 \times 10^3$.

$1.84 \times 10^2 = 184$ and $8.7 \times 10^3 = 8700$
$\therefore \quad 1.84 \times 10^2 + 8.7 \times 10^3 = 184 + 8700$
$\qquad\qquad\qquad\qquad\qquad = 8884$
$\qquad\qquad\qquad\qquad\qquad = 8.884 \times 10^3$

Key in 1.84 $\boxed{\times 10^x}$ $2 + 8.7$ $\boxed{\times 10^x}$ 3 $\boxed{=}$

The result displayed is 8884 which is 8.884×10^3.

Multiplying and dividing numbers in standard form

To multiply (or divide) numbers expressed in standard form, first multiply the 'a parts' and then multiply the numbers expressed as powers of 10.
The calculator is particularly useful in these operations.

Thus, $(3.8 \times 10^3)(9.4 \times 10^{-2}) = (3.8 \times 9.4) \times 10^3 \times 10^{-2}$
$\qquad\qquad\qquad\qquad\qquad\quad = 35.72 \times 10^1 \quad \ldots 3 - 2 = 1$
$\qquad\qquad\qquad\qquad\qquad\quad = 3.572 \times 10^2$

Or using a calculator, key in

3.8 $\boxed{\times 10^x}$ 3 $\boxed{\times}$ 9.4 $\boxed{\times 10^x}$ -2 $\boxed{=}$

The result is 357.2

$357.2 = 3.572 \times 10^2$

Chapter 14 Indices – Standard form – Surds

Example 2

Express each of these in standard form:

(i) $2.76 \times 10^3 - 5.9 \times 10^2$

(ii) $\dfrac{(6 \times 10^3) \times (4.5 \times 10^4)}{1.2 \times 10^4}$

(i) $2.76 \times 10^3 - 5.9 \times 10^2 = 2760 - 590$
$= 2170 = 2.17 \times 10^3$

[or key in 2.76 $\boxed{\times 10^x}$ 3 $\boxed{-}$ 5.9 $\boxed{\times 10^x}$ 2 $\boxed{=}$ The result is 2170.]

(ii) $\dfrac{(6 \times 10^3) \times (4.5 \times 10^4)}{1.2 \times 10^4} = \dfrac{6 \times 4.5 \times 10^3 \times 10^4}{1.2 \times 10^4}$

$= \dfrac{27 \times 10^7}{1.2 \times 10^4}$

$= \dfrac{27}{1.2} \times \dfrac{10^7}{10^4} = 22.5 \times 10^3$

$= 2.25 \times 10^4$

[or key in 6 $\boxed{\times 10^x}$ 3 $\boxed{\times}$ 4.5 $\boxed{\times 10^x}$ 4 $\boxed{\div}$ 1.2 $\boxed{\times 10^x}$ 4 $\boxed{=}$

The result is 22 500.
This is then converted to 2.25×10^4.]

Exercise 14.5

1. Which of the following numbers are written in standard form?
   (i) 3.6×10^2 (ii) 14.3×10^4 (iii) 0.8×10^3 (iv) 9.8×10^4

2. Write each of the following as a decimal number:
   (i) 6×10^2 (ii) 4.5×10^2 (iii) 6.8×10^3 (iv) 5.1×10^4
   (v) 6.7×10^4 (vi) 5.16×10^2 (vii) 7.05×10^3 (viii) 1.86×10^4

3. Write each of these numbers in standard form:
   (i) 400   (ii) 280   (iii) 840   (iv) 6200   (v) 8600
   (vi) 127   (vii) 827   (viii) 76 000   (ix) 146.8   (x) 72 400

4. Express these numbers in standard form:
   (i) 40×10^2 (ii) 320×10^3 (iii) 0.9×10^3 (iv) 94.3×10^2

5. Work these out and express your answers as decimal numbers:
   (i) $3.8 \times 10^2 + 1.7 \times 10^3$ (ii) $1.76 \times 10 + 6.43 \times 10^2$
   (iii) $8.4 \times 10^3 - 1.7 \times 10^2$ (iv) $6.64 \times 10^2 - 9.4 \times 10$

Text & Tests 2 Higher Level

6. Evaluate each of the following and give your answer in standard form:
   (i) $(3.6 \times 10^2) \times (1.5 \times 10^3)$
   (ii) $(4.6 \times 10^2) \times (3.7 \times 10^{-1})$
   (iii) $(3.64 \times 10^{-2}) \times (9 \times 10^4)$
   (iv) $(1.8 \times 10^{-4}) \times (8 \times 10^5)$

7. Change these numbers to decimal form:
   (i) 2.5×10^{-1}
   (ii) 6×10^{-2}
   (iii) 4.8×10^{-3}
   (iv) 9.2×10^{-4}

8. Write these numbers in standard form:
   (i) 0.04
   (ii) 0.062
   (iii) 0.007
   (iv) 0.0065

9. Write these numbers in standard form:
   (i) 0.008
   (ii) 0.0079
   (iii) 0.0006
   (iv) 0.00053

10. Write each of these in the form $a \times 10^n$, where $1 \leq a < 10, n \in Z$:
    (i) $\dfrac{8.4 \times 10^5}{1.2 \times 10^2}$
    (ii) $\dfrac{9 \times 10^4}{1.5 \times 10^2}$
    (iii) $\dfrac{4.48 \times 10^3}{8 \times 10^{-1}}$
    (iv) $\dfrac{8.4 \times 10^{-2}}{1.2 \times 10^3}$

11. Write these in standard form:
    (i) $\dfrac{1.4 \times 10^3 + 5.6 \times 10^2}{7 \times 10^{-1}}$
    (ii) $\dfrac{(6.4 \times 10^2) + (8.2 \times 10^4)}{1.033 \times 10^2}$

12. Express $\dfrac{1.2 \times 10^8 \times 3.6 \times 10^5}{1.8 \times 10^9}$ in standard form.

13. Calculate the value of $\dfrac{5.1 \times 10^8 + 1.9 \times 10^7}{1.4 \times 10^9}$ and write your answer as a decimal number.

14. Write each of these as a decimal number:
    (i) $\dfrac{6.8 \times 10^3 - 5.2 \times 10^2}{3.2 \times 10^2}$
    (ii) $\dfrac{1.12 \times 10^{-2} \times 9.8 \times 10^5}{1.4 \times 10^2}$

15. The Earth's diameter is 1.27×10^4 km and the diameter of Mars is 6.8×10^3 km.
    (i) Which planet has the larger diameter?
    (ii) What is the difference between their diameters?
    (iii) What is the total if the two diameters are added? Give your answer in standard form.

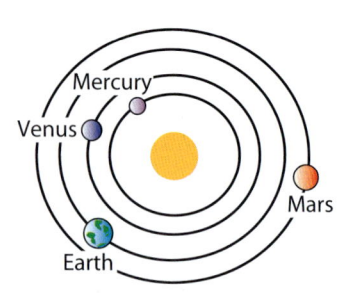

16. (a) If $speed = \dfrac{distance}{time}$, write an equation for time in terms of distance and speed.
    (b) The closest star to our sun is Proxima Centauri. It is 40 000 000 000 000 000 metres away from the Earth.
       (i) Write this distance in standard form.
       (ii) Light travels at a speed of 3×10^8 m/s. How many seconds does it take for light to travel from Proxima Centauri to Earth? Give your answer in standard form correct to 1 decimal place.

340

Chapter 14 Indices – Standard form – Surds

17. The length of the Amazon river is 7×10^6 metres long.
   The Shannon river is 3.6×10^5 metres long.
   How many 'times' longer, correct to the nearest whole number, is the Amazon?

18. The gross national income for Ireland in 2017 was €234 billion.
   The population of Ireland was 4.8 million for the same year.
   (i) Write each number in standard form.
   (ii) Calculate the income per capita (person) for 2017.

19. Cylinder A has a volume of 1.7×10^{12} cm³
   Cylinder B has a volume of 7.4×10^{13} cm³
   (i) If 1 litre = 1000 cm³, write the capacity of each cylinder in litres.
      Cylinder B is full of liquid.
   (ii) How many A-cylinders can be filled from cylinder B?

Section 14.6 Significant figures – Approximation

There are many occasions when it is either desirable or necessary to round off large or small numbers to a reasonable degree of accuracy. If there were 12 946 people at a football match, it would be reasonable to state that the attendance was about 13 000.
We say that 13 000 is given 'correct to the nearest thousand'.
Similarly, 1.823 could be rounded off to 1.8.

With the widespread use of calculators, it is important that we have some estimate of the answer we expect to get. Then we will know whether the answer shown on the calculator is reasonable or not. To make a rough estimate of a calculation, we generally give decimals correct to 1 or 2 decimal places and we round whole numbers to the nearest 10, 100 or 1000, as appropriate.

1. Decimal places

When writing a decimal correct to a given number of decimal places, count each digit, including zero, after the decimal point. If the last digit is 5 or more, increase the previous digit by 1. If the last digit is 4 or less, leave the previous digit as it is.

Thus, 6.8537 = 6.854, correct to 3 decimal places
           = 6.85, correct to 2 decimal places
           = 6.9, correct to 1 decimal place.

2. Significant figures

If the attendance at a football match was 34 176, it would be reasonable to write down 34 200 or 34 000.

   34 200 is written correct to 3 significant figures.
   34 000 is written correct to 2 significant figures.

When expressing a whole number correct to a given number of significant figures, zeros at the end of the number are not counted but must be included in the final result. All other zeros are significant.

Thus, 52 764 = 52 760, correct to 4 significant figures
= 52 800, correct to 3 significant figures
= 53 000, correct to 2 significant figures
= 50 000, correct to 1 significant figure.

The number 70 425 = 70 400, correct to 3 significant figures.
Notice here that the zero between the 7 and 4 is significant, but the two final zeros are not.

If a number is less than 1, then the zeros immediately after the decimal point are not significant.

Thus, (i) 0.07406 = 0.0741, correct to 3 significant figures.
(ii) 0.00892 = 0.0089, correct to 2 significant figures.

3. Making an Estimate

If a calculation involves a mixture of numbers greater than and less than 1, then to make an estimate of the answer,
(i) round numbers greater than 1 correct to one significant figure
(ii) round numbers less than 1 correct to one decimal place.

> **Example 1**
>
> Make a rough estimate of $\dfrac{10.25 + 29.83}{0.24 \times 46}$
>
> $\dfrac{10.25 + 29.83}{0.24 \times 46} \approx \dfrac{10 + 30}{0.2 \times 50} = \dfrac{40}{10} = 4$
>
> A rough estimate is 4.
> (The result using a calculator is 3.63…)

Exercise 14.6

1. Write each of these numbers correct to the nearest 10:
   (i) 76 (ii) 347 (iii) 1792 (iv) 7319 (v) 1608

2. Write these numbers to the nearest 100:
   (i) 87 (ii) 146 (iii) 1824 (iv) 2539 (v) 9829

3. Write each of these numbers correct to one decimal place:
   (i) 46.34 (ii) 8.753 (iii) 0.426 (iv) 0.456 (v) 0.074

Chapter 14 Indices – Standard form – Surds

4. How many significant figures are there in each of these numbers?
   (i) 3000   (ii) 28 000   (iii) 329 000   (iv) 309 000   (v) 607 100

5. Write each of these numbers correct to two significant figures:
   (i) 3184   (ii) 648   (iii) 2916   (iv) 28 936   (v) 40 673

6. Round these numbers to three significant figures:
   (i) 7136   (ii) 45 309   (iii) 3612   (iv) 159 762   (v) 700 713

7. Round these numbers to two significant figures:
   (i) 0.473   (ii) 0.06312   (iii) 2.384   (iv) 0.669   (v) 54.839

8. Round these numbers to three significant figures:
   (i) 0.7384   (ii) 8.372   (iii) 0.02843   (iv) 1.083   (v) 12.316

9. Write the number indicated by the arrow
   (i) correct to 3 significant figures
   (ii) correct to 2 significant figures
   (iii) correct to 1 significant figure.

10. Round each number correct to one significant figure and hence make an estimate of each of these:
   (i) $\dfrac{56 \times 18}{28}$ (ii) $\dfrac{19.48 + 43.2}{10.4 \times 2.8}$ (iii) $\dfrac{183 \times 46.4}{77.4}$

11. By rounding numbers less than 1 correct to one decimal place and other numbers to one significant figure, make a rough estimate of these calculations:
   (i) $\dfrac{807}{391.3 \times 0.37}$ (ii) $\dfrac{31.69 \times 6.25}{0.473}$ (iii) $\dfrac{324 \times 2.76}{196 \times 0.54}$

12. By rounding appropriately, estimate the value of
   (i) $\dfrac{518.6 \times 8.32}{98.5}$ (ii) $\dfrac{63.2 \times (9.8)^2}{48.7}$ (iii) $\dfrac{0.79 \times 28.4}{0.372}$

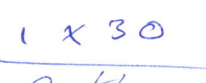

13. Sally estimates the value of $\dfrac{42.8 \times 63.7}{285}$ to be 8.

   Write down three numbers Sally could use to get her estimate: $\dfrac{\ldots \times \ldots}{\ldots}$

Text & Tests 2 Higher Level

Section 14.7 Using a calculator

The examples below show the procedure for finding powers and roots of numbers on your calculator.

Operation	Example
(i) To find the **square root** of a number, use the $\boxed{\sqrt{}}$ key.	To find $\sqrt{28}$, key in $\boxed{\sqrt{}}$ 28 $\boxed{=}$ The result is 5.29.
(ii) To find the **cube root** of a number, use the $\boxed{\sqrt[3]{}}$ key.	To find $\sqrt[3]{27}$, key in $\boxed{\text{SHIFT}}$ $\boxed{\sqrt[3]{}}$ 27 $\boxed{=}$ The result is 3.
(iii) To find the **square** of a number, use the $\boxed{x^2}$ key.	To find 24^2, key in 24 $\boxed{x^2}$ $\boxed{=}$ The result is 576.
(iv) To find 8^5 (or any power), use the $\boxed{x^{\blacksquare}}$ key.	To find 8^5, key in 8 $\boxed{x^{\blacksquare}}$ 5 $\boxed{=}$ The result is 32768.
(v) To find the **reciprocal** of 1.8 i.e. $\dfrac{1}{1.8} = 1.8^{-1}$ use the $\boxed{x^{-1}}$ key	To find 1.8^{-1}, key in 1.8 $\boxed{x^{-1}}$ $\boxed{=}$ The result is 0.555

> **Example 1**
>
> Use your calculator to evaluate $\dfrac{12.42 \times 23.47}{13.48 + 5.73}$, correct to two decimal places.
>
> Key in $\boxed{\frac{[\,]}{[\,]}}$ [12.42] $\boxed{\times}$ [23.47] $\boxed{\downarrow}$ [13.48] $\boxed{+}$ [5.73] $\boxed{=}$ 15.1742
>
> The answer is 15.17

344

Chapter 14 Indices – Standard form – Surds

Example 2

Use your calculator to evaluate, correct to 1 decimal place,

$$(2.59)^2 - \frac{31}{14.6} + \frac{78.4}{5 \times \sqrt{60.4}}.$$

Key in [2.59] $\boxed{x^2}$ $\boxed{-}$ $\boxed{\frac{[\ ]}{[\ ]}}$ [31] $\boxed{\downarrow}$ [14.6] $\boxed{\rightarrow}$ $\boxed{+}$ $\boxed{\frac{[\ ]}{[\ ]}}$ [78.4] $\boxed{\downarrow}$ [5] $\boxed{\times}$ $\boxed{\sqrt{[\ ]}}$ [60.4] $\boxed{=}$

The result is 6.6, correct to 1 decimal place.

Note: Always check that the numbers have been inputted correctly on the screen before pressing the $\boxed{=}$

Exercise 14.7

Correct each of the following answers to 2 places of decimals.

1. Write down the reciprocal of each of these numbers:
   (i) 6   (ii) $\frac{1}{2}$ (iii) $\frac{3}{4}$ (iv) $-\frac{2}{3}$ (v) $1\frac{1}{4}$

2. Use your calculator to work out the reciprocal of each of these, correct to 2 decimal places where necessary:
   (i) 2.6   (ii) 5.44   (iii) -2.8 (iv) 0.68   (v) -0.8

In the following questions, give all answers correct to two decimal places where necessary.

3. Use your calculator to verify that $\frac{48 \times 64}{16 + 24} = 76.8$.

4. Use your calculator to evaluate each of these:
   (i) $\frac{12.4 \times 5.9}{(3.7 \times 2.5)}$ (ii) $\frac{42.3 + 18.4}{16.7 \times 0.4}$ (iii) $\frac{81.73 - 21.4}{3.87 \times 1.25}$

5. Evaluate each of these:
   (i) $\sqrt{30.5}$ (ii) $\sqrt{348}$ (iii) $\sqrt{107.8}$ (iv) $(3.9)^2$ (v) $(16.34)^2$

6. Evaluate each of these:
   (i) $\frac{32}{14^2}$ (ii) $\frac{\sqrt{26}}{4}$ (iii) $\frac{2 \times \sqrt{40}}{3}$ (iv) $\frac{(12.8)^2}{3.7}$ (v) $\frac{15.4}{\sqrt{38}}$

7. Find the value of each of these:
   (i) $(3.4)^2 + \frac{3}{14.8} + \sqrt{108}$ (ii) $\sqrt{27} \times \frac{4}{3.8} + (9.62)^2$

   (iii) $\sqrt{73} + \frac{\sqrt{45}}{3} \times \frac{6.8}{14.9}$ (iv) $\frac{6}{15.9} \times \sqrt{136} - \frac{5}{18.7}$

345

8. Work out each of the following:

   (i) $\dfrac{4.9 - (1.8)^2}{3.5}$

   (ii) $6.84 + \dfrac{\sqrt{8.4}}{4.2}$

   (iii) $\dfrac{5.84 \times \sqrt{17}}{2.5 - \sqrt{3.5}}$

9. Work out the value of $\dfrac{\sqrt{(12.3)^2 + 7.9}}{1.8 \times 0.17}$.

10. Evaluate $\dfrac{19.6}{(9.7)^2} + \dfrac{\sqrt{281}}{3.4} \times \dfrac{(1.83)^2}{7.3}$.

11. Find the value of $(3.73)^2 + \dfrac{16}{\sqrt{28}} \times \dfrac{6.7}{19.4}$.

12. Evaluate $p^2 - \sqrt{2q} - \dfrac{1}{r}$, where $p = 4.256, q = 0.327$ and $r = 0.45$.

13. Using the formula $g = \dfrac{4 \times \pi^2 \times \ell}{T^2}$, Daniel repeated an experiment twice to find a value for g.
    Use his results to find an average value for g, correct to 1 place of decimals.
    Results (a) $\ell = 0.7, T = 1.68, \pi = 3.14$
    Results (b) $\ell = 0.8, T = 1.79, \pi = 3.14$

14. Evaluate $\dfrac{\sqrt{2a} + 3c}{b^2}$, where $a = 12.3, b = 7.1$ and $c = 4.5$, correct to 3 places of decimals.

Investigation:

If n is any whole positive number, explain why:
   (i) $n + 1$ might be an even or odd number.
   (ii) $2n + 1$ must **always** be odd.

If $2n + 1$ is an odd number:
   (i) Write down an expression for the **next three consecutive odd** numbers.
   (ii) Investigate why the **sum of** any **4 consecutive odd numbers** is always divisible by 8.
   (iii) Write down 2 examples of 4 consecutive odd number and show that their sum is divisible by 8.

Chapter 14 Indices – Standard form – Surds

Test yourself 14

1. (i) Find the value of $16^{\frac{1}{2}} + \sqrt{4^3}$.
   (ii) If $125^x = \frac{1}{5}$, find the value of x.

2. (i) Express $\sqrt{50} - \sqrt{32} + 2\sqrt{8}$ in the form $k\sqrt{2}$, where $k \in N$.
   (ii) Write down an irrational number between 6 and 7.

3. By rounding appropriately, estimate the value of $\frac{28.6 \times 2\sqrt{17.3}}{(4.12)^2 + 3.84}$.
   Now use your calculator to find its value, correct to two decimal places.

4. (i) Which **two** of the following have the same value?
   $$4^{\frac{1}{2}} \quad 4^{-\frac{1}{2}} \quad 16^{\frac{1}{4}} \quad 2^0$$
   (ii) Write 5300 in standard form.

5. (i) Express $3\sqrt{12} - \sqrt{27}$ in the form $k\sqrt{3}$, where $k \in N$.
   (ii) Find the value of $(8 \times 10^{-3})^{\frac{1}{3}}$ without using a calculator.

6. Find the value of the variable in each of these equations:
   (i) $2^x = 1$ (ii) $2^y = \frac{1}{4}$ (iii) $32^z = 2$ (iv) $16^{b+3} = 2^b$

7. (i) Which **two** of the following numbers are equal?
   $$16^{\frac{1}{2}} \quad 4^{-1} \quad 32^0 \quad (-2)^4 \quad 2^{-2}$$
   (ii) Find a value of x for which $\sqrt{2} \times \sqrt{x}$ is rational.

8. (i) Simplify $2x^4 \times 6x^3 \div 3x^5$.
   (ii) Express $\frac{8.4 \times 10^4}{2.8 \times 10^{-1}}$ in the form $a \times 10^n$, where $1 \leq a < 10, n \in Z$.

9. (i) Find the value of $25^{\frac{3}{2}}$.
   (ii) Find the value of x for which $16^x = \frac{1}{8}$.

10. Write each of these as a whole number or as a fraction:
    (i) 2^5 (ii) 3^{-2} (iii) $4^{\frac{1}{2}}$ (iv) 7^0 (v) $27^{\frac{1}{3}}$

11. (i) Express 0.04 in standard form.
    (ii) Solve the equation $4^x = 8$.

12. Decide if each of the following statements is true or false.
    If the statement is false, give an example to show why.
    (i) If $x^2 = x$, then the only possible value for x is 1.
    (ii) If $a^2 = 64$, then the only possible value for a is 8.

(iii) $a^0 \times a^0 \times a^0 \times a^0 > 2$
(iv) $2^{-n} = (0.5)^n$
(v) $2^n < 0$, where n is a negative integer.

13. Express each of these as a whole number or fraction:
    (i) $\dfrac{1}{4^{-2}}$ (ii) $\left(\dfrac{1}{4}\right)^{\frac{1}{2}}$ (iii) $125^{\frac{1}{3}}$ (iv) $\dfrac{\sqrt{8}}{\sqrt{2}}$.

14. (i) Express $\sqrt{40} \cdot \sqrt{5}$ in the form $p\sqrt{2}$, where $p \in N$.
    (ii) If $4^{2x+1} = 8$, find the value of x.

15. Express $\dfrac{8.4 \times 10^4}{1.2 \times 10^{-2} \times 2.8 \times 10^3}$ in the form $a \times 10^n$, where $1 \leq a < 10, n \in Z$.

16. (i) Find the value of $25^{\frac{1}{2}} + \left(\dfrac{1}{8}\right)^{\frac{1}{3}}$.
    (ii) If $16^n = \dfrac{1}{4}$, find the value of n.

17. If $x = \sqrt{a^2 + b^2}$, find the value of x when
    (i) $a = \sqrt{2}$ and $b = \sqrt{7}$
    (ii) $a = \dfrac{3}{7}$ and $b = \dfrac{4}{7}$

18. Express $\sqrt{125}$ as a power of 5.
    Hence find the value of x for which $25^x = \dfrac{\sqrt{125}}{5}$.

19. (i) $\sqrt{8} = k\sqrt{2}$, find the value of k.
    (ii) Write $\dfrac{3 + \sqrt{2}}{\sqrt{2}} + \dfrac{6 + \sqrt{8}}{\sqrt{8}}$ as a single fraction using a common denominator from (i).
    (iii) Hence show that $\dfrac{3 + \sqrt{2}}{\sqrt{2}} + \dfrac{6 + \sqrt{8}}{\sqrt{8}} = 3\sqrt{2} + 2$. Show clearly all the steps of your work.

20. There are 6.1×10^5 new computers made each month.
    2.6×10^4 computers are destroyed during the same period.
    Find, in standard form, the increase in the number of computers over a five-year period.

Chapter 14 Indices – Standard form – Surds

Assignment:

For loyal service, a king asked his servant how he could reward him.
The servant replied that he would be pleased with 1 grain of wheat for the first square of a chessboard, and then double that amount for next square and double that again for the next, etc.

Square	Grains of wheat	Power of 2	Total number of grains of wheat
1	1	2^0	1 …(2 − 1)
2	2	2^1	3 …(4 − 1)
3	4	2^2	7 …(8 − 1)
4	8	2^3	15 …(16 − 1)
…	…	…	…
10			

(i) Draw a large poster of a completed grid up to square 10.
(ii) By studying the first and third columns, write a formula for the number of grains of wheat on the *n*th square. *Number of grains of wheat on the nth square = _____*
(iii) By studying the pattern in the fourth column, write a formula for the total number of grains on the board. *Total number of grains on n squares = _____*
(iv) Use your formula to find:
 (a) the number of grains on the 64th square of the chessboard.
 (b) the total number of grains on the chessboard.
 Write each answer in standard form.
(v) Research in a library or on the internet the weight of grains of wheat and the current price of a kilogram of wheat.
(vi) Estimate the value of the reward asked for by the servant.
 Write a report on your findings.

349

chapter 15 Quadratic equations

From first year, you will recall how to:
- solve linear equations,
- rearrange equations,
- use algebra techniques to solve word problems.

In this chapter, you will learn to:
- solve a quadratic equation using factors,
- solve a quadratic equation using a formula,
- interpret the point of intersection of a quadratic curve and the x-axis,
- form a quadratic equation, given the two roots or solutions.

Section 15.1 Solving quadratic equations using factors

Equations such as $x^2 - 4x + 3 = 0$ or $2x^2 - x - 3 = 0$ contain a term in x^2. These are called **quadratic equations**.

Take the equation $x^2 - 5x + 6 = 0$.

When $x = 2$, then $x^2 - 5x + 6$ becomes
$(2)^2 - 5(2) + 6$, i.e., $4 - 10 + 6 = 0$

When $x = 3$, then $x^2 - 5x + 6$ becomes
$(3)^2 - 5(3) + 6$, i.e., $9 - 15 + 6 = 0$

> The **roots** of an equation are the values of x which satisfy the equation.

When $x = 2$ or $x = 3$, both sides of the equation are zero.
When this happens, we say that $x = 2$ and $x = 3$ are **solutions** or **roots** of the equation.

Multiplication by zero

Any number multiplied by zero is zero.
For example, $4 \times 0 = 0$ or $0 \times 6 = 0$.
This illustrates a very important property of real numbers which is given on the right.

> If the product of two numbers is zero, then at least one of them must be zero.
> e.g. if $ab = 0$, then $a = 0$ or $b = 0$.

Chapter 15 Quadratic equations

Thus if $(x - 3)(x + 5) = 0$, then $x - 3 = 0$ or $x + 5 = 0$
i.e. $x = 3$ or $x = -5$.

Steps for solving quadratic equations

> If necessary, rearrange the equation with one side being **zero**.
> Factorise fully the other side.
> Let each factor equal zero.
> Solve the resulting simple equations.

Example 1

Solve each of the following equations (a) $4x(x + 3) = 0$ (b) $(x - 2)(x + 5) = 0$

(a) $4x(x + 3) = 0$
$\therefore 4x = 0$ or $x + 3 = 0$
$\therefore x = 0$ or $x = -3$
i.e. $x = 0$ or -3

(b) $(x - 2)(x + 5) = 0$
$\therefore x - 2 = 0$ or $x + 5 = 0$
$\therefore x = 2$ or $x = -5$
i.e. $x = 2$ or -5

Example 2

Solve the equation $x^2 - 5x - 14 = 0$.

$x^2 - 5x - 14 = 0$
$(x - 7)(x + 2) = 0$ ... factorise the left-hand side
$x - 7 = 0$ or $x + 2 = 0$ ... let each factor $= 0$
$x = 7$ or $x = -2$
$\therefore x = 7$ or $x = -2$

	x	$+2$
x	x^2	$+2x$
-7	$-7x$	-14

	-14
$+1$	-14
$+2$	-7	$\rightarrow -5$

$\therefore x^2 - 5x - 15 = (x + 2)(x - 7)$

Example 3

Solve the equation $2x^2 = 9x$

$2x^2 = 9x$
$\therefore 2x^2 - 9x = 0$ ... rearranging the equation to have zero on one side
$\therefore x(2x - 9) = 0$ ... factorising the highest common factor from both terms.
$\therefore x = 0$ or $2x - 9 = 0$ ... let each factor $= 0$
$\therefore x = 0$ or $x = \frac{9}{2} = 4\frac{1}{2}$

351

Example 4

Solve the equation $4x^2 - 25 = 0$

$4x^2 - 25 = 0$
$(2x - 5)(2x + 5) = 0$ ... the difference of two squares
$2x - 5 = 0$ or $2x + 5 = 0$ ... both factors = 0
$2x = 5$ or $2x = -5$
$x = \frac{5}{2}$ or $x = -\frac{5}{2}$
$\therefore x = 2\frac{1}{2}$ or $x = -2\frac{1}{2}$

Investigation:

The curves on the right are called **parabolas**.

They are the graphs of
(i) $y = x^2 + x - 2$
(ii) $x = x^2 - 2x - 3$

A: By factorising $x^2 + x - 2$, solve the equation, $x^2 + x - 2 = 0$

B: By factorising $x^2 - x - 3$, solve the equation, $x^2 - 2x - 3 = 0$

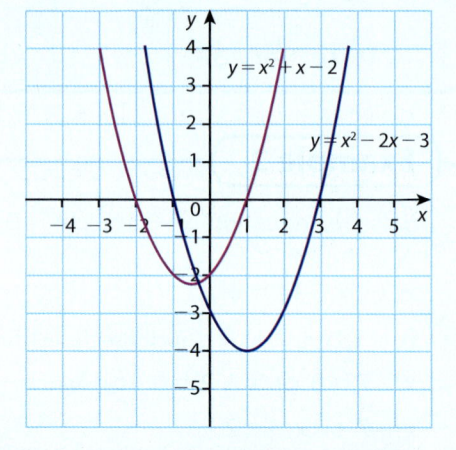

By investigating the graphs, find the connection between the roots (solutions) of the equations and the graphs of the equations.

Complete the sentence "the roots (solutions) of an equation are ..."

Exercise 15.1

Solve the following quadratic equations:

1. $(x - 2)(x - 4) = 0$
2. $(x - 4)(x + 2) = 0$
3. $(x - 6)(x + 4) = 0$
4. $(x - 4)(2x - 3) = 0$
5. $(x + 3)(6x - 9) = 0$
6. $(2x - 1)(x + 4) = 0$
7. $x(x - 3) = 0$
8. $x(x + 5) = 0$
9. $2x(x + 3) = 0$
10. $x^2 + 7x + 10 = 0$
11. $x^2 + 12x + 35 = 0$
12. $x^2 + 14x + 48 = 0$

Chapter 15 Quadratic equations

13. $x^2 - 5x + 6 = 0$
14. $x^2 - 8x + 15 = 0$
15. $x^2 - 10x + 21 = 0$
16. $x^2 - x - 12 = 0$
17. $x^2 - 3x - 10 = 0$
18. $x^2 + 3x - 28 = 0$
19. $2x^2 - 5x + 2 = 0$
20. $2x^2 - 3x - 2 = 0$
21. $2x^2 - x - 6 = 0$
22. $2x^2 + 5x + 2 = 0$
23. $3x^2 - 7x + 2 = 0$
24. $3x^2 + x - 10 = 0$
25. $3x^2 + 10x - 8 = 0$
26. $3x^2 - 13x - 10 = 0$
27. $3x^2 + 19x - 14 = 0$
28. $4x^2 - 12x + 5 = 0$
29. $5x^2 - 13x - 6 = 0$
30. $5x^2 - 13x + 6 = 0$
31. $x^2 - 6x = 0$
32. $2x^2 - 5x = 0$
33. $3x^2 - 4x = 0$
34. $4x^2 - x = 0$
35. $5x^2 - 6x = 0$
36. $3x^2 - 7x = 0$
37. $x^2 - 9 = 0$
38. $x^2 - 25 = 0$
39. $4x^2 - 1 = 0$
40. $4x^2 - 25 = 0$
41. $9x^2 - 16 = 0$
42. $4x^2 - 49 = 0$
43. $2x(x - 2) = 3(x + 10)$
44. $(x - 2)(x - 3) = 20$
45. $(2x - 5)(x - 2) = 15$

46. Solve the equation $(x - 8)(x - 2) = 2x(x - 5)$.

47. Write down the roots of the equation $x^2 + 2x - 3 = 0$ by referring to the graph shown.

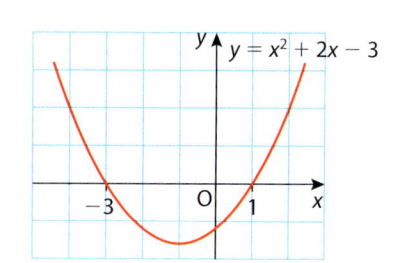

48. Write down the values of x where the graph of each of these functions crosses the x-axis. (You do not need to draw the graphs.)

(i) $y = (x - 4)(x + 5)$ (ii) $y = (x + 2)(x + 4)$ (iii) $y = (x - 5)(x - 6)$

49. Three parabolas are shown here.

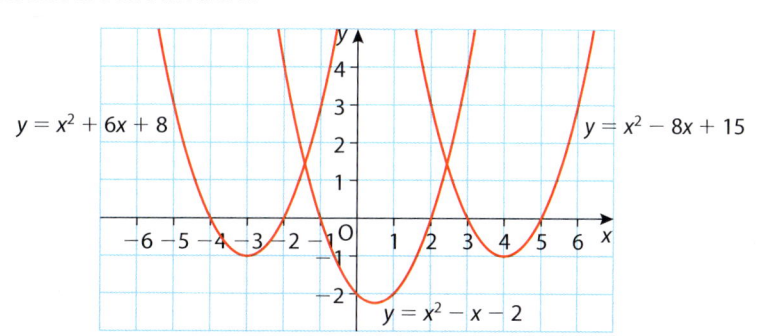

Use the graphs above to solve the following equations (each has two solutions).

(i) $x^2 - 8x + 15 = 0$ (ii) $x^2 + 6x + 8 = 0$ (iii) $x^2 - x - 2 = 0$

50. (i) How many values of x make $(x + 2)^2 = 0$?

(ii) One of these sketches shows $y = (x + 2)^2$.
Which one?
Explain your answer.

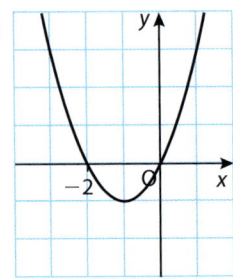

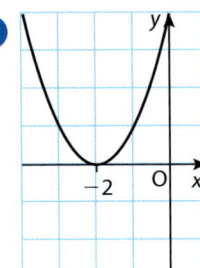

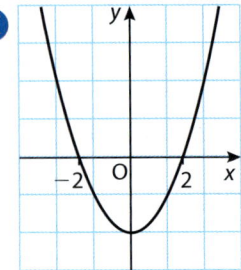

A   **B**   **C**

Section 15.2 Using the quadratic formula

In the previous section of this chapter, we used factors to solve quadratic equations of the form $ax^2 + bx + c = 0$.

If the expression $ax^2 + bx + c$ cannot be factorised, the equation can still be solved by using a special formula called the **quadratic formula**.
This formula is given below:

The quadratic formula

> The roots of the quadratic equation $ax^2 + bx + c = 0$ are
> $$x = \frac{-b \pm \sqrt{b^2 - 4ac}}{2a}$$

Example 1

Use the quadratic formula to find the roots of the equation $5x^2 + 7x - 3 = 0$, correct to two decimal places.

In the equation $5x^2 + 7x - 3 = 0$, $a = 5$, $b = 7$ and $c = -3$.

$$x = \frac{-b \pm \sqrt{b^2 - 4ac}}{2a}$$

$$= \frac{-7 \pm \sqrt{49 - 4(5)(-3)}}{2(5)}$$

$$= \frac{-7 \pm \sqrt{49 + 60}}{10}$$

$$= \frac{-7 \pm \sqrt{109}}{10} = \frac{-7 \pm 10.44}{10} = \frac{-17.44}{10} \text{ or } \frac{3.44}{10}$$

$\therefore$ $x = -1.744$ or $x = 0.344$

$\therefore$ $x = -1.74$ or $x = 0.34$

Chapter 15 Quadratic equations

Note: When using the quadratic formula to solve a quadratic equation, remember that all terms must be on the left-hand side and zero only on the right-hand side, that is, the equation must be in the form,
$$ax^2 + bx + c = 0.$$

Example 2

Solve the equation $x^2 - 2x - 4 = 0$.
Give your answer in (surd) form, $x = a \pm \sqrt{b}$, $a \in Z, b \in N$

In the equation $x^2 - 2x - 4 = 0$, $a = 1, b = -2$ and $c = -4$.

$$\therefore x = \frac{-b \pm \sqrt{b^2 - 4ac}}{2a}$$

$$\therefore x = \frac{-(-2) \pm \sqrt{(-2)^2 - 4(1)(-4)}}{2(1)}$$

$$\therefore x = \frac{2 \pm \sqrt{4 + 16}}{2} = \frac{2 \pm \sqrt{20}}{2}$$

$$\therefore x = \frac{2 \pm \sqrt{4 \times 5}}{2} = \frac{2 \pm \sqrt{4} \times \sqrt{5}}{2}$$

$$\therefore x = \frac{2 \pm 2\sqrt{5}}{2}$$

$$\therefore x = 1 \pm \sqrt{5}$$

Exercise 15.2

Solve the following equations using the formula $x = \frac{-b \pm \sqrt{b^2 - 4ac}}{2a}$

In questions **1–6** give your answers in surd form.

1. $x^2 + 4x + 2 = 0$
2. $x^2 + 6x + 4 = 0$
3. $x^2 + 2x - 5 = 0$
4. $x^2 - 2x - 7 = 0$
5. $4x^2 + 2x - 1 = 0$
6. $3x^2 - x - 1 = 0$

Solve the following equations, giving your answers correct to two decimal places.

7. $3x^2 - 6x + 2 = 0$
8. $3x^2 + 7x - 5 = 0$
9. $5x^2 - 4x - 2 = 0$
10. $3x^2 + 8x + 2 = 0$
11. $6x^2 - 9x - 4 = 0$
12. $3x^2 + 7x = 2$
13. $4x^2 + 3x = 5$
14. $2x^2 = 7x - 4$
15. $3x^2 + 5x = 3$
16. $7 = 2x^2 + x$

Text & Tests 2 Higher Level

Section 15.3 Problems leading to quadratic equations

When a problem expressed in words is changed to a mathematical sentence, it often results in a quadratic equation.

To find the equation to represent a problem,
> where relevant, draw a diagram and put all the information you are given on it
> use x to represent the unknown you are asked to find
> look for the information in the question to form an equation in x
> solve the equation to find the value or values for x; you may sometimes have to reject a negative answer.

Example 1

The length of a rectangle exceeds its width by 6 cm.
If the area of the rectangle is 160 cm², find its length and width.

Let the width of the rectangle be x cm.

∴ The length is $(x + 6)$ cm.

Area = 160 cm²

∴ $x(x + 6) = 160$ ... $A = \ell \times w$
$x^2 + 6x = 160$
$x^2 + 6x - 160 = 0$
$(x - 10)(x + 16) = 0$
$x - 10 = 0$ or $x + 16 = 0$
$x = 10$ or $x = -16$

Naturally in this case, we reject the negative number -16.

∴ $x = 10$

∴ the length $(x + 6)$ cm = 16 cm and the width x cm = 10 cm

Example 2

(i) Two numbers have a sum of 13. If one of them is x, what it the other number?
(ii) If the sum of their squares is 89, find the numbers.

(i) The other number is $(13 - x)$.

(ii) The two numbers are x and $(13 - x)$.
Sum of their squares = 89 $\Rightarrow x^2 + (13 - x)^2 = 89$
$x^2 + (13 - x)^2 = 89$
$x^2 + 169 - 26x + x^2 = 89$

$2x^2 - 26x + 169 - 89 = 0$
$2x^2 - 26x + 80 = 0$
$x^2 - 13x + 40 = 0$ ... divide both sides by 2
$(x - 8)(x - 5) = 0$
$x - 8 = 0$ or $x - 5 = 0$
$x = 8$ or $x = 5$

The two numbers are 8 and 5.

Exercise 15.3

1. When a number, x, is added to its square, the answer is 72.
   Write an equation in x and solve it to find two numbers.
   Verify that both numbers satisfy the equation.

2. If a positive number is subtracted from its square, the result is 90.
   What is the number?

3. One positive number is 3 bigger than another number. If the two numbers are multiplied together, the answer is 88. Find the two numbers.

4. When four times a positive number is taken from its square, the result is 60.
   Find the number.

5. One positive number is 3 greater than another positive number. When 12 is added to the square of the smaller number, the result is the same as four times the larger number. Find the two numbers.

6. When 5 is added to a certain positive number and the result is squared, the answer is 81. Find the number.

7. The area of the given rectangle is 77 cm². Find its length and width.

8. State the *Theorem of Pythagoras*.
   Now use this theorem to find the value of x in the given right-angled triangle.

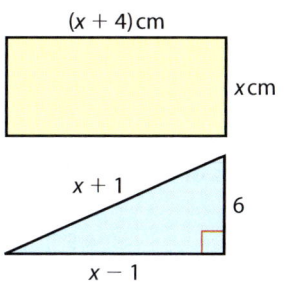

9. A rectangle has length 3 cm greater than its width.
   If it has an area of 28 cm², find the dimensions of the rectangle.

10. Alan is x years old. His mother's age is the square of his age.
    If Alan's father is two years older than his mother and the sum of all three ages is 80 years, how old is Alan?

Text & Tests 2 Higher Level

11. The sum of the squares of two consecutive integers is 41.
    (i) If x is one of the integers, show that $x^2 + x - 20 = 0$.
    (ii) Solve $x^2 + x - 20 = 0$ to find two pairs of consecutive integers.

    > 7 and 8 are consecutive integers.

12. The diagram shows a rectangular lawn surrounded on three sides by flower beds.
    Each flower bed is 2 m wide.
    The area of the lawn is 14 m².
    Find the length of the lawn.

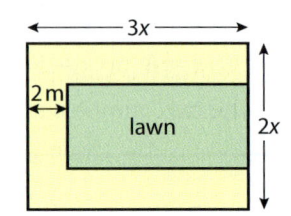

13. If the area of the given triangle is 40 square units, find the value of x.

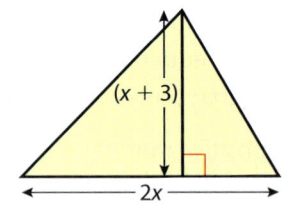

14. A baker making cakes finds that his profit per hour, €P, is given by the relationship $P = 20x - x^2$, where x is the number of cakes made per hour.
    Find the number of cakes baked when the company makes
    (i) €0 per hour profit
    (ii) €84 per hour profit.

15. When a cricket ball is hit directly upwards, its height (h) above the ground is given by $h = (30t - 5t^2)$ metres, where t is the time after the ball is hit (in seconds).
    After how many seconds is the ball at a height of:
    (i) 0 m above the ground
    (ii) 40 m?

16. (i) A decorator's logo is rectangular and measures 10 centimetres by 6 centimetres.
    It consists of three smaller rectangles: one red, one yellow and one blue.

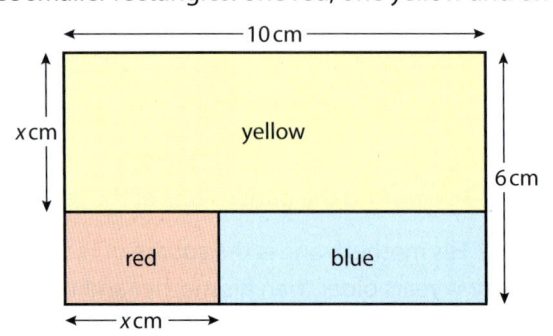

The yellow rectangles measures 10 centimetres by *x* centimetres.
The length of the red rectangle is *x* centimetres.
Show that the area, *A*, of the blue rectangle is given by the expression
$A = x^2 - 16x + 60$.

(ii) The area of the blue rectangle is equal to $\frac{1}{5}$ of the total area of the logo.
Calculate the value of *x*.

17. The weight, *W* kilograms, of a giraffe is related to its age, *M* months, by the formula
$W = \frac{1}{4}(M^2 - 4M + 272)$

At what age (in months) will a giraffe weigh 83 kilograms?

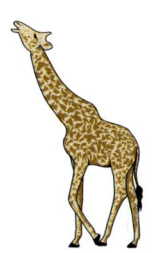

18. The closed rectangular box shown has a square base of side *x* cm.
The height of the box is 5 cm.
The total surface area of the box is 288 cm².
Write an equation in *x* to represent this information and use it to calculate *x*.

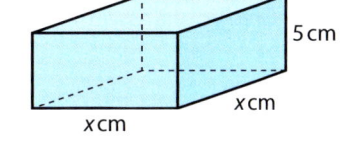

Section 15.4 Forming a quadratic equation given its roots

Examine the quadratic equation $x^2 + x - 6 = 0$.
The factors of the left-hand side are $(x + 3)(x - 2)$.
$\Rightarrow (x + 3)(x - 2) = 0$
$x + 3 = 0$ or $x - 2 = 0$
$\therefore \quad x = -3$ or $x = 2$
i.e. -3 and 2 are the roots of the equation.

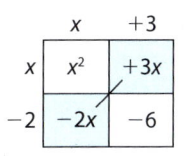

	x	+3
x	x^2	$+3x$
-2	$-2x$	-6

We can now use the reverse of this method to form a quadratic equation when we are given the roots.

Example 1

Form the quadratic equation with roots -4 and 5.

If the roots are -4 and 5, then

$(x + 4)(x - 5) = 0$ is the quadratic equation with these roots.

$\Rightarrow x^2 - x - 20 = 0$ is the equation

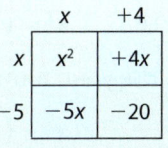

	x	+4
x	x^2	$+4x$
-5	$-5x$	-20

359

Text & Tests 2 Higher Level

Exercise 15.4

Form the quadratic equation, given the two roots, in each of the following:

1. 2, 4
2. 5, 1
3. 3, 2
4. 3, −1
5. 4, −2
6. −3, −4
7. 6, −2
8. 5, 0
9. −2, $\frac{1}{2}$
10. −5, −4
11. −$\frac{1}{2}$, 4
12. $\frac{1}{4}$, 8
13. 0, −4
14. $\frac{1}{2}$, −$\frac{1}{2}$
15. ±3
16. 0, $\frac{1}{4}$

17. If the roots of the equation $x^2 + ax + b = 0$ are 2 and −1, find the values of a and b.

18. Here is the graph of a quadratic function.
    Use the x-values of the points at which the graph crosses the x-axis to write the function that this graph represents.
    Give your answer in the form $y = \ldots\ldots$.

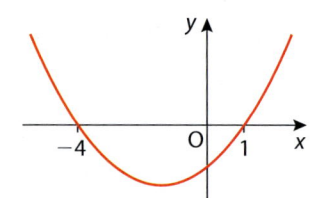

Investigation:

Copy and complete the chart below which compares the roots of an equation with the coefficients of the equation itself.

Roots ⟶	Equation
2, 3	$x^2 - 5x + 6 = 0$
(,)	$x^2 - 9x + 20 = 0$
6, 1	$x^2 - 7x + 6 = 0$
−2, −1	$x^2 + 3x + 2 = 0$
−3, −2	$x^2 + 5x + 6 = 0$
(,)	$x^2 + 12x + 20 = 0$
(,)	$x^2 + 3x - 4 = 0$
5, −3	$x^2 - 2x - 15 = 0$
−2, 7	$x^2 - 5x - 14 = 0$

Devise a quick formula which could be used to write an equation given its roots:

i.e. $x^2 - ($ $)x + ($ $) = 0$

Use your "formula" to write an equation whose roots are (3, −2).

$x^2 - ($ $)x + ($ $) = 0$

Test yourself 15

1. Solve the equation $x^2 - 2x - 35 = 0$.

2. Given that $x^2 + y^2 + z^2 = 29$, find the two possible values of y when $x = 2$ and $z = -3$.

3. The length of a rectangle is $(x + 4)$ cm.
   The width is $(x - 3)$ cm.
   The area of the rectangle is 78 cm².
   Use this information to write down an equation in x.
   Solve this equation to find the value of x.

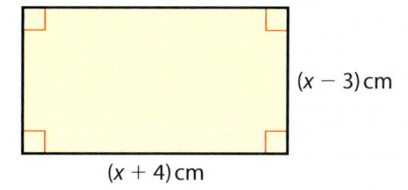

4. Solve the equation $3x^2 + 10x = 8$.

5. Solve the equation $2x^2 - 7x + 4 = 0$, giving your answers correct to two decimal places.

6. The length of a rectangle is 4 cm more than its width.
   If the area of the rectangle is 96 cm², write an equation and solve it to find the length and width.

7. If $x = 2$ is a root of the equation $x^2 - x + r = 0$, find the value of r.

8. The roots of a quadratic equation are -2 and 3.
   Write down an equation in x which has these 2 roots.

9. The diagram shows a shape in which all the corners are right angles.
   The area of the shape is 48 cm².

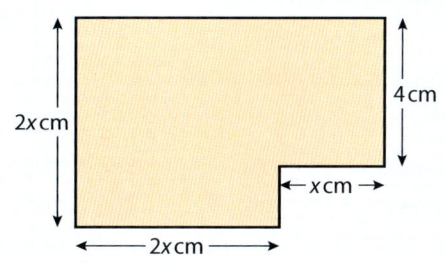

   (i) Form an equation, in terms of x, for the area of the shape.
   Show that the equation can be simplified to $x^2 + x - 12 = 0$.
   (ii) Solve the equation $x^2 + x - 12 = 0$ and hence calculate the perimeter of the shape.

10. Solve the equations (i) $2x^2 - 7x = 0$ (ii) $x^2 - 36 = 0$

11. Which of the two graphs on the right gives the solutions to the equation $x^2 + 2x - 3 = 0$? Explain your answer.

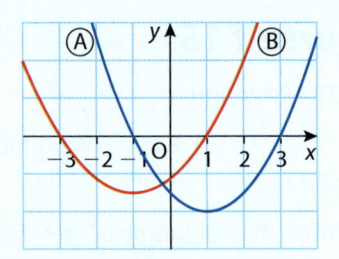

12. The diagram on the right shows a carpet 10 m by 8 m placed in the centre of a hotel lounge so that there is a uniform border, x metres in width, all the way round.
   (i) Express the area of the lounge in terms of x. 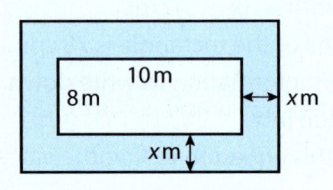
   (ii) If the area of the lounge is 168 m², find the value of x.

13. Solve the equation $x(x + 4) - (x - 2) = 20$.

14. The square of a number is subtracted from the original number and the result is -110.
Find the number.

15. Solve the equation $12x^2 - 4x - 5 = 0$.

16. Form the quadratic equation whose roots are 2 and -5.

17. A rectangle of area 72 cm² is divided into 4 smaller rectangles. The measurements of the sides are shown in the diagram. Write an equation in x to represent this information and hence solve the equation.

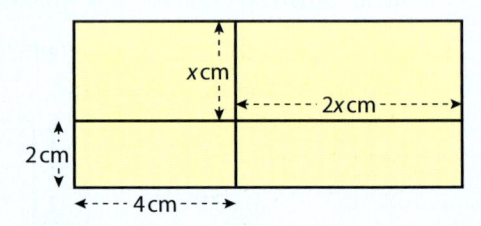

18. A hurley-maker finds that his profit, €P per day, is given by the formula $P = 100x - 4x^2$, where x is the number of hurleys made.
How many hurleys does he need to make in order to have a profit of €400 a day?

19. If the area of the pink section of this design is 20 m², show that $5x^2 - 9x - 18 = 0$ and hence find the value of x.

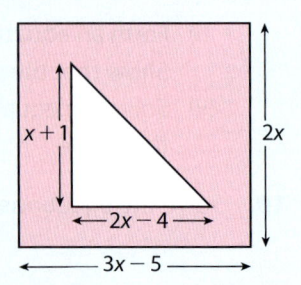

Chapter 15 Quadratic equations

Assignment:

The total area of a back garden plus path is 195 m².

The garden measures 12 m × 10 m.

Kevin, Edyta and Jack each work out the width "x" of the path using different methods.

Using the information below, work out the value of "x" each obtained and state which method you think is:

(a) quickest (b) more comprehensive.

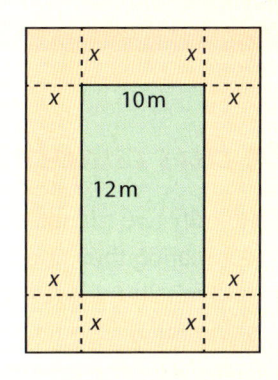

Kevin calculated the area of the path by subtraction.

He then created an equation in x for the area of the 8 sections of the path (4 squares and 4 rectangles) and let his answer equal the area he calculated for the path.

Finally he solved the equation for x and verified his answer.

Edyta calculated the area of the whole "garden + path" in terms of x.

She then let her answer = 195 m²

Finally, she solved the equation for x and verified her answer.

Jack used "trial and error" starting with "x = 1" to find the area of the garden. He then increased the value until 195 was exceeded. He then slowly reduced the value (by halves) until he got 195 m².

Chapter 16

Geometry 2: Similar Triangles – Circles – Theorems

In this chapter, you will learn to:

- identify two triangles as similar by comparing their angles,
- find missing sides in similar triangles using ratio,
- calculate missing lengths using transversals,
- work with parallel lines within triangles,
- justify that an angle inside a semicircle is a right angle,
- recognise the relationship between the angle at the centre of a circle and the angle at the circumference,
- find a variety of missing angles within circles and cyclical quadrilaterals,
- display an understanding of the proofs of theorems.

Section 16.1 Similar triangles

The shapes A and B are similar.
All the corresponding angles are the same and all the sides in shape B are twice as long as the corresponding sides in shape A.

When two figures are **similar**:
› their **shapes** are the same
› their **angles** are equal
› corresponding **lengths** are in the **same ratio**.

All the sides in figure B are $1\frac{1}{2}$ times longer than the corresponding sides in figure A.

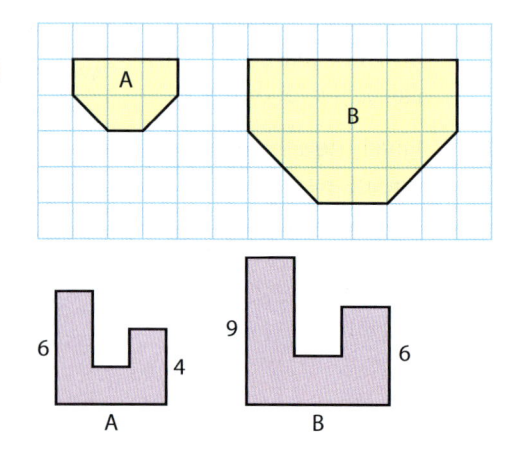

Similar triangles

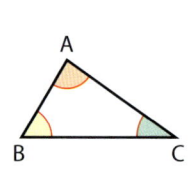

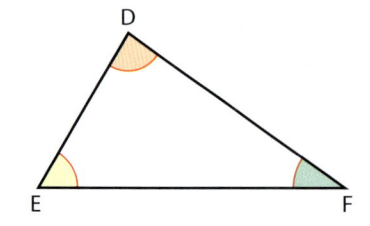

Similar triangles have the same shapes but different sizes.

Chapter 16 Geometry 2: Similar Triangles – Circles – Theorems

The triangles ABC and DEF above have equal angles.
Notice that they have the same shape but are different in size.
These triangles are said to be **similar** or **equiangular** triangles.
The sides [BC] and [EF] are said to be **corresponding sides** since they are opposite equal angles.
The sides [AB] and [DE] are also corresponding.

> Equiangular means all the corresponding angles are equal.

Since each side in the triangle DEF is twice the length of the corresponding side in the triangle ABC, we say that the sides are in the same **ratio** or are **proportional**.

In the triangles above, |AB| is half |DE|.
Similarly, $|BC| = \frac{1}{2}|EF|$ and $|AC| = \frac{1}{2}|DF|$.

Thus, $\dfrac{|AB|}{|DE|} = \dfrac{|BC|}{|EF|} = \dfrac{|AC|}{|DF|} = \dfrac{1}{2}$

> **Theorem**
> If two triangles ABC and DEF are similar, then their sides are proportional, in order
> $$\dfrac{|AB|}{|DE|} = \dfrac{|BC|}{|EF|} = \dfrac{|AC|}{|DF|}$$

The **converse** of this theorem is also true.

> If the sides of two triangles are proportional, in order, then the triangles are similar.

Note: Two triangles are similar if two angles in one triangle are equal to two angles in the other triangle. The triangles are equiangular or similar because the third angles must be equal.

Example 1

The given triangles ABC and DEF are similar.
Find the lengths of the sides
(i) [DE]
(ii) [DF]

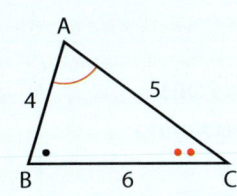

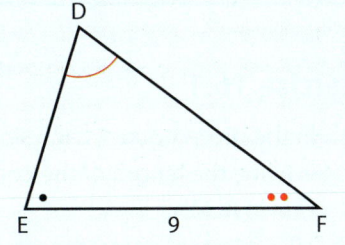

(i) [DE] corresponds to [AB].
Each side of the triangle DEF is $1\frac{1}{2}$ times the length of the corresponding side in the triangle ABC since 9 is $1\frac{1}{2}$ times 6.
∴ $|DE| = 1\frac{1}{2}|AB|$
$|DE| = 1\frac{1}{2}(4) = 6$

365

Text & Tests 2 Higher Level

(ii) $|DF| = 1\frac{1}{2}|AC|$
$|DF| = 1\frac{1}{2}(5) = 7\frac{1}{2}$

Example 2

(i) Show that triangle ABC is similar to triangle EFG.
(ii) Find the length of side [FG].

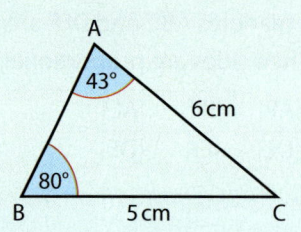

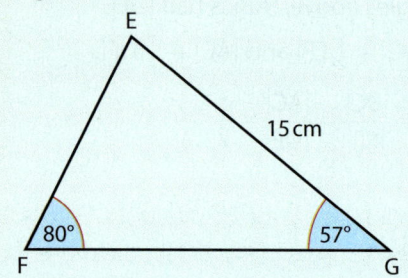

(i) Find the missing angles:
$|\angle ACB| = 180° - 80° - 43° = 57°$
$|\angle FEG| = 180° - 80° - 57° = 43°$

Since each triangle has angles measuring 80°, 57° and 43°, the triangles are similar.

(ii) [FG] corresponds to the side [BC].
Since $|EG| = 2\frac{1}{2}|AC| \Rightarrow |FG| = 2\frac{1}{2}|BC|$
$= 2\frac{1}{2}(5 \text{ cm})$
$|FG| = 12.5 \text{ cm}$

Exercise 16.1

1. In the given figures, each side in PQRS is twice the length of the corresponding side in KLMN.
   (i) What side corresponds to [NM]?
   (ii) What side corresponds to [QR]?
   (iii) If $|KL| = 4$, find $|PQ|$.
   (iv) If $|NM| = 8.2$, find $|SR|$.
   (v) If $|QR| = 15$, find $|LM|$.

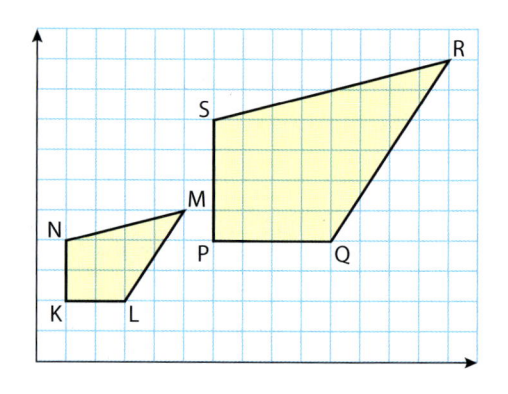

Chapter 16 Geometry 2: Similar Triangles – Circles – Theorems

2. The triangles ABC and DEF are similar.

 (i) Complete this ratio:
  |BC| : |EF| = 6 : 12 = … : …
 (ii) If |AC| = 7.2, find |DF|.
 (iii) If |DE| = 8, find |AB|.

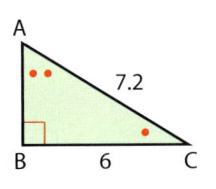

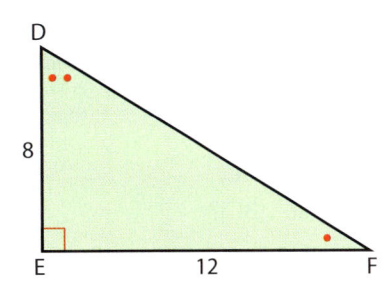

3. The given triangles are similar. Find the lengths of the sides marked x and y.

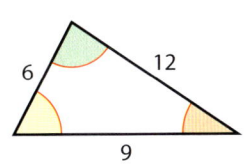

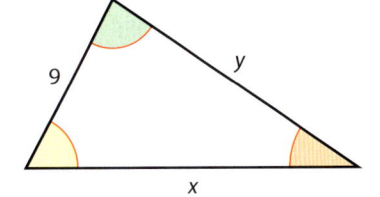

4. The shapes in (i) and (ii) below are similar. Find the lengths of the sides marked with letters.

 (i)

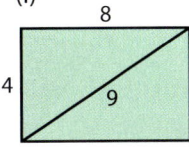

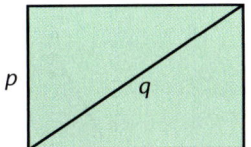

 (ii)

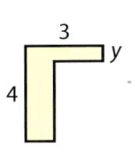

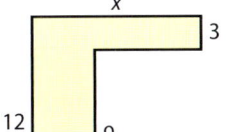

5. The two given triangles are similar.

 (i) Copy and complete this statement:
  'Each side of the bigger triangle is … times the length of the corresponding side of the smaller triangle'.
 (ii) Find the values of x and y.

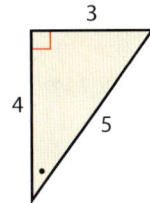

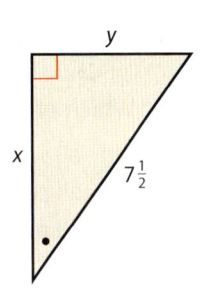

6. Explain why the triangles ABC and DEF are similar. Find the values of x and y.

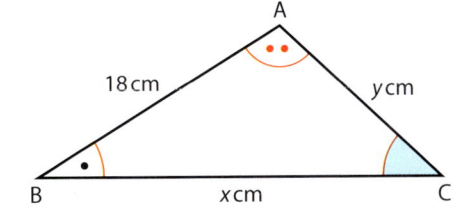

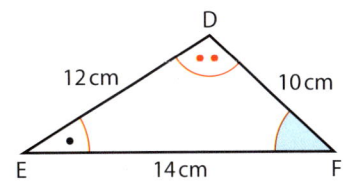

Text & Tests 2 Higher Level

7. The triangles ABC and PQR are similar.
   In the triangle PQR, which side corresponds to
   (i) [AB]
   (ii) [AC]
   (iii) [BC]?
   If |AC| = 8, |PR| = 12 and |BC| = 6, find |PQ|.

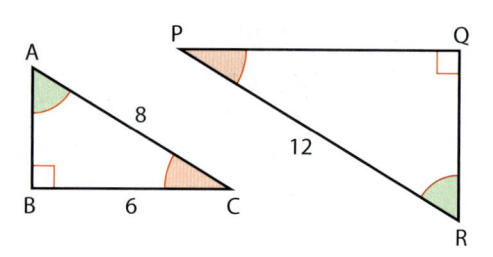

8. The triangles DEF and KLM are similar.
   (i) Which side corresponds to [DF]?
   (ii) Which side corresponds to [ML]?
   (iii) Find |KM|.

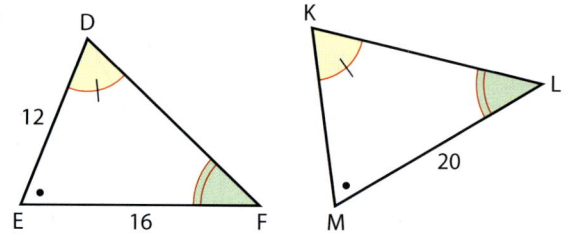

9. The triangles ABC and XYZ are similar.
   (i) Which side of the triangle XYZ corresponds to [AB]?
       Explain your answer.
   (ii) Find the values of d and e.

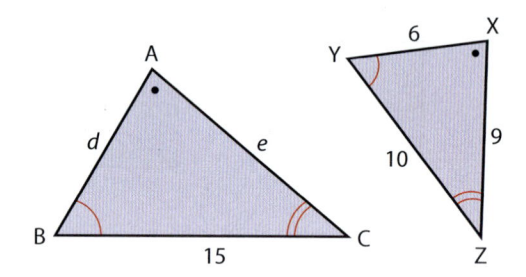

10. Which of these *shape families* are always similar?
    (i) all squares
    (ii) all rectangles
    (iii) all parallelograms
    (iv) all circles
    (v) all equilateral triangles
    (vi) all isosceles triangles

11. Find the length of the side marked x in the figure below:

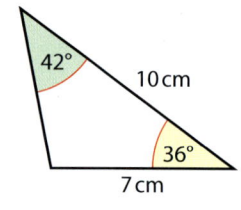

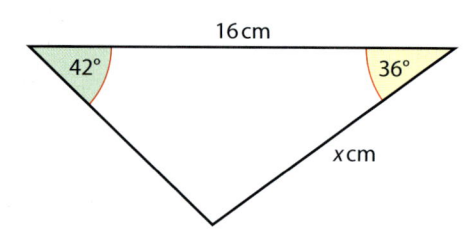

Chapter 16 Geometry 2: Similar Triangles – Circles – Theorems

12. In the given figure, BC∥DE.
Draw the triangles ABC and ADE as separate diagrams.
Mark in the lengths of the known sides in each triangle.

  (i) Explain why the triangles ABC and ADE are similar.
  (ii) Now find |DE|.

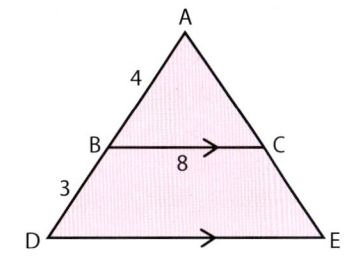

13. ABCD is a quadrilateral in which
AB∥DC and |∠DAB| = |∠CBD|.

  (i) Name two other equal angles in this figure.
  (ii) Now explain why the triangles ABD and DCB are similar.
  (iii) Which side in △DCB corresponds to [DB] in △ABD?
  (iv) Which side in △ABD corresponds to [BC] in △BCD?
  (v) If |DC| = 15 cm and |DB| = 12 cm, find |AB|.

14. In the given triangles, the arrows indicate that the lines are parallel.

Mark in the equal angles and hence use similar triangles to find the values of x and y.

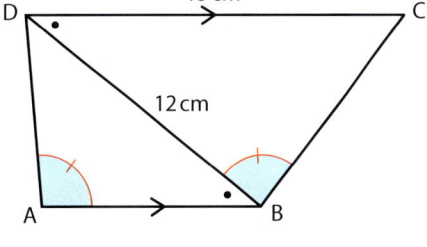

15. When James planted a tree 5 m from a window, the tree just blocked from view a building 50 m away.
If the building was 20 m tall, how tall was the tree?

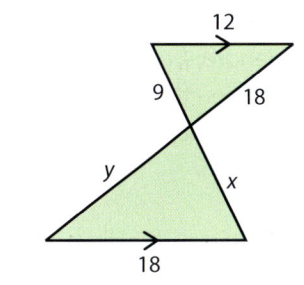

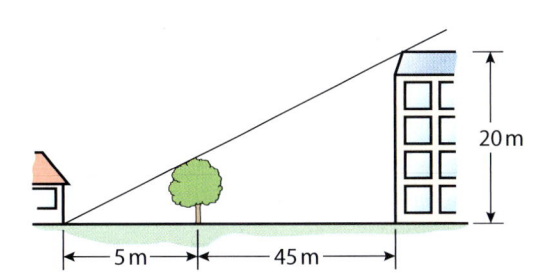

Text & Tests 2 Higher Level

16. A tall man, who is sitting up straight in his seat, is completely blocking John's view at the cinema.
John is 10 m from the 4 m high screen. The man is 1 m in front of John.
How far would the man need to lower his head and shoulders if John is to be able to see all of the screen?

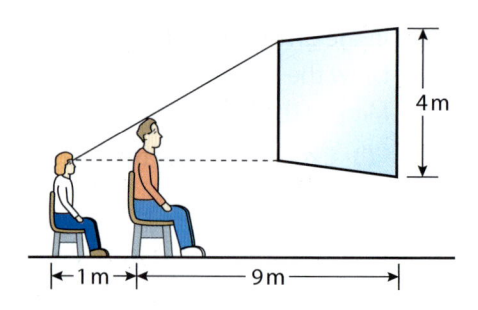

17. In the given figure, JK∥ML.
   (i) Explain why triangles JKM and KLM are similar.
   (ii) Find the length of [JK].

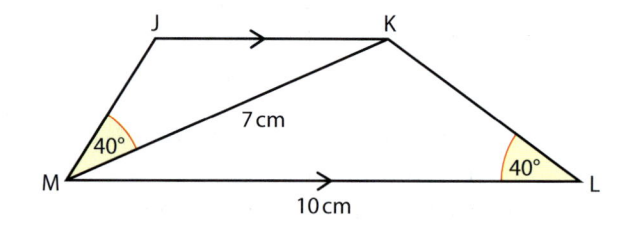

18. A swimming pool is being filled. Find the length, l, of the surface of the water when the pool has been filled to a depth of 2 m.

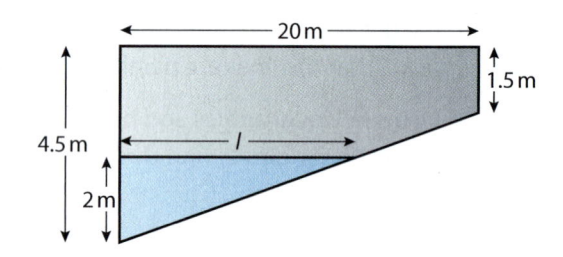

19. A surveyor wants to calculate the distance across a lake. The lake is surrounded by woods. Three paths have been constructed to provide access to the lake from a road AC as shown in the diagram.

The lengths of the paths from the road to the lake are as follows.
|AE| = 120 m
|BE| = 80 m
|CD| = 200 m
   (i) Explain how these measurements can be used to find |ED|.
   (ii) Calculate |ED|, the distance across the lake.

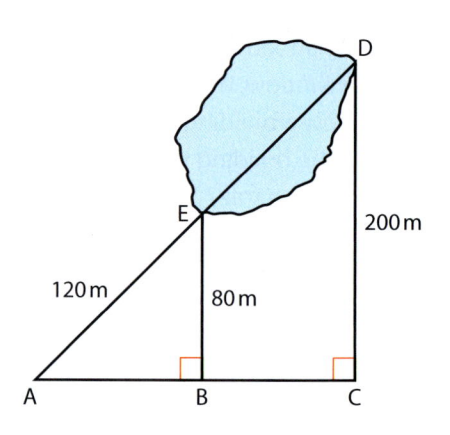

Chapter 16 Geometry 2: Similar Triangles – Circles – Theorems

Section 16.2 Transversals and triangles

1. Transversals

The diagram on the right shows a line p intersecting three parallel lines ℓ, m and n.
The line p is called a **transversal**.
Since $|AB| = |BC|$, we say that the parallel lines ℓ, m and n cut **equal segments** on the transversal.

If another line q is drawn, it can be shown that the parallel lines will also cut equal segments on the line q, that is, $|DE| = |EF|$.

The same property holds for all other transversals. This property is stated in the theorem below.

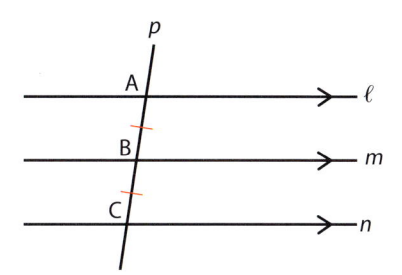

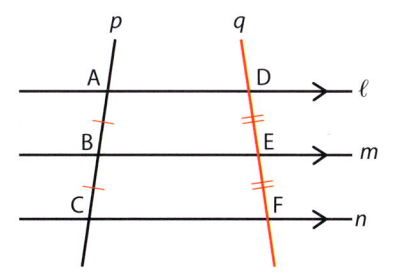

> **Theorem**
> If three parallel lines cut off equal segments on some transversal line, then they will cut off equal segments on any other transversal.

Example 1

In the given figure, the lines ℓ, m and n cut equal intercepts of 9 cm from the transversal p.
If q is another transversal, find the value of x.

The lines ℓ, m and n also cut equal intercepts on the line q.

$\therefore\ 12\,\text{cm} = (x + 5)\,\text{cm}$
$\quad x + 5 = 12$
$\quad\quad x = 12 - 5$
$\quad\quad x = 7$

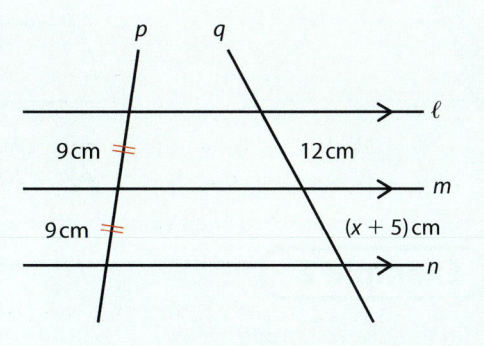

2. Line parallel to a side of a triangle

In the given triangle, the points D and E divide the side [AB] into 3 equal parts.

If lines through D and E are drawn parallel to [BC], then the points F and G will also divide the side [AC] into 3 equal parts.

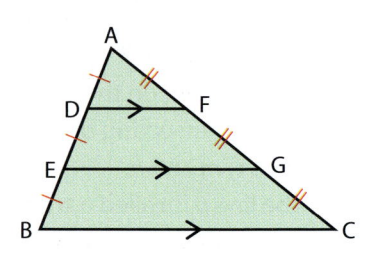

The example above can be extended to include any ratio $s:t$ as shown below.

In the given triangle, X divides the side [AB] in the ratio $s:t$.

If XY is parallel to BC, then Y will divide [AC] also in the ratio $s:t$.

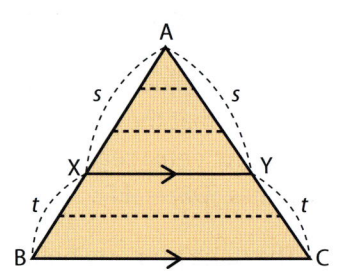

The diagram above illustrates a very important and useful geometric result which is given on the right.

Theorem
A line drawn parallel to one side of a triangle divides the other two sides in the same ratio.

In a triangle ABC in which XY∥BC, the following ratios are always true.

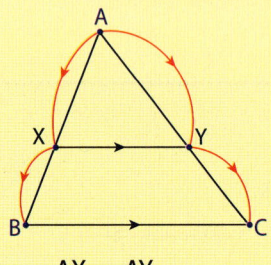

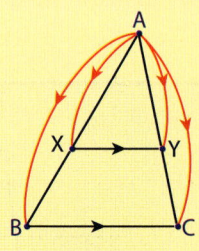

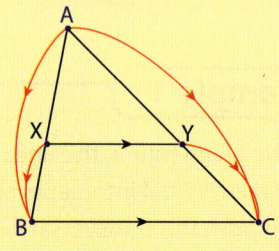

(i) $\dfrac{AX}{XB} = \dfrac{AY}{YC}$

(ii) $\dfrac{AB}{AX} = \dfrac{AC}{AY}$

(iii) $\dfrac{AB}{XB} = \dfrac{AC}{YC}$

Example 2

In the given triangle, DE∥BC.
If $|AD| = 8$, $|DB| = 4$ and $|AC| = 9$, find $|AE|$.

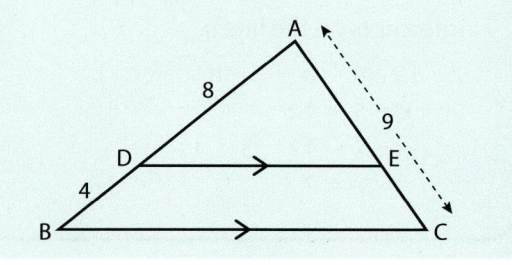

Chapter 16 Geometry 2: Similar Triangles – Circles – Theorems

Generally we start the ratio with the side that we require.

$$\frac{|AE|}{|AC|} = \frac{|AD|}{|AB|}$$

$$\frac{|AE|}{9} = \frac{8}{12} \quad \ldots \quad |AB| = 8 + 4 = 12$$

$$12|AE| = 8 \times 9$$

$$|AE| = \frac{8 \times 9}{12} = \frac{72}{12} = 6 \quad \text{i.e.} \quad |AE| = 6$$

The **converse** of the theorem on the previous page is also true and is stated on the right.

Converse of theorem
If a line cuts two sides of a triangle in the same ratio, then that line is parallel to the third side of the triangle.

Exercise 16.2

1. Find the value of x in each of the following figures where arrows indicate parallel lines.

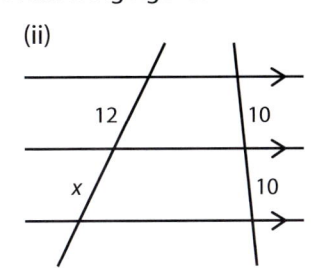

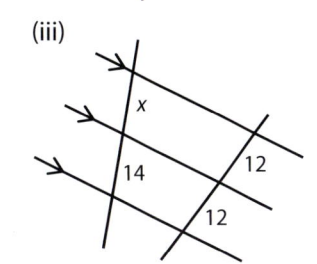

(i)   (ii)   (iii)

2. In each of the given figures, the parallel lines ℓ, m and n cut equal intercepts on the transversals p and q.
Find the values of x and y in each figure.

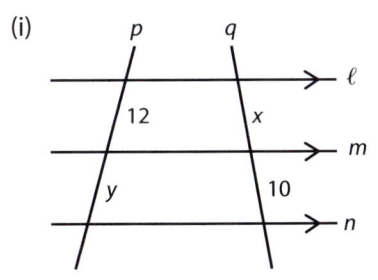

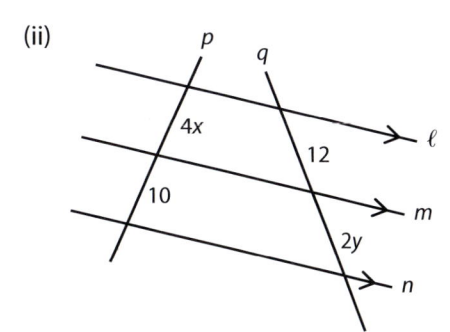

(i)   (ii)

373

Text & Tests 2 Higher Level

(iii) [diagram with parallel lines ℓ, m and transversals p, q showing segments x+4, y−3, 9, 12]

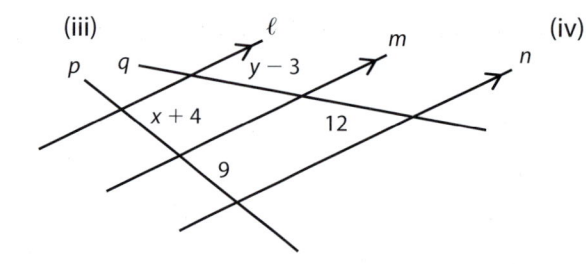

(iv) [diagram with transversals p, q and parallel lines ℓ, m, n showing segments 3x, 4x, 12, y−6]

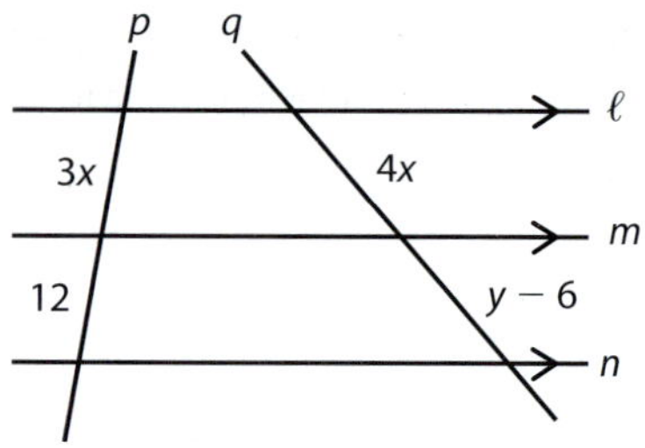

3. The given parallel lines ℓ, m and n cut equal intercepts on the transversals p and q, as shown.

   If $|BC| + |EF| = 3$ cm, find the value of a.

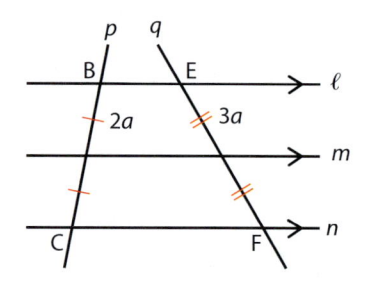

   [diagram showing segments 2a and 3a between parallel lines]

4. Examine the given diagram and then work out the values of x and y.

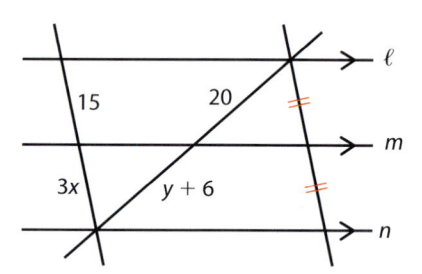

   [diagram showing segments 15, 20, 3x, y+6 between parallel lines ℓ, m, n]

5. a, b and c are parallel lines.
   p, q and r are three transversals intersecting a, b and c.
   $|DE| = |EF|$, $|GH| = 8$ cm and $|JK| = 7$ cm.

   Find   (i) $|HI|$ (ii) $|GJ|$.

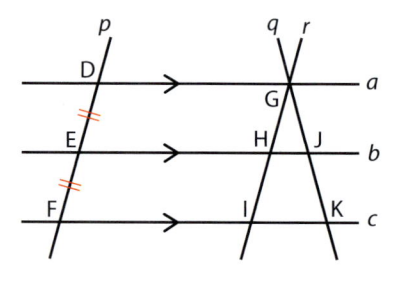

   [diagram showing points D, E, F on transversal p; G, H, I on transversal q; J, K on transversal r; across parallel lines a, b, c]

6. In each of the following triangles, the arrows indicate that the lines are parallel. Find the length of the line segment marked x in each triangle:

   (i) [triangle with sides 6, 5, 3 and segment x]

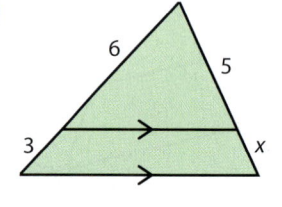

   (ii) [triangle with 6, x, 4, 6]

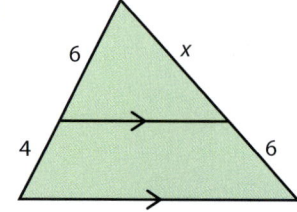

   (iii) [triangle with 4, 3, x, 5]

374

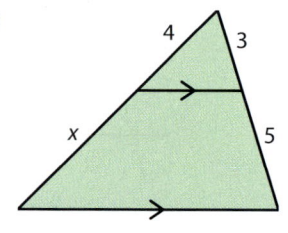

Chapter 16 Geometry 2: Similar Triangles – Circles – Theorems

7. Find the length of the line segment marked *a* in each of the following triangles, where the arrows indicate parallel lines:

   (i), (ii), 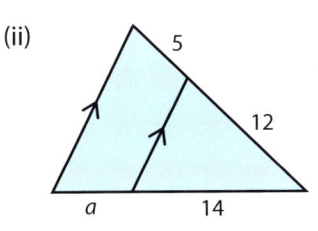 (iii)

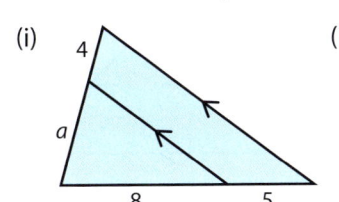

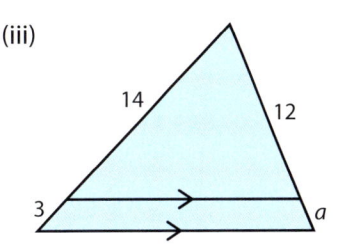

8. Find the values of *x*, *y* and *z* in the following triangles, where the arrows indicate parallel lines:

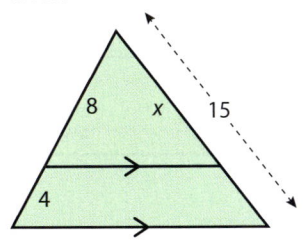

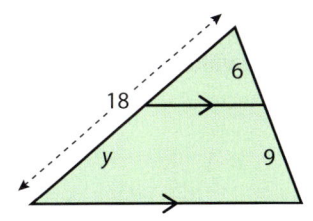

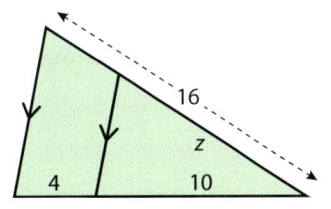

9. In the given triangle, DE∥BC.
   |AD| = 8,
   |DB| = 4,
   |AC| = 9.
   Find |AE|.

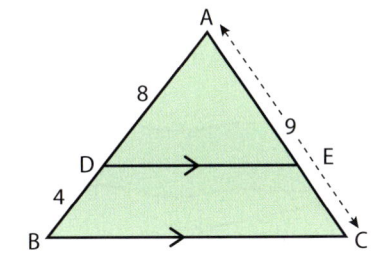

10. In the given diagram, DE∥BC.
    If $\dfrac{|AD|}{|DB|} = \dfrac{2}{1}$ and |AE| = 14 cm, find |EC|.

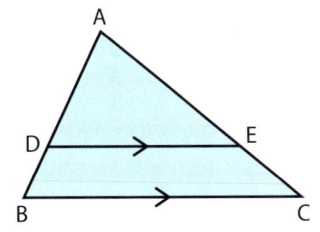

11. In the given triangle, XY∥BC.
    If $\dfrac{|AY|}{|YC|} = \dfrac{7}{3}$ and |AB| = 15 cm, find |AX|.

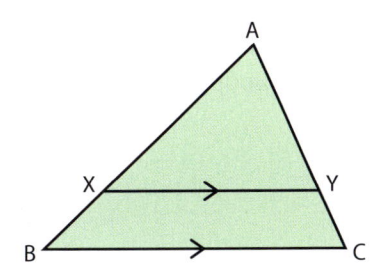

375

Text & Tests 2 Higher Level

12. In the given triangle, XY∥ST.

If |XS| = 5 cm, |YT| = 6 cm and |RS| = 12 cm, find |RT|.

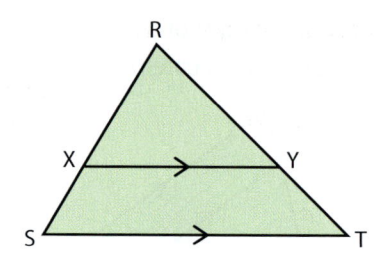

13. Explain why the triangles ABC and ADE are similar.

(i) Fill in the missing parts in these ratios:

$$\frac{|AD|}{|AB|} = \frac{|AE|}{\boxed{}} = \frac{|DE|}{\boxed{}}$$

(ii) Use these ratios to find the values of x and y.

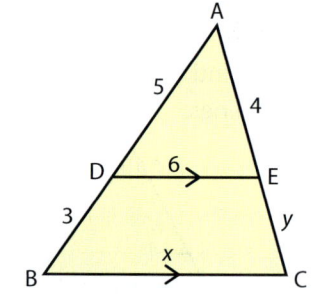

14. A group of students were trying to find the distance between two trees on opposite sides of a river using pegs, a measuring tape and a large amount of string. They align the pegs in a particular way, take several measurements and sketch this diagram. On the diagram, A and B are the trees and C, D and E are the pegs.

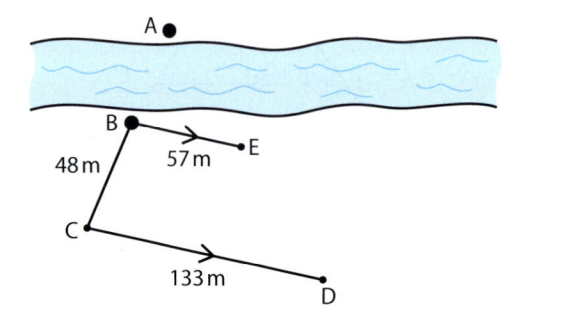

|BE| = 57 m
|BC| = 48 m
|CD| = 133 m

(i) In what way must the pegs and the trees be aligned if the students are to use these measurements to calculate |AB|?

(ii) Calculate the distance between the trees.

(iii) Another group of students repeats the activity. They have a similar diagram but different measurements. Their measurements are |BE| = 40 m and |BC| = 9 m. Based on the value of |AB| that the first group got, what measurement will this second group have for |CD|?

Chapter 16 Geometry 2: Similar Triangles – Circles – Theorems

Section 16.3 Angles and circles

The diagrams below will help you understand the meanings of the terms frequently used when dealing with circles.

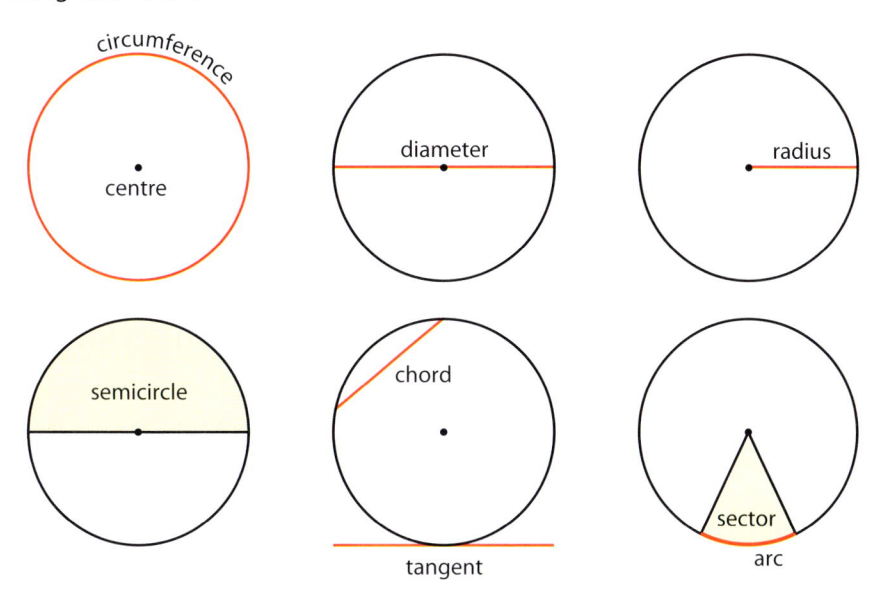

1. The angle in a semicircle

The shaded angle shown is called the angle in a semicircle because [AB] is a diameter. We will show below that the angle in a semicircle is a right angle.

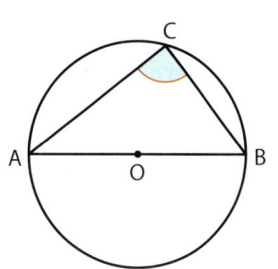

Explanation

In the given circle, |AB| is a diameter,

|OB| = |OA| = |OC| = radius.

The angles marked x are equal because the triangle AOB is isosceles.

Similarly, the angles marked y are equal.

$2x + 2y$ make up the three angles of the $\triangle$ABC.

$\therefore \quad 2x + 2y = 180°$
$\therefore \quad |\angle x| + |\angle y| = 90°$
Thus, $\quad |\angle BAC| = 90°$

> The angle in a semicircle is a right angle.

377

Text & Tests 2 Higher Level

> **Example 1**
>
> A, B and C are three points on a circle
> with centre O.
> If $|\angle OCB| = 65°$, find
>
> (i) $|\angle OBC|$ (ii) $|\angle AOB|$ (iii) $|\angle OBA|$. 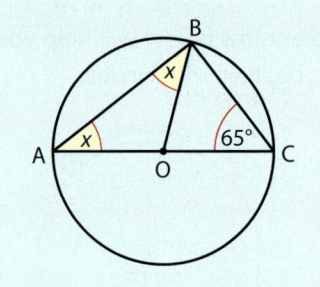
>
> (i) The triangle OCB is isosceles since $|OC| = |OB|$ = radius.
> $\therefore |\angle OBC| = |\angle OCB| = 65°$
> (ii) $|\angle BOC| = 180° - 65° - 65°$
> $\therefore |\angle BOC| = 50°$
> $\therefore |\angle AOB| = 180° - 50° = 130°$
> (iii) Since $|OA| = |OB|$ = radius, $|\angle OAB| = |\angle OBA| = x°$
> $\therefore x + x + 130° = 180°$ ... $|\angle AOB| = 130°$
> $2x = 50°$
> $x = 25°$
> $|\angle OBA| = 25°$

Note: Many of the problems dealing with angles in circles will involve identifying isosceles triangles. These isosceles triangles occur when the two equal sides consist of radii. Two isosceles triangles are shown in the given circle.

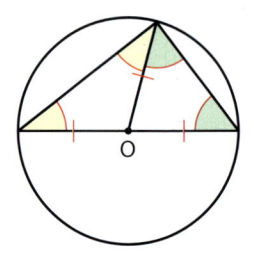

2. Angle at the centre of a circle and angle at the circumference

In the given diagram, O is the centre of the circle.
The angle AOB is said to be at the centre of the
circle and **standing on the arc AB**.
The angle ACB is at the circumference of the circle,
also standing on the arc AB.

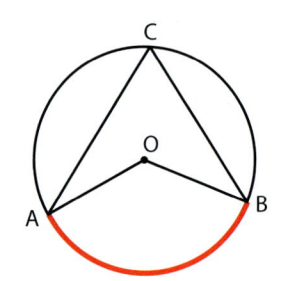

Chapter 16 Geometry 2: Similar Triangles – Circles – Theorems

A very important theorem linking the angle at the centre of a circle and the angle at the circumference is stated below.

Theorem 19
The angle subtended at the centre of a circle is twice the angle at the circumference.

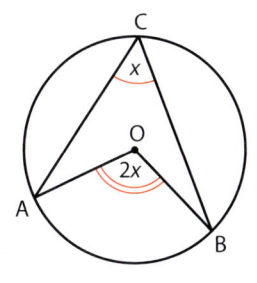

The formal proof of this theorem is given in Section 16.4.

$|\angle AOB| = 2|\angle ACB|$

Corollaries

Some very important deductions or corollaries result from the theorem above.

Corollary 1
All angles at a point of a circle, standing on the same arc, are equal.

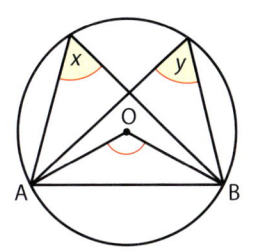

Explanation
The angles x and y are both standing on the arc AB.

$|\angle x| = \frac{1}{2}|\angle AOB|$ and $|\angle y| = \frac{1}{2}|\angle AOB|$

$\therefore |\angle x| = |\angle y|$

Cyclic quadrilaterals

The figure in the diagram on the right is called a **cyclic quadrilateral** because all the vertices are on the circle.

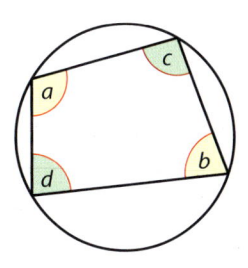

Corollary 2
The opposite angles of a cyclic quadrilateral add to 180°.

$a + b = 180°$
$c + d = 180°$

379

Explanation

The diagram shows that

$2x + 2y = 360°$

$\therefore x + y = 180°$

$\therefore |\angle ABC| + |\angle ADC| = 180°$

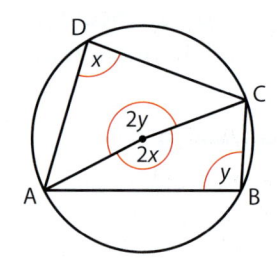

> **Corollary 3**
> The angle in a semicircle is a right angle.

Earlier in this section, we showed that the angle in a semicircle is a right angle.
Here is another way of showing the truth of this statement.

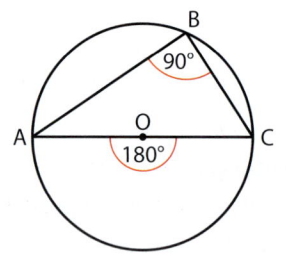

$|\angle ABC| = \frac{1}{2}|\angle AOC|$

$\therefore |\angle ABC| = \frac{1}{2}(180°)$

$|\angle ABC| = 90°$

> **Corollary 4**
> If the angle standing on a chord [BC] at some point of the circle is a right angle, then [BC] is a diameter.

Example 2

In the given diagram, O is the centre of the circle.
Find the measures of the angles a and b.

$|\angle a| = 48°$ ... angles standing on the same arc

$|\angle b| = 2 \times 48°$ ... angle at centre double angle at
$ = 96°$ circumference standing on the same arc

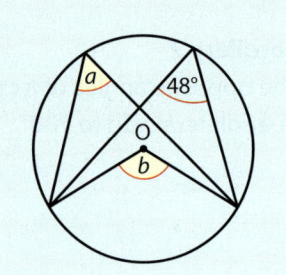

Chapter 16 Geometry 2: Similar Triangles – Circles – Theorems

Example 3

In the given figure, O is the centre of the circle and $|\angle AOB| = 80°$.

Find (i) $|\angle ACB|$ (ii) $|\angle ADB|$.

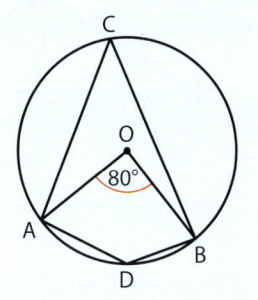

(i) $|\angle ACB| = \frac{1}{2}|\angle AOB|$ ... angle at centre
$= \frac{1}{2}(80°) = 40°$

(ii) $|\angle ADB| + |\angle ACB| = 180°$ ... ADBC is a cyclic quadrilateral
$|\angle ADB| + 40° = 180°$
$|\angle ADB| = 140°$

Example 4

In the given diagram, O is the centre of the circle, $|\angle AOB| = 110°$ and $|\angle OBC| = 30°$.

Find (i) $|\angle ACB|$ (ii) $|\angle OAC|$.

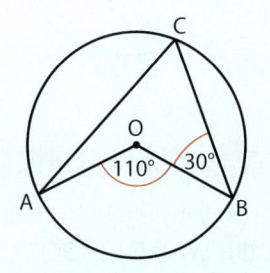

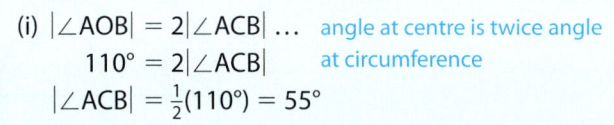

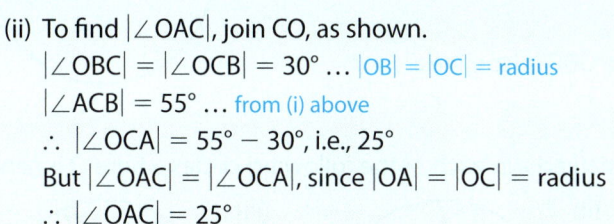

(i) $|\angle AOB| = 2|\angle ACB|$ ... angle at centre is twice angle
$110° = 2|\angle ACB|$ at circumference
$|\angle ACB| = \frac{1}{2}(110°) = 55°$

(ii) To find $|\angle OAC|$, join CO, as shown. 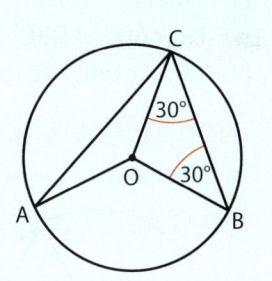
$|\angle OBC| = |\angle OCB| = 30°$ ... $|OB| = |OC|$ = radius
$|\angle ACB| = 55°$ ... from (i) above
$\therefore |\angle OCA| = 55° - 30°$, i.e., $25°$
But $|\angle OAC| = |\angle OCA|$, since $|OA| = |OC|$ = radius
$\therefore |\angle OAC| = 25°$

Exercise 16.3

1. [AB] is a diameter of the given circle.
   (i) Explain why $\angle ACB$ is a right angle.
   (ii) Find $|\angle CAB|$.
   (iii) Describe the triangle ABC in two ways.

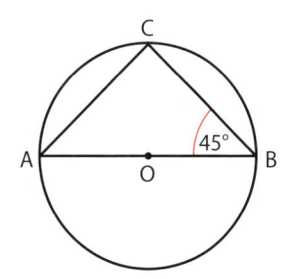

381

Text & Tests 2 Higher Level

2. Find the value of *x* in each of these circles where O is the centre:

(i) [circle with angle x at top, diameter through O]

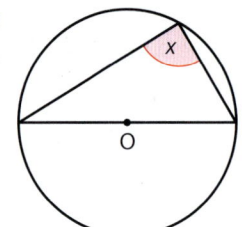

(ii) [circle with 60° and x angles, diameter through O]

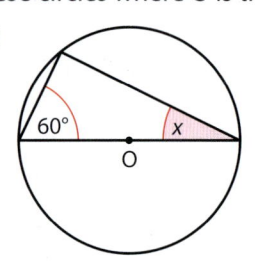

(iii) [circle with x and 50° angles, diameter through O]

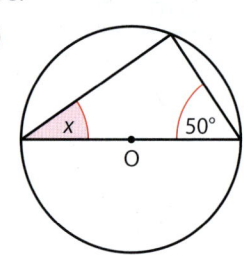

3. Write down the sizes of the angles marked with a letter in each of the following circles with O as centre:

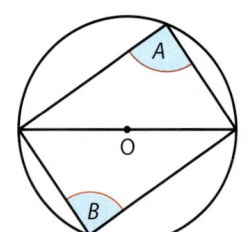

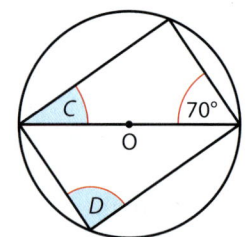

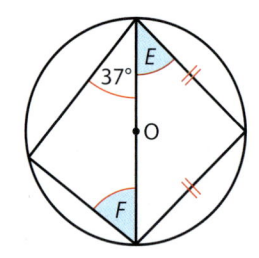

[circle with angles A and B marked, O centre]

[circle with angles C, D and 70° marked, O centre]

[circle with angles E (37°) and F marked, O centre]

4. In the given circle, O is the centre.
   (i) Why is |OA| = |OB|?
   (ii) What is |∠ABC|?
   (iii) What is |∠ABO|?
   (iv) Now find |∠OBC|.
   (v) Explain why the triangle OBC is isosceles.

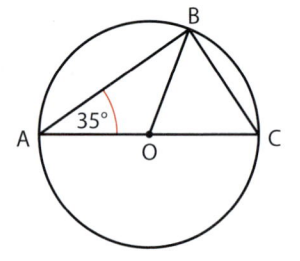

[circle with points A, B, C; angle 35° at O; O centre]

5. Find the value of the angle marked *x* in each of the following circles where O is centre:

(i) [circle with 140° and x, O centre]

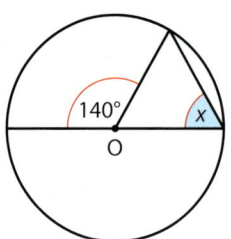

(ii) [circle with 30° and x, O centre]

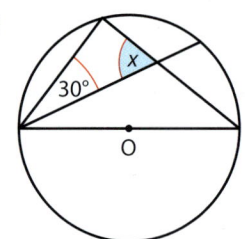

(iii) [circle with 35° and x, O centre]

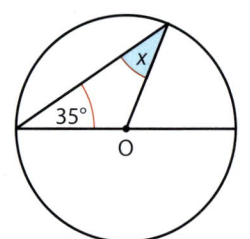

Chapter 16 Geometry 2: Similar Triangles – Circles – Theorems

6. Find the measure of the angle marked with a letter in each of the following circles where O is the centre:

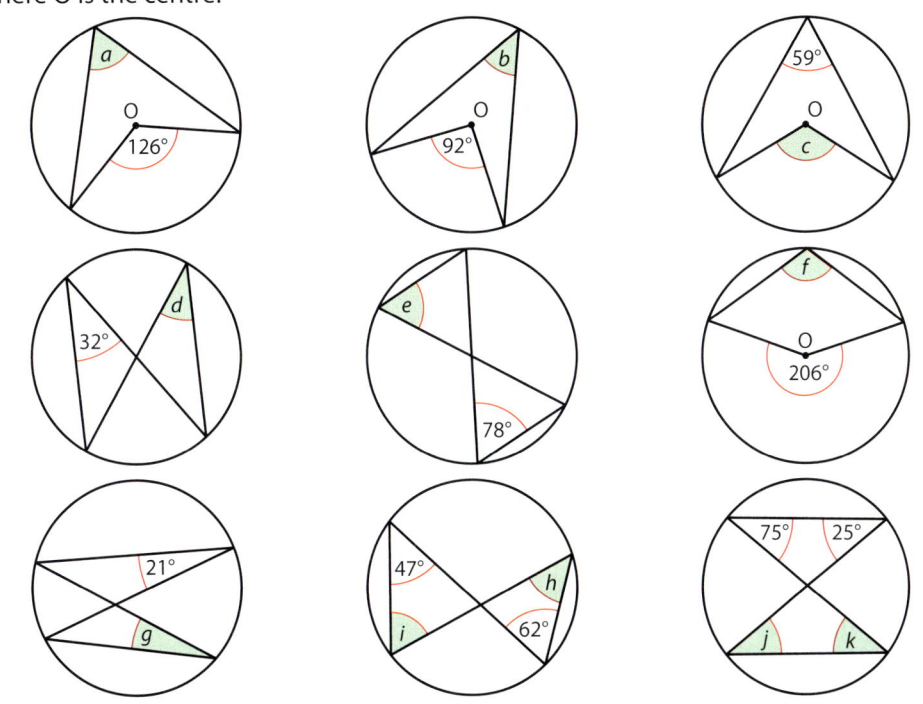

7. Find the measure of the angle marked with a letter in the following cyclic quadrilaterals:

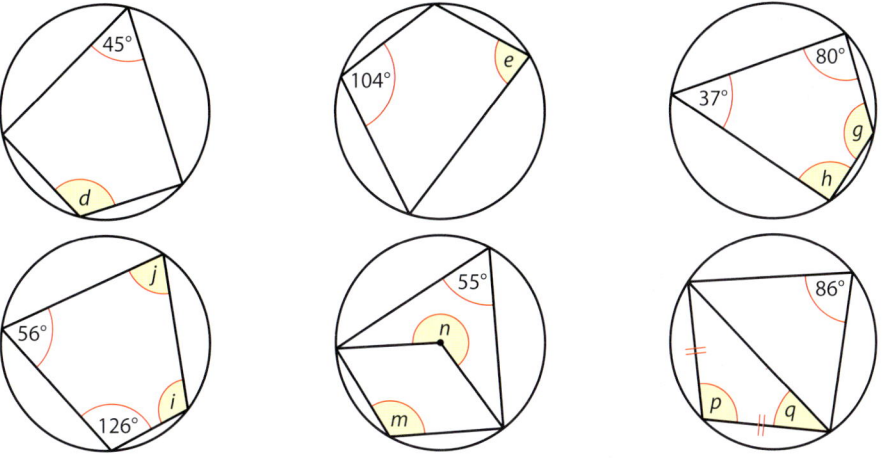

8. Find the measure of the angle marked with a letter in each of these circles.

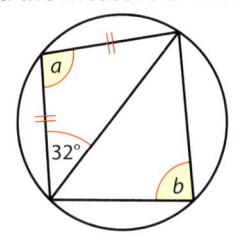

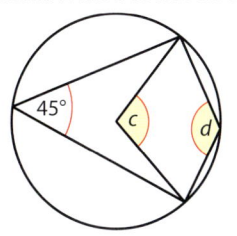

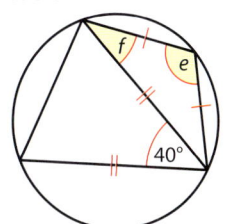

Text & Tests 2 Higher Level

9. In the given diagram, O is the centre of the circle, $|\angle AOB| = 140°$ and $|\angle OAC| = 30°$.

    Find (i) $|\angle ACB|$ (ii) $|\angle OCA|$
    (iii) $|\angle OCB|$ (iv) $|\angle OBC|$

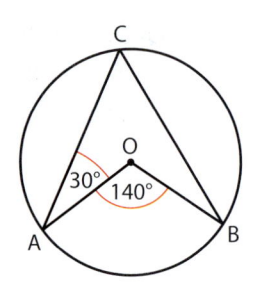

10. Find the measures of the angles marked *x* and *y* in the following circles with O as centre:

    (i)   (ii) 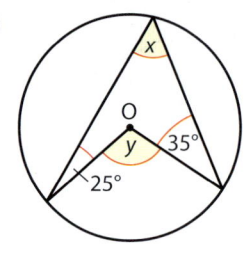   (iii)

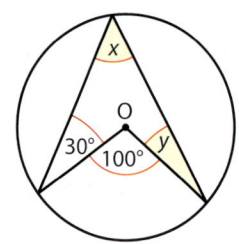

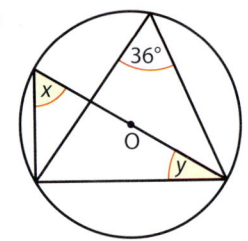

11. Calculate the measure of $\angle BDC$ in the given diagram.

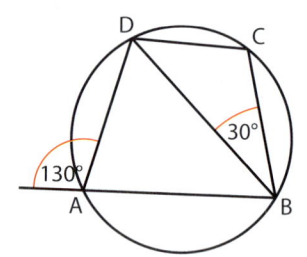

12. Find the measure of the angle marked *x* in each of the following circles with O as centre.

    (i)   (ii) 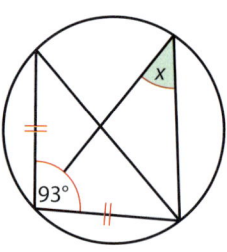   (iii)

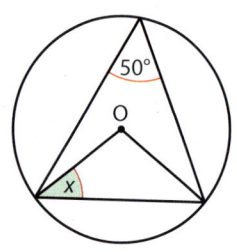

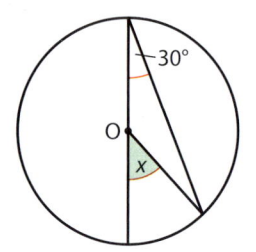

13. In the given diagram, $|\angle RPQ| = 30°$ and $|\angle PSQ| = 50°$.
    (i) Name another angle that is 30°.
    (ii) Hence find the measure of the angle marked *x*.

384

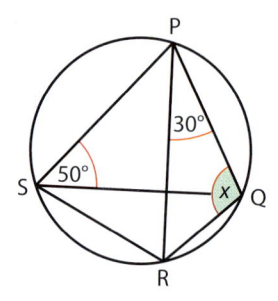

Chapter 16 Geometry 2: Similar Triangles – Circles – Theorems

14. PQRS is a cyclic quadrilateral with PQ∥SR.
If $|\angle QSR| = 33°$ and $|\angle SQR| = 81°$,
show that $|PS| = |PQ|$.

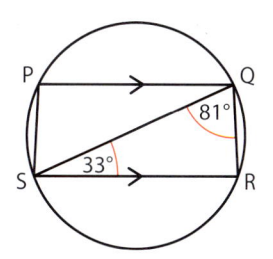

15. The diagonals of the cyclic quadrilateral shown on the right meet at the point X.
If $|AX| = |XB|$, prove that AB is parallel to DC.

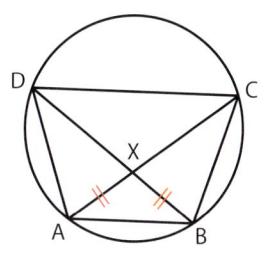

16. The indicated angles in the diagram are equal in measure.
Prove that $\angle QPS$ is a right angle.

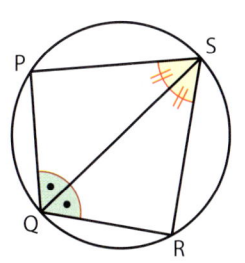

17. The chords [AC] and [BD] intersect at the point X, as shown.
Prove that the triangles AXB and CXD are similar.

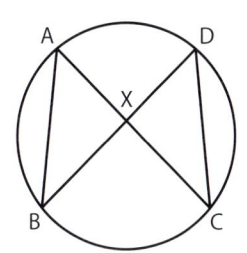

18. A, B, C and D are four points on a circle as shown.
[AD] bisects $\angle BAC$.
P is the point of intersection of AD and BC.
   (i) Show that the triangles ADB and APC are similar.
   (ii) Hence show that
      $|AC| \cdot |BD| = |AD| \cdot |PC|$.

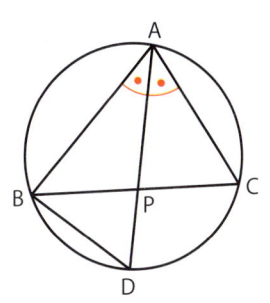

Text & Tests 2 Higher Level

19. In the given diagram, O is the centre of the circle.

Prove that $x + y = 90°$.

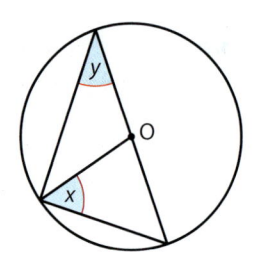

Section 16.4 Understanding proofs of theorems 4, 6, 9, 14, 19

In this section, the formal proofs of five theorems on your course are given. As stated already in section 9.6, the full formal proofs will **not** be examined; however, 'an understanding' of the proofs and corollaries will be tested. You will be familiar with the results of these theorems from the earlier sections of this chapter and also from Chapter 8. The various geometrical problems you solved used the results in these theorems.

Theorem 4	The angles in any triangle add to 180°.

Given: The triangle ABC with angles marked 1, 2 and 3.

To prove: $|\angle 1| + |\angle 2| + |\angle 3| = 180°$.

Construction: Draw a line ℓ through A parallel to BC. Mark the angles 4 and 5.

Proof: $|\angle 2| = |\angle 4|$ and $|\angle 3| = |\angle 5|$ ... alternate angles

$|\angle 4| + |\angle 1| + |\angle 5| = 180°$ ... straight angle

For $\angle 4$ and $\angle 5$, substitute $\angle 2$ and $\angle 3$.

$\therefore |\angle 2| + |\angle 1| + |\angle 3| = 180°$

i.e. $|\angle 1| + |\angle 2| + |\angle 3| = 180°$

Chapter 16 Geometry 2: Similar Triangles – Circles – Theorems

Theorem 6	Each exterior angle of a triangle is equal to the sum of the interior opposite angles.

Given: A triangle ABC with the side [BC] extended to the point D.
The angles marked 1, 2, 3 and 4 are also given.

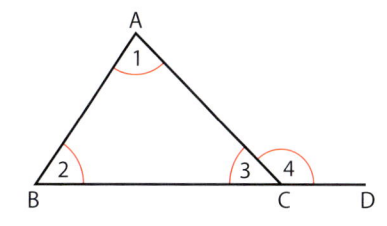

To prove: $|\angle 4| = |\angle 1| + |\angle 2|$

Proof: $|\angle 3| + |\angle 4| = 180°$ ... straight angle
$|\angle 1| + |\angle 2| + |\angle 3| = 180°$ ... angles in a triangle
∴ $|\angle 3| + |\angle 4| = |\angle 1| + |\angle 2| + |\angle 3|$
∴ $|\angle 4| = |\angle 1| + |\angle 2|$ ... subtract $\angle 3$ from each side

Theorem 9	In a parallelogram, opposite sides are equal and opposite angles are equal.

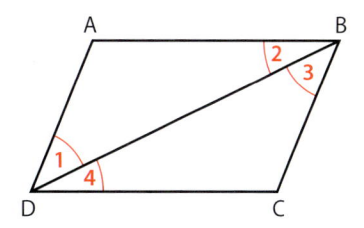

Given: A parallelogram ABCD.

To prove: $|AB| = |DC|$ and $|AD| = |BC|$.

Construction: Draw the diagonal [BD] and mark in the angles 1, 2, 3 and 4.

Proof: In the triangles ABD and BCD,
$|\angle 1| = |\angle 3|$ ... alternate angles as AB∥DC
$|\angle 2| = |\angle 4|$ ... alternate angles
$|DB| = |DB|$ ... common side
∴ △s ABD and BCD are congruent ... ASA
∴ $|AB| = |DC|$ and $|AD| = |BC|$ ... corresponding sides
Also, $|\angle DAB| = |\angle DCB|$ ... corresponding angles
and $|\angle ABC| = |\angle ADC|$ ... $|\angle 2| + |\angle 3| = |\angle 1| + |\angle 4|$

Thus, opposite sides and opposite angles of a parallelogram are equal.

Text & Tests 2 Higher Level

| **Theorem 14**
Theorem of
Pythagoras | In a right-angled triangle, the square of the hypotenuse is equal to the sum of the squares of the other two sides. |

Given: A triangle ABC in which A is a right angle.

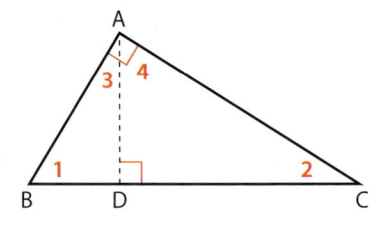

To prove: $|BC|^2 = |AB|^2 + |AC|^2$.

Construction: Draw AD ⊥ BC and mark in the angles 1, 2, 3 and 4.

Proof: Consider the triangles ABC and ABD.

∠1 is common to both △s

$|\angle BAC| = |\angle ADB| = 90°$

∴ △ABC and △ABD are similar.

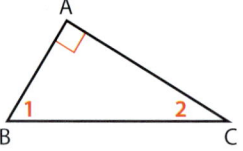

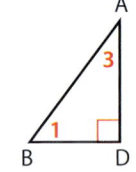

∴ $\dfrac{|BC|}{|AB|} = \dfrac{|AB|}{|BD|} \Rightarrow |AB|^2 = |BC| \cdot |BD|$ ... Ⓐ

Now consider the triangles ABC and ADC.

∠2 is common to both.

$|\angle BAC| = |\angle ADC| = 90°$

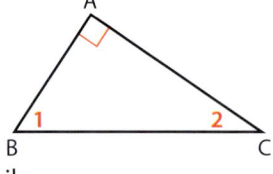

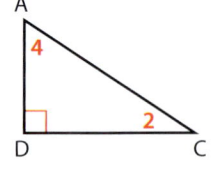

∴ △ABC and △ADC are similar.

∴ $\dfrac{|AC|}{|DC|} = \dfrac{|BC|}{|AC|} \Rightarrow |AC|^2 = |BC| \cdot |DC|$ ... Ⓑ

Adding Ⓐ and Ⓑ we get:

$|AB|^2 + |AC|^2 = |BC| \cdot |BD| + |BC| \cdot |DC|$

$\qquad\qquad\quad = |BC|[|BD| + |DC|]$

$\qquad\qquad\quad = |BC|[|BC|]$ ... $|BD| + |DC| = |BC|$

$|AB|^2 + |AC|^2 = |BC|^2$

i.e. $|BC|^2 = |AB|^2 + |AC|^2$

Chapter 16 Geometry 2: Similar Triangles – Circles – Theorems

Theorem 19	The angle at the centre of a circle standing on a given arc is twice the angle at any point of the circle standing on the same arc.

Given: A circle k with centre O.

A, B and C are three points on k.

∠AOB is at the centre and

∠ACB is at the circumference.

Both stand on the arc AB.

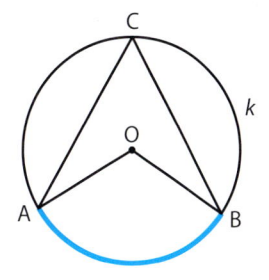

To prove: $|\angle AOB| = 2|\angle ACB|$.

Construction: Join C to O and extend to D.
Label the angles.

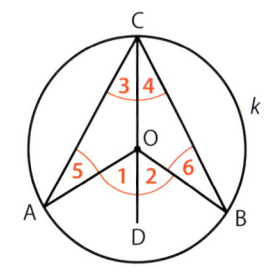

Proof: $|\angle 3| = |\angle 5|$ as △AOC is isosceles

and $|\angle 1| = |\angle 3| + |\angle 5|$ … *exterior angle is equal to the sum of interior opposite angles*

∴ $|\angle 1| = 2|\angle 3|$

Similarly, $|\angle 2| = 2|\angle 4|$

Adding: $|\angle 1| + |\angle 2| = 2|\angle 3| + 2|\angle 4|$

$|\angle 1| + |\angle 2| = 2[|\angle 3| + |\angle 4|]$

∴ $|\angle AOB| = 2|\angle ACB|$

Investigation:

Investigate the conditions necessary for a quadrilateral to be a rectangle.

Consider a circle with centre A. Two diameters BC and DE are drawn through A forming a quadrilateral BDCE.

List the number of different proofs you could use to show that BDCE is a rectangle.

Compare your proofs with other groups in the class.

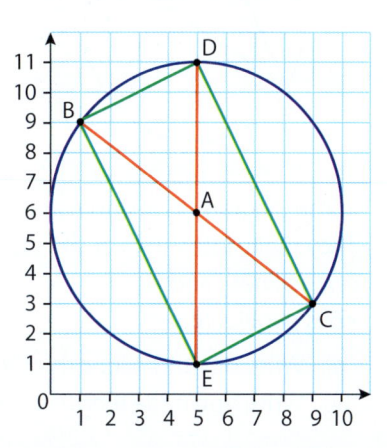

Text & Tests 2 Higher Level

Test yourself 16

1. In the given circle, O is the centre, $|\angle ACD| = 65°$ and $|AB| = |BC|$.
   - (i) Name two right angles in the figure.
   - (ii) Find $|\angle BAC|$.
   - (iii) Find $|\angle BAD|$.

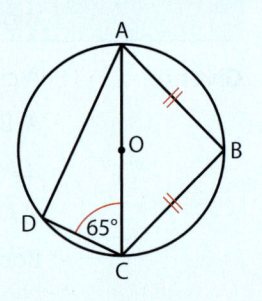

2. In the given triangles, the marked angles are equal.
   - (i) Explain why the two triangles are similar.
   - (ii) Find the values of x and y.

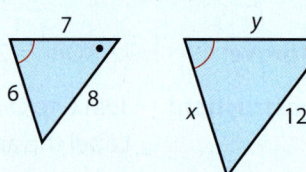

3. In the given diagram, the arrows indicate that the lines are parallel. Find the lengths of the line segments marked a and b.

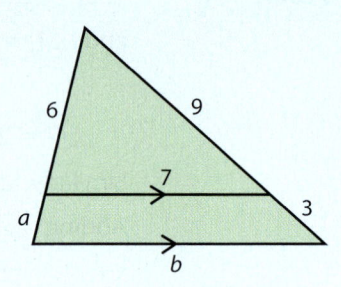

4. Find the measures of the angles marked by letters in each of these circles:

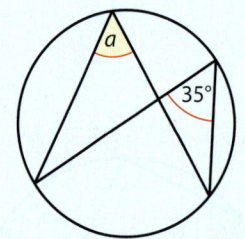

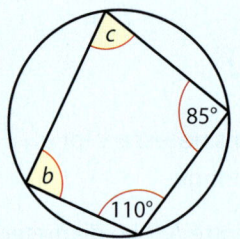

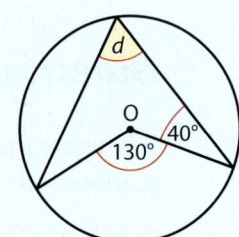

5. In the diagram, ℓ, m and n are parallel lines. They make intercepts of the indicated lengths on the lines j and k. AB is parallel to j.
   - (i) Write down the length of [AB].
   - (ii) Write down the length of [AC].

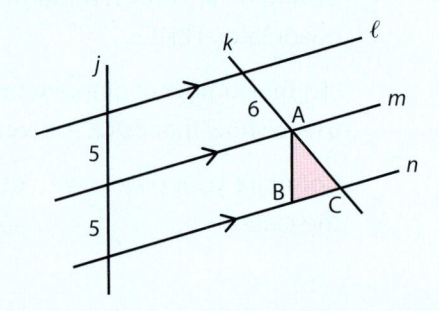

Chapter 16 Geometry 2: Similar Triangles – Circles – Theorems

6. In the diagram, PRS is an equilateral triangle and $|\angle PRQ| = 36°$. Find
   (i) $|\angle QRS|$
   (ii) $|\angle PQR|$
   (iii) $|\angle QPS|$.

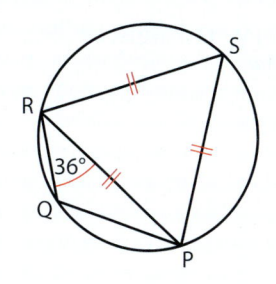

7. A 3.5 m ladder leans on a 2.4 m fence. One end is on the ground and the other end touches a vertical wall 2.9 m from the ground.
   How far is the bottom of the ladder from the fence?
   Give your answer in metres, correct to one decimal place.

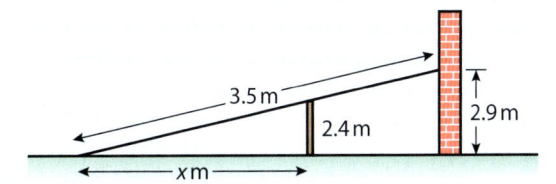

8. Find the value of x and the value of y in each of these circles with O as centre:
   (i)
   (ii)

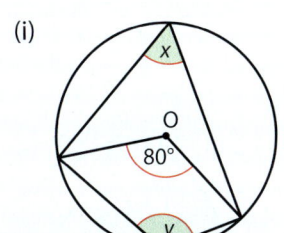

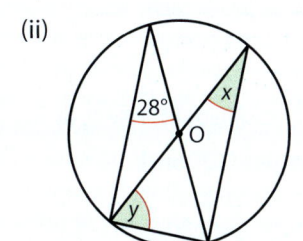

9. In the diagram, VZ is parallel to WY.
   Find (i) |WY|
        (ii) |VW|
        (iii) |VX|.

10. Colin calculated the width, w, of a river by taking the measurements shown and then using similar triangles.
    What answer should Colin get for the width?

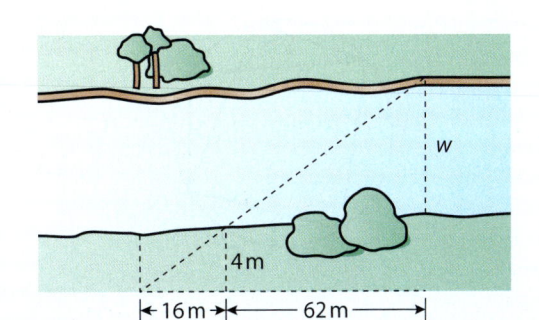

11. In the given triangle, DE∥BC. Find |DE|.

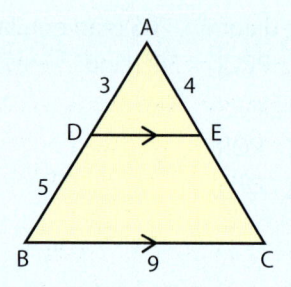

12. A path up to the carpark from the beach has a constant slope of 2 in 7.
This means that for every 7 m horizontally, the path rises 2 m.
The carpark is 60 m horizontally from the beach end of the path.
How high in the sand-dunes is the carpark?
Give your answer correct to the nearest whole number.

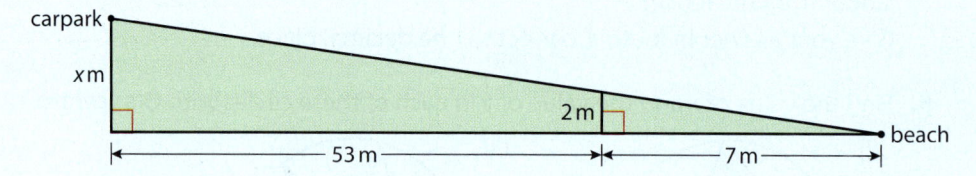

13. In this circle, chords [PR] and [QS] intersect at T.
   (i) Prove that the triangles PQT and SRT are similar.
   (ii) Hence find |TS|.

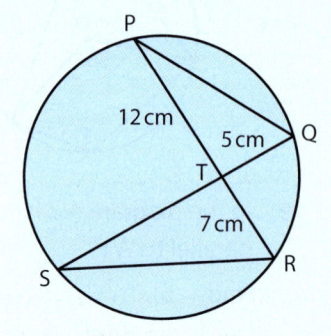

14. Find the measure of the angles marked x and y in each of the following diagrams.
   (i)
   (ii)

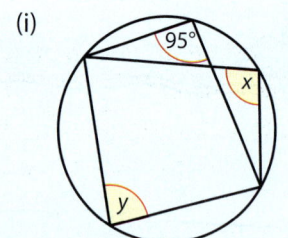

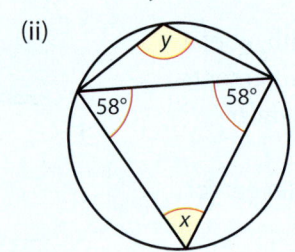

Chapter 16 Geometry 2: Similar Triangles – Circles – Theorems

15. Sarah found the height of a tree by placing a 30 cm ruler upright in the shadow of the tree. She placed the ruler so that the end of its shadow was at the same place as the end of the shadow of the tree.
    How high was this tree?
    Give your answer in metres, correct to one decimal place.

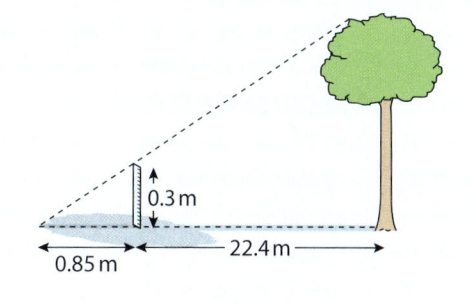

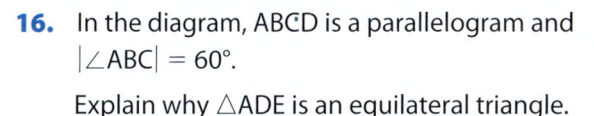

16. In the diagram, ABCD is a parallelogram and $|\angle ABC| = 60°$.
    Explain why △ADE is an equilateral triangle.

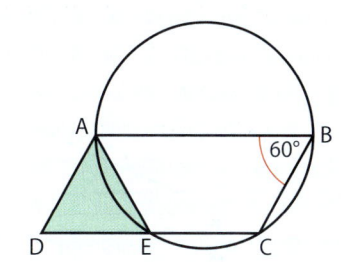

17. In the given figure, $|EC| = 9$ cm, $|AB| = 8$ cm and $|BE| = 15$ cm.
    Find $|DE|$.

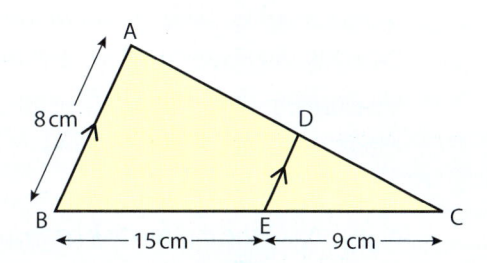

18. A, B and C are pegs on the bank of a canal which has parallel straight sides. C and D are directly opposite each other. $|AB| = 30$ m and $|BC| = 140$ m. When I walk from A directly away from the bank, I reach a point E, 25 m from A, where E, B and D line up. How wide is the canal?

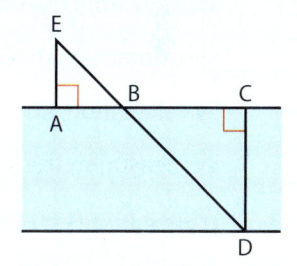

19. Two surveyors estimate the height of a nearby hill. One stands 5 m away from the other on horizontal ground, holding a 3 m stick vertically. The other surveyor finds a "line of sight" to the top of the hill, and observes that this line passes the vertical stick at 2.4 m. The distance from the stick to the top of the hill is 1500 m (as measured by laser equipment).
    How high, correct to the nearest metre, is their estimate of the height of the hill?

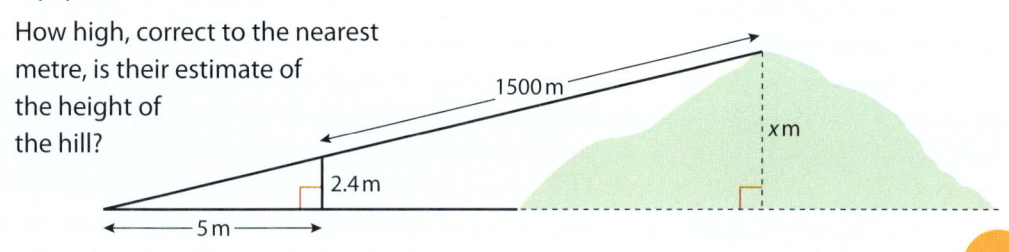

Text & Tests 2 Higher Level

Assignment:

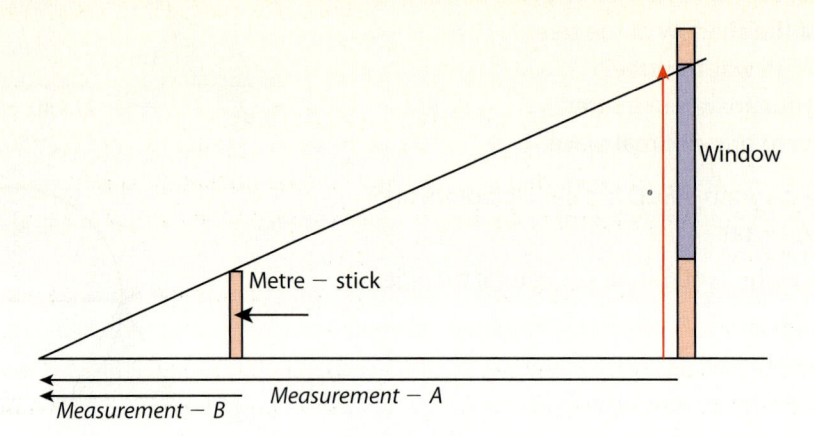

Using the light of a classroom window, a large triangle is made by the wall / window, floor and the ray of light from the top of the window.

Measure from the wall to the point on the floor where the image of the top of the window ends. *Measurement – A.*

Holding a metre-stick vertically to the floor, move it along the floor until the image of the top of the metre-stick corresponds to the image of the top of the window.

Measure from the bottom of the metre-stick to end of the shadow. *Measurement – B.*

Show mathematically that the height of the window $= \dfrac{A}{B}$

By calculation, find the height of the window.

By measuring the height of the window, check the accuracy of your calculation.

Write a report on your results.

Note: This method can be adapted to estimate the height of trees or school buildings once a shadow and level ground can be found to create similar triangles.

Cylinder – Sphere

chapter 17

In this chapter, you will learn to:

- find the volume of a cylinder,
- find the curved and total surface area of a cylinder,
- find the volume of a sphere and hemisphere,
- find the curved surface area of a sphere and hemisphere,
- find missing dimensions of shapes when given their volume or surface area,
- solve problems involving rates of flow,
- solve problems involving partial, or multiple cylinders, spheres and rectangular solids.

Section 17.1 The cylinder

When dealing with prisms in an earlier chapter, we found that the volume of a prism is the area of the base (cross-section) multiplied by the height.

Volume of prism = Area of base × height
$$= A \times h$$

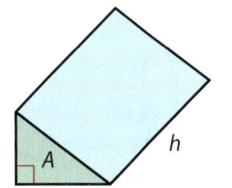

› A cylinder can be thought of as a prism whose cross-section is a circle.
› Since we know how to find the area of a circle, we can use the above formula to find the volume of a cylinder.
› The formula $V = Ah$ becomes $V = \pi r^2 h$, since $A = \pi r^2$.

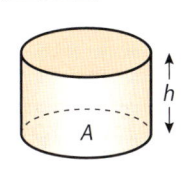

Curved surface area of cylinder

To calculate the area of the curved surface, imagine that the cylinder is hollow. If we cut the curved surface along the dotted line and flattened it out, it would form a rectangle.

The area of this rectangle would be the same as the area of the curved surface.

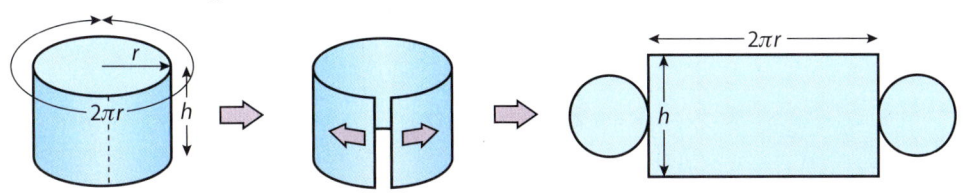

Text & Tests 2 Higher Level

From the series of diagrams on the previous page, we see that the curved surface area is equivalent to a rectangle that has a length equal to the circumference of the circle and a width equal to the height of the cylinder. Using the formula for the area of a rectangle, we obtain:

Curved surface area = $2\pi rh$

The total surface area = curved surface area + area of 2 circles
$= 2\pi rh + 2\pi r^2$

Cylinder

> Volume = $\pi r^2 h$
>
> Curved surface area = $2\pi rh$
>
> Total surface area = $2\pi rh + 2\pi r^2$

Example 1

Find (i) the volume
(ii) the total surface area
of the cylinder shown, taking $\pi = 3.14$.

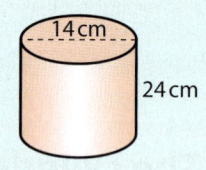

14 cm
24 cm

Correct each answer to 3 significant figures.

Volume = $\pi r^2 h$
$= 3.14 \times 7^2 \times 24$ ... $r = \frac{14 \text{ cm}}{2}$, i.e. 7 cm
$= 3692.64$ cm³

Volume = 3690 cm³

Total surface area = $2\pi rh + 2\pi r^2$
$= 2 \times 3.14 \times 7 \times 24 + 2 \times 3.14 \times 7^2$
$= 1362.76$ cm²

Total surface area = 1360 cm²

Example 2

The volume of a cylinder is 1232 cm³.
If its height is 8 cm, find the length of its radius taking $\pi = 3.14$.
Give your answer correct to the nearest centimetre.

Volume = 1232 cm³ $\Rightarrow \pi r^2 h = 1232$
$3.14 \times r^2 \times 8 = 1232$
$r^2 = \frac{1232}{3.14 \times 8}$
$r^2 = 49.04$
$r = \sqrt{49.04} = 7.0029$
$r = 7$ cm

The radius = 7 cm

Chapter 17 Cylinder – Sphere

Exercise 17.1

1. Taking $\pi = 3.14$, find, correct to 2 decimal places, the volume of each of the cylinders shown below:

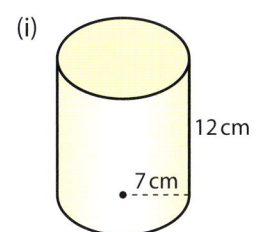

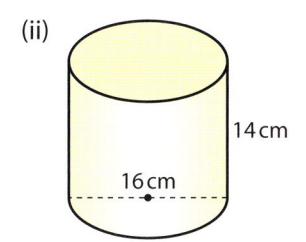

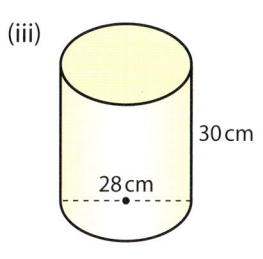

   (i) 12 cm, 7 cm

   (ii) 14 cm, 16 cm

   (iii) 30 cm, 28 cm

2. Find, correct to 2 decimal places, the total surface areas of the solid cylinders in Question 1 above, taking $\pi = 3.14$.

3. Taking $\pi = 3.14$, find the volume of each of these cylinders. Give your answers correct to the nearest whole numbers.

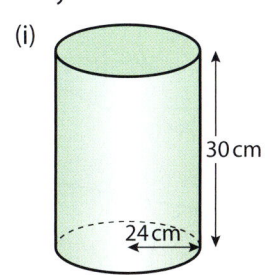

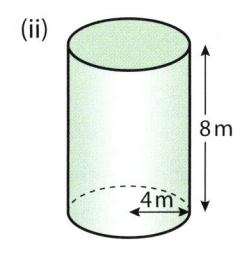

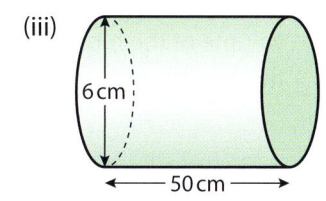

   (i) 30 cm, 24 cm

   (ii) 8 m, 4 m

   (iii) 6 cm, 50 cm

4. Taking $\pi = 3.14$, find the volume of the cylinder shown on the right.

   If 1 litre = 1000 cm³, find the capacity of the cylinder, correct to the nearest litre.

   40 cm, 28 cm

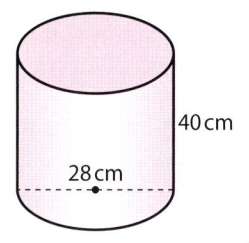

5. The figure on the right shows a solid cylinder cut along its diameter.
   Taking $\pi = 3.14$, find the volume of the figure in cm³.

   5 cm, 18 cm

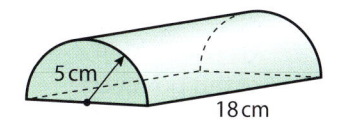

6. The volume of the given cylinder is 350π cm³.
   (i) Write down the formula for the volume of a cylinder.
   (ii) Write in all the known values in the formula, given that the height is 14 cm.
   (iii) Now find the length of the radius of the cylinder.

   14 cm, Volume = 350π cm³

7. The volume of a cylinder is 288π cm³.
   If the height of the cylinder is 8 cm, find its radius.

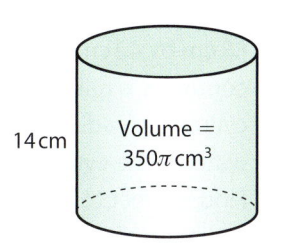

397

Text & Tests 2 Higher Level

8. The volume of a cylinder is 360π cm³.
   If the radius of the cylinder is 6 cm, find its height.

9. Write down the formula for the curved surface area of a cylinder.
   The curved surface area of a certain cylinder is 110 cm².
   If the height of the cylinder is 5 cm, find the length of the radius correct to 1 decimal place.

10. The area of the base of a cylinder is 154 cm².
    If the volume of the cylinder is 770 cm³, find its height.

11. The volume of a cylinder is 1848 cm³.
    If the height of the cylinder is 12 cm, find, correct to 2 decimal places, its radius, taking $\pi = 3.14$.

12. A hole of radius 4 cm is bored through this rectangular solid, as shown.
    Using the π key on your calculator, find the volume of the remaining solid, correct to the nearest cm³.

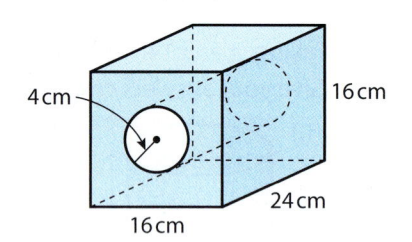

13. A cylindrical metal pipe has an external diameter of 6 cm and an internal diameter of 4 cm, as shown.
    The pipe is 1 m long.
    Taking $\pi = 3.14$, find, correct to 2 decimal places:
    (i) the volume of the pipe in cm³
    (ii) the mass of the pipe, in kg, if 1 cm³ of the metal has a mass of 9 g.

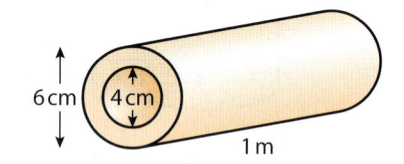

14. A cylindrical pencil holder has a diameter 4 cm and height 14 cm. Taking $\pi = 3.14$, find the volume of the holder in cm³.
    Eight pencil holders are packed tightly into a rectangular box as shown.
    Find, correct to 2 decimal places, the volume of this box in cm³.

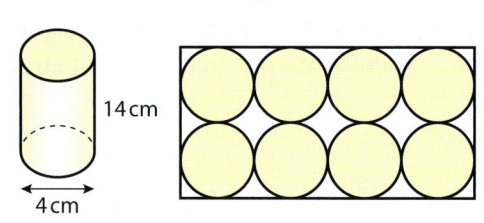

15. Rain falls into a flat rectangular container 88 cm by 42 cm by 6 cm. When the container is full, it is poured into an empty cylinder of radius 21 cm. The depth of water in the cylinder is h cm.
    Find, correct to 2 decimal places, the value of h.
    Take $\pi = 3.14$.

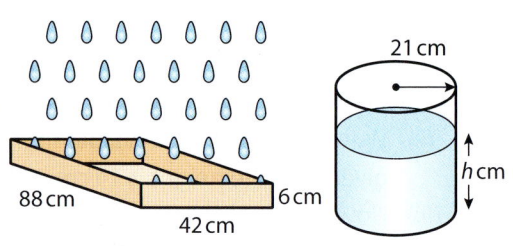

Chapter 17 Cylinder – Sphere

16. This is the metal frame of a greenhouse.
    It consists of semicircles mounted on
    rectangular frames.
    (i) Find the area of the material needed
        to cover this greenhouse.
        Exclude the floor and door.
    (ii) Calculate the volume of the greenhouse in
        cubic metres.
        Use the π key on your calculator and give
        each answer to the nearest whole number.

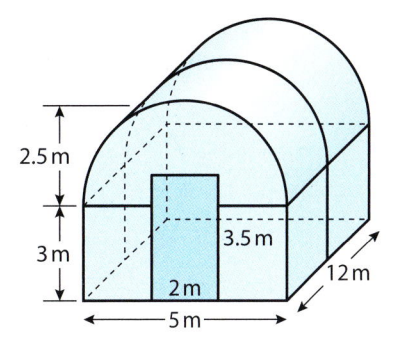

17. A semicircular shape of radius 9 cm is
    cut from a solid cube of side 18 cm. Take $\pi = 3.14$.

    Find (i) the volume of the remaining solid
          (ii) the surface area of the remaining solid.

    Give each answer correct to the nearest whole number.

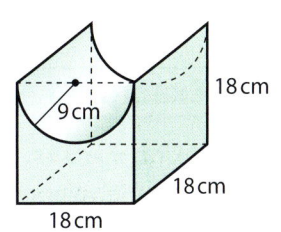

Section 17.2 The sphere and hemisphere

The figure on the right is a sphere of radius r.
The Greek mathematician and engineer, **Archimedes** (born 287 BC),
found that the volume of a sphere is equal to two thirds the volume
of the smallest cylinder which encloses it.

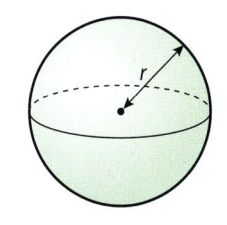

Here is how Archimedes made his discovery.
He used a sphere of radius r and a cylinder of base radius r and height $2r$.

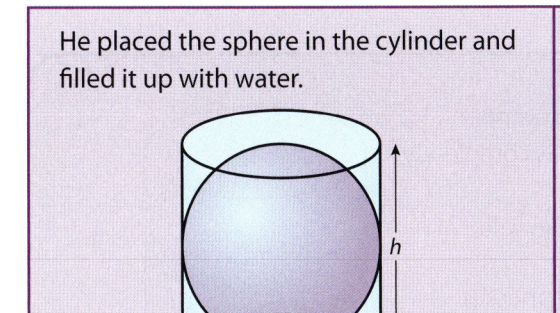

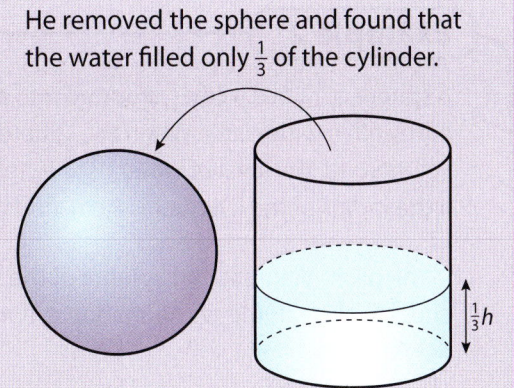

He placed the sphere in the cylinder and filled it up with water.	He removed the sphere and found that the water filled only $\frac{1}{3}$ of the cylinder.

Volume of sphere $= \frac{2}{3}$ volume of cylinder
$= \frac{2}{3} \times \pi r^2 h$
$= \frac{2}{3} \times \pi r^2 (2r)$ ... $h = 2r$
$= \frac{4}{3} \pi r^3$

399

Text & Tests 2 Higher Level

1. **The sphere**

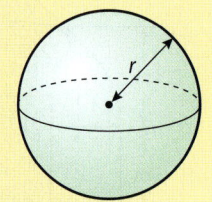

   Volume = $\frac{4}{3}\pi r^3$
   Surface area = $4\pi r^2$

2. **The hemisphere**

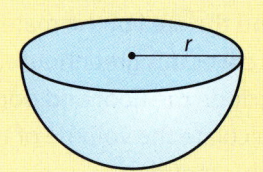

   Volume = $\frac{2}{3}\pi r^3$
   Surface area of solid hemisphere = $3\pi r^2$

Example 1

Taking $\pi = 3.14$, find correct to 1 place of decimals,
(i) the volume
(ii) the surface area, of the given sphere.

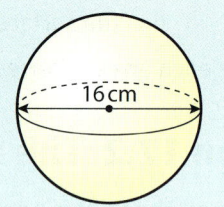

16 cm

(i) Volume = $\frac{4}{3}\pi r^3$
       = $\frac{4}{3} \times 3.14 \times 8^3$ ... $r = 8$ cm
       = 2143.57 cm³
       = 2143.6 cm³

(ii) Surface area = $4\pi r^2$
         = $4 \times 3.14 \times 8^2$
         = 803.84 cm²
         = 803.8 cm²

Example 2

A sphere of radius 4 cm is dropped into a cylinder partly filled with water. When the sphere is completely submerged, the level of water rises h cm.
If the radius of the cylinder is 8 cm, find the value of h.

In the given diagram, the volume of the sphere is equal to the volume of the shaded cylinder of height h cm.

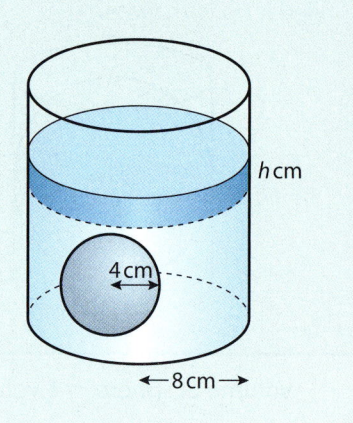

h cm

4 cm

← 8 cm →

Chapter 17 Cylinder – Sphere

Volume of sphere = Volume of cylinder

$\Rightarrow \quad \frac{4}{3}\pi r^3 = \pi r^2 h$

$\Rightarrow \quad \frac{4}{3}\pi(4)^3 = \pi(8)^2 h$

$\Rightarrow \quad \frac{4}{3} \times 64 = 64h \quad$ ... divide both sides by π

$\Rightarrow \quad \frac{4}{3} = h \quad$ ... divide both sides by 64

$\therefore \quad h = \frac{4}{3} = 1\frac{1}{3}$ cm

Note: In example 2 above, we are given two solids of equal volume, i.e., the volume of the sphere equals the volume of the cylinder.

$\Rightarrow \frac{4}{3}\pi(4)^3 = \pi(8)^2 h$

Here both sides of the equation contain π.
When this occurs, we divide both sides by π and so there is no need to substitute a value for π.

Exercise 17.2

1. Find the volume of each of these solids in cm³.
Take $\pi = 3.14$ and give each answer correct to 1 decimal place.

(i) 18 cm   (ii) 11 cm   (iii) 7 cm

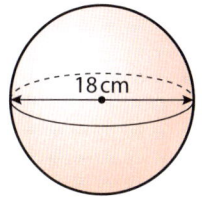

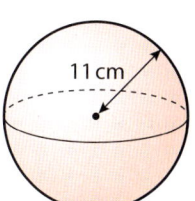

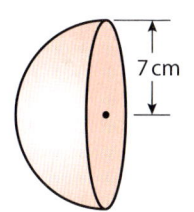

2. Find the surface area of each of the figures above.
Use the π key on your calculator and give each answer correct to the nearest whole number.

3. The length of the radius of a solid hemisphere is 5 cm.
Find, in terms of π, (i) the volume
(ii) the total surface area
of the hemisphere.

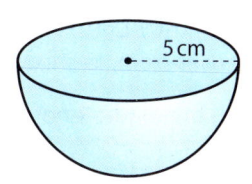

4. The volume of a sphere is 288π cm³.
(i) Find the length of the radius of the sphere.
(ii) Find, in terms of π, its total surface area.

5. The surface area of a sphere is 616 cm². Taking $\pi = 3.14$, find, correct to 2 places of decimals,
(i) the radius of the sphere
(ii) the volume of the sphere.

Text & Tests 2 Higher Level

6. The surface area of a sphere is 36π cm².
   Find the volume of the sphere in terms of π.

7. A container is in the shape of a cylinder on top of a hemisphere, as shown. The cylinder has a radius of length 3 cm and the container has a total height of 15 cm.

   Calculate the volume of the container in cm³, correct to the nearest whole number.

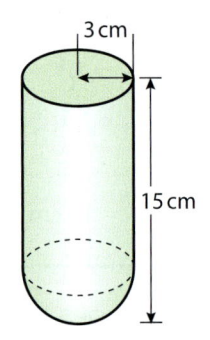

8. The cylinder and the sphere shown on the right have equal volumes.

   Find the length of the radius of the cylinder, correct to the nearest centimetre.

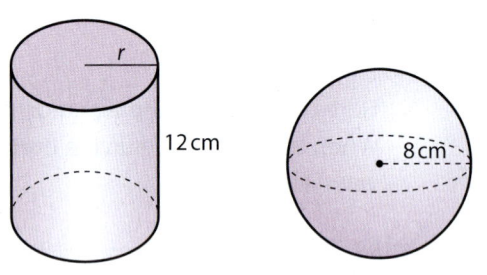

9. A cylinder has height $4\frac{1}{2}$ cm and radius length 2 cm. This cylinder has the same volume as a hemisphere. Find the radius of the hemisphere.

10. A basketball fits exactly into a cube which has sides equal in length to the diameter of the basketball. What percentage of the cube's volume does the basketball occupy?

    Use the π key on your calculator and give your answer correct to the nearest whole number.

11. When a solid sphere of radius 6 cm is dropped into a cylinder partly filled with water, the level of the water rises h cm, as shown on the right.

    If the diameter of the cylinder is 16 cm, find the value of h.

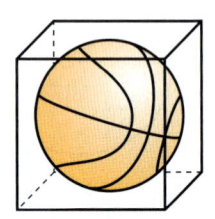

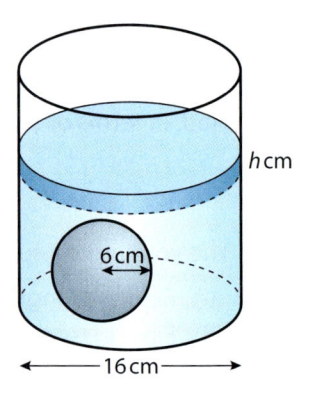

Chapter 17 Cylinder – Sphere

12. Three tennis balls, each of diameter 6 cm, just fit into a cylindrical can, as shown.

Find, in terms of π,
  (i) the volume of a tennis ball
  (ii) the volume of the cylindrical can
  (iii) the volume of the can not occupied by the tennis balls.

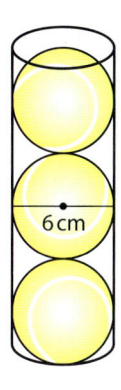

13. A sphere with radius of length 3 cm has a volume equal to eight times the volume of a sphere with radius of length *r* cm. Calculate *r*.

14. The height of a cylinder is equal to the length of its diameter.
The curved surface area of the cylinder is 100π cm². Calculate the height.

15. A wine glass is in the form of a hemisphere of radius 4 cm, as shown.
Find its volume in terms of π.

A full cylindrical container of wine is just sufficient to fill 21 of these wine glasses.
If the radius of the base of the cylinder is 8 cm, find its height.

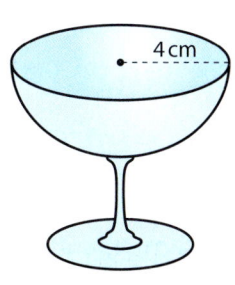

16. Nine solid metal spheres, each of radius $1\frac{1}{2}$ cm, are dropped into a cylinder partly filled with water. If the spheres are totally immersed, find the increase in the height of the water if the radius of the cylinder is 3 cm.

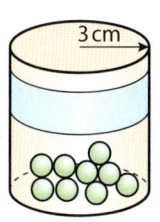

17. (i) A container is in the shape of a cylinder on top of a hemisphere as shown. The cylinder has a radius of length 3 cm and the container has a total height of 15 cm. Calculate the volume of the container in terms of π.

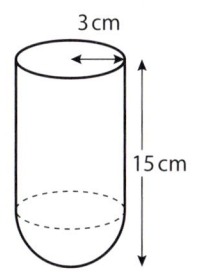

403

Text & Tests 2 Higher Level

(ii) If half the volume of the container is filled with liquid, calculate the height, h cm, of liquid in the container.

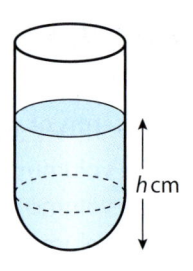

Investigation:

If $A = 3ab$, then $15ab = 5(3ab) = 5A$.
We say that $15ab$ is written 'in terms of' A.

Write each of the following 'in terms of' A.

(i) $6ab$ (ii) $4a(3b)$ (iii) $\frac{a}{2} \times \frac{b}{3}$ (iv) $8a \times \frac{5b}{4}$

Emilia was asked to work out the ratio of (a) the curved surface area
              (b) the total surface area
              (c) the volume
of the cylinders shown.

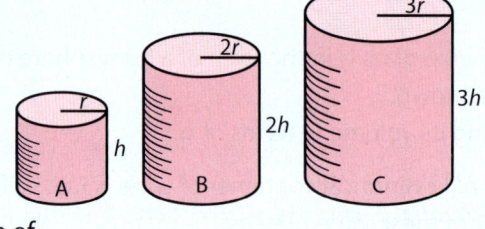

She presented her results in the form of a chart, writing each result 'in terms of' her result for A.

Copy and complete a poster sized diagram of her results.

		In terms of CS_A
Curved surface area of A	$CS_A =$	$CS_A =$
Curved surface area of B	$CS_B =$	$CS_B =$
Curved surface area of C	$CS_C =$	$CS_C =$
		In terms of S_A
Total surface area of A	$S_A =$	$S_A =$
Total surface area of B	$S_B =$	$S_B =$
Total surface area of C	$S_C =$	$C_C =$
		In terms of V_A
Volume of A	$V_A =$	$V_A =$
Volume of B	$V_B =$	$V_B =$
Volume of C	$V_C =$	$V_C =$

Chapter 17 Cylinder – Sphere

Section 17.3 Rates of flow

Some problems involve liquid flowing at a steady rate from one container to another. In these cases we use the formulae for volume and find the volume passing in 1 second to find the rate of flow.

e.g.

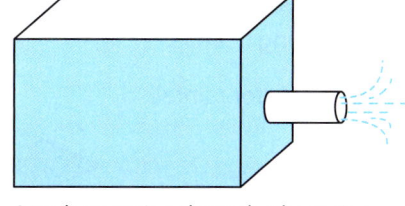

Rainfall into a cylinder

A tank emptying through a hosepipe

A basin emptying into a pipe

Example 1

A cylindrical mains pipe, with diameter of 10 cm, is delivering water at a rate of 30π litres per minute. If 1 litre = 1000 cm³, find the rate at which the water is passing through the pipe in cm/s.

30π litres per minute = $30\,000\pi$ cm³ per minute ...1 litre = 1000 cm³
$\qquad\qquad\qquad\qquad\quad = 500\pi$ cm³ per second ... 60s = 1 minute

In 1 second: $\quad \pi r^2 h = 500\pi$ cm³

$\pi \times 5^2 \times h = 500\pi \ ... \ r = \dfrac{10}{2} = 5$ cm

$h = \dfrac{(500 \times \pi)}{(25 \times \pi)} = 20$ cm per second

Exercise 17.3

(Take $\pi = 3.14$ in the following exercise)

1. Water drops into a graduated cylinder, of diameter 10 cm, at a rate of 20 cm³/min. How high will the level have risen in 10 minutes?

2. An overflow tank with dimensions 80 cm × 60 cm × 60 cm, has water pouring into it at a rate of 20ℓ per minute. How long does it take the tank to fill? (I litre = 1000 cm³)

Text & Tests 2 Higher Level

3. A rectangular oil tank with dimensions 60 cm × 100 cm × 100 cm, as shown, has a hole in it and is losing oil at a rate of 3.6 litres per hour.

   Find the rate at which the oil level is falling in cm/min.

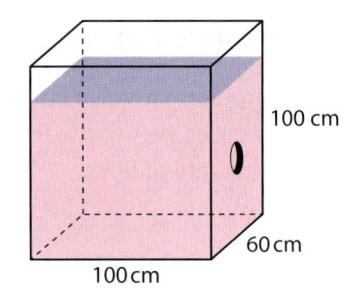

4. Water is flowing at a rate of 10 cm³ per second into a cylindrical can of diameter 30 cm. Find the rate at which the water is rising in cm/s.

5. A small carpark has a drain at its centre for rainfall. The carpark measures 18 m × 60 m.
   During a storm, 10 cm of rain falls in 1 hour.
   Find how many litres of rain per second must pass through the drain to prevent flooding. (1 litre = 1000 cm³)

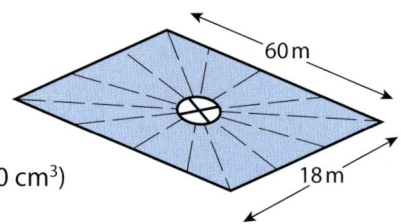

6. Water is flowing from a cylindrical tube of radius 2 cm into a larger cylinder of radius 8 cm.
   If the rate of flow from the smaller cylinder is 4 cm/s, find the rate at which the level is rising in the larger cylinder.

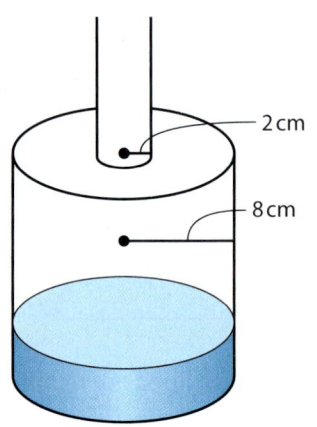

7. Finn said it took 1 minute 20 seconds for a sink of water to empty completely.
   The radius of the (hemispherical) sink was 18 cm.
   The radius of the waste pipe was 3 cm.
   Find:
   (i) The volume of water in the sink.
   (ii) The volume of water passing into the waste pipe per second.
   (iii) The rate at which the water is passing through the pipe in cm/s.

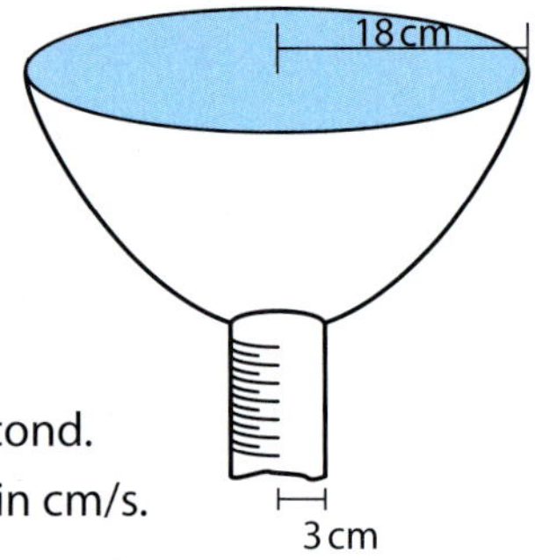

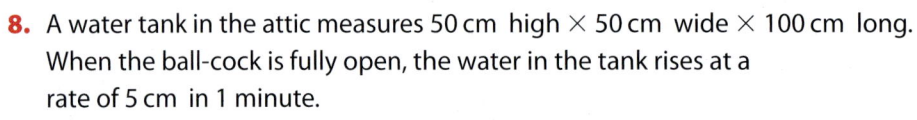

8. A water tank in the attic measures 50 cm high × 50 cm wide × 100 cm long.
   When the ball-cock is fully open, the water in the tank rises at a rate of 5 cm in 1 minute.
   Find how many litres are passing through the inlet pipe per second.
   (1 litre = 1000 cm³)

Chapter 17 Cylinder – Sphere

9. A cylindrical tank of radius 30 cm and depth 20 cm completely empties through a cylindrical pipe in 2 minutes.

   If the liquid passes through the outlet pipe at a rate of 6 cm/s, find the radius of the pipe.

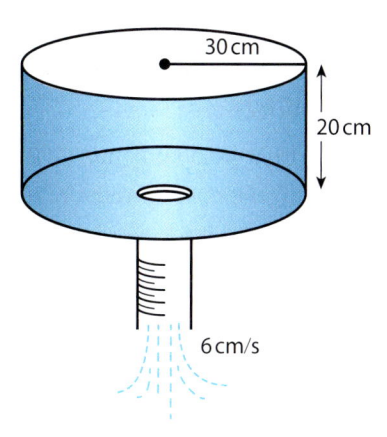

Test yourself 17

1. Using $\pi = 3.14$, find
   (i) the volume
   (ii) the curved surface area of the given cylinder, correct to the nearest whole number.

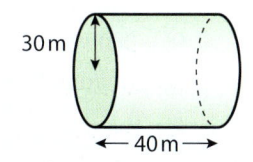

2. The cylinder and the sphere, shown below, have the same volume.

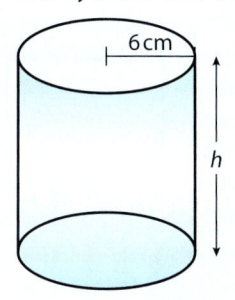

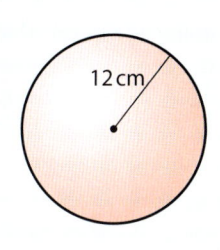

   (i) Find the volume of the sphere in terms of π.
   (ii) Calculate h, the height of the cylinder.

3. (i) Soup is contained in a cylindrical saucepan which has an internal radius of length 12 cm. The depth of the soup is 18 cm.
   Calculate, in terms of π, the volume of soup in the saucepan.
   (ii) A ladle, in the shape of a hemisphere with internal radius of length 6 cm, is used to serve the soup.
   Calculate, in terms of π, the volume of soup contained in one full ladle.
   (iii) How many full ladles of soup does the saucepan contain?

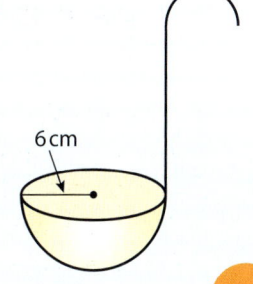

407

Text & Tests 2 Higher Level

4. A pipe delivers 500 litres of oil per minute into a cylindrical tank of height 9 m and curved surface area 90 m².
   (i) Find, in terms of π, the radius of the cylinder.
   (ii) Find, in terms of π, the area of a lid needed to cover the tank.
   (iii) Find the time taken, correct to the nearest minute, to fill the tank.
   ($\pi = 3.14$, 1 m³ = 1000 litres)

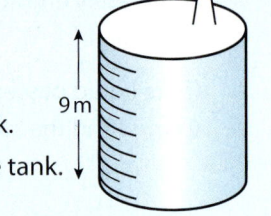

5. A machine part consists of a rectangular block of metal with two cylindrical holes drilled through as shown.

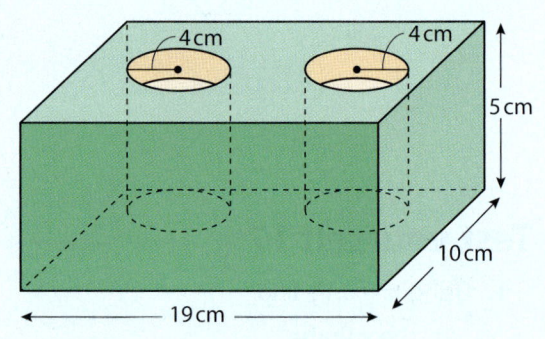

   Using the measurements given, find the volume of metal in the block, correct to the nearest cm³.

   If each cm³ of the metal has a mass of 6 g, find
   (a) the mass of the original block
   (b) the mass of the drilled block.
   ($\pi = 3.14$)

6. A solid is made of a cube, of side 24 cm, with a hemispherical top. 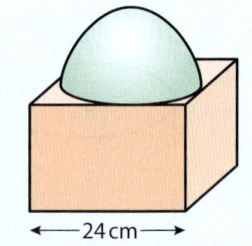
   (i) Calculate the volume of the solid, correct to the nearest cm². ($\pi = 3.14$)
   (ii) Find the ratio of the volume of the hemisphere to the volume of the cube, in terms of π.

7. (i) The volume of a sphere is 36π cm³. Find the radius of the sphere.

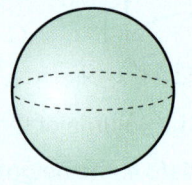

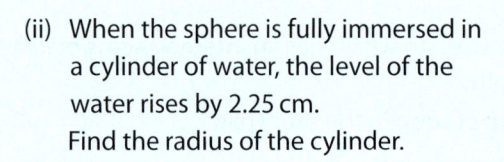

   (ii) When the sphere is fully immersed in a cylinder of water, the level of the water rises by 2.25 cm. Find the radius of the cylinder.

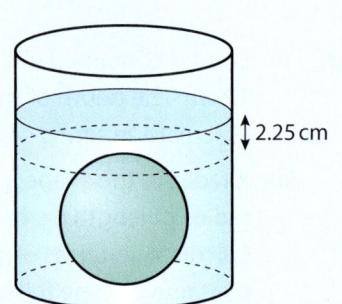

Chapter 17 Cylinder – Sphere

8. Find the total surface area of each of the following correct to 1 decimal place.

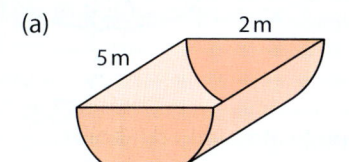

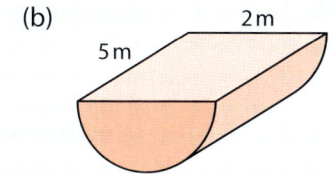

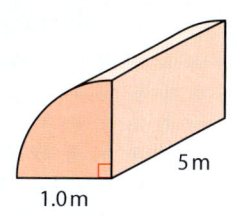

   (a) 2 m, 5 m

   (b) 2 m, 5 m

   (c) 1.0 m, 5 m

9. Find the volume and the total surface area of the following solid. ($\pi = 3.14$)

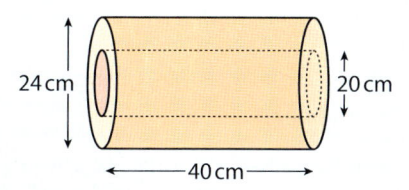

   24 cm, 20 cm, 40 cm

10. The diagram below shows a solid rectangular block of metal, 75 cm by 11 cm by 6 cm. It is melted down and recast into cylindrical rods of length 25 cm and radius of length 1 cm, as shown.
    Calculate the number of complete rods that can be made from the block.

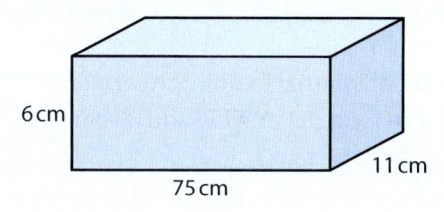

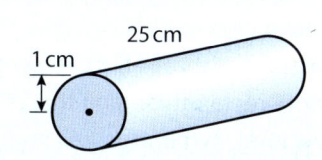

    6 cm, 75 cm, 11 cm, 1 cm, 25 cm

11. A cylindrical water tank has internal diameter 40 cm and height 50 cm.
    A cylindrical mug has internal diameter 8 cm and height 10 cm.

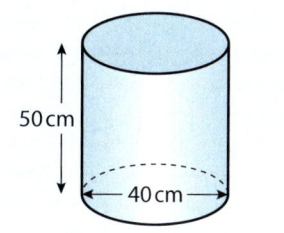

    (i) Find the volume of the tank in terms of π.

    (ii) Find the volume of the mug in terms of π.

    (iii) How many mugs can be filled from a full tank?

    50 cm, 40 cm, 10 cm, 8 cm

12. A horse's drinking trough is 2 m long and has a cross-section as shown alongside.
    How long will it take to fill the trough if water flows into it at a rate of 12 litres per minute?
    Give your answer to the nearest minute.

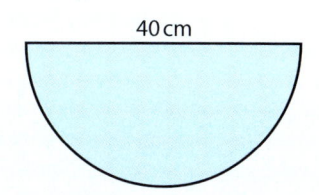

    40 cm

409

13. (i) What is the volume, correct to the nearest cm³, of this cylindrical can?

(ii) Will it hold 1 litre of water? Explain your answer.

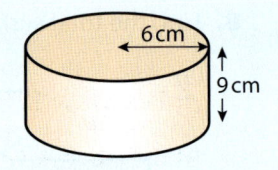

(iii) If the height is doubled to 18 cm, how many complete litres would it hold?

(iv) If the height was 9 cm, but the radius was doubled to 12 cm, how many complete litres would it then hold?

14. A vitamin capsule is in the shape of a cylinder with hemispherical ends. The length of the capsule is 20 mm and the diameter is 6 mm.

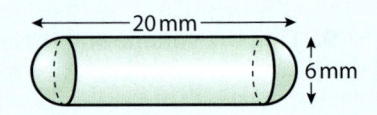

(i) Calculate the volume of the capsule, giving your answer correct to the nearest mm³.

A course of these vitamins consists of 24 capsules.
The capsules are stacked in three rows of eight in a box, as shown in the diagram.

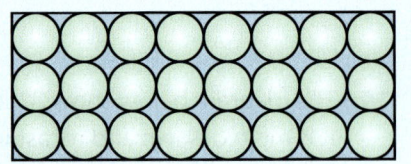

(ii) How much of the internal volume of the box is not occupied by the capsules?

15. Calculate the volume of a cylinder of height 7 cm and of radius 2 cm, correct to the nearest cm³.
Water flows through a circular pipe of internal radius 2 cm at a rate of 7 cm/sec into an empty rectangular tank that is 1.2 m long, 1.1 m wide and 30 cm high.
How long, in minutes, will it take to fill the tank?

Chapter 17 Cylinder – Sphere

Assignment:

A: This assignment tries to find out the relationship between (a) the surface area (b) the volume of a sphere as its radius is doubled, tripled, etc.

On a separate sheet of paper, find the values that are missing from each of the following open brackets.

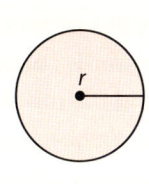

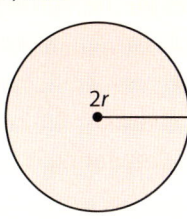

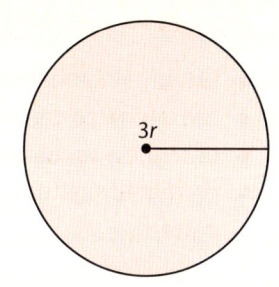

Make a poster of your results.

Radius	r	2r	3r	......nr
Surface area of sphere	$4\pi r^2$	$(\ )(4\pi r^2)$	$(\ )(4\pi r^2)$	$(\ )(4\pi r^2)$
Volume of sphere	$\frac{4}{3}\pi r^3$	$(\ )\left(\frac{4}{3}\pi r^3\right)$	$(\ )\left(\frac{4}{3}\pi r^3\right)$	$(\ )\left(\frac{4}{3}\pi r^3\right)$

Conclusion: _____.

B: To investigate whether young children dehydrate more quickly than older children.
Let a cube of side 2 cm represent a 1-year old child.
Two cubes stacked one on top of another a 6-year old.
Three cubes a 12-year old etc. Using the chart below, find the ratio of Surface Area to Volume for each age.

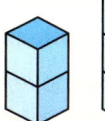

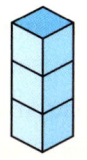

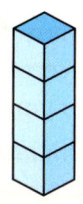

Cube of side 2 cm	1-yr old	6-yr old	12-yr old	18-yr old
Surface area of cube				
Volume of cube				
$\frac{\text{Surface Area}}{\text{Volume}}$				

Discuss in your group how this ratio might influence the rate of dehydration.

Discuss the limitations of this 'model'.

Conclusion: _____.

Chapter 18: Patterns and Sequences

In this chapter, you will learn to:

- identify a number pattern or sequence,
- use a term-to-term rule,
- describe a sequence in words,
- predict future terms in a repeating pattern,
- identify a linear sequence,
- find the nth term of a linear sequence,
- create a linear sequence from shapes,
- identify a quadratic sequence,
- find the nth term of a quadratic sequence,
- identify an exponential sequence,
- graph linear, quadratic and exponential sequences.

Section 18.1 Sequences

If we start at 0 and keep adding 4, we get this pattern:

    0, 4, 8, 12, 16, 20, 24, 28, 32, 36, 40, 44, …

If we take the last digit in each of these numbers, we get another pattern, as follows:

    0, 4, 8, 2, 6, 0, 4, 8, 2, 6, 0, 4, …

The first pattern continues on with each number 4 bigger than the number before it.
The second pattern is a little more complex.
The numbers repeat in **blocks** of 5 with a particular pattern in each block.

The number patterns above are called **sequences**.
A sequence is a set of numbers in a particular order.

    1, 3, 5, 7, 9, … is a sequence

1st term 4th term the dots indicate that the sequence continues on.

Each number is called a **term**.
Each number's place in the sequence is called its **position**.

Chapter 18 Patterns and Sequences

The pattern below is made of squares.

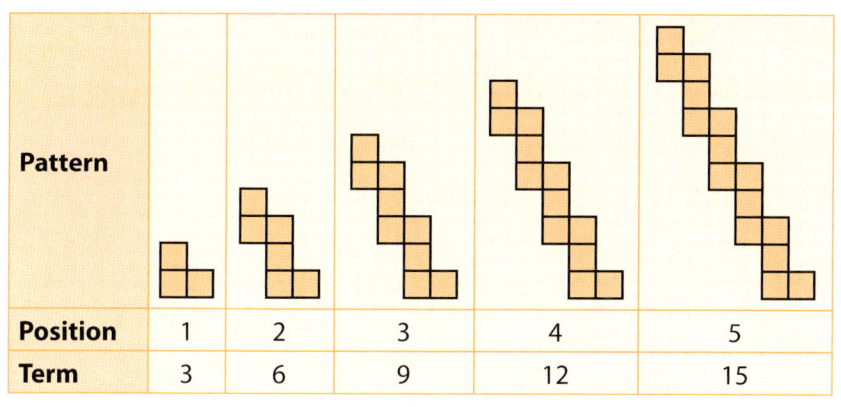

Pattern					
Position	1	2	3	4	5
Term	3	6	9	12	15

The terms form the sequence.

The fifth term is 15. It is made of 15 squares.
The pattern increases by 3 each time.
The sixth pattern in the sequence is made of 18 squares.
Thus, the sixth term in the sequence is 18.

The **term-to-term rule** describes how to get from one term to the next.

The term-to-term rule for 4, 8, 12, 16, 20, … is 'add 4'.
The term-to-term rule for 2, 6, 18, 54, … is 'multiply by 3'.
The term-to-term rule for 30, 25, 20, 15, … is 'subtract 5'.

A sequence is generally **described in words** by giving the first term and then the term-to-term rule.

> ### Example 1
>
> (i) A sequence starts at 7 and increases in steps of 4.
>   Write down the first six terms of the sequence.
>
> (ii) Describe in words this sequence:
>   27, 24, 21, 18, …
>
> (i) The first six terms of the sequence are: 7, 11, 15, 19, 23, 27.
>
> (ii) The sequence begins at 27 and goes down in steps of 3.

Working backwards

Starting with the number 3, the rule 'subtract 2 and then multiply by 4', gives the sequence

   3, 4, 8, 24, …

413

Given any starting number then this rule would give;

Starting number ⟶ subtract 2 ⟶ multiply by 4

If we need to find a number that went before in this sequence we work backwards by;

The original number ⟵ add 2 ⟵ divide by 4 (Start)

If we start with 24, $24 \div 4 = 6$ then $6 + 2 = 8$, the number before 24.

Example 2

Gary made a sequence of numbers using the rule 'multiply by 3, then add 1'.

He wrote his sequence as ▇, 22, 67, 202, … but he spilled some ink on the first two terms.

Find the first two terms.

Working backwards the rule becomes 'subtract 1 then divide by 3'

Starting with 22, $22 - 1 = 21$ then $21 \div 3 = 7$

Starting with 7, $7 - 1 = 6$ then $6 \div 3 = 2$

His sequence was 2, 7, 22, 67, 202, …

Exercise 18.1

1. Write down the next four terms of each of these sequences:
   (i) 3, 5, 7, 9, 11, …
   (ii) 2, 5, 8, 11, 14, …
   (iii) 4, 8, 12, 16, 20, …
   (iv) 20, 18, 16, 14, …
   (v) 50, 45, 40, 35, …
   (vi) 12, 8, 4, …

2. Write down the next three terms of each of these sequences:
   (i) 1, 1.5, 2, 2.5, …
   (ii) $-10, -8, -6, -4, \ldots$
   (iii) 2, 6, 18, 54, …
   (iv) $-\frac{1}{2}, 1, 2\frac{1}{2}, 4, \ldots$
   (v) $-40, -20, -10, \ldots$
   (vi) 6, 3, 0, …

3. Write down the first four terms of these sequences:
   (i) Start with 2 and count forwards in steps of 4.
   (ii) Start with 5 and count forwards in steps of 3.
   (iii) Start with 3 and count forwards in steps of 5.
   (iv) Start with 30 and count back in steps of 4.
   (v) Start with -10 and count forwards in steps of 3.

4. Describe in words each of these sequences:
   (i) 3, 6, 9, 12, …
   (ii) 0, 4, 8, 12, …
   (iii) 10, 15, 20, 25, …
   (iv) 16, 14, 12, 10, …
   (v) $-6, -3, 0, 3, \ldots$
   (vi) $-2\frac{1}{2}, -2, -1\frac{1}{2}, -1, \ldots$

Chapter 18 Patterns and Sequences

5. Write the term-to-term rule for each of these sequences:
   (i) 4, 8, 12, 16, …
   (ii) 1, 4, 7, 10, …
   (iii) 2, 6, 10, 14, …
   (iv) 22, 20, 18, 16, …
   (v) $\frac{3}{4}$, 1, $\frac{5}{4}$, $\frac{3}{2}$, …
   (vi) −12, −9, −6, −3, …

6. Copy and complete this table:

1st term	Term-to-term rule	2nd, 3rd, 4th and 5th terms
8	+5	
	+4	9, 13, 17, 21
		12, 15, 18, 21
0	−3	
−12		−7, −2, 3, 8
		$\frac{1}{7}, \frac{2}{7}, \frac{3}{7}, \frac{4}{7}$
$5\frac{1}{4}$	$-\frac{1}{4}$	

7. The first term of a sequence is 4.
   The term-to-term rule is 'add 4'.
   (i) What is the second term of the sequence?
   (ii) What is the fifth term?

8. The sixth term of a sequence is 11.
   The term-to-term rule is 'subtract 3'.
   (i) What is the fifth term of the sequence?
   (ii) What is the first term?

9. Each table below shows patterns in a sequence.
   Each term in the sequence is the number of squares in the pattern.
   Copy and complete each table.

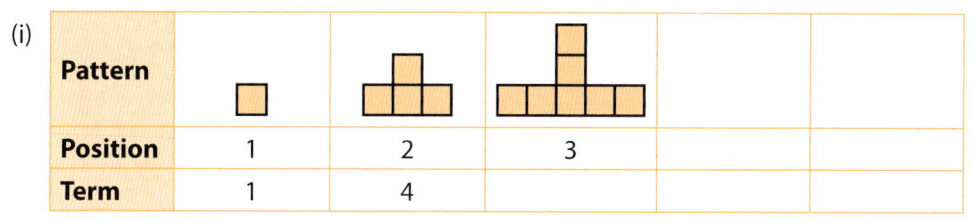

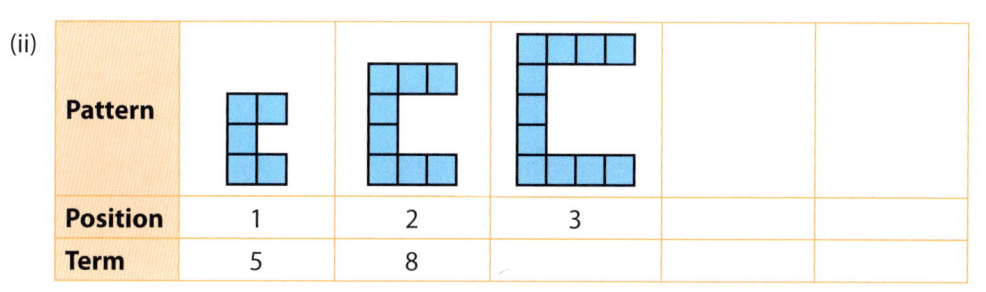

(i)

Pattern					
Position	1	2	3		
Term	1	4			

(ii)

Pattern					
Position	1	2	3		
Term	5	8			

Text & Tests 2 Higher Level

(iii)

Pattern					
Position	1	2	3		
Term	3	7			

10. Write down the first six terms of this sequence:

I am thinking of a sequence.
The 3rd term is 4.
The rule is 'multiply by 2'.

11. In each of the sequences below, the difference between the terms is constant.
Copy each sequence and fill in the missing numbers.

(i) 4, 6, ___, ___, ___, 14, …
(ii) 25, ___, 19, ___, 13, 10, …
(iii) 1, ___, 11, ___, 21, ___, …
(iv) ___, 10, ___, ___, 19, ___, …

12. Examine these number patterns.
Write down the next line in each pattern without using a calculator.
Now use a calculator to check that you are correct.

(i) $3 \times 11 = 33$ (ii) $9 \times 1 = 9$ (iii) $7 \times 7 = 49$
     $33 \times 11 = 363$ $9 \times 12 = 108$ $67 \times 67 = 4489$
     $333 \times 11 = 3663$ $9 \times 123 = 1107$ $667 \times 667 = 444889$
     $3333 \times 11 = 36663$ $9 \times 1234 = 11106$ $6667 \times 6667 = 44448889$

--------------------   --------------------   --------------------

13. A bus leaves for town every 10 minutes.
One leaves at 2:15 p.m..
Write down the times of the next 6 buses.

14. Lucille made a sequence using the rule 'multiply by 2 then subtract 2'.
Find x, and y, if the first six terms of her sequence were; $x, y, 10, 18, 34, 66, …$

15. A rule 'subtract 3 then divide by 2' is used to write a sequence of numbers.
If 17 is the second term of the sequence find (i) the first term (ii) the third term.

16. Max made a sequence of numbers using the rule 'multiply the last term by 2 then subtract 1'.
If the 11th term is 3073, use the information above to find the 10th and the 9th terms.

17. Part of a sequence is …, 4, 7, 11, 18, … .
The rule for this sequence is 'add together the last two numbers to find the next number'.
Write down two numbers that come (i) after 18 (ii) before 4, in this sequence.

Chapter 18 Patterns and Sequences

Investigation:

In your group, create a chart of different sequences.
Keep the rule hidden and share with other groups. Try to discover the rules.

e.g.						Rule
1	4	6	10	18	34	?
2	1	3	4	7	11	?
3						
4						
5						

Section 18.2 Repeating patterns

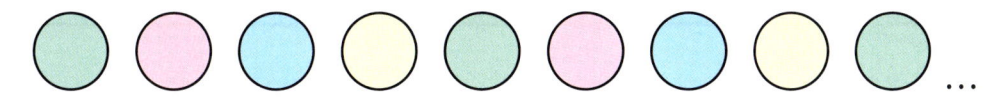

The pattern of the coloured circles above is green, pink, blue, yellow, green, …
The pattern repeats in blocks of 4.
The pattern of green circles is 1, 5, 9, …
The pattern of yellow circles is 4, 8, 12, …

What colour is the 35th circle?
Since the pattern repeats every 4 circles, we find how many blocks of 4 there are in 35 and then how many circles are left over.

$35 \div 4 = 8$ and remainder 3

When the remainder is 3, we look for the colour of the 3rd circle in the block of 4.
This colour is blue.

Example 1

A repeating pattern is made up of letters as follows:

A B C D E A B C D E A …

(i) What is the 25th letter?
(ii) What is the 43rd letter?
(iii) What is the 61st letter?

(i) The pattern repeats in blocks of 5.
   To find the 25th letter, divide 25 by 5.
   25 ÷ 5 = 5, i.e., five complete blocks.
   The 25th letter is therefore the last letter in the block.
   Thus, the 25th letter is E.
(ii) The 43rd letter is 43 ÷ 5. This is 8 and remainder 3.
   Remainder 3 means it is the 3rd letter in the block.
   This letter is C.
   The 43rd letter is C.
(iii) The 61st letter is 61 ÷ 5. This is 12 and remainder 1.
   Remainder 1 means the first letter in the block.
   The 61st letter is A.

Exercise 18.2

1. Here is a repeating pattern of geometric shapes:

□ ○ △ □ □ ○ △ □ ...

   (i) What are the next two shapes?
   (ii) List the positions of the first three circles. Is there a pattern?
   (iii) Which shape forms the pattern 3, 7, …?
   (iv) What is the 21st shape?
   (v) What is the 37th shape?
   (vi) If the 61st shape is a square, what is the 62nd shape?

2. Here is a repeating pattern of coloured tiles:

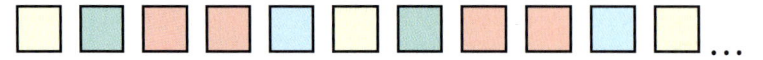

   (i) What is the next colour in the pattern?
   (ii) What colour is the 30th tile?
   (iii) What colour is the 48th tile?
   (iv) If the 63rd tile is red, what colour is the 65th tile?
   (v) Write down the pattern formed by the blue tiles.
   (vi) In what position is the 6th blue tile?

3. The pattern below is the multiples of 6.

   6, 12, 18, 24, 30, 36, 42, 48, 54, 60, 66, 72, …

The last digit in each number forms this pattern:

   6, 2, 8, 4, 0, 6, 2, 8, 4, 0, 6, 2, …

Notice that this is a repeating pattern.

(i) What are the next two numbers of this pattern?
(ii) What is the 24th number of the pattern?
(iii) What is the 51st number of the pattern?
(iv) What is the position of the fifth 8 of the pattern?

4. Write down the first ten multiples of 8.

(i) Show that the last digits of these multiples form a repeating pattern.
(ii) After how many digits does the pattern start repeating?
(iii) What number appears in the 100th position in the pattern?

Investigation:

A gardener is planting trees and flowers. She has **735 trees** to plant and uses the pattern below for her flowers which she plants between the trees.

Question: How many flowers does she need?

In your group, devise a strategy to find the number of flowers the gardener needs for this pattern.

Draw a poster showing your method.

Compare your method with other groups in your class.

Section 18.3 Linear sequences

Look at this sequence:

12, 9, 6, 3, …   The term-to-term rule is −3 or 'subtract 3'.

When the term-to-term rule involves adding or subtracting a constant (a fixed number), it is known as a **linear sequence**.

A linear sequence is also known as an **arithmetic sequence**.

The following sequences are not linear because the term-to-term rule does not involve adding or subtracting a constant.

(i) 2, 4, 8, 16, 32, …   The term-to-term rule is ×2.
(ii) 27, 9, 3, 1, $\frac{1}{3}$, …   The term-to-term rule is ÷3.

Text & Tests 2 Higher Level

How to find any term of a linear sequence

Question: What is 20th term of the sequence 7, 10, 13, 16, 19, 22, … ?

We could keep adding 3 until we got to the 20th term; however, this is very time consuming and impractical if we need to find a term a large distance along the sequence.

Examine how the following sequence is formed:

Position ⟶ ×3 ⟶ +4

Position	1	2	3	4	5	…n
Term	$(3 \times 1) + 4$	$(3 \times 2) + 4$	$(3 \times 3) + 4$	$(3 \times 4) + 4$	$(3 \times 5) + 4$	…$(3n + 4)$
	7	10	13	16	19	

The 2nd term is given by $T_2 = 3(2) + 4 = 10$

The 5th term is given by $T_5 = 3(5) + 4 = 19$

The ***n*th** term is given by $T_n = 3n + 4$.

> The position-to-term rule is generally called the **nth term** rule.

∴ the 20th term is $T_{20} = 3(20) + 4 = 64$.

The position-to-term rule for a sequence can be given by writing an expression for T_n, the *n*th term.

When we know T_n we can write down any term of the sequence.

Example 1

The *n*th term of a sequence is given by $T_n = 3n - 4$.
  (i) Write down the first three terms of the sequence and also T_{20}.
  (ii) Explain why the sequence is linear.

(i) $T_n = 3n - 4$
  $T_1 = 3(1) - 4 = 3 - 4 = -1$ … substitute 1 for *n*.
  $T_2 = 3(2) - 4 = 6 - 4 = 2$
  $T_3 = 3(3) - 4 = 9 - 4 = 5$
  $T_{20} = 3(20) - 4 = 60 - 4 = 56$

  The first three terms are $-1, 2, 5$ and $T_{20} = 56$.

(ii) Since the difference between the terms is a constant, i.e. 3, the sequence is linear.

Chapter 18 Patterns and Sequences

Exercise 18.3

1. The nth terms of some sequences are given.
Write out the first four terms of each sequence.

(i) $T_n = 2n$ (ii) $T_n = 3n + 1$ (iii) $T_n = 4n - 3$
(iv) $T_n = 2n + 5$ (v) $T_n = 5n - 4$ (vi) $T_n = 7 - 2n$

2. Write out the first three terms of these sequences defined by the given nth term:

(i) $T_n = 1 - 3n$ (ii) $T_n = n^2 + 1$ (iii) $T_n = \dfrac{n+1}{4}$

3. The nth term of a sequence is $T_n = 2n + 3$.

(i) Write down the first five terms of the sequence.
(ii) Find T_{20} and T_{100}.

4. If $T_n = 2n - 6$, show that $T_1 + T_5 = 0$.

5. Explain why each of these sequences is linear:

(i) 3, 8, 13, 18, …   (ii) 18, 14, 10, 6, …

6. Investigate whether each of these sequences is linear:

(i) $-8, -10, -12, -14, \ldots$ (ii) 1, 3, 9, 27, …
(iii) $20, 10, 5, 2\frac{1}{2}, \ldots$ (iv) 0.1, 0.3, 0.5, 0.7, …

7. The nth terms of six different sequences are:

A $7n - 2$ **B** $10 - n$ **C** $\frac{1}{2}n - 3$ **D** $n^2 + 1$ **E** $\dfrac{60}{n}$ **F** 2^n

(i) Calculate the first four terms of each sequence.
(ii) Calculate the 20th term of each sequence.
(iii) Which of these sequences are linear?

8. The nth term of a sequence is $3n + 2$.

(i) Write down the first six terms of the sequence.
(ii) Calculate the 100th term.

9. Linear sequences can be found on this grid.
Two are shown on the diagram.

(i) Find seven more linear sequences that have four terms or more.

Write down each sequence as an **increasing** sequence and find its next term.

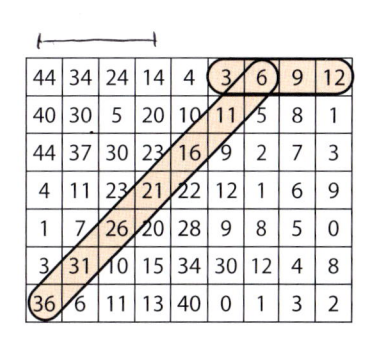

44	34	24	14	4	3	6	9	12
40	30	5	20	10	11	5	8	1
44	37	30	23	16	9	2	7	3
4	11	23	21	22	12	1	6	9
1	7	26	20	28	9	8	5	0
3	31	10	15	34	30	12	4	8
36	6	11	13	40	0	1	3	2

Text & Tests 2 Higher Level

(ii) The expressions below give the nth terms of these sequences.
Match each expression to its sequence.

| $3n$ | $6n - 2$ | $10n - 6$ | $2n + 1$ | $4n$ |

| $3n + 1$ | $n + 2$ | $5n + 1$ | $7n - 5$ |

Section 18.4 Finding the nth term, T_n, of a linear sequence

To find the nth term of a linear sequence, we look at the differences between terms.

$$7 \quad 10 \quad 13 \quad 16 \quad 19$$
$$+3 \quad +3 \quad +3 \quad +3$$

The sequence is linked to 3-times tables because the terms go up in 3s.
So $3n$ will be part of the nth term.
T_n will be $3n \pm$ some number.

To work out what to add to or subtract from $3n$, we compare the terms of $T_n = 3n$ with the given sequence:

If $T_n = 3n$, then sequence is 3, 6, 9, 12, 15, ...

compare this sequence with the given sequence 7, 10, 13, 16, 19, ...

We can see that, 4, needs to be added to each term of the sequence, $T_n = 3n$, to get our given sequence i.e. $7 - 3 = 4$.

∴ $T_n = 3n + 4$ is the nth term of the sequence 7, 10, 13, 16, 19, ...

Example 1

Find the nth term of the sequence 3, 7, 11, 15, ...

In the sequence 3, 7, 11, 15, ..., the difference between the terms is $+4$.
So $T_n = 4n \pm$ some number.
If $T_n = 4n$, then $T_1 = 4(1) = 4$.
What do I need to add to or subtract from 4 to get the first term 3 of the given sequence?
I need to subtract 1, since $4 - 1 = 3$.
So $T_n = 4n - 1$.

Note: It is only necessary to compare the first term of each sequence but it is good practice having found T_n to check T_2, T_3 also.

Note: A second method to find the nth term is to set up a table format as the next example indicates.

Example 2

Find the nth term of the sequence 10, 7, 4, 1, −2, …
Hence work out T_{20} of the sequence.

	$T_{n=1}$	$T_{n=2}$	$T_{n=3}$	$T_{n=4}$	$T_{n=5}$	…
Sequence	10	7	4	1	−2	
Difference =		−3	−3	−3	−3	
∴ −3n =	−3	−6	−9	−12	−15	
$T_n = -3n + 13$	10	7	4	1	−2	

From the table we can see that (+13) needs to be added to the terms of −3n to form the given sequence.

∴ $T_n = -3n + 13$

∴ $T_{20} = -3(20) + 13 = -60 + 13 = -47$

If we know the nth term of a sequence, we can use this information to find which term of the sequence any given number is.

Example 3

The nth term of a sequence is given by $T_n = 5n - 4$.
Which term of the sequence is 21?

Let $T_n = 21$
∴ $5n - 4 = 21$
$5n = 25$
$n = 5$

Thus 21 is the 5th term of the sequence.

Exercise 18.4

1. A given sequence is 5, 9, 13, 17, …
   (i) Write down the constant difference between the terms.
   (ii) If $T_n = \boxed{}n \pm$ number, what number goes in the box?
   (iii) Now find an expression for T_n, the nth term.
   (iv) Write down the value of T_{20}.

Text & Tests 2 Higher Level

2. Find an expression for the *n*th term of each of these sequences:
   (i) 5, 7, 9, 11, …
   (ii) 4, 7, 10, 13, …
   (iii) 6, 10, 14, 18, …

3. Find an expression for the *n*th term of this sequence:
   7, 11, 15, 19, …
   Use the expression for the *n*th term to find T_{10} and T_{20}.

4. Consider the sequence 12, 10, 8, 6, … .
   (i) What is the term-to-term rule for this sequence?
   (ii) If $T_n = \boxed{} n \pm$ a number, what number goes in the box?
   (iii) Use this to find an expression for T_n.
   (iv) Find T_{10} of the sequence.
   (v) Which term of the sequence is -14?

5. Find an expression for the *n*th term of these sequences:
   (i) $-3, 0, 3, 6, 9, \ldots$
   (ii) 20, 15, 10, 5, …

6. Find an expression for T_n of the sequence 8, 5, 2, …
   For what value of *n* is $T_n = -34$?

7. Three linear sequences A, B and C are given. Copy the table and fill in the missing terms.

A	8	11		17	20	23
B		2			14	18
C		3				35

8. Show that the sequence,
   $2a + 3b - 2c, \ 2a + 4b - c, \ 2a + 5b, \ 2a + 6b + c, \ 2a + 7b + 2c$ is linear.

Section 18.5 Sequences (linear) formed from shapes

So far in this chapter, we have dealt only with number patterns.

In this section, we will examine some geometric figures and the patterns they form.

Chapter 18 Patterns and Sequences

Example 1

The figure on the right shows some photo frames made with rods.

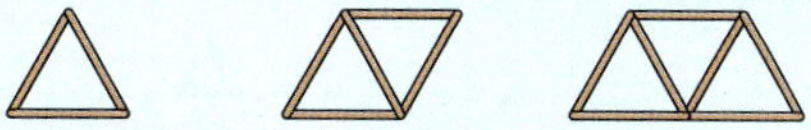

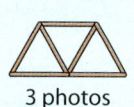

1 photo   2 photos   3 photos

(i) Draw the frame that holds 4 photos.
(ii) How many rods are there in the frame that holds 5 photos?
(iii) Find an expression for the number of rods in the nth frame.
(iv) Which frame uses 41 rods?
(v) Is it possible to make one of these frames using exactly 56 rods?

(i) This is the frame that holds 4 photos: 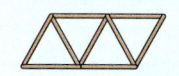
(ii) The sequence is 3, 5, 7, 9, 11, …
The 5th frame has 11 rods.
(iii) The difference between the terms is $+2$.
Thus, the nth term will be $2n \pm$ a number.
If $T_n = 2n$, $T_1 = 2$ and so 1 must be added to get the first term 3.
$\therefore T_n = 2n + 1$
(iv) Let $T_n = 41 \Rightarrow 2n + 1 = 41$
$2n = 40$
$n = 20$
The 20th frame uses 41 rods.
(v) Let $T_n = 56$
$2n + 1 = 56$
$2n = 55$
$n = 27\frac{1}{2}$
Since $27\frac{1}{2}$ is not a whole number, no frame uses exactly 56 rods.

Exercise 18.5

1. Here is a pattern made from sticks.

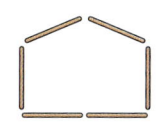

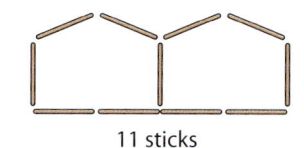

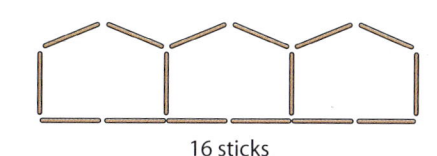

6 sticks   11 sticks   16 sticks

(i) Draw the 4th pattern in this sequence.
(ii) Write down the sequence of numbers generated by the sticks in the first six patterns.
(iii) Show that the number of sticks in the nth pattern is given by $T_n = 5n + 1$.
(iv) How many sticks are required for the 20th pattern?
(v) For which pattern are 51 sticks required?

Text & Tests 2 Higher Level

2. Here are three diagrams made with triangles.

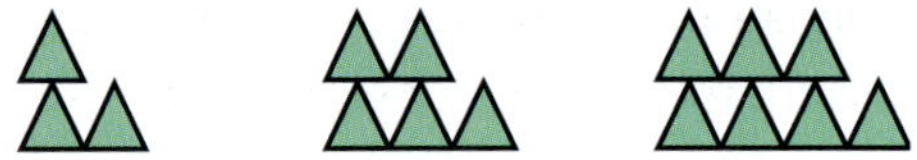

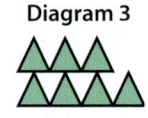

   Diagram 1 — 3 triangles
   Diagram 2 — 5 triangles
   Diagram 3 — 7 triangles

   (i) Draw diagram 4.
   (ii) How many triangles will be in diagram 7?
   (iii) Find an expression for the number of triangles in the nth diagram.
   (iv) Which diagram will contain 33 triangles?

3. Complete the table of values for this sequence of matchstick patterns.

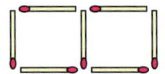

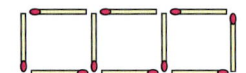

Number of squares	1	2	3	4	5
Number of matchsticks	4	7			

   (i) How many matchsticks are required for the 6th pattern?
   (ii) Find an expression in n for the number of matchsticks in the nth pattern.
   (iii) Use the expression found to ascertain the number of matchsticks required for the 50th pattern.

4. Here is a pattern made with matchsticks.

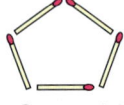

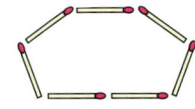

   Pattern 1   Pattern 2   Pattern 3

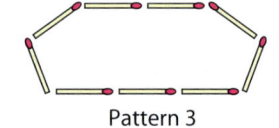

   (i) How many matchsticks will be in Pattern 5?
   (ii) Find an expression for the number of matchsticks in the nth pattern.
   (iii) In which pattern are there 51 matchsticks?

5. Here is another pattern made with matchsticks.

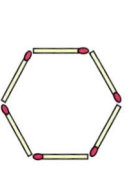

   Pattern 1   Pattern 2   Pattern 3

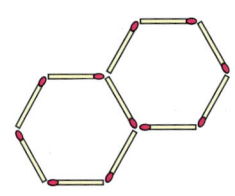

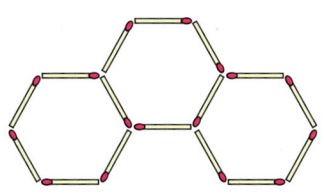

Chapter 18 Patterns and Sequences

(i) How many matchsticks will there be in pattern 4?
(ii) What is the term-to-term rule for the pattern?
(iii) How many matchsticks will there be in the nth pattern?
(iv) Which pattern will contain exactly 66 matchsticks?
(v) Will any pattern use exactly 88 matchsticks?

6. Sharon drew these shapes on her bedroom wall.

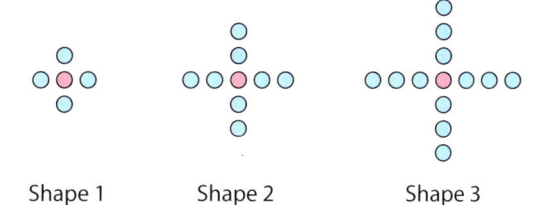

Shape 1   Shape 2   Shape 3

(i) Draw shape 4.
(ii) Copy and complete this table.

Shape number	1	2	3	4	5
Total number of circles	5	9			

(iii) Describe in words the sequence formed.
(iv) Find an expression for the nth term of the sequence.
(v) Which shape will contain exactly 81 circles?
(vi) Will any shape contain exactly 89 circles?

7. Tommy builds fences of different lengths using pieces of wood.

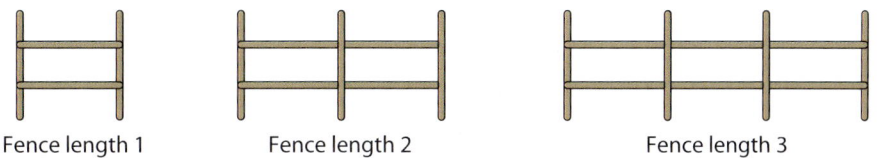

Fence length 1   Fence length 2   Fence length 3

(i) Sketch fence length 5.
Tommy counted how many pieces he needed to make each fence length. He then drew up the table below.

Fence length	1	2	3	4	5	6
Number of pieces	4	7	10			

(ii) Complete the table to show how many pieces of wood he would use for fence lengths 4, 5 and 6.
(iii) Write down, in terms of n, an expression for the number of pieces of wood needed for fence length n.
(iv) How many pieces of wood are needed for fence length 40?
(v) If 91 pieces of wood are needed, what is the number of the fence length?

Text & Tests 2 Higher Level

Section 18.6 Quadratic sequences

1, 4, 9, 16, 25, ... is the sequence of square numbers.
Since $T_1 = 1^2, T_2 = 2^2, T_3 = 3^2, T_n = n^2$.

Sequences that have an nth term containing n^2 as the highest power are called **quadratic sequences**.

Let us examine the first seven terms of the sequence $T_n = n^2$.

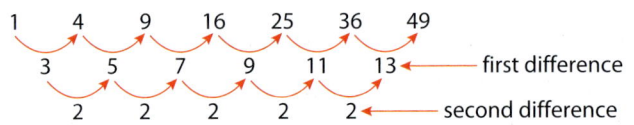

```
 1    4    9   16   25   36   49
   3    5    7    9   11   13  ← first difference
     2    2    2    2    2  ← second difference
```

Notice that the second difference is a constant, i.e. 2.
Quadratic sequences always have a constant second difference.

Now let us look at the sequence with nth term, $T_n = 2n^2 - n$.
The first five terms of this sequence are

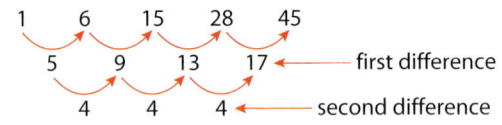

```
 1    6   15   28   45
   5    9   13   17  ← first difference
     4    4    4  ← second difference
```

Here again the second differences are all the same, i.e., 4.

Notice that in each of the quadratic sequences above, the coefficient of n^2 in the nth term is half the second difference.

> In a quadratic sequence, the coefficient of n^2 in the nth term is half the second difference.

Investigation:

Design a poster showing the connection between the value of the second difference and the coefficient of the squared term, n^2.

Write the nth term, T_n, of your own quadratic into the 3rd column.

	$T_n = 4n^2 - 2$	$T_n = 2n^2 + 3n$	$T_n =$
First 5 terms			
First difference			
Second difference			
Coefficient of n^2			

Conclusion: In a quadratic sequence the …

Finding the *n*th term of a quadratic sequence

The *n*th term of a quadratic sequence will always be of the form

$T_n = an^2 + bn + c$

We now use a difference table to find the values of *a*, *b* and *c*, as shown in the following example.

Example 1

Find the *n*th term of the sequence 3, 10, 21, 36.

The terms and the 1st and 2nd differences are shown on the right.

Terms	3	10	21	36
1st differences		7	11	15
2nd differences			4	4

T_n will be of the form $T_n = an^2 + bn + c$
$a = 2$ … half the value of the second difference, i.e., $4 \div 2$.

$\therefore T_n = 2n^2 + bn + c$

We now express T_1 and T_2 in terms of *b* and *c*.

$T_n = 2n^2 + bn + c \Rightarrow T_1 = 2 + b + c = 3$
$\therefore b + c = 1$

Also $T_2 = 8 + 2b + c = 10$
$\therefore 2b + c = 2$

We now solve the simultaneous equations ① and ②.

$b + c = 1$ … ①　　　　$b + c = 1$
$2b + c = 2$ … ②　　　$\Rightarrow 1 + c = 1$
$-b = -1 \Rightarrow b = 1$　　$\Rightarrow c = 0$

$\therefore T_n = 2n^2 + n$ … $a = 2, b = 1, c = 0$

Investigation:

Remember　(i)　for a **linear** sequence the **'first difference'** is constant.
　　　　　(ii)　for a **quadratic** sequence the **'second difference'** is constant.

1. Build a linear sequence of 6 terms, if 3, 6, …. must be the first two terms.

2. Build a quadratic sequence of 6 terms, if 3, 6, … must be the first two terms and the second difference is 2.

3. Build a quadratic sequence of 6 terms, if 3, 6, … must be the first two terms and the second difference is 5.

Text & Tests 2 Higher Level

Exercise 18.6

1. Work out the first four terms of each of these quadratic sequences:

   (i) $T_n = n^2 + 4$ (ii) $T_n = n^2 - 2$ (iii) $T_n = 2n^2 - 1$ (iv) $T_n = 3n^2 - 4$

2. Find the next two terms of these quadratic sequences by finding the first and second differences:

   (i) 3, 4, 6, 9, 13, ...   (ii) 3, 6, 11, 18, 27, ...   (iii) 2, 7, 14, 23, 34, ...

3. Which of these sequences are quadratic?

   (i) 6, 8, 12, 18, 26, 36, ...   (ii) 6, 8, 10, 12, 14, 16, ...
   (iii) 3, 4, 7, 12, 19, 28, ...   (iv) 0, 3, 8, 15, 24, ...

4. If $T_n = n^2 + 2n - 4$, work out the tenth term.

5. The value of the second difference can tell us something about the formula for the nth term of a quadratic sequence.

   (i) Copy and complete this table.

nth term	First five terms	First differences	Second differences
$2n^2$	2, 8, 18, 32, 50, ...	6, 10, 14, 18, ...	4, 4, 4, ...
$3n^2$	3, 12, __, __, __, __, ...		
$4n^2$	4, __, __, __, __, __, ...		
$5n^2$	5, __, __, __, __, __, ...		

   (ii) What do you notice about the second difference and how it is connected to the quadratic formula for each sequence?

   (iii) If the second difference in a quadratic sequence is 12, and $T_n = an^2 + bn$, find the value of a.

6. Write the sequence 4, 7, 12, 19, 28, ... as follows

   $$4 \quad 7 \quad 12 \quad 19 \quad 28$$

   first difference
   second difference

   If $T_n = an^2 + bn + c$, use the second difference to write down the value of a. Hence find the expression for T_n.

7. Find an expression for the nth term of each of the quadratic sequences:

   (i) 7, 10, 15, 22, 31, ...   (ii) 2, 7, 14, 23, ...   (iii) 2, 8, 18, 32, 50, ...

8. Show that the nth term of the quadratic sequence 8, 15, 26, 41, 60, ... is given by $T_n = 2n^2 + n + 5$.

9. The given figures show a pattern of square tiles.

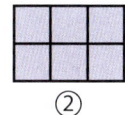

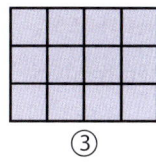

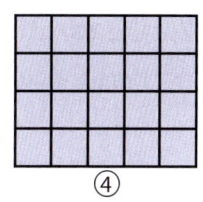

   ① ② ③ ④

   (i) How many tiles will there be in the fifth pattern?
   (ii) Explain why the numbers of tiles in the pattern do not form a linear sequence.
   (iii) Is the sequence of tiles used a quadratic sequence? Explain your answer.
   (iv) Use the second differences to find an expression for the nth term of the sequence.
   (v) Use the expression for the nth term that you found to work out the number of tiles in the twentieth pattern.

10. Here are the first 3 diagrams of a matchstick pattern.
    (i) How many matchsticks will there be in Diagram 4?
    (ii) Using the sequence formed, write down the number of matchsticks in Diagram 5.

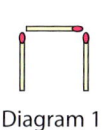

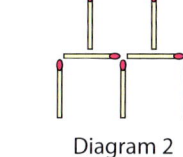

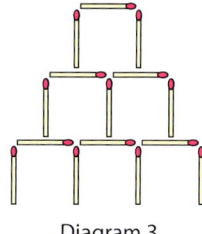

    Diagram 1   Diagram 2   Diagram 3

    (iii) Explain why the sequence is quadratic.
    (iv) Find an expression for the nth term of the sequence.
    (v) Use the nth term to find the number of matchsticks in Diagram 10.

Section 18.7 Graphing sequences

1. Linear sequences

Here is a linear pattern: 1, 4, 7, 10, 13, …
It can be seen that $T_1 = 1, T_2 = 4, T_3 = 7, …$

These may be written as ordered pairs as follows:
$(T_1, 1), (T_2, 4), (T_3, 7), (T_4, 10), …$

On the right, we have plotted the terms on the horizontal axis and the values of the terms on the vertical axis.
When the term and its value are plotted and the points joined, the result is a straight line.

This illustrates why the sequence is called **linear**.

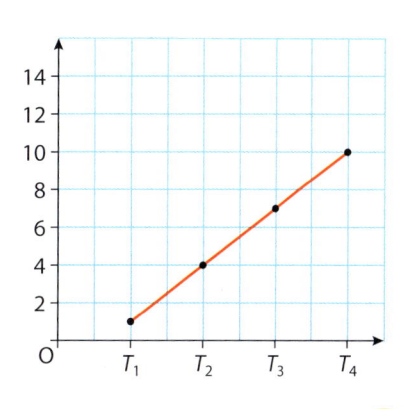

431

2. Quadratic sequences

Here is a quadratic sequence:
3, 4, 6, 9, 13, ...

We will now start to plot these ordered pairs – $(T_1, 3)$, $(T_2, 4)$, $(T_3, 6)$, $(T_4, 9)$, $(T_5, 13)$ – on a graph.

When the points are joined, the resulting curve forms part of a **quadratic graph**.

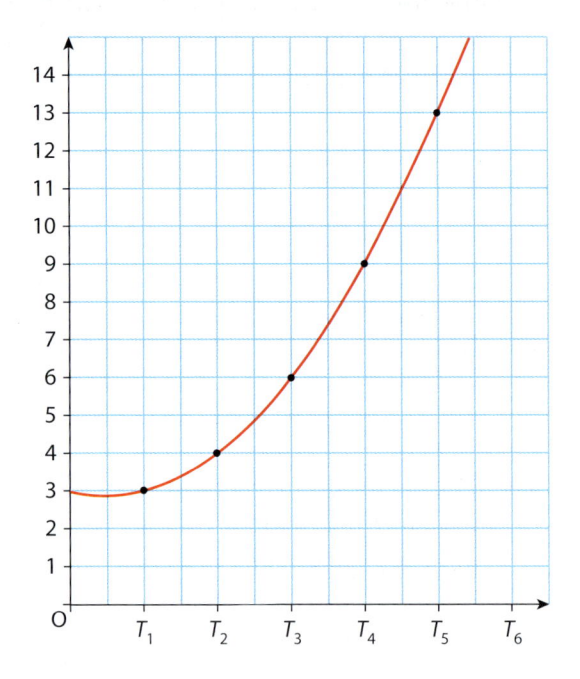

A quadratic graph takes one of the two shapes shown on the right.

3. Exponential sequences

Here is a special type of sequence formed by powers of 2:

$$2^1, 2^2, 2^3, 2^4, 2^5, \ldots \quad \text{or} \quad 2, 4, 8, 16, 32, \ldots$$

Notice that the values of the terms increase very quickly. This is an example of an **exponential sequence**.

If $T_n = 3^n$, then the sequence is

$$3^1, 3^2, 3^3, 3^4, 3^5, \ldots \quad \text{or} \quad 3, 9, 27, 81, 243, \ldots$$

> Exponent is another word for power.

In everyday language, **exponential growth** is used to indicate 'very fast growth'.

Chapter 18 Patterns and Sequences

When the sequence 2, 4, 8, 16, ... is plotted on a graph, it can be seen that the curve rises very steeply.

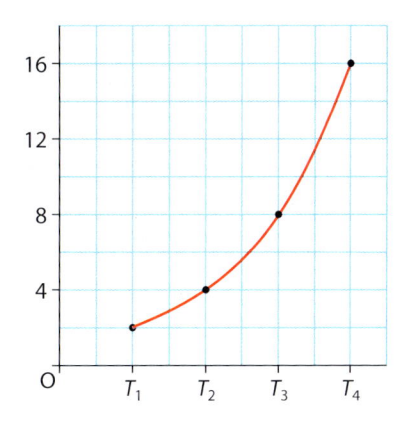

Investigation:

Quadratic sequences take the form $T_n = an^2 + bn + c$

Exponential sequences take the form $T_n = 2^n, 3^n$ etc.

Investigate the graphs of the sequences, $T_n = n^2$, $T_n = 2^n$ and $T_n = 3^n$.

Draw a large labelled graph of these sequences.

(Scale the x – axis from 0 to 5 (i.e. 0 < n < 5) and y – axis in units of 10 from 0 to 250)

Example 1

Here are the fare structures of two taxi companies.

Company A has a fixed charge of €4 plus €2 per kilometre
Company B has no fixed charge but charges €2.50 per kilometre travelled.

Draw a graph to represent these two companies' charges.
Put the charges on the x-axis and the distances on the y-axis.
Use your graph to find

(i) how much Company A charges for a journey of 10 km
(ii) how far you could travel with Company B for €16
(iii) the distance for which both companies charge the same amount
(iv) the difference in the charges when the distance is 4 km.

Find the slope of the line that represents company B and explain its meaning.

We set out a table of charges for each company.

433

Text & Tests 2 Higher Level

Ⓐ	Distance (km)	0	1	2	3	Ⓑ	Distance (km)	0	1	2	3
	Cost (€)		4	6	8	10		Cost (€)	0	2.5	5	7.5

We now plot these charges on the same graph.

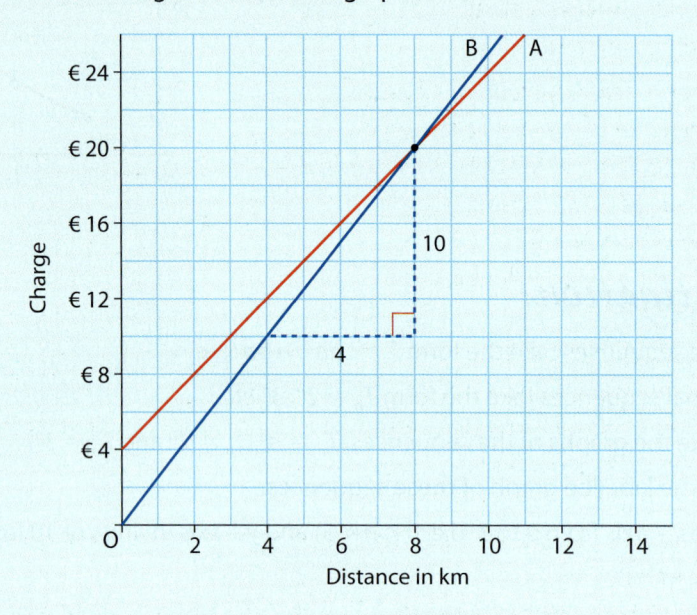

(i) Company A charges €24 for a journey of 10 km.
(ii) You could travel 6.4 km with company B for €16.
(iii) Both charges are equal where the lines intersect.
    This happens at 8 km.
(iv) For 4 km, Company A charges €12.
    For 4 km, Company B charges €10.
    The difference in the charges is €2.

The slope of the line B is $\frac{10}{4}$, as shown on the graph.

$\frac{10}{4} = \frac{5}{2} = 2\frac{1}{2}$ and €$2\frac{1}{2}$ is the charge for 1 km travelled.

Thus, the slope of the line B is the charge in euro for 1 km travelled.

Exercise 18.7

1. The table on the right shows the first four terms of a sequence and the values of these terms.

Term	1	2	3	4
Value	4	7	10	13

    Putting the terms on the horizontal axis and the values on the vertical axis, draw a graph of the sequence.
    Explain why the sequence is linear.

Chapter 18 Patterns and Sequences

2. If $T_n = 2n + 1$, write out the first five terms of the sequence.
Illustrate this sequence on a graph, putting the term numbers on the horizontal axis.
Explain why the graph is a straight line.

3. The graph on the right shows a plumber's charges when called to do a repair job on a boiler. 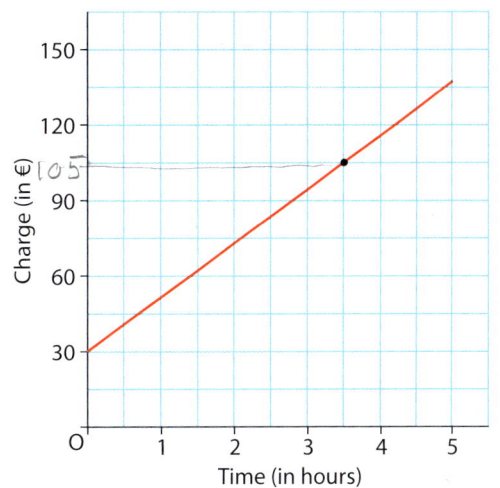
  (i) What is the initial or 'call out' charge?
  (ii) How much does he charge for a job that lasts for $3\frac{1}{2}$ hours?
  (iii) If he charges €135, how many hours has he worked?
  (iv) Do his charges form a linear sequence?
    Explain your conclusion.
  (v) Use the graph to work out what the plumber charges for each hour of actual work (i.e. excluding the 'call out' charge).
  (vi) Investigate if the slope of the line is the same as the rate he charges for each hour's work.
  (vii) If the work lasted 10 hours, use the sequence to work out what the charge would be.

4. The table on the right shows the total amounts of money Cara has saved after weeks 1, 2, 3, ….
Draw a graph to illustrate these savings, putting the week number on the x-axis.

Week number	Amount saved
1	€10
2	€20
3	€30
4	€40
5	€50
……	……

  (i) Is the graph linear?
  (ii) Use the pattern to find the amount she will have saved at the end of the 12th week.
  (iii) Find the equation of the line you have drawn.
  (iv) Use the equation to find what Cara will have saved at the end of the 20th week.

5. This pattern is made from cubes.
The outside faces of the cubes in each block are painted.

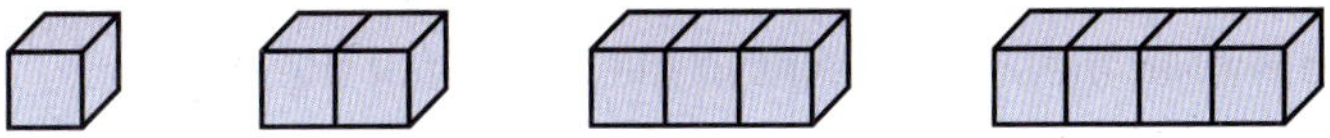

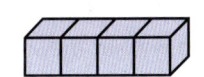

435

Text & Tests 2 Higher Level

The table below shows the number of faces painted in each block.

Block number (n)	1	2	3	4
Number of painted faces	6	10	14	18

    (i) Explain why the sequence formed by the numbers of faces painted forms a linear sequence.
    (ii) Now find an expression for the nth term of the sequence.
    (iii) Draw a graph of the sequence, putting the block numbers on the horizontal axis.

6. A fast-growing plant is 4 cm in height when purchased. It grows 2 cm per day each day afterwards.
Copy and complete the table on the right showing the height of the plant in its first seven days.

Day	Height (cm)
1	4
2	6
3	8
……	……

    (i) Draw a graph to show the height of the plant for Day 1 ….. Day 7.
    (ii) How many days will it take for the plant to reach a height of 30 cm?
    (iii) The plant will stop growing when it reaches a height of 60 cm. How many days will this take?
    (iv) What is the slope of the line you have drawn?
    (v) What is the rate of change of growth per day in the table?
    (vi) What is the connection between your answers in (iv) and (v) above?

7. The numbers of edges for the numbers of hexagons are shown in the pattern and table below:

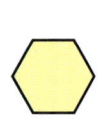

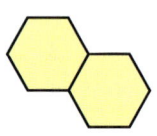

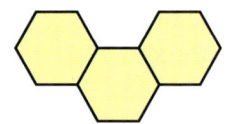

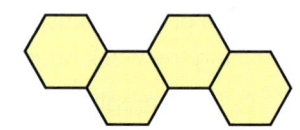

Number of hexagons (n)	1	2	3	4
Number of edges (E)	6	11	16	21

    (i) Find the number of edges when there are 5 hexagons.
    (ii) Explain why the pattern in the numbers of edges is linear.
    (iii) Find an expression for the nth term of the sequence 6, 11, 16, …
    (iv) Draw a graph of the pattern, putting the numbers of hexagons on the x-axis.
    (v) Find the equation of the line you have drawn in the form $E = \square n + \square$.
    (vi) What is the slope of this line?
    (vii) Explain what the slope means in the context of the pattern.

Chapter 18 Patterns and Sequences

8. A sequence of numbers begins 4, 7, 12, 19, 28, …

   (i) Explain why this is a quadratic pattern.
   (ii) What is the second difference between the terms?
   (iii) Draw a graph of this pattern using the scales shown on the right.
   (iv) Describe the shape of the graph.

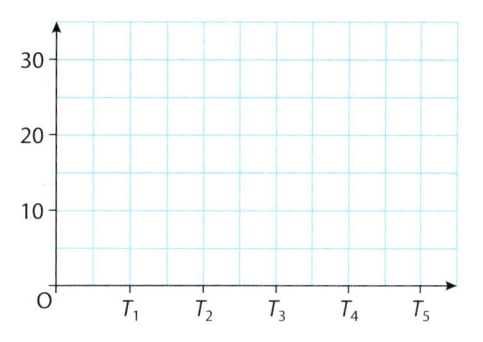

9. Here are the first three terms of an exponential sequence:

   3, 9, 27, …

   (i) Write down the next three terms.
   (ii) Investigate if the second difference is a constant.
   (iii) Explain why the sequence is not quadratic.
   (iv) Describe one feature of an exponential graph.

10. Here are three graphs and three sequences.

Which sequence does each graph represent?

A: 2, 4, 8, 16, …

B: 3, 6, 10, 15, 21, …

C: 2, 5, 8, 11, …

State which of sequences is linear. Explain your answer.

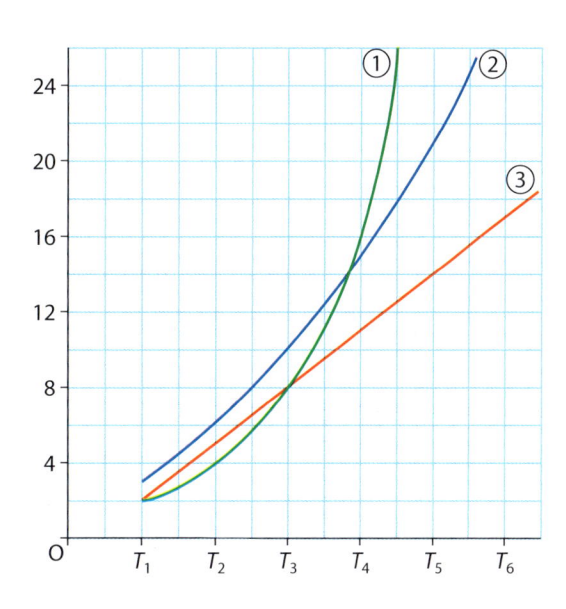

437

Text & Tests 2 Higher Level

Test yourself 18

1. Describe in words each of these three sequences:
   (i) 3, 7, 11, 15, ...
   (ii) −1, −3, −5, −7, ...
   (iii) 3, 6, 12, ...

2. Write out the first three terms of each of these sequences where T_n is the nth term:
   (i) $T_n = 3n + 1$
   (ii) $T_n = 1 - 2n$
   (iii) $T_n = 2n^2 - 1$

3. Look at the sequence of these triangle patterns:

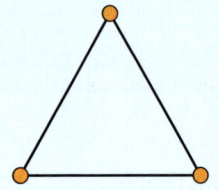

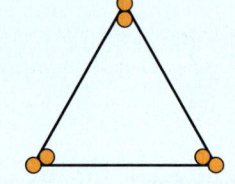

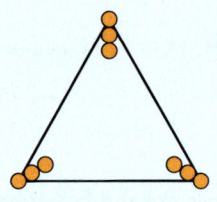

   (i) Draw the next triangle in the sequence.
   (ii) How many dots will there be in the 5th pattern?
   (iii) Find an expression for the nth term for this sequence.
   (iv) Use the expression for the nth term to find which pattern has 63 dots.

4. Write the next three terms of these sequences:
   (i) 7, 4, 1, −2, ...
   (ii) 40, 20, 10, ...
   (iii) 1, 2, 4, 7, 11, ...

5. Here is a repeating pattern of coloured tiles:

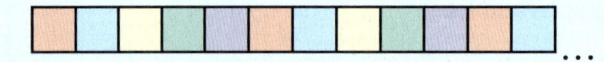

   (i) What are the colours of the next two tiles?
   (ii) Write down the sequence formed by the positions of the yellow tiles in the pattern.
   (iii) In what position is the 10th yellow tile?
   (iv) What is the colour of the 72nd tile?

6. (i) Write down the first three terms of the sequence if its nth term is given by $T_n = 2n^2 + 2$.
   (ii) 2, 5, 10, 17, 26, ... are the first five terms of a sequence.
   Work out the second difference between the terms.
   Explain why the sequence is quadratic.

7. Which **one** of the following sequences is linear?
   (i) 6, 4, 0, ...
   (ii) −3, −1, 3, 5, ...
   (iii) −5, −3, −1, 1, ...

Chapter 18 Patterns and Sequences

8. Look at these matchstick shapes.

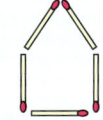

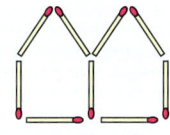

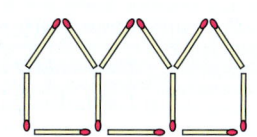

   5 matchsticks   9 matchsticks

   (i) Copy and complete the table below:

Shape number	1	2	3	4	5
Number of matchsticks	5	9	…	…	…

   (ii) How many matchsticks are there in Shape 7?
   (iii) Find an expression for the number of matchsticks in Shape n?
   (iv) Which shape contains exactly 101 matchsticks?

9. What number goes in the box in each of these sequences:
   (i)   10, 7, 4, 1, ☐, …
   (ii) −2, 1, ☐, 7, …
   (iii) 81, 27, ☐, 3, …
   (iv) 3, 5, 9, ☐, 23, …

10. The first four terms of a sequence are 4, 7, 10, 13, …
    (i)   Explain why the sequence is linear.
    (ii) Find an expression for the nth term of the sequence.
    (iii) Use the expression you have found to work out the 40th term of the sequence.

11. The first term of a quadratic sequence is 12.
    The first 1st difference is 3 and the second difference is 2.
    Write down the first six terms of the sequence.

12. Write down the next three terms of each of these sequences, where the first two terms and the term-to-term rules are given:
    (i)   1, 3, …   Double the previous term and add 1.
    (ii) 1, 3, …   Multiply the previous term by 4 and take away 1.
    (iii) 1, 3, …   Add the two previous terms together.

13. Tess made this pattern with buttons around the hem of her dress.

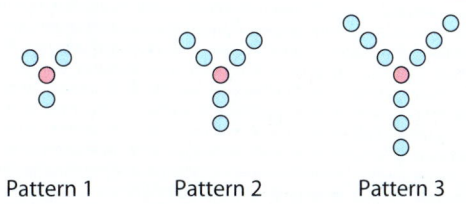

    Pattern 1   Pattern 2   Pattern 3

Pattern number	1	2	3	4	…
Number of buttons	4	7	10	?	…

439

(i) Draw pattern 4.
How many buttons are in pattern 4?
(ii) Describe the pattern and how it continues.
(iii) Find an expression for the number of buttons in the *n*th pattern.
(iv) Use the expression to find which pattern uses 25 buttons.

14. 2, 6, 12, 20, … are the first four terms of a quadratic sequence.
    (i) Work out the second difference between the terms.
    (ii) Use this second difference to find an expression for the *n*th term of the sequence.

15. (i) Write the next two terms in the sequence: 4, 5, 7, 10, 14, …
    (ii) Describe in words this sequence: 2, 6, 18, 54, …

16. The first two terms of a sequence are 3, 9, … .
    (i) If the sequence is linear, write down the next three terms.
    (ii) If the sequence is quadratic, write down what the next three terms could be.
    (iii) If the sequence is exponential, write down the next three terms.
    (iv) If the graphs of these sequences were drawn, which graph would rise the fastest?
    (v) Explain why there is more than one quadratic sequence that satisfies the pattern 3, 6, … .

17. A particular type of bacteria starts as a single cell and grows by doubling.

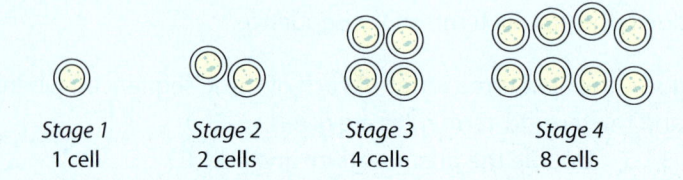

    Stage 1   Stage 2   Stage 3   Stage 4
    1 cell   2 cells   4 cells   8 cells

    (i) How many cells will be present at stage 6?
    (ii) By studying the pattern, write down an expression in *n* for the number of cells present at stage *n*.

Chapter 18 Patterns and Sequences

Assignment:

1. (a) Study the chart over and copy and complete the patterns up to 10.
   (b) Check that the sum in second column is equal to the product in the third column.
   (c) By studying the patterns in the rows, find an *n*th term, T_n, for Row *n*.
   (d) Using the formula, show how to find the sum of,
      (i) the first 100 natural numbers
      (ii) the first 200 natural numbers.

Row 1	1	$= \dfrac{1 \times 2}{2}$
Row 2	1 + 2	$= \dfrac{2 \times 3}{2}$
Row 3	1 + 2 + 3	$= \dfrac{3 \times 4}{2}$
Row 4	1 + 2 + 3 + 4	$= \dfrac{4 \times 5}{2}$
Row 5	1 + 2 + 3 + 4 + 5	$= \dfrac{5 \times 6}{2}$
Row 6	1 + 2 + 3 + 4 + 5 + 6	=
Row 7		=
Row 8		=
Row 9		=
Row 10		=
Row *n*	1 + 2 + 3 + 4 + ... *n*	=

2. Patricia said that if you add the first *n* odd numbers, the answer is always n^2.
By designing a chart similar to the one above, show why Patricia made this hypothesis.

Chapter 19 Functions

In this chapter, you will learn to:

- recognise that a function is a rule that produces one output value only for each input value,
- understand the terms input and output in relation to a function,
- use the terms domain, range, co-domain and couple, when describing functions,
- calculate missing operations in a function,
- draw and understand mapping diagrams,
- correctly identify a function,
- understand the notation used to write functions,
- evaluate functions for given values,
- find the coefficients of a function when given couples belonging to that function.

Section 19.1 Functions

Each term in the number sequence below is found by adding 4 to the previous term:

3, 7, 11, 15, 19
+4 +4 +4 +4 ... 'Add 4' is the rule for finding the next term.

Now consider this sequence:

2, 6, 18, 54
×3 ×3 ×3 ... Here the rule is 'multiply by 3'

The next number in the sequence is 54×3, i.e., 162.
When the operation '×3' is applied to 54, we get 162.
We use the term **input** for 54 and **output** for 162.

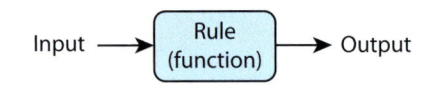

Input → Rule (function) → Output

The chain of diagrams below shows how we can find the output if we are given the input by means of a **function machine** or **flow chart**.

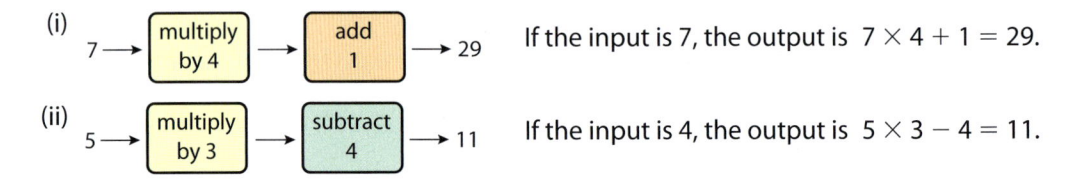

(i) 7 → [multiply by 4] → [add 1] → 29   If the input is 7, the output is $7 \times 4 + 1 = 29$.

(ii) 5 → [multiply by 3] → [subtract 4] → 11   If the input is 4, the output is $5 \times 3 - 4 = 11$.

442

Chapter 19 Functions

If we call the input number *x* and the output number *y*, we can then write the 'rule' in terms of *x* and *y*.

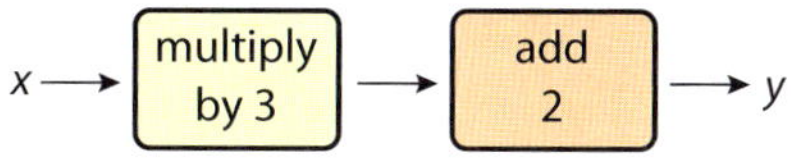

$$x \rightarrow \boxed{\text{multiply by 3}} \rightarrow \boxed{\text{add 2}} \rightarrow y$$

The rule for this function machine is 'multiply by 3, then add 2'.

We can write this as $x \times 3 + 2 = y$ or $y = 3x + 2$.

Here are the rules for these function machines:

(i) $x \rightarrow \boxed{\text{multiply by 2}} \rightarrow \boxed{\text{add 4}} \rightarrow y$ Rule: $y = 2x + 4$

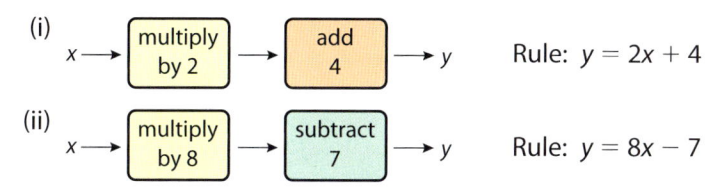

(ii) $x \rightarrow \boxed{\text{multiply by 8}} \rightarrow \boxed{\text{subtract 7}} \rightarrow y$ Rule: $y = 8x - 7$

The rule $y = 2x + 4$ may also be written as $x \rightarrow 2x + 4$.

Exercise 19.1

1. Find the output for each of these:

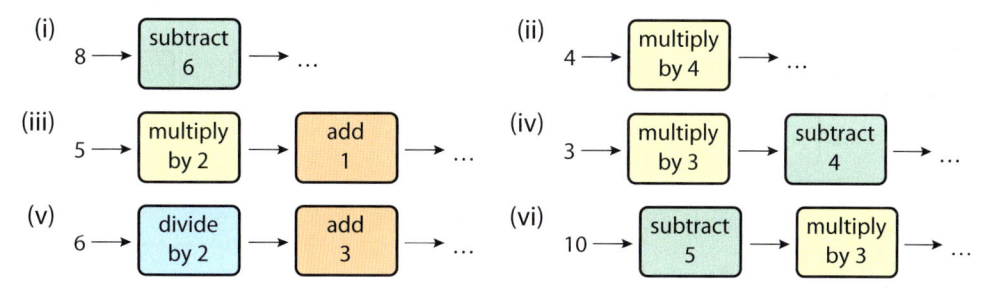

(i) $8 \rightarrow \boxed{\text{subtract 6}} \rightarrow \ldots$

(ii) $4 \rightarrow \boxed{\text{multiply by 4}} \rightarrow \ldots$

(iii) $5 \rightarrow \boxed{\text{multiply by 2}} \rightarrow \boxed{\text{add 1}} \rightarrow \ldots$

(iv) $3 \rightarrow \boxed{\text{multiply by 3}} \rightarrow \boxed{\text{subtract 4}} \rightarrow \ldots$

(v) $6 \rightarrow \boxed{\text{divide by 2}} \rightarrow \boxed{\text{add 3}} \rightarrow \ldots$

(vi) $10 \rightarrow \boxed{\text{subtract 5}} \rightarrow \boxed{\text{multiply by 3}} \rightarrow \ldots$

2. Describe in **words** what each function machine does to the input in Question 1 above.

3. Find the outputs for these:

(i) $3, 7, 8 \rightarrow \boxed{\text{multiply by 2}} \rightarrow \boxed{\text{subtract 4}} \rightarrow \ldots$

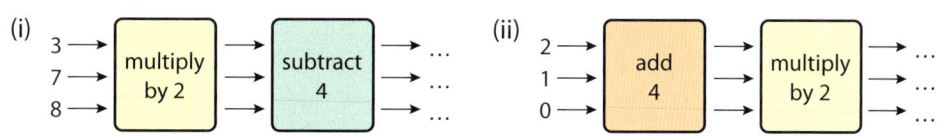

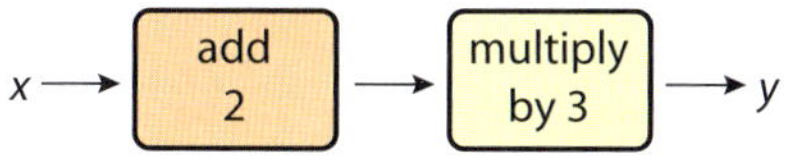

(ii) $2, 1, 0 \rightarrow \boxed{\text{add 4}} \rightarrow \boxed{\text{multiply by 2}} \rightarrow \ldots$

4. $x \rightarrow \boxed{\text{add 2}} \rightarrow \boxed{\text{multiply by 3}} \rightarrow y$ is a function machine.

Use a copy of this table and fill in the values for *y*.

x	1	2	3	4	5
y					

Write in words what this function machine does.

443

5. Write the rules for these function machines as $y = \ldots$

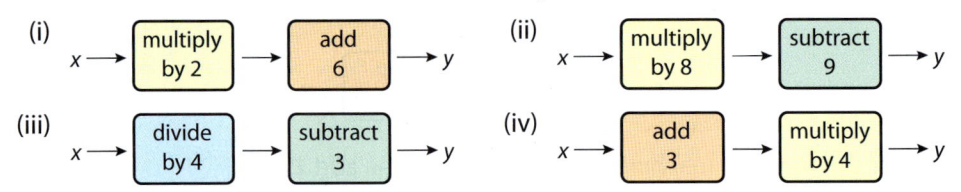

(i) $x \to$ [multiply by 2] $\to$ [add 6] $\to y$

(ii) $x \to$ [multiply by 8] $\to$ [subtract 9] $\to y$

(iii) $x \to$ [divide by 4] $\to$ [subtract 3] $\to y$

(iv) $x \to$ [add 3] $\to$ [multiply by 4] $\to y$

6. Find the missing operation in each of these:

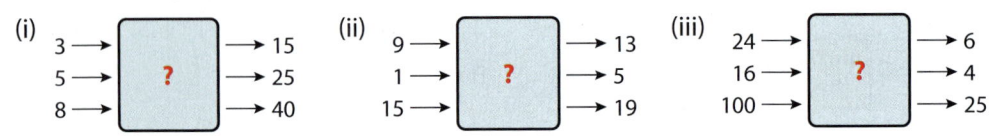

(i)
$3 \to$ [?] $\to 15$
$5 \to$ [?] $\to 25$
$8 \to$ [?] $\to 40$

(ii)
$9 \to$ [?] $\to 13$
$1 \to$ [?] $\to 5$
$15 \to$ [?] $\to 19$

(iii)
$24 \to$ [?] $\to 6$
$16 \to$ [?] $\to 4$
$100 \to$ [?] $\to 25$

7. Find the missing operations in these function machines:

(i)
$3 \to$
$2 \to$ [multiply by 2] $\to$ [?] $\to 5, 3, 1$
$1 \to$

(ii)
$0 \to$
$1 \to$ [multiply by 3] $\to$ [?] $\to 1, 4, 16$
$5 \to$

8. What numbers went into each of these function machines?

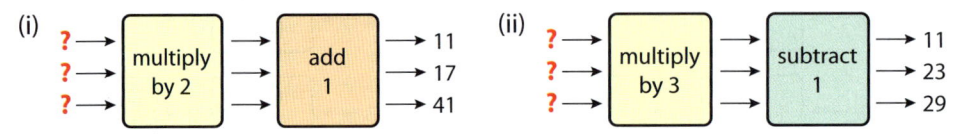

(i)
$? \to$
$? \to$ [multiply by 2] $\to$ [add 1] $\to 11, 17, 41$
$? \to$

(ii)
$? \to$
$? \to$ [multiply by 3] $\to$ [subtract 1] $\to 11, 23, 29$
$? \to$

Section 19.2 Mapping diagrams

Consider this function machine: $\ldots \to$ [multiply by 3] $\to$ [subtract 4] $\to \ldots$

We will input all the numbers from the set $\{1, 3, 5, 7, 9\}$.

The output numbers are: $\{-1, 5, 11, 17, 23\}$.

The set of input numbers is called the **domain**.

The set of output numbers is called the **range**.

The input numbers and output numbers can be represented by a special type of diagram called a **mapping diagram**.

Each input number is mapped onto its output number.

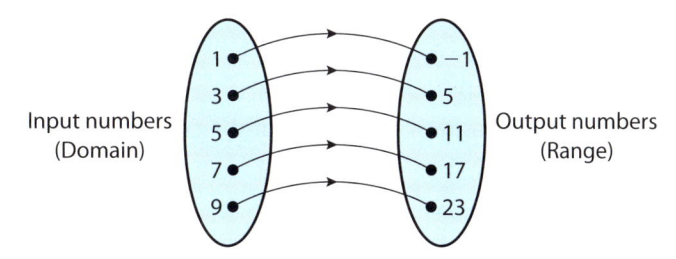

Input numbers (Domain) → Output numbers (Range)

In the mapping diagram above, notice that there is one and only **one output number for each input number**.

> In mathematics, we use the word **function** for any rule that produces one output value only for each input value.

Notation for a function

Consider this rule for a function: "Double the number and add 4".
If we input x, the output will be $2x + 4$.
The rule for this function may be written in any one of these three ways:

(i) $f(x) = 2x + 4$
(ii) $f: x \rightarrow 2x + 4$
(iii) $y = 2x + 4$.

These three notations tell us that if the input is 3, the output $(2x + 4)$ is $[(2 \times 3) + 4]$, i.e. 10.
This can be written as $f(3) = 10$.

The codomain

Take the two sets $A = \{1, 2, 3\}$ and $B = \{1, 3, 5, 7, 9, 11\}$.
If we are asked to list the couples of the function $f: x \rightarrow 2x - 1$, where the input numbers come from set A and the output numbers come from set B, we could set up a mapping diagram as follows:

The couples are (1, 1), (2, 3) and (3, 5).

The set A is the **domain**, i.e. $\{1, 2, 3\}$.

The **range** is $\{1, 3, 5\}$.

The set B is called the **codomain**, that is, the set of allowable outputs.
∴ the codomain $= \{1, 3, 5, 7, 9, 11\}$.

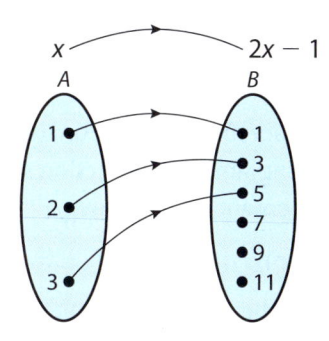

> The set of inputs is called the **domain**.
>
> The set of outputs is called the **range**.
>
> The set of possible outputs is called the **codomain**.

445

Example 1

A function f is defined as $f: x \rightarrow 3x - 2$.
The domain of f is $\{0, 1, 2, 3, 4\}$.
Represent f on a mapping diagram and write out the couples generated.
What is the range of f?

x	$3x - 2$	$f(x)$
0	$0 - 2$	-2
1	$3 - 2$	1
2	$6 - 2$	4
3	$9 - 2$	7
4	$12 - 2$	10

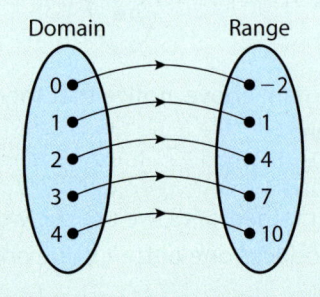

The couples are: $\{(0, -2), (1, 1), (2, 4), (3, 7), (4, 10)\}$.
The range is $\{-2, 1, 4, 7, 10\}$.

Identifying functions

When a function is represented by a mapping diagram, each element of the domain maps onto **one and only one** element of the range.

Consider these two mapping diagrams:

(i)   (ii)

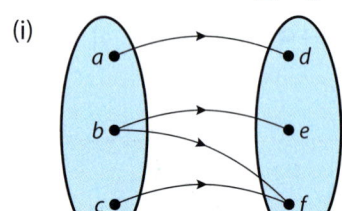

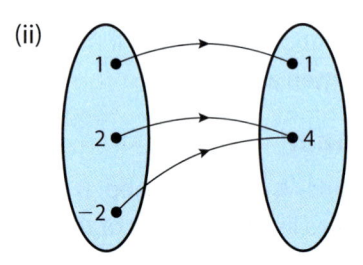

Diagram (i) is not a function since the element b is paired with 2 elements in the range.
Diagram (ii) is a function since each element in the domain is mapped onto one and only one element in the range.

Couples

We have already seen that a function can be written as a set of **couples** or **ordered pairs**, i.e. (input, output).
In notation form the couple or ordered pair is written as (x, y) or $(x, f(x))$
When a function is written as a set of couples, no two distinct couples will have the same input.

> $\{(1, 4), (2, 5), (3, 6), (4, 7)\}$ is a function as no two couples have the same input.

> $\{(2, 7), (3, 8), (3, 9), (4, 12)\}$ is **not** a function as the input 3 has two different outputs.

Exercise 19.2

1. Use the given mapping diagram to write down
  (i) the domain
  (ii) the range
  (iii) the set of couples formed
  (iv) the rule that gives the outputs.

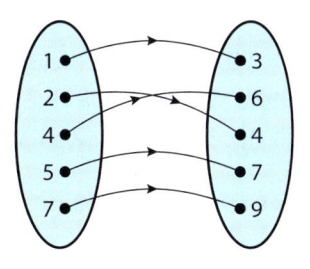

2. Copy and complete the mapping diagrams below.
Write down the domain and range of each function.

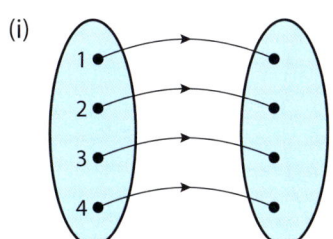

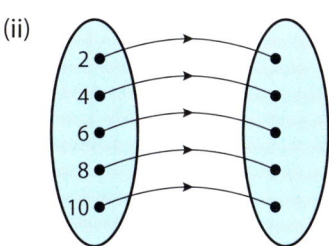

(i) Rule: Add 5

(ii) Rule: $x \rightarrow 2x + 1$

3. State whether each of the following mapping diagrams is a function.
Give a reason for your answer in each case:

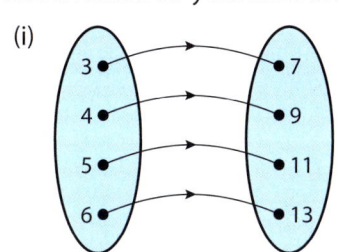

(i)

(ii)

(iii)

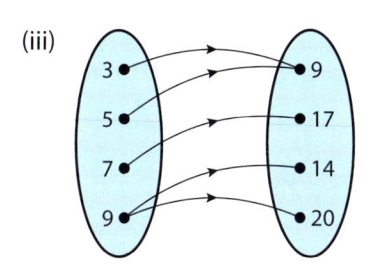

(iv)

4. Say why the following set of couples is a function:
{(1, 4), (2, 5), (3, 6), (4, 7)}.

5. Say why the following set of couples is not a function:
{(2, 5), (3, 6), (5, 8), (2, 10)}.

6. Investigate if each of these sets of couples represents a function.
If it is not a function, state the reason why.

  (i) {(0, 0), (1, 1), (2, 4), (3, 9), (4, 16)}
  (ii) {(−2, 1), (−1, 3), (−2, 5), (1, 6), (2, 9)}
  (iii) {(−3, 4), (0, 7), (2, 9), (4, 11)}

7. For each of the mapping diagrams below, write down

  (i) the domain
  (ii) the range
  (iii) the codomain.

(a) Domain: {0, 1, 3, 5}, Codomain: {3, 4, 5, 6, 8}

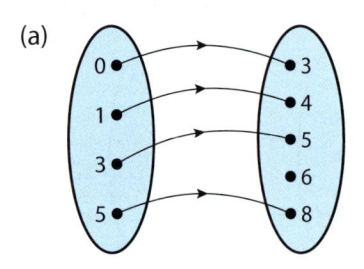

(b) Domain: {−2, 2, 3, 7}, Codomain: {−4, 2, 6, −3, 4, 9}

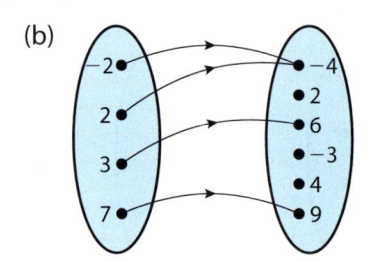

8. The rule for a function is: 'Multiply by 2 and add 3'.
If the domain of the function is {0, 1, 3, 5}, write down

  (i) the range
  (ii) the couples generated.

9. A function f is defined as $f: x \rightarrow 3x - 1$.
The domain of the function is {1, 2, 4, 6}.
Write down the range of the function.

10. A function f is defined as $f(x) = 4x - 5$.
The domain of the function is {−2, 0, 2, 4}.

  (i) What is the range of f?
  (ii) Write f as a set of couples.

11. Make a copy of this table.
Fill it in for the function machine shown below.

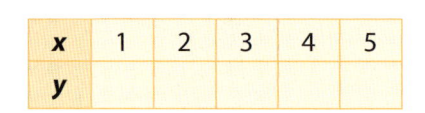

x	1	2	3	4	5
y					

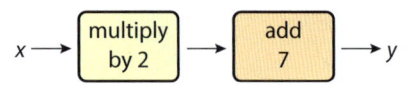

$x \rightarrow$ [multiply by 2] $\rightarrow$ [add 7] $\rightarrow y$

Write the function in the form $y = \ldots$.

12. This is a function machine:

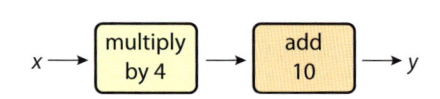

$x \rightarrow$ [multiply by 4] $\rightarrow$ [add 10] $\rightarrow y$

Write the function in the form $y = \ldots$.
If the input is 5, what is the output?
Use the function rule to find the input when the output is 22.

13. x → [multiply by 2] → [add 4] → y describes a function.

Copy the table on the right and fill in the missing input and output numbers.

Input	Output
3	
−2	
	14
	−8

14. In the three tables below, some input and output numbers are given.
By 'trial and error' or guessing, find the rule for each function in the form y = …….

(i)
Input	Output
3	2
7	10
5	6
11	18

(ii)
Input	Output
1	5
3	11
5	17
10	32

(iii)
Input	Output
1	4
3	10
6	19
8	25

15. $f: x \to 6x - 2$ defines a function.
If the couples $(2, a)$, $(-4, b)$, $(c, 16)$ and $(d, -14)$ are all couples of f, work out the values of a, b, c and d.

Section 19.3 Notation for functions

We have already seen that a function can be written in any of these ways:

(i) $f(x) = 3x - 2$ (ii) $f: x \to 3x - 2$ (iii) $y = 3x - 2$

In each case, the output is $(3x - 2)$ when the input is x.

The notation **f(3)** is used to represent the output number when 3 is the input number.
If $f(x) = 3x - 2$, then $f(3) = 3(3) - 2 = 9 - 2 = 7$.
Thus, $f(3) = 7$.

While f(x) is generally used to describe a function, other letters such as g(x) and h(x) are used when we are dealing with more than one function.

Example 1

The functions f and g are defined on R such that
$f: x \to x + 5$ and $g: x \to x^2 - 1$.
Find (i) f(3) (ii) g(−3) (iii) f(2k) (iv) f(k + 1) (v) g(3k) (vi) g(k + 1)

(i) $f(x) = x + 5$
$f(3) = 3 + 5$
$= 8$

(ii) $g(x) = x^2 - 1$
$g(-3) = (-3)^2 - 1$
$= 9 - 1 = 8$

Text & Tests 2 Higher Level

(iii) $f(x) = x + 5$
       $f(2k) = 2k + 5$

(iv) $f(x) = x + 5$
       $f(k + 1) = (k + 1) + 5$
               $= k + 6$

(v) $g(x) = x^2 - 1$
       $g(3k) = (3k)^2 - 1$
              $= 9k^2 - 1$

(vi) $g(x) = x^2 - 1$
       $g(k + 1) = (k + 1)^2 - 1$
               $= k^2 + 2k + 1 - 1$
               $= k^2 + 2k$

Example 2

A function is defined by $f : x \rightarrow 4x - 5$.
(i) Find $f(3)$
(ii) Find the value of k for which $kf(3) = f(10)$.

(i) $f(x) = 4x - 5$
       $f(3) = 4(3) - 5$
           $= 12 - 5$
           $= 7$

(ii) $f(3) = 7$ ... from (i)
       $kf(3) = 7k$
       $f(10) = 4(10) - 5 = 40 - 5 = 35$
       $kf(3) = f(10)$
     $\Rightarrow$ $7k = 35$
            $k = 5$

Exercise 19.3

1. If $f(x) = 2x - 3$, find
   (i) $f(1)$ (ii) $f(0)$ (iii) $f(2)$ (iv) $f(-1)$ (v) $f(-3)$.

2. If $f(x) = 4x - 5$, find
   (i) $f(2)$ (ii) $f(0)$ (iii) $f(-3)$ (iv) $f\left(\frac{1}{2}\right)$ (v) $f\left(\frac{1}{4}\right)$.

3. If $f(x) = x^2 - 3$, find
   (i) $f(0)$ (ii) $f(1)$ (iii) $f(2)$ (iv) $f(-2)$ (v) $f(-4)$.

4. If $f(x) = 5 - 2x$, find
   (i) $f(0)$ (ii) $f(2)$ (iii) $f(-3)$ (iv) $f\left(-\frac{1}{2}\right)$ (v) $f(k)$.

5. If $f(x) = 5x - 2$, solve the following equations:
   (i) $f(x) = 8$ (ii) $f(x) = 3$ (iii) $f(k) = -12$.

Chapter 19 Functions

6. If $f(x) = 3x - 2$ and $g(x) = 2 - 4x$, solve these equations:
   (i) $f(x) = 4$
   (ii) $g(x) = -10$
   (iii) $g(x) = f(4)$.

7. Given $f(x) = 5x - 1$, find
   (i) $f(-3)$
   (ii) $f\left(\frac{1}{5}\right)$
   (iii) $f(k)$
   (iv) $f(2k)$
   (v) $f(2k - 1)$.

8. The function f is defined as $f: x \rightarrow 2 - 3x$.
   Find the value of the number k if $kf(3) = 7f(2)$.

9. If $f(x) = 2x - 3$ and $g(x) = 3 - 5x$, solve these equations:
   (i) $f(x) = 7$
   (ii) $g(x) = -7$
   (iii) $f(x) = g(-3)$.

10. A function is defined by $f: x \rightarrow 5x - 7$.
   (i) Find $f(4)$.
   (ii) Find the value of k for which $f(-3) = kf(3)$.

11. The function f is defined by $f: x \rightarrow 3x - 4$.
   For what value of k is $f(k) + f(2k) = 0$?

12. $f: x \rightarrow 4x$ and $g: x \rightarrow x + 1$ define two functions.
   If $g(3) + k[f(3)] = 8$, find the value of k.

13. $f: x = 2x^2 - 1$ and $g(x) = x + 2$ define two functions.
   Solve these equations:
   (i) $f(x) = 3$
   (ii) $g(x) = f(3)$
   (iii) $f(x) = g(x)$.

14. $h: x \rightarrow 2x + a$ and $k: x \rightarrow b - 5x$ are two functions where a and b are real numbers.
   If $h(1) = -5$ and $k(-1) = 4$, find the value of a and the value of b.

15. A function $f(x)$ is defined by $f(x) = 1 + \frac{2}{x}$.
   (i) Evaluate $f(-4)$ and $f\left(\frac{1}{5}\right)$.
   (ii) Find the value of x for which $f(x) = 2$.
   (iii) Find the value of k if $kf(2) = f\left(\frac{1}{2}\right)$.

16. $g(x) = 1 - 4x$ defines a function.
   (i) Find $g(k + 1)$.
   (ii) Solve the equation $g(k + 1) = g(-3)$.

17. Given that $f(x) = 2^x$, find
   (i) $f(4)$
   (ii) $f(-2)$
   (iii) the value of x for which $f(x) = \frac{\sqrt{2}}{2}$.

Investigation:

Addition is the inverse of Subtraction, Multiplication is the inverse of Division. Inverses in mathematics are very important and help us to reverse any operation.

If the set $\{1, 2, 3, 4, …\}$ is input into the function $f(x) = x + 5$, the output is $\{6, 7, 8, 9, …\}$.

If the set $\{6, 7, 8, 9, …\}$ is the input set, the function $g(x) = x - 5$, will bring us back to $\{1, 2, 3, 4, …\}$. $\therefore g(x)$ is the **inverse function** of $f(x)$.

Investigate each of the following functions and make a chart of their inverses. Create your own function and its inverse on the last line.

By creating your own input set, you can check your inverse function.

Function	Inverse
$f(x) = x - 6$	$g(x) =$
$f(x) = 4x$	$g(x) =$
$f(x) = 2x + 1$	$g(x) =$
$f(x) = 3x + 1$	$g(x) =$
$f(x) = 2(x - 1)$	$g(x) =$
$f(x) = 4 - 2x$	$g(x) =$
$f(x) = 3(2x + 1)$	$g(x) =$
$f(x) =$	$g(x) =$

Section 19.4 Finding coefficients of functions

In a later chapter we will learn how to draw the graphs of functions such as $f(x) = 2x + 4$ or $f(x) = x^2 + 2x - 4$.

The function $f(x) = 2x + 4$ represents a straight line.

The function $f(x) = x^2 + 2x - 4$ represents a shape like that shown on the right.
This smooth curve is called a **parabola**.

Consider the function $f(x) = ax + b$.
If we are told that $(2, 4)$ is on this line, then 2 is the input and 4 is the output
i.e. $(x, y) = (2, 4) \therefore f(2) = 4$

Similarly, if $(3, 0)$ is on the line, then $f(3) = 0$.

Chapter 19 Functions

The following example illustrates how to find unknown coefficients of a function when given some couples of the function.

> **Example 1**
>
> The given diagram shows part of the graph of the function
> $y = ax + b$.
> Find the values of a and b. 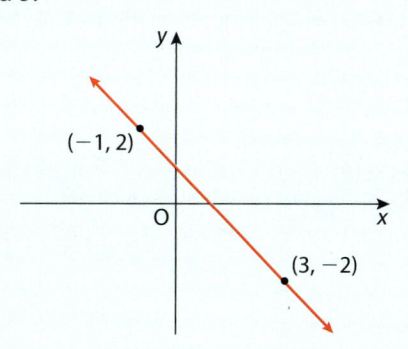
>
> $(3, -2) \in y = ax + b$
> → when $x = 3, y = -2$.
> ∴ $-2 = 3a + b$
> $(-1, 2) \in y = ax + b$
> → when $x = -1, y = 2$.
> ∴ $2 = -a + b$
>
> i.e. $3a + b = -2$ ...①
> i.e. $-a + b = 2$ ...②
> subtracting: $4a = -4$
> ⇒ $a = -1$
>
> From ①: $3(-1) + b = -2$
> ⇒ $-3 + b = -2 \Rightarrow b = 1$
> ∴ $a = -1$ and $b = 1$

Quadratic functions

A function such as $f(x) = x^2 - 3x + 2$ which contains a term in x^2 is called a **quadratic function**.

The diagram on the right shows a curve crossing the x-axis at the points where $x = -3$ and $x = 2$.

These numbers are the roots of the equation

$(x + 3)(x - 2) = 0$
i.e. $x^2 + x - 6 = 0$

Thus, the equation of the curve is

$f(x) = x^2 + x - 6$

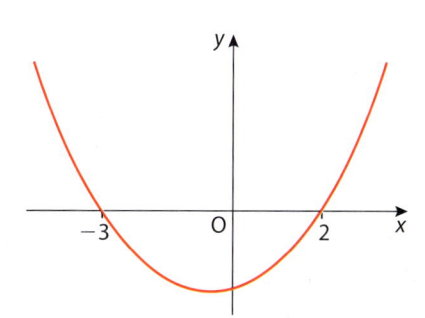

453

Text & Tests 2 Higher Level

> **Example 2**
>
> The graph of the quadratic function
> $f(x) = x^2 + bx + c$ is shown.
> Find the values of b and c.
> Hence write down the coordinates of p and q.
>
> $(-1, 0) \in$ the curve $\Rightarrow f(-1) = 0$
> $f(-1) = 1 - b + c \Rightarrow 1 - b + c = 0$
> $\qquad \Rightarrow -b + c = -1 \ldots$ ①
> $(4, 5) \in$ the curve $\Rightarrow f(4) = 5$
> $f(4) = 16 + 4b + c \Rightarrow 16 + 4b + c = 5$
> $\qquad \Rightarrow 4b + c = -11 \ldots$ ②
> We now solve equations ① and ②
> ①: $-b + c = -1$
> ②: $4b + c = -11$
> $\overline{-5b \quad = \quad 10} \Rightarrow b = -2$
> From ①: $2 + c = -1 \Rightarrow c = -3$
> $\therefore \ b = -2$ and $c = -3$ i.e. $f(x) = x^2 - 2x - 3$.
>
> To find the coordinates of p, we solve the equation $f(x) = 0$.
> $f(x) = 0 \Rightarrow x^2 - 2x - 3 = 0$
> $\qquad \Rightarrow (x - 3)(x + 1) = 0$
> $\qquad \Rightarrow x = 3 \ \text{ or } \ x = -1$
> $\therefore$ the coordinates of p are $(3, 0)$
>
> > The coordinates of p are $(x, 0)$
> > The coordinates of q are $(0, y)$
>
> To find the coordinates of the point where a curve crosses the y-axis, we let $x = 0$.
> $x = 0 \Rightarrow f(x) = 0 - 0 - 3$ i.e. $f(x) = -3 \Rightarrow y = -3$
> $\therefore$ the coordinates of q are $(0, -3)$

Exercise 19.4

1. $f(x) = 3x + k$ is a function.
   If $f(4) = 10$, find the value of k.

2. If $(1, 5)$ is a couple of the function $f(x) = kx + 4$, find the value of k.

3. $f(x) = ax - 6$ is a function.
   If $f(2) = -2$, find the value of a.

4. $f : x \rightarrow x^2 - 2x + k$ is a function.
   If $(1, 2)$ is a couple of the function, find the value of k.

5. (−3, 2) is a point on the line $y = ax + 11$. Find the value of a.

6. $f(x) = kx^2 + 3$ is a function.
If (−1, −1) is a couple of this function, find the value of k.

7. The graph of the linear function
$$f(x) = ax + b \text{ is shown.}$$
Find the values of a and b.

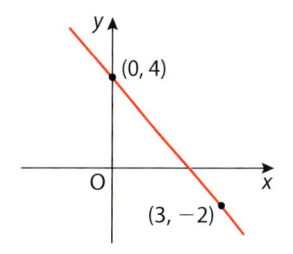

8. A function f is defined as $f: x \rightarrow 2x - 1$.
If the mapping diagram on the right represents f, find the values of a, b and c.

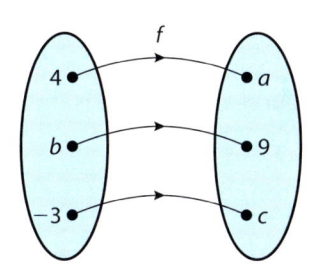

9. $g: x \rightarrow ax^2 + bx + 1$ defines a function.
If $g(1) = 0$ and $g(2) = 3$, write down two equations in a and b.
Solve these equations to find the values of a and b.

10. A function is defined by $f: x \rightarrow ax^2 + bx + 1$.
If $f(1) = 0$ and $f(-1) = 0$, find the value of a and the value of b.

11. $f: x \rightarrow x^2 + px + q$ defines a function.
Given that $f(3) = 4$ and $f(-1) = 4$, find the values of p and q.
Using these values for p and q, solve the equation $x^2 + px + q = 0$.

12. The function $f(x) = x^2 + bx + c$ is graphed on the right.
  (i) Use $f(0)$ to find the value of c.
  (ii) Use the graph to find another equation in b and c.
  Use this equation and the value for c found in (i) to find the value of b.
  (iii) Using these values for b and c, solve the equation $x^2 + bx + c = 0$ to find the coordinates of the point d.

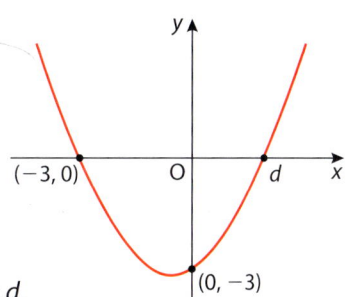

Text & Tests 2 Higher Level

13. Functions *f* and *g* are defined as follows:

    $f: x \to x^2 + 1$ and $g: x \to ax + b$, where *a* and *b* are constants.
    If $f(0) = g(0)$ and $g(2) = 15$, find the values of *a* and *b*.

14. The diagram shows part of the graph of the function

    $f: x \to x^2 + bx + c.$

    The named couples are elements of the function.
    (i) Find the values of *b* and *c*.
    (ii) If (2, *y*) is a point on the graph, find the value of *y*.

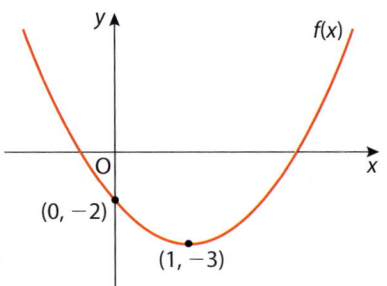

    (0, −2), (1, −3)

15. The curve on the right is the graph of the function

    $y = x^2 + 2x - 3.$

    Find the coordinates of the points *a*, *b* and *c*.

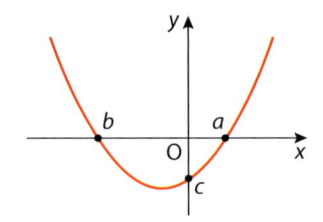

16. $f(x) = 2x^2$ and $g(x) = 3x - 1$ are two functions.
    Find (i) $f(3)$ (ii) $g(1)$ (iii) $g\left(\frac{1}{3}\right)$.
    If $f(3) = kg(1)$, find *k*.

17. Given that $f(x) = 3^x$, find
    (i) $f(4)$ (ii) $f(-2)$ (iii) $f\left(\frac{1}{2}\right)$ (iv) the value of *x* for which $f(x) = \frac{\sqrt{3}}{3}$.

456

Investigation:

The graph below shows the height (H), measured in metres, of a ball kicked directly upwards where t is measured in seconds.

Using English sentences, investigate the connection between the graph and the following three mathematical statements.

A: $20t - 5t^2 = 0 \rightarrow t = 0$ (s) and $t = 4$ (s)
B: $20t - 5t^2 = 15 \rightarrow t = 1$ (s) and $t = 3$ (s)
C: $20t - 5t^2 = 20 \rightarrow t = 2$ (s)

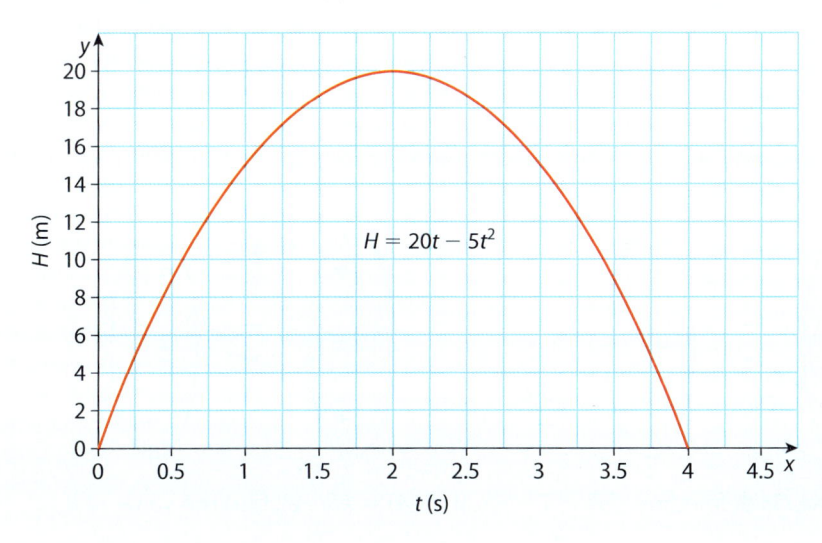

Verify **A** and **C** above mathematically.

Test yourself 19

1. Complete the ordered pairs below and hence draw a graph of the line $y = 2x - 4$.
   $(-2, \ldots), (0, \ldots), (2, \ldots)$.

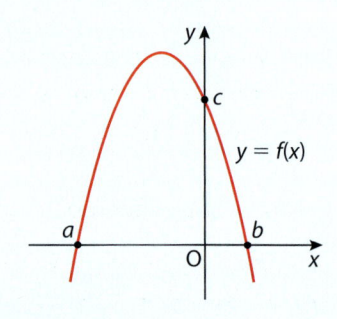

2. A function f is defined by $f: x \rightarrow 5x - 1$.
   If the domain of $f = \{0, 1, 2, 3\}$, find the range of f.

3. The curve on the right is the graph of the function
   $$f(x) = 8 - 2x - x^2.$$
   Find the coordinates of the points marked a, b and c.

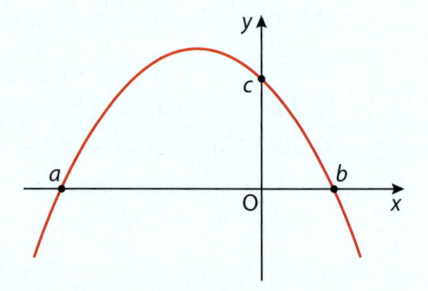

4. State whether each of these mapping diagrams represents a function, giving a reason for your answers:
   (i)   (ii)

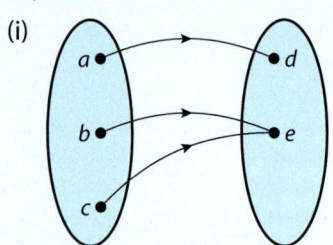

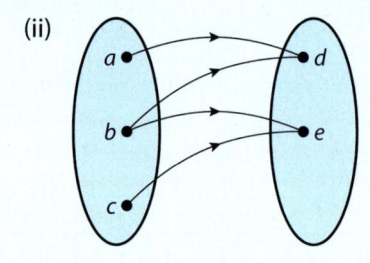

5. The function f is defined by $f(x) = 7 - 3x$. If $f(24) = kf(-2)$, find the value of k.

6. $f(x) = 2x - 1$ and $g(x) = 1 - 3x$ are two functions.
   (i) For what value of k is $f(k) + f(2k) = 4$?
   (ii) For what value of t is $tf(3) = g(t)$?

7. State why the set of couples $\{(1, 3), (2, 7), (3, 10), (1, 12)\}$ is not a function.

8. The function f is defined by $f: x \rightarrow 3x - 4$.
   For what value of k is $f(k) + f(2k) = 1$?

9. The curve on the right is the graph of the function
   $$f(x) = 10 - 3x - x^2.$$
   Find the coordinates of the points marked a, b and c.

Chapter 19 Functions

10. A function f is defined by $f: x \rightarrow 5x - 3$.
    Copy and complete these three couples of f:
    $(1, *), (3, *), (0, *)$.
    Hence draw a graph of the function $f: x \rightarrow 5x - 3$.

11. The function f is defined on R such that $f: x \rightarrow 3x - 1$.
    Find (i) $f(2)$ (ii) $f\left(\frac{1}{2}\right)$.
    Find the value of $k \in N$ such that $f(2) = kf\left(\frac{1}{2}\right)$.
    Investigate if $f(h) = kf\left(\frac{1}{h}\right)$.

12. The function $f(x) = x^2 + bx + c$ is graphed on the right. The curve crosses the x-axis at $(-1, 0)$ and it contains the point $(3, -4)$.
    (i) Write down two equations in b and c.
    (ii) Solve these equations to find the values of b and c.
    (iii) Use these values for b and c to write down the function $f(x)$.
    (iv) Use this function to find the coordinates of d and e.

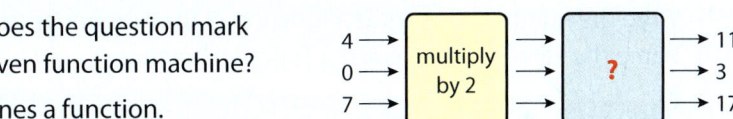

13. (i) What operation does the question mark stand for in the given function machine?

    $4 \rightarrow$ multiply by 2 $\rightarrow$? $\rightarrow 11$
    $0 \rightarrow$ multiply by 2 $\rightarrow$? $\rightarrow 3$
    $7 \rightarrow$ multiply by 2 $\rightarrow$? $\rightarrow 17$

    (ii) $f(x) = 3x - 4$ defines a function.
    If the domain of $f(x)$ is $\{-3, -2, -1, 0\}$, what is the range of $f(x)$?

14. A function is defined by $f(x) = ax^2 + bx + 1$.
    If $f(-1) = 6$ and $f(1) = 2$, write down two equations in a and b.
    Solve these equations to find the values of a and b.

15. A function is defined by $f(x) = \sqrt{x^2 + 8}$.
    (i) Evaluate $f(2)$ and $f(8)$.
    (ii) Given that $f(2) \times f(8) = k\sqrt{6}$, find k, where $k \in N$.

16. $y = 3x - 2$ defines a function.
    Copy and complete the given table for this function and hence draw its graph.

x	−1	0	1	2
y				

17. A function is defined as $f(x) = \sqrt{\frac{12}{x}}$, where $x > 0$.
    (i) Express $f(27)$ as a fraction in its simplest form.
    (ii) If $f(x) = 4\sqrt{3}$, find the value of x.

Text & Tests 2 Higher Level

Assignment:

Study the cutting of a very large sheet of paper and creating a pile by laying one half on the other.

A: By completing the table below, find out how many layers are created when, after each cut, one half is piled on top of the other side.

Folds	Number of layers	Exponent form
1st cut		
2nd cut		
3rd cut		
4th cut		
⋮		
⋮		
10th cut		
20th cut		
nth cut		

$f(n) = (\ \ )^{(\ \ )}$

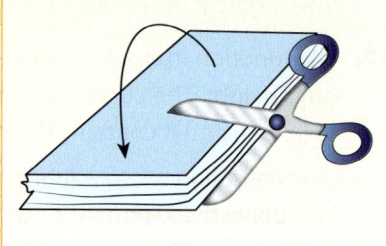

B:
Write the number of layers as a function of the number of cuts, n.
Name the category to which this function belongs.

C:
Sally has cut her sheet, k times.
Eoin has cut his sheet $(k - 2)$ times.
When they place their layers side by side on a table, how do the heights of their separate piles compare?

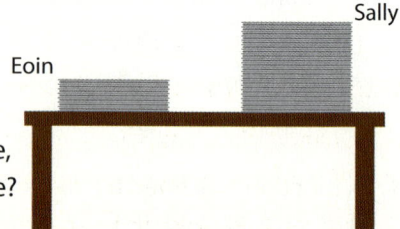

D:
Assume the height of a ream of A4 paper (500 sheets) is 5cm. Calculate the height (thickness) of a single sheet (a very small number).
Imagine a very, very, large sheet of this paper was cut 50 times.
Estimate the height of the final pile of paper.
Get an average estimate of the height from your group.

Estimate:

E:
Using the function above, the thickness of a single sheet and a calculator with an $x^{(\ )}$ function, find the true height of the layers of paper after 50 cuts.
Compare this distance with some well-known distance.

F:
Write a report on this type of function.

460

Drawing and interpreting real-life graphs

chapter 20

From first year, you will recall how to:

- draw x and y axes, and label them,
- plot points onto a coordinated plane.

In this chapter, you will learn to:

- draw distance–time graphs,
- read information from a distance–time graph,
- recognise a directly proportional graph as a straight line through the origin,
- draw directly proportional graphs,
- interpret information from directly proportional graphs,
- compare graphs that represent liquid being poured at a steady rate into various containers,
- Interpret graphs that represent a variety of real-world scenarios.

Section 20.1 Distance–time graphs

› A distance–time graph (or travel graph) is a special type of line graph used to describe a journey.

› The vertical axis represents the distance from a certain point, while the horizontal axis represents time.

The distance–time graph below shows the journey of a cyclist who set out from town A.

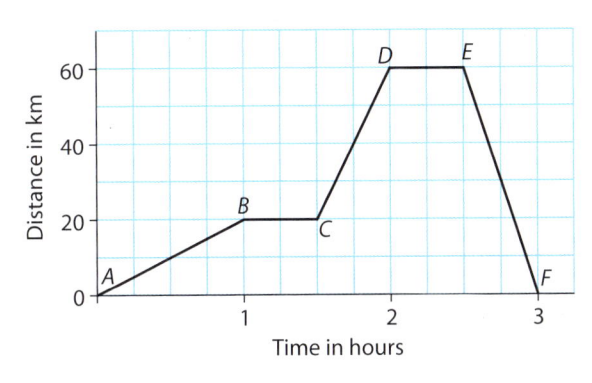

Text & Tests 2 Higher Level

(i) From A to B he cycled a distance of 20 km in 1 hour.

(ii) At B he stopped for half an hour which is represented by [BC].

(iii) At C he took a lift on a lorry and travelled to D, a distance of 40 km. This part of the journey took half an hour.

(iv) He then rested for half an hour. This is represented by [DE].

(v) He then took a train back to the town he originally left and completed the 60 km return journey in half an hour. This is represented by [EF].

[Note that both A and F represent town A with a time-gap of 3 hours.]

Distance–time graphs

> A change in speed represents a change in steepness.
> The steeper the line, the faster the speed.
> The flatter the line, the slower the speed.
> A horizontal line indicates that the person or object is stopped.

The formulae that connect distance (D), time (T) and average speed (S) are given below:

$$D = S \times T \qquad S = \frac{D}{T} \qquad T = \frac{D}{S}$$

Exercise 20.1

1. This travel graph gives the distance of a boy from home.

    (i) When did the boy leave home? When did he return?
    (ii) How far was he from home at 1.00 p.m.?
    (iii) At what times was he 15 km from home?
    (iv) At what times did he rest?
    (v) When was he travelling most quickly?

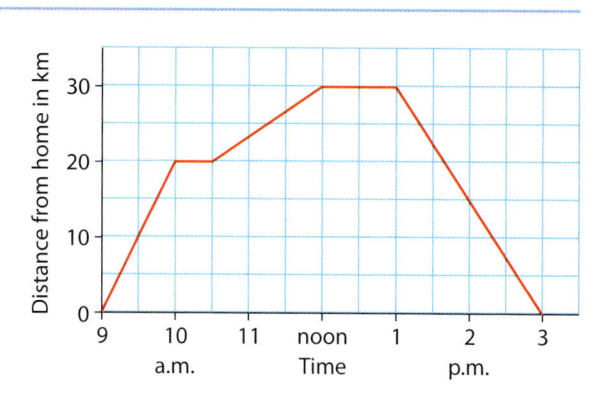

Chapter 20 Drawing and interpreting real-life graphs

2. The distance–time graph given shows Olivia's 3-hour journey.
   (i) How far did she travel in the first hour?
   (ii) For how long was she stopped?
   (iii) How far did she travel in the third hour?
   (iv) What was the total length of the journey?

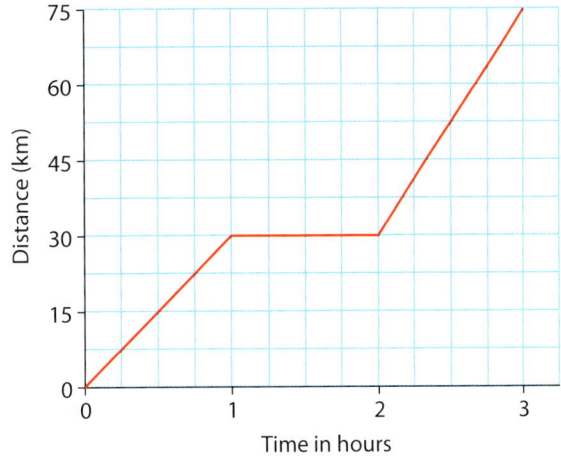

3. The travel graph shows the distance of a cyclist from his home between the times of 10. a.m. and 4.30 p.m.
   (i) How far does the cyclist travel in the first 2 hours?
   (ii) How far from home is he when he stops to rest?
   (iii) At what time does he commence the return journey?
   (iv) At 3.00 p.m. his speed changes. Does it increase or decrease? How can you tell without calculating the actual speeds?
   (v) How far does he travel?

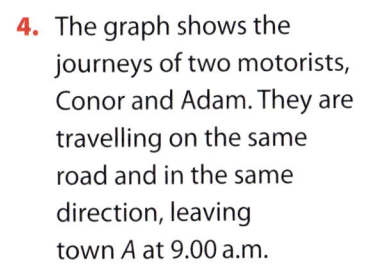

4. The graph shows the journeys of two motorists, Conor and Adam. They are travelling on the same road and in the same direction, leaving town A at 9.00 a.m.
   (i) Who travels faster in the first hour?
   (ii) How many times do they pass each other?

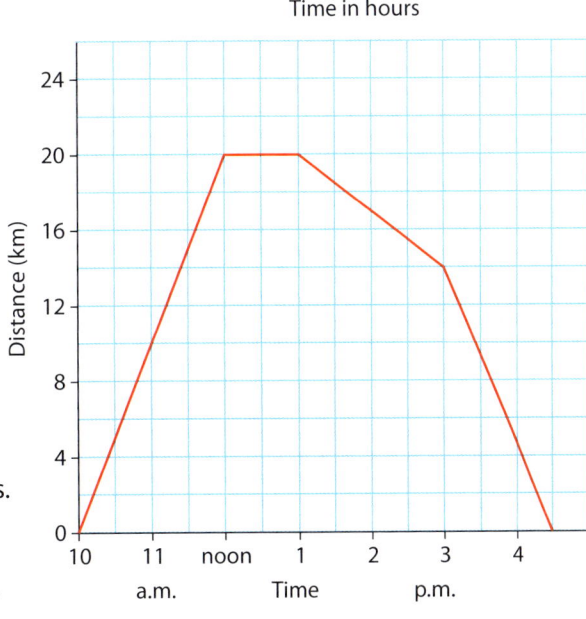

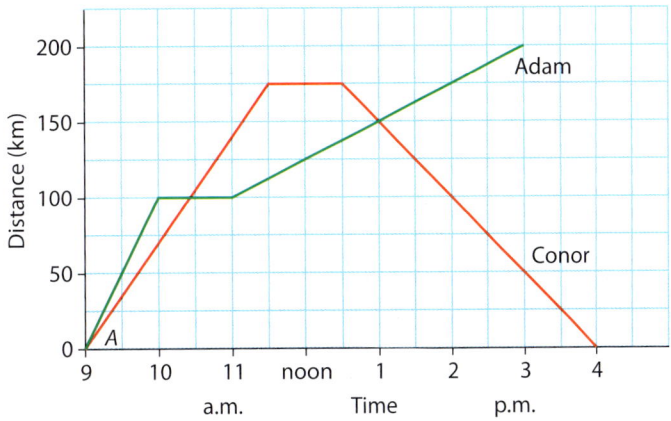

Text & Tests 2 Higher Level

  (iii) At what time do they pass the second time?
  (iv) How far apart are they at 3.00 p.m.?
  (v) How far does each man travel altogether?

5. The given graph indicates the distance a cyclist must travel to work.
   Use the graph to determine:
   (i) the distance to work
   (ii) the time taken to get to work
   (iii) the distance travelled after
      (a) 10 minutes
      (b) 17 minutes
   (iv) the time taken to travel
      (a) 6 km
      (b) 11 km
   (v) the average speed for the whole distance. (Exclude the two minute stop.)

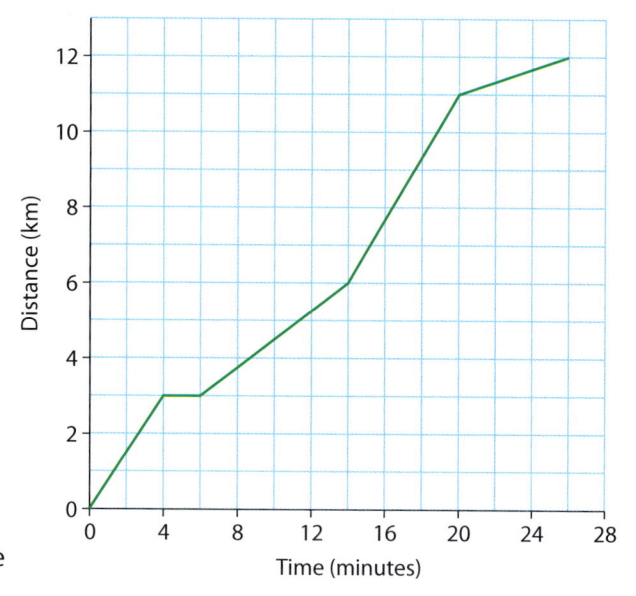

6. The graph shows the journeys of two motorists and gives their distances from their home town.
   (i) How far is David from the town when Darren starts his journey?
   (ii) At approximately what times do their paths cross?
   (iii) At what time does David begin his return journey?
   (iv) How far is Darren from town when David begins his return journey? 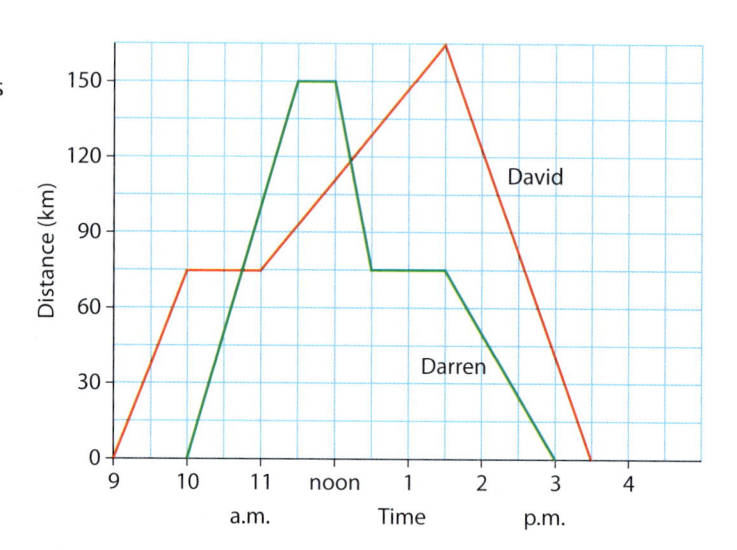
   (v) Who returns to town first? What time elapses before the other motorist arrives?

Chapter 20 Drawing and interpreting real-life graphs

7. Two aircraft were flying the air route from *A* to *B* but in opposite directions. The distance from *A* is shown on the graph alongside. Use the graph to determine:
  (i) the distance from *A* to *B*
  (ii) in which direction the flight was completed more rapidly, and by how much
  (iii) how long into the flight the planes were when they crossed
  (iv) the average speed of the flight in each direction.

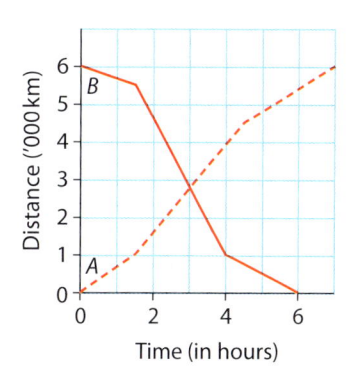

8. The given distance–time graph describes the journey of a family travelling from a French ferry-port to their campside for a holiday. The distance is 590 km.

Describe which line segment or point is appropriate for these statements:
  (i) "We will have lunch now."
  (ii) "This is the fastest section."
  (iii) "At last we have arrived."
  (iv) "We are only stopping for petrol."
  (v) "This is the slowest section."
  (vi) "This is the longest section."

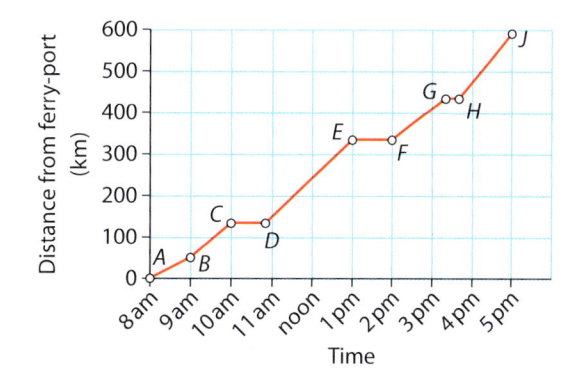

Estimate the average speed for the whole journey, excluding stops.

9. Noel cycled to his friend's place. He started at 8.00 a.m. and covered 15 km in the first hour. After resting for half an hour, he then covered the next 20 km to his friend's place in two hours.
  (i) At what time did he reach his friend's place?
  (ii) How far was it from his home to his friend's place?
  (iii) Using a scale 1 cm : 5 km on the distance axis and 1 cm : $\frac{1}{2}$ hr on the time axis, make a travel graph for Noel's trip.

10. Abdul is going to college, 1.25 km from his home.
He walks 250 metres to the bus stop. This takes him 4 minutes.
A bus arrives after 5 minutes and the journey takes 6 minutes.
  (i) Draw a distance–time graph for his journey.
  (ii) Work out the speed of the bus in
    (a) metres/minute   (b) km/hour.

Investigation:

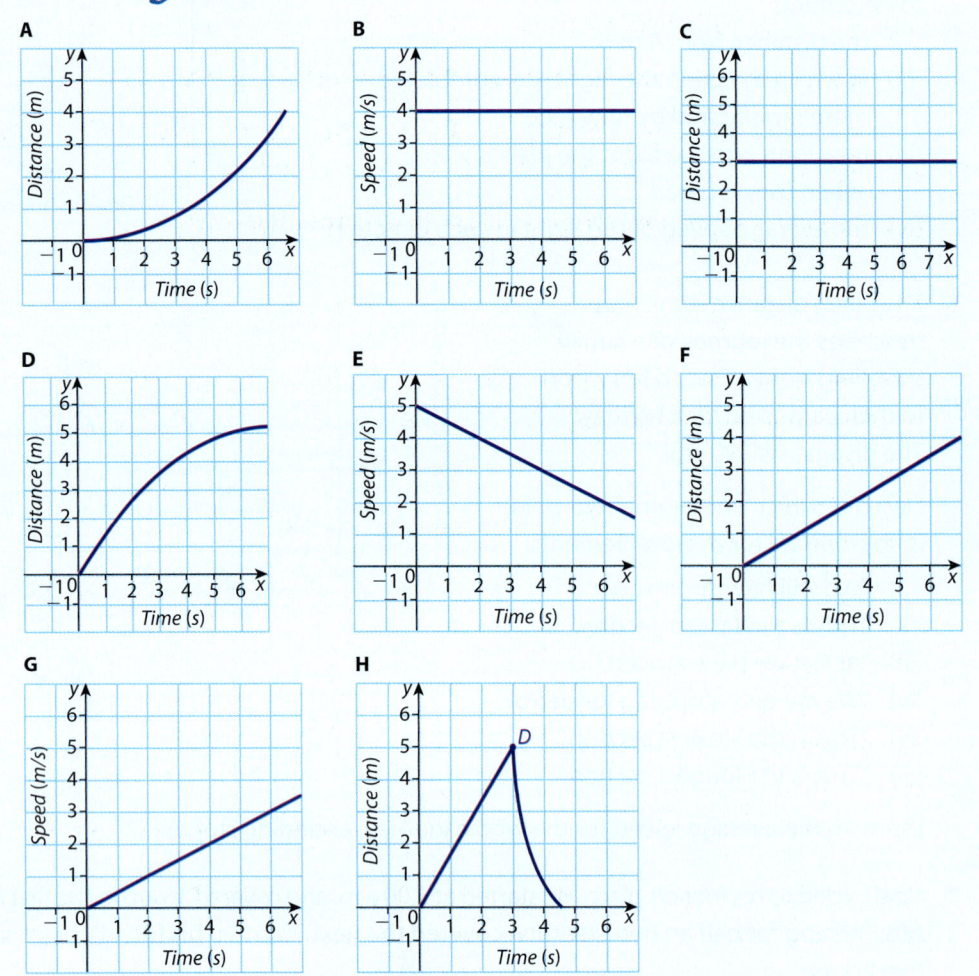

A — Distance (m) vs Time (s): curve increasing (concave up)

B — Speed (m/s) vs Time (s): constant horizontal line at 4

C — Distance (m) vs Time (s): constant horizontal line at 3

D — Distance (m) vs Time (s): curve increasing (concave down)

E — Speed (m/s) vs Time (s): straight line decreasing from 5

F — Distance (m) vs Time (s): straight line increasing from 0

G — Speed (m/s) vs Time (s): straight line increasing from 0

H — Distance (m) vs Time (s): rises to peak D at 5, then decreases

The 8 graphs above, track the motion of a car.

(i) By investigating each of the graphs, describe the motion indicated.
(Pay particular attention to quantity measured on the vertical axis)

(ii) State, giving reasons, which 3 pairs of graphs are linked.

Chapter 20 Drawing and interpreting real-life graphs

Section 20.2 Directly proportional graphs

Lucy is paid for the hours that she works at the rate of €12 per hour.
If she works 2 hours, she is paid €12 × 2 = €24.
If she works 5 hours, she is paid €12 × 5 = €60.

The hours worked and the pay received are said to be **directly proportional**.

When two quantities are in direct proportion, a graph is particularly useful for illustrating how one quantity increases (or decreases) relative to the second quantity.

Directly proportional graphs are always **straight lines through the origin**.

Example 1

The graph below shows the relationship between kilograms and pounds.

Use the graph to approximately convert
- (i) 20 pounds to kilograms (kg)
- (ii) 14 pounds to kilograms
- (iii) 4 kg to pounds
- (iv) 7.5 kg to pounds.

From the graph,
- (i) 20 pounds = 9.1 kg
- (ii) 14 pounds = 6.4 kg
- (iii) 4 kg = 8.8 pounds
- (iv) 7.5 kg = 16.5 pounds

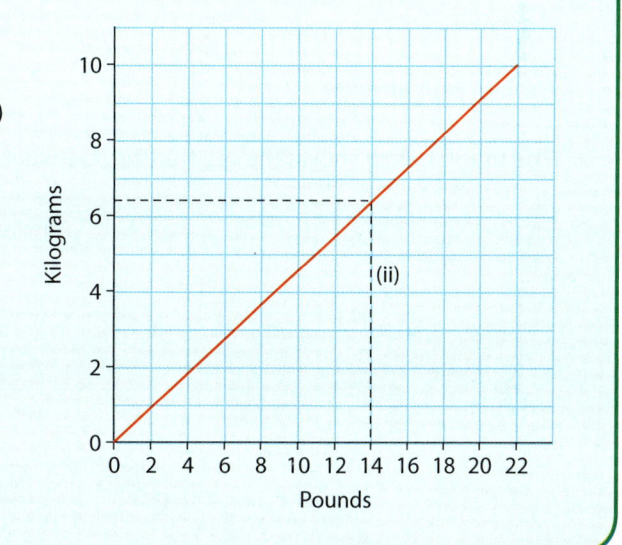

Note:

(i) If y is **directly proportional** to x

$$\therefore y = mx$$

(ii) If y is **proportional** to x

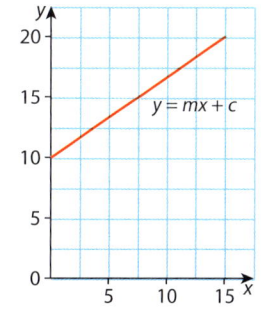

$$\therefore y = mx + c$$

m is the constant of proportionality.

Text & Tests 2 Higher Level

Exercise 20.2

1. In which of these graphs is h directly proportional to t?

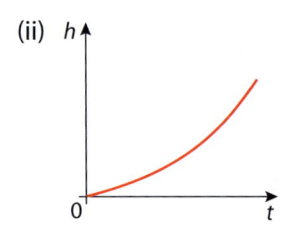

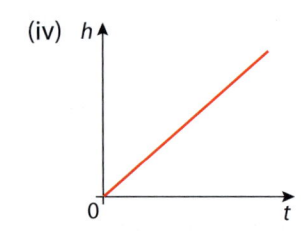

(i), (ii), (iii), (iv)

Explain your answer.

2. The graph below shows the relationship between kilometres and miles.

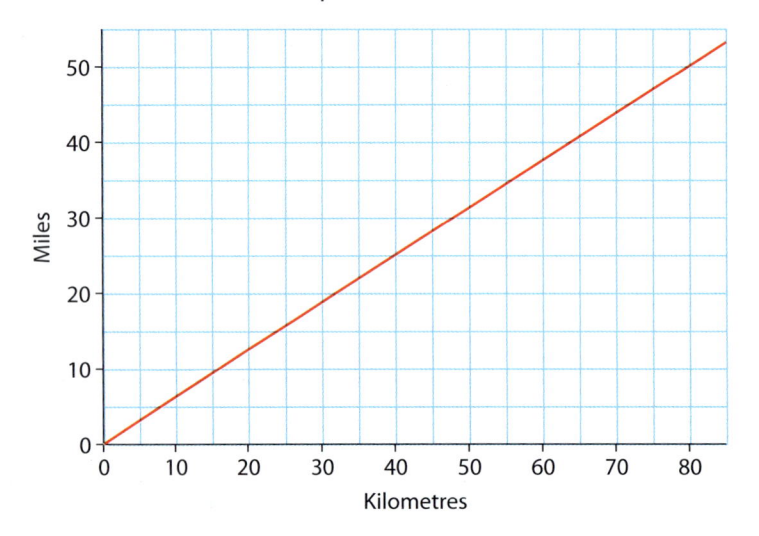

Use the graph to convert approximately

(i) 60 km to miles (ii) 80 km to miles
(iii) 30 miles to km (iv) 15 miles to km.

Is the given graph a directly proportional one?

Chapter 20 Drawing and interpreting real-life graphs

3. The graph below shows the relationship between degrees Celsius (°C) and degrees Fahrenheit (°F).

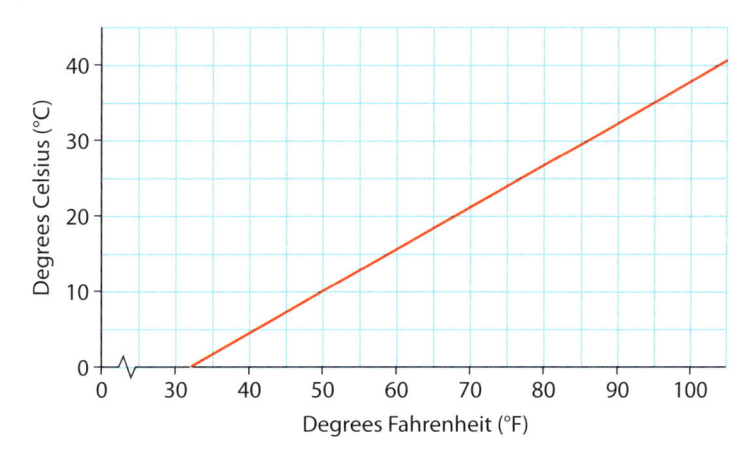

   Is this a directly proportional graph? Explain your answer.
   Use the graph to convert approximately
   (i) 35°C to Fahrenheit
   (ii) 15°C to Fahrenheit
   (iii) 50°F to Celsius
   (iv) 100°F to Celsius.

   If the temperature in a city on a particular day ranges between 55°F and 90°F, express this range in °C.

4. Television repair charges depend on the length of time taken for the repair, as shown on the graph.

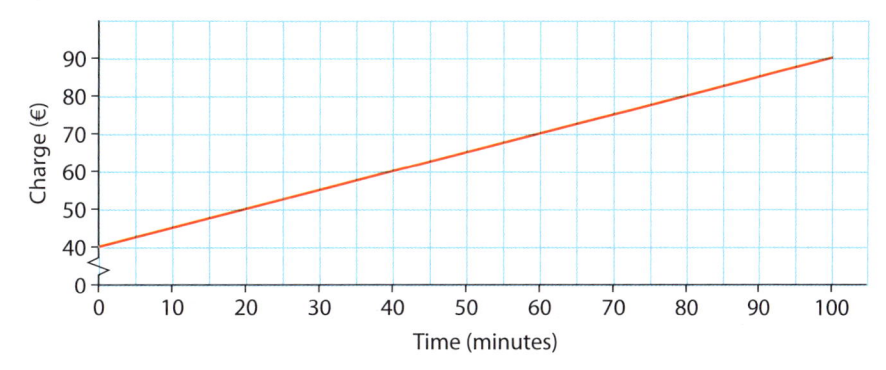

   (i) What is the charge for a repair that took 60 minutes?
   (ii) What is the charge for a repair that took 30 minutes?
   (iii) If the charge was €80, how long did the repair take?
   (iv) If the charge was €60, how long did the repair take?

   The standing charge is the basic charge before the time charge is added.
   (v) What is this standing charge?

Text & Tests 2 Higher Level

5. The given diagram shows that the length of the shadow cast by a tree at midday is directly proportional to the height of the tree.

 (i) What is the length of the shadow when the tree is 8 m in height?
 (ii) By using two points on the line, find the equation of the line in terms of s and h.
 (iii) Use the equation you have found to write down the length of the shadow when the tree is 15 metres in height.

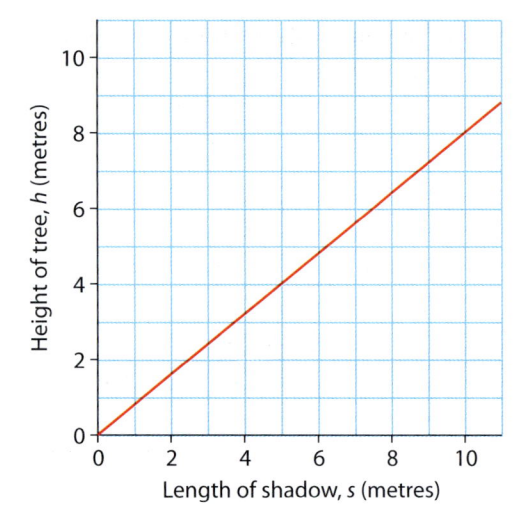

6. Is each of these statements true or false?

 (i) The cost of petrol is directly proportional to the quantity purchased.
 (ii) The height of a person is directly proportional to their age.
 (iii) The area of a square is directly proportional to the length of the side.
 (iv) The distance travelled in a certain time by a car travelling at constant speed is directly proportional to the speed of the car.
 (v) The time taken for a journey is directly proportional to the speed of travel.

7. The graph below shows the cost of using broadband internet for one month on three different tariffs.

The three tariffs are:
Tariff 1: Rental €30 + 10c/GB
Tariff 2: No rental but 30c/GB
Tariff 3: Rental €37.50 + 5c/GB with the first 60GB free

 (i) Match each tariff with the letter of its graph.

Carol downloads more than 140 Gigabytes of data each month.

 (ii) Explain which tariff would be the cheapest for her to use.

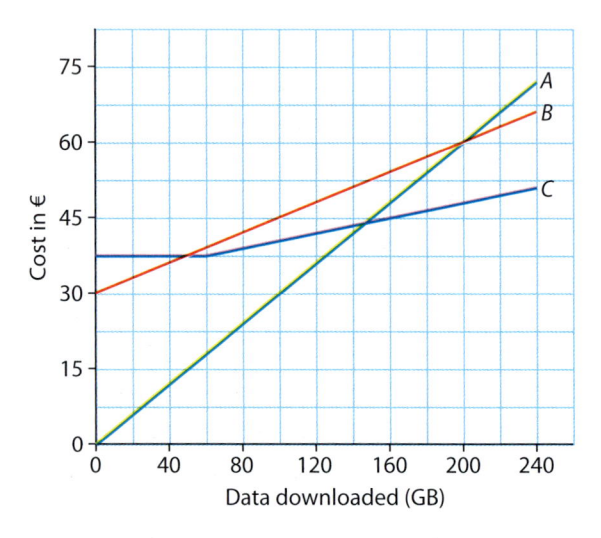

Chapter 20 Drawing and interpreting real-life graphs

8. This graph shows how much petrol two cars use.

    ———————— David's car
    - - - - - - - - Stephen's car

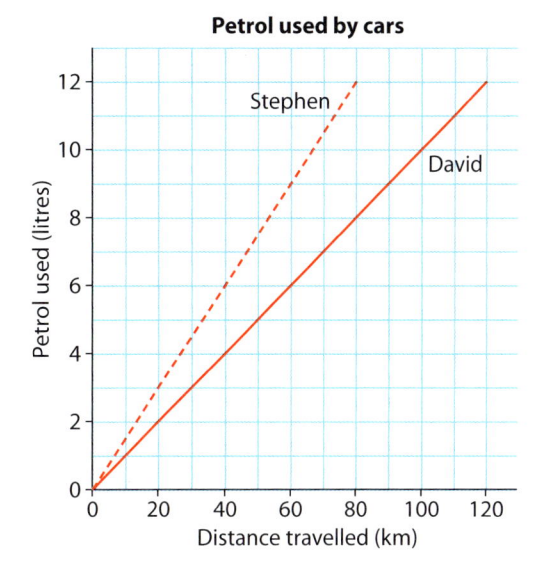

    (i) David's car travelled 80 km. How much petrol did it use?
    (ii) Stephen's car used 9 litres of petrol one day. How far did it go?
    (iii) How much more petrol does Stephen's car use than David's car when each car travels 60 km?
    (iv) Is each line graph directly proportional? Explain your answer.
    (v) Find the equation of the broken red line in the form $y = mx$.
    Now use this equation to find the number of litres used when the car travels 300 km.

Investigation:

In a fitness test, a student runs from a baseline in the gym to a halfway line and back again. This is called a lap. The result of student A's test is shown.

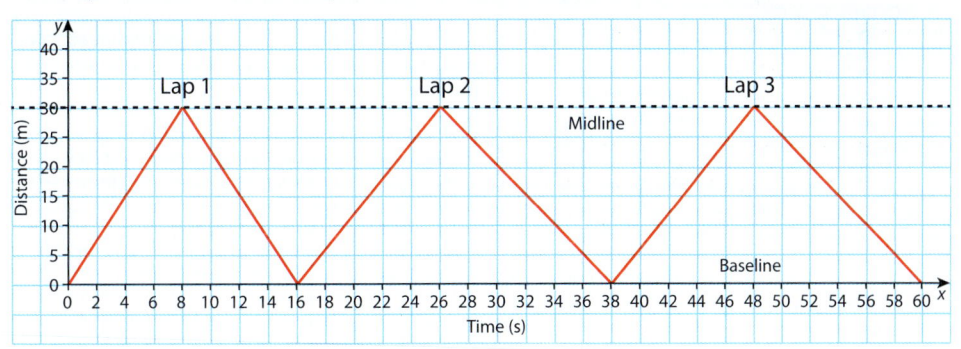

Answer the following questions about his test:

1. How far is the baseline from the halfway line?
2. How long did each lap take?
3. Write down the average speed of the student for each lap in m/s.

Using a stopwatch and a fixed distance in the gym, draw a real-life fitness graph for each student in your group. Find out how many laps each student can complete in 40 seconds and write down the average speed for each lap.

Text & Tests 2 Higher Level

Section 20.3 Real-life graphs

When water is poured into the vessel below **at a steady rate**, the water will rise in the vessel also at a steady rate.
The graph of the water's height as time passes is shown on the right below.

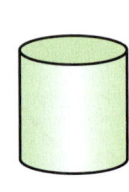

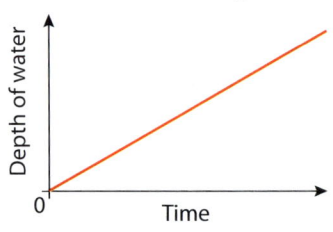

The graph is a straight line because the water rises at a **constant rate**.

Containers with sides that bulge out have a curved line graph. They may start steep, get less steep and then get steep again.
The graph of the water's height for the given container is shown on the right.
The top part of the graph is a straight line because the top part rises at a constant rate.

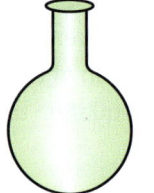

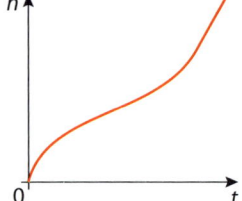

Example 1

Match these containers to their graphs when they are filled with liquid at a constant rate.

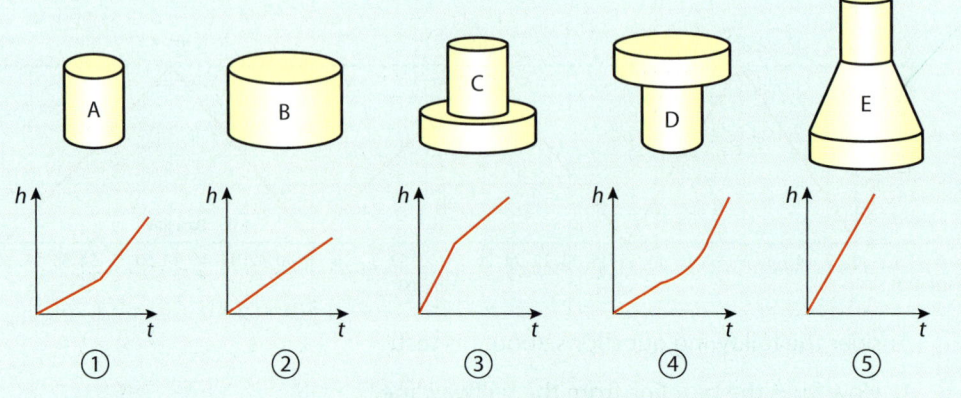

A is matched to ⑤ since A has straight sides and is thin.
B is matched to ② since B has straight sides but is wider than A.
C is matched to ① since C is initially wide with straight sides and then narrow with straight sides – hence two line segments.
D is matched to ③ since D is initially narrow with straight sides and then wide with straight sides.
E is matched to ④ since E has three sections which can be identified on the graph.

Chapter 20 Drawing and interpreting real-life graphs

Exercise 20.3

1. Water is poured at the same rate into each of these containers.
Match these containers with their graphs showing the rate at which the water is rising.

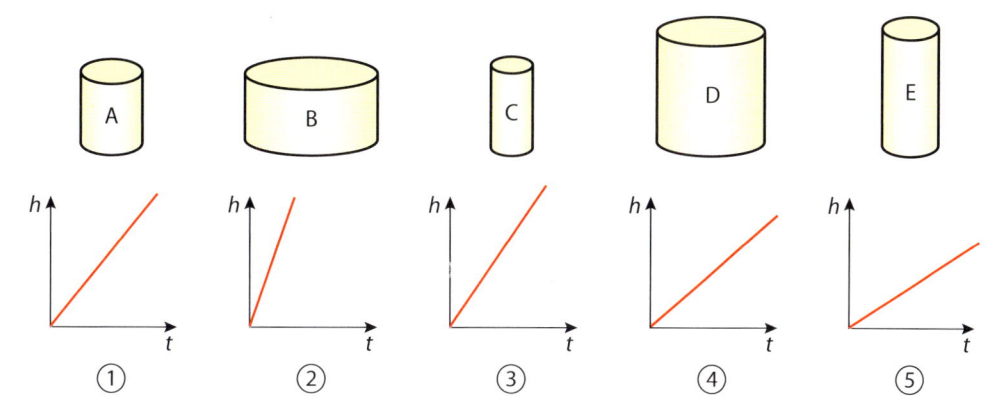

2. Water is added to the tank shown at a steady rate.
Which graph best represents the increase in the water level h?

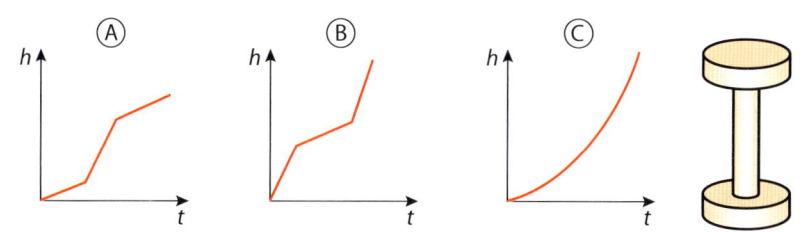

3. Here are three different-shaped bowls.

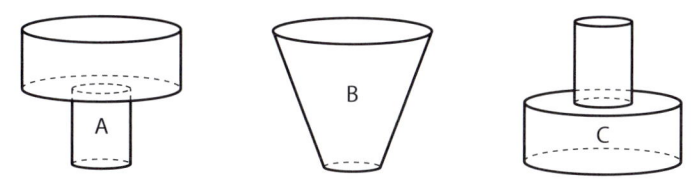

(i) Which description of filling the bowls with water goes with which bowl?
(a) The water level goes up fast at first and then suddenly goes up more slowly.
(b) The water level goes up slowly at first, then changes to go up more quickly.
(c) The water level starts by going up quickly, but gets slower and slower.

(ii) Which graph goes with which bowl?

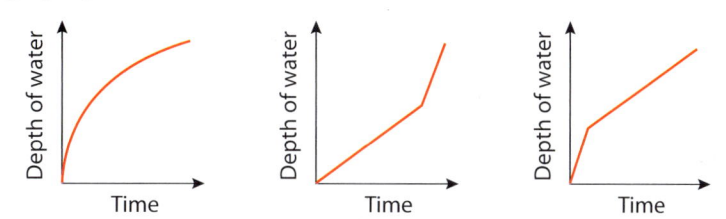

Text & Tests 2 Higher Level

4. Match the graph to the story.

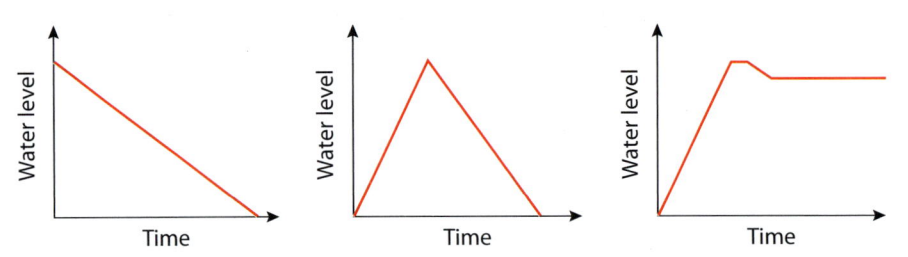

   (i) I fill a bucket with water. After a few minutes, my dog drinks some of the water. I decide to leave the water in the bucket in case he wants a drink later.
   (ii) I quickly fill a bucket with water but the bucket is spilt and the water runs out.
   (iii) I start with a full bucket of water and pour the water slowly over my seedlings until the bucket is empty.

5. Liquid is poured at a constant rate into these five containers.
   The height, h cm, of the liquid in the containers is plotted against time, t seconds.
   Match these containers with their graphs.

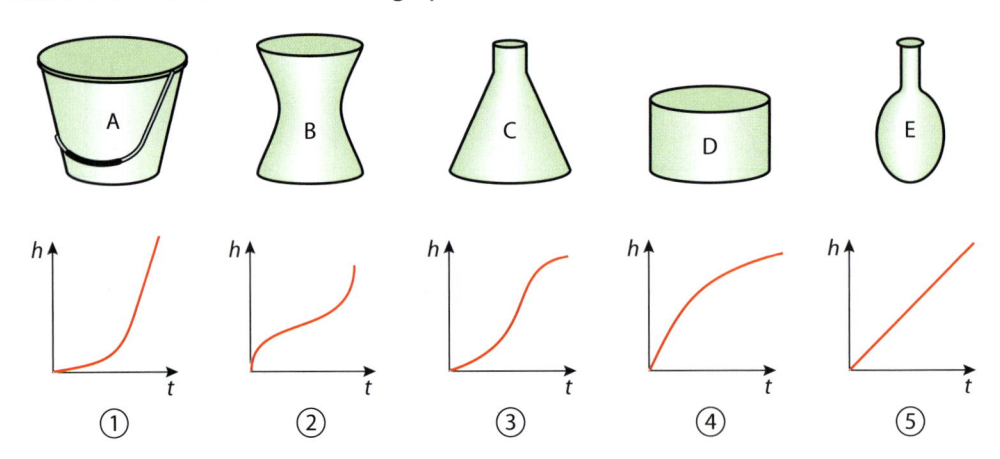

6. Liquid is poured into each of these containers at a constant rate.
   Draw, for each container and on the same graph, the height of the liquid h against the time t in seconds.

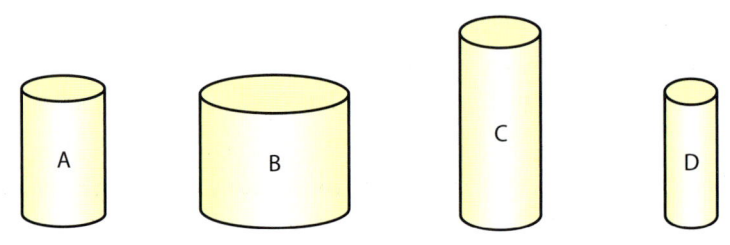

Chapter 20 Drawing and interpreting real-life graphs

7. Here are three containers.
   For each one, sketch a graph showing how it fills up with water.

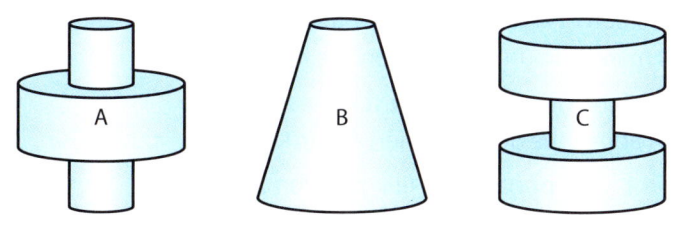

8. Liquid is poured into each of these receptacles at a constant rate.
   Draw, on the same graph, the height of the liquid h, against time t, in seconds.

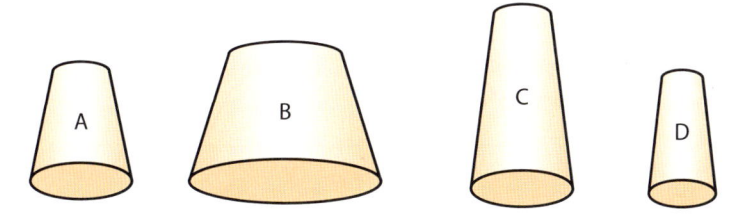

9. The graph shows the temperature inside a new fridge.
   The temperature was taken every minute over a two-hour period.

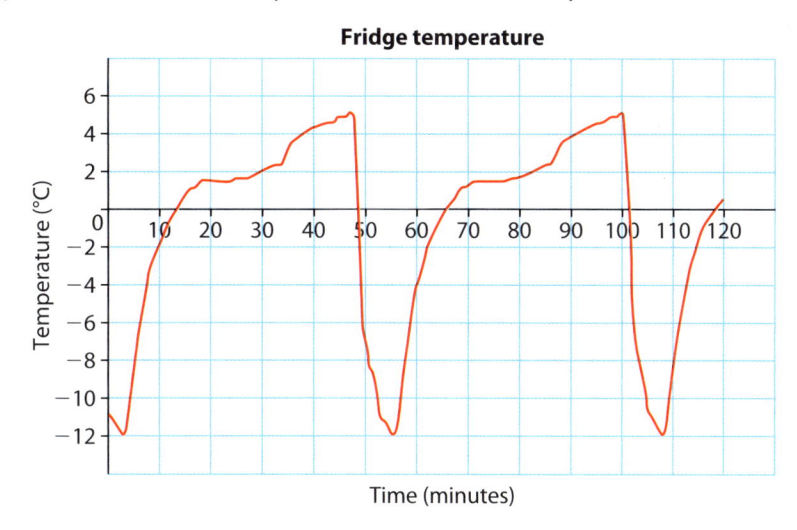

   The fridge has a motor which cools down the inside.
   The motor is switched on and off by a thermostat.
   (i) What happens to the temperature in the fridge when the motor is running?
   (ii) At what temperature does the thermostat switch the motor on?
   (iii) What happens to the temperature when the motor is not running?
   (iv) At what temperature does the thermostat switch the motor off?
   (v) For about how long does the motor run each time it is switched on?

Text & Tests 2 Higher Level

10. A point *A* is on the circumference of a wheel. The wheel completes one revolution where the starting position of *A* can be at any of the points 1, 2, 3 or 4 marked in the diagram on the right.

    Which one of the graphs below best represents the height of *A* above the ground when *A* starts at:

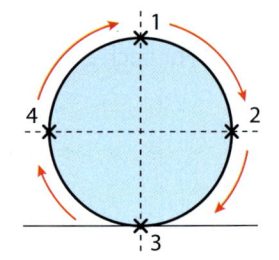

    (i) position 1   (ii) position 3   (iii) position 2 ?

    Note: You will need to know that the wheel is rolled from left to right.

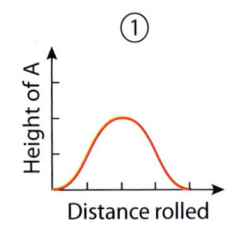

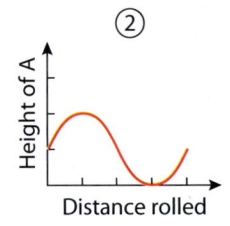

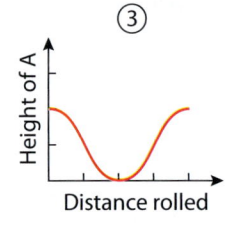

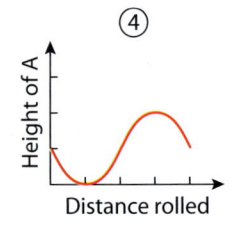

11. Each of the four containers pictured is filled with water at a steady rate. When the level of water in each container was plotted, the graphs ① to ④ were obtained.
    Match each container to its graph.

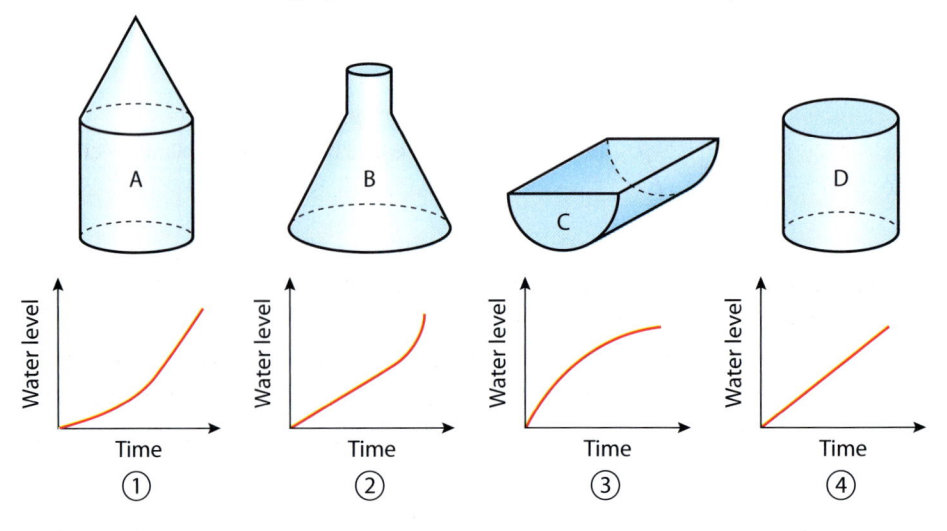

Chapter 20 Drawing and interpreting real-life graphs

Assignment:

A: Alva and Sean travel on the same road between town A and town B.

Based on the information given below, copy and complete a large distance–time graph for their journeys. Then write in the answers to the questions in the panel provided.

Compare your answers with other groups in your class.

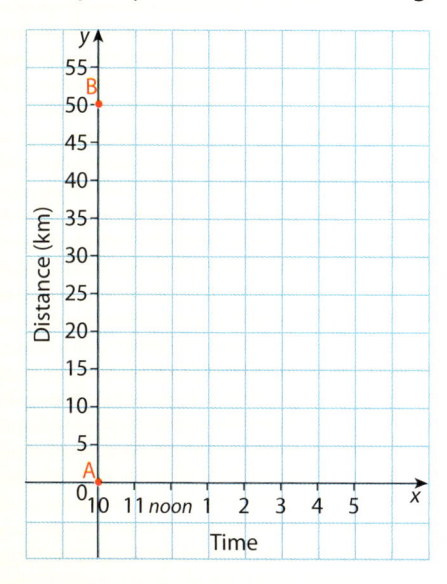

Answers

(a) _____

(b) _____

(c) _____

(d) _____

(e) _____

(f) _____

Sean:
Sean leaves A at 10 o'clock and travels 25 km in 2.5 hours. He then rests until 2 o'clock before continuing his journey arriving in B, 3 hours later.

Alva:
Alva lives 10 km away from A on the road to B. She also starts her journey at 10 o'clock. After 1 hour, when she has travelled 15 km, she realises that she forgot to collect something from a friend's house 10 km back down the road. It takes her 30 minutes for the return journey. Alva stays with her friend until 12.30 before travelling to A, a journey which takes 2 hours. Finally, she travels directly to B at 75 km/hour.

From your graph find:

(a) Who arrives at B first?
(b) When do Sean and Alva first meet?
(c) How far is Sean form B at 2.30 pm?
(d) How far does Sean travel?
(e) How far are Alva and Sean apart when Alva is at town A?
(f) How far does Alva travel?

Text & Tests 2 Higher Level

B1: Copy and complete the following:

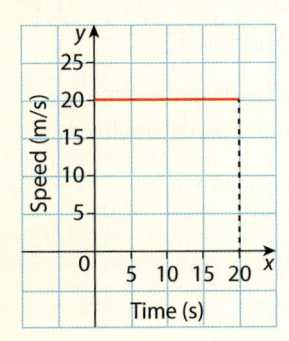

A car travels at 20 m/s for 20 s, the distance travelled = _____ m

The area under the speed-time graph = _____ m

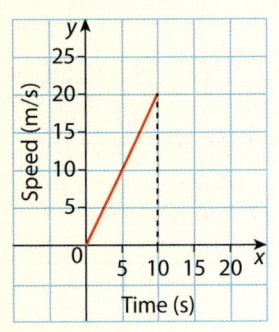

A car starts from 0 m/s and accelerates to 20 m/s in 10 s, the average speed is _____ m/s
The distance travelled at the average speed = _____ m

The area under the speed-time graph = _____ m

What conclusion can you deduce from this exercise?

Conclusion: _____

B2:
It can be shown that the area under a speed-time graph is equal to the distance travelled.

The following graph shows the speed of a car as it travels between two sets of traffic lights.

(a) Describe the motion of the car between the sets of traffic lights.

(b) Make a poster of the graph indicating the area under each section of the graph.

(c) Calculate the total **distance** travelled.

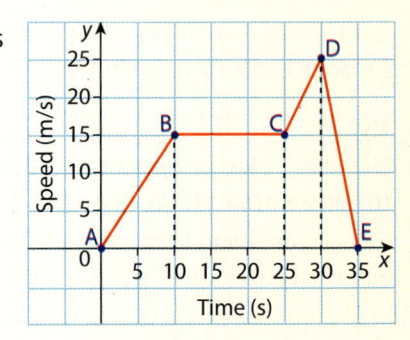

(d) For varying speeds, the
  Average speed = $\frac{Total\ distance}{Total\ time}$, hence find the average speed of the car.

Average speed = _____

Algebra 2

chapter 21

From first year, you will recall how to:

- add and subtract fractions,
- solve a linear equation,
- substitute values into an expression.

In this chapter, you will learn to:

- simplify algebraic fractions,
- add and subtract algebraic fractions,
- solve equations involving fractions,
- create and solve word problems resulting in equations with fractions,
- rearrange a formula to change the subject,
- evaluate a formula using substitution,
- derive and use a formula that describes a given situation.

Section 21.1 Adding algebraic fractions

To add $\frac{3}{4} + \frac{4}{5}$, we find the LCM of 4 and 5, i.e. 20.
We now express each fraction with 20 as denominator.

$$\therefore \frac{3}{4} + \frac{4}{5} = \frac{5(3)}{20} + \frac{4(4)}{20} = \frac{15}{20} + \frac{16}{20} = \frac{15 + 16}{20} = \frac{31}{20}$$

Similarly, $\frac{6}{7} - \frac{2}{3} = \frac{3(6) - 7(2)}{21} = \frac{18 - 14}{21} = \frac{4}{21}$

Algebraic fractions can be added or subtracted in the same way as numerical fractions.

Example 1

Express as a single fraction: $\frac{5x - 3}{2} - \frac{2x + 1}{3}$

The LCM of 2 and 3 is 6.

$$\frac{5x - 3}{2} - \frac{2x + 1}{3} = \frac{3(5x - 3) - 2(2x + 1)}{6}$$

$$= \frac{15x - 9 - 4x - 2}{6} = \frac{11x - 11}{6}$$

Note: the use of brackets in the example above.

Simplifying algebraic terms

The fraction $\frac{8}{12}$ can be simplified by dividing the numerator and denominator by 4, as shown.

$$\frac{^2\cancel{8}}{_3\cancel{12}} = \frac{2}{3}$$

Similarly, the algebraic fraction $\frac{4ab}{2b}$ can be simplified by dividing the numerator and denominator by any common factors.

Thus, $\frac{4ab}{2b} = \frac{^2\cancel{4} \times a \times \cancel{b}^1}{_1\cancel{2} \times \cancel{b}_1} = 2 \times a = 2a$

Example 2

Simplify each of the following:

(i) $\dfrac{9x^2y}{3x}$ (ii) $\dfrac{12a^3b}{ab^2}$

(i) $\dfrac{9x^2y}{3x} = \dfrac{^3\cancel{9} \times \cancel{x}^1 \times x \times y}{_1\cancel{3} \times \cancel{x}_1}$

$= 3xy$

(ii) $\dfrac{12a^3b}{ab^2} = \dfrac{12 \times a \times a \times \cancel{a}^1 \times \cancel{b}^1}{_1\cancel{a} \times b \times \cancel{b}_1}$

$= \dfrac{12a^2}{b}$

Example 3

Simplify $\dfrac{3}{4x-2} - \dfrac{1}{2x-1}$

The LCM of $(4x-2)$ and $(2x-1)$ is $(4x-2)(2x-1)$

$\therefore \dfrac{3}{4x-2} - \dfrac{1}{2x-1} = \dfrac{3(2x-1)}{(4x-2)(2x-1)} - \dfrac{(4x-2)}{(4x-2)(2x-1)}$

$= \dfrac{3(2x-1) - (4x-2)}{(4x-2)(2x-1)}$

$= \dfrac{6x - 3 - 4x + 2}{(4x-2)(2x-1)} = \dfrac{(2x-1)^1}{(4x-2)(2x-1)_1}$

$= \dfrac{1}{4x-2}$

Chapter 21 Algebra 2

Exercise 21.1

1. Simplify each of the following expressions:

(i) $\dfrac{10ab}{2b}$ (ii) $\dfrac{8xy}{4x}$ (iii) $\dfrac{15cd}{5d}$ (iv) $\dfrac{18ab}{6a}$

(v) $\dfrac{8x^2y}{4xy}$ (vi) $\dfrac{16b^2c}{2c}$ (vii) $\dfrac{14x^3y}{2x^2y}$ (viii) $\dfrac{28ab^2}{7ab}$

2. Simplify these expressions:

(i) $\dfrac{3}{x} \times \dfrac{4x}{9}$ (ii) $\dfrac{km}{4n} \times \dfrac{2n}{m}$ (iii) $\dfrac{ab}{3} \times \dfrac{6b}{a}$ (iv) $\dfrac{2ab \times 6a}{3a}$

(v) $\dfrac{x}{3} \div \dfrac{x}{6}$ (vi) $\dfrac{3}{2x} \div \dfrac{1}{3x}$ (vii) $\dfrac{3ab^2}{2} \div \dfrac{ab}{6}$ (viii) $\dfrac{8a \times 3ak}{2a \times 6k}$

3.

A	E	G	L	M	N	O	P	R
$2b$	$4bc$	bc^2	$4d$	cd	$2b^2$	$3bd$	$3c$	$2b^2d$

Simplify each expression below as far as you can.
Use the code above to find a letter for each expression.
Rearrange each set of letters to spell a fruit.

(i) $\dfrac{8cd}{2c}$ $\dfrac{12bc}{3}$ $\dfrac{15cd}{5d}$ $\dfrac{4bc}{2c}$ $\dfrac{9c^2b}{3cb}$

(ii) $\dfrac{18b^2d}{6b}$ $\dfrac{10ab^2}{5a}$ $\dfrac{20b^2c^2}{5bc}$ $\dfrac{12cd^5}{3cd^4}$ $\dfrac{5c^2d}{5c}$

4. Express each of the following as a single fraction:

(i) $\dfrac{1}{2} + \dfrac{2}{3}$ (ii) $\dfrac{3}{4} + \dfrac{3}{5}$ (iii) $\dfrac{5}{12} + \dfrac{2}{12} + \dfrac{1}{12}$

(iv) $\dfrac{7}{8} - \dfrac{3}{4}$ (v) $\dfrac{x}{2} + \dfrac{x}{3}$ (vi) $\dfrac{x}{5} + \dfrac{x}{3}$

Express each of these as a single fraction.

5. $\dfrac{3x}{4} + \dfrac{5x}{2}$ **6.** $\dfrac{3x}{5} + \dfrac{2x}{3}$

7. $\dfrac{x}{4} - \dfrac{x}{6}$ **8.** $\dfrac{x}{2} - \dfrac{x}{5}$

9. $\dfrac{7x}{5} - \dfrac{x}{2}$ **10.** $\dfrac{3x}{4} - \dfrac{2x}{5}$

Text & Tests 2 Higher Level

11. $\dfrac{3x-4}{5} + \dfrac{5x-2}{5}$

12. $\dfrac{3x-2}{4} + \dfrac{5x+6}{4}$

13. $\dfrac{2x+1}{3} + \dfrac{2x-3}{3}$

14. $\dfrac{2x-1}{6} + \dfrac{x-3}{4}$

15. $\dfrac{5x-1}{4} - \dfrac{2x-4}{5}$

16. $\dfrac{2x-3}{2} + \dfrac{x-1}{4} - \dfrac{5}{6}$

17. $\dfrac{x-6}{3} + \dfrac{3}{4} - \dfrac{3x-4}{2}$

18. $\dfrac{3x-1}{4} - \dfrac{x}{10} - \dfrac{4x+2}{5}$

19. $\dfrac{3x+5}{6} - \dfrac{1}{12} - \dfrac{2x+3}{4}$

20. $\dfrac{3}{5} - \dfrac{2x-1}{10} + \dfrac{3x-2}{4}$

21. Express in its simplest form the perimeter of the given triangle.

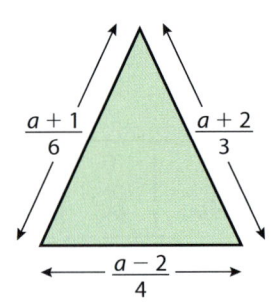

    (Triangle with sides $\dfrac{a+1}{6}$, $\dfrac{a+2}{3}$, and base $\dfrac{a-2}{4}$)

22. Simplify each of the following:

    (a) $\dfrac{-2}{x-1} + \dfrac{3}{x-1}$

    (b) $\dfrac{2}{4x-2} - \dfrac{1}{2x-1}$

    (c) $\dfrac{3}{x-2} + \dfrac{1}{2x-1}$

23. Simplify:

    (a) $\dfrac{3}{x+1} - \dfrac{2}{x-1}$

    (b) $\dfrac{3}{x-3} + \dfrac{4}{2x+1}$

    (c) $\dfrac{2}{3x-1} + \dfrac{1}{3x+1}$

24. $R = \dfrac{r}{a} + \dfrac{r}{3}$, find r in terms of R and a.
    Hence evaluate r when $R = 4$ and $a = 2$.

Section 21.2 Solving equations involving fractions

Consider the equation $\dfrac{x-1}{5} = 4$.

To get rid of the fraction, we multiply both sides by 5.

$\therefore \dfrac{{}^1\cancel{5}(x-1)}{\cancel{5}_1} = 4 \times 5$

$x - 1 = 20$

$x - 1 + 1 = 20 + 1$

$x = 21$

> If an equation contains more than one fraction, we multiply each part by the lowest common multiple (LCM) of the denominators.

482

Chapter 21 Algebra 2

Example 1

Solve each of these equations:

(i) $\dfrac{3x}{4} - \dfrac{x}{2} = 3$ (ii) $\dfrac{2x-5}{3} = \dfrac{x-2}{2}$

(i) The LCM of 4 and 2 is 4.
Multiply each term by 4.

$$\dfrac{4(3x)}{4} - \dfrac{4(x)}{2} = 3 \times 4$$
$$3x - 2x = 12$$
$$x = 12$$

(ii) The LCM of 3 and 2 is 6.
Multiply each term by 6.

$$\dfrac{6(2x-5)}{3} = \dfrac{6(x-2)}{2}$$
$$2(2x-5) = 3(x-2)$$
$$4x - 10 = 3x - 6$$
$$4x - 3x - 10 = 3x - 6 - 3x$$
$$x - 10 = -6$$
$$x - 10 + 10 = -6 + 10$$
$$x = 4$$

Example 2

Solve the equation: $\dfrac{3x-1}{6} - \dfrac{x-3}{4} = \dfrac{4}{3}$

The LCM of 6, 4 and 3 is 12.
We now multiply each term by 12.

$$\dfrac{12(3x-1)}{6} - \dfrac{12(x-3)}{4} = \dfrac{12(4)}{3}$$
$$2(3x-1) - 3(x-3) = 4(4)$$
$$6x - 2 - 3x + 9 = 16$$
$$3x + 7 = 16$$
$$3x + 7 - 7 = 16 - 7$$
$$3x = 9$$
$$x = 3$$

Exercise 21.2

Solve the following equations:

1. $\dfrac{2x}{3} = 6$

2. $\dfrac{3x}{5} = 3$

3. $\dfrac{x}{2} = \dfrac{6}{4}$

4. $\dfrac{3x}{4} = \dfrac{9}{2}$

5. $\dfrac{5x}{3} = 10$

6. $\dfrac{x-3}{2} = 4$

Text & Tests 2 Higher Level

7. $\dfrac{3x-1}{4} = 2$

8. $\dfrac{3x-1}{4} = 8$

9. $\dfrac{2x+1}{3} = \dfrac{1}{2}$

10. $\dfrac{2x-5}{3} = \dfrac{x-2}{3}$

11. $\dfrac{x-3}{4} = \dfrac{x-2}{5}$

12. $\dfrac{x+2}{6} = \dfrac{2x-5}{3}$

13. $\dfrac{2x}{5} + \dfrac{x}{2} = \dfrac{9}{2}$

14. $\dfrac{2x}{3} - \dfrac{x}{4} = \dfrac{5}{6}$

15. $\dfrac{3x}{4} - \dfrac{5x}{8} = \dfrac{1}{2}$

16. $\dfrac{2x}{3} - \dfrac{x}{4} = \dfrac{5}{2}$

17. $\dfrac{2x-1}{3} + \dfrac{x}{4} = \dfrac{6}{4}$

18. $\dfrac{x-3}{6} = \dfrac{x}{5} - \dfrac{3}{2}$

19. $\dfrac{x+2}{4} + \dfrac{x-3}{2} = \dfrac{1}{2}$

20. $\dfrac{x+2}{4} - \dfrac{x-3}{3} = \dfrac{1}{2}$

21. $\dfrac{3x-1}{6} - \dfrac{x-3}{4} = \dfrac{4}{3}$

22. $\dfrac{x-2}{5} + \dfrac{2x-3}{10} = \dfrac{1}{2}$

23. $\dfrac{2x-3}{5} + \dfrac{1}{20} = \dfrac{x-1}{4}$

24. $\dfrac{3x-1}{2} - \dfrac{2x-5}{3} = 2$

25. $\dfrac{x-2}{3} + \dfrac{x-3}{4} = \dfrac{x-1}{2}$

26. $\dfrac{2x-1}{4} - \dfrac{x-1}{5} = 1$

27. $\dfrac{3x-2}{6} - \dfrac{3x+1}{4} = \dfrac{2}{3}$

28. $\dfrac{3(x-4)}{5} + 3 = \dfrac{3(x-5)}{2}$

29. $\dfrac{4x+5}{5} + \dfrac{2x+7}{2} = \dfrac{3x}{10}$

30. The diagram shows an isosceles triangle ABC.

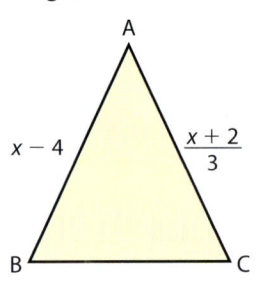

    [Triangle ABC with side AB labelled $x - 4$ and side AC labelled $\dfrac{x+2}{3}$]

    If $|AB| = |AC|$,

    (i) write down an equation in terms of x.
    (ii) work out the length of [AB].

Section 21.3 Solving problems involving fractions

The ability to change a problem expressed in words into a mathematical sentence is very important in mathematics.

You will already have changed statements like that shown on the right into mathematical sentences.

> I think of a number.
> I take off 5.
> I multiply the result by 3.
> My answer is 21.
> What is my number?

Chapter 21 Algebra 2

Discuss which of these equations you would use to solve this puzzle.

| $3x - 5 = 21$ | $3(x - 5) = 21$ | $x - 5 \times 3 = 21$ |

In this section we will deal with some simple problems that involve the use of fractions.

Example 1

If the sum of a quarter of a number and a fifth of the same number is 18, find the number.

Let x be the number.

$\frac{1}{4}$ of the number $= \frac{x}{4}$ $\frac{1}{5}$ of the number $= \frac{x}{5}$

The equation is: $\frac{x}{4} + \frac{x}{5} = 18$

Multiply each term by 20, the LCM of 4 and 5.

$$\frac{20(x)}{4} + \frac{20(x)}{5} = \frac{20(18)}{1}$$
$$5x + 4x = 360$$
$$9x = 360$$
$$x = 40$$

The required number is 40.

Example 2

One number is 4 bigger than another number.
One quarter of the smaller number and one third of the larger sum to 6.
Find the numbers.

Let x and $(x + 4)$ be the numbers.

$\frac{1}{4}$ of the smaller number $= \frac{x}{4}$ $\frac{1}{3}$ of the larger number $= \frac{x + 4}{3}$

Equation: $\frac{x}{4} + \frac{x + 4}{3} = \frac{6}{1}$

485

Text & Tests 2 Higher Level

> Multiply each term by 12, the LCM of 4, 3 and 1.
>
> $$\frac{12(x)}{4} + \frac{12(x+4)}{3} = 12(6)$$
>
> $$3x + 4(x + 4) = 72$$
> $$3x + 4x + 16 = 72$$
> $$7x + 16 = 72$$
> $$7x + 16 - 16 = 72 - 16$$
> $$7x = 56$$
> $$x = 8$$
>
> The two numbers x and $(x + 4)$ are 8 and 12.

Exercise 21.3

1. The sum of a number and half the number is 12. Find the number.

2. If the sum of half a number and a third of the same number is 15, find the number.

3. The sum of half and three quarters of a certain number is 20. Find the number.

4. When half a certain number is taken from three quarters of the number, the result is 5. Find the number.

5. One number is 5 bigger than another number. When one third of the smaller number is added to half the bigger number, the answer is 10. Find the smaller number.

6. When 5 is added to a number and the result is divided by 4, the answer is 3. Find the number.

7. When 3 is taken from four times a certain number and the result is divided by 7, the answer is 3. Find the number.

8. I think of a number x. I add 8 to the number and then divide the total by 3. The result is the same as half the number I thought of. Find the value of x.

9. One number is 3 greater than another number. When one sixth of the bigger number is taken from one third of the smaller one, the result is 2. Find the two numbers.

10. x and $x + 1$ are two consecutive natural numbers. When one fifth of the smaller number is added to one quarter of the larger one, the result is 7. Find the value of x.

11. A father is 30 years older than his son. When one fifth of the father's age is added to one third of the son's age, the result is 14 years. Find the son's age.

12. The length of a rectangle is $(2x + 3)$ cm.
    The width of the rectangle is $\frac{1}{2}(x + 3)$ cm.
    If the perimeter of the rectangle is 49 cm, find the value of x.

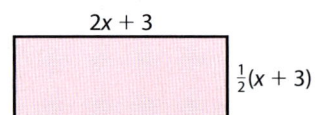

Section 21.4 Rearranging formulae

Examine the box on the right to see how the letters in the formula $a = 6b + 5$ have been changed around.

We have changed the formula from

$a = 6b + 5$ to $b = \dfrac{a-5}{6}$.

$a = 6b + 5$
$a - 5 = 6b + 5 - 5$
$a - 5 = 6b$
$\dfrac{a-5}{6} = b$ or $b = \dfrac{a-5}{6}$

In the formula $b = \dfrac{a-5}{6}$, we have expressed b in terms of a.

This is known as **rearranging the formula** to make b the **subject of the formula**.

The process of changing the subject of a formula is very similar to the steps we use when solving an equation.

> An equation remains unchanged if the same operation is performed on both sides.

The following examples will illustrate the basic rules for changing the subject of a formula.

Example 1

If $bc - d = a$, make c the subject of the formula.

$bc - d = a$
$\therefore \quad bc = a + d$ ... add d to both sides
$\therefore \quad c = \dfrac{a+d}{b}$ ... divide both sides by b

Example 2

If $a = \dfrac{b}{c} + bd$, make b the subject of the formula

$a = \dfrac{b}{c} + bd$
$ac = b + bcd$ ... multiply each term by c
$ac = b(1 + cd)$ ... factorise b out of each term.
$\dfrac{ac}{(1+cd)} = b$
$b = \dfrac{ac}{(1+cd)}$

Text & Tests 2 Higher Level

> **Example 3**
>
> If $y = \dfrac{c - ax}{b}$, make x the subject of the formula.
>
> $$y = \dfrac{c - ax}{b}$$
> $$by = c - ax \quad \text{... multiply each term by } b$$
> $$by + ax = c$$
> $$ax = c - by$$
> $$x = \dfrac{c - by}{a}$$

Exercise 21.4

1. Change the following equations to the form $y = \ldots$
   - (i) $2x + y - 4 = 0$
   - (ii) $2x + y = -7$
   - (iii) $3x + y - 7 = 0$

2. Make the underlined letter the subject of the formula in each of the following:
   - (i) $2\underline{x} - 4 = y$
   - (ii) $a = 8\underline{b} - 6$
   - (iii) $c = 4\underline{d} - 1$
   - (iv) $h = 2\underline{k} - 2$

3. Rearrange each of these formulas to make the underlined letter the subject:
   - (i) $a = 3\underline{b} - 5$
   - (ii) $b = 4\underline{w} + 2$
   - (iii) $d = 6\underline{e} - 12$
   - (iv) $g = 18 - 5\underline{h}$

4. Which of the following are correct rearrangements of $a = 2b - 10$?

   A $b = \dfrac{a - 10}{2}$ **B** $b = \dfrac{a}{2} + 5$ **C** $b = \dfrac{a + 10}{2}$ **D** $b = \dfrac{a + 2}{10}$ **E** $b = \dfrac{a - 2}{10}$ **F** $b = \dfrac{10 + a}{2}$

5. Copy and complete each of the following:
   - (i) $v = u + at$
     $v - \square = at$
     $t = \ldots$
   - (ii) $ap + bq = k$
     $ap = k - \square$
     $p = \dfrac{k - \square}{\square}$
   - (iii) $p = \dfrac{g}{5} + 3h$
     $p - \square = \dfrac{g}{5}$
     $\square\,(p - \square) = g$
     $g = \ldots$

6. Make x the subject of the formula in each of these:
   - (i) $x - y = 2z$
   - (ii) $3x - b = 4c$
   - (iii) $6y + 3x = 7$
   - (iv) $\dfrac{x}{3} - 2y = 8$

7. Make a the subject of the formula in each of these:
   - (i) $2a - b = \tfrac{1}{2}$
   - (ii) $ab - 3a = 5$
   - (iii) $7(a - 3) = 4b$

8. Make the letter in brackets the subject of the formula in each of the following:

(i) $c = \dfrac{a}{2} - 4b \ldots (a)$
(ii) $2(a - 2b) = 3c \ldots (a)$
(iii) $2x - \dfrac{1}{3} = \dfrac{y}{3} \ldots (x)$

(iv) $5(b - 3) = \dfrac{a}{2} \ldots (b)$
(v) $x = \dfrac{y - 2z}{3} \ldots (z)$
(vi) $a = \dfrac{b}{2} - \dfrac{3c}{4} \ldots (b)$

9. Make x the subject of the formula in each of these:

(i) $xa + xb = 3c$
(ii) $ax - 3x = 5$
(iii) $y + \dfrac{2}{3} = \dfrac{x - 1}{3}$

10. If $k = s(a - b)$, make b the subject of the formula.

11. The formula $h = \dfrac{a}{k} + j$ gives h in terms of a, k and j.

Which of the following are correct rearrangements of the formula?

A $a = hk - j$ **B** $a = k(h - j)$ **C** $a = jk - kh$ **D** $a = \dfrac{k}{h - j}$ **E** $a = hk - jk$

12. Make the letter in brackets the subject of the formula in each of the following:

(i) $x = \dfrac{2y - 3z}{4} \ldots (z)$
(ii) $\dfrac{b}{3} + \dfrac{3c}{4} = 2a \ldots (b)$
(iii) $\dfrac{3x}{4} = 5(y + z) \ldots (y)$

(iv) $\dfrac{ab}{3} = \dfrac{b}{2} + c \ldots (b)$
(v) $t = \dfrac{x - 2y}{z} \ldots (y)$
(vi) $\dfrac{p}{q} = \dfrac{q}{t} + 1 \ldots (t)$

(vii) $y = \dfrac{3x + 4}{x - 1} \ldots (x)$
(viii) $p = \dfrac{qr}{q - r} \ldots (r)$

13. Given that $z = \dfrac{3y + 2}{y - 1}$, express y in terms of z.

Hence find the value of y when $z = \dfrac{1}{2}$.

14. The area A of a trapezium can be written $A = \dfrac{(a + b)h}{2}$.

(i) Rearrange this formula to make h the subject.
(ii) Work out the height of a trapezium whose area is 100 cm² and whose parallel sides are 6.5 cm and 7.8 cm. Give your answer to the nearest whole number.

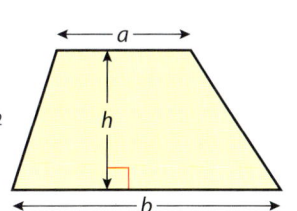

Section 21.5 Evaluating and writing formulae

A **formula** describes the relationship between two or more variables.
For example, the formula for the area of a rectangle is
$$A = \ell \times b$$
If $\ell = 6$ and $b = 4$, then $A = 6 \times 4 = 24$.
For different values of ℓ and b, you get the corresponding value for A.

Text & Tests 2 Higher Level

> **Example 1**
>
> If $V = \pi r^2 h$, find V when $r = 3$ and $h = 8$.
>
> $V = \pi r^2 h$
> $V = \pi \times 3^2 \times 8$
> $V = 226.19$ … use the π key on your calculator

Writing formulae

It is important to be able to **derive a formula** from information that you are given. Here is an example:

> If the cost (€C) of hiring a car consists of a fixed daily charge of €F and €k for each kilometre travelled, then the cost of hiring a car for 12 days, having travelled 800 km, is given by the formula
> €$C = 12F + 800k$.

> **Example 2**
>
> The number of children at a party is four times the number of adults.
> Three teenagers are helping with the party.
> If a represents the number of adults at the party, find a formula for N, the number of people at the party.
>
> If there are a adults at the party, there are $4a$ children.
> The number of people at the party is adults + children + teenagers
> $\therefore \quad N = a + 4a + 3$ … for every 1 adult, there are 4 children
> $\quad N = 5a + 3$

Exercise 21.5

1. (i) If $V = \dfrac{AH}{3}$, find V when $A = 12$ and $H = 4$.
    (ii) If $s = ut + \frac{1}{2}at^2$, find s when $u = 10$, $t = 5$ and $a = 8$.
    (iii) If $A = \dfrac{h}{2}(a + b)$, find A when $h = 12$, $a = 10$ and $b = 9$.
    (iv) If $A = \frac{1}{2}h(x + y)$, find A when $h = 12$, $x = 6$ and $y = 3$.

2. The formula $C = \frac{5}{9}(F - 32)$ changes degrees Celsius into degrees Fahrenheit.
   Find C when
   (i) $F = 212°$ (ii) $F = 32°$ (iii) $F = -40°$ (iv) $F = 14°$ (v) $F = -13°$.

490

3. If $v = u + at$, find
   (i) v when $u = 5, a = 4$ and $t = 6$
   (ii) u when $v = 25, a = 3$ and $t = 5$
   (iii) a when $v = 15, u = 5$ and $t = 3$.

4. If $V = \sqrt{u^2 - 2as}$, find V when $u = 0, a = -10$ and $s = 5$.

5. The general equation of a straight line is $y = mx + c$.
   (i) Find the value of y when $m = \frac{1}{2}, x = 4$ and $c = -2$.

   Rearrange the formula to make m the subject.
   (ii) Now find the value of m when $x = 3, y = 5$ and $c = -4$.

6. Write down a formula for P, the perimeter of each of these figures:
   (i) rectangle with length ℓ and width b
   (ii) L-shaped figure with sides 8, 5, x, y

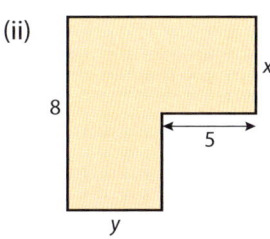

7. Given that $T = \frac{ab}{6} + C$, find the value of T when $a = 4, b = 12$ and $C = 5$.
   Rearrange the formula to make b the subject.
   Now find the value of b when $T = 15, a = 5$ and $C = 4$.

8. The cost of hiring a taxi from the airport is $C = 3 + 1.5k$, where C is the cost in euro and k is the number of kilometres driven.
   (i) Find the cost of a journey of 12 km.
   (ii) Joe hired a taxi from the airport to his house. The cost was €33. How far from the airport does Joe live?

9. The time taken T, in minutes, to complete my homework consists of 15 minutes to get my books organised and then 40 minutes to do each assignment, a.
   Write down a formula, making T the subject.

10. The members of the school social committee calculate that the profit, in euro, made on the school disco is given by
   $$P = 5T - 900,$$
   where T represents the number of tickets sold. Find:
   (i) the profit made when 195 tickets are sold
   (ii) the number of tickets sold if the profit is €870
   (iii) the number of tickets that must be sold in order to break even (i.e., no profit made).

11. The cost of hiring a minibus is given by the formula $C = 20 + 12d + 2k$, where C is the cost in euro, d is the number of days the minibus is hired for, and k is the number of kilometres the minibus travels.

    (i) The minibus is hired for 8 days and travels 300 km.
Calculate the total cost of hiring the minibus.

    (ii) Margaret hires the bus for 6 days and the total bill comes to €452.
How many kilometres did she travel?

12. On each long side of a table at a restaurant, the number of seats is equal to the length of the table (in metres) multiplied by 2.
Two more people can sit at each end of the table.

    (i) Write a formula that gives the number of people at a table of length ℓ metres.

    (ii) Find the number of people who can sit at a table 6 m long.

    (iii) What length of table would have 32 seats?

13. The diagram shows a trapezium.

    (i) Show that the area, A, of the trapezium is given by $A = 2x^2$.

    (ii) Rearrange this formula to make x the subject.

    (iii) Find the value of x for a trapezium of area 20 cm².

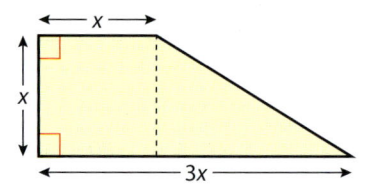

14. $C = 180R + 2000$ is the formula which gives the capacity, C litres, of the tank needed to supply water to R hotel rooms.

    (i) If $R = 5$, work out the value of C.

    (ii) If $C = 3440$, work out the value of R.

    (iii) A water tank has a capacity of 3800 litres.
Work out the greatest number of hotel rooms it could supply.

15. A taxi driver charges a fare (F) of €4 added to €1.50 per kilometre (k) added to €2 per passenger (p).

    (i) Write a formula that relates the fare to the number of kilometres travelled and the number of passengers.

    (ii) Find the fare for 4 passengers if the journey was 18 km in length.

    (iii) If 3 passengers paid a total of €28, how long was the journey?

16. The volume of this cuboid is 216 m³.

    (i) Write a formula for the volume of a cuboid.

    (ii) Using the formula in (i) show that the volume of this cuboid is given by, $x^2 + 3x - 54 = 0$

    (iii) Write down the actual dimensions of the cuboid.

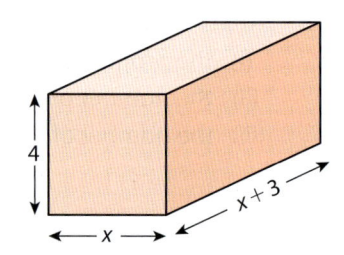

Chapter 21 Algebra 2

Test yourself 21

1. Simplify each of these as much as possible:
   (i) $\dfrac{8x^3}{2x}$
   (ii) $\dfrac{12xy^2}{3xy}$
   (iii) $\dfrac{10x^2}{7} \times \dfrac{14y^2}{5xy}$

2. If $y = \dfrac{2x - 6}{3x - 4}$, express x in terms of y.

3. Solve the equation $\dfrac{x}{3} + \dfrac{2x - 2}{5} = 4$

4. Evaluate $\dfrac{ab}{a - b}$ when $a = \tfrac{1}{2}$ and $b = \tfrac{1}{3}$.

5. If $7a - \dfrac{ab}{c} = c$, express b in terms of a and c.
   Hence find the value of b when $a = -1$ and $c = -3$.

6. The given figure consists of a square and a rectangle.
   (i) If the perimeter of the figure is P cm, express P in terms of x, y and z.
   (ii) If $x = 2y$, $y = 2z$ and $P = 55$, find the value of x.

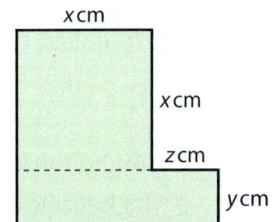

7. The number of hours (H) of sleep that children need depends on their age (A) in years and is given by the formula $H = 17 - \dfrac{A}{2}$.
   (i) Find the number of hours of sleep needed when a child is 14 years old.
   (ii) Find how old the child is who needs 8 hours sleep.

8. Solve the equation $\dfrac{x + 1}{4} - \dfrac{x}{3} = \dfrac{1}{12}$

9. Evaluate $\dfrac{2}{x + 2} + \dfrac{3}{2x + 1}$ when $x = \tfrac{1}{2}$

10. (i) If $\dfrac{b}{2x} = b - a$, express x in terms of a and b.
    (ii) Simplify as far as possible:
    $\dfrac{3a^2 b}{5c} \div \dfrac{9ab}{10}$

11. In the given triangle, the two equal sides are marked.
    If the perimeter of the triangle is 26 cm, write an equation in x and solve it to find its value.

    $\left(\dfrac{2x}{3} - 5\right)$ cm

    $\left(\dfrac{x}{2} + 3\right)$ cm

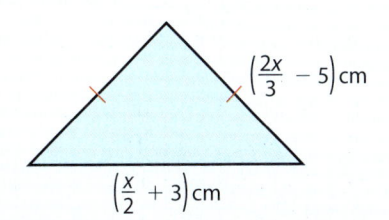

12. Express $\dfrac{3x - 1}{3} + \dfrac{x + 5}{4}$ as a single fraction in its simplest form.

493

Text & Tests 2 Higher Level

13. The charge C, in euro, for hiring a hall for an event is $C = 150 + 2N$, where N stands for the number of people at the event.
    (i) Find the charge when 250 people are present.
    (ii) Find the number of people at the event when the charge is €790.

14. If $\dfrac{3a - 2b}{3} = \dfrac{1}{2}$, express a in terms of b.
    Use your result to show that $6a - 4b$ can be expressed as a single number k, where $k \in N$ and write down this number.

15. If $\dfrac{1}{x} = \dfrac{1}{y} + \dfrac{2}{z}$, find the value of x when $y = \dfrac{1}{3}$ and $z = 4$.

16. Solve the equation $\dfrac{x-2}{3} - \dfrac{x+1}{6} = \dfrac{x-1}{10}$.

17. To convert temperatures between Celsius and Fahrenheit, you can use one of these formulas.
    $$C = \dfrac{5(F - 32)}{9} \qquad F = \dfrac{9C}{5} + 32$$
    C stands for the temperature in °C, F stands for the temperature in °F.
    (i) The freezing point of water is 0°C. What is it in Fahrenheit?
    (ii) The boiling point of water is 100°C. What is it in Fahrenheit?
    (iii) A comfortable room temperature is about 72°F. What is it in Celsius?
    (iv) The temperature in a domestic fridge should be about 36°F. What is this in Celsius?

18. If $\dfrac{ap}{3} = \dfrac{p}{2} + c$, express p in terms of a and c.
    Hence, find the value of p when $a = -1\dfrac{1}{2}$ and $c = 3$.

19. These two rectangles have equal perimeters.
    Form an equation and solve it to find x.

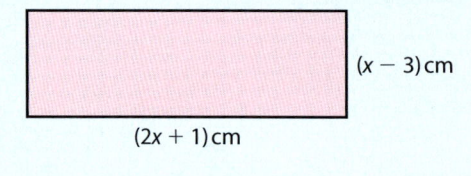

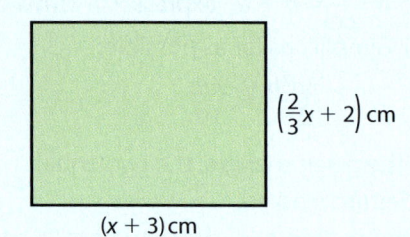

    $(x - 3)$ cm
    $(2x + 1)$ cm
    $\left(\dfrac{2}{3}x + 2\right)$ cm
    $(x + 3)$ cm

20. Solve each of the following equations.
    (i) $\dfrac{1}{x} + \dfrac{4}{x} = \dfrac{1}{2}$
    (ii) $a = 1 + \dfrac{2}{a}$

Chapter 21 Algebra 2

21. A group of people agree to pay €360 for a day's rock climbing.
    Each person pays an equal share.
    When 4 people pull out, the remaining members of the group each must pay an extra €3.
    If x is the original number of people, write:
    (i) an expression for the original amount each member had agreed to pay.
    (ii) an expression for the amount each member had to pay when the 4 people pulled out.
    (iii) an equation for the difference between the two amounts in (i) and (ii) and show that
    $$x^2 - 4x - 480 = 0$$
    By solving this equation, find the original number of people in the group.

22. Colin thinks of a number. He divides 60 by his number and then adds his answer to one tenth of his number. This results in the number 5.
    Write an equation to represent this information.
    By simplifying, form a quadratic equation and solve it to show that Colin could have used two different numbers to get the same result.

23. Express b in terms of a and c, given that,
    $$\frac{1}{abc} = \frac{1}{a} + \frac{1}{b} + \frac{1}{c}.$$
    Find the value of b when $a = \frac{1}{2}$ and $c = \frac{1}{3}$

Text & Tests 2 Higher Level

Assignment:

Three friends *Jane*, *Alice* and *Tom* went on holiday together to Nice. *Jane* had €x and *Alice* had double that amount. *Jane* then gave *Alice* €40 (that she owed her).

Soon afterwards, *Tom* lost all his money, so *Jane* gave him one third of her money. At the same time, *Alice* gave one fifth of her money to *Tom*. *Tom* then had €310.

By completing the following chart, show how to form an equation based on the information given, then solve the equation to find out how much *Alice* had to begin with.

Information	Algebra
Jane had €x	*Jane*:
Alice had twice that amount	*Alice*:
Jane gave *Alice* €40	*Jane*: *Alice*:
Tom had no money	*Tom*:
Jane gave *Tom* one third of her money	*Jane*: *Tom*:
Alice gave *Tom* one fifth of her money	*Alice*: *Tom*:
Tom then had €310.	*Tom*:
	Equation: ∴ $x =$

∴ *Alice* had € _____ to begin with.

Trigonometry

chapter 22

In this chapter, you will learn to:

- use the Theorem of Pythagoras,
- identify the three sides of a right-angled triangle,
- use the three trigonometric ratios: sin, cos and tan,
- apply inverse trigonometric functions to find missing angles,
- solve right-angled triangles,
- use trigonometry to solve real life problems.

Section 22.1 The Theorem of Pythagoras

As you begin the study of trigonometry, you will recall the **Theorem of Pythagoras** from chapter 8. It is perhaps the best-known theorem in mathematics.

The diagram below illustrates his theorem.

Theorem of Pythagoras
In a right-angled triangle, the area of the square drawn on the hypotenuse is equal to the sum of the squares drawn on the other two sides.

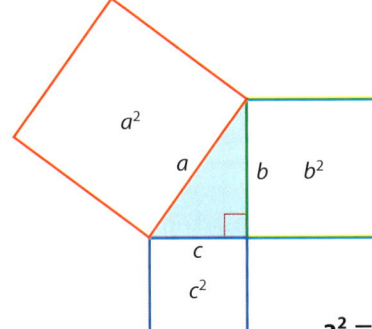

$$a^2 = b^2 + c^2$$

Example 1

Find the length of the side marked x in the given right-angled triangle.

$x^2 = 8^2 + 6^2$
$x^2 = 64 + 36$
$x^2 = 100$
$x = \sqrt{100}$
$x = 10$

497

Text & Tests 2 Higher Level

Exercise 22.1

1. Find the missing areas of the squares on these right-angled triangles.

    (i) ? , 4 cm², 8 cm²

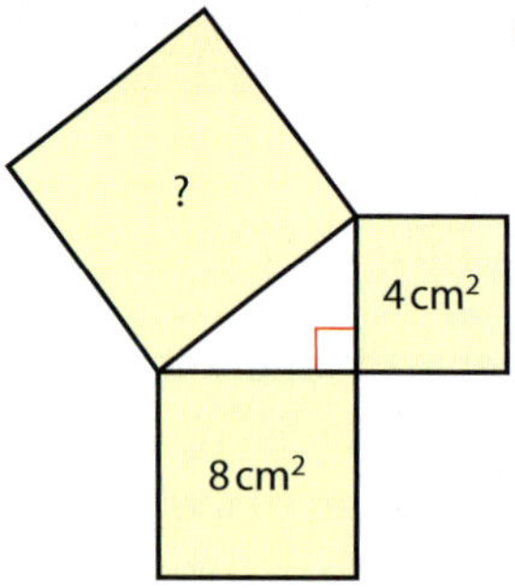

    (ii) 16 cm², ?, 28 cm²

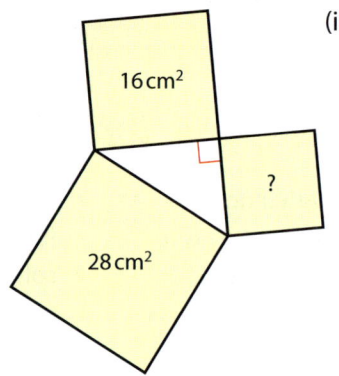

    (iii) 14 cm², ?, 6 cm²

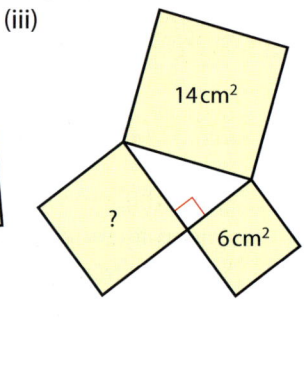

2. What is the area of the square drawn here?

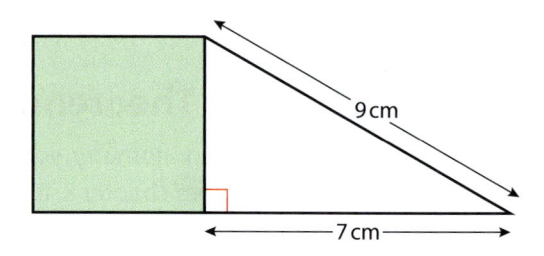

    9 cm, 7 cm

3. Use Pythagoras' theorem to find the length of the side [AC].

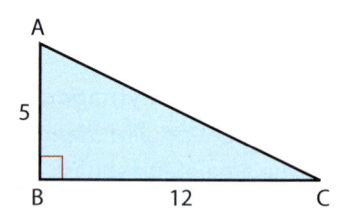

    AB = 5, BC = 12

4. Calculate the length of the side marked with a letter in each of the following triangles. You may leave your answer in surd ($\sqrt{}$) form, where necessary.

    (i) a, 3 cm, 2 cm

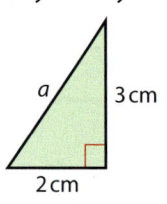

    (ii) b, 7 cm, 3 cm

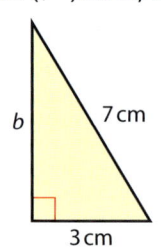

    (iii) 2 cm, 7 cm, c

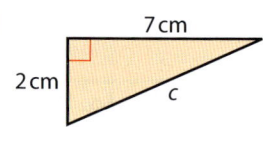

    (iv) d, 4 cm, 6 cm

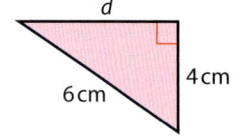

    (v) e, 12 cm, 9 cm

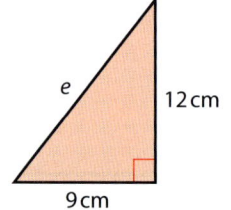

    (vi) f, 13 cm, 5 cm

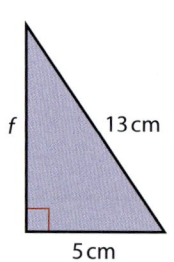

5. Find the length of the side marked *x* in each of these triangles.
Give each answer correct to 1 decimal place.

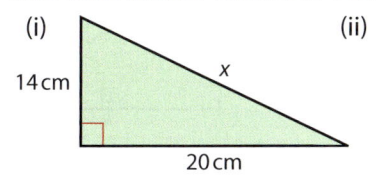

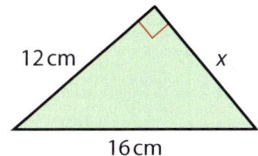

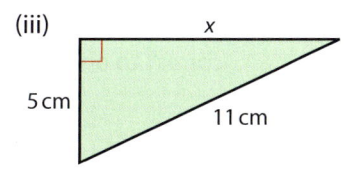

(i) Triangle with sides 14 cm, 20 cm, and hypotenuse *x*.

(ii) Triangle with legs 12 cm and 16 cm, hypotenuse *x*.

(iii) Triangle with legs 5 cm and *x*, hypotenuse 11 cm.

6. A rectangle is 10 cm long and 8 cm wide.
Calculate the length of the diagonal.
Give your answer in centimetres, correct to one decimal place.

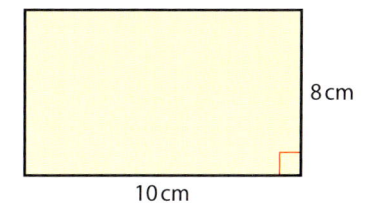

7. Use the given grid to write down the lengths of [PR] and [QR].
Hence find the length of [PQ], correct to one decimal place.

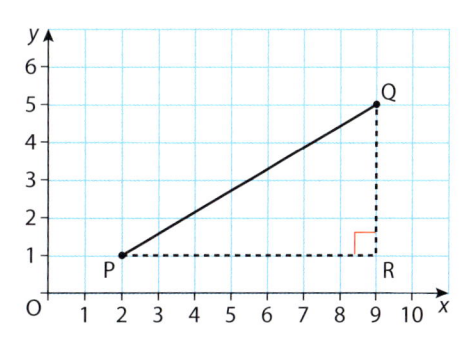

8. The diagram shows a ladder leaning against a vertical wall.
The foot of the ladder is on horizontal ground, 3.6 m from the wall. The length of the ladder is 5 m.
Work out how far up the wall the ladder reaches.
Give your answer in metres, correct to 1 decimal place.

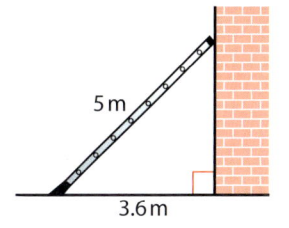

9. In the given figure, |AB| = 10 cm, |AD| = 5 cm and |DC| = 6 cm.
The angles at A and D are right angles.
Find the length of [BC], correct to one decimal place.

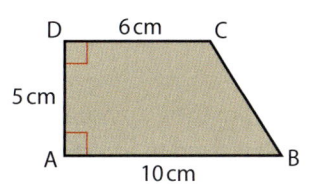

Text & Tests 2 Higher Level

10. The diagram shows a right-angled triangle ABC.
    (i) Find the length of [BD].
    (ii) Find the length [AD] in centimetres, correct to one decimal place.

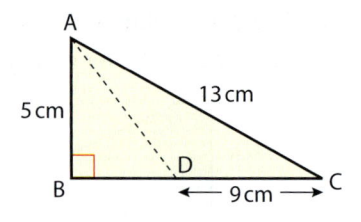

11. Use the grid and the Theorem of Pythagoras to work out the lengths of the sides of the given figure.
    Give your answer correct to one decimal place.

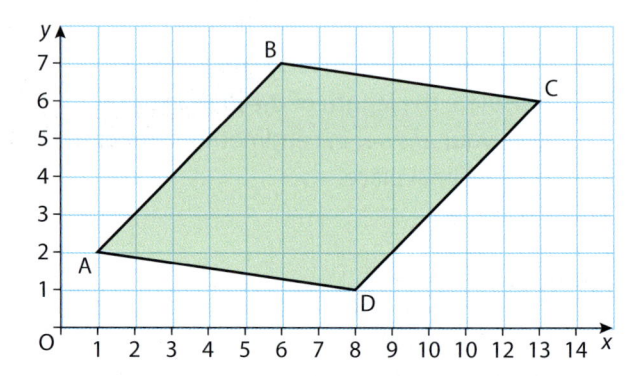

12. Calculate the lengths of the sides marked x and y in the given right-angled triangles.

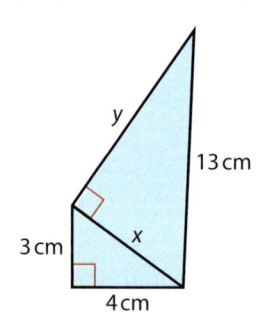

13. In the given figure, the two right angles are marked.
    Find the lengths of c and d.

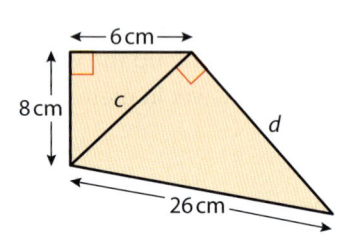

14. The diagram shows a horizontal shelf [AB]. The shelf is fixed to a vertical wall at A.
    The support [CD] is fixed to the wall at C and to the shelf at D.
    $|AB| = 23$ cm, $|AC| = 20$ cm and $|BD| = 8$ cm.
    Calculate the length of [CD].

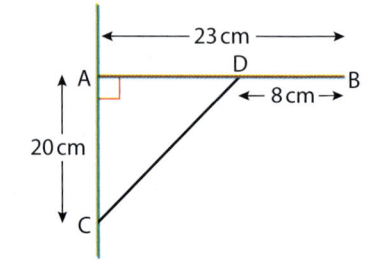

15. The area of a square drawn on the hypotenuse of a right-angled, isosceles triangle is 24 cm². Work out the area of the square drawn on each of the other two sides.

16. The given television has a rectangular screen with a diagonal of length 74 cm.
The sides of the screen are in the ratio 5 : 3.
Work out the lengths of these sides, in centimetres, correct to 1 decimal place.

17. Explain why a triangle of sides 12 cm, 13 cm and 18 cm is not right-angled.

Section 22.2 Sine, Cosine and Tangent ratios

One of the most common uses of trigonometry is in working out lengths and angles in right-angled triangles. Three very special ratios connecting angles and sides are given below.

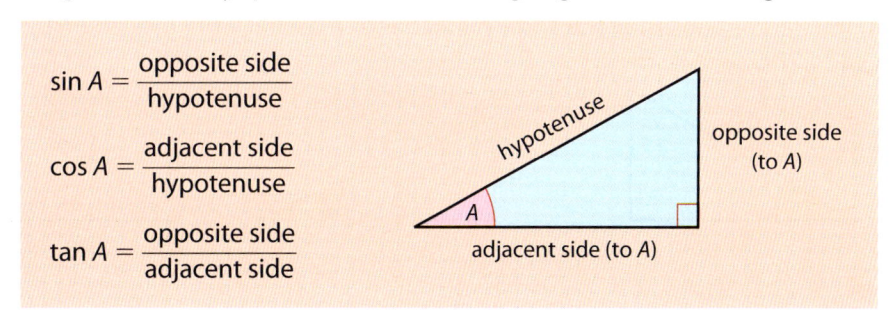

$$\sin A = \frac{\text{opposite side}}{\text{hypotenuse}}$$

$$\cos A = \frac{\text{adjacent side}}{\text{hypotenuse}}$$

$$\tan A = \frac{\text{opposite side}}{\text{adjacent side}}$$

In the given triangle,

$\sin A = \frac{1}{\sqrt{5}}$ $\sin B = \frac{2}{\sqrt{5}}$

$\cos A = \frac{2}{\sqrt{5}}$ $\cos B = \frac{1}{\sqrt{5}}$

$\tan A = \frac{1}{2}$ $\tan B = \frac{2}{1} = 2$

If we are given $\cos A = \frac{3}{4}$, we can draw a sketch of a right-angled triangle in which the side adjacent to A is 3 and the hypotenuse is 4.

We now find the third side by using the Theorem of Pythagoras.

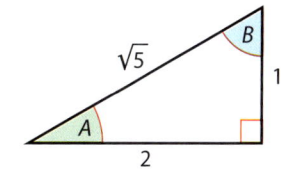

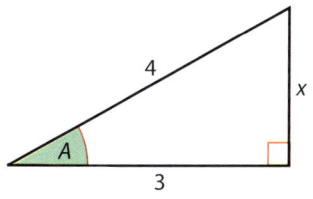

Let the third side $= x$.
$$x^2 + 3^2 = 4^2$$
$$x^2 + 9 = 16$$
$$x^2 = 7$$
$$x = \sqrt{7}$$

501

Text & Tests 2 Higher Level

> **Example 1**
>
> If $\tan B = \frac{\sqrt{5}}{2}$, find the value of sin B and cos B.
>
> $\tan B = \frac{\sqrt{5}}{2} \Rightarrow$ opposite side to B is $\sqrt{5}$ and adjacent side is 2.
>
> Now draw a rough sketch of a right-angled triangle.
> Let x be the length of the hypotenuse.
>
> $x^2 = 2^2 + (\sqrt{5})^2$
> $x^2 = 4 + 5 \ldots (\sqrt{5})^2 = 5$
> $x^2 = 9 \Rightarrow x = 3$
>
> From the triangle: $\sin B = \frac{\sqrt{5}}{3}$ and $\cos B = \frac{2}{3}$.

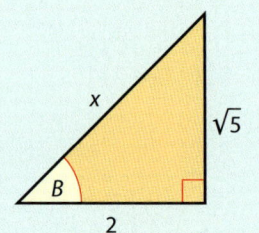

Exercise 22.2

1. Find the sin, cos and tan of the angle marked with a capital letter in each of the following triangles:

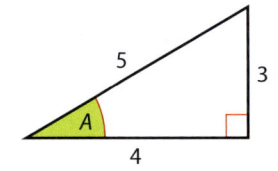

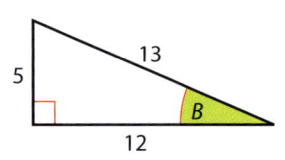

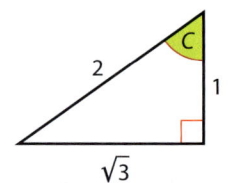

2. In the given triangle, state which of the ratios sine, cosine or tangent
   (i) connects 3, 4 and the angle A
   (ii) connects 4, 5 and the angle A
   (iii) connects 3, 5 and the angle A.

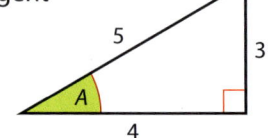

3. Write down what should be inserted into each of the following coloured boxes:

   (i) $\sin \square = \frac{5}{13}$ (ii) $\tan \square = \frac{12}{5}$

   (iii) $\cos \square = \frac{5}{13}$ (iv) $\square A = \frac{12}{13}$

   (v) $\square B = \frac{5}{13}$ (vi) $\square A = \frac{5}{12}$

4. Find the length of the side marked x in the given right-angled triangle.
Hence write down the value of
(i) sin A (ii) cos A (iii) tan A.

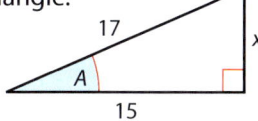

5. Find the value of a in the given right-angled triangle.
Hence write down the value of
(i) sin B (ii) cos B (iii) tan B.

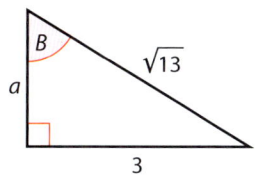

6. The angle θ and three sides of a right-angled triangle are shown in the given diagram.
State whether each of these ratios represents sin θ, cos θ or tan θ.
(i) $\frac{4}{5}$ (ii) $\frac{4}{\sqrt{41}}$ (iii) $\frac{5}{\sqrt{41}}$

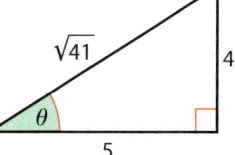

7. Given that $\cos B = \frac{5}{13}$, draw a rough sketch of a right-angled triangle and use it to write down the ratios sin B and tan B.

8. (i) If $\tan A = \frac{1}{2}$, find sin A. (ii) If $\cos B = \frac{2}{5}$, find tan B.

9. If $\tan C = \frac{1}{\sqrt{3}}$, find the values of sin C and cos C.

10. Using Pythagoras's theorem, find, in surd form, the length of the third side (c) of the right-angled triangle shown.
Using your value for c, find:
(a) (i) sin A (ii) cos A
(b) (i) sin B (ii) cos B.

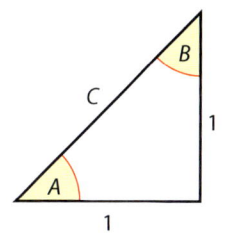

11. Given that in a right-angled triangle $\sin A = \frac{1}{2}$, draw a rough sketch of the triangle and use it to write down the ratios, cos A, tan A.

12. In a right-angled triangle, $\tan C = \frac{8}{15}$. Draw a rough sketch of the triangle and hence find, in fraction form, the value of sin C and cos C.

503

Investigation:

From the given triangle, find the values of sin A, cos A, sin B, cos B.

Using these values, find the value of:

(a) $\sin^2 A + \cos^2 A$
(b) $\sin^2 B + \cos^2 B$

Conclusion: _____

(Note: $\sin^2 A = (\sin A)^2$)

Using a set square, draw a large diagram of right-angled triangle.

Measure the lengths of the sides of the triangle a, b and c as accurately as possible.

Place the measurements on the diagram.

Using these values, verify your conclusion above.

Compare your results with other groups in your class.

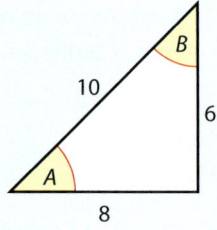

Section 22.3 Using a calculator to find ratios and angles

Angles are generally measured in degrees. A right angle, which is a quarter of a full rotation, measures 90°.

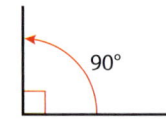

We can find the value of the sine, cosine or tangent of any angle by using the $\boxed{\sin}$, $\boxed{\cos}$ and $\boxed{\tan}$ keys on an electronic calculator.

To find sin 35°, key in $\boxed{\sin}$ 35 $\boxed{=}$.

The result is 0.573576 … = 0.5736, correct to 4 decimal places.

To find tan 37.4°, key in $\boxed{\tan}$ 37.4 $\boxed{=}$.

The result is 0.7646.

Using the $\boxed{\sin^{-1}}$ $\boxed{\cos^{-1}}$ and $\boxed{\tan^{-1}}$ keys

Given a trigonometric ratio, a calculator can be used to work backwards to find the angle.

If we are given that sin A = 0.8661, we can find the angle A by using the $\boxed{\sin^{-1}}$ key.

Chapter 22 Trigonometry

The $\boxed{\sin^{-1}}$ key is got by keying in $\boxed{\text{SHIFT}}$ $\boxed{\sin}$.

Thus if sin A = 0.8661, we find A by keying in $\boxed{\text{SHIFT}}$ $\boxed{\sin}$ 0.8661 $\boxed{=}$.

The result is 60.008° = 60°.

Similarly, if tan $B = \dfrac{6}{6} = 1$,

then $B = \tan^{-1}(1)$

we find the angle B by keying in $\boxed{\text{SHIFT}}$ $\boxed{\tan}$ 1 $\boxed{=}$.

The result is 45°.

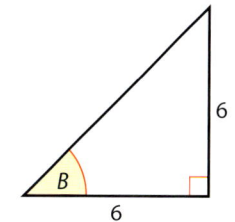

Example 1

If sin A = 0.5216, find A correct to the nearest degree.

If sin A = 0.5216, we find A by keying in

$\boxed{\text{SHIFT}}$ $\boxed{\sin}$ 0.5216 $\boxed{=}$

The result is 31.44°. ⇒ A = 31°, to the nearest degree.

Note: From the given triangle, the sin $B = \dfrac{4}{7}$.

To find the angle B, we write $B = \sin^{-1}\left(\dfrac{4}{7}\right)$

and using a calculator key in $\boxed{\text{SHIFT}}$ $\boxed{\sin}$ $\boxed{\dfrac{[\;]}{[\;]}}$ 4 ↓ 7 → $\boxed{=}$

The result is 34.8°.

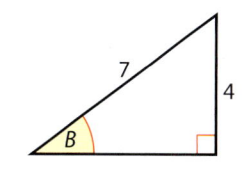

Exercise 22.3

1. Find the measure of the angle A in the given triangle.

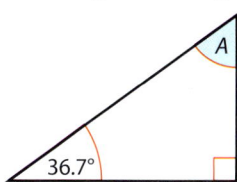

2. Use your calculator to evaluate each of the following, correct to 4 decimal places:
   (i) sin 48°   (ii) cos 74°   (iii) tan 15°   (iv) sin 72°   (v) cos 28.5°

3. Use your calculator to find the measure of each of these angles, correct to the nearest degree:
   (i) sin A = 0.7453   (ii) cos B = 0.3521   (iii) tan C = 1.4538
   (iv) cos A = 0.2154   (v) tan B = 0.8923   (vi) sin C = 0.2132

Text & Tests 2 Higher Level

4. Find the value of A in each of the following.
   Give your answer in degrees, correct to one decimal place.
   (i) sin A = 0.6
   (ii) cos A = 0.7534
   (iii) tan A = 3.84
   (iv) cos A = 0.2715

5. Find the measure of the angle θ, correct to the nearest degree, in each of the following:
   (i) $\sin \theta = \frac{2}{3}$
   (ii) $\cos \theta = \frac{3}{5}$
   (iii) $\tan \theta = \frac{7}{8}$
   (iv) $\sin \theta = \frac{2}{5}$
   (v) $\tan \theta = \frac{6}{11}$
   (vi) $\sin \theta = \frac{1}{5}$
   (vii) $\cos \theta = \frac{9}{11}$
   (viii) $\tan \theta = 1\frac{3}{5}$

6. If cos A = 0.5484 and A < 90°, find A and hence find the value of sin A, correct to 2 decimal places.

7. If tan A = 1.3462, find A in degrees correct to 2 places of decimals.

8. Write down which trigonometric ratio is needed to calculate the angle θ in each of these triangles:

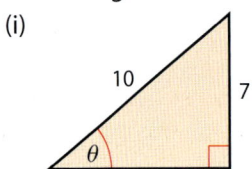

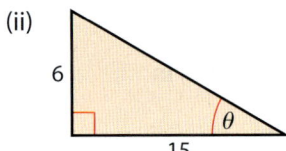

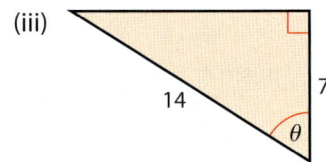

9. Find, correct to the nearest degree, the sizes of the angles marked A, B and C in the triangles below:

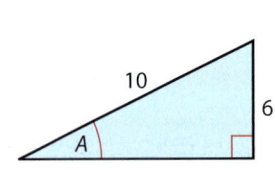

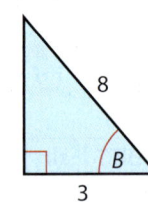

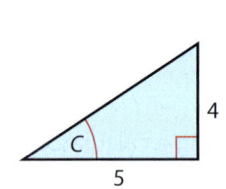

10. In the given triangles, all of the lengths are in cm.
    Calculate the value of each angle marked with a letter, correct to the nearest degree.

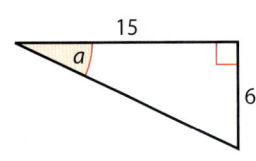

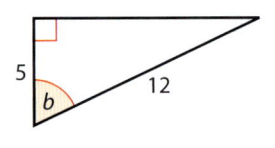

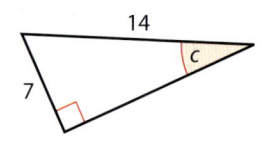

11. By using the appropriate ratio, work out the measure of each of the marked angles in degrees, correct to one decimal place:

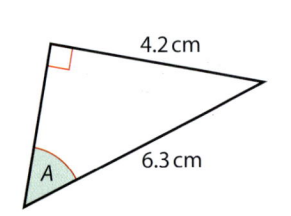

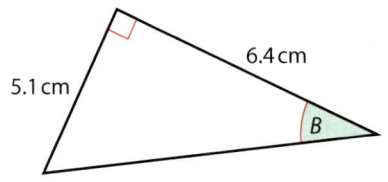

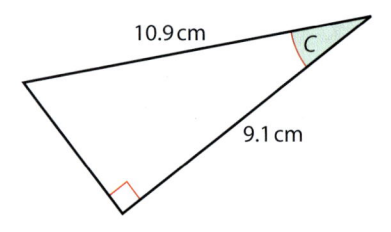

12. Find the value of the angle θ in each of these:
  (i) $2 \sin \theta = 1$
  (ii) $5 \cos \theta = 2$
  (iii) $2 \tan \theta = 1$
  Give each angle correct to the nearest degree.

13. The diagram shows a vertical mast of height 12 metres.
  The length of the mast's shadow on horizontal ground is 30 metres.
  Calculate the measure of the angle marked x, correct to the nearest degree.

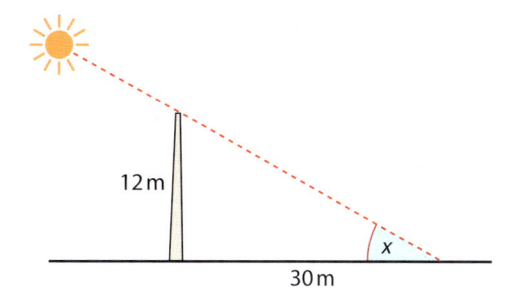

Investigation:

During a trigonometry lesson, a group of students write down some statements about what they expected to happen when they look at values of the trigonometric functions of some angles.

They then find the Sin, Cos and Tan of some angles, up to 360°, correct to three places of decimals, to test their ideas. Here are some of the things they wrote down.

(a) The value of any of these trigonometric functions will **always** be less than 1.
(b) If the size of the angle is doubled, then the value from the trigonometric functions will **not** double.
(c) The value of all trigonometric functions will **increase** if the size of the angle is increased.

State whether you **agree** or **disagree** with each of the statements.

Give examples to justify your answers.

Section 22.4 Solving right-angled triangles

In this section we will use the sine, cosine and tangent ratios to find an unknown side or an unknown angle in a right-angled triangle.

When using your calculator to find the sine, cosine or tangent of an angle, write the value correct to 4 decimal places.

Text & Tests 2 Higher Level

Example 1

Find the lengths of the sides marked x and y in the given triangle.

Give your answers correct to 1 decimal place.

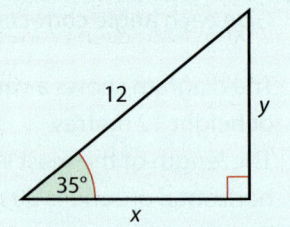

$\dfrac{x}{12} = \cos 35°$ $\qquad$ $\dfrac{y}{12} = \sin 35°$

$\dfrac{x}{12} = 0.8192$ $\qquad$ $\dfrac{y}{12} = 0.5736$

$x = 12(0.8192)$ $\qquad$ $y = 12(0.5736)$

$x = 9.8304$ $\qquad$ $y = 6.8832$

$x = 9.8$ $\qquad$ $y = 6.9$

Example 2

In the given triangle, |AB| = 9 and |BC| = 13.
Find |∠ACB|, correct to the nearest degree.

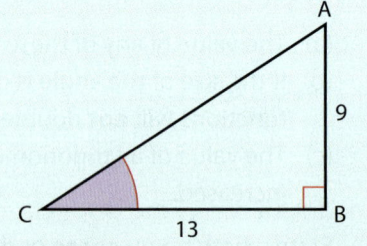

$\tan \angle ACB = \dfrac{9}{13}$

$|\angle ACB| = \tan^{-1} \dfrac{9}{13}$

$|\angle ACB| = 34.695°$ $\qquad$ Key in [SHIFT] [tan] $\dfrac{[\;]}{[\;]}$ 9 ↓ 13 → [=]

$= 35°$, correct to the nearest degree.

Chapter 22 Trigonometry

Exercise 22.4

1. Write down which trigonometric ratio is needed to calculate the length of the side marked *x* in each of these triangles:

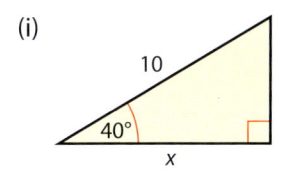

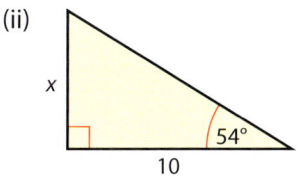

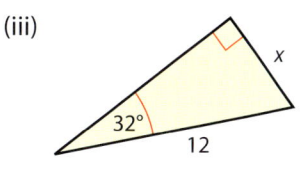

(i) [triangle: hypotenuse 10, angle 40°, adjacent x]

(ii) [triangle: opposite x, angle 54°, adjacent 10]

(iii) [triangle: angle 32°, hypotenuse 12, opposite x]

2. In each of the following triangles, work out the length of the side marked with a letter. Give each answer correct to 1 decimal place.

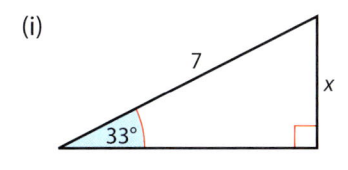

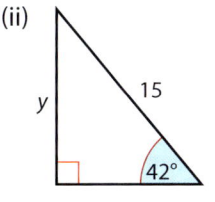

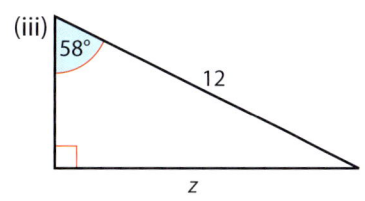

(i) [triangle: hypotenuse 7, angle 33°, opposite x]

(ii) [triangle: hypotenuse 15, angle 42°, y]

(iii) [triangle: angle 58°, hypotenuse 12, z]

3. Find the length of the side marked *x* in these triangles. Give your answers correct to one decimal place.

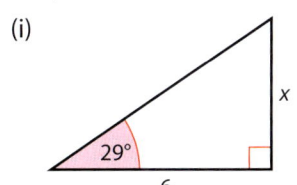

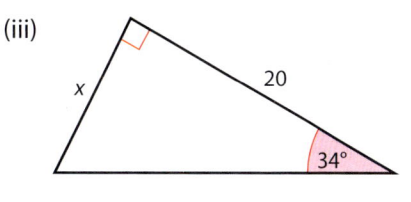

(i) [triangle: angle 29°, adjacent 6, hypotenuse x]

(ii) [triangle: angle 48°, 15, x]

(iii) [triangle: 20, angle 34°, x]

4. Find the size of the angle marked A in each of these triangles. Give your answers correct to the nearest degree.

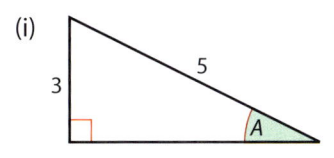

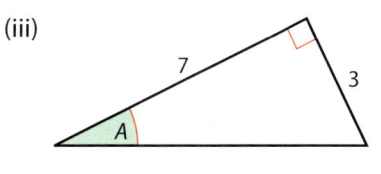

(i) [triangle: 3, 5, angle A]

(ii) [triangle: 10, 7, angle A]

(iii) [triangle: 7, 3, angle A]

5. Find the measure of the angles marked *p*, *q* and *r* in each of these triangles. Give each answer correct to the nearest degree.

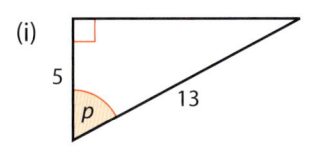

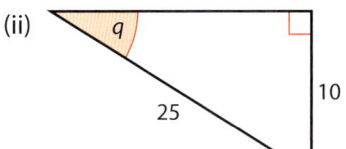

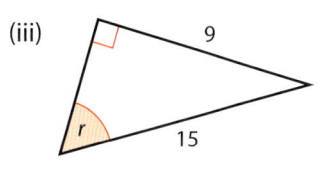

(i) [triangle: 5, 13, angle p]

(ii) [triangle: angle q, 25, 10]

(iii) [triangle: 9, 15, angle r]

Text & Tests 2 Higher Level

6. Copy and complete the following to find the length of the side marked *x*.

   $$\frac{8}{x} = \cos 32°$$

   $$x \times \cos 32° = 8$$

   $$x = \frac{8}{\cos 32°}$$

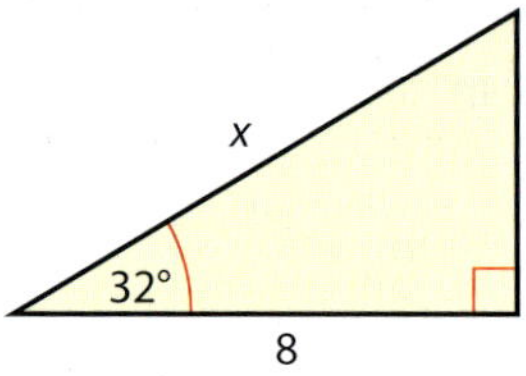

   Give your answer correct to 1 decimal place.

7. Find the length of the hypotenuse marked *x* in each of these triangles:

   (i)   (ii) 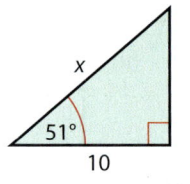   (iii)

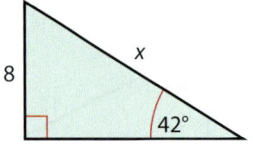

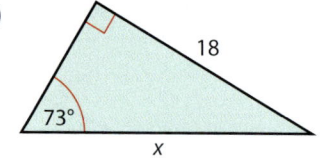

   Give each answer correct to 1 decimal place.

8. Find the values of *x* and *y*, correct to the nearest whole number, in the given triangle.

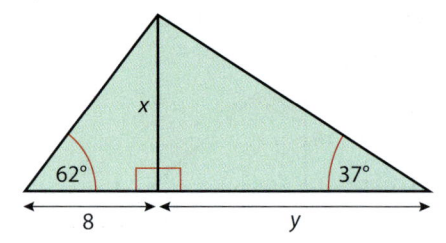

9. Work out the length of the side marked with a letter in each of the following triangles. Give each answer correct to 1 decimal place.

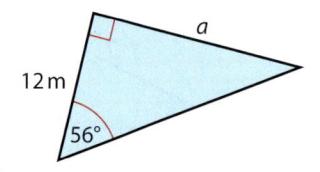

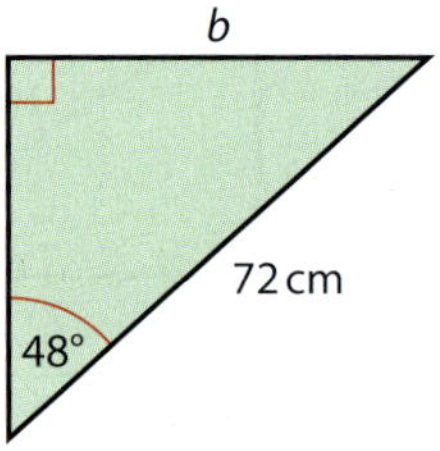

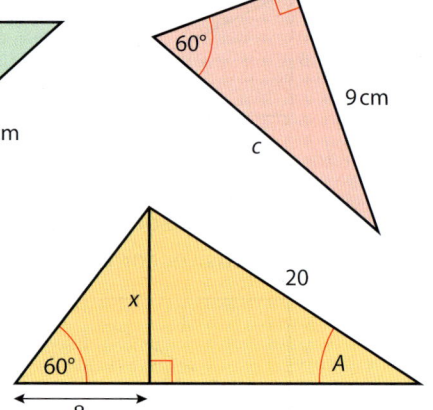

10. In the given triangle, find
    (i) *x*, correct to 1 decimal place
    (ii) the angle *A*, correct to the nearest degree.

510

11. ABCD is a rectangle as shown.
If $|DC| = 11$ cm and $|\angle BDC| = 28°$, find the length of the diagonal [DB].
Give your answer in centimetres, correct to one decimal place.

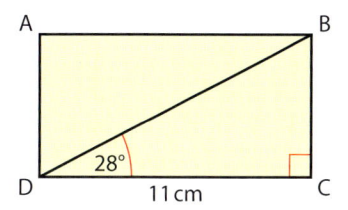

12. The diagram represents the frame, PQRS, of a roof.

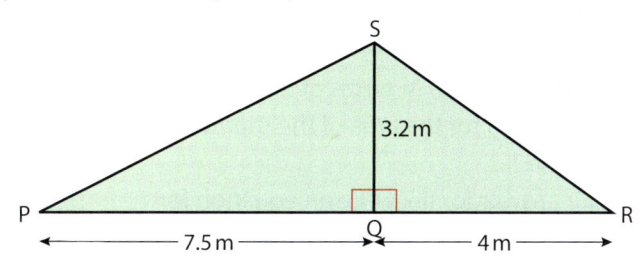

$|PQ| = 7.5$ m, $|QR| = 4$ m and $|SQ| = 3.2$ m.
(i) Calculate the length of [PS].
(ii) Find $|\angle SRQ|$, correct to the nearest degree.

13. In the given diagram, $|AD| = 6$ cm, $|DB| = 9$ cm, $|\angle CAD| = 35°$ and $CD \perp AB$.

Find (i) $|CD|$, correct to 1 decimal place
(ii) $|\angle CBD|$, correct to the nearest degree.

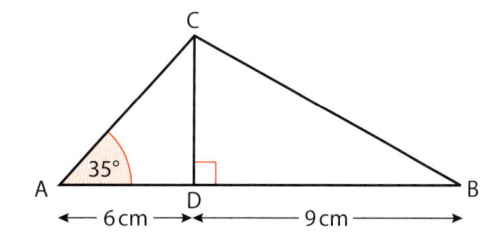

14. Find the value of: (i) $\cos^2 45°$ (ii) $\tan^2 30°$ (iii) $\sin^2 60°$

Note: $\sin^2 A = (\sin A)^2$

15. Show that (i) $1 - \sin^2 30° = \cos^2 30$ (ii) $\sin 60° = 2 \sin 30° \cos 30°$

16. Using your knowledge of trigonometric ratios, write an equation for h, the perpendicular height of the equilateral triangle shown.

Hence find the area of the triangle, leaving your answer in surd form.

Based on the symmetry of the triangle, describe a second method for calculating the perpendicular height, h.

Use the second method to find h, leaving your answer in surd form.

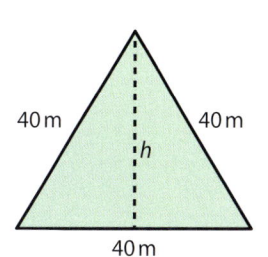

Investigation:

Examine the triangle given with sides *a* and *b* and the angle *C* contained between these sides.
h is the perpendicular height of the triangle.
In the chart:

(i) Write down the ratio for sin *C*.
Hence:
(ii) Write an equation for *h* in terms of *a* and sin *C*.
(iii) Write an equation for the area of the triangle in terms of *b* and *h*.
(iv) Using your answer for (ii), write an equation for the area of a triangle in terms of *a*, *b* and sin *C*.

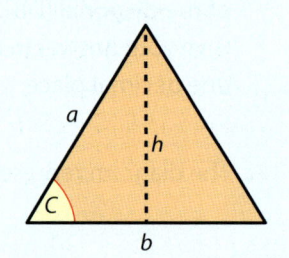

(i) sin *C* =
(ii) *h* =
(iii) Area =
(iv) Area =

Conclusion: _____

Section 22.5 Using trigonometry to solve problems

The terms **angle of elevation** and **angle of depression** will occur frequently when dealing with trigonometric problems.
The diagrams below illustrate what these terms mean.

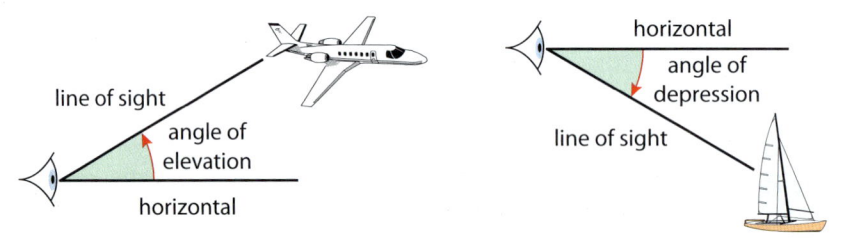

A **clinometer** is generally used to measure angles of elevation and depression.

Chapter 22 Trigonometry

Example 1

Alan stands at A, directly under the end of a crane. From A, he walks 10 m to B. At B, he measures the angle of elevation of the end of the crane as 73°.

How high is the end of the crane?

We will use the tangent of 73° to find h.

$$\frac{h}{10} = \tan 73°$$

$$h = 10 \times \tan 73°$$

$$h = 10\,(3.2709)$$

$$h = 32.709 \text{ m}$$

∴ the height of the end of the crane is 32.7 m.

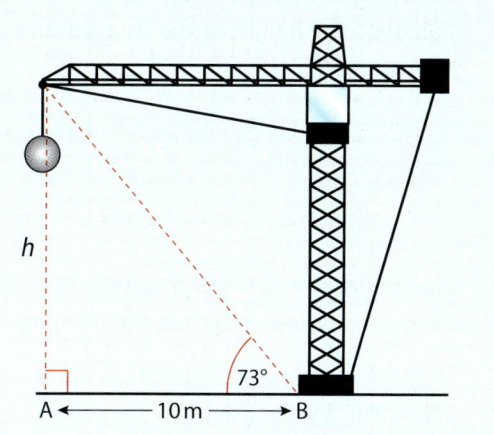

Note: The tan of an angle in a right-angled triangle is defined as, $\tan \theta = \dfrac{\text{Opposite}}{\text{Adjacent}} = \dfrac{h}{d}$

In chapter 11, when studying coordinate geometry, the slope of a line, ℓ, was given as,

slope $= \dfrac{\text{Rise}}{\text{Run}} = \dfrac{h}{d}$

Trigonometry provides another method for finding the slope of a line, e.g. a roof.

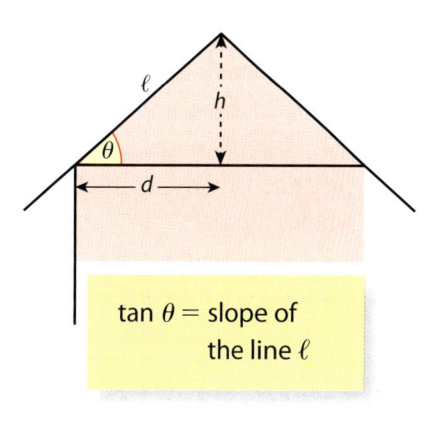

$\tan \theta =$ slope of the line ℓ

Exercise 22.5

1. A ladder makes an angle of 70° with the ground. The foot of the ladder is 1.2 m from the wall. How long is this ladder?

   Give your answer correct to 1 decimal place.

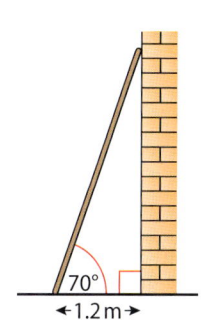

Text & Tests 2 Higher Level

2. From a point on the ground 20 m from the base of a tree, the angle of elevation to the top of the tree is 47°. Calculate the height of the tree, correct to the nearest metre.

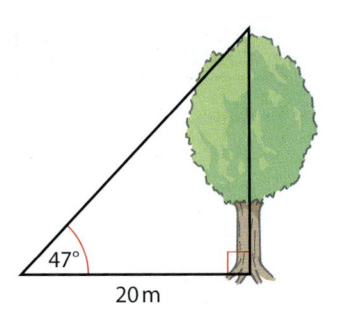

3. The diagram shows a lighthouse, 30 m in height, standing on horizontal ground.

    Work out the angle of elevation of the top of the lighthouse from the point A on the ground, correct to the nearest degree.

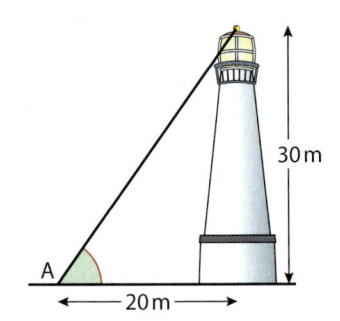

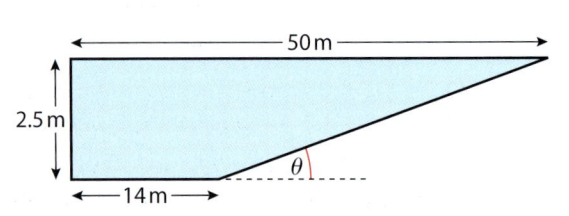

4. Two yachts sail into a harbour at R. Their positions are shown in the given diagram where PQ is perpendicular to PR.
    (i) Find the distance from Q to R.
    (ii) Find the measure of the angle PRQ.
    Give each answer correct to the nearest whole number.

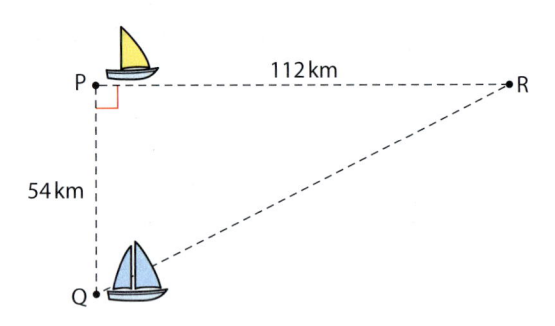

5. Paula stands at point P on the bank of a river. Vertically across from her on the other bank is a tree, T.
    She walks 25 metres along the bank to a point Q. She measures the angle between QT and QP and finds that it is 38°.
    Find the width of the river, correct to the nearest metre.

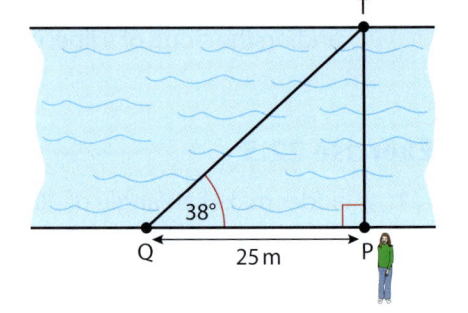

6. The diagram shows the cross-section of a swimming pool.
    θ is the angle the sloping part makes with the horizontal.
    Find θ, correct to the nearest degree.

Chapter 22 Trigonometry

7. From the top of a 25 m high cliff, the angle of depression of a canoe is 28°. How far is this canoe from the foot of the cliff? Give your answer correct to the nearest metre.

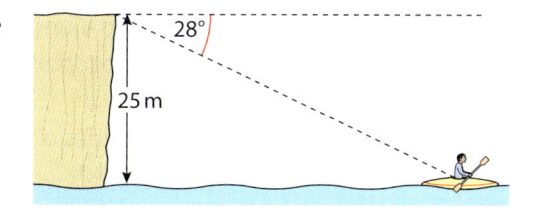

8. Andy stood 5 m from the foot of a tree. He measured the angle of elevation of the top of the tree as 59° and the angle of depression of the foot of the tree as 20°.
    (i) What is the length of [GH]?
    (ii) Work out the length of [TH], correct to 1 decimal place.
    (iii) What other calculations need to be made to find the height of the tree?
    (iv) What is the height of the tree, in metres, correct to 1 decimal place?

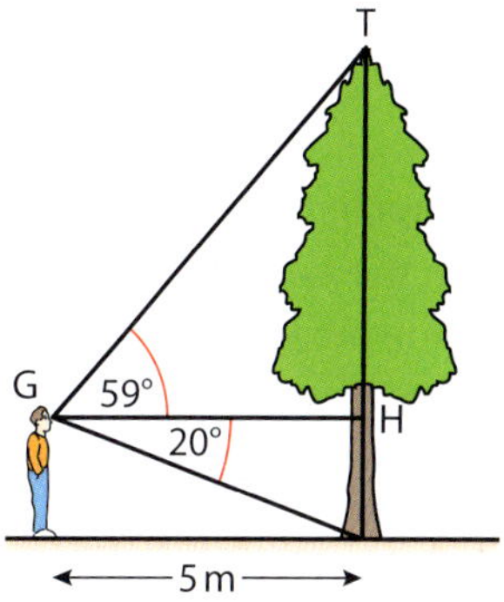

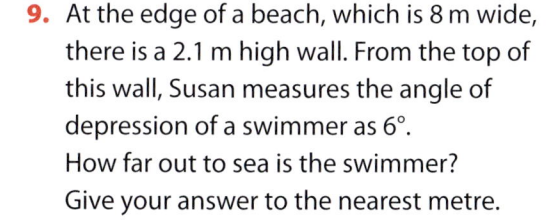

9. At the edge of a beach, which is 8 m wide, there is a 2.1 m high wall. From the top of this wall, Susan measures the angle of depression of a swimmer as 6°.
   How far out to sea is the swimmer? Give your answer to the nearest metre.

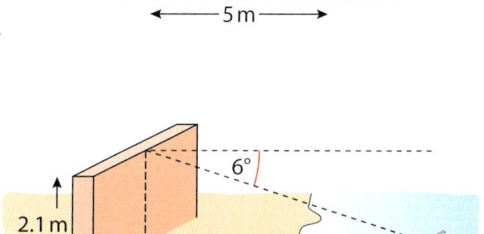

10. The diagram shows a vertical building standing on horizontal ground.
    The points A, B and C are in a straight line on the ground.
    The point T is at the top of the building so that TC is vertical.
    The angle of elevation of T from A is 40°, as shown in the diagram.

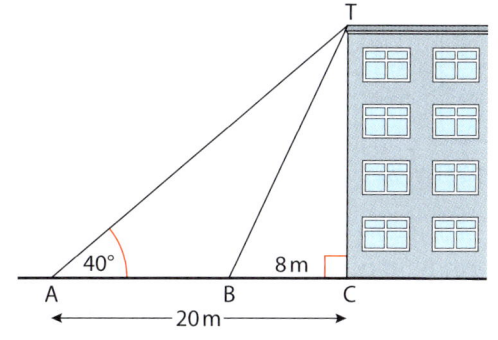

    (i) Work out the height, |TC|, of the building.
    (ii) Work out the size of the angle of elevation of T from B.
    (iii) Work out the size of angle ATB.
    Give all answers correct to the nearest whole number.

515

Text & Tests 2 Higher Level

11. Drainage pipes were being laid along the diagonal of a rectangular paddock, as shown in this diagram.
At what angle, to the shorter sides of this paddock, were the pipes laid?
Give your answer correct to the nearest degree.

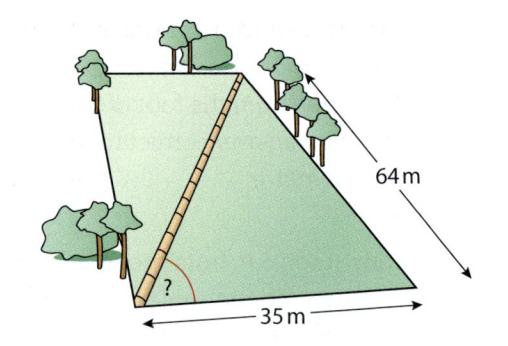

12. A flagpole is on the top of a government building. From the point D, 4 m from the base of the building, Joanne measures the angles of elevation of the top, A, and the bottom, B, of the flagpole.
Her measurements are shown on the diagram.

(i) Find the length [AC].
(ii) Find the length [BC] and the height, h, of the flagpole.
Give all answers correct to 1 decimal place.

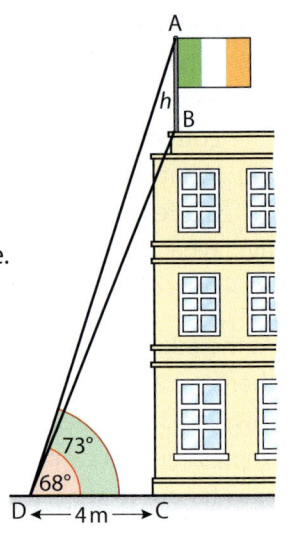

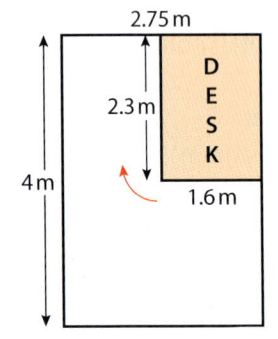

13.

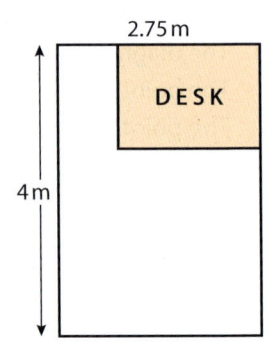

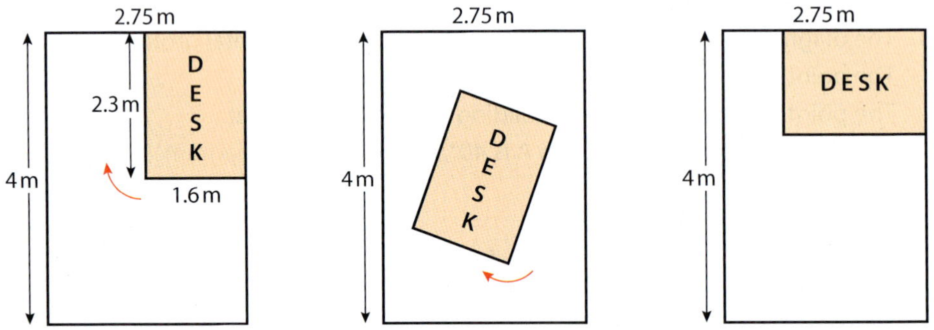

Is it possible to turn a 2.3 m by 1.6 m desk in a room that is 4 m by 2.75 m? Explain your answer.

14. The guidelines for preventing occupational overuse syndrome say that you should sit with your eyes 55 cm from the centre of the screen and at an angle of depression of 15°.

(i) What height should your eyes be above the centre of the screen?
(ii) What horizontal distance should you sit from the screen?
Give each answer in centimetres, correct to 1 decimal place.

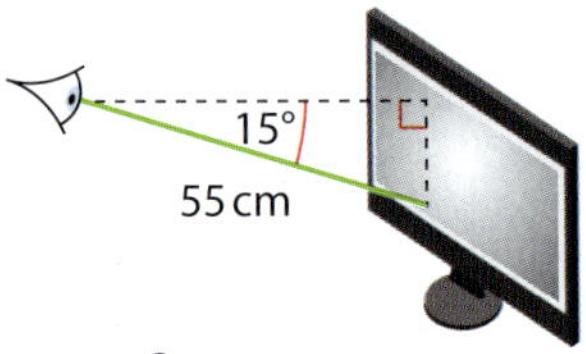

15. Marguerite finds the distance between two boats, P and R, on the other side of the river, as follows.
She begins at A, opposite boat P.
From A she walks to B, a distance of 54 m.
She measures the angle ABP as 43° and angle CBR as 47°.
From these measurements, she is able to find the distance, |PR|, between the two boats.
  (i) Calculate w, the width of the river, using the triangle APB.
  (ii) Using triangle CBR, calculate the distance |BC|. Hence find the distance between the boats.
Give each answer in metres, correct to 1 decimal place.

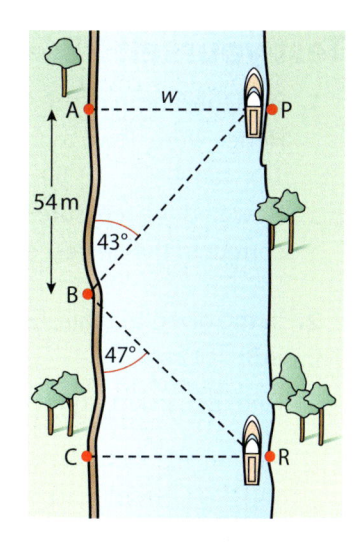

16. The diagram shows a vertical cliff face, PZ, standing on a horizontal beach, XYZ.
The angle of elevation of P from a rock on the beach at X is 44°, as shown in the diagram.
  (i) Work out the height, PZ, of the cliff face.
  (ii) Work out the angle of elevation of P, from the point Y on the beach, to the nearest degree.
  (iii) Work out the size of angle XPY to the nearest degree.

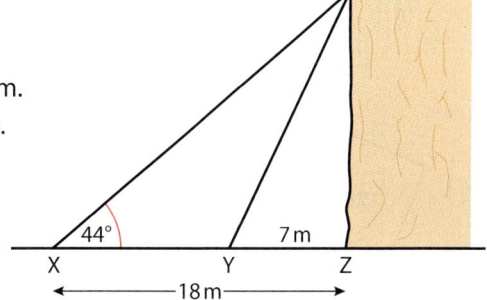

17. Harry wants to refelt the roof of his lean-to shed.
Felt is sold in 5 m rolls that are 1 m wide.
They cost €40 each.
  (i) How many rolls will he need to buy?
The felt is stuck on with an adhesive which costs €18 for a 2.5 litre tin. It will cover 6 m².
  (ii) How much will Harry have to pay for the materials to do the job?

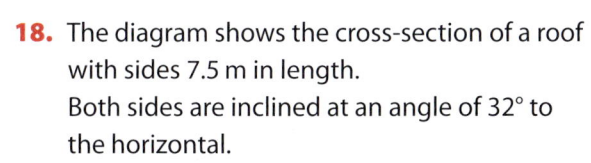

18. The diagram shows the cross-section of a roof with sides 7.5 m in length.
Both sides are inclined at an angle of 32° to the horizontal.
  (i) Find the height marked h.
  (ii) Find the width, w, of the roof support.
  (iii) Find the slope of the roof correct to 3 places of decimals.
Give each answer in metres, correct to 1 decimal place.

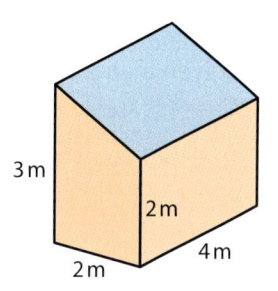

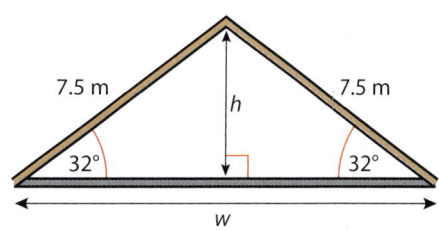

Text & Tests 2 Higher Level

Test yourself 22

1. Find the length of the side marked *x* in the given triangle.
   Hence write down as fractions
      (i) tan A   (ii) sin A   (iii) cos A.
   Now find the measure of the angle A,
   correct to the nearest degree.

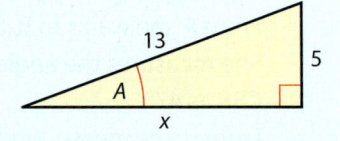

2. In the given triangle, $|\angle ACB| = 34°$, $|\angle ABC| = 90°$ and $|AB| = 12$ cm.

   Find $|BC|$, in cm, correct to one decimal place.

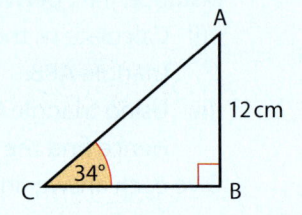

3. Find the missing area in each of the following figures:
   (i)   (ii)   (iii)

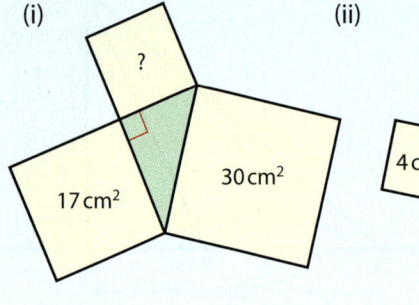

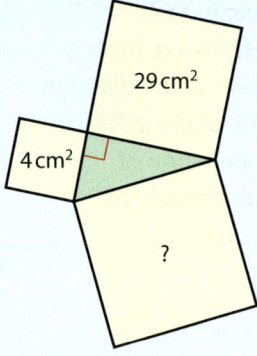

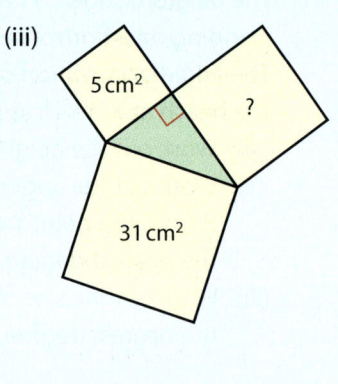

4. In the given triangle, $|AB| = 12$ cm, $|CD| = 20$ cm, $|\angle ABC| = 43°$ and $|\angle ACD| = 90°$.

   (i) Find $|AC|$, correct to the nearest cm.
   (ii) Find $|\angle ADC|$, correct to the nearest degree.

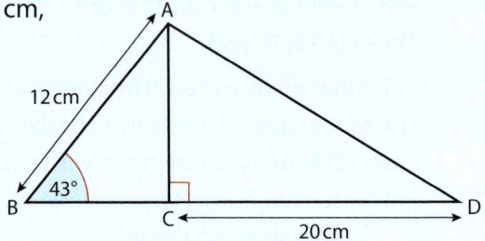

5. A plane, which took off from Shannon Airport, had gained an altitude of 2.1 km after it had travelled 8 km.

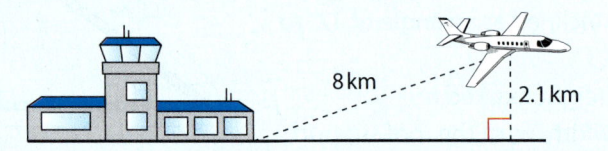

   At what angle was this plane climbing?
   Give your answer to the nearest degree.

518

Chapter 22 Trigonometry

6. In the given diagram, |AD| = 6 cm, |DB| = 9 cm, |∠CAD| = 35° and CD is perpendicular to AB.

   (i) Find |CD|, in cm, correct to one decimal place.
   (ii) Find |∠CBD|, correct to the nearest degree.

7. Use the triangle on the right to write the value of $\sin^2 60° + \cos^2 30°$ in the form $\frac{a}{b}$, where $a, b \in \mathbb{N}$.

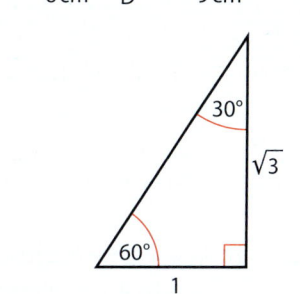

8. The diagram shows the design for a logo that is to be hung outside a company's headquarters. It comprises triangles ABC and ADE. The angles ACB and ADE are both 90°.

   (i) Work out the length of [AC], correct to the nearest whole number.
   (ii) Find |∠DAE|, correct to the nearest degree.

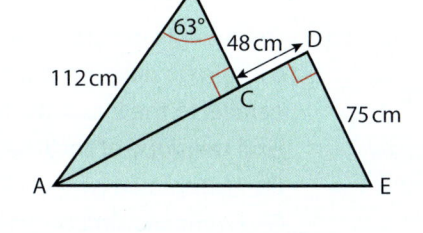

9. The dimensions for the side of a bird box are shown in the diagram on the right. Calculate the length of the side [PS]. Give your answer in cm, correct to 1 decimal place.

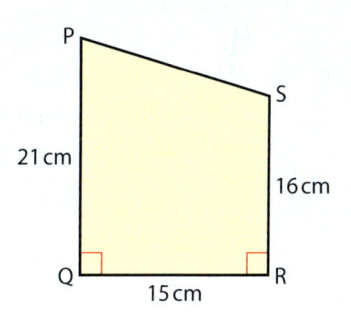

10. Find the missing length in each of the following figures:

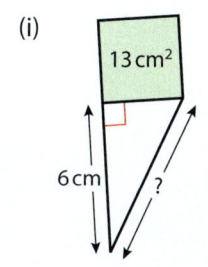

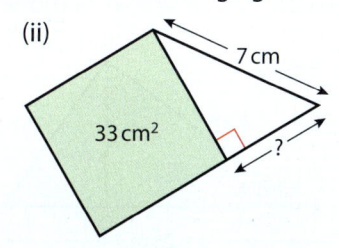

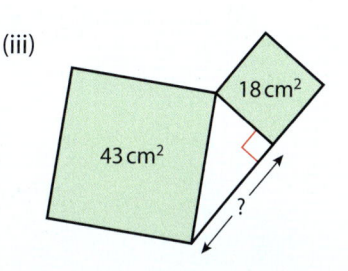

    (i)   (ii)   (iii)

Text & Tests 2 Higher Level

11. By how many degrees is the angle *x* bigger than the angle *y*?

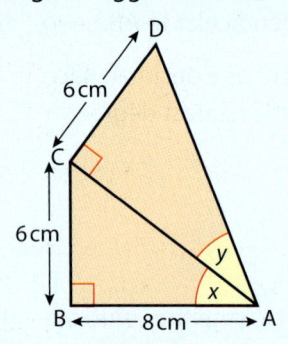

Give your answer correct to the nearest degree.

12. (i) In the given right-angled triangle, one of the acute angles is four times as large as the other acute angle.
Find the measures of the two acute angles.

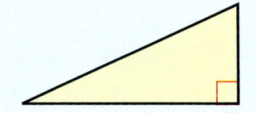

(ii) The triangle in part (i) is placed on a coordinate diagram. The base is parallel to the *x*-axis, as shown.
Find the slope of the line ℓ that contains the hypotenuse of the triangle.
Give your answer correct to two decimal places.

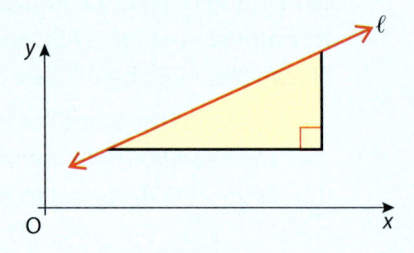

13. The given triangle ABC is right-angled at B.
(i) Calculate the area of triangle ABC.

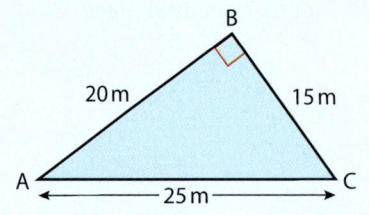

(ii) |BD|, the height of triangle ABC, is drawn as shown.

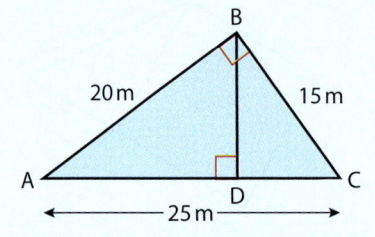

Use your answer to part (i) to calculate the height |BD|.

Chapter 22 Trigonometry

14. A group of students wish to calculate the height of the Millennium Spire in Dublin. The Spire stands on flat, level ground. Maria, who is 1.72 m tall, looks up at the top of the Spire using a clinometer and records an angle of elevation of 60°. Her feet are 70 m from the base of the Spire. Ultan measures the circumference of the base of the Spire as 7.07 m.
   (i) Explain how Ultan's measurement will be used in the calculation of the height of the Spire.
   (ii) Draw a suitable diagram and calculate the height of the Spire, to the nearest metre, using the measurements obtained by the students.

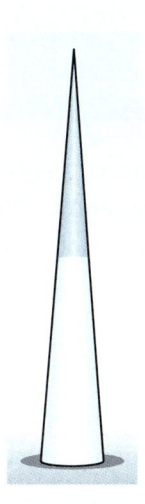

15. Mary is thinking of buying a new television. The television is advertised as having a "40 inch" screen. This refers to the diagonal measurement of the screen. The *aspect ratio* of a television screen is the ratio of its width to its height. For this television, the aspect ratio is 16 : 9 (sixteen units wide for every nine units in height).
   (i) Convert 40 inches to centimetres if
       1 inch = 2.54 cm.
   (ii) Find the width and height of the screen in cm.
       Give your answers correct to the nearest cm.
   (iii) A different 40-inch television screen has an aspect ratio of 4 : 3.
       Which of the two television screens has the greater area, and by how much?

16. Find the values of *a* and *b* in the given diagram, where the right angles are indicated.
Give each answer as a surd.

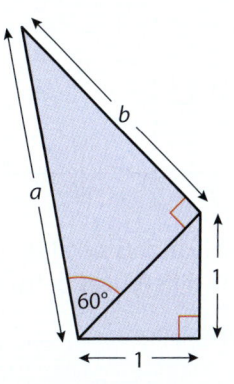

521

Assignment:

Consider a right-angled triangle with hypotenuse of length 1 unit.

As the base angle *A* in this triangle increases, the value of each trigonometric ratio changes.

Copy and complete the chart below, giving each ratio correct to two places of decimals.

On a large sheet of squared paper, graph each set of points in a different colour.

Join and label each set of points.

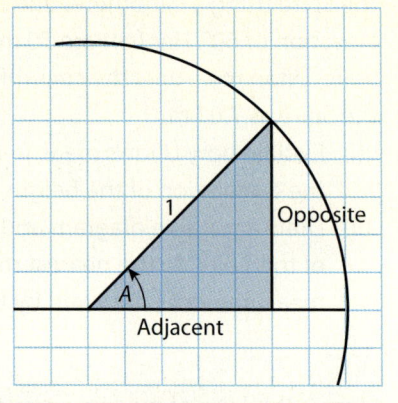

Ratio\angle	0°	10°	20°	30°	40°	50°	60°	70°	80°	90°	100°
Sin											
Cos											
Tan											

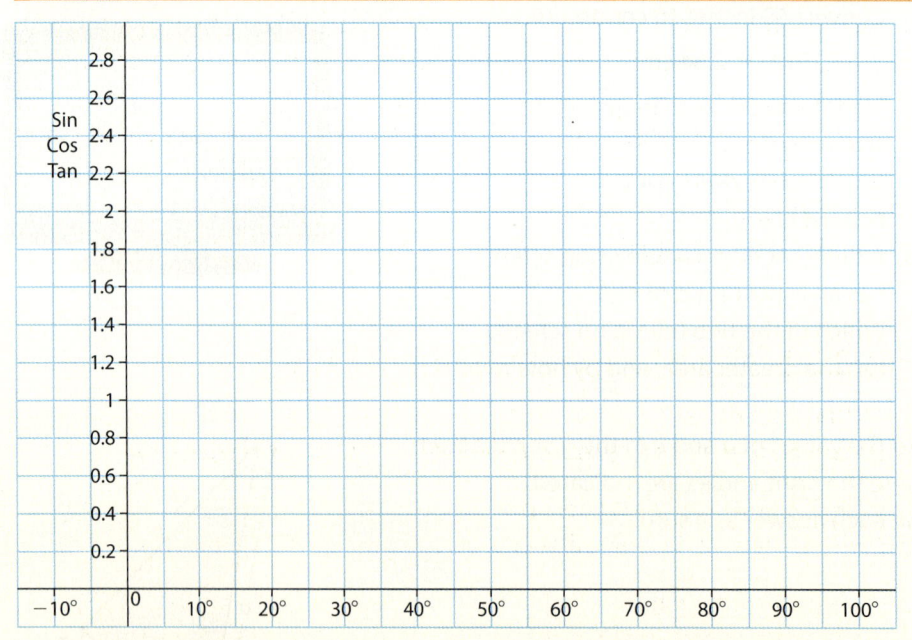

Based on this small sample of angles, what observation could you make about the main differences between the graphs of sine, cosine and tangent?

Observations: _____

_____.

Graphing functions

chapter 23

From first year, you will recall how to:

- draw x and y axes, and label the origin,
- plot points onto a coordinated plane.

In this chapter, you will learn to:

- input various values from a given domain into a function,
- plot the resulting couples onto a coordinated plane,
- create a straight-line graph from a linear function,
- create a ∪ or ∩ shaped graph from a quadratic function,
- use a quadratic graph to solve a quadratic equation,
- identify the maximum or minimum point of a quadratic graph,
- create a rapidly increasing or decreasing graph from an exponential function,
- use graphs to find the point of intersection of two functions,
- make connections between the shape of a graph and an associated word problem,
- understand how to map a function around the coordinated plane.

Section 23.1 Graphing linear functions

Consider the function $f(x) = x + 3$.
This function can be written as a set of couples by taking different values for x.

$f(1) = 1 + 3 = 4 \Rightarrow (1, 4)$ is one couple.
$f(2) = 2 + 3 = 5 \Rightarrow (2, 5)$ is another couple.

Other couples are $(0, 3), (-3, 0), \ldots$
When these couples are plotted and joined, they will form a line, as shown.

Since the graph of $f(x) = x + 3$ is a line, we say f(x) is a **linear function**.

A line is the most straightforward function to graph as we need only two points to plot it.

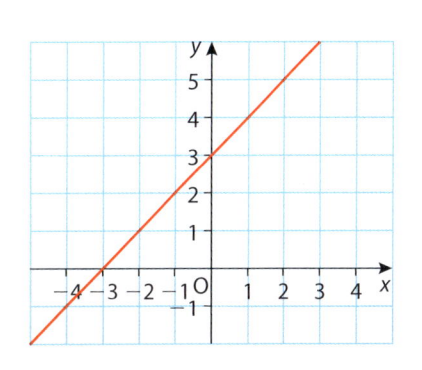

523

Usually we are given the domain in which to draw any function.
The domain $x = -2$ to $x = 3$, both included, is written as $-2 \leq x \leq 3$.

When plotting a line, two points are sufficient to plot but we generally take three points in case any errors are made.

> ### Example 1
>
> Graph the function $f(x) = 2x - 4$ in the domain $-1 \leq x \leq 4$.
> Use your graph to find
> (i) $f(3)$ (ii) the value of x for which $f(x) = -2$.
>
> To find three points, we select the smallest and largest x-values in the given domain and one value for x in between those two.
>
> | x | 2x − 4 | y |
> |----|--------|----|
> | −1 | −2 − 4 | −6 |
> | 0 | 0 − 4 | −4 |
> | 4 | 8 − 4 | 4 |
>
> The three points are $(-1, -6)$, $(0, -4)$ and $(4, 4)$.
> Join these points to give a line.
>
> (i) $f(3)$ represents the y-value when $x = 3$.
>   From the graph, this is 2, i.e., $f(3) = 2$.
>
> (ii) $f(x) = -2 \Rightarrow y = -2$
>   The value of x in the graph when $y = -2$ is $x = 1$.

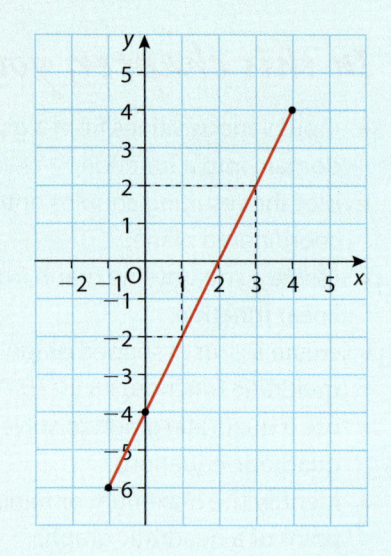

The intercept method for drawing a line

If the equation of a line is in a form such as $3x - 4y = 12$, it is more convenient to find the two points where the line intersects the x-axis and y-axis.

$3x - 4y = 12$

$x = 0 \Rightarrow 0 - 4y = 12 \Rightarrow y = -3$

∴ $(0, -3)$ is one point on the line.

$y = 0 \Rightarrow 3x = 12 \Rightarrow x = 4$

∴ $(4, 0)$ is a second point on the line.

These points are joined to give the required line.

This method is generally called the **intercept method**.

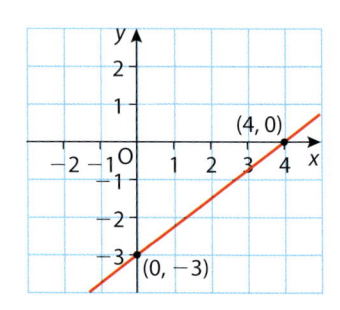

Chapter 23 Graphing functions

Remember

1. **Horizontal lines**, i.e. lines parallel to the x-axis are written as $y = ?$

2. **Vertical lines**, i.e. lines parallel to the y-axis are written as $x = ?$

Exercise 23.1

1. Copy and complete the table on the right and use the table to draw a graph of the line $y = 2x - 3$ in the domain $-1 \leqslant x \leqslant 4$.

x	2x − 3	y
−1		
0		
1		
2		
3		
4		

2. Draw the graph of $f(x) = 2x - 5$ in the domain $0 \leqslant x \leqslant 5$.

3. Copy and complete the table on the right and hence draw a graph of the function $f(x) = 3x - 4$ in the domain $-1 \leqslant x \leqslant 3$.

x	3x − 4	y
−1		
0		
3		

4. Draw the graph of the function $f(x) = 6 - x$ in the domain $0 \leqslant x \leqslant 6$ by finding only three points on the line.

5. Draw the graph of the function $f(x) = 2x - 2$ in the domain $-2 \leqslant x \leqslant 3$.

525

6. Drawn on the right is the graph of a function $y = f(x)$.

   Use this graph to write down

   (i) $f(3)$ (ii) $f(0)$ (iii) $f(-4)$

   (iv) the value of x when $f(x) = -2$

   (v) the value of x when $f(x) = 6$.

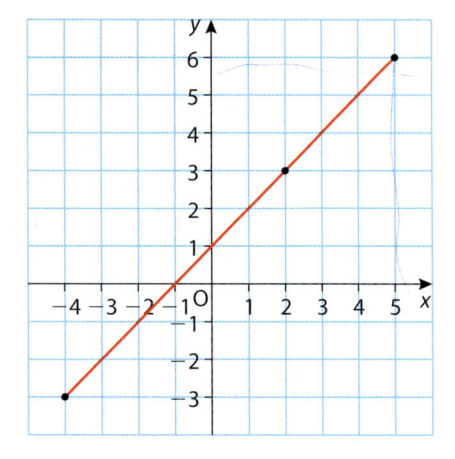

7. The given diagram shows the graphs of two lines,
   $$f(x) = x + 1 \text{ and } g(x) = 2x - 2.$$

   (i) Write down the point of intersection of the two lines.

   (ii) What is the meaning of the equation $f(x) = g(x)$ in this situation? 3

   (iii) Solve the equation $x + 1 = 2x - 2$. Is there any connection between the value you found for x and the point of intersection of the two lines?

   (iv) Is there another way of finding the point of intersection of two lines besides drawing their graphs?

   (v) If $f(k)$ has the same value as $g(k)$, write down the value of k.

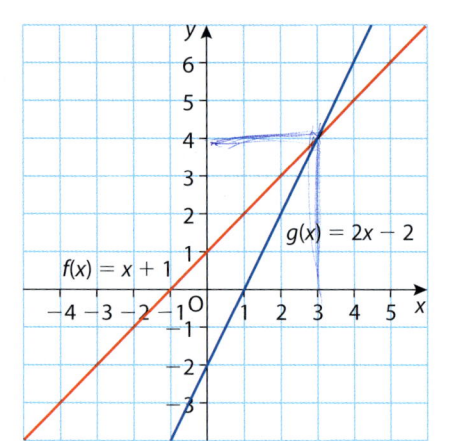

8. On the same diagram, draw the lines $y = 5 - x$ and $y = 2x - 4$, in the domain $0 \leq x \leq 4$.

   Use your graph to write down the point of intersection of the two lines.

9. By finding the couples $(*, 0)$ and $(0, *)$, draw a graph of the line $y = 4 - 2x$.

10. Use the intercept method to draw the graph of the line $3x + 2y = 6$.

11. Use the intercept method to draw the following two lines on the same graph:
    $$2x + y = 4 \text{ and } x - y = 2.$$

    Where do the two lines intersect?

Chapter 23 Graphing functions

12. The lines $y = x + 2$, $y = -x + 2$ and $y = 2x + 2$ have been graphed on the same axes on the right.

   (i) How are the lines similar?
   (ii) How are the linear equations similar?
   (iii) How are the lines different?
   (iv) How are the linear equations different?

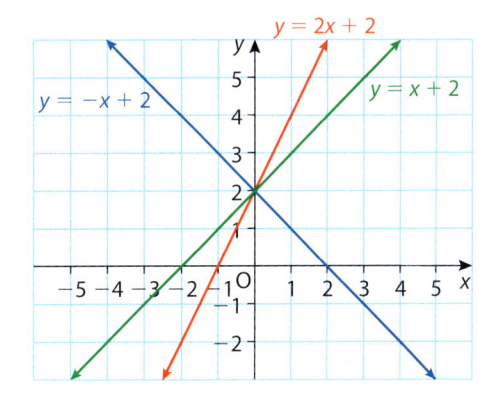

13. Write down the next three points of the pattern started below:

$(1, 8), (0, 6), (-1, 4) \ldots$

Now plot these points to show that they lie on a straight line.

14. Penguins survive in freezing climates. The temperature $T\,°C$ at a penguin colony, t hours after midnight, is given by the rule $T = -0.5t - 1$.

t	0	1	2	3	4	5	6
T							

   (i) Complete the table, which gives the temperatures up to 6 a.m.
   (ii) Plot the points whose coordinates are given by the values in the table on a set of axes of your own.
   (iii) Join the plotted points with a straight line. Do not extend the line.
   (iv) From your graph, read off the temperature at 5.30 a.m..
   (v) Use the rule that relates T to t to find the exact temperature at 5.30 a.m..

15. Ian and Liz decide to walk to the local swimming pool which is half a kilometre away.
Liz begins to walk at a speed of 40 metres per minute.
Ian starts 2 minutes later and walks at a speed of 50 metres per minute.

   (i) Copy and complete the following table which shows how many metres Liz has walked after various minutes:

t (min)	0	1	2	3	4	5	6	7	8	9	10
d (metres)	0	40	80								

   (ii) On a set of axes of your own, plot the points given in this table.
Set out t values along the horizontal axis and d values up the vertical axis.
Join the plots with a straight line.
Label and scale your axes clearly.

(iii) Copy and complete this table which shows how many metres Ian has walked after various minutes:

t (min)	0	1	2	3	4	5	6	7	8	9	10
d (metres)	0	0	0	50							

(iv) Using a different colour, plot these values on the same set of axes.
Join the plotted points to form a straight line.

(v) From the two graphs, find out when Ian meets up with Liz.
How far has each walked when they meet?

Section 23.2 Graphs of quadratic functions

The curve on the right is called a **parabola**.
The name parabola comes from the Greek word for throw, because when a ball, for example, is thrown high in the air, its path makes a parabolic shape.

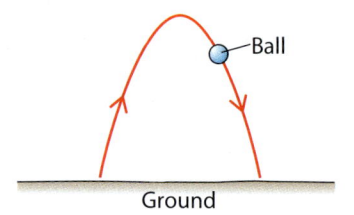

Suspension bridges, such as the Golden Gate bridge in San Francisco, form parabolic curves.

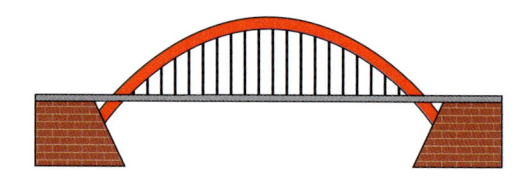

The simplest quadratic function is $y = x^2$.
Its graph can be drawn from a table of values from $x = -3$ to $x = 3$.

x	−3	−2	−1	0	1	2	3
y	9	4	1	0	1	4	9

The points shown on this curve are:
$(-3, 9), (-2, 4), (-1, 1), (0, 0), (1, 1), (2, 4), (3, 9)$

When these points are joined, a smooth curve called a parabola is formed.
Notice that this curve is symmetrical about the y-axis.
Hence the y-axis is called **the axis of symmetry**.

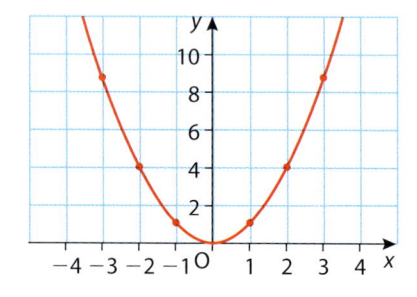

The function shown above may be written in one of these ways:

(i) $y = x^2$ (ii) $f(x) = x^2$ (iii) $f : x \to x^2$

A function in the form $f(x) = ax^2 + bx + c$, where a, b and c are constants and $a \neq 0$, is called a **quadratic function**.

Chapter 23 Graphing functions

It is called a quadratic function because it contains a term in x^2.

To draw the **graph of a quadratic function**, we take a given number of x values (domain) and find the corresponding f(x) values (or y-values) and plot the resulting points.

When asked to draw the graph of a function, we are usually given the x-values we are to use. The values of x from -2 to 3 inclusive are written as $-2 \leqslant x \leqslant 3$.

The steps used in drawing a quadratic graph are given in the following example.

Example 1

Draw the graph of the function $f(x) = x^2 - 2x - 3$ in the domain $-2 \leqslant x \leqslant 4$.

We set out a table of ordered pairs as follows:

x	$x^2 - 2x - 3$	y
-2	$4 + 4 - 3$	5
-1	$1 + 2 - 3$	0
0	$0 + 0 - 3$	-3
1	$1 - 2 - 3$	-4
2	$4 - 4 - 3$	-3
3	$9 - 6 - 3$	0
4	$16 - 8 - 3$	5

Plotting these ordered pairs, we get the following curve:

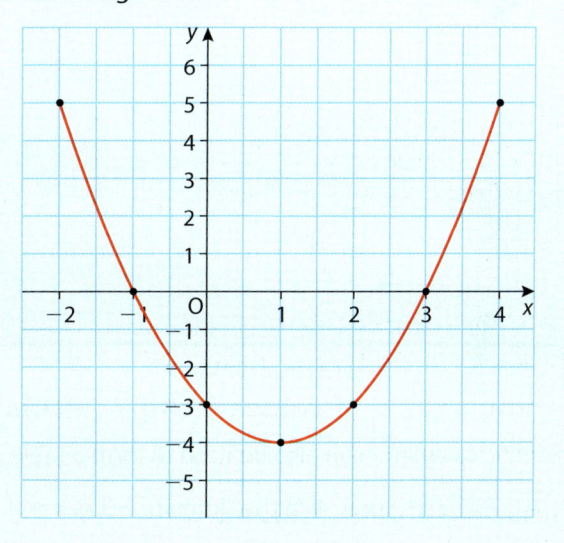

The ordered pairs found are:
$(-2, 5), (-1, 0), (0, -3), (1, -4),$
$(2, -3), (3, 0), (4, 5)$.

Graphing functions when the coefficient of x^2 is negative

If the coefficient of x^2 is negative in a quadratic function, e.g., $f(x) = -3x^2 + 4$, then the graph of the function will take the shape shown on the right.

x^2 negative

529

Example 2

Draw the graph of the function $f(x) = -x^2 + 3x + 4$ in the domain $-2 \leq x \leq 5$.

The table of values is set out below:

x	$-x^2 + 3x + 4$	y
−2	−4 − 6 + 4	−6
−1	−1 − 3 + 4	0
0	0 + 0 + 4	4
1	−1 + 3 + 4	6
2	−4 + 6 + 4	6
3	−9 + 9 + 4	4
4	−16 + 12 + 4	0
5	−25 + 15 + 4	−6

The required points are:
(−2, −6), (−1, 0), (0, 4), (1, 6), (2, 6), (3, 4), (4, 0), (5, −6).
The graph of the function is shown below:

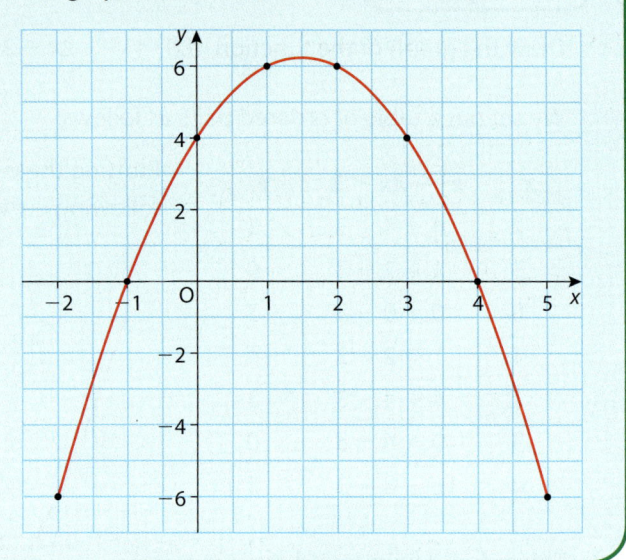

Forming a table of values using a calculator

A scientific calculator can also be used to form a table of values for a given function.

e.g. $f(x) = x^2 + x - 4$, in the domain, $-3 \leq x \leq 4$

Press mode on the calculator, a window opens with 4 options.

Press 3 for table and $f(x)$ appears on the screen.

The variable 'x' is added to the function line by **Pressing Alpha** then **)** keys.

Now the main keys for 'x^2', +, −, etc are used to complete the function.

The domain of the function is entered by **Pressing the '='** key. The calculator asks for the lowest value to **Start?** (−3)

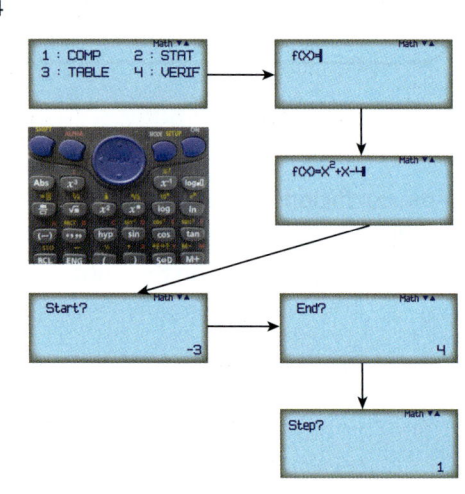

Chapter 23 Graphing functions

Pressing '=' again the calculator asks for the highest value to **End?** (4).

Pressing '=' the calculator now asks what **Step?** we want to use between (−3) and (4). The default 1 means the calculator will find values of the function for x = −3, −2, −1, 0, 1, 2, 3, 4 (in steps of 1 unit)

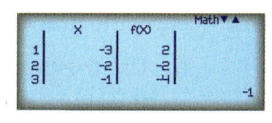

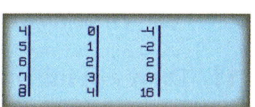

Pressing '=' finally a table of values is created in column form.

The points on the curve are:

(−3, 2), (−2, −2), (−1, −4), (0, −4), (1, −2), (2, 2), (3, 8), (4, 16).

(**Note**: Based on Casio fx-85GT.)

Exercise 23.2

1. Complete the table on the right and hence draw a graph of the function $f(x) = x^2 - 4$ in the domain $-3 \leq x \leq 3$.

x	$x^2 - 4$	y
−3		
−2		
−1		
0		
1		
2		
3		

2. Draw the graph of the function $f: x \to x^2 - 4x$ in the domain $-1 \leq x \leq 4$.

3. Draw the graph of the function $f(x) = x^2 + x - 2$ in the domain $-3 \leq x \leq 3$.

4. Draw the graph of the function $f(x) = 2x^2 - x - 3$ in the domain $-2 \leq x \leq 3$.

5. Draw the graph of the function $f(x) = 2x^2 + 3x - 4$ in the domain $-3 \leq x \leq 2$.

6. Draw the graph of the function $f(x) = 2x^2 - 5x - 3$ in the domain $-2 \leq x \leq 4$.
   Use your graph to write down the coordinates of the points at which the graph crosses the x-axis.
   Now write down the coordinates of the point where the graph crosses the y-axis.

7. Draw the graph of the function $y = -x^2$ in the domain $-2 \leq x \leq 2$.

8. Draw the graph of the function $f: x \to -x^2 + 2x + 3$ in the domain $-2 \leq x \leq 4$.
   Use your graph to find the coordinates of the points where the graph crosses the x-axis.

9. Draw the graph of the function $f: x \to -2x^2 + x + 3$ in the domain $-2 \leq x \leq 3$.
   Write down the values of x at which the curve crosses the x-axis.

Text & Tests 2 Higher Level

10. Graph the function $f(x) = -2x^2 + 7x - 3$ in the domain $-1 \leqslant x \leqslant 4$.
    (i) Use the graph to write down the coordinates of the points at which the graph intersects the x-axis.
    (ii) Write down the coordinates of the point at which the graph crosses the y-axis.

11. Draw a graph of the function $A(x) = x(8 - x)$ in the domain $0 \leqslant x \leqslant 10$.
    Write an equation for the axis of symmetry of the resulting curve.

12. A garage is x metres wide. It is 5 metres longer than it is wide. The area of the garage floor is 24m². Using this information, write a quadratic equation for the area of the floor. Draw a graph of the equation in the domain $-8 \leqslant x \leqslant 3$
    (i) What is significant about the two values $x = -8$ and $x = 3$, on the curve?
    (ii) What is the only valid value of x? Explain your answer.

Investigation:

Investigate each of the graphs of the function $f(x) = x^2 + x - 4$, below.

Sketch each of the graphs and write in the missing piece of information needed to explain the differences between the graphs.

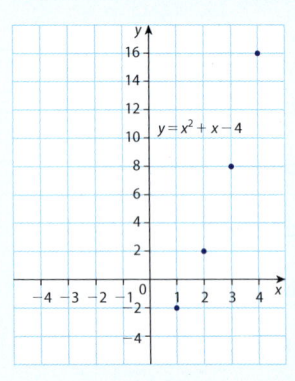

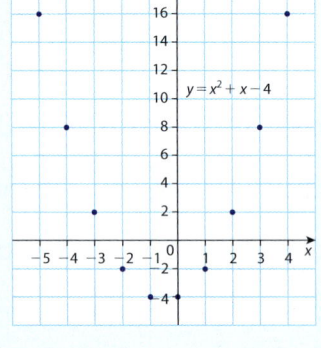

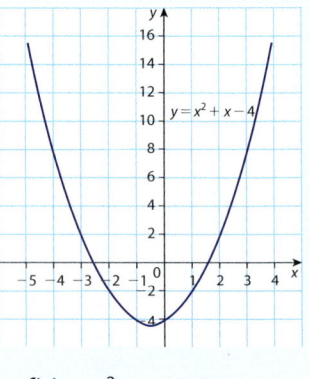

$f(x) = x^2 + x - 4,$ _____ $f(x) = x^2 + x - 4,$ _____ $f(x) = x^2 + x - 4,$ _____

Section 23.3 Using quadratic graphs

1. Solving the equation $f(x) = 0$

The graph on the right shows the curve $f(x) = x^2 - 2x - 3$ intersecting the x-axis at a and b.

The x-values of these points are the roots of the associated quadratic equation $x^2 - 2x - 3 = 0$.

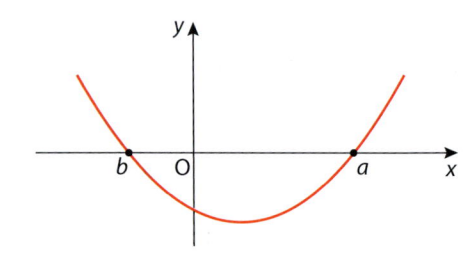

Chapter 23 Graphing functions

Why is this?

$f(x) = x^2 - 2x - 3$ may be also written as $y = x^2 - 2x - 3$.
When $y = 0$, then $x^2 - 2x - 3 = 0$.
$y = 0$ is another name for the x-axis.

Thus the solution of the equation $x^2 - 2x - 3 = 0$, gives the x-values of the points at which $y = x^2 - 2x - 3$ meets $y = 0$ i.e. where the curve crosses the x-axis.

The values are $x = 3$ and $x = -1$ (when $y = 0$).

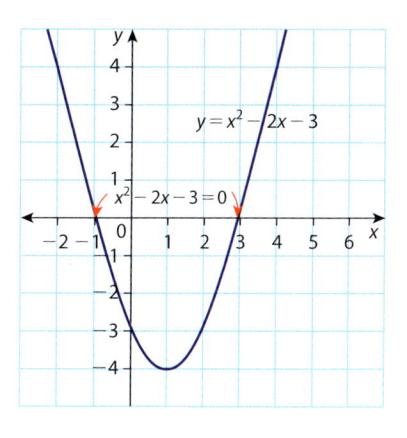

2. Solving the equation $f(x) = k$, where $k \in R$

The graph of the function $f(x) = x^2 - 3x$ is drawn below.

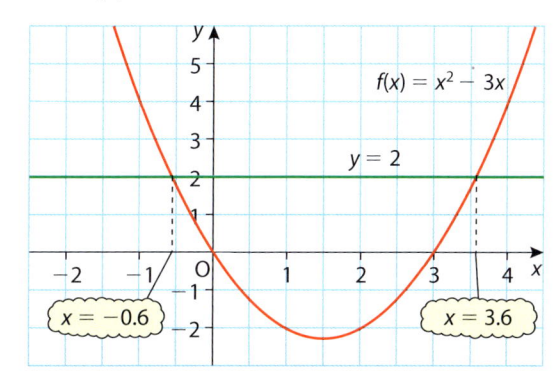

This graph can be used to solve the equation $f(x) = 2$ or $y = 2$ by drawing the line $y = 2$ and then reading from the graph the x-values of the points where the line $y = 2$ intersects the curve.

These values are $x = -0.6$ or $x = 3.6$.

3. When is a function negative?

On the right is a graph of the function $f(x) = x^2 + x - 2$.

The function is said to be **negative** when the curve is **below** the x-axis. It is negative because the $f(x)$ values (or y-values) are negative.

Thus, the function is negative for $-2 < x < 1$.

The function is **positive** when $x > 1$ or $x < -2$.

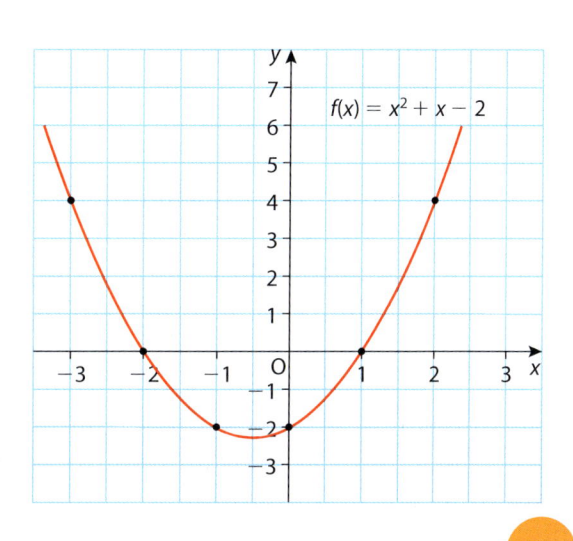

533

Text & Tests 2 Higher Level

4. Intersecting graphs

Graphed below are the functions,

$f(x) = x^2$ (i.e. $y = x^2$) and $g(x) = x + 2$ (i.e. $y = x + 2$)

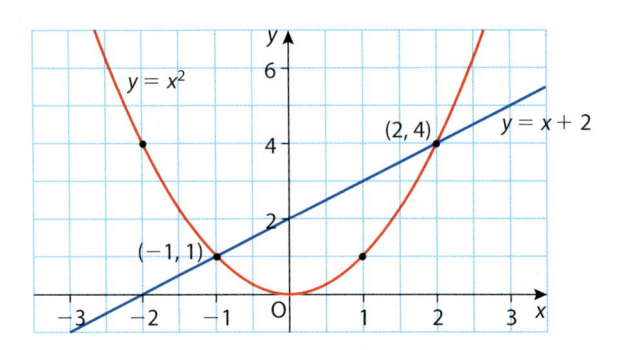

Notice that the curve $f(x)$ and the line $g(x)$ intersect at the points $(-1, 1)$ and $(2, 4)$.

We will now solve the equation $f(x) = g(x)$ to find the points of intersection.

$$\text{i.e. } x^2 = x + 2$$
$$\Rightarrow x^2 - x - 2 = 0$$
$$\Rightarrow (x + 1)(x - 2) = 0$$
$$\Rightarrow x + 1 = 0 \text{ or } x - 2 = 0$$
$$\therefore x = -1 \text{ or } x = 2.$$

Notice that these are the *x*-values of the points where the two graphs intersect.

> **Remember**
> If $f(x)$ and $g(x)$ are two functions, then the equation $f(x) = g(x)$ can be solved by drawing the graphs of the functions, using the same axes and same scales, and then writing down the *x*-values of the points of intersection of the graphs.

We can also use the curve above to solve the inequality $f(x) < g(x)$.

$f(x) < g(x)$ represents that part of the graph where the curve $f(x)$ is below the line $g(x)$.

From the graph, the curve is below the line from $x = -1$ to $x = 2$.

Thus, $f(x) < g(x)$ for $-1 < x < 2$.

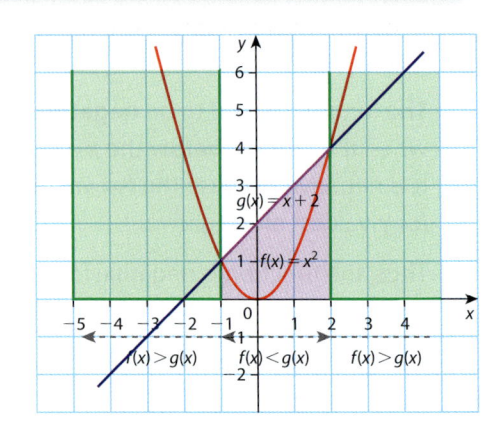

5. Maximum and minimum values

On the right is a graph of the function

$$y = x^2 - 2x - 3$$

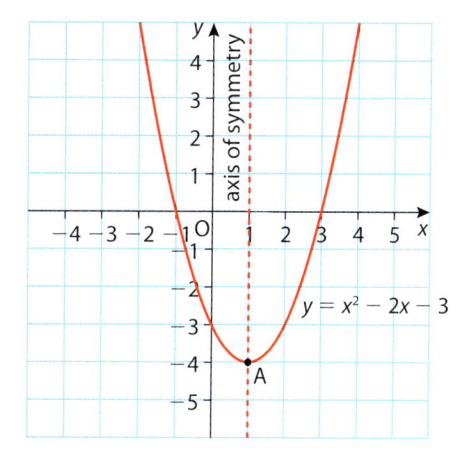

The point marked A is called the **minimum point** or **minimum turning point** of the curve.
This point is (1, −4).

The y-value of this point is called the **minimum value**.
In this graph, the minimum value is −4.

The broken red line is called the **axis of symmetry** of the curve.
The equation of this axis of symmetry is **x = 1**.

A quadratic curve with a shape like the one shown will have a **maximum turning point**.

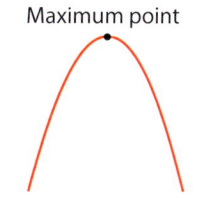

Maximum point

6. Finding f(k) from a graph

The graph of the function $f(x) = x^2 + 5x - 1$ is shown.

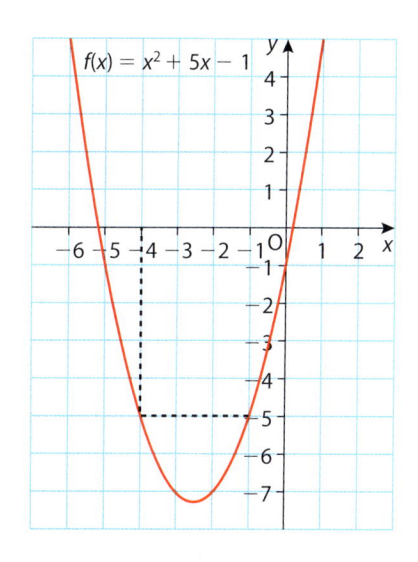

$f(-4)$ is the value of y when $x = -4$.
To find $f(-4)$, we draw the line $x = -4$ and then read the y-value of the point where this line intersects the curve.

This y-value is −5.
Thus, $f(-4) = -5$.

7. When is a function increasing or decreasing?

The given graph shows that the function is **decreasing** (i.e. the y-value is decreasing) from $x = -5$ to $x = -1$.

The function is **increasing** from $x = -1$ to $x = 3$.

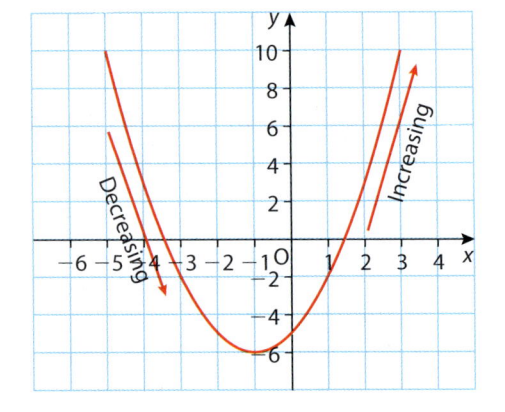

Remember

1. **Given x, to find f(x)**, draw a line vertically from the given value of x on the x-axis until it intersects the curve, then horizontally until it intersects the f(x) axis.

2. **Given f(x), to find x**, draw a line parallel to the x-axis at the given value of f(x), until it intersects the curve and then vertically until it intersects the x-axis.

(Note: this normally results in two answers)

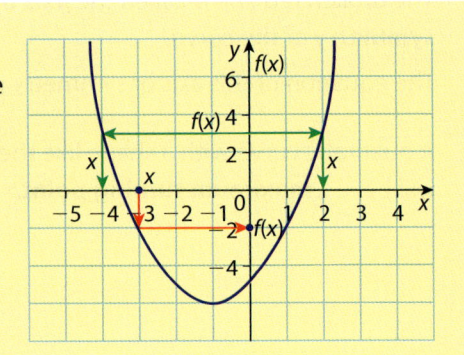

Exercise 23.3

1. The curve on the right is the graph of the function
   $$y = x^2 - 4x + 3.$$
   From the graph, write down
   (i) the coordinates of the points where the curve crosses the x-axis
   (ii) the value of y when $x = 2$
   (iii) the values of x when $y = 8$
   (iv) the minimum point of the curve.

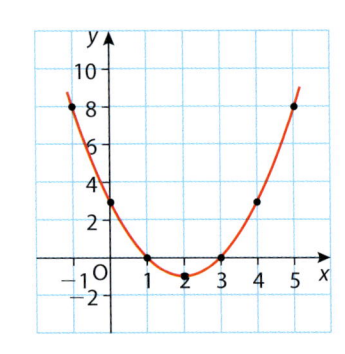

Chapter 23 Graphing functions

2. The curve on the right is the graph of the function

   $f(x) = x^2 - 1$

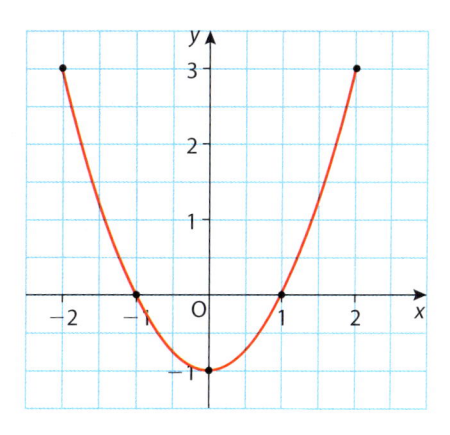

   Use the graph to find
   - (i) the value of $f(x)$ when $x = 2$
   - (ii) the value of $f(x)$ when $x = -2$
   - (iii) the minimum point of the curve
   - (iv) the values of x when $f(x) = 0$
   - (v) the values of x when $f(x) = 3$.

3. Shown below is the graph of the function

   $f(x) = x^2 - 3x - 4$ in the domain $-2 \leq x \leq 5$.

   Use the graph shown to write down
   - (i) the values of x for which $f(x) = 0$
   - (ii) the values of x for which $f(x) = 6$
   - (iii) the values of x for which $f(x) = -4$
   - (iv) the value of $f(2)$
   - (v) the value of $f\left(\frac{1}{2}\right)$
   - (vi) the coordinates of the minimum point of the curve
   - (vii) the minimum value of $f(x)$.

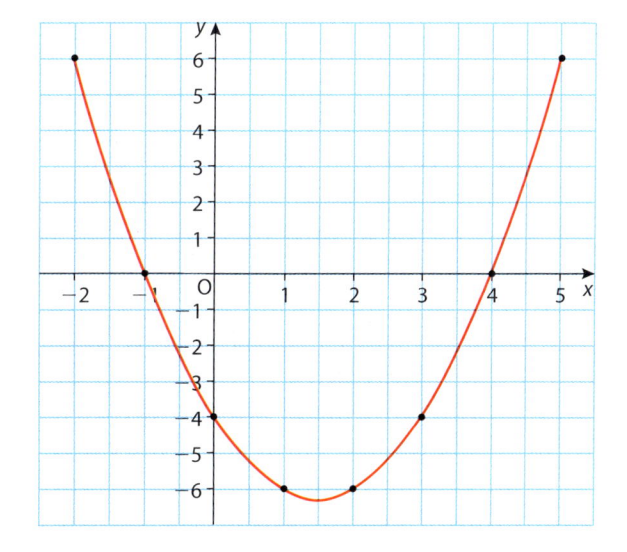

4. The graph of $f(x) = x^2 - 2x - 5$ is given on the right.
   Use this graph to write down
   - (i) $f(-3)$ and $f(1)$
   - (ii) the values of x for which $f(x) = 0$
   - (iii) the values of x for which $f(x) = 6$
   - (iv) the minimum point of the curve
   - (v) the minimum value of $f(x)$.
   - (vi) the range of values of x for which $f(x)$ is negative.

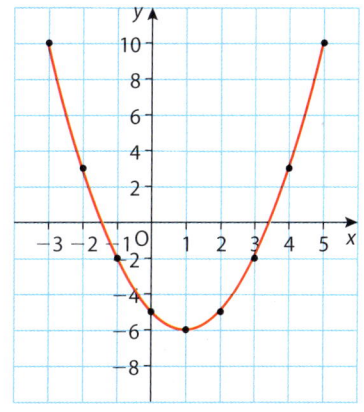

537

Text & Tests 2 Higher Level

5. Drawn below is a graph of the function:
   $f: x \rightarrow 3 + 2x - x^2$, for $-2 \leqslant x \leqslant 4, x \in R$.

   Use the graph to write down
   (i) the roots of the equation $f(x) = 0$
   (ii) the values of x for which $f(x) = 3$
   (iii) the value of $f\left(2\frac{1}{2}\right)$
   (iv) the maximum value of $f(x)$
   (v) the coordinates of the maximum point of $f(x)$
   (vi) the range of values of x for which $f(x)$ is increasing
   (vii) the range of values of x for which $f(x)$ is positive
   (viii) the equation of the axis of symmetry of the curve.

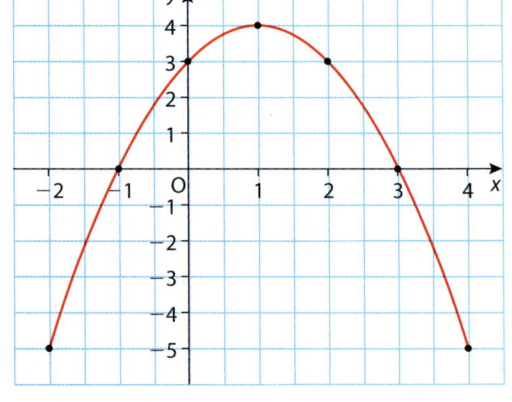

6. Draw the graph for the function $f(x) = 2x^2 - x - 3$ in the domain $-2 \leqslant x \leqslant 3$.
   Use your graph to find
   (i) the values of x for which $f(x) = 0$
   (ii) the values of x for which $f(x) = 6$
   (iii) the coordinates of the minimum point of the curve
   (iv) the values of x for which $f(x) < 0$.

7. The graphs of the functions $f(x) = x^2$ and $g(x) = 2x + 3$ are shown below.

   (i) Write down the coordinates of the points where the curve and line meet.
   (ii) Solve the equation $x^2 = 2x + 3$.
   (iii) What is the connection between the answers in (i) and (ii) above?
   (iv) Explain the meaning of the equation $f(x) = g(x)$.

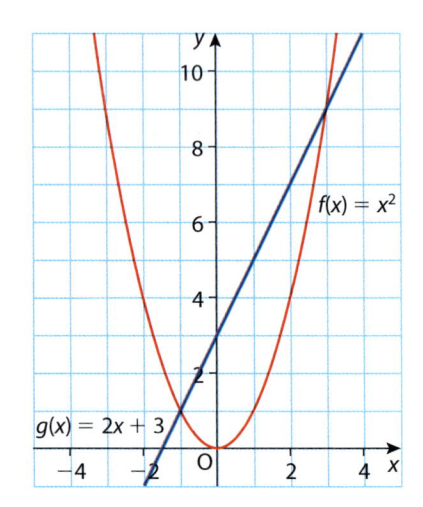

8. Drawn below are the graphs $f(x) = x^2 + x - 6$ and $g(x) = 3x - 3$.

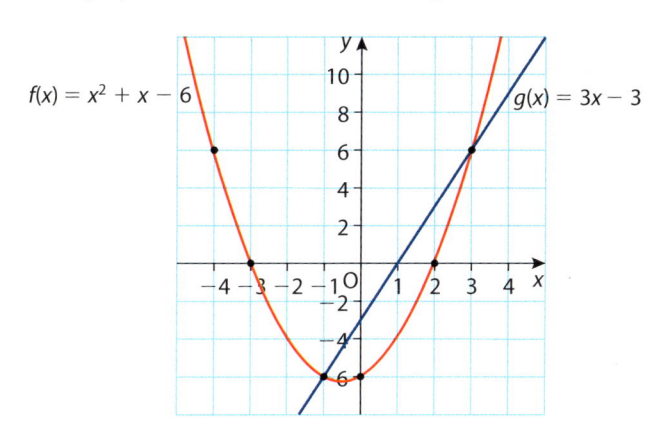

Use the graph to estimate
  (i) $f(-2)$ and $g(3)$
  (ii) the roots of the equation $f(x) = 0$
  (iii) the roots of the equation $f(x) = 4$
  (iv) the roots of the equation $f(x) = g(x)$
  (v)   the range of values of x for which $f(x) \leq g(x)$
  (vi) the range of values of x for which $f(x) \leq 0$.

9. Here are two graphs:

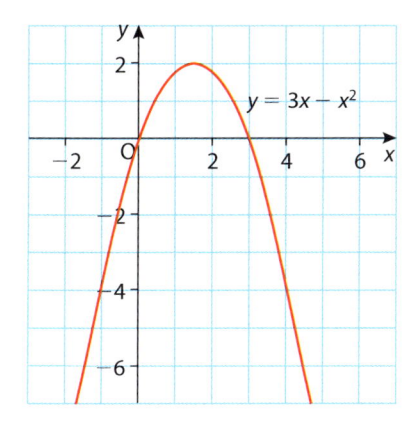

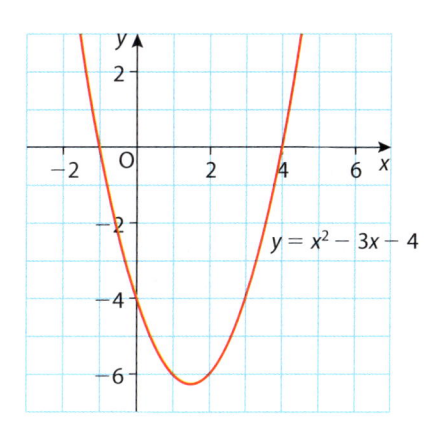

Use the graphs to solve these equations:
  (i) $3x - x^2 = 0$
  (ii) $x^2 - 3x - 4 = 0$
  (iii) $3x - x^2 = -3$
  (iv) $x^2 - 3x - 4 = -2$.

Text & Tests 2 Higher Level

10. This is the graph of $y = 3x^2 - 5$.

Use the graph to solve these equations:
  (i) $3x^2 - 5 = 0$
  (ii) $3x^2 - 5 = 20$.

For what values of x is $3x^2 - 5 < 20$?

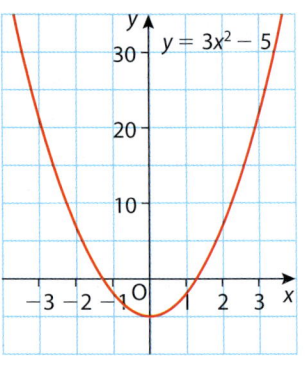

11. Drawn below are the graphs of $f(x) = x^2 - 2x$ and $g(x) = x - 1$ in the domain $-1 \leqslant x \leqslant 3$.

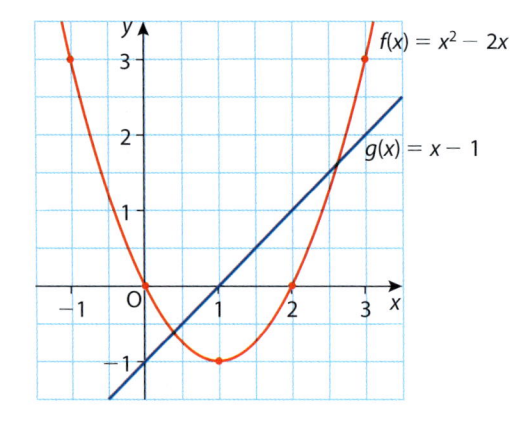

Use the graph to write down
  (i) the roots of the equation $f(x) = 0$
  (ii) the roots of the equation $f(x) = 3$
  (iii) the roots of the equation $f(x) = g(x)$
  (iv) the range of values of x for which $f(x) < 0$
  (v) the range of values of x for which $g(x) < f(x)$.

Explain how the graph could be used to solve the equation
$$x^2 - 2x - 2 = 0.$$

12. Using the same axes and the same scales, graph the functions,
$$f: x \rightarrow x^2 + 3x - 3 \quad \text{and} \quad g: x \rightarrow x - 2 \text{ in the domain } -4 \leqslant x \leqslant 2, x \in R.$$

Use the graph to estimate
  (i) the roots of the equation $x^2 + 3x - 3 = 0$
  (ii) the roots of the equation $x^2 + 3x - 3 = -2$
  (iii) the roots of the equation $f(x) = g(x)$
  (iv) the minimum value of $f(x)$.

What is the meaning of $f(x) < g(x)$?
Now use your graph to find the range of values of x for which $f(x) < g(x)$.

Chapter 23 Graphing functions

13. The equation of the given curve is $y = (x + 2)^2$.
  (i) Solve the equation $(x + 2)^2 = 0$.
  (ii) Did you get one or two values for x?
  (iii) If you got one value only, the value for x that you found is called a **repeated root**.
  Explain how the graph shows this repeated root.

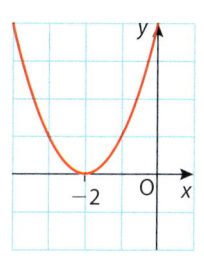

14. The diagram below shows the graphs of
$$f(x) = x^2 - 6x + 9 \qquad g(x) = x^2 - 3x + 3.$$

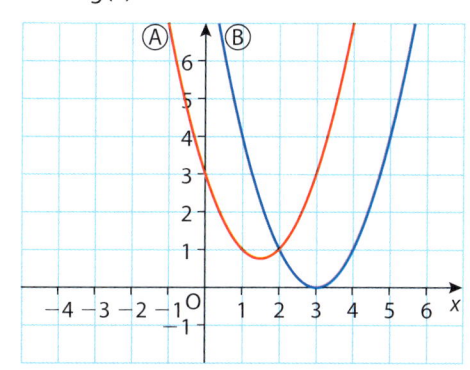

  (i) By substituting $x = 0$ (or any other value of x) into each equation, work out which graph corresponds to which equation.
  (ii) Use the graph to find one value of x for which $f(x) = g(x)$.
  (iii) Why has the equation $f(x) = 0$ only one root?

Section 23.4 Quadratic graphs and real-life problems

Many real-life situations such as the flight of a golf ball or maximising the area of a rectangle with a given perimeter can be modelled by quadratic equations.

The graph on the right shows the height of a ball as it is thrown through the air.
From the graph, it can be seen that
 (i) the ball reaches a height of 12 m
 (ii) the ball lands 50 m away from the position from which it was thrown.

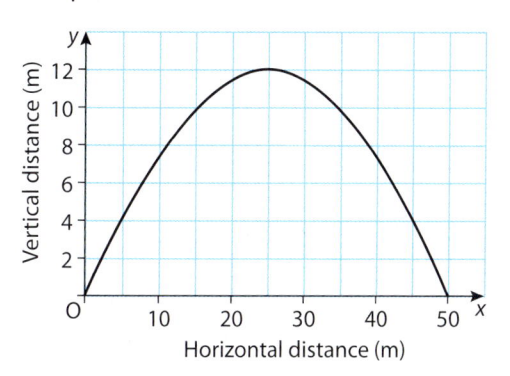

541

Example 1

Graphed on the right is the function

$$f(x) = 7 + 5x - 2x^2$$

in the domain $-1 \leq x \leq 4$.

Use your graph to solve

$$7 + 5x - 2x^2 = 0.$$

$f(x)$ is the height, in metres, reached by a particle fired from level ground at the point where $x = -1$, the x-axis representing level ground. From the time of firing until it hits the ground again, the particle was in flight for exactly 4.5 seconds.

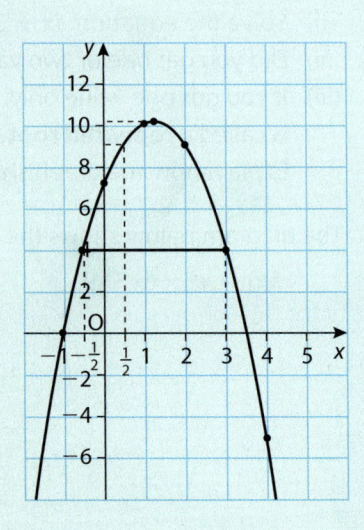

Use your graph to estimate

(i) the maximum height reached by the particle
(ii) the height reached by the particle after 1.5 seconds of flight
(iii) the number of seconds the particle is 4 m or more above the ground.

From the graph, the roots of the equation $7 + 5x - 2x^2 = 0$ are

$$\Rightarrow x = -1 \quad \text{or} \quad x = 3.5$$

(i) The maximum height reached by the particle is 10.3 m.

(ii) The height reached after 1.5 seconds is found by drawing a vertical line from $x = \frac{1}{2}$ until it meets the curve.
The corresponding y-value (i.e. the height) is 9 metres.

(iii) To find the number of seconds the particle is 4 m or more above the ground, draw the line $y = 4$ and then read the x-values of the points where it intersects the curve.
These x-values are -0.5 and 3.
∴ the number of seconds is 3.5.

Exercise 23.4

1. On the following page is the graph of the function $f(x) = -x^2 + 4x + 12$.
   Use the graph to write down
   (i) $f(1)$
   (ii) the values of x for which $f(x) = 12$
   (iii) the equation of the axis of symmetry.

Chapter 23 Graphing functions

$f(x)$ represents the number of taxis at a taxi-rank from 6 a.m. ($x = -2$) to 10 p.m. ($x = 6$). Each unit on the x-axis represents 2 hours and each unit on the y-axis represents one taxi.

Use the graph to estimate
(iv) the number of taxis at the rank at 12 noon
(v) the times when there were 14 taxis at the rank
(vi) the number of hours when there were 10 taxis or more at the rank.

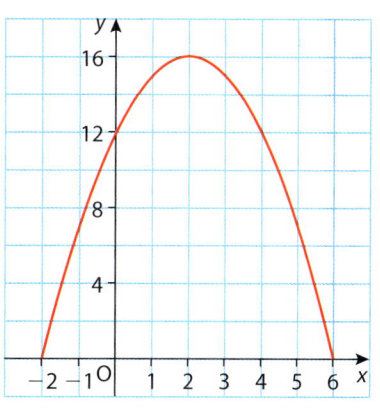

2. A ball is thrown into the air.
The formula $y = 20x - 4x^2$ shows its height, y metres above the ground, x seconds after it is thrown.
   (i) Copy and complete the table of values to show the height of the ball during its first five seconds.
   (ii) Use the table to plot a graph to show the ball's height against time.
   (iii) Use your graph to find
      (a) the maximum height reached by the ball and the time at which it reaches this height
      (b) two times when the ball is 12 metres above the ground
      (c) the interval of time when the ball is above 15 metres.

x	20x − 4x²	y
0	0 − 0	0
1	20 − 4	16
2		
3		
4		
5		

3. Given that $f(x) = 4 - 3x - x^2$, $x \in R$, copy and complete the given table.

Draw the graph of $f(x)$ in the domain $-5 \leqslant x \leqslant 2$.

If the graph represents the temperature, in °C, taken every two hours between 6 a.m. ($x = -5$) and 8 p.m. ($x = 2$) in a certain city, use the graph to estimate
   (i) the temperature at 11 a.m.
   (ii) the time when the temperature was highest
   (iii) the times when the temperature was 3°C
   (iv) the number of hours the temperature was at or above freezing point.

x	4 − 3x − x²	y
−5	4 + 15 − 25	−6
−4		
−3		
−2		
−1		
0		
1	4 − 3 − 1	0
2		

4. A farmer has 16 metres of fencing with which to make a rectangular enclosure for sheep. If one side of the enclosure is x metres long, show that the area A is given by $A(x) = 8x - x^2$.

Draw the graph of $A(x)$ in the domain $0 \leqslant x \leqslant 8$.

543

Text & Tests 2 Higher Level

Use your graph to estimate

   (i) the area of the enclosure when $x = 2.5$.
   (ii) the maximum possible area and the value of x when this occurs
   (iii) the two values of x for which the area is 12 m².

5. Draw the graph of the function $f: x \to 6x - x^2$ in the domain $0 \leq x \leq 6$.

    $f(x)$ represents the height, in metres, reached by a golf ball from the time it was hit $(x = 0)$ to the time it hit the ground $(x = 6)$.

    If each unit on the x-axis represents 1 second and each unit on the y-axis represents 5 metres, use your graph to estimate

      (i) the greatest height reached by the golf ball
      (ii) the height of the golf ball after $1\frac{1}{2}$ seconds
      (iii) after how many seconds the ball was 10 metres above ground
      (iv) after how many seconds the ball reached its maximum height.

6. The area of a circle is given roughly by the formula $A = 3r^2$.

      (i) Copy and complete the table given on the right and draw a graph of the function for $0 \leq r \leq 3$.
      (ii) Use your graph to find an estimate for the area of a circle of radius 2.5 m.
      (iii) If a circle has an area of 10 m², use the graph to estimate the length of its radius.
      (iv) Check your answers to parts (ii) and (iii) using the accurate version of the formula for the area of a circle.

r	$3r^2$	A
0		
1	3(1)	3
2		
3		

7. A farmer has 20 metres of fencing.
    He wishes to use it to form a rectangular enclosure in the corner of a field, as in the diagram.

      (i) Write down an expression for the area, A m², enclosed by the fencing.
      (ii) Plot the graph of A for values of x between 0 and 20.
      (iii) For what values of x is the area 40 m²?
      (iv) What values of x give an enclosed area greater than 90 m²?
      (v) What is the maximum area the farmer can enclose?
          What are the lengths of the fencing for this maximum area?

Section 23.5 Graphs of exponential functions

$f(x) = 2^x$ is a function.
Notice that the power is the variable x.

A function of x in which x appears as a power is called an **exponential function**.
$f(x) = 3^x$ and $g(x) = 4.3^x$ are other exponential functions.

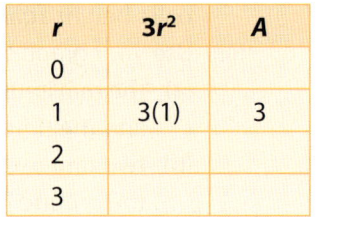

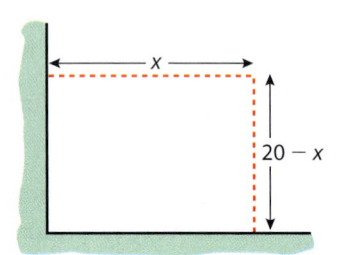

Chapter 23 Graphing functions

To draw the graph of $f(x) = 2^x$, we set out a table of inputs and outputs from $x = -2$ to $x = 3$, for example.

x	2^x	y
-2	$2^{-2} = \frac{1}{4}$	$\frac{1}{4}$
-1	$2^{-1} = \frac{1}{2}$	$\frac{1}{2}$
0	$2^0 = 1$	1
1	$2^1 = 2$	2
2	$2^2 = 4$	4
3	$2^3 = 8$	8

The graph of $f(x) = 2^x$ is shown below.

> Any number to the power of zero is 1.

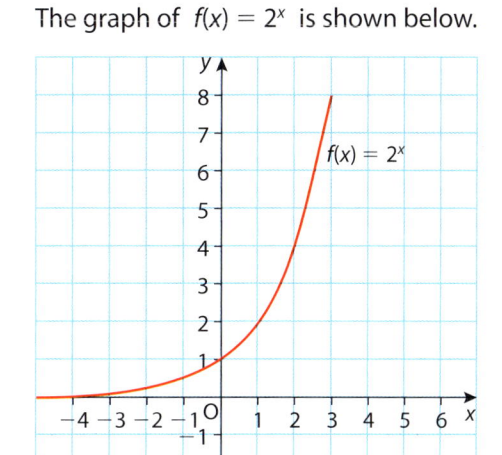

Example 1

Draw a graph of the function $f(x) = 2.3^x$ in the domain $-2 \leq x \leq 3$.
 (i) Use your graph to find an estimate for $f(2.5)$.
 (ii) Use your graph also to estimate the value of x for which $f(x) = 7$.

We set out a table of values for $f(x) = 2.3^x$, $-2 \leq x \leq 3$.

x	2.3^x	y
-2	2.3^{-2}	$\frac{2}{9}$
-1	2.3^{-1}	$\frac{2}{3}$
0	2.3^0	2
1	2.3^1	6
2	2.3^2	18
3	2.3^3	54

The graph is shown on the right.

 (i) To find $f(2.5)$, draw a vertical line from $x = 2.5$ until it meets the curve.
    The y-value of the point of intersection is 30.
    $\therefore f(2.5) = 30$
 (ii) To find the value of x for which $f(x) = 7$, draw the line $y = 7$ and read the x-value of the point of intersection of this line and the curve.
    This value is $x = 1.1$.

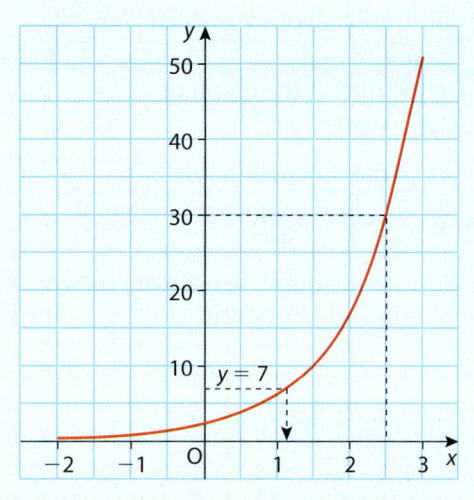

Text & Tests 2 Higher Level

Note: A calculator can also be used to produce a table of values for any exponential function.
When f(x) appears, use the $\boxed{x^\blacksquare}$ key to find 2^x, 3^x etc.

Exercise 23.5

1. This is the graph of $f(x) = 2^x$.

    Use the graph to write down
    (i) $f(0)$ (ii) $f(1)$ (iii) $f(1.5)$.

    $f(3)$ is not shown on the graph.
    (iv) What is $f(3)$?
    (v) For what value of x is $f(x) = 5$?

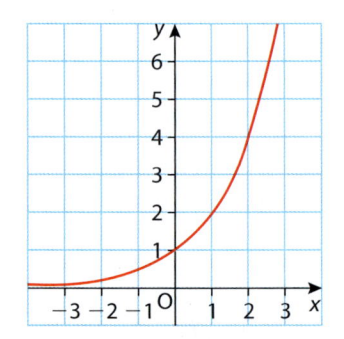

2. Copy and complete the table below and then draw the graph of the function $f(x) = 3^x$.

x	−2	−1	0	1	2	3
3^x		$\frac{1}{3}$				

    Use your graph to write down
    (i) $f(1.5)$
    (ii) the value of x for which $f(x) = 4$.

3. On the right is the graph of $f(x) = k \cdot 2^x$, where $k \in N$.

    (i) Write down the value of k.
    (ii) $f(2)$ is not shown on the graph. What is $f(2)$?
    (iii) Use the graph to estimate the value of x for which $f(x) = 1$.

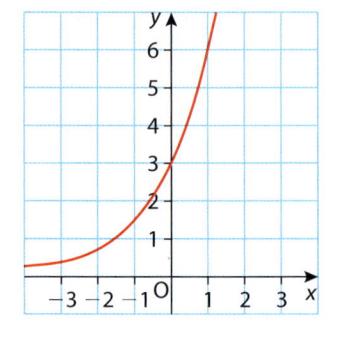

4. Copy and complete the table below:

x	−2	−1	0	1	2
2^x	$\frac{1}{4}$				
4.2^x	1				

    Use the table to draw a sketch of the function $f(x) = 4.2^x$ in the domain $-2 \leqslant x \leqslant 2$.
    Use your graph to find an estimate for $f(0.5)$.

Chapter 23 Graphing functions

5. Three graphs – Ⓐ, Ⓑ and Ⓒ – are sketched on the right.

   Associate each graph with one of the functions given below:

   $f(x) = 2^x$ $f(x) = 3^x$ $f(x) = 3.3^x$

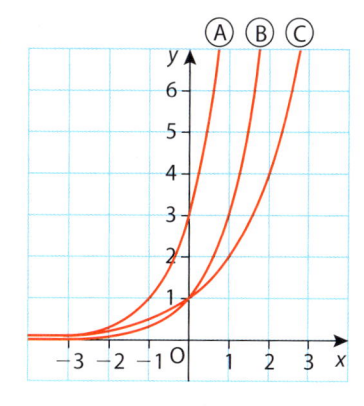

6. The diagram shows a sketch of the curve $y = 3^x$.
   (i) Write down the coordinates of the point where the curve cuts the y-axis.
   (ii) Copy the diagram and add sketches of the curves
       (a) 2×3^x (b) 5×3^x.

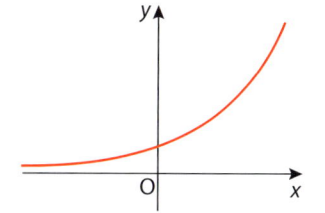

7. Niamh is told that the given curve is the graph of either
   (a) $f(x) = k \cdot 2^x$ or   (b) $f(x) = k \cdot 3^x$.
   (i) Find the value of k.
   (ii) Write down which of the two functions the curve represents.

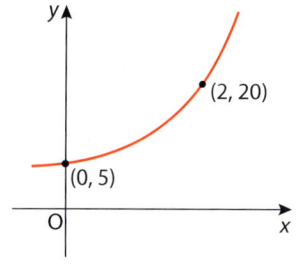

8. Draw the graph of the function $f(x) = 2^x$ in the domain $-2 \leqslant x \leqslant 3$.
   $g(x)$ is another function where $g(x) = x + 3$.

   Draw a sketch of $g(x)$ on the same axes and using the same scales.

   Use your graph to estimate the positive solution of the equation $2^x = x + 3$.

547

Text & Tests 2 Higher Level

Test yourself 23

1. The graph of the function $f(x) = 2x + 5$ is shown.

Use the graph to write down

(i) $f(0)$ (ii) $f(1)$ (iii) $f(-1)$
(iv) the value of x for which $y = 3$
(v) the value of y when $x = -2.5$.

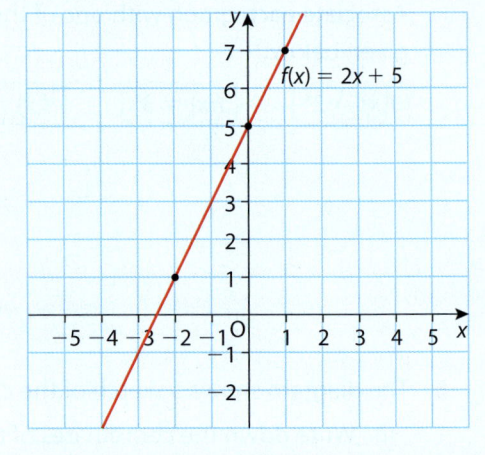

2. On the right is the graph of the function $f(x) = x^2 - 4x$.

Use the curve to write down

(i) $f(3.5)$
(ii) the values of x for which $f(x) = -3$
(iii) the minimum value of $f(x)$.
(iv) the equation of the axis of symmetry of the curve.

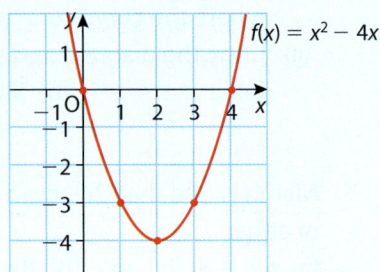

3. Match each of the graphs below with one of the equations given. In each equation, k is a positive number.
(One of the equations is not needed.)

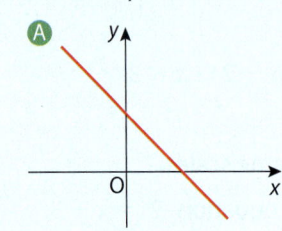

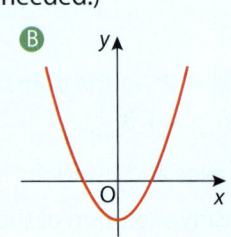

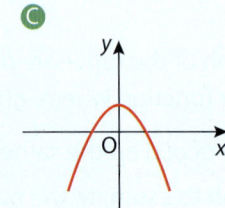

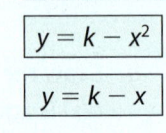

$y = kx$

$y = x^2 - k$

$y = k - x^2$

$y = k - x$

4. Draw the graph of the function $f(x) = 3x - 1$ in the domain $-2 \leq x \leq 3$.
Use your graph to estimate

(i) $f(-1.5)$ (ii) the value of x when $y = 3.5$.

5. The curve on the right is the graph of the function

$f(x) = x^2 + 2x - 3.$

(i) Find the coordinates of a, b and c.
(ii) Write down the values of x for which $f(x) \leq 0$.
(iii) If $f(k) = -3$, find two values for k.

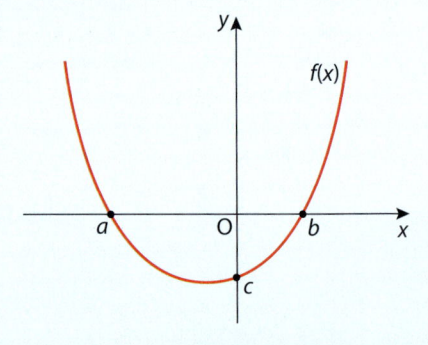

548

Chapter 23 Graphing functions

6. Copy and complete the following table.

x	−3	−2	−1	0	1	2	3	4	5
2^x	0.125			1		4			

(i) Use the values in your table to draw the graph of $y = 2^x$ using a scale of 1 cm for 1 unit on the x-axis and 1 cm for 5 units on the y-axis.

(ii) Use your graph to solve the equation $2^x = 6$.

7. Draw the graph of the function
$$f : x \rightarrow 2x^2 - x - 6 \text{ for } -3 \leqslant x \leqslant 4, x \in R.$$

Use the graph to estimate

(i) the values of x for which $f(x) = 0$
(ii) the minimum value of $f(x)$
(iii) the value of $f(2.5)$
(iv) the range of values of x for which $f(x)$ is less than zero.

8. Three times one number plus twice another is 9.
Twice the first number less the second number is 13.
If x is one number and y is the other, form two equations in x and y.
By drawing a sketch of the two equations, find the two numbers.

9. The graph of $y = x^2 − 2x$ has been drawn on the given grid.

Use the graph to find estimates for the solution of these equations:

(i) $x^2 - 2x = 0$
(ii) $x^2 - 2x = 3$.

Write down the equation of the axis of symmetry of the curve.

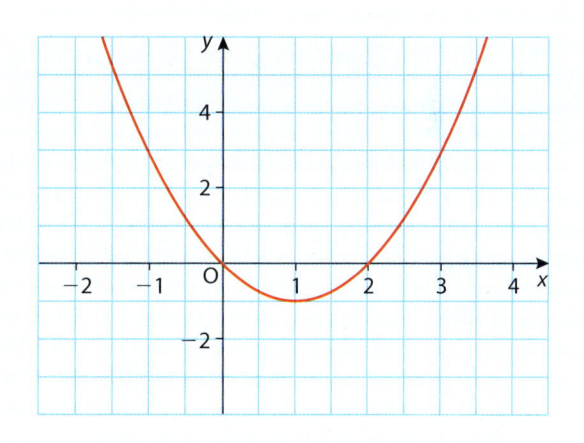

10. Which sketch graph fits which equation?
Give reasons for your answers.

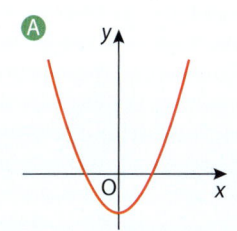

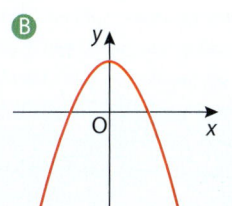

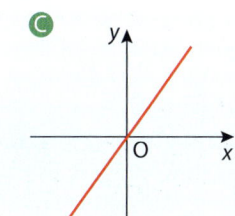

Ⓐ Ⓑ Ⓒ

$y = 2x$

$y = x^2 − 2$

$y = 2 − x^2$

$y = x^2 + 2$

549

Text & Tests 2 Higher Level

11. A gardener has 18 metres of timber fencing to enclose a rectangular vegetable patch using a straight stone wall as one of the sides as shown. The width is x metres.

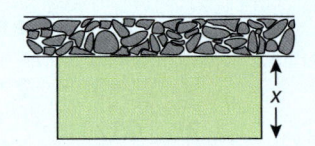

    Show that the area of the enclosure is given by the function

    $A(x) = 18x - 2x^2$.

    Draw the graph of the function $y = A(x)$ in the domain $0 \leqslant x \leqslant 9$.
    (i) Find the area of the enclosure when $x = 3$.
    (ii) Find the two values of x for which the area is 30 m^2.
    (iii) Find the length and breadth of the enclosure of maximum area.
    (iv) What is the maximum area?

12. The following table gives the cost of hiring a surfboard for a number of days:

Days t	3	4	5	6
Cost €C	50	60	70	80

    (i) By using any two couples, write down the equation of the line that relates the cost €C to the number of days t.
    (ii) Use the equation to find the cost of hiring a surfboard for two weeks.

13. Two functions, f and g, are defined as follows:

    $f: x \rightarrow 2^x$, $g: x \rightarrow 9x - 3x^2 - 1$.

    Complete the table below and use it to draw the graphs of f and g for $0 \leqslant x \leqslant 3$.

x	0	0.5	1	1.5	2	2.5	3
f(x)							
g(x)							

    (i) Use your graph to estimate the value(s) of x for which $2^x = 9x - 3x^2 - 1$.
    (ii) If $2^k = 6$, use your graph to estimate the value of k.

Chapter 23 Graphing functions

Assignment:

By using a graphing package or otherwise, identify each of the following graphs.

(a) $f(x) = x$
(b) $f(x) = x + 2$
(c) $f(x) = x - 3$

What conclusion can be made about the position of a linear graph when a constant is added or subtracted from the original function?
Conclusion:

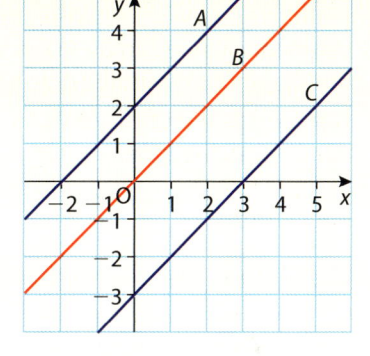

(d) $f(x) = x$
(e) $f(x) = 2x$
(f) $f(x) = -4x$
(g) $f(x) = \dfrac{x}{2}$

What conclusion can be made about the shape of a linear graph when you change the coefficient of x in the original function?
Conclusion:

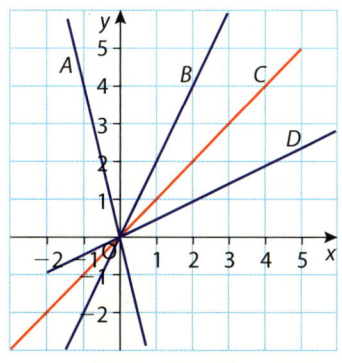

Using both conclusions above, draw the following graphs on the same scaled axes.

(i) $f(x) = x$ (ii) $f(x) = 2x$ (iii) $f(x) = 2x + 3$ (iv) $f(x) = -2x + 3$

(h) $f(x) = x^2$
(i) $f(x) = x^2 + 3$
(j) $f(x) = x^2 - 2$

What conclusion can be made about the position of a quadratic graph when you add or subtract a constant to/from the original function?

Conclusion:

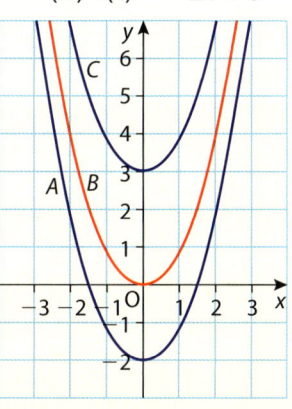

551

(k) $f(x) = x^2$
(l) $f(x) = 3x^2$
(m) $f(x) = \dfrac{x^2}{5}$

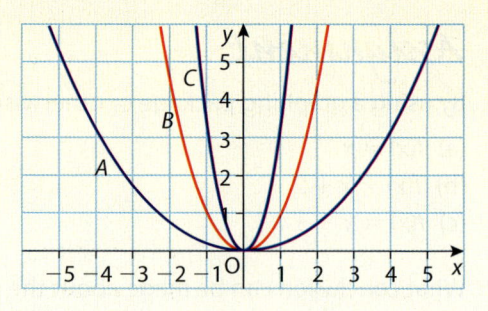

What conclusion can be made about the shape of a quadratic graph when you change the coefficient of x^2 of the original function?

Conclusion:

Study and identify each of the following graphs.
Write out the coordinates of the minimum value of each graph.

(n) $f(x) = x^2$
(o) $f(x) = (x + 2)^2$
(p) $f(x) = (x - 3)^2$

(q) $f(x) = x^2$
(r) $f(x) = (x - 4)^2 + 2$
(s) $f(x) = (x + 3)^2 - 1$

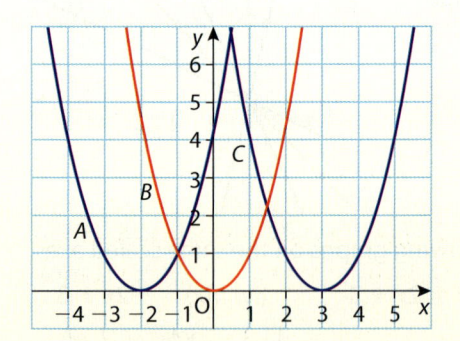

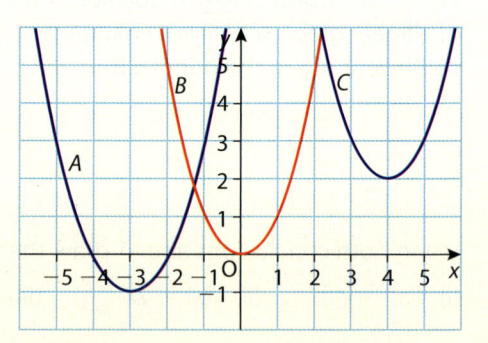

Write a report on how the minimum value of a quadratic function is found when it is written in the form, $f(x) = (x \pm a)^2 \pm b$.

Geometry 3: Transformations – Constructions

chapter 24

From first year, you will recall how to:

- construct an image using translations,
- identify axes and centres of symmetry,
- construct an image using axial and central symmetry,
- bisect an angle and line segment,
- draw parallel and perpendicular lines,
- divide a line segment into 3 equal parts.

In this chapter, you will learn to:

- perform a rotation of given points and objects,
- construct different types of triangles including SSS, SAS, ASA and RHS,
- construct rectangles,
- divide a line segment into any number of equal parts.

Section 24.1 Transformation geometry

The figure marked A in the diagram below has been moved to different positions. All the figures have the same shape and size. Some are upside-down and some are back-to-front.

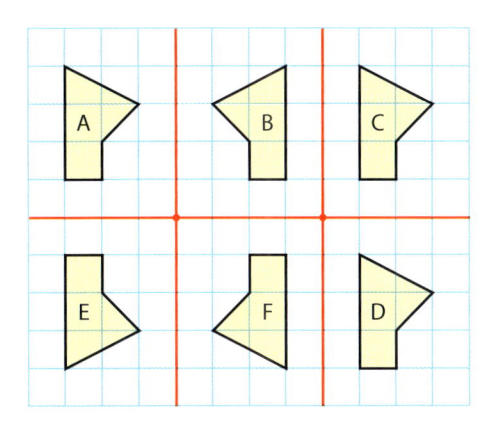

Text & Tests 2 Higher Level

Each of the figures B, C, D, E and F is an **image** of the figure A under a **transformation**.
The original figure A is called the **object**.
The new position is called the **image**.
In this section, we consider four transformations.
These are **translations, axial symmetry, central symmetry** and **rotation**

1. Translations

A translation is movement in a straight line.
It may also be described as a 'sliding movement'.

The shape A on the left has been moved in the direction PQ and by a distance equal to |PQ|.
The translation PQ is written $\overrightarrow{PQ}$.

The image of the given figure is found by moving 4 units to the right and 3 units up.
Notice that the size and shape of the figure is unchanged.

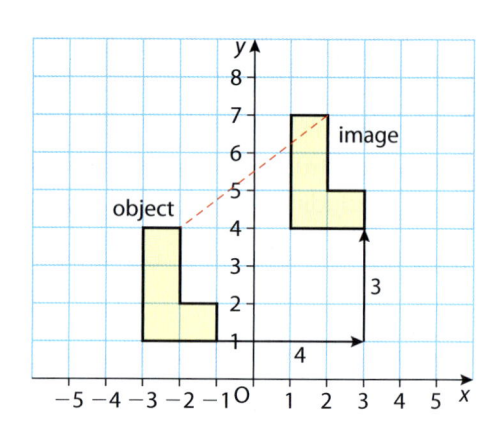

Here is the image of a line segment [AB] under the translation $\vec{t}$.
The image is labelled A'B'.

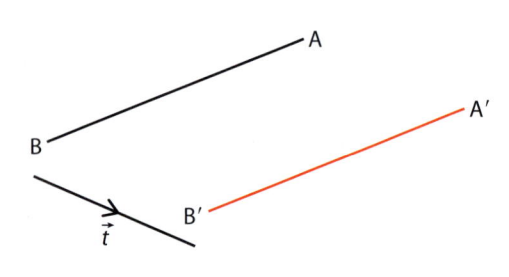

The image of the triangle ABC under the translation $\overrightarrow{BC}$ is shown on the right.

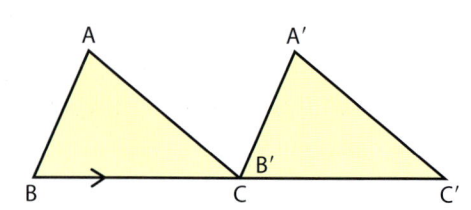

554

Chapter 24 Geometry 3: Transformations – Constructions

Exercise 24.1

1. Describe the translation that maps the blue shape onto the red shape in each of the following. Use words such as right, left, up and down.

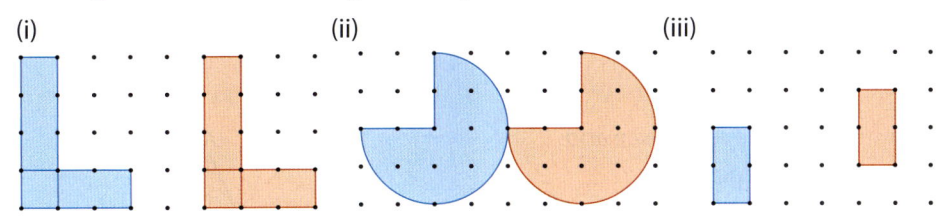

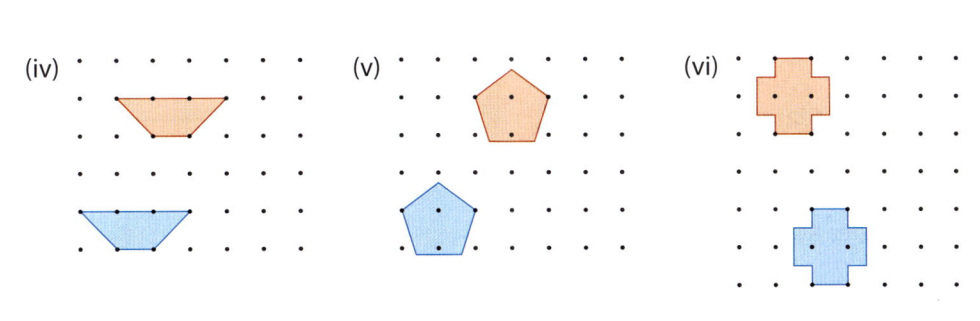

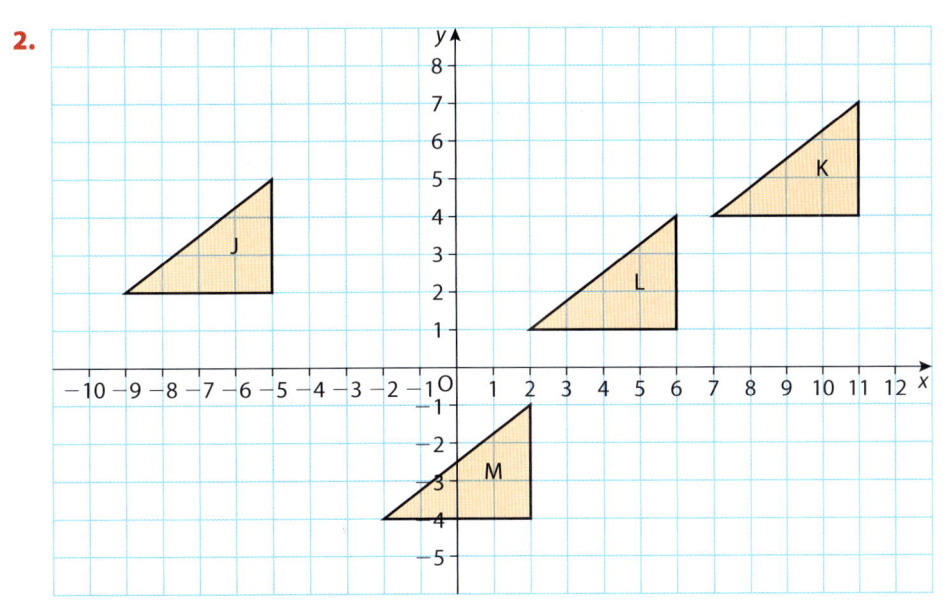

   (i) (ii) (iii)

   (iv) (v) (vi)

2.

   Describe fully the translation that maps
   (i) shape L onto shape K
   (ii) shape J onto shape L
   (iii) shape M onto shape L
   (iv) shape J onto shape M
   (v) shape L onto shape M.

Text & Tests 2 Higher Level

3. Construct the image of the letter T under the given translation $\vec{AB}$.

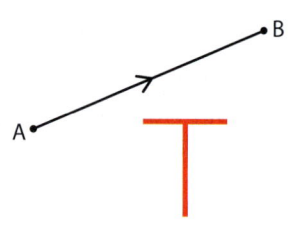

4. Draw the triangle ABC twice and construct its image under
   - (i) $\vec{BC}$
   - (ii) $\vec{AC}$.

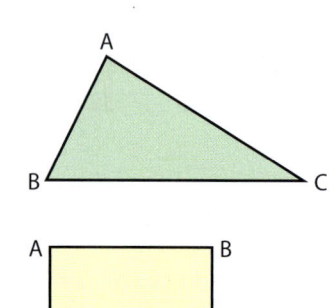

5. ABCD is a square, as shown. Copy the diagram and draw a rough sketch of the image of ABCD
   - (i) under $\vec{AB}$
   - (ii) under $\vec{DB}$.

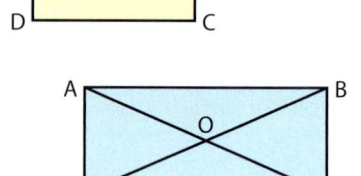

6. ABCD is a rectangle with the diagonals intersecting at the point O. Find each of the following:
   - (i) the image of A under $\vec{DC}$
   - (ii) the image of [AB] under $\vec{BC}$
   - (iii) the image of D under $\vec{OB}$
   - (iv) the image of [DC] under $\vec{DA}$.

7. ABCD and ABEC are parallelograms. Under the translation $\vec{CE}$, write down the image of
   - (i) the point A
   - (ii) [AD]
   - (iii) △ADC
   - (iv) [AC].

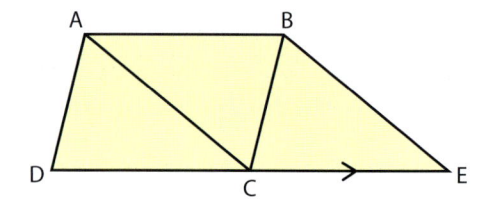

8. In the given figure, ABCD is a square and BECD is a parallelogram.
   - (i) What is the image of [BD] under $\vec{DC}$?
   - (ii) What is the image of C under $\vec{DB}$?
   - (iii) What is the image of △ABD under $\vec{BE}$?
   - (iv) Of what point is B the image under $\vec{CE}$?
   - (v) Of what line segment is [BC] its image under $\vec{DC}$?
   - (vi) Of what triangle is ABD the image under $\vec{CD}$?

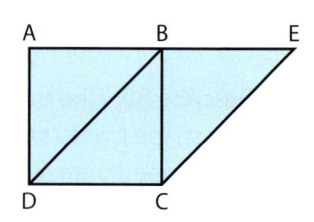

Chapter 24 Geometry 3: Transformations – Constructions

9.

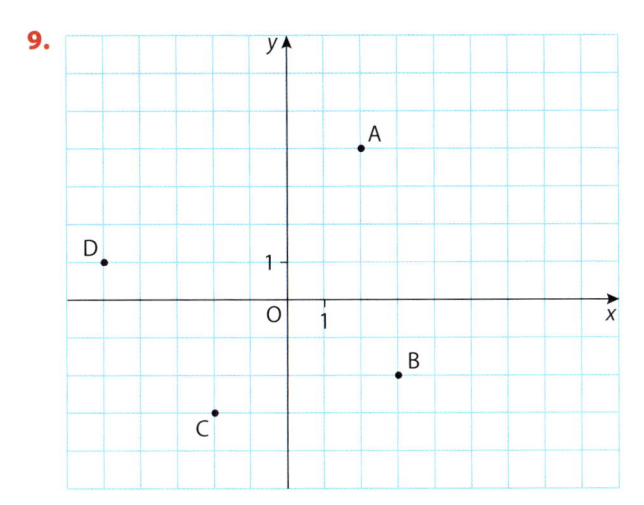

(i) Write down the coordinates of A, B, C and D.

(ii) Each point is translated 5 units to the right and 2 units up.
What are the coordinates of the image points A′, B′, C′ and D′?

Section 24.2 Symmetries

1. Symmetrical shapes

Each of the figures below is **symmetrical**.
The broken line in each figure is called an **axis of symmetry**.
A figure will have an axis of symmetry if it can be reflected in that line so that each half of the figure is reflected exactly onto the other half of the figure.

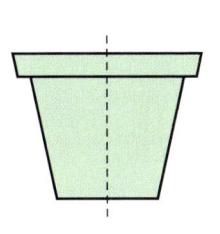

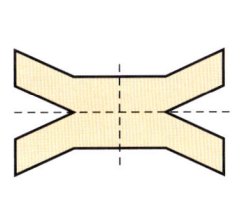

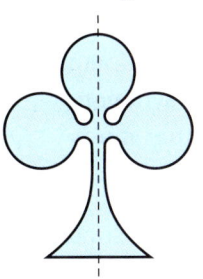

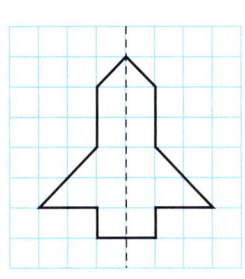

Text & Tests 2 Higher Level

Here are some well-known geometrical figures and their axes of symmetry.

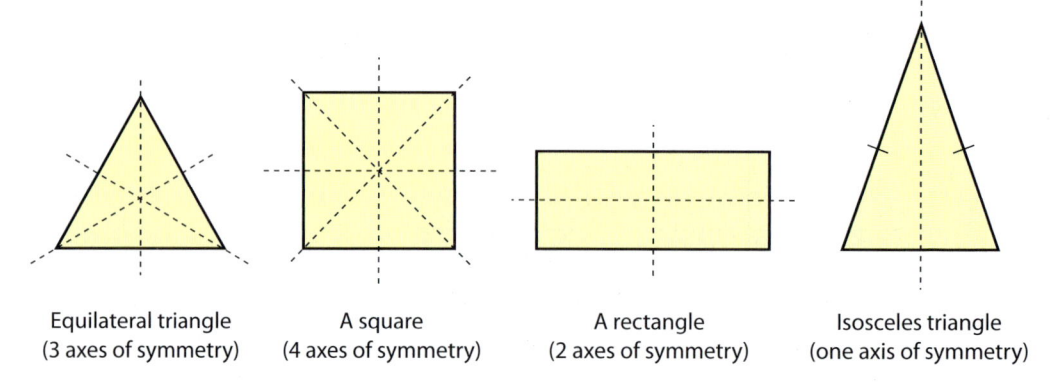

Equilateral triangle
(3 axes of symmetry)

A square
(4 axes of symmetry)

A rectangle
(2 axes of symmetry)

Isosceles triangle
(one axis of symmetry)

A parallelogram with unequal sides and no right angle has no axis of symmetry.

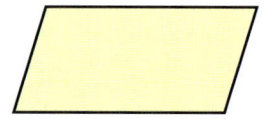

2. Axial symmetry

In the given diagram, the blue figure is the image of the green figure under reflection in the broken line ℓ.

We name the image figure A'B'C'D'.

Here is another reflection in the horizontal broken red line.

The word MAM has line symmetry. Can you think of any other words that have line symmetry?

The diagram on the right illustrates how the image of a figure is constructed under reflection in a line.

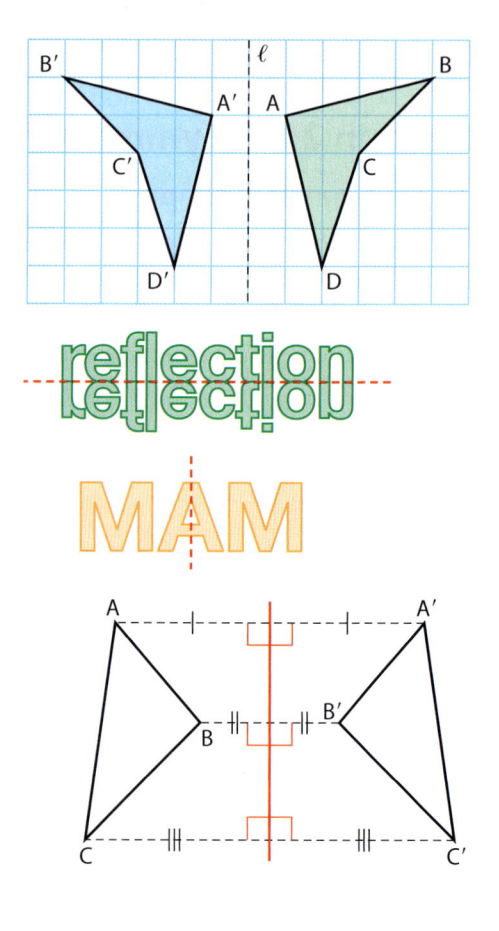

558

Chapter 24 Geometry 3: Transformations – Constructions

3. Central symmetry

In the diagram on the right, the point A is joined to the point X and produced to A′ such that
$|XA'| = |AX|$.
We say that the point A′ is the image of A under reflection in the point X or **central symmetry** in X.

The diagram on the right shows the letter F and its image under central symmetry in the point X.

Notice that the image appears **upside-down and back-to-front** in relation to the given figure.

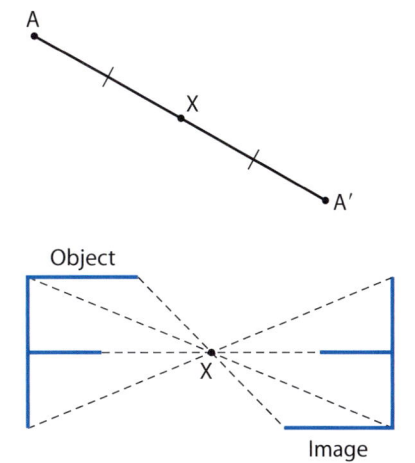

4. Centre of symmetry

All the figures below are mapped onto themselves under central symmetry in the point X.

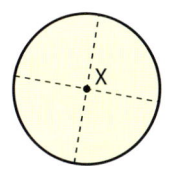

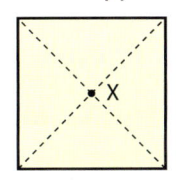

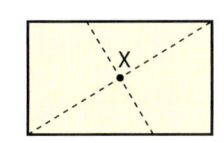

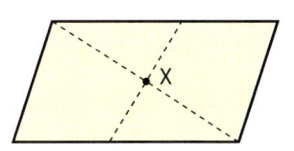

In each case, the point X is the centre of symmetry.

Exercise 24.2

1. Use a set square and ruler to construct the image of the point X under reflection in the line ℓ in each of the following:

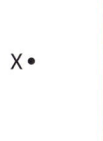

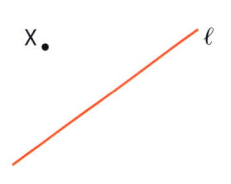

2. Use a set square and ruler to draw a rough sketch of the images of these triangles under reflection in the line *m*.

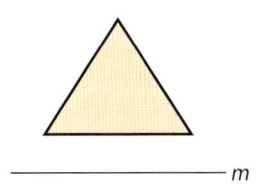

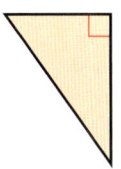

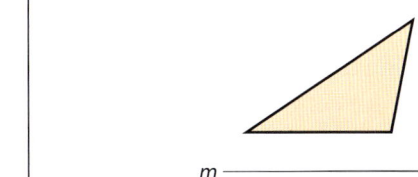

Text & Tests 2 Higher Level

3. The rectangle DCFE is the image of the rectangle ABCD under axial symmetry in the line *k*.

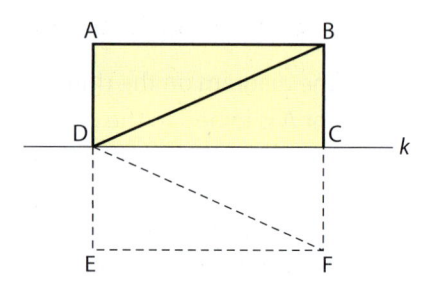

    Write down the image of each of the following under reflection in the line *k*.

    (i) the point B (ii) [AB] (iii) [DB]
    (iv) △DCB (v) △ABD (vi) [CB]

4. Which of the following transformations represent reflection in a line?

    (i) (ii) 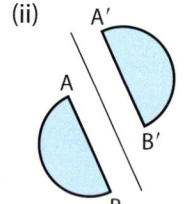 (iii) 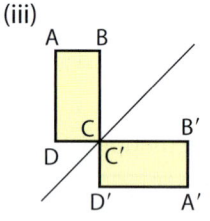 (iv)

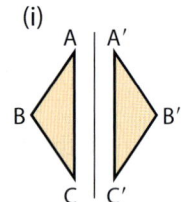

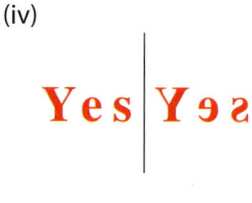

5. Which of the letters in the word below have an axis of symmetry?

    MONDAY

6. Sketch the image of the triangle ABC under central symmetry in the point C in each of the following.

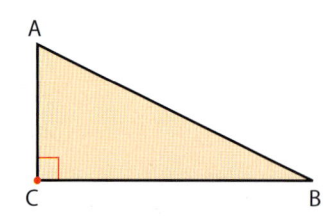

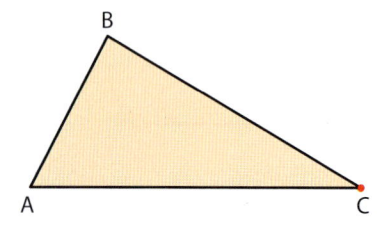

7. ABCD is a rectangle with the diagonals intersecting at the point O.

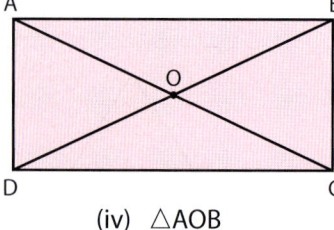

    Find the image of each of the following under central symmetry in the point O.

    (i) D (ii) C (iii) [BC] (iv) △AOB
    (v) [AO] (vi) △ADB (vii) [OC] (viii) ABCD.

Chapter 24 Geometry 3: Transformations – Constructions

8. Which of the four faces shown below could be the image of the face shown on the right under a central symmetry?

Ⓐ   Ⓑ   Ⓒ   Ⓓ

9. Which of the four faces in question 8 could be the image of the given face under
   (i) reflection in a vertical line
   (ii) a translation?

10. In the diagram on the right, describe fully the single transformation which will map
   (i) shape P onto shape P_1
   (ii) shape P_1 onto shape P_2
   (iii) shape P onto shape P_2.

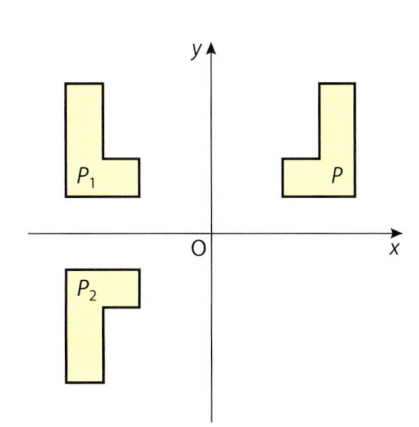

11. On the right is a circle of centre C. Name two transformations, each of which maps the circle onto itself.

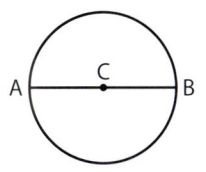

12. The diagram on the right shows a pattern and a line n.

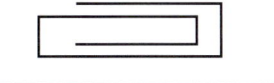

Which one of the following diagrams is the reflection of the pattern in n?
   A   B   C   D

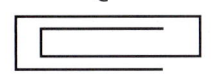

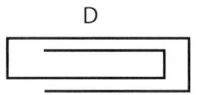

Text & Tests 2 Higher Level

13. The diagram on the right shows the triangle ABC.
    The image of ABC under reflection in the y-axis is A′B′C′.

    (i) Find the coordinates of A′, B′ and C′.

    A″, B″ and C″ are the images of A, B and C under reflection in the x-axis.

    (ii) Find the coordinates of A″, B″ and C″.

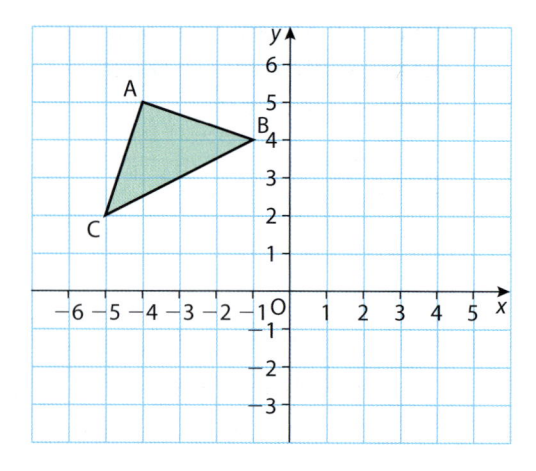

14. How many axes of symmetry has each of the following figures?

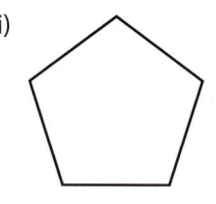

    (i)   (ii)   (iii)   (iv)

15. Which of the figures in question 14 have a centre of symmetry?

16.

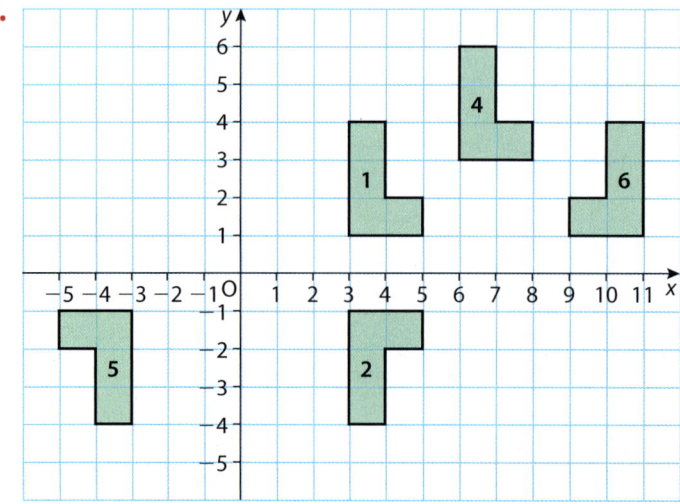

    Which of the transformations – axial symmetry, central symmetry or translation – will map
    (i) L_1 onto L_2
    (ii) L_1 onto L_4
    (iii) L_5 onto L_2
    (iv) L_1 onto L_6
    (v) L_1 onto L_5?

Chapter 24 Geometry 3: Transformations – Constructions

17. For these triangles, describe fully the single transformation that maps

  (i) A onto B
  (ii) B onto D
  (iii) B onto C.

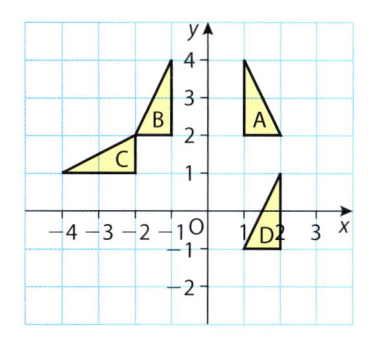

18. (i) Draw a shape which has exactly three axes of symmetry. Show the axes on the diagram.
  (ii) Draw a shape which has exactly four axes of symmetry. Show the axes on the diagram.

19. ABCD is a rectangle with the diagonals intersecting at the point O.
ℓ is a line that contains O and ℓ is perpendicular to DC.
Find the image of each of the following under the indicated transformation.

  (i) the image of △AOD under central symmetry in O
  (ii) the image of △AOB under central symmetry in O
  (iii) the image of △BOC under axial symmetry in ℓ
  (iv) the image of △DOF under axial symmetry in ℓ
  (v) the image of [AD] under the translation $\overrightarrow{DF}$.

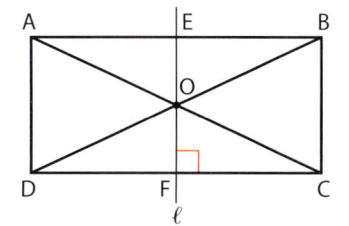

Investigation:

A: Sophie drew a detailed symmetrical design on her computer.

The design has 4 dotted-lines of axial symmetry as shown.

She then deleted most of the lines leaving just 3 segments of the design.

Using your knowledge of reflection, copy and recreate Sophie's design.

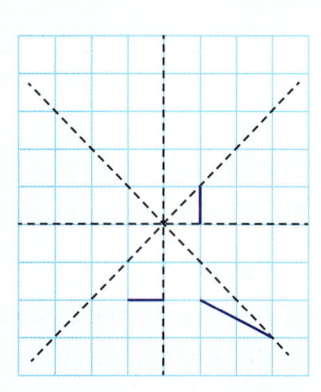

Text & Tests 2 Higher Level

B: Folding a piece of paper twice as shown, cut any design with a scissors.
Open the paper and investigate the symmetries produced.

Cut along this line

Section 24.3 Rotation

Rotations are transformations in which one point is fixed and all other points in the plane rotate, through the same angle, around this point. An **image** of the original set of points is made.

This diagram shows the **rotation** of the triangle S through $\frac{1}{4}$ turn in an anti-clockwise direction, about O.

The point O is called the **centre of rotation**.

There are two directions of rotation:

1. anticlockwise ↺
2. clockwise ↻

In this diagram, triangle T is rotated through 90°, about the origin O, in a clockwise direction.

1. When a shape is rotated its **size** and **shape** remain the same but its **position** on the plane changes.
2. All points on the shape are turned through the same angle about the same point.

   i.e. $\angle EOE' = \angle FOF' = 90°$

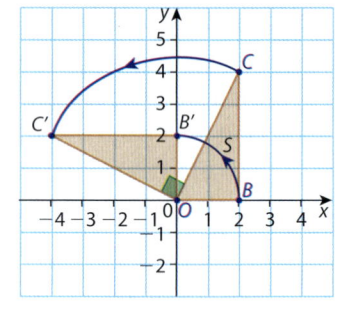

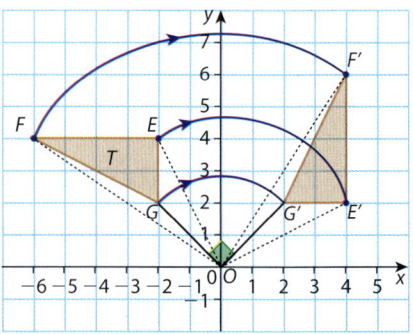

To describe a **Rotation**, you need:

1 the centre
2 the angle (degrees or fraction of a turn)
3 the direction (clockwise or anticlockwise)

Notation:

The image of A is usually labelled A'.

We say that:
The set ABC is "mapped onto" the set $A'B'C'$

564

Chapter 24 Geometry 3: Transformations – Constructions

Example 1

Find the coordinates of the image of (4, 1) under a rotation about O(0, 0) through:

(i) 90° anticlockwise   (ii) 180°   (iii) 90° clockwise

(i) (4, 1) becomes (−1, 4)
(ii) (4, 1) becomes (−4, −1)
(iii) (4, 1) becomes (1, −4)

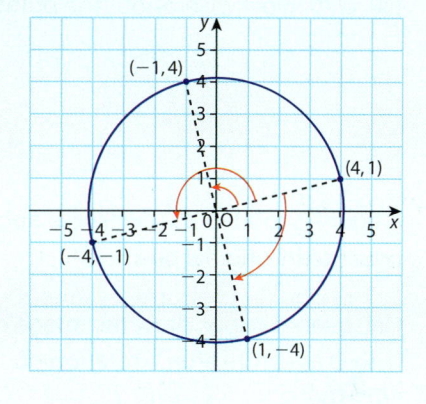

Exercise 24.3

1. Copy the diagram of the rectangle and draw its image by a rotation of 180° clockwise about the origin O.

Write down the coordinates of the image of points B, C and D, under this rotation.

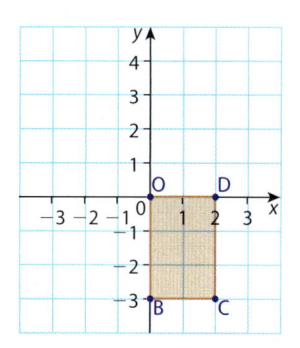

2. Describe each of the following rotations:
  (i) ABC ⟶ DEC
  (ii) ABC ⟶ IHC
  (iii) ABC ⟶ GFC

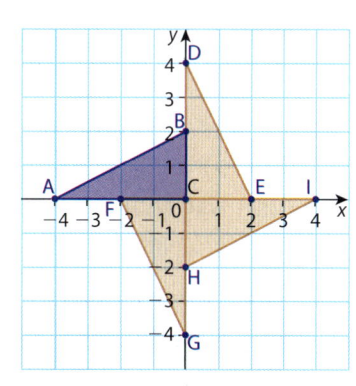

Text & Tests 2 Higher Level

3. Copy the following shape onto squared paper.

   Draw the new position of the shape after a rotation of:
   (i) 90° clockwise
   (ii) 180°
   (iii) 270° clockwise, about the point (0, 0).

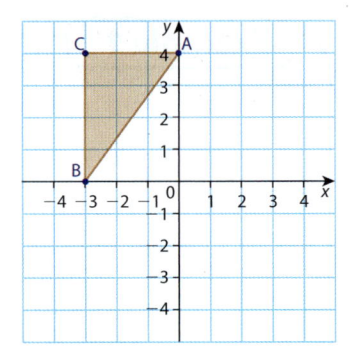

4. A figure is rotated 85° clockwise about a point O. Describe a rotation that will return the figure to its original position.

5. On squared paper, draw the image of this shape with O as centre after a rotation of:
   (i) 180°
   (ii) 90° clockwise
   (iii) 90° anticlockwise.

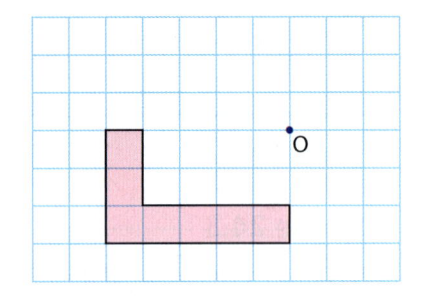

6. Rotate each of the following figures, about O, through the angle given.

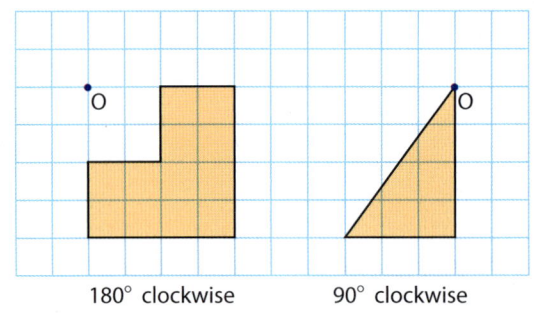

   180° clockwise   90° clockwise

7. Draw the image of this shape after a rotation of
   (i) 90° anticlockwise
   (ii) 180° anticlockwise
   (iii) 270° anticlockwise

   Is the image formed by a rotation of 180° clockwise the same as the image formed due to a rotation of 180° anticlockwise?
   What other rotation is equivalent to a rotation of 270° anticlockwise?

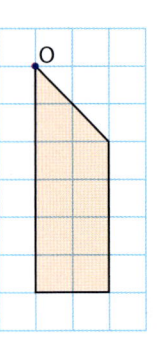

8. Rotate this figure about O, through:
   (i) 90° clockwise
   (ii) 180°

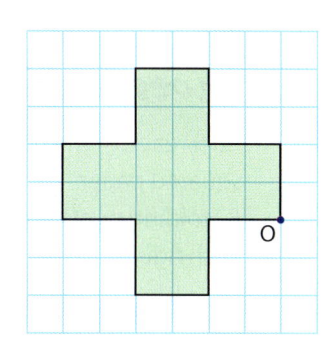

9 Find the coordinates of the images of these points under an anticlockwise rotation of 90° about O.
   (i) (5, 1)   (ii) (5, −3)   (iii) (−5, 0)   (iv) (−5, −2)

10. Find the coordinates of the images of these points under a rotation of 180° about O.
   (i) (3, 2)   (ii) (3, −3)   (iii) (−3, 1)   (iv) (−3, −2)

11. Find the coordinates of the images of the following points under a clockwise rotation of 90° about O.
   (i) (2, 2)   (ii) (2, −3)   (iii) (−2, 0)   (iv) (−2, −4)

12. ABC is an equilateral triangle.
Copy this diagram onto squared paper and draw its three axes of symmetry.
Mark the point where the axes cross, O.
This point is called the centre of symmetry.
Describe the rotation needed for each of the following maps about O:
   (i) ABC mapped onto BCA
   (ii) ABC mapped onto CAB.

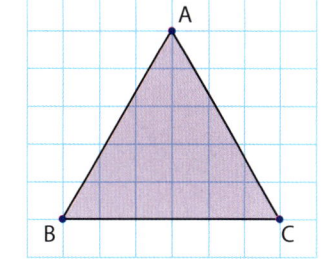

13. D is the midpoint of AC.
Copy the diagram onto squared paper and draw the image of ABC after a rotation of 180°, about D.
Name the resulting figure made up of ABC and its image.
What geometrical property is shown by your result?

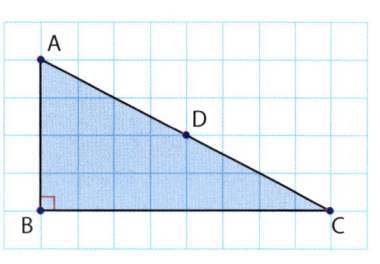

Investigation:

Copy each of the figures shown onto a large sheet of squared paper.
By folding or otherwise, find the centre of symmetry of each figure.

Investigate the smallest angle you need to rotate through, about this centre, so that the image appears the same as the original.

	parallelogram	square	hexagon
angle			

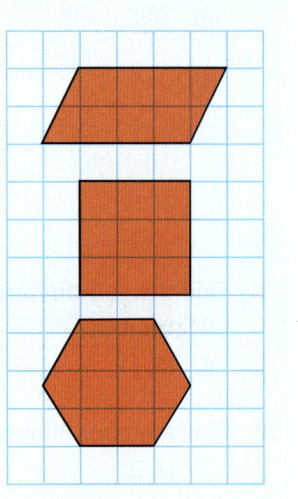

Section 24.4 Constructions 1

1. Bisector of a given angle using only compass and straightedge

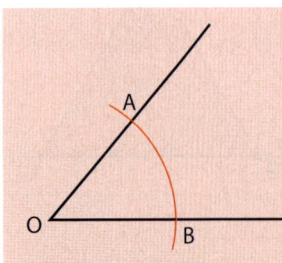

To bisect the given angle, place the point of the compass at O and draw an arc to cut both arms of the angle at A and B.

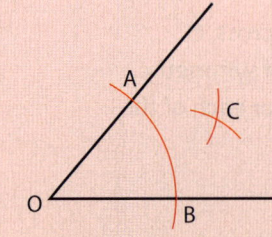

With the point of the compass at A and with the same radius, draw an arc between the arms of the angle. Repeat at B, cutting the first arc at C.

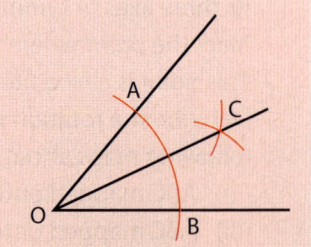

Join the point O to C. OC is the bisector of the angle AOB.

Chapter 24 Geometry 3: Transformations – Constructions

2. How to construct the perpendicular bisector of a line segment

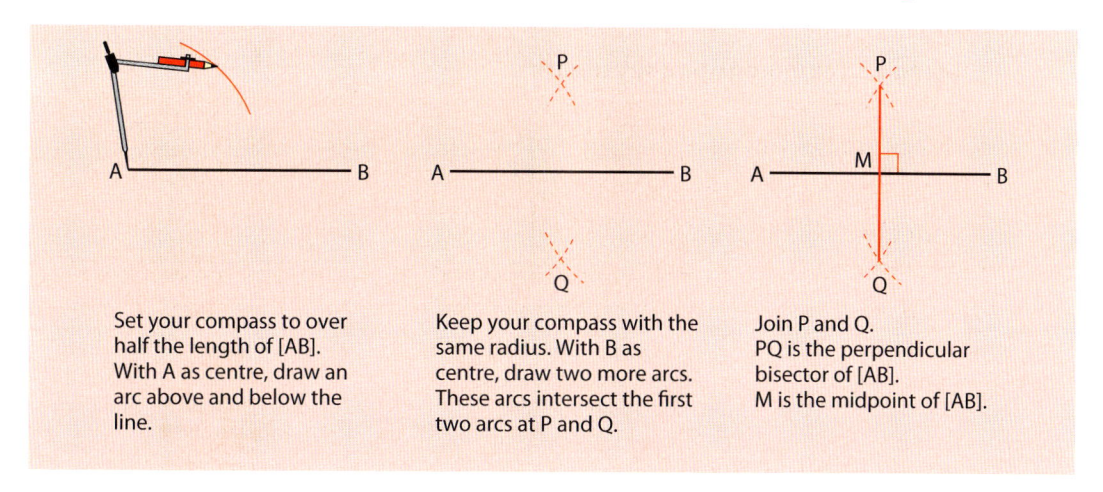

Set your compass to over half the length of [AB]. With A as centre, draw an arc above and below the line.

Keep your compass with the same radius. With B as centre, draw two more arcs. These arcs intersect the first two arcs at P and Q.

Join P and Q.
PQ is the perpendicular bisector of [AB].
M is the midpoint of [AB].

3. Line perpendicular to a given line ℓ, passing through a given point on ℓ

(i) Using a set square and straightedge

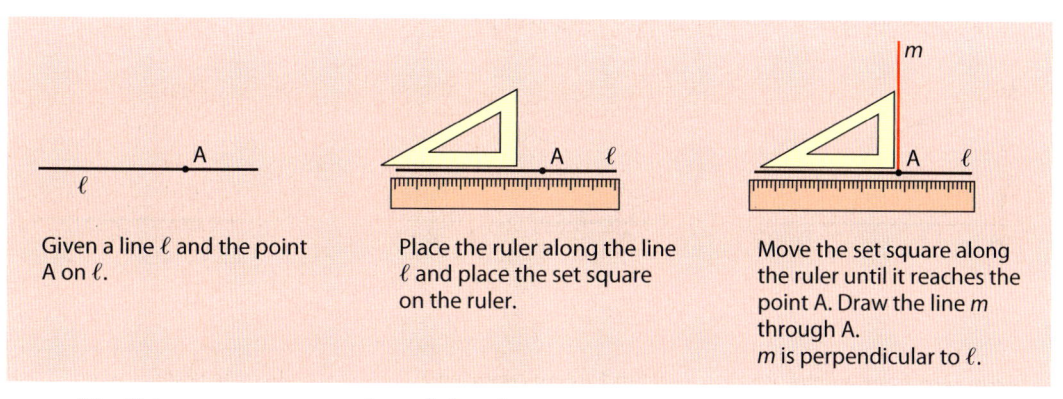

Given a line ℓ and the point A on ℓ.

Place the ruler along the line ℓ and place the set square on the ruler.

Move the set square along the ruler until it reaches the point A. Draw the line m through A.
m is perpendicular to ℓ.

(ii) Using a compass and straightedge

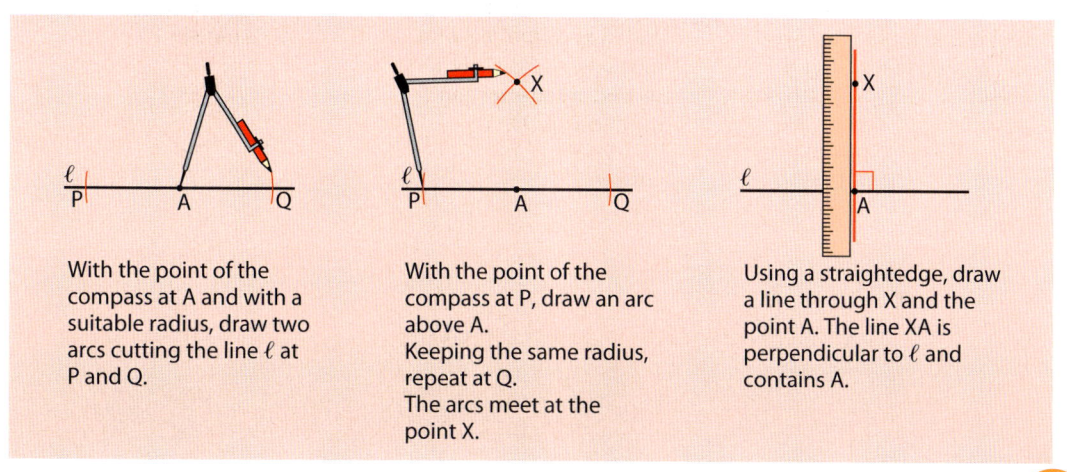

With the point of the compass at A and with a suitable radius, draw two arcs cutting the line ℓ at P and Q.

With the point of the compass at P, draw an arc above A.
Keeping the same radius, repeat at Q.
The arcs meet at the point X.

Using a straightedge, draw a line through X and the point A. The line XA is perpendicular to ℓ and contains A.

Text & Tests 2 Higher Level

4. Line perpendicular to a given line ℓ, passing through a given point not on ℓ

(i) Using a straightedge and set square

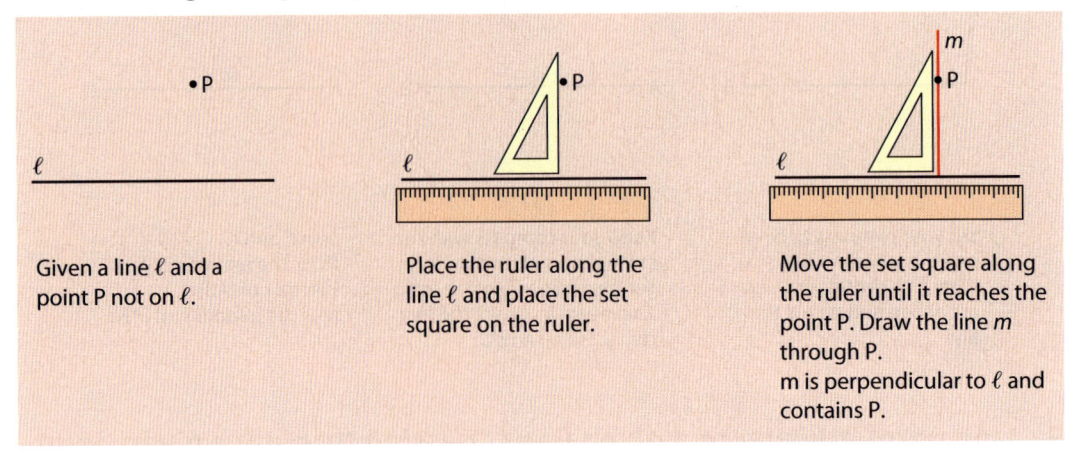

Given a line ℓ and a point P not on ℓ.

Place the ruler along the line ℓ and place the set square on the ruler.

Move the set square along the ruler until it reaches the point P. Draw the line m through P.
m is perpendicular to ℓ and contains P.

(ii) Using only a compass and straightedge

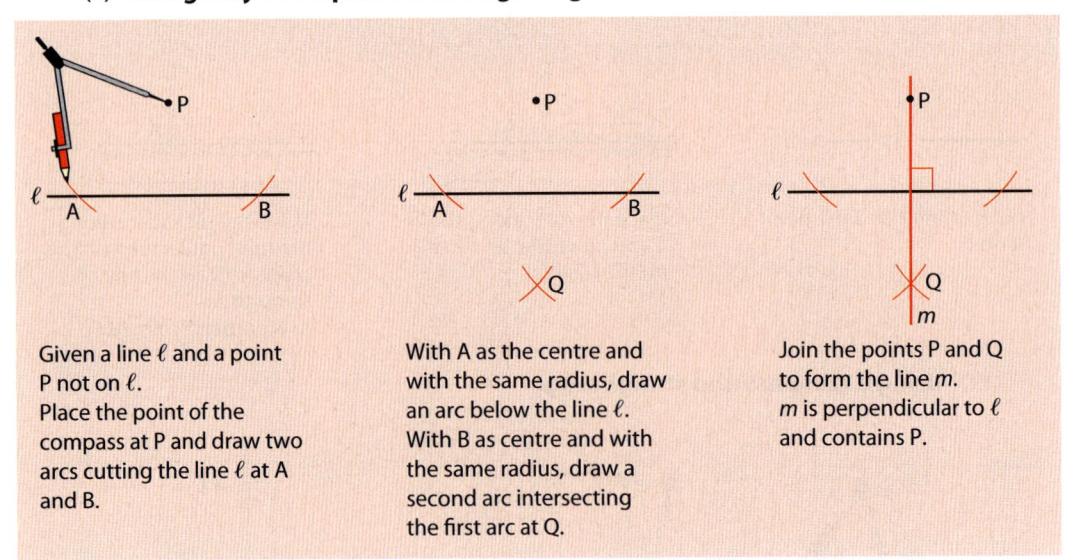

Given a line ℓ and a point P not on ℓ.
Place the point of the compass at P and draw two arcs cutting the line ℓ at A and B.

With A as the centre and with the same radius, draw an arc below the line ℓ.
With B as centre and with the same radius, draw a second arc intersecting the first arc at Q.

Join the points P and Q to form the line m.
m is perpendicular to ℓ and contains P.

570

Chapter 24 Geometry 3: Transformations – Constructions

5. How to draw a line parallel to a given line, through a given point

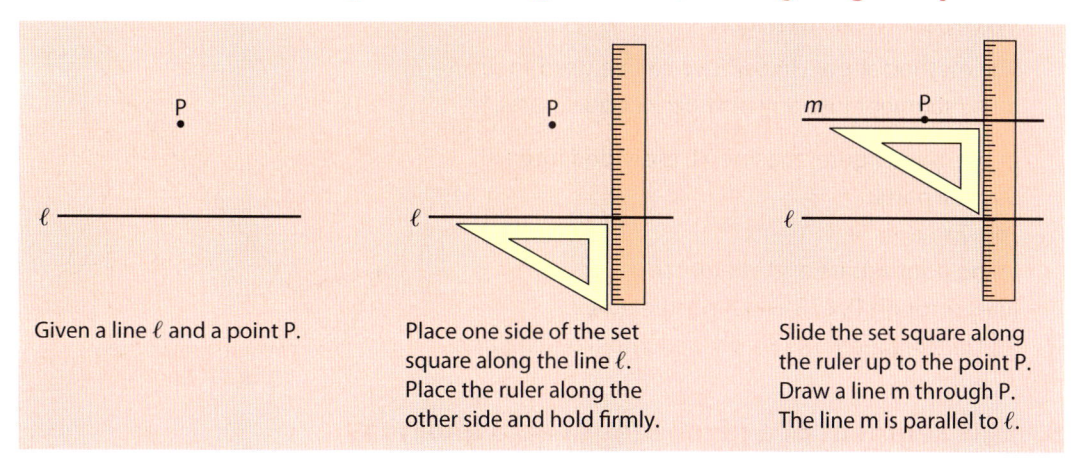

Given a line ℓ and a point P.

Place one side of the set square along the line ℓ. Place the ruler along the other side and hold firmly.

Slide the set square along the ruler up to the point P. Draw a line m through P. The line m is parallel to ℓ.

6. Division of a line segment into three equal parts

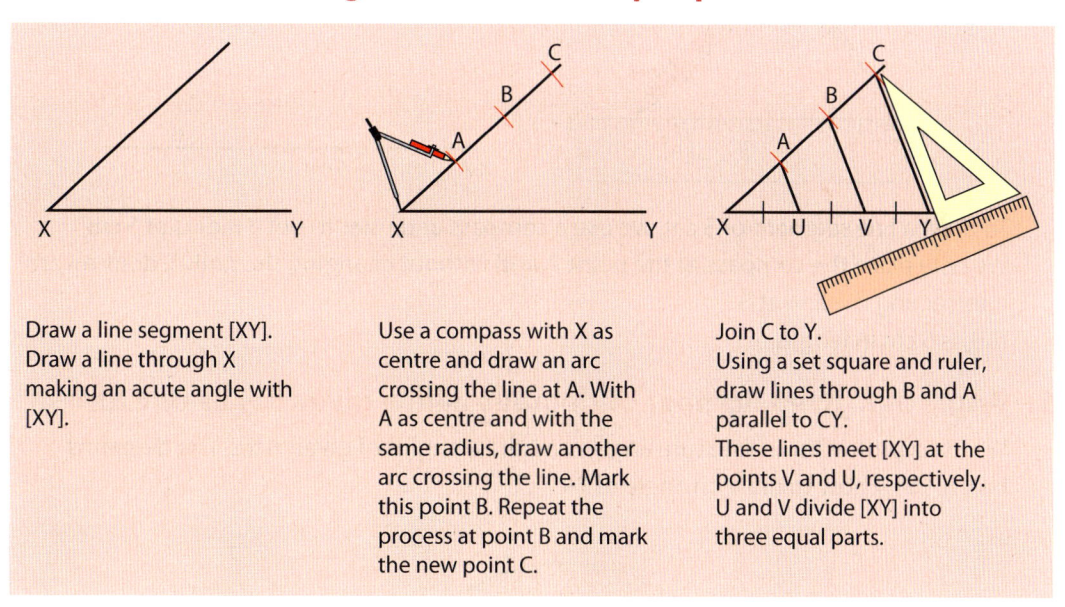

Draw a line segment [XY]. Draw a line through X making an acute angle with [XY].

Use a compass with X as centre and draw an arc crossing the line at A. With A as centre and with the same radius, draw another arc crossing the line. Mark this point B. Repeat the process at point B and mark the new point C.

Join C to Y. Using a set square and ruler, draw lines through B and A parallel to CY. These lines meet [XY] at the points V and U, respectively. U and V divide [XY] into three equal parts.

571

7. Division of a line segment into any number of equal segments, without measuring it

The method shown in 6 above can be used to divide a line segment into any number of equal parts.

In the given figure, the line XE is divided into 5 equal parts.
Join EY.
Using a set square and straightedge, draw lines through D, C, B and A parallel to EY.
The line segment [XY] is divided into 5 equal parts.

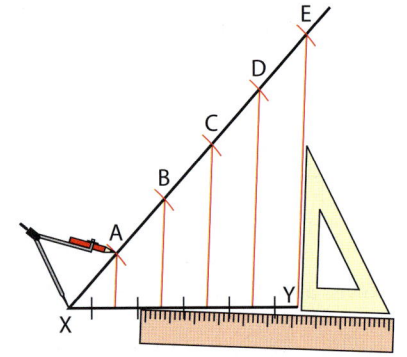

8. Line segment of a given length on a given ray

We use a compass, ruler and straightedge to draw a line segment of a given length on a given ray.

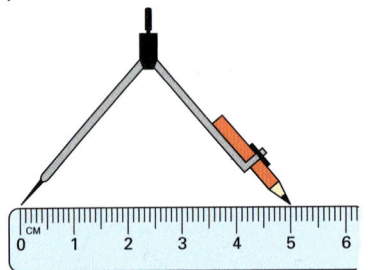

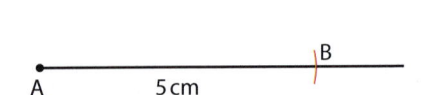

To draw a line segment of 5 cm, we use a compass and ruler to get a radius of 5 cm. We now place the compass at the point A and without changing the radius, draw an arc intersecting the line at B.
[AB] is 5 cm in length.

9. Angle of a given number of degrees with a given ray as one arm

We use a protractor to measure angles and draw angles of given sizes. The diagrams below show how to draw an angle of 74°.

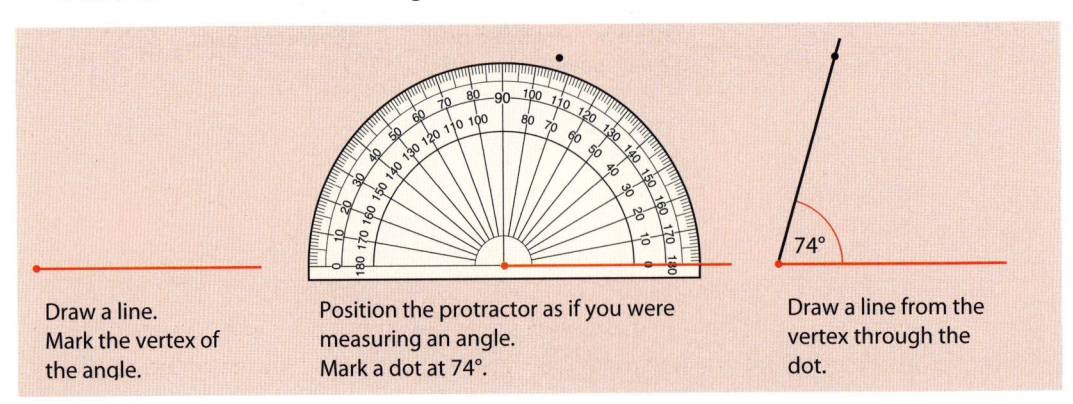

Draw a line.
Mark the vertex of the angle.

Position the protractor as if you were measuring an angle.
Mark a dot at 74°.

Draw a line from the vertex through the dot.

Chapter 24 Geometry 3: Transformations – Constructions

Exercise 24.4

1. Using only a compass and straightedge, construct the bisector of each of the angles shown below:

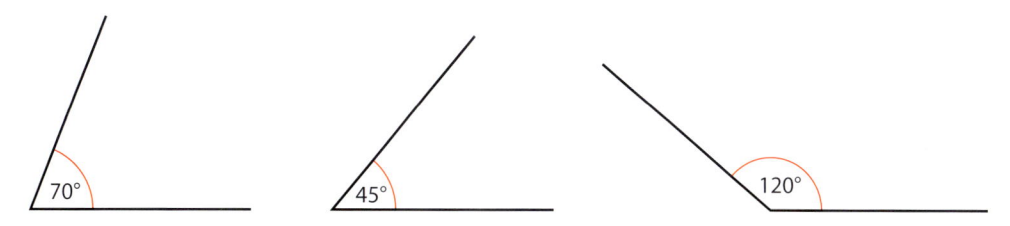

   70°   45°   120°

2. Use your set square to draw a right angle.
   Now use your compass and straightedge to divide the angle into two equal parts.
   Use your protractor to verify that each part is 45°.

3. Draw a line segment 6 cm in length.
   Use your compass and straightedge to construct the perpendicular bisector of this line segment.
   Verify that each half is 3 cm in length.

4. Draw a line segment 7 cm in length.
   Bisect the line and verify that both halves are equal in length.

5. Draw a line segment [AB], 8 cm in length.
   Use a compass and straightedge to construct the perpendicular bisector of this line segment.
   Pick any point on the perpendicular bisector and verify that it is the same distance from A and B.

6. Using a set square and straightedge, construct a line perpendicular to the given line through the given point for each of the lines shown below:

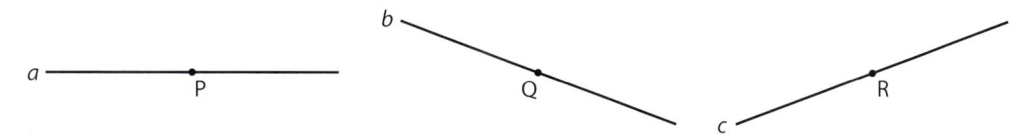

   a — P   b — Q   c — R

7. Using diagrams similar to those in question 6 above, construct a line perpendicular to the given line through the given point using only a compass and straightedge.

573

Text & Tests 2 Higher Level

8. In each of the following, construct a line perpendicular to the given line and through the given point, using
   (i) a set square and straightedge only
   (ii) a compass and straightedge only.

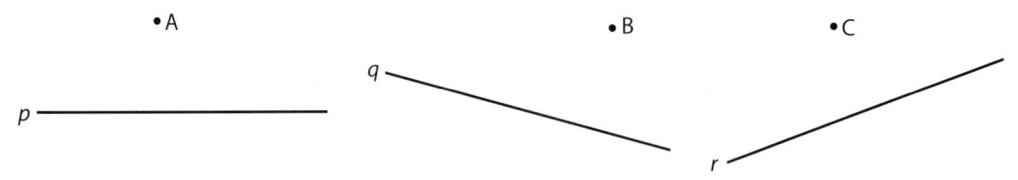

   • A   • B   • C

   q

   p

   r

9. Using a set square and straightedge, draw a line through the point P parallel to the line ℓ.

   P

   ℓ

10. Draw any other line segment and plot a point P not on the line.
    Now, using a set square and straightedge, draw a line through P parallel to the line segment you have drawn.

11. The diagram on the right shows a line segment [AB] and a line AY in which $|AX| = |XY|$.
    Use your set square and ruler to draw XM parallel to YB.
    Verify that M is the midpoint of [AB].

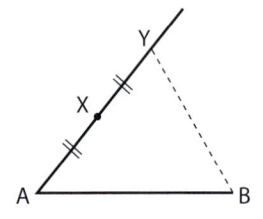

12. Draw a line segment 9 cm in length.
    Now use your compass, ruler and set square to divide the line into 3 equal parts.
    Use your ruler to verify that each part is 3 cm in length.

13. Draw a line segment 10 cm in length.
    Now use your compass, ruler and set square to divide the line into 4 equal parts.

14. Use your protractor to draw an angle of 65° ($\angle$BAC).
    Now use a compass and straightedge to construct the bisector of this angle.
    If X is any point on the bisector of the angle BAC and XB $\perp$ AB and XC $\perp$ AC, use congruent triangles to show that $|XB| = |XC|$.

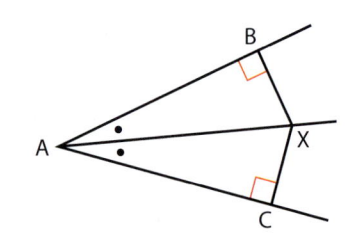

574

Chapter 24 Geometry 3: Transformations – Constructions

15. Copy the given diagram and then construct the shortest line segment from P to the line *m*.

16. Construct a right-angled triangle with the same dimensions as the given triangle.
    Verify that |AB| = 5 cm.

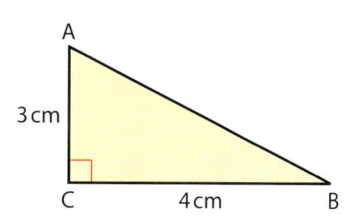

    Now construct the perpendicular bisectors of [AC] and [AB].
    If your constructions are accurate, the two bisectors should meet on [AB].

17. The given parallelogram has these dimensions:
    |DC| = 8 cm, |AD| = 3 cm and |DB| = 10 cm.

    Using a compass and ruler only, construct this parallelogram.

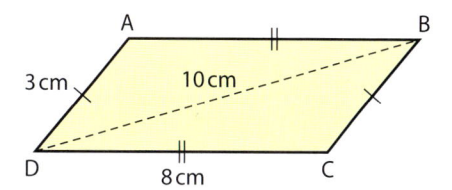

Section 24.5 Constructing triangles and rectangles
1. Triangle given lengths of the three sides

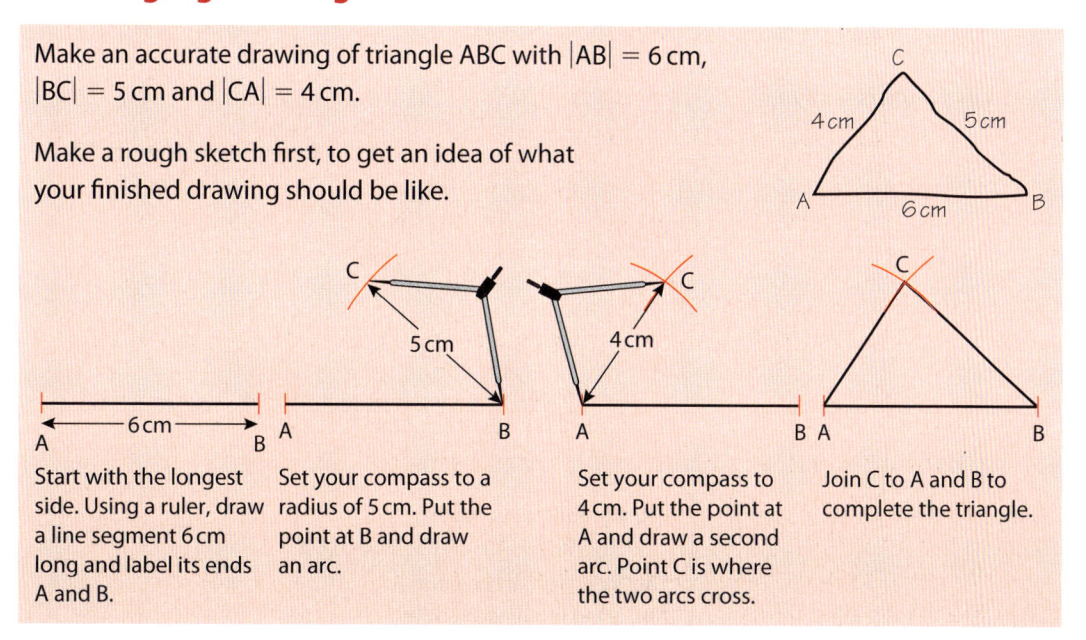

Make an accurate drawing of triangle ABC with |AB| = 6 cm, |BC| = 5 cm and |CA| = 4 cm.

Make a rough sketch first, to get an idea of what your finished drawing should be like.

Start with the longest side. Using a ruler, draw a line segment 6 cm long and label its ends A and B.	Set your compass to a radius of 5 cm. Put the point at B and draw an arc.	Set your compass to 4 cm. Put the point at A and draw a second arc. Point C is where the two arcs cross.	Join C to A and B to complete the triangle.

575

Text & Tests 2 Higher Level

2. Triangle given side, angle and side measurements

Construct a triangle ABC with [BC] as base, where |BC| = 4 cm, |AB| = 3 cm and |∠ABC| = 60°. Measure the side [AC].

A rough sketch is shown on the right.

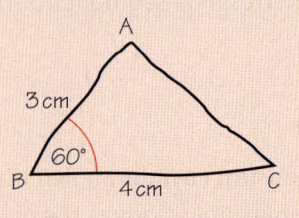

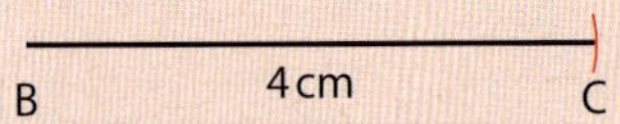

| Draw a horizontal line and use your compass to mark off 4 cm. This gives the base [BC] = 4 cm. | Use your protractor to measure ∠CBA = 60° and draw the line BA. Place the point of your compass at B and draw an arc using a radius of 3 cm. The point where the arc cuts the line BA gives us the required point A. | Join A to C. ABC is the required triangle. If we measure |AC|, we get 3.6 cm. |

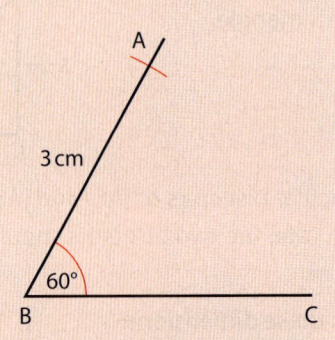

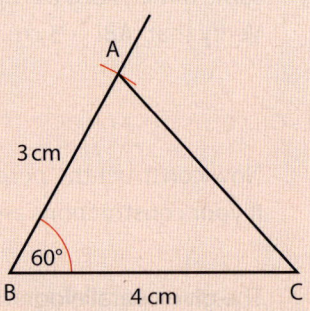

3. Triangle given angle, side, angle measures

Construct a triangle ABC with |BC| = 5 cm, |∠ABC| = 40° and |∠ACB| = 50°.

A rough sketch is shown.

| Draw a line segment [BC], 5 cm in length. | Use a protractor to make |∠ABC| = 40° and |∠BCA| = 50° The lines meet at the point A. ABC is the required triangle. |

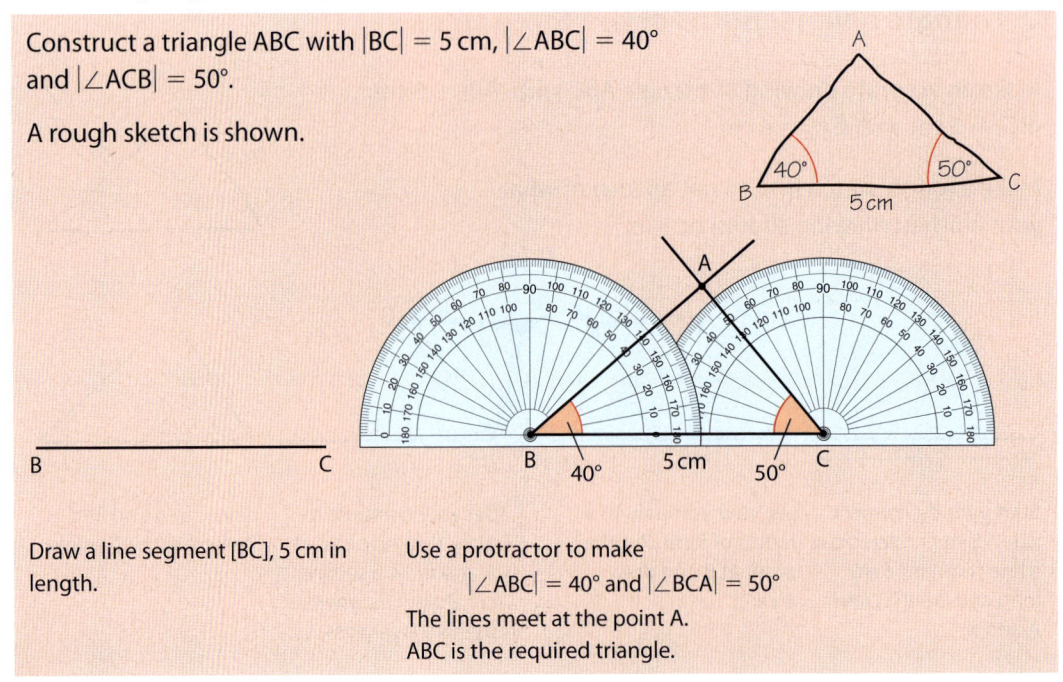

576

Chapter 24 Geometry 3: Transformations – Constructions

4. Right-angled triangle, given the length of the hypotenuse and one other side

Construct the triangle ABC so that $|\angle ABC| = 90°$, $|BC| = 5$ cm and $|AC| = 6$ cm.
A rough sketch of the triangle is shown.

Draw a line segment [BC], 5 cm in length.

Use a protractor to make an angle of 90° at B.
Draw a vertical line BA.
Set your compass to a radius of 6 cm.
With C as centre, draw an arc cutting the vertical line.
Mark this point A and join AC.
ABC is the required triangle.

5. Right-angled triangle, given one side and one of the acute angles

Construct the triangle ABC so that the base $[BC] = 5$ cm, $|\angle ABC| = 90°$ and $|\angle ACB| = 40°$.
A rough sketch is shown.

Draw a line segment [BC], 5 cm in length.

Use a protractor to make an angle of 90° at B.
Draw a vertical line BA.
Now use your protractor to make an angle of 40° at C.
Mark the point A where the arm of the angle meets the vertical line.
ABC is the required triangle.

577

Text & Tests 2 Higher Level

6. Constructing rectangles

Construct a rectangle of sides 5 cm and 3 cm in length.

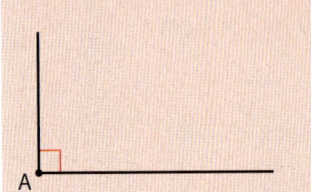

| Draw a horizontal line and mark a point A on it. Use a set square or protractor to draw a line perpendicular to given line at A. | Use a compass to measure 5 cm on the horizontal line and 3 cm on the vertical line. Mark the points D and B, respectively. | Draw a line through B parallel to AD. Draw a line through D parallel to AB. These lines meet at the point C. ABCD is the required rectangle. |

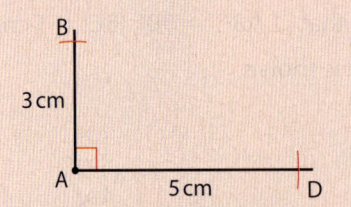

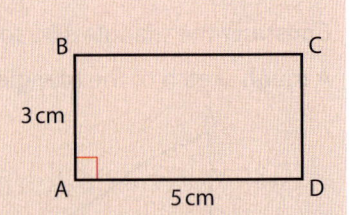

Exercise 24.5

1. Draw an accurate construction of each of the following triangles. All construction lines must be shown.

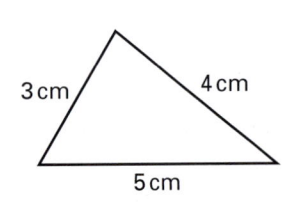

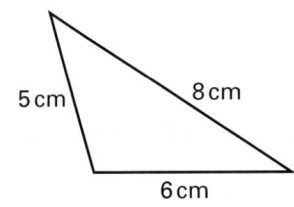

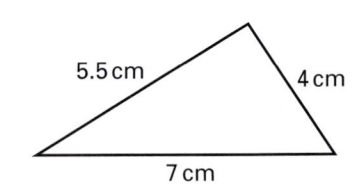

2. Draw a rough sketch of each of the following triangles.
   Use [BC] as base in each case.
   Now draw an accurate construction of each triangle.
   (i) △ABC in which $|BC| = 6$ cm, $|AB| = 5$ cm and $|AC| = 4$ cm.
   (ii) △ABC in which $|BC| = 8$ cm, $|AB| = 5.5$ cm and $|AC| = 6$ cm.

3. Draw a triangle of sides 3 cm, 5 cm and 6 cm.
   Measure the three angles and verify that
   (i) the smallest angle is opposite the shortest side
   (ii) the largest angle is opposite the longest side.

Chapter 24 Geometry 3: Transformations – Constructions

4. Construct the following triangles based on the dimensions shown in the rough sketches below.

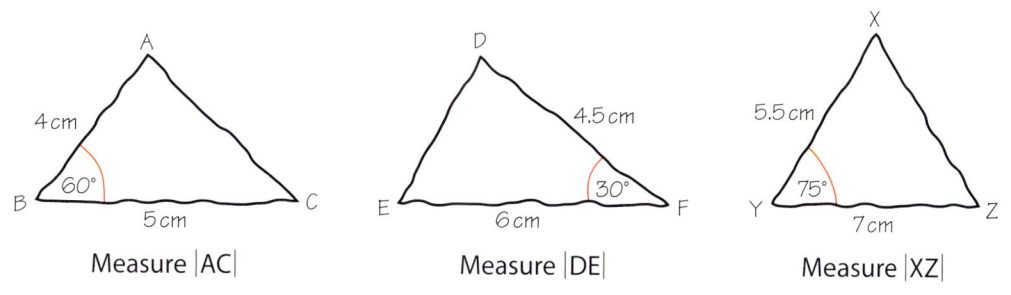

Measure |AC| (triangle ABC: AB = 4 cm, BC = 5 cm, ∠B = 60°)

Measure |DE| (triangle DEF: DF = 4.5 cm, EF = 6 cm, ∠F = 30°)

Measure |XZ| (triangle XYZ: XY = 5.5 cm, YZ = 7 cm, ∠Y = 75°)

5. Construct a triangle ABC, with [BC] as base, in each of the following cases. (First draw a rough sketch.)
Measure the third side in each triangle.

(i) |BC| = 4 cm, |AB| = 3 cm and |∠ABC| = 50°.
(ii) |BC| = 6 cm, |∠BCA| = 60° and |AC| = 4.5 cm.

6. Draw accurate diagrams of the sketches shown below:

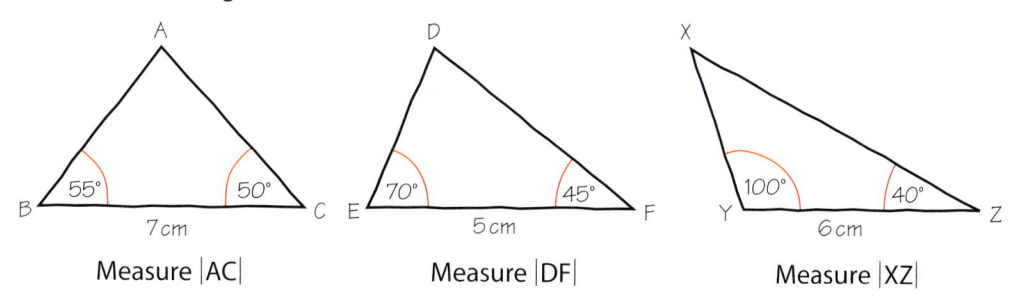

Measure |AC| (triangle ABC: BC = 7 cm, ∠B = 55°, ∠C = 50°)

Measure |DF| (triangle DEF: EF = 5 cm, ∠E = 70°, ∠F = 45°)

Measure |XZ| (triangle XYZ: YZ = 6 cm, ∠Y = 100°, ∠Z = 40°)

7. Draw an accurate construction of each of the following right-angled triangles:

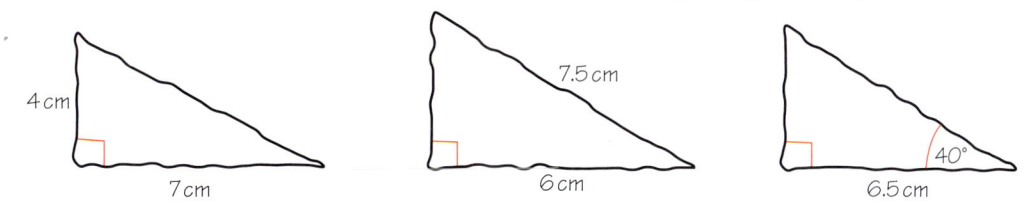

(triangle with legs 4 cm and 7 cm, right angle between them)

(right-angled triangle with hypotenuse 7.5 cm and one leg 6 cm)

(right-angled triangle with one leg 6.5 cm and angle 40°)

8. Construct the triangle DEF, with base [EF], in which |DE| = 5 cm, |EF| = 6.5 cm and |∠DEF| = 90°.

9. Construct the triangle ABC, with [BC] as base, in which |BC| = 7 cm, |∠ABC| = 90° and |∠ACB| = 50°.
Measure |AC|.

Text & Tests 2 Higher Level

10. Draw a rectangle of sides 6 cm and 4 cm in length.
    Verify that both diagonals are equal in length.

11. Draw a rectangle of sides 7 cm and 4.5 cm in length.
    Measure the length of the diagonal.

12. Construct the rectangle ABCD with base [AB] = 7 cm in length if the area of the rectangle is 28 cm².

13. Draw a triangle ABC having the same measurements as those shown on the right.
    Use your compass to perpendicularly bisect the three sides of the triangle.
    If your drawing is accurate, the three lines should intersect at the same point.
    Now use this point as the centre to draw a circle through A, B and C.
    This circle is called the **circumcircle** of the triangle.

14. Draw a triangle with base 7 cm and other sides of length 5 cm and 6 cm.
    Bisect the three angles using a compass and ruler.
    The three bisectors should meet at the one point.
    Using this point as centre, draw a circle which touches the three sides of the triangle.
    This circle is called the **incircle** of the triangle.

Investigation:

Construct a square ABCD

Mark the points E, F, G, H so that |AE| = |BF| = |CG| = |DH| = a

Let |ED| = |HC| = |GB| = |FA| = b

Join points E, H, G, F. Prove that EFGH is a square.

Copy and complete each of the following lines:

1. The area of each triangle = $\frac{1}{2}$( )( ).
2. The area of the 4 triangles = ( )( )( ).
3. The area of the small square = ( )²
4. The area of the small square + 4 triangles =
5. The area of the large square = (   )²

By equating lines 4 and 5, prove that $a^2 + b^2 = c^2$.

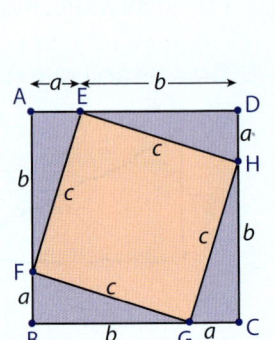

Chapter 24 Geometry 3: Transformations – Constructions

Test yourself 24

1. How many axes of symmetry has each of the following letters?
   (i) T   (ii) E   (iii) A   (iv) M

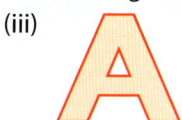

2. Copy the diagram on the right and then use a ruler and set square to draw a line through P perpendicular to ℓ.

3. Describe in full the transformation that maps each of these:
   (i) F onto G
   (ii) D onto F
   (iii) A onto B
   (iv) A onto H
   (v) E onto B
   (vi) E onto C.

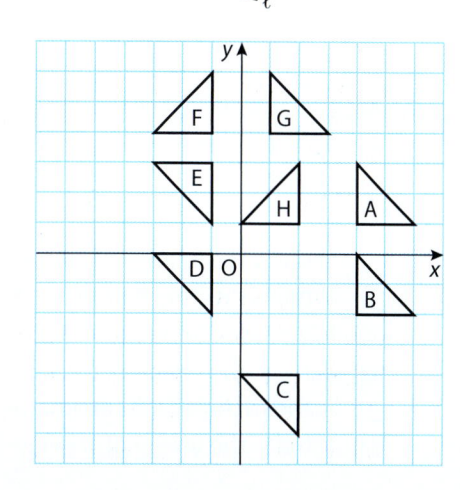

4. Construct the triangle based on the dimensions shown in the rough sketch on the right.

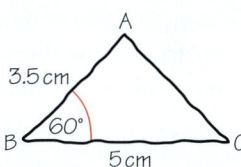

5. Which of the four fish in the boxes below could be the image of the fish shown on the right under
   (i) a translation
   (ii) an axial symmetry
   (iii) a central symmetry?

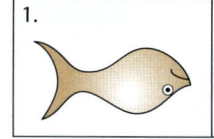

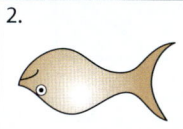

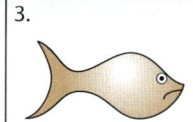

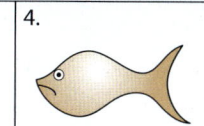

6. (i) A'B'C'D' is the image of the figure ABCD under reflection in the y-axis.
   Write down the coordinates of A', B', C' and D'.
   (ii) Find the image of ABCD by a rotation of 90° about O, in an anticlockwise direction.

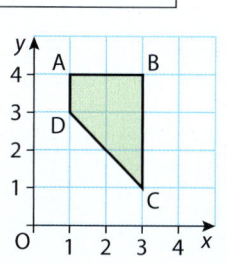

581

7. Use your protractor to draw an angle of 70°.
   Now use your compass and straightedge only to construct the bisector of this angle.

8. Copy these diagrams onto squared paper.
   Shade **two more squares** in each diagram to make the dashed line an axis of symmetry.

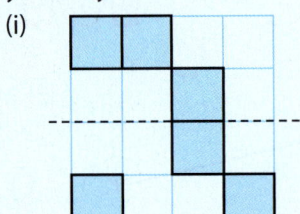

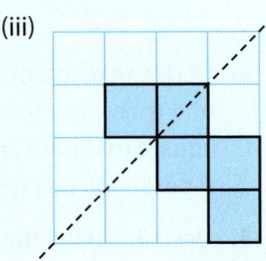

   (i)   (ii)   (iii)

9. ABCD is a parallelogram with the diagonals intersecting at the point O.

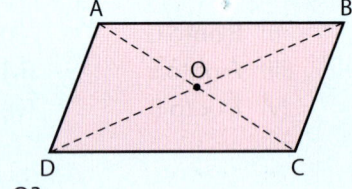

   (i)   What is the image of D under $\vec{AB}$?
   (ii) What is the image of [AD] under central symmetry in O?
   (iii) What is the image of △AOB under central symmetry in O?
   (iv) What is the image of [DC] under $\vec{CB}$?
   (v)   Is the triangle DCB the image of the triangle DAB under reflection in the line DB?
   (vi) What is the image of 'triangle' BOC by a rotation of 180° about O.

10. Use a compass and ruler only to construct a line through P perpendicular to the line k.

11. Describe the transformation that will map

    (i)   shape T onto shape S
    (ii) shape P onto shape Q
    (iii) shape A onto shape B.

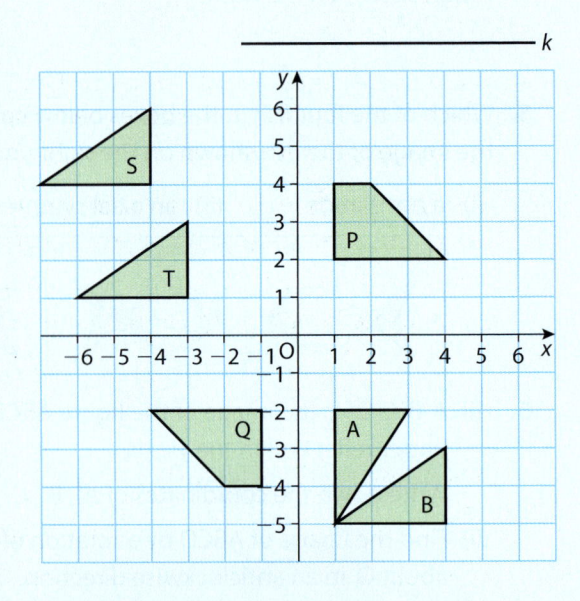

Chapter 24 Geometry 3: Transformations – Constructions

12. (a) Find the coordinates of the image of the triangle ABC by a rotation of:
  (i) 90°
  (ii) 180° about O in an anticlockwise direction.
  (b) Find the image of ABC by central symmetry through the point O.

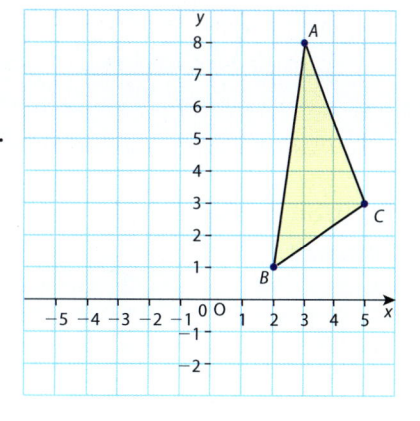

13. On squared paper draw the parallelogram DEFG.
Using a compass, draw an arc of 180° with O as centre, from each of the points DEFG.
Draw the image of DEFG.
Write down the coordinates of D'E'F'G'.

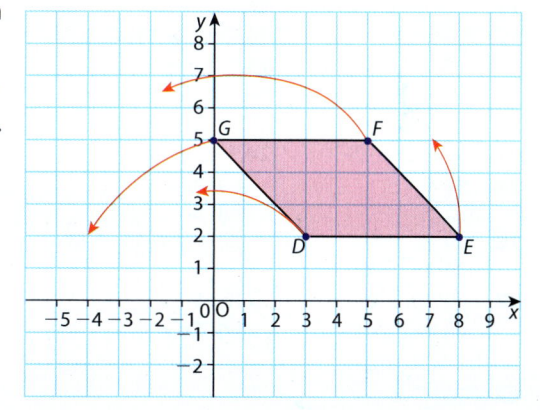

Assignment

Computer programs can be used to rotate images about points. These programs require mathematical 'rules' to locate each image.

By studying the images of the point, A, as it rotates about the origin (0, 0) create a rule for finding the image of (x, y) by a rotation about the origin for each of the given rotations.

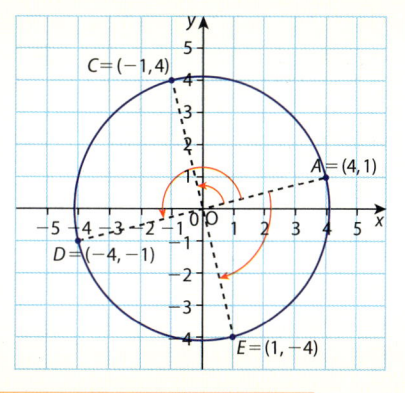

Rotation	90° anticlockwise	180°	90° clockwise
(x, y)			

583

Answers

Chapter 1: Algebra 1

Exercise 1.1
1. $5x$
2. $11a + 9$
3. $3x + 5y$
4. $3a - 2b$
5. $15a + 6b$
6. $7x + 5y + 4$
7. $7x + 4$
8. $4x + 3$
9. $8a + 3b + 2$
10. $6x + 1$
11. $5a + 4b$
12. $5ab + 2$
13. $3p - q + r$
14. $2k + 5$
15. $7ab - 3c$
16. $4xy + 11z$
17. $5ab + 5cd$
18. $11x - 8xy$
19. $-x^2 + 2x + 1$
20. $4x^2 - 11x + 7$
21. $7a^2 - 8a - 3$
22. $-2y^2 - 6y - 3$
23. $3x^2 - 2x - 5$
24. $2a^2 - a + 6$
25. (i) 4   (ii) 4   (iii) 2   (iv) 8
26. (i) $7p + 8q$ (ii) $6a + 4b + 13$ (iii) $4a + 4b + 4c$
27. (i) $4p + 2$ (ii) 3   (iii) $2x$ (iv) $5x + 4$

Exercise 1.2
1. (i) $12a$ (ii) $15a^2$ (iii) $2ab$ (iv) $12xy$ (v) $-6a^2$ (vi) $8ab^2$ (vii) $2a^3b^2$ (viii) $24a^3$
2. $11x + 7$
3. $8x + 7$
4. $13x - 8$
5. $x + 2$
6. $18x - 20$
7. $3x - 14$
8. $a - 1$
9. $a - 5$
10. $4x^2 - 4x - 6$
11. $x^2 + x - 24$
12. $6x^2 - x - 12$
13. $6x^2 + 16x + 8$
14. $6x^2 - 10x - 4$
15. $10x^2 + 11x - 6$
16. $2x^2 - 13x + 15$
17. $15x^2 - 12x - 3$
18. $3x^3 + 7x^2 + 5x + 1$
19. $4x^3 + 6x^2 - 10x - 12$
20. $5x^3 - 7x^2 + 22x - 8$
21. $6x^3 - 13x^2 + 27x - 14$
22. $4x^3 - 17x^2 + 28x - 6$
23. $8x^3 - 18x^2 + 17x - 6$
24. $6a^3 - 17a^2 + 18a - 8$
25. $2y^3 - y^2 - 19y - 7$
26. (i) $2xy$ (ii) $2km + nm$ (iii) $15a^2 + ac$
27. (i) $\boxed{d + 5}$ (ii) $\boxed{n - 4}$ (iii) $\boxed{5 - p}$ (iv) $\boxed{4 + k}$

28. (i) $2q$ (ii) $3m$ (iii) $3b$ (iv) $5x^2$ (v) $5c^2$ (vi) $4v^2w$

Exercise 1.3
1. (i) 12   (ii) 14   (iii) 3   (iv) 19   (v) 33
2. (i) 4   (ii) 3   (iii) 22   (iv) -10
3. (i) 4   (ii) 3   (iii) 33   (iv) 10   (v) 12   (vi) 26   (vii) 5   (viii) 2   (ix) 2
4. (i) 7   (ii) 5   (iii) 1   (iv) 6
5. (i) 19   (ii) 1   (iii) 30   (iv) 24
6. 7
7. (i) -11 (ii) 34   (iii) 180
8. (i) 30   (ii) 15   (iii) 1   (iv) $\frac{9}{2}$ (v) 180
9. (i) 24   (ii) 36   (iii) 25
10. (i) 125 cm^2 (ii) 96 cm^2
11. (i) 125 cm^2 (ii) 242 cm^2
12. A and F, B and G, C and E, D and H
13. $1\frac{1}{2}$

Exercise 1.4
1. (i) 7   (ii) 4   (iii) 10   (iv) 4   (v) 3   (vi) 6
2. (i) $x = 4$ (ii) $x = 9$ (iii) $x = 7$ (iv) $x = 7$ (v) $x = 7$
3. $x = 3$
4. $x = 6$
5. $x = 6$
6. $x = 4$
7. $x = 1$
8. $x = 4$
9. $x = 6$
10. $x = 5$
11. $x = 3$
12. $x = 8$
13. $x = 6$
14. $x = 7$
15. $x = 7$
16. $x = 5$
17. $x = 9$
18. $x = 2$
19. $x = 5$
20. $x = 1$
21. $x = 10$
22. $x = 4$
23. $x = 5$
24. $x = 5$
25. $x = 2$
26. $m = 2$
27. $x = -6$
28. $x = 3$
29. $y = 2$
30. $k = 4$
31. $x = 2$
32. (i) $x = 2$ (ii) $x = 2$
33. $x = 2\frac{3}{11}, f = 3\frac{3}{8}$

Exercise 1.5
1. 5
2. 2
3. 6 and 11
4. 14 yrs old
5. (i) $6x + 1$ (ii) 9
6. 7
7. 12
8. 51
9. (i) 15   (ii) $9\frac{1}{2}$ (iii) 10
10. $\frac{7}{12}$

Answers

11. (i) 8   (ii) 5
12. (i) As $20 - x + x = 20$
    (ii) $15 - x$ (iii) 8
13. $(7x - 4)$ cm^2; 6
14. (i) $(x - 6)$ yrs   (ii) $(x + 12)$ yrs
    (iii) 15 yrs
15. 48
16. Air – 2 hours, Sea – 5 hours 20 min, Train – 3 hours 20 min
17. 55, 56, 57
18. (i) $x = 41°$ (ii) $x = 31°$
19. €6
20. $4S + 2P = €322$, $S = €46$, $P = €69$
21. 12

Exercise 1.6

1. $x + 2$ **2.** $x + 3$
3. $x + 7$ **4.** $2x + 1$
5. $3x + 1$ **6.** $x - 2$
7. $2x - 4$ **8.** $2x + 1$
9. $x - 7$ **10.** $3x - 5$
11. $5x + 4$ **12.** $3x - 4$
13. $x^2 + 2x + 3$ **14.** $x^2 + 3x + 5$
15. $x^2 + 6x + 8$ **16.** $x^2 - x - 6$
17. $x^2 + x - 2$ **18.** $x^2 - 4x + 4$
19. $x^2 + 7x - 10$ **20.** $x^2 - 4$
21. $x^2 + 5x + 6$ **22.** $2x^2 + 3x - 1$
23. $3x^2 - 8x + 4$ **24.** $3x^2 - 3x + 12$
25. (i) $2x - 3$ (ii) $5x - 2$

Exercise 1.7

1. (i) T (ii) T (iii) F (iv) T
    (v) F (vi) F (vii) T (viii) T
2. (i) $>$ (ii) $<$ (iii) $>$ (iv) $<$
3. (i) $x < 4$ (ii) $2 > -3$
    (iii) $S \leq 40$ km/hr (iv) $b \leq -5$
    (v) $A \geq 18$ (vi) $A \leq 60$
4. (i) 1, 2, 3 (ii) 1, 2, 3, 4, 5
    (iii) 1, 2, 3, 4, 5, 6 (iv) 3, 4, 5, 6
    (v) 1, 2, 3, 4 (vi) 2, 3, 4, 5, 6, 7
5. (i) $-2, -1, 0, 1$ (ii) 0, 1, 2, 3, 4
    (iii) $-3, -2, -1, 0$ (iv) $-4, -3, -2$
    (v) $-4, -3, -2, -1, 0, 1$
    (vi) $-2, -1, 0, 1, 2, 3$
7. (i) $x > 3$ (ii) $x < 3$
    (iii) $x = 3$ (iv) $x \leq 3$
8. (i) $x \geq 1$ (ii) $x \leq -1$ (iii) $x < 4$
    (iv) $x > -6$ (v) $x > 6$ (vi) $x < 2$
10. (i) $x \geq 1, x \in N$ (ii) $x \geq -1, x \in Z$
    (iii) $x \leq 0, x \in Z$ (iv) $x \leq 1, x \in R$
    (v) $x \geq -2, x \in R$ (vi) $x < 15, x \in R$

11. $\sqrt{9}, \sqrt{20}$ **12.** 12, 16, 20, 24
13. 9, -4, 0
14. (i) $n \geq 6$ (ii) $n \leq 5°C$
    (iii) $n \leq 10$ kg (iv) $n > 5$
    (v) $20 \leq n \leq 30$ (vi) $5n - 12 > -7$

Exercise 1.8

1. A, B, D, E   **2.** A, C, D, E   **3.** $x \leq 5$
4. $x \leq 4$ **5.** $x \leq 4$ **6.** $x \leq 3$
7. $x \leq -2$ **8.** $x \leq 4$ **9.** $x < -3$
10. $x \leq 2$ **11.** $x \leq 4$ **12.** $x \leq 3$
13. $x < 2$ **14.** $x \geq -1$ **15.** $x \leq 6$
16. $x < 3$ **17.** {3, 4, 5}   **18.** (iii)
19. $-4, -3, -2, -1, 0, 1, 2, 3, 4$
20. (i) $350 < c < 500$
    (iii) $120 \leq c \leq 200$
    (v) $12 \leq c \leq 20$

Test yourself 1

1. (i) $6x^2 + x - 3$ (ii) $x = 3$
2. $x \geq 2, x \in R$.
    0   1   2   3   4   5
3. $16x - 12$; $x = 3$
4. (i) $10(x + 3)$ (ii) $2 - 4x^2$
5. (i) $(x + 3)$ cm (ii) $(x - 1)$ cm
    (iii) $(3x + 2)$ cm
    (iv) $3x + 2 = 44$; $|AB| = 14$
    $|BC| = 17$ cm
6. (i) x ... units

Chapter 2: Factors

Exercise 2.1
1. (i) 3 (ii) 6 (iii) 7 (iv) 7
2. (i) $4x$ (ii) $3n$ (iii) $5x$ (iv) $3a$ (v) $3x$ (vi) $2ab$
3. (i) $(x + 2y)$ (ii) $(2a + 3b)$ (iii) $(a + c)$ (iv) $(a + 2)$ (v) $(x - 3y)$ (vi) $(2x - 3z)$ (vii) $(3x + 2y)$ (viii) $(3a - 4b + 2)$
4. $6(x + 3y)$
5. $3b(a + c)$
6. $6a(x - 2y)$
7. $6a(a - 2)$
8. $7x(x - 4)$
9. $5x(3x + 5y)$
10. $3x^2(1 - 2y)$
11. $3ab(b - 2)$
12. $3p(p - 2q)$
13. $2x(2x - 3y + 4z)$
14. $5xy(y - 4x)$
15. $4xy(xy - 2)$
16. $2ab(a - 2b + 6c)$

Exercise 2.2
1. $(2a + 3)(x + y)$
2. $(3x - 4)(2a - b)$
3. $(3a - 4)(2b - c)$
4. $(2x + b)(5y - z)$
5. $(2a - 1)(x - 2y)$
6. $(a + c)(a + b)$
7. $(x + 3)(x - a)$
8. $(a - 5)(b + c)$
9. $(a + 5)(b + 3)$
10. $(3x + 4y)(x - z)$
11. $(c - 2d)(2c + 1)$
12. $(2a - 3)(x - 3y)$
13. $(2a + b)(c - 2d)$
14. $(3xy + 2z)(1 - z)$
15. $(4a - 3b)(2x + y)$
16. $(3a - 4)(2x^2 + 3)$
17. $(2y - z)(x - 1)$
18. $(n - 5)(a + b)$
19. $(2x - 3)(xy - z)$
20. $(7y + 2a)(y - 3b)$
21. $(2a + b)(2ab - 3)$
22. $(3a - 2b)(4a + 3c)$
23. $(ax - y)(3bx - 5y)$
24. $(3a + 2c)(3a^2 - 2b)$
25. $(x - 2a)(x + b)$
26. $(2x - 3y)(3x - 2a)$

Exercise 2.3
1. $(x + y)(x - y)$
2. $(a + b)(a - b)$
3. $(x + 2y)(x - 2y)$
4. $(x + 4y)(x - 4y)$
5. $(2x + y)(2x - y)$
6. $(3x + 4y)(3x - 4y)$
7. $(2a + 5b)(2a - 5b)$
8. $(6x + 7y)(6x - 7y)$
9. $(8x + 3y)(8x - 3y)$
10. $(6 + 11y)(6 - 11y)$
11. $(7a + 2b)(7a - 2b)$
12. $(xy + 2)(xy - 2)$
13. $(ab + 5)(ab - 5)$
14. $(xy + 4)(xy - 4)$
15. $(ab + 7)(ab - 7)$
16. $(5xy + 6)(5xy - 6)$
17. $(4ab + 5)(4ab - 5)$
18. $(3xy + 1)(3xy - 1)$
19. $(2ab + 7cd)(2ab - 7cd)$
20. $(11a + 8bc)(11a - 8bc)$
21. $(9hk + 5pq)(9hk - 5pq)$
22. (i) $3(x + 3y)(x - 3y)$ (ii) $3(2x + y)(2x - y)$ (iii) $3(3x + y)(3x - y)$ (iv) $5(3 + x)(3 - x)$ (v) $5(3k + 2)(3k - 2)$ (vi) $4(ax + 3y)(ax - 3y)$
23. $2(9x^2 - 4y^2)$; $2(3x + 2y)(3x - 2y)$
24. $(3x + y)(3x - y)$

Exercise 2.4
1. $(x + 2)(x + 3)$
2. $(x + 2)(x + 6)$
3. $(x + 7)(x + 2)$
4. $(x + 3)(x + 8)$
5. $(x + 2)(x + 10)$
6. $(x + 3)(x + 9)$
7. $(x + 5)(x + 6)$
8. $(x + 4)(x + 11)$
9. $(x + 2)(x + 18)$
10. $(2x + 1)(x + 2)$
11. $(2x + 7)(x + 2)$
12. $(5x + 1)(x + 4)$
13. $(x - 3)(x - 4)$
14. $(x - 3)(x - 6)$
15. $(x - 4)(x - 5)$
16. $(x - 2)(x - 12)$
17. $(x - 3)(x - 9)$
18. $(x - 4)(x - 9)$
19. $(2x - 1)(x - 3)$
20. $(3x - 2)(x - 5)$
21. $(5x - 2)(x - 3)$
22. $(3x - 5)(x - 4)$
23. $(5x - 3)(x + 6)$
24. $(3x - 5)(x - 3)$
25. $(x + 2)(x - 6)$
26. $(x + 2)(x - 5)$
27. $(x - 2)(x + 9)$
28. $(x - 3)(x + 10)$
29. $(x + 2)(x - 15)$
30. $(x + 2)(x - 20)$
31. $(4x - 5)(3x + 1)$
32. $(3x + 5)(2x - 3)$
33. $(4x - 1)(2x - 3)$
34. $(3x - 2)(x + 5)$
35. $(3x + 4)(3x + 4)$
36. $(5x - 1)(x - 6)$
37. $(3x - 7)(x + 2)$
38. $(3x - 1)(2x - 3)$
39. $(4x - 5)(3x - 2)$
40. $(9x - 2)(x + 3)$
41. $(6x - 11)(x + 2)$
42. $(9x - 10)(x + 1)$
43. $(4x - 3)(x - 2)$
44. $(5x + 4)(2x - 5)$
45. $(9x - 4)(4x + 1)$
46. $(4x - 3)(3x - 2)$
47. $(3x - 4)(5x + 2)$
48. $(6x + 5)(4x - 3)$

Exercise 2.5
1. (i) $\frac{2}{5}$ (ii) $\frac{x}{2}$ (iii) $3x$ (iv) $4p$ (v) $3x$
2. (i) $x + y$ (ii) 4 (iii) $\frac{3}{x}$ (iv) $\frac{4}{3}$
3. $x - 1$
4. $2(y + 3)$
5. $x + 7$
6. $\frac{1}{x - 2}$
7. $\frac{1}{x + 7}$
8. $\frac{3}{x - 1}$
9. $\frac{2}{x + 4}$
10. $x + 6$
11. $\frac{a}{3}$
12. $x + 3$
13. $\frac{a + 4}{3}$
14. $\frac{1}{n + 9}$
15. $\frac{4}{x + 2}$
16. $x + 3$
17. $x + 3$
18. a
19. -1
20. $\frac{3}{a + 1}$

Test yourself 2
1. (i) $(x - 3y)$ (ii) $(x - 4)(x - 6)$
2. (i) $(a + b)(7 + x)$ (ii) $(5a + 9)(5a - 9)$
3. $\frac{4x + 1}{4x}$
4. (i) $(3x - 2)(2x + 1)$ (ii) $(3a + b)(2a + c)$
5. (i) $3ax(2a + x - 3)$ (ii) $3(x + 4)(x - 4)$

Answers

6. $\dfrac{3x+2}{2x+5}$
7. (i) $2ab(4a+b)$ (ii) $(3x-7)(x-3)$
8. (i) $2(x+2y)(x-2y)$ (ii) $(x-1)(2y-z)$
9. $12(x+a)(x-a)$
10. (i) $3c(5b-c)$ (ii) $(8x+3)(3x-1)$
11. (i) $2(2x+y)(2x-y)$ (ii) $(a-b)(x-2y)$
12. $\dfrac{5x-2}{2x+5}$
13. (i) $(3x-4)(x+2)$ (ii) $(a-2)(a+b)$
14. (i) $5(a+5b)(a-5b)$
    (ii) $(2x+3)(x+y)(x-y)$
15. $\dfrac{2x-3}{x(x+6)}$

Chapter 3: Sets

Exercise 3.1
1. (i) {1, 3, 4, 5, 6, 7}
   (ii) {1, 7, 8, 9, 10, 11}
   (iii) {1, 7}
   (iv) {1, 3, 4, 5, 6, 7, 8, 9, 10, 11}
2. (i) {1, 3, 5, 7, 8} (ii) {3, 7}
   (iii) {2, 4, 9, 10} (iv) {1, 2, 5, 8, 10}
   (v) {2, 10} (vi) {4, 9}
3. (i) 7 (ii) 7 (iii) 14
   (iv) 11 (v) 3 (vi) 3
4. 22
6. (i) 33 (ii) 24 (iii) 9
8. (i) 5 (ii) 30 (iii) 11 (iv) 7
9. (i) 6 (ii) 10
10. 10
11. (a) (i) Natural numbers
        (ii) Integer numbers
        (iii) Rational numbers
    (b) (i) N (ii) Z (iii) Q (iv) Z
12. $U = 30$

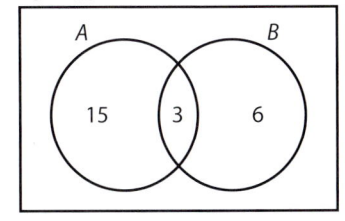

13. (i) (−1, 0, 1, 2, 3, 4, 5, 6, 7, 8)
    (ii) (2, 4)
    (iii) (2, 5, 8, 11, 14)
    (iv) (−5, −1, 3)
14. (i) (−4, −2, 0, 2)
    (ii) (−4, −3, −2, −1, 0, 1, 2, 3, 4, 6)
15. $32 = 24 + 18 - x$; $x = 10$
16. (i) 6 (ii) 18 (iii) 11
17. (i) 16 (ii) 46 (iii) 30

Exercise 3.2
1. (i) {1, 2, 4, 5, 7, 8} (ii) {3, 9, 10}
   (iii) {1, 3, 5, 7} (iv) { } (or ∅)
2. (i) {a, c, e} (ii) {f, g, h}
   (iii) {f, g, h, i, j} (iv) {a, c, e, f, g, h, i, j}
3. (i) T (ii) F (iii) T (iv) F
   (v) T (vi) T (vii) T (viii) F
4. (i) {2, 4, 8, 10}
   (ii) {3, 9, 15}; No; Set diff. not commutative
5. (i) 3 (ii) 4 (iii) 2 (iv) 7
7. (i) All the people who live in Newtown excluding car owners
   (ii) All the people who live in Newtown excluding retired people
   (iii) Car owners who live in Newtown that are not retired
   (iv) Retired people who live in Newtown that do not own a car
   (v) Car-owning, retired people who live in Newtown
8. (i) R: Real numbers, Q: Rational numbers, Z: Integer numbers, N: Natural numbers
   (ii) (a) Negative whole numbers and zero.
        (b) Irrational numbers.
   (iii)

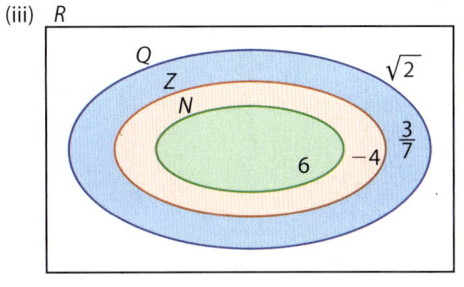

   (iv) In Z/N

Exercise 3.3
1. (i) {1, 3, 4, 5, 9, 12} (ii) {4, 6, 7, 8, 9, 10, 12}
   (iii) {4, 9, 12} (iv) {9}
   (v) {1, 3, 5} (vi) {8, 10}
2. (i) {2, 8} (ii) {1, 2, 8}
   (iii) {3, 7} (iv) {1}
   (v) {12, 13} (vi) {14, 15}
3. (i) 15 (ii) 17 (iii) 7 (iv) 3 (v) 2
4. (i) T (ii) T (iii) F (iv) T
   (v) F (vi) F (vii) T (viii) F
5. (i) 21 (ii) 3 (iii) 17
6. (i) $A \cup B \cup C$ (ii) $A \cap B \cap C$
   (iii) $A \cap C$
8. (i) T (ii) T
   (iii) Not true; $3 \div 4 \neq 4 \div 3$
   (iv) Not true; $2 - 3 \neq 3 - 2$

(v) Not true; $(11 - 12) - 13 \neq 11 - (12 - 13)$
(vi) Not true; $4 \div (6 \div 8) \neq (4 \div 6) \div 8$

9. (i) Addition is commutative
   (ii) Multiplication is associative
   (iii) Subtraction is not commutative
   (iv) Subtraction is not associative
   (v) Division is not associative
11. Set difference is not associative
12. (i) Union of sets is commutative
    (ii) Intersection of sets is associative
    (iii) Union of sets is associative
    (iv) Set difference is not associative
13. (i) $(A \cup B \cup C) \setminus (A \cap B \cap C)$
    (ii) $\cup \setminus (B \cup C)$
14. U

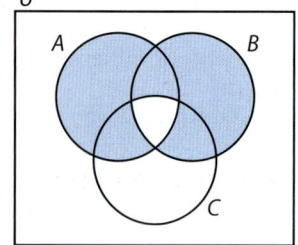

Exercise 3.4
1. (i) 28   (ii) 9   (iii) 4   (iv) 10
   (v) 22   (vi) 18   (vii) 14; 100
2. (i) 139   (ii) 113   (iii) 13
3. (i) 1   (ii) 7   (iii) 2   (iv) 81
4. (i) 6   (ii) 26   (iii) 4
5. (i) 16   (ii) 14   (iii) 8   (iv) 21
6. $x = 2$
7. (i) 4   (ii) 37
8. (i) 15   (ii) 17   (iii) 40
9. (i) 12   (ii) 7   (iii) 4

Test yourself 3
1. (i) {5, 7}   (ii) {2, 4, 6, 10}
3. (i) 19   (ii) 9   (iii) 7   (iv) 22
4. (i) {2, 3, 4, 5, 7}   (ii) {3, 5, 7}
   (iii) {1, 6, 9, 10, 11}   (iv) {1, 9}
5. (i) 34   (ii) 3   (iii) 6
6. (i) 27   (ii) 11   (iii) 4   (iv) 30
7. (i) #P = 6   (ii) #Q = 18
8. (i) 56   (ii) 38   (iii) 12
9. Intersection of sets is distributive over union
10. From left: 55, 5, 10, 30
11. (i) 40   (ii) 10   (iii) 30   (iv) 14
12. (i) $u = a + b - c + d$
    (ii) $d = u - a - b + c$
    (iii) $B \subset A$
    (iv) a

13. 9
14. (iv) is true
15. (i) 4   (ii) 26   (iii) 8   (iv) 34
16. 25

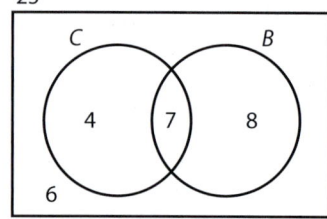

17. 11

Chapter 4: Applied Arithmetic
Exercise 4.1
1. (i) 0.07   (ii) 0.035   (iii) 0.12   (iv) 0.15
   (v) 0.165   (vi) 1.04   (vii) 1.1   (viii) 1.14
   (ix) 1.25   (x) 0.875
2. (i) 132   (ii) 159   (iii) 570   (iv) 717.5
3. (i) €29.12   (ii) €35
4. €25   5. €639.60   6. €800
7. €180   8. €1600
9. (i) €245   (ii) €240
10. (i) €320   (ii) 17%
11. (i) €125   (ii) €125   (iii) 100%
12. (i) €125   (ii) €625   (iii) 20%
13.

Cost	Selling price	Profit	Mark-up	Margin
€1104	€1150	€230	25%	20%

14. 20%   15. $21\frac{1}{3}$%
16. Store C; €6.15 cheaper than Store A
17. $16\frac{2}{3}$%   18. Equates to a $57\frac{1}{2}$% reduction
19. (i) proof   (ii) 4.8%

Exercise 4.2
1. €356.72
2. Maher – €161.27; O'Gorman – €223.71
3. 480   4. €232.24   5. €106.13
6. (i) €900   (ii) 2275 km
7. (i) 8   (ii) €640   (iii) 5
8. (i) 30c   (ii) 75c   (iii) €1.20
9. (i) €12.60   (ii) €31.52   (iii) 152
10. (i) €77.50   (ii) 234 km
11. Tariff 3

Exercise 4.3
1. €730   2. €29 729   3. €115.50
4. €424   5. €5640
6. (i) €174   (ii) €876
7. (i) €11 340   (ii) €8140

Answers

8. (i) €256.2 (ii) €212.2
9. €7800
10. (i) €1887.97 (ii) €29.74
    (iii) €2157.97 (iv) €40.99
11. 22
12. €1000
13. €4950
14. €35 000
15. (i) €168.00 (i) €27.49
    (iii) €36 (ii) €668.51
16. (i) €10 100 (iii) €1752.97
    (iii) €2160 (iv) €39 987.03
    (v) 74%
17. (i) €520 (ii) €67.20
    (iii) €10.39 (iv) €26
    (v) €416.41
18. (i) €11 200 (ii) €5600
    (iii) €5600 (iv) €14 000
    (v) €42 000
19. (i) €33 160 (ii) €41 200

Exercise 4.4

1. (i) $585 (ii) €615.38
2. (i) 108 000 yen (ii) €75
3. (i) £960 (ii) €750
4. €400
5. (i) C$4900 (ii) €4000
6. €2970
7. 41 600 baht
8. (i) 101 600 yen (ii) €16
9. €57.89
10. €1625
11. 2%
12. €29 931; €3975 gain
13. Mexico, €16.86

Exercise 4.5

1. €49.44
2. €133.12
3. €92.25
4. €188.10
5. €57.12
6. €178.50
7. (i) €661.50 (ii) €2138.58
8. €423.20
9. €1606.80
10. €9235.20
11. (i) 1.08 (ii) 1.08
12. €6400
13. 4.5%
14. €800
15. €8200
16. €8904; 4%
17. $11\frac{1}{2}$%
18. (i) 1.05 (ii) 1.04; €8500
19. €11 475; 4%
20. €10 837.50
21. (i) €11 776 (ii) €18 000
22. 16%
23. (i) €5090 (ii) 3.5%

Test yourself 4

1. €255.49
2. €7570
3. €6675.20
4. €651.60
5. 2.5%
6. (i) €420 (ii) $31\frac{1}{4}$%
7. €2.10
8. 64 g
9. (i) €5040 (ii) 5%
10. 7
11. €4650
12. €6000
13. €445.48
14. 2%
15. €23 000
16. Offer A
17. 4500
18. €45 000
19. €112.10
20. (i) €5090 (ii) 4%
21. (i) €33 160 (ii) €41 200

Chapter 5: Statistics 1 – Collecting Data

Exercise 5.1

1. (i) N (ii) C (iii) C (iv) N
   (v) N (vi) C (vii) C (viii) N
2. (i) P (ii) P (iii) S (iv) S
4. (i) Overlap between 'not very often' and 'sometimes'; Not specific enough; no time-frame provided
5. Q(i) is the one to use as Q(ii) is a leading question.
6. (i) Month / Day / Date
   (ii) categorical
7. Numerical 24 players, 26 years of age
   Categorical Premier / first team / Country
8. (i) Too personal
   (ii) May cause embarrassment
   (iii) Biased
   (iv) Leading question
   (v) Too personal/embarrassing/shaming
   (vi) Too personal
   (vii) Leading question
9. (i) Too personal, first name would suffice
   (ii) 'Often' and 'sometimes' are too vague
10. (i) Question is too personal and response boxes aren't specific enough/are too subjective
12. QA – Too subjective/potentially embarrassing
    QB – Biased question which encourages a positive response
13. (i) A (ii) A (iii) C (iv) B
15. (i)

12	13	14	15	16	17	18
3	6	7	9	5	3	1

   (ii) 6 years (iii) 15 years
   (iv) 18 years (v) 53%
17.

64	65	66	67	68	69	70	71	72	73	74
1	0	3	1	4	4	11	3	2	0	1

   (i) 10 shots (ii) 70 (iii) 20%
18. Those surveyed were already members of the club.

Exercise 5.2
1. (i) 820   (ii) 40
2. 40, 4 is not representative, 400 would take too long
3. (a), (b), (e) population (c), (d) sample
4. (i) • People already at a cinema are much more likely to be regular "cinema-goers"
   • No men surveyed
5. These people are likely to be "sporty", i.e. not representative
6. B
7. B; this sample best represents the community at large.
8. Method 2

Test yourself 5
1. (i) C   (ii) N   (iii) N   (iv) C   (v) C   (vi) N
2. (i) P   (ii) S   (iii) S   (iv) S
4. (ii) is better
6. Sample 4 is a good sample
7. (i) only positive options
   (ii) too limited, no scope for answer under €6
   (iii) Too vague
8.

7	8	9	10	11	12	13
1	1	3	6	6	3	4

9. (i)

1	2	3	4	5	6
8	10	6	3	2	1

(ii) 20%
(iii) There had to be at least 1 child in each family.

Chapter 6: Perimeter – Area – Volume

Exercise 6.1
1. (i) 46 cm   (ii) 42 cm   (iii) 55 cm
2. (i) 126 cm^2 (ii) 104 cm^2 (iii) 178.5 cm^2
3. (i) 7 cm   (ii) 16 cm   (iii) 22 cm
4. (i) 58 cm   (ii) 54 cm   (iii) 58 cm
5. (i) 5 cm   (ii) 12 m   (iii) 25 cm
6. (i) 56 cm^2 (ii) 120 cm^2 (iii) 120 cm^2
7. (i) 31.5 cm^2 (ii) 60 cm^2 (iii) 240 cm^2
8. (i) 10 cm   (ii) 14 cm   (iii) 12 cm
9. (i) 121 cm^2 (ii) 182 cm^2 (iii) 420 cm^2
10. (i) 12 cm^2 (ii) 24 cm^2 (iii) 8 cm
11. 20 m^2; 25 m^2 12. 440 cm^2
13. $x = 4, y = 16, z = 3$
14. 11.5 cm^2

15. (i) etc. (P = 160 cm)
    (ii) (P = 120 cm)

Exercise 6.2
1. (i) 240 cm^2 (ii) 63 cm^2 (iii) 165 cm^2
2. (i) 60 cm^2 (ii) 52.5 cm^2 (iii) 30 cm^2
3. (i) 6 cm   (ii) 7 cm   (iii) 4.5 cm
4. 308 cm^2; $x = 17\frac{1}{9}$
5. (i) 10 cm^2 (ii) 5 cm^2 (iii) 2 : 1
6. (i) 5 cm   (ii) 6.5 cm   (iii) 12 cm
7. (i) 1.5 cm   (ii) 1.6 cm   (iii) 4 cm
8. 20 cm^2; $1\frac{2}{3}$ cm
9. (i) 784 m^2 (ii) 440 m^2
10. 154 cm^2
11. (i) 747.5 m^2 (ii) 85.43%

Exercise 6.3
1. (i) radius   (ii) chord
   (iii) diameter   (iv) arc
   (v) semicircle   (vi) sector
   (vii) segment   (viii) tangent
2. (i) 62.8 cm   (ii) 25.12 cm
   (iii) 75.36 cm   (iv) 56.52 cm
3. (i) (a) 201.1 cm^2 (b) 50.3 cm
   (ii) (a) 1385.4 cm^2 (b) 131.9 cm
   (iii) (a) 380.1 cm^2 (b) 69.1 cm
   (iv) (a) 254.5 cm^2 (b) 56.5 cm
4. (i) 81.64 cm   (ii) 94.2 cm   (iii) 251.2 cm
5. (i) $\frac{1}{4}$ (ii) $\frac{1}{3}$ (iii) $\frac{1}{6}$ (iv) $\frac{1}{8}$
6. (i) 32.97 cm   (ii) 10.99 cm   (iii) 58.61 cm
7. (i) 346.19 cm^2 (ii) 76.93 cm^2 (iii) 820.59 cm^2
8. (i) 71.96 cm^2 (ii) 42.65 cm   (iii) 46.97 cm
9. (i) 38.99 cm   (ii) 168.56 cm^2
10. (i) 190.0 cm^2 (ii) 150.8 cm^2 (iii) 244.5 cm^2
11. (i) 399.82 m
    (ii) 406 m, 412.38 m, 418.66 m, 424.94 m
    (iii) 6.28 m
    (iv) 25
12. (i) 91.4 cm   (ii) 301.6 cm^2
13. (i) 5 cm   (ii) 11 cm   (iii) 13 cm
14. (i) 7 cm   (ii) 44 cm
15. (i) 2500 m   (ii) 796
16. Both the same length
17. 42 cm^2
18. (i) 98 cm^2 (ii) 56 cm^2

Answers

19. (i) 2 m (ii) 75.4 m² (iii) 79%
20. 37%
21. Alan; 25 m

Exercise 6.4
1. (i) 32 cm³ (ii) 144 cm³
2. (i) 64 cm² (ii) 180 cm²
3. (a) (i) 288 cm³ (ii) 80 cm³ (iii) 176 cm³
    (b) (i) 288 cm³ (ii) 136 cm³ (iii) 208 cm³
4. 88 **5.** 270 cm²
6. (i) 900 cm³ (ii) 368 cm³ (iii) 532 cm³
7. €652.80
8. (i) 288 cm³ (ii) 384 cm²
9. $a = 5$ cm, $b = 7$ m, $c = 20$ cm
10. proof
11. If the 22 × 7 face is used; Yes (2700 needed).
    If the 10 × 7 face is used; No (5760 needed)
12. (i) 4 cm (ii) 96 cm²
13. 5 o'clock on Tuesday
14. 1000
15. (i) 8 cm (ii) 1.5 (iii) 157 cm²
16. (i) F (ii) [CB] (iii) [KL]
17. (i) 820 cm² (iv) 240 cm³
18. A – 5, B – 3, C – 6
19. $x^3 = 6x^2$; 6 cm
20. (i) 6 ℓ (ii) 1.6 ℓ (iii) 6.75 ℓ
21. (i) 4800 cm³ (ii) 8 cm
22. 1000 litres
23. 30 litres, 15 cm × 40 cm × 50 cm,
    30 cm × 20 cm × 50 cm.

Exercise 6.5
1. (i) 2112 cm³ (ii) 1116 cm³ (iii) 156 cm³
2. (i) 28 cm² (ii) 252 cm³
3. 54 cm³
4. (i) 450 m³ (ii) 1440 cm³ (iii) 48 cm³
    (iv) 48 cm³ (v) 264 mm³ (vi) 1512 m³
5. (i) 5 (ii) 2 (iii) 84 cm²
6. (i) 152 cm² (ii) 300 sq. units
    (iii) 241 cm²
7. (i) 780 cm² (ii) 120 mm² (iii) 200 cm²
8. (i) (a) 480 m³ (b) 432 m²
    (ii) (a) 270 m³ (b) 330 m²
    (iii) (a) 337.5 m³ (b) 335 m²
9. (i) 84 cm² (ii) 480 cm²
10. (i) 32.31 m² (ii) €650
11. (i) 410.4 cm³ (ii) 441.6 cm²
13. • Star opposite yellow circle with red border
    • Square with green border opposite square with circle in it
    • Triangle opposite red and green square
14. (i) triangular prism (ii) 6

Exercise 6.6
1. (i) 1 : 40 (ii) 1 : 100 (iii) 1 : 60 000
    (iv) 1 : 2000 (v) 1 : 10 000 (vi) 1 : 10 000
2. Kangaroo – 1.2 m, giraffe – 3.6 m, horse – 1.35 m
3. (i) 5 m (ii) 11 m (iii) 8.5 m
    (iv) 14.8 m
4. (i) 6 m (ii) 40 m
    (iii) 28.8 m (iv) 14.375 m
5. 6.2 m; 2.7 m
6. (i) (a) 500 m (b) 1.25 km
    (c) 2.125 km (d) $1687\frac{1}{2}$ m
    (ii) (a) 40 cm (b) 16 cm
    (c) 26 cm (d) 51 cm
7. (i) 17 km (ii) 4.4 cm
8. (i) (a) 12 cm (b) 8.5 cm
9. 1 : 40 000; 75 cm
10. (i) |CB| = 5 cm; 1 : 200 (ii) 6 m
    (iii) 30 m²

Test yourself 6
1. (i) 96 cm³ (ii) 144 cm²
2. 37.68 cm² **3.** 7.2
4. (i) 324 cm³ (ii) 342 cm²
5. (i) 89.1 cm² (ii) 36.6 cm
6. (i) 50 cm (ii) 1 : 25
7. (i) both 18 m³
    (ii) Not the same (iii) €1323
8. 56 cm²
9. 375 cm²
10. 11.60 cm
11. (i) 165 m² (ii) €6680
12. (i) 1 km (ii) 14 cm
13. 14
14. Yes (€90 000 > €88 128)
15. A triangular prism;
    (i) 6.8 cm³ (ii) 27.4 cm²
16. 64.5 cm²
17. (i) 96 m²
    (ii) Min: 144 m² Max: 168 m²

Chapter 7: Statistics 2 – Averages and Variability

Exercise 7.1
1. (i) 12 (ii) 45 (iii) 5.7
    (iv) 7 (v) bus (vi) $\frac{1}{4}$
2. 5
3. 3, 3, 5, 7, 7, 7, 8, 8, 9, 11, 12;
    (i) 7 (ii) 7

Text & Tests 2 Higher Level

4. (i) 2, 3, 5, 6, 7, 8, 9; 6
   (ii) 6, 7, 8, 9, 10, 12, 14, 18; 9.5
5. (i) 14   (ii) 14
6. (i) 9   (ii) 9
7. (i) 9   (ii) 9
8. 6
9. €12.80
10. $a = 2, 4$
11. (i) 32   (ii) Size 6   (iii) No
    (iv) No; In general, boys wear larger shoes.

Exercise 7.2

1. (i) 5   (ii) 14   (iii) 7   (iv) 19.75
2. 61   3. 26   4. 84
5. (i) 36   (ii) 5
6. 13 cm   7. 12   8. 25
9. (i) 18   (ii) 12   (iii) 0
10. €1.73
11. ⟨4⟩⟨4⟩⟨5⟩⟨8⟩⟨9⟩ etc.
12. (i) 13.2 m   (ii) $165\frac{1}{3}$ cm
13. 19
14. (i) 2   (ii) 17
15. (i) 195 (ii) 19
16. 4, 6
17. (i) A – 16.4, B – 25.3
    (ii) The final value
    (iii) The outlier (91) has a big effect on mean
18. (i) 44   (ii) 44   (iii) 40
    (iv) Increase; $40\frac{1}{6}$ points
19. 7, 9
20. 40

Exercise 7.3

1. (i) 2   (ii) 1
   (iii) As 6 of the 8 values are well below the mean (6.9) due to the two outliers
2. Mean – 17, Median – 3; Median
3. (i) 25   (ii) 15; Median
4. (i) $30\frac{4}{7}$ °C
   (ii) The data is tightly grouped with no outliers
5. (i) 27
   (ii) The mode (37) is the highest data value
6. (i) Denim
   (ii) As the data is categorical it is the only average that can be used
7. (i) Mean   (ii) Mode
   (iii) Median/mean (use median if there is an outlier)
   (iv) Mode   (v) Median

8. Mean – 3.3, Mode – 0, Median – 2.5; Median
9. Mean (65) as it is the highest of the three averages.
10. (i) 28   (ii) 38   (iii) 63.9   (iv) Mean

Exercise 7.4

1. (i) 4   (ii) 3   (iii) 2; 6 marks
2. (i) 1   (ii) 4   (iii) 2
   (iv) 150 (v) 3
3. (i) 8   (ii) 2   (iii) 180   (iv) 3
4. (i) 3   (ii) 1   (iii) 25%   (iv) 26
5. 3.6
6. (i) 30   (ii) 7   (iii) 13   (iv) 13
7. (i) 19   (ii) (41–60)   (iii) (61–80)
   (iv) Exact mean cannot be found from table
8. (i) (4–6)   (ii) 6.5
9. 12
10. (i) because the value 16 was in 2 categories.
    (ii) 18.6
    (iii) 14 – 16, includes values from 14 up to but not including 16
11. (i) (0–4)   (ii) 9   (iii) 45   (iv) 7
12. (i) 250 cm (ii) 240 cm
    (iii) 100 cm (iv) 251 cm

Exercise 7.5

1. (i) 11   (ii) 21
2. (i) has bigger range
3. (i) Saskia – 44, John – 20; John far more consistent
   (ii) Saskia
4. (i) Emer – 82, Anna – 83
   (ii) Emer – 20, Anna – 12
   (iii) Anna; Marginally inferior mean score but more consistent
5. 5, 9
6. (i) 6   (ii) 8; boys did better
7. (i) ⟨3⟩⟨4⟩⟨6⟩⟨6⟩⟨7⟩ etc.
   (ii) ⟨4⟩⟨6⟩⟨6⟩⟨7⟩
8. (i) Impossible (ii) Possible (iii) True
9. A: range 7°C, median 1°C, B: range 7°C, median 0°C.
10. 8, 9, 13, 15, 25
11. (i) 105 g   (ii) 19 g
    (iii) The mean weight of a South African apple is higher but the variability of the apples is the same.

Answers

Test yourself 7
1. 12
2. (i) 8.1
   (ii) 6; Median as it has the same number of values above and below it.
3. Mean 17, Median 3. The median.
4. 1.73 m
5. (i) 5
   (ii) 14.5
   (iii) The boys had a higher mean score and were more consistent.
6. 6, 15, 18
7. (i)

Mark (x)	40–54	55–69	70–84	85–99
Mid-interval value	47	62	77	92
Frequency (f)	5	8	7	4
(fx)	235	496	539	368

   (ii) 68.25
8. (i) 8   (ii) 13
9. (i) Impossible   (ii) Possible
   (iii) Possible
10. Mean – 27.1; Mode = 19. The mode is not representative of the other values
11. 14.8
12. (i) 8.17; 22.87   (ii) 6.67; 21.33
13. (i) €376.67   (ii) €245
    (iii) No two data values (wages) the same; Median
14. 45, 2   15. 12   16. 37
17. (a) False   (b) Could be true
    (c) False   (d) Could be true

Chapter 8: Geometry 1 – Triangles and Quadrilaterals

Exercise 8.1
1. (i) Line segment [AB]   (ii) Line AB
   (iii) Ray [BA
2. $A = 117°, B = 85°, C = 45°, D = 140°, E = 70°, F = 23°$
3. $A = 70°, B = 110°, C = 150°, D = 30°, E = 140°, F = 40°$
4. (i) 4   (ii) 7   (iii) 4
5. $a = 110°, b = 70°, c = 46°, d = 134°, e = 60°, f = 120°$
6. $p = 80°, q = 80°, r = 75°, s = 105°$
7. $a = 96°, b = 96°, c = 84°, d = 72°, e = 68°, f = 112°, g = 68°$
8. (i) 15°   (ii) 29°   (iii) 19°

Exercise 8.2
1. $a = 50°, b = 86°, c = 111°, d = 50°, e = 60°, f = 43°, g = 85°, h = 95°, i = 37°, j = 143°, k = 79°$
2. $a = 70°, b = 70°, c = 71°, d = 71°, e = 62°, f = 56°$
3. $a = 65°, b = 40°, c = 52.5°, d = 60°, e = 30°$
4. $p = 106°, q = 37°, r = 37°, d = 25°, e = 130°, f = 50°, v = 59°, w = 31°, x = 59°, y = 121°$
5. $a = 50°, b = 58°, c = 25°$
6. $a = 62°, b = 110°, c = 55°, d = 34°$
7. (i) $x = 55°$; ∠CAB and ∠EBD are corresponding angles
   (ii) $y = 45°$; angles in a △ sum to 180°
8. $x = 82°, y = 16°, a = 48°, b = 114°$
9. $d = 35°, e = 35°, f = 110°$
10. $a = 95°, b = 115°, c = 39°, d = 85°$
12. As |∠BCA| = 49°
13. $x = 126°$

Exercise 8.3
1. $A = 78°, B = 102°, C = 60°, D = 120°, E = 60°, F = 120°$
2. $A = 66°, B = 72°, C = 80°, D = 45°, E = 75°, F = 55°, G = 55°$
3. $A = 42°, B = 100°, C = 35°, D = 65°, E = 28°, F = 112°, G = 52°$
4. $x = 70°, y = 40°, z = 40°, r = 70°$
5. (i) 8   (ii) 11   (iii) 10   (iv) 7
6. $x = 55°, y = 55°, z = 70°$
7. $g = 67.5°, h = 45°$
8. $a = 121°, b = 89°, c = 129°, d = 51°$
9. (i) $x = 80°$ (ii) $x = 77°$ (iii) $x = 55°$
10. (i) $y = 86°$ (ii) $y = 64°$

Exercise 8.4
1. SAS
2. (i) SSS   (ii) SAS   (iii) SAS
   (iv) ASA   (v) RHS   (vi) ASA
3. A and D; SSS
4. (i) Yes; ASA
   (ii) No; not the same size (sides don't correspond)
5. Yes; SSS
6. SAS (|∠AOB| = |∠COD| … vertically opposite)
7. ASA; (i) [EF]   (ii) [AB]   (iii) 35°
8. $x = 70°, y = 10$ cm
9. Corresponding angles, both opposite [AC].

593

Exercise 8.5

1. (i) 5   (ii) 10   (iii) 17
2. $a = 7, b = 12, c = 21$
3. (i) 3   (ii) 5   (iii) 8
4. $P = 44\,cm^2, Q = 46\,cm^2, R = 50\,cm^2$
5. (i) $2\sqrt{19}$ (ii) $4\sqrt{2}$ (iii) $2\sqrt{11}$
6. 6; 13.5 sq. units
7. (i) $x = 13\,cm, y = \sqrt{394}\,cm$
   (ii) $x = 6\,cm, y = \sqrt{145}\,cm$
   (iii) $x = 9\,cm, y = \sqrt{2581}\,cm$
8. $x = 5, y = 12$
9. 74 cm
10. $x = 10, y = 8$
11. (i) 2.47 m   (ii) 10.17 m   (iii) 6.21 m^2
12. No; the diagonal is 100 cm, i.e. less than 105 cm.
13. (i) No   (ii) Yes
14. As $|AD|^2 = |CD|^2 + |AC|^2$
15. (i) 13 cm   (ii) 15.3 cm
16. Yes, equal
18. 100

Test yourself 8

1. $a = 110°, b = 70°, c = 140°, d = 55°, e = 125°$
2. $A = 50°, B = 70°, C = 73°$
3. $a = 63°, b = 30°$
4. $A = 35°, B = 67°, C = 40°, D = 65°, E = 33°, F = 107°, G = 45°$
5. $a = 74°, b = 53°, c = 142°, d = 68°, e = 38°, f = 74°$
6. $x = 56$; isosceles $\triangle$
7. $a = 23.5°, b = 83.5°, c = 23.5°$
8. $a = 55°, b = 50°$
9. 1 and 4; SAS
10. (ii) No; As $|\angle ABC| \neq |\angle ACB| \Rightarrow |\angle DAE| \neq |\angle CAE|$
11. (i) 124°   (ii) 63°   (iii) 32°
12. 0.9 m
14. (i) $x = 140°, y = 100°$
    (ii) $x = 20°, y = 140°$
    (iii) $x = 69°, y = 37°$
15. (i) 6.4 m   (ii) 7 m

Chapter 9: Probability

Exercise 9.1

1. 12
2. HH, HT, TH, TT
3. (i) 18   (ii) 6   (iii) 3
4. 36   5. 24   6. 27
7. (i) 36   (ii) 12

8. (i) [tree diagram: H branches to 1,2,3,4,5,6; T branches to 1,2,3,4,5,6]
   (ii) 3   (iii) 3
9. (i) 4   (ii) 128
10. [tree diagram: a.m → P→E,S,M; N→E,S,M; p.m → P→E,S,M; N→E,S,M]

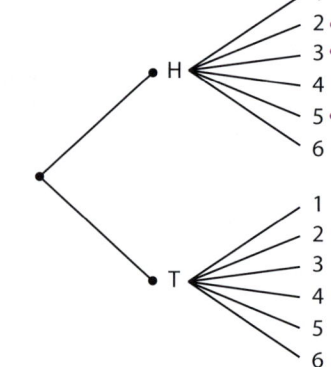

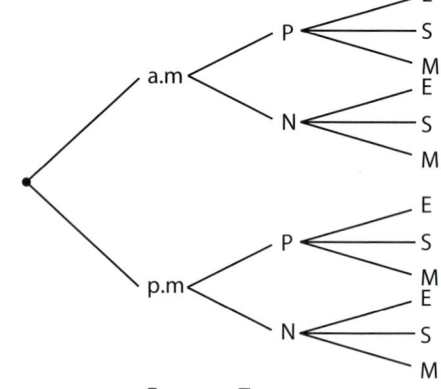

F	T
a.m.-P-E	p.m.-P-E
a.m.-P-S	p.m.-P-S
a.m.-P-M	p.m.-P-M
a.m.-N-E	p.m.-N-E
a.m.-N-S	p.m.-N-S
a.m.-N-M	p.m.-N-M

11. (i)

	Swimming	Tennis	Football	Totals
Boys	12	(9)	(25)	(46)
Girls	16	(13)	11	40
Totals	(28)	22	36	(86)

(ii) 86   (iii) Tennis
(iv) Football   (v) $\dfrac{11}{43}$ (vi) 40%

Exercise 9.2

1. (i) E.C.   (ii) Certain   (iii) Impossible
   (iv) Unlikely   (v) Likely   (vi) E.C.
   (vii) Likely   (viii) Unlikely   (ix) E.C.
   (x) Likely

Answers

2. (i) Event 1: Unlikely (ii) Event 1: Likely
   Event 2: E.C.   Event 2: Certain
   Event 3: E.C.   Event 3: Impossible
   Event 4: Impossible Event 4: Unlikely
   Event 5: Certain   Event 5: Likely
3. (i) B (ii) C (iii) C (iv) A (v) B (vi) C
4. (i) (b), (a), (c)   (ii) (b), (a), (c)
5. Green − (a), Red − (b), Blue − (c)
6. (i) 6   (ii) 8   (iii) 2

Exercise 9.3

1. (i) (a) Red, blue
      (b) Red, blue, yellow, green
      (c) Red, blue
   (ii) (a) $\frac{1}{2}$ (b) $\frac{1}{4}$ (c) $\frac{1}{2}$
2. (i) $\frac{1}{4}$ (ii) $\frac{1}{2}$ (iii) $\frac{1}{4}$; $\frac{3}{4}$
3. (i) $\frac{1}{6}$ (ii) $\frac{1}{3}$ (iii) $\frac{1}{2}$ (iv) $\frac{1}{2}$ (v) $\frac{1}{3}$ (vi) $\frac{1}{2}$
4. (i) $\frac{3}{10}$ (ii) $\frac{2}{5}$ (iii) $\frac{7}{10}$ (iv) $\frac{3}{5}$ (v) $\frac{3}{10}$ (vi) $\frac{3}{10}$
5. (i) $\frac{1}{11}$ (ii) $\frac{2}{11}$ (iii) $\frac{2}{11}$ (iv) $\frac{4}{11}$ (v) $\frac{4}{11}$
6. (i) $\frac{1}{4}$ (ii) $\frac{1}{9}$ (iii) $\frac{4}{9}$ (iv) $\frac{1}{36}$ (v) $\frac{1}{18}$ (vi) $\frac{1}{6}$
7. (i) $\frac{1}{13}$ (ii) $\frac{1}{13}$ (iii) $\frac{3}{13}$ (iv) 1 (v) 0 (vi) $\frac{2}{13}$
8. (i) $\frac{1}{4}$ (ii) $\frac{1}{2}$ (iii) $\frac{1}{2}$ (iv) $\frac{1}{13}$ (v) $\frac{3}{13}$ (vi) $\frac{2}{13}$
9. (i) $\frac{10}{13}$ (ii) $\frac{7}{13}$ (iii) $\frac{7}{13}$ (iv) 0
10. (i) Red and any colour other than red or black
    (ii) Red and any colour other than red or blue
11. (i) $\frac{1}{6}$ (ii) $\frac{3}{8}$ (iii) $\frac{1}{6}$ (iv) $\frac{1}{12}$
13. (i) $\frac{1}{7}$ (ii) $\frac{2}{7}$ (iii) $\frac{1}{6}$
14. (i) $\frac{5}{12}$ (ii) $\frac{1}{6}$ (iii) $\frac{1}{12}$ (iv) $\frac{1}{12}$ (v) $\frac{5}{12}$
    (vi) $\frac{7}{12}$; Every disc is either even or odd, i.e. every outcome covered
15. (i) $\frac{3}{10}$ (ii) $\frac{7}{20}$ (iii) $\frac{13}{20}$ (iv) $\frac{7}{20}$
16. (i) $\frac{2}{5}$ (ii) $\frac{3}{10}$ (iii) $\frac{11}{25}$; $\frac{1}{6}$
17. (i) $\frac{1}{100}$ (ii) $\frac{1}{10}$ (iii) $\frac{1}{20}$ (iv) $\frac{21}{25}$
    (v) 30 (vi) 20 (vii) 25 (viii) 100
18. $\frac{3}{7}$
19. (i) $\frac{4}{13}$ (ii) $\frac{4}{13}$ (iii) $\frac{5}{13}$ (iv) $\frac{9}{13}$
20. (i) 30 (ii) (a) $\frac{3}{10}$ (b) $\frac{1}{2}$ (iii) $\frac{1}{5}$
21. (a)

	French	German	Spanish	Total
Boys	(18)	25	12	(55)
Girls	22	(18)	(30)	70
Totals	(40)	(43)	42	125

   (b) 40 (c) 55 (d) $\frac{43}{125}$
   (e) (i) $\frac{8}{25}$ (ii) $\frac{6}{25}$ (iii) $\frac{1}{5}$

Exercise 9.4

1. (i) $\frac{1}{4}$ (ii) $\frac{1}{4}$ (iii) $\frac{1}{2}$
2. (i) $\frac{3}{16}$ (ii) $\frac{1}{2}$ (iii) $\frac{3}{16}$ (iv) $\frac{3}{16}$
3. (i) $\frac{1}{18}$ (ii) $\frac{1}{9}$ (iii) $\frac{1}{6}$ (iv) $\frac{1}{3}$ (v) $\frac{2}{9}$ (vi) $\frac{5}{18}$
4. (ii) (a) $\frac{3}{16}$ (b) $\frac{1}{2}$ (c) $\frac{5}{8}$
5. (i) $\frac{1}{16}$ (ii) 1 (iii) $\frac{3}{8}$ (iv) $\frac{1}{4}$ (v) $\frac{7}{16}$ (vi) $\frac{9}{16}$
6. HHH, HHT, HTH, THH, TTT, TTH, THT, HTT;
   (i) $\frac{1}{8}$ (ii) $\frac{3}{8}$ (iii) $\frac{1}{8}$ (iv) $\frac{7}{8}$
7. (i) $\frac{1}{9}$ (ii) $\frac{1}{12}$ (iii) $\frac{1}{12}$ (iv) $\frac{5}{36}$
8. (i)
   A — R, L, D
   E — R, L, D
   I — R, L, D
   (ii) $\frac{1}{9}$ (iii) $\frac{1}{9}$ (iv) $\frac{2}{9}$
9. (A) R — R, W, W; R — R, W, W; W — R, W, W
   (B) (R,R), (R,W), (R,W), (R,R), (R,W), (R,W), (W,R), (W,W), (W,W)
   (i) $\frac{2}{9}$ (ii) $\frac{4}{9}$ (iii) $\frac{5}{9}$

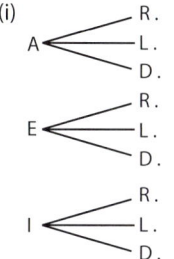

Exercise 9.5

1. 50
2. (i) 10 (ii) 10 (iii) 30
3. (i) 160 (ii) 240
4. $\frac{3}{10}$
5. (i) $\frac{1}{2}$ (ii) $\frac{3}{4}$
   (iii) Nicky's result as it involved a greater number of trials
6. (i) $\frac{3}{8}$ (ii) $\frac{27}{32}$
7. (ii) 0.6 (iii) 180
8. (i) $\frac{1}{6}$ (ii) $\frac{1}{2}$ (iii) $\frac{1}{2}$
9. (i) 4 (relative frequency of 0.525)
   (ii) 2 (relative frequency of 0.23)
10. Ben's (relatively even spread of outcomes as between the 6 faces); Joe's (relative frequency of a "6" was $\frac{1}{72}$)

11. Red – 1, White – 2, Blue – 3
12. (i) $\frac{12}{25}$ (ii) 48
13. (i) Red – $\frac{7}{50}$, Green – $\frac{12}{25}$
    (ii) Red – one side, Green – three sides;
    $\frac{7}{50} \simeq \frac{1}{6}$, $\frac{12}{25} \simeq \frac{1}{2}$
14. 100
15. (i) $\frac{3}{10}$ (ii) $\frac{14}{25}$

Exercise 9.6

1. (i) $\frac{13}{41}$ (ii) $\frac{6}{41}$ (iii) $\frac{13}{41}$ (iv) $\frac{26}{41}$ (v) $\frac{15}{41}$
2. (i) 30 (ii) 7 (iii) $\frac{1}{10}$
   (iv) $\frac{11}{30}$ (v) $\frac{2}{15}$ (vi) $\frac{8}{15}$
3. (i) 12 (ii) $\frac{3}{5}$ (iii) $\frac{1}{10}$ (iv) $\frac{21}{25}$ (v) $\frac{37}{50}$
4. (i) U 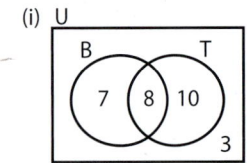
   B / T Venn diagram: 7, 8, 10, 3
   (ii) $\frac{5}{14}$ (iii) $\frac{3}{28}$
5. (i) 24
   (ii) They liked both chocolate and ice-cream
   (iii) $\frac{3}{20}$ (iv) $\frac{3}{4}$
6. (i) 100 (ii) $\frac{7}{25}$ (iii) $\frac{9}{100}$ (iv) $\frac{1}{25}$
   (v) $\frac{1}{10}$ (vi) $\frac{9}{50}$ (vii) $\frac{7}{50}$
7. (i) U 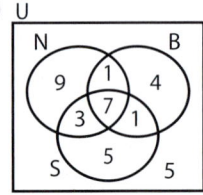
   N / B Venn diagram with S: 9, 1, 4, 7, 3, 1, 5, 5
   (ii) $\frac{1}{7}$ (iii) $\frac{9}{35}$ (iv) $\frac{5}{7}$ (v) $\frac{2}{5}$

Exercise 9.7

1. (i) $\frac{1}{4}$ (ii) $\frac{1}{2}$
2. (i) $\frac{8}{15}$ (ii) $\frac{7}{15}$
3. (i) $\frac{13}{18}$ (ii) $\frac{5}{36}$
4. (ii) (a) $\frac{2}{9}$ (b) $\frac{4}{9}$ (c) $\frac{5}{9}$
5. (ii) $\frac{12}{25}$
6. (ii) $\frac{12}{25}$
7. (ii) (a) $\frac{1}{36}$ (b) $\frac{5}{18}$
8. (i) $\frac{1}{4}$ (ii) $\frac{3}{8}$
9. (i) $\frac{4}{9}$ (ii) $\frac{4}{9}$ (iii) $\frac{8}{9}$

Test yourself 9

1. (i) B (ii) C (iii) A
2. (i) $\frac{7}{10}$ (ii) $\frac{1}{10}$ (iii) $\frac{1}{20}$
   (iv) $\frac{3}{10}$ (v) $\frac{3}{20}$
3. (i) $\frac{2}{5}$ (ii) $\frac{6}{25}$ (iii) $\frac{16}{25}$
4. Spinner A; Experimental probabilities v. close to true probabilities
5. (i) (3, 2), (3, 4), (3, 7), (6, 2), (6, 4), (6, 7), (8, 2), (8, 4), (8, 7)
   (ii) $\frac{4}{9}$ (iii) $\frac{4}{9}$
6. $\frac{7}{10}$ 7. 10
8. (i) $\frac{19}{30}$ (ii) $\frac{3}{10}$ (iii) $\frac{9}{10}$
   (iv) $\frac{1}{15}$ (v) $\frac{1}{10}$ (vi) $\frac{14}{15}$
9. (i) Event cannot happen
   (ii) Event has a '50-50 chance' of happening
   (iii) Event will occur three times out of four, i.e., it's likely to occur
   (iv) Event will definitely happen
10. (i) 0.2 (ii) 0.4
11. (i) $\frac{1}{2}$ (ii) $\frac{1}{52}$ (iii) $\frac{5}{13}$
    (iv) $\frac{3}{26}$ (v) $\frac{1}{13}$ (vi) $\frac{7}{13}$
12. (i) (a) $\frac{1}{10}$ (b) $\frac{13}{30}$ (c) $\frac{1}{3}$
    (ii) Similar results – yes, identical results – no.
13. U 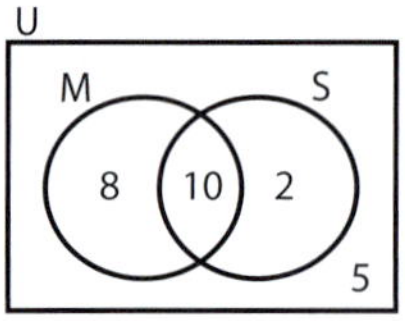
    M / S Venn diagram: 8, 10, 2, 5
    (i) $\frac{8}{25}$ (ii) $\frac{2}{25}$ (iii) $\frac{4}{5}$ (iv) $\frac{2}{5}$
14. 80   15. Graph C
16. (ii) $\frac{4}{15}$
17.
	Milk	Water	Orange Juice	Total
Boys	24	(17)	(16)	57
Girls	(8)	27	(8)	(43)
Totals	(32)	(44)	24	100

(ii) $\frac{11}{25}$ (iii) $\frac{17}{57}$
18. (a) $U = ( )$ (b) 60
    G / S / F Venn diagram: (8), 2, (15), 1, 2, (2), (10), (20)
    (c) $\frac{1}{3}$ (d) $\frac{7}{10}$ (e) $\frac{1}{20}$ (f) $\frac{1}{6}$
19. (i) $\frac{6}{21}$ (ii) $\frac{5}{7}$
    (iii) 2R-5B, 4R-10B, 6R-15B (iv) $\frac{15}{28}$

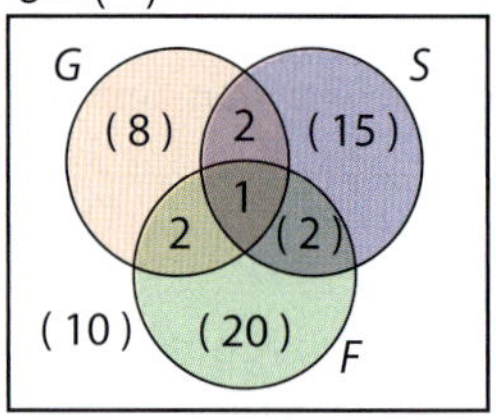

Answers

Chapter 10: Simultaneous Equations

Exercise 10.1
1. $x = 2, y = 4$
2. $x = 4, y = 2$
3. 1, 4
4. 3, 5
5. 2, 3
6. 4, 2
7. 3, 4
8. 6, 3
9. 2, 3
10. 4, -2
11. 1, 2
12. 5, -2
13. 6, 3
14. 7, 2
15. 2, 2
16. 6, -4
17. 15, 12
18. $-3, 8$
19. 9, 4
20. 6, 1
21. 2, 10
22. 4, 10
23. 3, 5
24. 6, $1\frac{1}{2}$

Exercise 10.2
1. (i) (2, 1) (ii) $x = 2, y = 1$ (iii) Same
2. (2, 3)
3. (i) $-2, -3$ (ii) 3, 5
4. (i) 4, 2 (ii) 2, 1
5. (i) 3, 7 (ii) 1, 3 (iii) 11, -1
6. (i) (a) 0, 4 (b) 1, 3
   (ii) Parallel lines, therefore no point of intersection
7. 12, -3
8. 10, 3
9. $x = 5, y = 2$
10. 14 g
11. (i) Ⓒ (ii) $b = 55$ g, $e = 75$ g
12. Twenty 5c coins and fourteen 10c coins
13. Small mug – 196 g, large mug – 366 g
14. $x = 4, y = 7$ cm
15. (i) $2a + b = 8, 4a - 3b = 1$
    (ii) $a = 2\frac{1}{2}, b = 3$
16. €50, 40 c
17. 40, 12
18. 42, 36
19. □ = 4, ♡ = 20, ◇ = 2
20. $x = 12, y = 9$

Test yourself 10
1. 7, 3
2. (i) $4b + 3r = 58, 5b + 6r = 86$
   (ii) blue – 10 g, red – 6 g
   (iii) 66 g
3. 1, -2
4. (i) $\frac{1}{2}, 2\frac{1}{2}$ (ii) $6\frac{1}{2}$ cm
5. 4, 3
6. (i) $-2, 7$
   (ii) $2x - y = 4, x + y = 5$
7. $x = 18, y = 24$
8. 15, 12
9. $a =$ €45, $b =$ €75; €1170
10. (2, -1)
11. 10, 4
12. $x = 3, y = 1$
13. Mother – 45, son – 13
14. $\frac{2}{3}$
15. 16 × 30

Chapter 11: Coordinate Geometry – The Line

Exercise 11.1
1. A(2, 3), B(4, 2), C(2, 1), D(-3, 3), E(-2, 2), F(-4, 1), G(-3, 0), H(-4, -2), I(-2, -3), J(0, -3), K(2, -3), L(3, -2), M(5, -3)
3. (i) First (ii) Third (iii) Fourth
   (iv) Second (v) Fourth (vi) Third
4. (i) x-axis (ii) x-axis (iii) y-axis
   (iv) y-axis (v) both
5. (i) $\sqrt{34}$ (ii) $\sqrt{50}$ (iii) $\sqrt{53}$; No
6. (i) $\sqrt{10}$ (ii) $\sqrt{5}$ (iii) $\sqrt{13}$
   (iv) $\sqrt{89}$ (v) $\sqrt{53}$ (vi) 5
8. $\sqrt{53}$
9. (i) $\sqrt{18}$ (ii) $\sqrt{34}$; No
10. (i) |FE| = 6, |ED| = 3 (ii) $\sqrt{45}$
11. (i) (4, 3) (ii) (1, 3) (iii) (3, 1)
    (iv) (1, 1) (v) (1, -2) (vi) (-2, 0)
12. (0, $\frac{11}{2}$); y-axis
13. (2, 4)
14. (1, $\frac{1}{2}$)
15. ($-1, -1$)
16. (5, 8)
17. (-1, 6)

Exercise 11.2
1. (i) b, c (ii) a, d
2. a: $\frac{3}{2}$, b: 1, c: $\frac{1}{3}$, d: -1
3. (i) b (ii) $\frac{2}{3}$ (iii) 2
4. The line is falling (from left to right); $-\frac{3}{2}$
5. (i) 1 (ii) $-\frac{3}{2}$ (iii) 8 (iv) 1
6. Parallel lines
7. Yes, parallel
9. a: $\frac{1}{2}$, b: 1, c: 2
10. (i) $\frac{3}{4}$ (ii) $-\frac{4}{3}$
11. (i) $-\frac{3}{2}$ (ii) $-\frac{5}{4}$ (iii) $\frac{4}{3}$ (iv) $\frac{5}{2}$ (v) 2
12. (i) -1 (ii) 1
13. (i) 1 (ii) -1
14. 5
15. $\frac{-8}{3}$
16. (i) $\frac{1}{2}$ (ii) $\frac{2}{k-1}$ (iii) 5
17. Ramps A and C are suitable

Exercise 11.3
1. (i) $2x - y - 2 = 0$ (ii) $4x - y + 1 = 0$
   (iii) $5x + y + 17 = 0$ (iv) $2x - 3y - 9 = 0$
2. (i) $3x - 4y - 19 = 0$ (ii) $3x - 5y + 22 = 0$
3. (i) $4x - y + 11 = 0$ (ii) $2x + y + 1 = 0$
   (iii) $3x - 4y + 18 = 0$ (iv) $2x + 3y - 5 = 0$
4. $3x + y = 0$
5. (i) $3x - y = 0$ (ii) $5x + y = 0$
   (iii) $x - 3y = 0$
   (iv) $3x + 2y = 0$; no constant number

597

6. -3; $3x + y - 5 = 0$
7. (i) $3x - 2y = 0$ (ii) $2x + y = 0$
   (iii) $x + 6y - 1 = 0$ (iv) $4x + 5y - 7 = 0$
8. $5x + 4y - 2 = 0$
9. (i) 3, $3x - y - 6 = 0$
   (ii) $\frac{1}{3}$, $x - 3y + 6 = 0$

Exercise 11.4
1. (i) 3 (ii) 2 (iii) $\frac{1}{2}$
2. (i) (0, 5) (ii) (0, -3) (iii) (0, 4)
3. (i) $y = -x + 4$; -1 (ii) $y = -3x + 5$; -3
   (iii) $y = -\frac{2}{3}x + \frac{7}{3}$; $-\frac{2}{3}$ (iv) $y = \frac{5}{2}x + \frac{3}{2}$; $\frac{5}{2}$
   (v) $y = -\frac{3}{4}x + \frac{1}{2}$; $-\frac{3}{4}$ (vi) $y = \frac{3}{4}x + \frac{3}{2}$; $\frac{3}{4}$
4. $y = -\frac{2}{3}x + \frac{7}{3}$; (i) $-\frac{2}{3}$ (ii) $-\frac{2}{3}$ (iii) $\frac{3}{2}$
5. -2
7. (i) $y = 3x + c$ (ii) $y = -\frac{1}{3}x + c$
8. Yes, parallel
9. (i) A & E, B & F, C & I, D & G
   (ii) H
10. (i) $\frac{2}{3}$ (ii) $y = \frac{2}{3}x + 1$
11. $r - \boxed{y = 2x + 5}$ $p - \boxed{y = x + 5}$
    $q - \boxed{y = x - 2}$
12. $y = \frac{1}{2}x + 1$
13. (i) a&f (ii) e&f and a&e and b&d (iii) e (iv) a
14. 4   15. 2
16. (i) $y = 2x + 3$ (ii) $y = x + 2$
    (iii) $y = 3x - 3$
17. A & C

Exercise 11.5
1. -2; $2x + y - 8 = 0$
2. $3x - y - 9 = 0$
3. $\frac{2}{3}$; $-\frac{3}{2}$; $3x + 2y - 10 = 0$
4. $2x - 3y + 7 = 0$
5. $3x - y + 12 = 0$
6. (i) Slope a: 2, Slope b: $-\frac{1}{2}$
   (ii) Yes, perpendicular
   (iii) $2x - y - 8 = 0$
7. $2x + y - 5 = 0$ 8. C
9. (2, 4); $5x - y - 6 = 0$
10. (i) Slope: 2, P(0, 5) (ii) $x + 2y - 10 = 0$
11. $\frac{1}{3}$; $y = \frac{1}{3}x + 2$; P(3, 3); $y = -3x + 12$

Exercise 11.6
1. a: $y = 1$, b: $y = 3$, c: $x = 3$, d: $x = -1$
3. (i) 3 (ii) (0, 6) (iii) 4
   (iv) 2 (v) 9 sq. units

4. (i) (0, 5) (ii) (5, 0)
5. (6, 0), (0, -3) 6. (5, 0), (0, $-2\frac{1}{2}$)
7. Same slope, i.e. all parallel to each other
8. 9 sq. units
9. (i) a (ii) b
   (iii) Not perpendicular (iv) $\frac{15}{2}$ sq. units
10. (i) A(0, 2), B(-4, 0) (ii) $\frac{1}{2}$
12. (i) d (ii) c (iii) a (iv) b
13. (iv) Not on this line
14. -6 15. 3
16. (i) 2 (ii) 5

Exercise 11.7
1. (4, 1) 2. (1, 3) 3. (1, 4)
4. (2, 3) 5. (3, 1) 6. (-2, 1)
7. (-1, -2) 8. (3, -4) 9. (-2, 5)
11. P(0, 6), Q(-7, 0)

Exercise 11.8
1. (i) (a) 10 ℓ/min (b) 3 ℓ/min
   (ii) 10, 3
   (iii) Slope = rate of flow
2. (i) (a) $\frac{7}{4}$ ℓ/sec (b) 2 ℓ/sec
   (ii) $\frac{7}{4}$, 2
   (iii) Both the same value
3. (i) $\frac{1}{2}$ (ii) C is true
4. (i) -8
   (ii) Goes from forty gallons to zero gallons
   (iii) 8 gallons/min
   (iv) Slope means that the rate of flow is -8 gallons per minute
5. (i) (a) 9.1 kg (b) 8.8 lb
   (ii) $\frac{5}{11}$
   (iii) Slope means that 5 kg = 11 lb
   2.2 lb = 1 kg (rate of change)
   (iv) $5x - 11y = 0$ (or $5k - 11\ell = 0$)
   (v) 44 lb
6. (i) (a) €182 (b) €125
   (ii) (a) 24 days (b) 47 days
   (iii) $\frac{19}{5}$
   (iv) Value of slope = daily hire charge (€3.80)
   (v) €30
7. (i) ℓ_1: 11, ℓ_2: $\frac{17}{2}$
   (ii) That the fuel consumptions are 11 km/ℓ and 8.5 km/ℓ respectively.
   (iii) €7.76

Answers

Test yourself 11
1. (i) 2 (ii) (0, −4) (iii) (2, 0) (iv) $-\frac{1}{2}$
2. $\frac{1}{2}$; $y = \frac{1}{2}x + 1$ 3. B *it's right*
4. (i) (0, 5); y-axis (ii) $\frac{4}{3}$
   (iii) $-\frac{3}{4}$ (iv) $3x + 4y = 0$
5. (a) A: $2x − y + 3 = 0$, B: $2x − y − 2 = 0$
   (b) $2x − y + c = 0$
6. (2, 2)   7. 2
8. A(3, 0), B(0, 2); 3 sq. units
9. $a = \frac{-3}{5}, b = 3$
10. (i) b & c (ii) 2 (iii) D & a, E & b, F & c
11. $3x − y − 1 = 0$
12. (a) 0.675
    (b) Yes as the slope is 0.675, i.e. under 0.7
14. $-\frac{1}{2}$
15. (i) $2x − y + 1 = 0$
    (ii) By checking whether the product of their slopes is −1 (which it isn't)
16. (i) 7070 m (ii) 3 km
    (iii) $3x − 4y + 31 = 0$
    (iv) $4x + 3y − 92 = 0$
    (v) (11, 16)
    (vi) Up North St. to Tangent St. and then follow Tangent St. directly to the museum; 21.5 km

Chapter 12: Ratio – Time – Speed

Exercise 12.1
1. (i) 1 : 3 (ii) 5 : 9 (iii) 2 : 7
   (iv) 1 : 4 (v) 1 : 3 (vi) 1 : 8
   (vii) 1 : 7 (viii) 2 : 9
2. (i) 2 : 1 (ii) 3 : 1 (iii) 2 : 3
   (iv) 4 : 3 (v) 4 : 5 (vi) 6 : 7
   (vii) 7 : 3 (viii) 1 : 3
3. Ann – €180, David – €108
4. €1600, €800, €400
5. €390, €910
6. €225
7. (i) B and C, A and E
   (ii) One quarter of the class are girls OR The ratio of boys to girls is 3 : 1
8. 210   9. €5508
10. (i) 10 kg (ii) 15 kg
11. 250
12. (i) 15 apples, 125 g br. sugar, 1 kg flour, 250 g c. sugar, 5 tbsp water
    (ii) 20 ppl
13. 3 : 7   14. $16\frac{1}{5}$ c
15. (i) 50 cm (ii) 16 m
16. (i) Butter – 400 g, Flour – 600 g
    (ii) 500 g (iii) 1875 g
17. 10 days
18. (i) 9 days (ii) 18
19. 1 : 2   20. 13 : 47
21. 3 : 2   22. 2 : 1
23. (a) (i) $\frac{2}{1}$ (ii) $\frac{5}{3}$ (iii) $\frac{\sqrt{89}}{5}$
    (b) (i) $\frac{13}{7}$ (ii) $\frac{10}{3}$
    (c) $\frac{20}{3} \times \frac{15}{3}$
24. (i) $x − 4$ (ii) 6.47

Exercise 12.2
1. (i) 8 hr 24 min (ii) 2 hr 36 min
   (iii) 4 hr 58 min (iv) 1 hr 41 min
2. (i) 204 min (ii) 336 min
   (iii) 474 min
3. (i) 1.25 am (ii) 10.30 pm
   (iii) 6.50 am (iv) 4.45 pm
4. (i) 11.40 am (ii) 3.35 pm
   (iii) 12.20 pm (iv) 12.30 am
   (v) 10.15 pm
5. (i) 06.00 (ii) 10.45
   (iii) 16.00 (iv) 22.12
   (v) 12.00
6. (i) 4 hr 30 min (ii) 7 hr 5 min
   (iii) 8 hr 15 min (iv) 8 hr 28 min
7. (i) 4 hr 10 min (ii) 3 hr 32 min
   (iii) 8 hr 9 min
8. A and (i), B and (iv), C and (ii), D and (iii)
9. 36 hr 15 min   10. 10.55 pm
11. 3 hr 48 min   12. 14.26
13. (i) 3 hr 35 min (ii) 19 min
    (iii) 1 hr 53 min (iv) Train 2
    (v) 2 hr 55 min (vi) 2 min
    (vii) 38 min (viii) Train 2

Exercise 12.3
1. (i) 225 km (ii) 198 km
2. (i) 2 hr 30 min (ii) $\frac{3}{4}$ hr
3. (i) 60 km/hr (ii) 60 km/hr
   (iii) 50 km/hr (iv) 135 km/hr
4. 180 km/hr   5. 70 km/hr
6. $4\frac{1}{2}$ hours   7. 72 km/hr
8. 5 hr 12 min   9. $53\frac{1}{3}$ km/hr
10. (i) 86 km/hr (ii) 67 ℓ
11. 8 km/hr
12. Cheetah is faster; 469.4 m/min
13. 8.35 am
14. Cheetah, Antelope, Racehorse, Deer
15. 125 km/hr   16. 1418 hours

599

Text & Tests 2 Higher Level

Test yourself 12
1. (i) 4 : 5   (ii) 1 : 5
   (iii) 1 : 12   (iv) 1 : 5
2. (i) 2.5 hr   (ii) 88 km/hr
3. 3 : 11   4. 6
5. 9 ℓ 6. 192 cm
7. (i) 5 : 7 : 10 : 3   (ii) 0.8 kg
8. 40 min each   9. 1625
10. (i) 240 km   (ii) 3 hours
    (iii) 80 km/hr
11. 81 kg
12. (i) 19.17   (ii) 23.49
13. €2080   14. 12.24 pm
15. 7 : 23   16. $\frac{1}{4}$
17. 56
18. (i) 3 hr   (ii) 8 km/hr
19. 25.2 m

Chapter 13: Statistics 3 – Presenting Data

Exercise 13.1
1. (i) 15   (ii) 1
   (iii) 0 to 5 (i.e. 5)   (iv) 20%
2. (i) 18°C   (ii) 28°C   (iii) 3
   (iv) $53\frac{1}{3}$%   (v) $\frac{4}{15}$
3. (i) 42   (ii) 3   (iii) 10
   (iv) 29.2%   (v) $\frac{1}{13}$
4. (i) 25   (ii) 10
   (iii) 3   (iv) 5–10 (i.e. 5)
   (v) 9   (vi) 169
   (vii) 6.76
5. (i) 7   (ii) 12   (iii) 13   (iv) 4
   (v) 30   (vi) $16\frac{2}{3}$%   (vii) $\frac{1}{10}$
6. (i) 60   (ii) 115   (iii) 1.9
7. (i) 4   (ii) 5   (iii) 3   (iv) 0.225

Exercise 13.2
1. (i) 105°   (ii) 120°   (iii) 125°
2. (i) 45°   (ii) 40   (iii) Spain
   (iv) France   (v) Spain and Portugal
3. (i) 90°   (ii) 45°   (iii) 165°
4. (i) Bus – 120°, Car – 90°, Train – 72°,
   Walk – 48°, Bicycle – 30°
5. (i) €1800   (ii) (a) 120°   (b) €600
6. Pie chart Ⓒ

7.

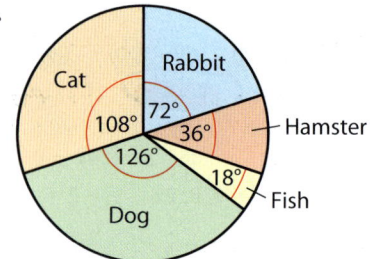

8. (i) 150
   (ii) Slightly larger % of cards at *Cardworld* are c'ions cards but there are 3 times as many cards (in total) at *Card Den*.
9. 90
10. (i) 20%   (ii) $x = 126°, y = 79°$
11. 250

Exercise 13.3
1. (i) 20   (ii) 16
   (iii) (6–9) km   (iv) 62
2. (i) 7.30 am   (ii) 45
   (iii) Breakfast   (iv) 10.30 am–11.30 am
   (v) Elevenses
3. (ii) 28   (iii) 12
4. (i) 32   (ii) (30–40) sec
   (iii) 25%   (iv) 23   (v) $\frac{9}{32}$
5. (ii) 12   (iii) (20–40) km
   (iv) (20–40) km   (v) 38 km
6. (i) 2   (ii) (€20 000–€30 000)
   (iii) 7   (iv) 20   (v) $\frac{3}{20}$
7. (i) 12   (ii) 60   (iii) (50–60) yrs
   (iv) $\frac{1}{10}$ (v) 21   (vi) $43\frac{1}{2}$ yrs
8. (i) chart   (ii) $150 \leqslant h < 160$
   (iii) 32   (iv) $150 \leqslant h < 160$
   (v) 5020   (vi) 156.875
   (vii) 87.5%

Exercise 13.4
1. (i) 4   (ii) 27 yrs   (iii) 8   (iv) 36 yrs
2. (i) 20   (ii) 5   (iii) 43   (iv) 76
3. (i) 50   (ii) $75\frac{1}{2}$ (iii) 45%
4. (ii) 8   (iii) 16   (iv) 15
5. (i) chart
   (ii) the actual score of each student is represented.
6. (ii) mean; 29.14 km/hr   median; 29 km/hr
   mode; 29 km/hr
7. (i) Before – 48, After – 45
   (ii) Before – 66, After – 79
   (iii) The pulse rates were consistently higher after PE

Answers

8. (i) 23
   (ii) Dynamo – 37 hours, Energy Plus – 29 hours
   (iii) Dynamo better as it has a much higher median though is less predictable (much larger range)
9. (ii) Male median – 53 yrs
   Female median – 56 yrs
   Male range – 32 yrs
   Female range – 36 yrs
10. (i) 10 (ii) 5 (iii) 2 (iv) 6
11. (i) 7
    (ii) (a) 19 (b) 21
    (iii) 25.35
    (iv) (a) 19 (b) 23
    (v) 82
12. (i)

Geography		History
	2	5 7
6	3	0 8
8 7 5 0	4	5 5 7
8 5 1	5	2 3 4 5 9
9 7 5 4 4 2	6	5 7 9
6 5 4 2	7	1 3
5 3	8	3 6
	9	1 Key: 6|5 = 65

   (ii) There is a greater number of higher percentages in Geography.

Exercise 13.5

1. (i) 2 (ii) 4 (iii) 8
   (iv) 3 (v) 9 (vi) 27
2. Graph only shows part of the scale
3. (i) Area of column for "fish 2" increased dramatically by larger width
   (ii) Increased width and depth (and by extension, volume) of carton B creates illusion of greater production despite the actual productions being the same.
   (iii) Scale doesn't start at 0
   (iv) "Creative" cubes (area and volume) mislead
4. (i) Graph shows only part of the vertical scale
5. (i) Graph A (ii) No (iii) No, untrue

Test yourself 13

1. (i) 45° (ii) 60 (iii) $12\frac{1}{2}$%
2. (i) 36 (ii) 28
   (iii) 20%
3. (i) As the continuous data is grouped
   (ii) 7 (iii) 8
   (iv) 16 (v) 11.94 seconds

4. (ii) Mode – 3.7 kg, Median – 4.15 kg
5. No; Greendale has >60, Nevin has <50
6. (i) 60° (ii) 84°
7. (i) No vertical scale
   (ii) Increased width of mobile phone on right distorts the actual increase
8. (ii) 49 kg (iii) 75
9. (i) €1133.33 (ii) €400
   (iii) €666.67 (iv) €200
10. (i) S – $92\frac{1}{2}$, D – $99\frac{1}{2}$
    (ii) S – 49, D – 23
    (iii) Dynamos; much smaller range
    (iv) While they did achieve 3 v. high scores, they also got the 4 lowest scores (Erratic scoring)
11. (ii) 24
    (iii) 1st Test – 33   2nd Test – 29
    (iv) Yes; higher mean, higher median, higher starting point (27 → 33)
    (v) Slightly better-than-average improvement (3 compared to 2.83)
12. (iii) 3 (iv) $22\frac{1}{2}$% (v) 70%

Chapter 14: Indices – Scientific Notation – Surds

Exercise 14.1

1. (i) 49 (ii) 64 (iii) 16
   (iv) 25 (v) 36
2. (i) 2^3 (ii) 2^4 (iii) 4^5
   (iv) 5^6 (v) a^6 (vi) $6x^3$
   (vii) $8x^5$ (viii) a^3
3. (i) 3^2 (ii) 5^2 (iii) 3^3
   (iv) 2^5 (v) 10^3 (vi) 20^2
4. (i) 5^2 (ii) 3^4 (iii) 7^2
   (iv) 3^4 (v) 5^7 (vi) 4^4
5. (i) F (ii) T (iii) F (iv) F
6. (i) 8 (ii) 16 (iii) 9 (iv) 343
   (v) 9
7. (i) $\frac{1}{9}$ (ii) 8 (iii) 12 (iv) $\frac{1}{12}$
   (v) 1
8. (i) 8 (ii) 3 (iii) 4 (iv) 8
9. A – 27 (3^3); B – $\frac{1}{9}$ (3^{-2}); C – $\frac{1}{64}$ (2^{-6});
   D – $\frac{1}{216}$ (6^{-3}); E – 1 (7^0); F – $\frac{1}{4}$ (2^{-2}); G – 9 (3^2);
   H – 3125 (5^5)
10. (i) 36 (ii) $\frac{1}{8}$ (iii) $\frac{4}{9}$
    (iv) a^3b^3 (v) $\frac{4a^2}{9b^2}$
11. (i) $3^8 \times 5^7$ (ii) $2^6 \times 9^5$
    (iii) $3^8, 4^8$ (iv) $11^3 \times 3^1$
12. C

13. (i) 4^6 (ii) $(2^4)^3$ (iii) 2^{4n} (iv) $(5^x)^4$
14. (i) 3^2 (ii) 3^4 (iii) 3^9 (iv) 3^8
    (v) 3^{2n}
15. A and I; B and H; C and G; D and F
16. (i) $\frac{1}{a}$ (ii) 1 (iii) $6a^2$ (iv) a^4
17. (i) 3^8 (ii) 4^4 (iii) a^{-1}

Exercise 14.2

1. (i) 5 (ii) 12 (iii) 3
   (iv) 4 (v) 4 (vi) 5
2. (i) 5 (ii) 4 (iii) 6
   (iv) $\frac{2}{3}$ (v) $\frac{4}{5}$ (vi) $\frac{2}{3}$
3. (i) $x^{\frac{1}{2}}$ (ii) $x^{\frac{1}{3}}$ (iii) $a^{\frac{1}{4}}$
   (iv) $a^{\frac{2}{3}}$ (v) $a^{\frac{3}{2}}$ (vi) $a^{\frac{3}{4}}$
4. (i) $\frac{1}{2}$ (ii) $\frac{1}{3}$ (iii) $\frac{1}{4}$
   (iv) 3 (v) $\frac{1}{10}$ (vi) 0.1
5. (i) $\sqrt{a}$ (ii) $\sqrt[4]{a}$ (iii) $\sqrt[3]{a^2}$
   (iv) $\sqrt{a^5}$ (v) $\sqrt[4]{a^3}$ (vi) $\sqrt{\frac{a}{x}}$ or $\frac{\sqrt{a}}{\sqrt{x}}$
6. (i) 9 (ii) 4 (iii) 8
   (iv) 8 (v) 9 (vi) 64
   (vii) 16 (viii) 1000 (ix) 27
   (x) 25
7. (i) $\frac{1}{3}$ (ii) $\frac{1}{16}$ (iii) $\frac{1}{2}$
   (iv) 2 (v) $\frac{1}{4}$
8. (i) $\frac{1}{4}$ (ii) 4 (iii) $\frac{1}{8}$
   (iv) $\frac{1}{1000}$ (v) $\frac{1}{8}$
9. (i) $\frac{9}{4}$ (ii) 16 (iii) $\frac{25}{9}$
   (iv) $\frac{3}{2}$ (v) $\frac{5}{3}$
10. (i) $\frac{1}{343}$ (ii) $\frac{125}{27}$ (iii) $\frac{27}{8}$
    (iv) $\frac{25}{9}$ (v) 5
11. $a = 16, b = \frac{1}{9}$; 12
12. (i) $\frac{4}{9}$ (ii) $\frac{1}{125}$
13. 5 14. 4^{-2} 16. 3^{-2}
17. proof 18. $a = 2, b = 2$

Exercise 14.3

1. (i) 2^3 (ii) 2^4 (iii) 2^{-2}
   (iv) 2^{-3} (v) 2^{-5}
2. (i) 3^2 (ii) 3^3 (iii) 3^4
   (iv) 3^{-3} (v) 3^{-4}
3. (i) $2^{\frac{3}{2}}$ (ii) $2^{\frac{7}{2}}$ (iii) $2^{\frac{3}{2}}$
   (iv) $2^{\frac{7}{2}}$ (v) $2^{\frac{-5}{2}}$

4. (i) $x = 3$ (ii) $x = 3$ (iii) $x = \frac{3}{2}$
   (iv) $x = \frac{5}{2}$ (v) $x = \frac{5}{2}$ (vi) $x = \frac{3}{2}$
   (vii) $x = \frac{3}{2}$ (viii) $x = \frac{5}{4}$
5. (i) $x = -2$ (ii) $x = -3$ (iii) $x = \frac{-3}{2}$
   (iv) $x = 3$
6. (i) $x = \frac{4}{3}$ (ii) $x = -3$ (iii) $x = \frac{-5}{2}$
   (iv) $x = 3$
7. (i) $x = 6$ (ii) $x = 3$ (iii) $x = -\frac{3}{2}$
   (iv) $x = \frac{-1}{2}$
8. (i) $5^{\frac{1}{2}}$ (ii) $5^{\frac{3}{2}}$ (iii) $5^{\frac{3}{2}}$
   (iv) $5^{\frac{7}{2}}$ (v) $5^{\frac{-5}{2}}$
9. (i) $\frac{-1}{2}$ (ii) $\frac{-1}{2}$ (iii) $\frac{5}{2}$
   (iv) $\frac{-3}{2}$
10. $3^{\frac{7}{2}}$; $x = \frac{3}{4}$ 11. $3^{\frac{5}{2}}$; $x = \frac{13}{4}$
12. $2^{\frac{5}{2}}$; $x = \frac{9}{4}$ 13. $3^{\frac{-5}{2}}$; $x = \frac{17}{4}$
14. (i) 2^4 (ii) $2^{\frac{3}{2}}$; $x = \frac{7}{4}$

Exercise 14.4

1. (i), (ii), (iv), (vi) all rational
2. (i), (iii), (v), (vi) all irrational
3. (i) 5 (ii) 20 (iii) 12
   (iv) 5 (v) 29 (vi) 10
4. (i) $\sqrt{10}$ (or π) (ii) $\sqrt{17}$ (iii) $\sqrt{109}$
   (iv) $\sqrt{0.8}$
5. (i) $\sqrt{10}$ (ii) $\sqrt{21}$ (iii) $\sqrt{24}$
   (iv) $\sqrt{55}$
6. (i) 5 (ii) 6 (iii) 12
   (iv) 4 (v) 4
7. (i) $2\sqrt{2}$ (ii) $2\sqrt{3}$ (iii) $3\sqrt{2}$
   (iv) $3\sqrt{3}$ (v) $3\sqrt{5}$
8. (i) $5\sqrt{3}$ (ii) $5\sqrt{5}$ (iii) $4\sqrt{2}$
   (v) $12\sqrt{3}$ (v) $8\sqrt{3}$
9. A and K, F and G, B and H, E and J, C and I; D
10. (i) $8\sqrt{3}$ (ii) $5\sqrt{2}$ (iii) $5\sqrt{2}$
    (iv) $7\sqrt{2}$ (v) $7\sqrt{3}$ (vi) $3\sqrt{3}$
11. 4 times
12. (i) 10 (ii) 18 (iii) 60 (iv) 21
13. (i) $5 - 2\sqrt{5}$
    (ii) $6 - 4\sqrt{3}$ [or $2(3 - 2\sqrt{3})$]
    (iii) $6 - \sqrt{6}$
14. (i) $2(\sqrt{10} - 5)$ (ii) 1 (iii) 22
    (iv) -9 (v) -11 (vi) -3
15. (i) 2 (ii) $-7 - 13\sqrt{2}$
    (iii) 1
16. $24 - 8\sqrt{5}$ 17. $4\sqrt{15}$ 18. 6
19. (i) (a) $2\sqrt{3}$ (b) Irrational
    (ii) (a) 1 (b) Rational

Answers

Exercise 14.5
1. (i), (iv)
2. (i) 600 (ii) 450
   (iii) 6800 (iv) 51 000
   (v) 67 000 (vi) 516
   (vii) 7050 (viii) 18 600
3. (i) 4×10^2 (ii) 2.8×10^2
   (iii) 8.4×10^2 (iv) 6.2×10^3
   (v) 8.6×10^3 (vi) 1.27×10^2
   (vii) 8.27×10^2 (viii) 7.6×10^4
   (ix) 1.468×10^2 (x) 7.24×10^4
4. (i) 4×10^3 (ii) 3.2×10^5
   (iii) 9×10^2 (iv) 9.43×10^3
5. (i) 2080 (ii) 660.6
   (iii) 8230 (iv) 570
6. (i) 5.4×10^5 (ii) 1.702×10^2
   (iii) 3.276×10^3 (iv) 1.44×10^2
7. (i) 0.25 (ii) 0.06
   (iii) 0.0048 (iv) 0.00092
8. (i) 4×10^{-2} (ii) 6.2×10^{-2}
   (iii) 7×10^{-3} (iv) 6.5×10^{-3}
9. (i) 8×10^{-3} (ii) 7.9×10^{-3}
   (iii) 6×10^{-4} (iv) 5.3×10^{-4}
10. (i) 7×10^3 (ii) 6×10^2
    (iii) 5.6×10^3 (iv) 7×10^{-5}
11. (i) 2.8×10^3 (ii) 8×10^2
12. 2.4×10^4 13. 0.3779
14. (i) 19.625 (ii) 78.4
15. (i) Earth
    (ii) 5900 km (5.9×10^3)
    (iii) (1.95×10^4) km
16. (a) $\frac{distance}{speed}$
    (b) (i) 4×10^{16} (ii) 1.3×10^8 s
17. 19
18. (i) 2.34×10^{11}, 4.8×10^6 (ii) €48 750
19. (i) A: 1.7×10^9 ℓ, B: 7.4×10^{10} ℓ
    (ii) 43

Exercise 14.6
1. (i) 80 (ii) 350 (iii) 1790
   (iv) 7320 (v) 1610
2. (i) 100 (ii) 100 (iii) 1800
   (iv) 2500 (v) 9800
3. (i) 46.3 (ii) 8.8 (iii) 0.4
   (iv) 0.5 (v) 0.1
4. (i) 1 (ii) 2 (iii) 3
   (iv) 3 (v) 4
5. (i) 3200 (ii) 650 (iii) 2900
   (iv) 29 000 (v) 41 000
6. (i) 7140 (ii) 45 300 (iii) 3610
   (iv) 160 000 (v) 701 000
7. (i) 0.47 (ii) 0.063 (iii) 2.4
   (iv) 0.67 (v) 55
8. (i) 0.738 (ii) 8.37 (iii) 0.0284
   (iv) 1.08 (v) 12.3
9. (i) 72 700 (ii) 73 000 (iii) 70 000
10. (i) 40 (ii) 2 (iii) 125
11. (i) 5 (ii) 360 (iii) 9
12. (i) 40 (ii) 120 (iii) 60
13. $\frac{40 \times 60}{300}$

Exercise 14.7
1. (i) $\frac{1}{6}$ (ii) 2 (iii) $\frac{4}{3}$
   (iv) $-\frac{3}{2}$ (v) $\frac{4}{5}$
2. (i) 0.38 (ii) 0.18 (iii) -0.36
   (iv) 1.47 (v) -1.25
4. (i) 7.91 (ii) 9.09 (iii) 12.47
5. (i) 5.52 (ii) 18.65 (iii) 10.38
   (iv) 15.21 (v) 267.00
6. (i) 0.16 (ii) 1.27 (iii) 4.22
   (iv) 44.28 (v) 2.50
7. (i) 22.16 (ii) 98.01 (iii) 9.56
   (iv) 4.13
8. (i) 0.47 (ii) 7.53 (iii) 38.27
9. 41.23
10. 2.47 11. 14.96 12. 15.08
13. 9.8 14. 0.366

Test yourself 14
1. (i) 12 (ii) $x = \frac{-1}{3}$
2. (i) $5\sqrt{2}$ (ii) $\sqrt{37}$
3. 12; 11.43
4. (i) $4^{\frac{1}{2}}$ and $16^{\frac{1}{4}}$ (ii) 5.3×10^3
5. (i) $3\sqrt{3}$ (ii) 0.2 (2×10^{-1})
6. (i) $x = 0$ (ii) $y = -2$
   (iii) $z = \frac{1}{5}$ (iv) $b = -4$
7. (i) 4^{-1} and 2^{-2} (ii) $x = 2$ (8, 18…)
8. (i) $4x^2$ (ii) 3×10^5
9. (i) 125 (ii) $x = \frac{-3}{4}$
10. (i) 32 (ii) $\frac{1}{9}$ (iii) 2 (iv) 1 (v) 3
11. (i) 4×10^{-2} (ii) $x = \frac{3}{2}$
12. (i) F($0^2 = 0$) (ii) F$[(-8)^2 = 64]$
    (iii) F($1 < 2$) (iv) T
    (v) F$\left(2^{-4} = \frac{1}{16}$ and $\frac{1}{16} > 0\right)$
13. (i) 16 (ii) $\frac{1}{2}$ (iii) 5 (iv) 2
14. (i) $10\sqrt{2}$ (ii) $\frac{1}{4}$
15. 2.5×10^3
16. (i) $5\frac{1}{2}$ (ii) $-\frac{1}{2}$
17. (i) 3 (ii) $\frac{5}{7}$
18. $5^{\frac{3}{2}}$; $\frac{1}{4}$
19. (i) $k = 2$, (ii) $\frac{4\sqrt{2} + 12}{2\sqrt{2}}$ (iii) proof
20. 3.5×10^7

Chapter 15: Quadratic Equations

Exercise 15.1
1. $x = 2, 4$
2. $x = -2, 4$
3. $x = -4, 6$
4. $\frac{3}{2}, 4$
5. $-3, \frac{3}{2}$
6. $-4, \frac{1}{2}$
7. $0, 3$
8. $-5, 0$
9. $-3, 0$
10. $-5, -2$
11. $-7, -5$
12. $-8, -6$
13. $2, 3$
14. $3, 5$
15. $3, 7$
16. $-3, 4$
17. $-2, 5$
18. $-7, 4$
19. $\frac{1}{2}, 2$
20. $\frac{-1}{2}, 2$
21. $\frac{-3}{2}, 2$
22. $-2, -\frac{1}{2}$
23. $\frac{1}{3}, 2$
24. $-2, \frac{5}{3}$
25. $-4, \frac{2}{3}$
26. $\frac{-2}{3}, 5$
27. $-7, \frac{2}{3}$
28. $\frac{1}{2}, \frac{5}{2}$
29. $\frac{-2}{5}, 3$
30. $\frac{3}{5}, 2$
31. $0, 6$
32. $0, \frac{5}{2}$
33. $0, \frac{4}{3}$
34. $0, \frac{1}{4}$
35. $0, \frac{6}{5}$
36. $0, \frac{7}{3}$
37. ± 3
38. ± 5
39. $\pm \frac{1}{2}$
40. $\pm \frac{5}{2}$
41. $\pm \frac{4}{3}$
42. $\pm \frac{7}{2}$
43. $\frac{-5}{2}, 6$
44. $-2, 7$
45. $\frac{-1}{2}, 5$
46. ± 4
47. $-3, 1$
48. (i) $-5, 4$ (ii) $-4, -2$ (iii) $5, 6$
49. (i) $x = 3, 5$ (ii) $x = -4, -2$ (iii) $x = -1, 2$
50. (i) one ($x = -2$) (ii) B

Exercise 15.2
1. $-2 \pm \sqrt{2}$
2. $-3 \pm \sqrt{5}$
3. $-1 \pm \sqrt{6}$
4. $1 \pm 2\sqrt{2}$
5. $\frac{-1 \pm \sqrt{5}}{4}$
6. $\frac{1 \pm \sqrt{13}}{6}$
7. $0.42, 1.58$
8. $-2.91, 0.57$
9. $-0.35, 1.15$
10. $-2.39, -0.28$
11. $-0.36, 1.86$
12. $-2.59, 0.26$
13. $-1.55, 0.80$
14. $0.72, 2.78$
15. $-2.14, 0.47$
16. $-2.14, 1.64$

Exercise 15.3
1. $x^2 + x = 72; -9, 8$
2. 10
3. $8, 11$
4. 10
5. $4, 7$
6. 4
7. length – 11 cm, breadth – 7 cm
8. 9
9. length – 7 cm, breadth – 4 cm
10. 6 years old
11. (ii) $4, 5$ or $-5, -4$
12. 7 m
13. 5
14. (i) When 0 or 20 cakes an hour are baked (ii) When 6 or 14 cakes are baked
15. (i) 0 sec or 6 sec (ii) 2 sec or 4 sec
16. (ii) 4
17. 10 months
18. $x^2 + 10x - 144 = 0; x = 8$

Exercise 15.4
1. $x^2 - 6x + 8 = 0$
2. $x^2 - 6x + 5 = 0$
3. $x^2 - 5x + 6 = 0$
4. $x^2 - 2x - 3 = 0$
5. $x^2 - 2x - 8 = 0$
6. $x^2 + 7x + 12 = 0$
7. $x^2 - 4x - 12 = 0$
8. $x^2 - 5x = 0$
9. $2x^2 + 3x - 2 = 0$
10. $x^2 + 9x + 20 = 0$
11. $2x^2 - 7x - 4 = 0$
12. $4x^2 - 33x + 8 = 0$
13. $x^2 + 4x = 0$
14. $4x^2 - 1 = 0$
15. $x^2 - 9 = 0$
16. $4x^2 - x = 0$
17. $a = -1, b = -2$
18. $y = x^2 + 3x - 4$

Test yourself 15
1. $x = -5, 7$
2. ± 4
3. $x^2 + x - 90 = 0; x = 9$
4. $x = -4, \frac{2}{3}$
5. $x = 0.72, 2.78$
6. length – 12 cm, breadth – 8 cm
7. -2
8. $x^2 - x - 6 = 0$
9. (ii) $x = 3$; Perimeter $= 30$ cm
10. (i) $x = 0, \frac{7}{2}$ (ii) $x = \pm 6$
11. Ⓑ
12. (i) $A = (10 + 2x)(8 + 2x)$ (ii) $x = 2$
13. $x = -6, 3$
14. 11 or -10
15. $x = \frac{-1}{2}, \frac{5}{6}$
16. $x^2 + 3x - 10 = 0$
17. $2x^2 + 8x + 8 = 72; x = 4$
18. Either 5 or 20 hurleys
19. $x = 3$

Chapter 16: Geometry 2: Similar Triangles – Circles – Theorems

Exercise 16.1
1. (i) [SR] (ii) [LM] (iii) 8 (iv) 16.4 (v) 7.5
2. (i) 1 : 2 (ii) 14.4 (iii) 4
3. $x = 13.5, y = 18$

Answers

4. (i) $p = 6, q = 13.5$ (ii) $x = 9, y = 1$
5. (i) $1\frac{1}{2}$ (ii) $x = 6, y = 4.5$
6. As they have equal angles and corresponding sides of different lengths (i.e. not congruent △s); $x = 21$ cm, $y = 15$ cm
7. (i) [RQ] (ii) [RP] (iii) [QP]; 9
8. (i) [KL] (ii) [EF] (iii) 15
9. (i) [XY]; opposite equal angles
   (ii) $d = 9, e = 13.5$
10. (i), (iv), (v)
11. 11.2 cm
12. (i) Same angles (corresponding angles, e.g. $|\angle ABC| = |\angle ADE|$)
    (ii) 14
13. (i) $|\angle BDC| = |\angle ABD|$
    (iii) [CD] (iv) [AD] (v) 9.6 cm
14. $x = 13.5, y = 27$
15. 2 m
16. 40 cm
17. (i) $|\angle JKM| = |\angle KML|$ … alternate angles
    (ii) 4.9 cm
18. $13\frac{1}{3}$ m
19. (i) Use similar △s, namely △ABE and △ACD
    (ii) 180 m

Exercise 16.2

1. (i) 10 (ii) 12 (iii) 14
2. (i) $x = 10, y = 12$ (ii) $x = 2.5, y = 6$
   (iii) $x = 5, y = 15$ (iv) $x = 4, y = 22$
3. $a = 0.3$ cm
4. $x = 5, y = 14$
5. (i) 8 cm (ii) 7 cm
6. (i) $2\frac{1}{2}$ (ii) 9 (iii) $6\frac{2}{3}$
7. (i) $6\frac{2}{5}$ (ii) $5\frac{5}{6}$ (iii) $2\frac{4}{7}$
8. $x = 10, y = 10\frac{4}{5}, z = 11\frac{3}{7}$
9. 6
10. 7 cm
11. 10.5 cm
12. $14\frac{2}{5}$ cm
13. (i) $|AC|, |BC|$ (ii) $x = 9\frac{3}{5}, y = 2\frac{2}{5}$
14. (i) A, B, C must be collinear and the same for A, E, D with BE ∥ CD
    (ii) 36 m
    (iii) 50 m

Exercise 16.3

1. (i) Angle in semicircle (ii) 45°
   (iii) Right-angled, isosceles
2. (i) 90° (ii) 30° (iii) 40°

3. A = 90°, B = 90°, C = 20°, D = 90°, E = 45°, F = 53°
4. (i) both radii (ii) 90° (iii) 35°
   (iv) 55° (v) As $|OB| = |OC|$ = radius
5. (i) 70° (ii) 60° (iii) 35°
6. $a = 63°, b = 46°, c = 118°, d = 32°, e = 78°, f = 103°, g = 21°, h = 47°, i = 62°, j = 75°, k = 25°$
7. $d = 135°, e = 76°, g = 143°, h = 100°, i = 124°, j = 54°, m = 125°, n = 250°, p = 94°, q = 43°$
8. $a = 116°, b = 64°, c = 90°, d = 135°, e = 110°, f = 35°$
9. (i) 70° (ii) 30° (iii) 40° (iv) 40°
10. (i) $x = 50°, y = 20°$
    (ii) $x = 60°, y = 120°$
    (iii) $x = 36°, y = 54°$
11. 20°
12. (i) 40° (ii) 43.5° (iii) 60°
13. (i) $\angle RSQ$ (ii) 100°
14. △SPQ is isosceles (each base angle = 33°)
15. △AXB and △DXC are similar ⇒ $|\angle XAB| = |\angle XCD|$;
    As these are alternate angles ⇒ AB ∥ DC
16. $2|\triangle| + 2|\angle| = 180° \Rightarrow |\triangle| + |\angle| = 90° \Rightarrow |\angle QPS| = 90°$ (angles in △ sum to 180°)
17. $|\angle AXB| = |\angle DXC|$ (vertically opposite), $|\angle BAX| = |\angle CDX|$ and $|\angle ABX| = |\angle DCX|$
18. (i) $|\angle ACP| = |\angle BDA|$ (angles standing on same arc) ⇒ △s similar
    (ii) Corresponding sides are proportional
19. Isosceles triangle, $x + y$ = Angle in semicircle, i.e. 90°

Test yourself 16

1. (i) $\angle ADC$ and $\angle ABC$
   (ii) 45° (iii) 70°
2. (ii) $x = 9, y = 10.5$
3. $a = 2, b = 9\frac{1}{3}$
4. $a = 35°, b = 95°, c = 70°, d = 65°$
5. (i) 5 (ii) 6
6. (i) 96° (ii) 120° (iii) 84°
7. 1.6 m
8. (i) $x = 40°, y = 140°$
   (ii) $x = 28°, y = 62°$
9. (i) 6 cm (ii) 5 cm (iii) 15 cm
10. 15.5 m
11. $3\frac{3}{8}$
12. 17 m
13. (ii) 16.8 cm
14. (i) $x = 95°, y = 85°$
    (ii) $x = 64°, y = 116°$

605

Text & Tests 2 Higher Level

15. 8.2 m
16. $|\angle ADE| = 60°$ and $|\angle AEC| = 120° \Rightarrow$
    $|\angle AED| = 60° \Rightarrow |\angle DAE| = 60°$
17. 3 cm 18. $116\frac{2}{3}$ m 19. 652 m

Chapter 17: Cylinder – Sphere
Exercise 17.1
1. (i) 1846.32 cm³ (ii) 2813.44 cm³
   (iii) 18 463.2 cm³
2. (i) 835.24 cm² (ii) 1105.28 cm²
   (iii) 3868.48 cm²
3. (i) 54 259 cm³ (ii) 402 cm³
   (iii) 1413 cm³
4. (i) 24617.6 cm³ (ii) 25 ℓ
5. 707 cm³
6. (i) $V = \pi r^2 h$ (ii) $350\pi = \pi r^2 14$
   (iii) 5 cm
7. 6 cm 8. 10 cm 9. 3.5 cm
10. 5 cm 11. 7 cm 12. 4938 cm³
13. (i) 1570 cm³ (ii) 14.13 kg
14. 175.84 cm³; 1792 cm³
15. 16.01 cm
16. (i) 209 m² (ii) 298 m³
17. (i) 3542 cm³ (ii) 1874 cm²

Exercise 17.2
1. (i) 3052.1 cm³ (ii) 5572.5 cm³
   (iii) 718.0 cm³
2. (i) 1018 cm² (ii) 1521 cm²
   (iii) 462 cm²
3. (i) $\frac{250\pi}{3}$ cm³ (ii) 75π cm²
4. (i) 6 cm (ii) 144π cm²
5. (i) 7 cm (ii) 1436.03 cm³
6. 36π cm³ 7. 396 cm³ 8. 8 cm
9. 3 cm 10. 52% 11. $4\frac{1}{2}$
12. (i) 36π cm³ (ii) 162π cm³ (iii) 54π cm³
13. 1.5 cm 14. 10 cm
15. $\frac{128\pi}{3}$ cm³; 14 cm 16. $4\frac{1}{2}$ cm
17. (i) 126π cm³ (ii) 8 cm

Exercise 17.3
1. 2.55 cm 2. 14.4 min
3. 0.6 cm/min 4. 0.014 cm/s
5. 30 ℓ/s 6. 0.25 cm/s
7. (i) 12208.32 cm³ (ii) 152.6 cm³
   (iii) 5.4 cm/s
8. 0.416 ℓ/s 9. 5 cm

Test yourself 17
1. (i) 113040 m³ (ii) 7536 m²
2. (i) 2304π cm³ (ii) 64 cm
3. (i) 2592π cm³ (ii) 144π cm³
   (iii) 18
4. (i) $\frac{5}{\pi}$ m (ii) $\frac{25}{\pi}$ m²
   (iii) 143 min
5. 447.6 cm³ (a) 5700 g (b) 2685.6 g
6. (i) 17441.28 cm³ (ii) $\frac{\pi}{12}$
7. (i) 3 cm (ii) 4 cm
8. (i) 37.68 m² (ii) 28.84 m² (iii) 19.42 m²
9. (i) 5526.4 cm³ (ii) 5802.72 cm²
10. 63
11. (i) $20 000\pi$ cm³ (ii) 160π cm³
    (iii) 125
12. 10 mins
13. (i) 1018 cm³
    (ii) Yes; 1018 cm³ > 1000 cm³
    (iii) 2 (iv) 4
14. (i) 509 mm³ (ii) 5064 mm³
15. 88 cm³; 75 mins

Chapter 18: Patterns & Sequences
Exercise 18.1
1. (i) 13, 15, 17, 19 (ii) 17, 20, 23, 26
   (iii) 24, 28, 32, 36 (iv) 12, 10, 8, 6
   (v) 30, 25, 20, 15 (vi) 0, −4, −8, −12
2. (i) 3, 3.5, 4 (ii) −2, 0, 2
   (iii) 162, 486, 1458 (iv) $5\frac{1}{2}$, 7, $8\frac{1}{2}$
   (v) −5, −2.5, −1.25 (vi) −3, −6, −9
3. (i) 2, 6, 10, 14 (ii) 5, 8, 11, 14
   (iii) 3, 8, 13, 18 (iv) 30, 26, 22, 18
   (v) −10, −7, −4, −1
4. (i) Start with 3 and count forwards in steps of 3
   (ii) Start with 0 and increase in steps of 4
   (iii) Start with 10 and increase in steps of 5
   (iv) Start with 16 and count backwards in steps of 2
   (v) Start with −6 and count forwards in steps of 3
   (vi) Start with $-2\frac{1}{2}$ and count forwards in steps of $\frac{1}{2}$
5. (i) 'add 4' (ii) 'add 3' (iii) 'add 4'
   (iv) 'subtract 2' (v) 'add a $\frac{1}{4}$' (vi) 'add 3'

606

Answers

6.

1st term	Term-to-term rule	2nd, 3rd, 4th and 5th terms
8	+5	13, 18, 23, 28
5	+4	9, 13, 17, 21
9	+3	12, 15, 18, 21
0	−3	−3, −6, −9, −12
−12	+5	−7, −2, 3, 8
0	$+\frac{1}{7}$	$\frac{1}{7}, \frac{2}{7}, \frac{3}{7}, \frac{4}{7}$
$5\frac{1}{4}$	$-\frac{1}{4}$	$5, 4\frac{3}{4}, 4\frac{1}{2}, 4\frac{1}{4}$

7. (i) 8   (ii) 20
8. (i) 14   (ii) 26
10. 1, 2, 4, 8, 16, 32
11. (i) 4, 6, 8, 10, 12, 14, …
    (ii) 25, 22, 19, 16, 13, 10, …
    (iii) 1, 6, 11, 16, 21, 26, …
    (iv) 7, 10, 13, 16, 19, 22, …
12. (i) 33333 × 11 = 366663
    (ii) 9 × 12345 = 111105
    (iii) 66667 × 66667 = 4444488889
13. 2:25, 2:35, 2:45, 2:55, 3:05, 3:15
14. $y = 6, x = 4$
15. (i) 37   (ii) 7
16. 1537, 769
17. (i) 29, 47   (ii) 1, 3

Exercise 18.2

1. (i) □, ○   (ii) 2, 6, 10; Yes
  (iii) △   (iv) □   (v) □   (vi) ○
2. (i) green   (ii) blue
  (iii) red   (iv) blue
  (v) 5, 10, 15, 20 …   (vi) 30th
3. (i) 8, 4   (ii) 4   (iii) 6   (iv) 23rd
4. 8, 16, 24, 32, 40, 48, 56, 64, 72, 80;
  (i) |8, 6, 4, 2, 0|, |8, 6, 4, 2, 0|, …
  (ii) 5   (iii) 0

Exercise 18.3

1. (i) 2, 4, 6, 8   (ii) 4, 7, 10, 13
  (iii) 1, 5, 9, 13   (iv) 7, 9, 11, 13
  (v) 1, 6, 11, 16   (vi) 5, 3, 1, −1
2. (i) −2, −5, −8   (ii) 2, 5, 10
  (iii) $\frac{1}{2}, \frac{3}{4}, 1$
3. (i) 5, 7, 9, 11, 13   (ii) 43, 203
5. As the difference between the terms is a constant
6. (i) Yes   (ii) No
  (iii) No   (iv) Yes

7. (i) A – 5, 12, 19, 26
    B – 9, 8, 7, 6
    C – $-2\frac{1}{2}, -2, -1\frac{1}{2}, -1$
    D – 2, 5, 10, 17
    E – 60, 30, 20, 15
    F – 2, 4, 8, 16
  (ii) A – 138
    B – −10
    C – 7
    D – 401
    E – 3
    F – 1048576
  (iii) A, B, C are linear
8. (i) 5, 8, 11, 14, 17, 20   (ii) 302

Exercise 18.4

1. (i) +4   (ii) 4
  (iii) $4n + 1$ (iv) 81
2. (i) $2n + 3$ (ii) $3n + 1$
  (iii) $4n + 2$
3. $4n + 3$; 43, 83
4. (i) Subtract 2   (ii) −2
  (iii) $-2n + 14$ (iv) −6
  (v) T_{14}
5. (i) $3n - 6$ (ii) $-5n + 25$
6. $-3n + 11$; 15
7.

A	8	11	14	17	20	23
B	−2	2	6	10	14	18
C	−5	3	11	19	27	35

8. First difference $= b + c$

Exercise 18.5

1. (ii) 6, 11, 16, 21, 26, 31
  (iv) 101   (v) 10th
2. (ii) 15   (iii) $2n + 1$ (iv) Diagram 16
3. (i) 19   (ii) $3n + 1$ (iii) 151
4. (i) 13   (ii) $2n + 3$ (iii) Pattern 24
5. (i) 21   (ii) Add 5   (iii) $5n + 1$
  (iv) 13   (v) No
6. (iii) Start at 5 and add 4   (iv) $T_n = 4n + 1$
  (v) Shape 20
  (vi) Yes; Shape 22
7. (iii) $3n + 1$ (iv) 121   (v) 30

Exercise 18.6

1. (i) 5, 8, 13, 20   (ii) −1, 2, 7, 14
  (iii) 1, 7, 17, 31   (iv) −1, 8, 23, 44
2. (i) 18, 24   (ii) 38, 51   (iii) 47, 62
3. (i), (iii), (iv)
4. 116

Text & Tests 2 Higher Level

5. (ii) The coefficient of n^2 in the nth term is the 2nd diff. $\div 2$
   (iii) 6
6. $a = 1$; $T_n = n^2 + 3$
7. (i) $T_n = n^2 + 6$ (ii) $T_n = n^2 + 2n - 1$
   (iii) $T_n = 2n^2$
8. (i) 30
   (ii) As the term-to-term rule does not involve adding or subtracting a constant
   (iii) Yes; 2nd differences all the same
   (iv) $T_n = n^2 + n$ (v) 420
10. (i) 24   (ii) 35
    (iv) $T_n = n^2 + 2n$ (v) 120

Exercise 18.7
1. Constant difference between outputs
2. 3, 5, 7, 9, 11
3. (i) €30   (ii) €105
   (iii) 5   (iv) Yes
   (v) €21   (vi) Yes, both 21
   (vii) €240
4. (i) Yes   (ii) €120
   (iii) $y = 10x$ (or $a = 10w$)   (iv) €200
5. (ii) $T_n = 4n + 2$
6. (ii) 14   (iii) 29   (iv) 2
   (v) 2 cm per day
   (vi) The slope of the line equals the rate of growth of the plant
7. (i) 26   (iii) $T_n = 5n + 1$
   (v) $E = 5n + 1$ (vi) 5
   (vii) The increase in the number of edges from one pattern to the next
8. (ii) 2
   (iv) The graph is curved (parabola)
9. (i) 81, 243, 729
   (ii) It is not
   (iii) 2nd differences are not all the same
   (iv) The curve rises very steeply
10. A and 1, B and 2, C and 3: C is linear

Test yourself 18
1. (i) The sequence begins at 3 and goes up in steps of 4
   (ii) The sequence begins at -1 and goes down in steps of 2
   (iii) The sequence begins at 3 and after that, each term is double the previous term
2. (i) 4, 7, 10   (ii) $-1, -3, -5$ (iii) 1, 7, 17
3. (ii) 15   (iii) $T_n = 3n$ (iv) 21st
4. (i) $-5, -8, -11$ (ii) $5, \frac{5}{2}, \frac{5}{4}$
   (iii) 16, 22, 29
5. (i) Yellow, green   (ii) 3, 8, 13, 18 …
   (iii) 48th   (iv) blue

6. (i) 4, 10, 20
   (ii) 2; 2nd differences are all the same or 2nd difference is constant (2)
7. (iii)
8. (ii) 29   (iii) $T_n = 4n + 1$
   (iv) Shape 25
9. (i) -2 (ii) 4   (iii) 9   (iv) 15
10. (ii) $T_n = 3n + 1$ (iii) $T_{40} = 121$
11. 12, 15, 20, 27, 36, 47
12. (i) 7, 15, 31   (ii) 11, 43, 171   (iii) 4, 7, 11
13. (i) 13   (iii) $T_n = 3n + 1$
    (iv) Pattern 8
14. (i) 2   (ii) $T_n = n^2 + n$
15. (i) 19, 25
    (ii) The sequence starts at 2 and each term after that is treble the previous term
16. (i) 15, 21, 27   (ii) 17, 27, 39
    (iii) 27, 81, 243
    (iv) The exponential one
    (v) As any number of 2nd differences are possible
17. (i) 32   (ii) $T_n = 2^{n-1}$

Chapter 19: Functions
Exercise 19.1
1. (i) 2   (ii) 16   (iii) 11   (iv) 5   (v) 6   (vi) 15
3. (i) 2, 10, 12   (ii) 12, 10, 8
4.

x	1	2	3	4	5
y	9	12	15	18	21

5. (i) $y = 2x + 6$ (ii) $y = 8x - 9$
   (iii) $y = \frac{x}{4} - 3$ (iv) $y = 4(x + 3)$
6. (i) 'Multiply by 5'   (ii) 'Add 4'
   (iii) 'Divide by 4'
7. (i) 'Subtract 1'   (ii) 'Add 1'
8. (i) 5, 8, 20   (ii) 4, 8, 10

Exercise 19.2
1. (i) {1, 2, 4, 5, 7}   (ii) {3, 4, 6, 7, 9}
   (iii) {(1, 3), (2, 4), (4, 6), (5, 7), (7, 9)}
   (iv) 'Add 2' [or $f: x \to x + 2$]
2. (i) {1, 2, 3, 4}; {6, 7, 8, 9}
   (ii) {2, 4, 6, 8, 10}; {5, 9, 13, 17, 21}
3. (i) Yes   (ii) No   (iii) No   (iv) Yes
4. As no two couples have the same input.
5. The input 2 has two different outputs
6. (i) Yes   (ii) No   (iii) Yes
7. (a) (i) {0, 1, 3, 5}   (ii) {3, 4, 5, 8}
       (iii) {3, 4, 5, 6, 8}
   (b) (i) {$-2, 2, 3, 7$}   (ii) {$-4, 6, 9$}
       (iii) {$-4, -3, 2, 4, 6, 9$}

Answers

8. (i) {3, 5, 9, 13}
   (ii) {(0, 3), (1, 5), (3, 9), (5, 13)}
9. {2, 5, 11, 17}
10. (i) {−13, −5, 3, 11}
    (ii) {(−2, −13), (0, −5), (2, 3), (4, 11)}
11.

x	1	2	3	4	5
y	9	11	13	15	17

; $y = 2x + 7$

12. $y = 4x + 10$; 30; 3
13.

Input	Output
3	10
−2	0
5	14
−6	−8

14. (i) $y = 2x − 4$ (ii) $y = 3x + 2$
    (iii) $y = 3x + 1$
15. 10, −26, 3, −2

Exercise 19.3

1. (i) −1 (ii) −3 (iii) 1 (iv) −5 (v) −9
2. (i) 3 (ii) −5 (iii) −17 (iv) −3 (v) −4
3. (i) −3 (ii) −2 (iii) 1 (iv) 1 (v) 13
4. (i) 5 (ii) 1 (iii) 11
   (iv) 6 (v) $5 − 2k$
5. (i) $x = 2$ (ii) $x = 1$ (iii) $k = −2$
6. (i) $x = 2$ (ii) $x = 3$ (iii) $x = −2$
7. (i) −16 (ii) 0 (iii) $5k − 1$
   (iv) $10k − 1$ (v) $10k − 6$
8. $k = 4$
9. (i) $x = 5$ (ii) $x = 2$ (iii) $x = \frac{21}{2}$
10. (i) 13 (ii) $k = \frac{-11}{4}$
11. $k = \frac{8}{9}$ 12. $k = \frac{1}{3}$
13. (i) $x = \pm\sqrt{2}$ (ii) $x = 15$
    (iii) $x = -1, \frac{3}{2}$
14. $a = −7, b = −1$
15. (i) $\frac{1}{2}$, 11 (ii) 2 (iii) $\frac{5}{2}$
16. (i) $−4k − 3$ (ii) $k = −4$
17. (i) 16 (ii) $\frac{1}{4}$ (iii) $-\frac{1}{2}$

Exercise 19.4

1. −2   2. 1   3. 2
4. 3   5. 3   6. −4
7. $a = −2, b = 4$
8. $a = 7, b = 5, c = −7$
9. $a + b = −1, 2a + b = 1; a = 2, b = −3$
10. $a = −1, b = 0$
11. $p = −2, q = 1; x = 1$
12. (i) $c = −3$ (ii) $b = 2$ (iii) (1, 0)
13. $a = 7, b = 1$

14. (i) $b = −2, c = −2$ (ii) $y = −2$
15. $a(1, 0), b(−3, 0), c(0, −3)$
16. (i) 18 (ii) 2 (iii) 0; $k = 9$
17. (i) 81 (ii) $\frac{1}{9}$ (iii) $\sqrt{3}$ (iv) $-\frac{1}{2}$

Test yourself 19

1. (−2, −8), (0, −4), (2, 0)
2. {−1, 4, 9, 14}
3. $a(−4, 0), b(2, 0), c(0, 8)$
4. (i) Yes (ii) No
5. −5
6. (i) $k = 1$ (ii) $t = \frac{1}{8}$
7. As the input 1 has two different outputs
8. $k = 1$
9. $a = (−5, 0), b = (2, 0), c = (0, 10)$
10. (1, 2), (3, 12), (0, −3)
11. (i) 5 (ii) $\frac{1}{2}$; $k = 10$; No
12. (i) $−b + c = −1, 3b + c = −13$
    (ii) $b = −3, c = −4$
    (iii) $f(x) = x^2 − 3x − 4$
    (iv) $d(4, 0), e(0, −4)$
13. (i) 'add 3'
    (ii) {−13, −10, −7, −4}
14. $a = 3, b = −2$
15. (i) $\sqrt{12}$ $(2\sqrt{3})$, $\sqrt{72}$ $(6\sqrt{2})$ (ii) $k = 12$
16.

x	−1	0	1	2
y	−5	−2	1	4

17. (i) $\frac{2}{3}$ (ii) $\frac{1}{4}$

Chapter 20: Drawing and interpreting Real-life Graphs

Exercise 20.1

1. (i) 9 am; 3 pm
   (ii) 30 km
   (iii) 9.45 am, 2 pm
   (iv) 10 am–10.30 am, Noon–1 pm
   (v) From 9 am to 10 am (20 km/hr)
2. (i) 30 km (ii) 1 hour (iii) 45 km (iv) 75 km
3. (i) 20 km (ii) 20 km (iii) 1 pm
   (iv) Increase; The steepness of the line
   (v) 40 km
4. (i) Adam (ii) twice (iii) 1 pm
   (iv) 150 km
   (v) Adam – 200 km   Conor – 350 km
5. (i) 12 km (ii) 26 min
   (iii) (a) $4\frac{1}{2}$ km (b) $8\frac{1}{2}$ km
   (iv) (a) 3 min (b) 20 min
   (v) 30 km/hr

609

Text & Tests 2 Higher Level

6. (i) 75 km
   (ii) 10.45 am and 12.12 pm
   (iii) 1.30 pm
   (iv) 75 km
   (v) Darren; 30 min
7. (i) 6000 km (ii) B → A; 1 hour
   (iii) 3 hr
   (iv) A → B : 857 km/hr   B → A : 1000 km/hr
8. (i) [EF] (ii) [HJ] (iii) J (iv) [GH]
   (v) [AB] (vi) [DE]; 87 km/hr
9. (i) 11.30 am (ii) 35 km
10. (i) 240 km (ii) 10.02 am; 158 km
    (iii) Sam
    (iv) 9.00 am to 9.15 am, 10.15 am to 11.15 am
    (v) Sam − 96 km/hr   Bob − $53\frac{1}{3}$ km/hr
11. (ii) (a) $166\frac{2}{3}$ m/min (b) 10 km/hr

Exercise 20.2

1. (iv); straight line graph through the origin
2. (i) $37\frac{1}{2}$ miles (ii) 50 miles
   (iii) 48 km (iv) 24 km; Yes
3. No; it doesn't go through the origin;
   (i) 95°F (ii) 59°F (iii) 10°C
   (iv) 38°C; 13°C to 32°C
4. (i) €70 (ii) €55 (iii) 80 min
   (iv) 40 min (v) €40
5. (i) 10 m (ii) $4s - 5h = 0$
   (iii) 18.75 m
6. (i) T (ii) F (iii) F (iv) T (v) F
7. (i) T1 and B, T2 and A, T3 and C
   (ii) Tariff A
8. (i) 8ℓ (ii) 60 km (iii) 3ℓ
   (iv) Yes (v) $\ell = \frac{3}{20}k$; 45ℓ

Exercise 20.3

1. ① and A, ② and C, ③ and E, ④ and D, ⑤ and B
2. Graph Ⓐ
3. (i) (a) and A, (b) and C, (c) and B
   (ii) 1st graph − B
        2nd graph − C
        3rd graph − A
4. (i) and 3rd graph, (ii) and 2nd, (iii) and 1st
5. A and ④, B and ③, C and ①, D and ⑤, E and ②
9. (i) It drops (ii) 5°C (iii) It rises
   (iv) −12°C (v) 8 min
10. (i) ③ (ii) ① (iii) ④
11. A and ②, B and ①, C and ③, D and ④

Chapter 21: Algebra 2

Exercise 21.1

1. (i) $5a$ (ii) $2y$ (iii) $3c$ (iv) $3b$
   (v) $2x$ (vi) $8b^2$ (vii) $7x$ (viii) $4b$
2. (i) $1\frac{1}{3}$ (ii) $\frac{k}{2}$ (iii) $2b^2$ (iv) $4ab$
   (v) 2 (vi) $4\frac{1}{2}$ (vii) $9b$ (viii) $2a$
3. (i) APPLE (ii) LEMON or (MELON)
4. (i) $\frac{7}{6}$ (ii) $\frac{27}{20}$ (iii) $\frac{2}{3}$
   (iv) $\frac{1}{8}$ (v) $\frac{5x}{6}$ (vi) $\frac{8x}{15}$
5. $\frac{13x}{4}$ 6. $\frac{19x}{15}$ 7. $\frac{x}{12}$ 8. $\frac{3x}{10}$
9. $\frac{9x}{10}$ 10. $\frac{7x}{20}$ 11. $\frac{8x-6}{5}$
12. $\frac{8x+4}{4}$ 13. $\frac{4x-2}{3}$ 14. $\frac{7x-11}{12}$
15. $\frac{17x+11}{20}$ 16. $\frac{15x-31}{12}$ 17. $\frac{9-14x}{12}$
18. $\frac{-3x-13}{20}$ 19. 0
20. $\frac{11x+4}{20}$ 21. $\frac{9a+4}{12}$
22. (a) $\frac{1}{x-1}$ (b) 0 (c) $\frac{7x-5}{(x-2)(2x-1)}$
23. (a) $\frac{x-5}{(x+1)(x-1)}$ (b) $\frac{10x-9}{(x-3)(2x+1)}$
    (c) $\frac{9x+1}{(3x-1)(3x+1)}$
24. $r = \frac{3aR}{3+a}$, $r = 4.8$

Exercise 21.2

1. $x = 9$ 2. $x = 5$ 3. $x = 3$
4. 6 5. 6 6. 11 7. 3 8. 11
9. $\frac{1}{4}$ 10. 3 11. 7 12. 4 13. 5
14. 2 15. 4 16. 6 17. 2 18. 30
19. 2 20. 12 21. 3 22. 3 23. 2
24. 1 25. 11 26. $3\frac{1}{2}$ 27. −5 28. 9
29. −3 30. (i) $x - 4 = \frac{x+2}{3}$ (ii) $|AB| = 3$

Exercise 21.3

1. 8 2. 18 3. 16 4. 20
5. 9 6. 7 7. 6 8. 16
9. 15, 18 10. 15
11. 15 years old 12. 8

Exercise 21.4

1. (i) $y = 4 - 2x$ (ii) $y = -2x - 7$
   (iii) $y = 7 - 3x$
2. (i) $x = \frac{y+4}{2}$ (ii) $b = \frac{a+6}{8}$
   (iii) $d = \frac{c+1}{4}$ (iv) $k = \frac{h+2}{2}$

610

Answers

3. (i) $b = \dfrac{a+5}{3}$ (ii) $w = \dfrac{b-2}{4}$
   (iii) $e = \dfrac{d+12}{6}$ (iv) $h = \dfrac{18-g}{5}$
4. B, C, F
5. (i) $u, \dfrac{v-u}{a}$ (ii) bq, bq, a
   (iii) $3h, 5, 3h, 5(p-3h)$
6. (i) $x = y + 2z$ (ii) $x = \dfrac{b+4c}{3}$
   (iii) $x = \dfrac{7-6y}{3}$ (iv) $x = 3(2y+8)$
7. (i) $a = \dfrac{2b+1}{4}$ (ii) $a = \dfrac{5}{b-3}$
   (iii) $a = \dfrac{4b+21}{7}$
8. (i) $a = 2(4b+c)$ (ii) $a = \dfrac{4b+3c}{2}$
   (iii) $x = \dfrac{y+1}{6}$ (iv) $b = \dfrac{a+30}{10}$
   (v) $z = \dfrac{y-3x}{2}$ (vi) $b = \dfrac{4a+3c}{2}$
9. (i) $x = \dfrac{3c}{a+b}$ (ii) $x = \dfrac{5}{a-3}$
   (iii) $x = 3y + 3$
10. $b = \dfrac{as-k}{s}\left(=a-\dfrac{k}{s}\right)$ 11. B, E
12. (i) $z = \dfrac{2y-4x}{3}$ (ii) $b = \dfrac{24a-9c}{4}$
    (iii) $y = \dfrac{3x-20z}{20}$ (iv) $b = \dfrac{6c}{2a-3}$
    (v) $y = \dfrac{x-tz}{2}$ (vi) $t = \dfrac{q^2}{p-q}$
    (vii) $x = \dfrac{y+4}{y-3}$ (viii) $\dfrac{pq}{p+q}$
13. $y = \dfrac{z+2}{z-3}; -1$
14. (i) $h = \dfrac{2A}{a+b}$ (ii) 14 cm

Exercise 21.5
1. (i) 16 (ii) 150 (iii) 114 (iv) 54
2. (i) 100° (ii) 0° (iii) −40°
   (iv) −10° (v) −25°
3. (i) 29 (ii) 10 (iii) $\dfrac{10}{3}$
4. 10 5. (i) O; $m = \dfrac{y-c}{x}$ (ii) 3
6. (i) $P = 2(\ell + b)$ (ii) $P = 2y + 26$
7. 13; $b = \dfrac{6(T-C)}{a}$; $13\dfrac{1}{5}$
8. (i) €21 (ii) 20 km
9. $T = 15 + 40a$
10. (i) €75 (ii) 354 (iii) 180
11. (i) €716 (ii) 180 km
12. (i) $N = 4\ell + 4$ (ii) 28 (iii) 7 m
13. (ii) $x = \sqrt{\dfrac{A}{2}}$ (iii) $\sqrt{10}$ cm
14. (i) 2900ℓ (ii) 8 (iii) 10
15. (i) $F = 4 + 1.5k + 2p$
    (ii) €39 (iii) 12 km
16. (i) Volume = length × width × height
    (ii) proof
    (iii) 4 × 6 × 9

Test yourself 21
1. (i) $4x^2$ (ii) $4y$ (iii) $4xy$
2. $x = \dfrac{4y-6}{3y-2}$
3. $x = 6$
4. 1
5. $b = \dfrac{c(7a-c)}{a}; -12$
6. (i) $P = 2(2x+y+z)$ (ii) 10
7. (i) 10 hrs (ii) 18 years old
8. $x = 2$
9. $\dfrac{23}{10}$
10. (i) $x = \dfrac{b}{2(b-a)}$ (ii) $\dfrac{2a}{3c}$
11. $x = 18$
12. $\dfrac{15x+11}{12}$
13. (i) €650 (ii) 320
14. $a = \dfrac{4b+3}{6}; 3$
15. $\dfrac{2}{7}$
16. $x = 11$
17. (i) 32°F (ii) 212°F
    (iii) $22.\dot{2}$°C (iv) $2.\dot{2}$°C
18. $p = \dfrac{6c}{2a-3}; -3$
19. $x = 5\dfrac{1}{4}$
20. (i) $x = 10$ (ii) $a = -1, a = 2$
21. (i) $\dfrac{360}{x}$ (ii) $\dfrac{360}{x-4}$
    (iii) $\dfrac{360}{x-4} - \dfrac{360}{x} = 3; x = 24$
22. $\dfrac{60}{x} + \dfrac{x}{10} = 5; x^2 - 50x + 600 = 0; x = 30$ or 20
23. $b = \dfrac{(1-ac)}{(a+c)}, 1$

Chapter 22: Trigonometry
Exercise 22.1
1. (i) 12 cm² (ii) 12 cm² (iii) 8 cm²
2. 32 cm² 3. 13
4. (i) $\sqrt{13}$ cm (ii) $2\sqrt{10}$ cm (iii) $\sqrt{53}$ cm
   (iv) $2\sqrt{5}$ cm (v) 15 cm (vi) 12 cm

Text & Tests 2 Higher Level

5. (i) 24.4 cm (ii) 10.6 cm (iii) 9.8 cm
6. 12.8 cm
7. 7, 4; 8.1
8. 3.5 m
9. 6.4 cm
10. (i) 3 cm (ii) 5.8 cm
11. All sides are 7.1 units
12. $x = 5$ cm, $y = 12$ cm
13. $c = 10$ cm, $d = 24$ cm
14. 25 cm
15. each 12 cm^2
16. 63.5 cm, 38.1 cm
17. $18^2 \neq 12^2 + 13^2$

Exercise 22.2

1. $\frac{3}{5}, \frac{4}{5}, \frac{3}{4}; \frac{5}{13}, \frac{12}{13}, \frac{5}{12}; \frac{\sqrt{3}}{2}, \frac{1}{2}, \sqrt{3}$
2. (i) Tangent (ii) Cosine (iii) Sine
3. (i) A (ii) B (iii) B
   (iv) Cos (v) Cos (vi) Tan
4. $x = 8$; (i) $\frac{8}{17}$ (ii) $\frac{15}{17}$ (iii) $\frac{8}{15}$
5. $a = 2$; (i) $\frac{3}{\sqrt{13}}$ (ii) $\frac{2}{\sqrt{13}}$ (iii) $\frac{3}{2}$
6. (i) Tan θ (ii) Sin θ (iii) Cos θ
7. $\frac{12}{13}, \frac{12}{5}$
8. (i) $\frac{1}{\sqrt{5}}$ (ii) $\frac{\sqrt{21}}{2}$
9. $\frac{1}{2}, \frac{\sqrt{3}}{2}$
10. $\sqrt{2}$; (a) (i) $\frac{1}{\sqrt{2}}$ (ii) $\frac{1}{\sqrt{2}}$ (b) (i) $\frac{1}{\sqrt{2}}$ (ii) $\frac{1}{\sqrt{2}}$
11. $\cos A = \frac{\sqrt{3}}{2}$; $\tan A = \frac{1}{\sqrt{3}}$
12. $\sin C = \frac{8}{17}$; $\cos C = \frac{15}{17}$

Exercise 22.3

1. 53.3°
2. (i) 0.7431 (ii) 0.2756 (iii) 0.2679
   (iv) 0.9511 (v) 0.8788
3. (i) 48° (ii) 69° (iii) 55°
   (iv) 78° (v) 42° (vi) 12°
4. (i) 36.9° (ii) 41.1° (iii) 75.4° (iv) 74.2°
5. (i) 42° (ii) 53° (iii) 41° (iv) 24°
   (v) 29° (vi) 12° (vii) 35° (viii) 58°
6. $A = 56.74°$; Sin $A = 0.84$
7. 53.4°
8. (i) Sin (ii) Tan (iii) Cos
9. $A = 37°, B = 68°, C = 39°$
10. $a = 22°, b = 65°, c = 30°$
11. $A = 41.8°, B = 38.6°, C = 33.4°$

12. (i) 30° (ii) 66° (iii) 27°
13. 22°

Exercise 22.4

1. (i) Cos (ii) Tan (iii) Sin
2. (i) 3.8 (ii) 10.0 (iii) 10.2
3. (i) 3.3 (ii) 16.7 (iii) 13.5
4. (i) 37° (ii) 46° (iii) 23°
5. (i) 67° (ii) 24° (iii) 37°
6. $x = 9.4$
7. (i) 12.0 (ii) 15.9 (iii) 18.8
8. $x = 15, y = 20$
9. $a = 17.8$ m, $b = 53.5$ cm, $c = 10.4$ cm
10. (i) 13.9 (ii) 44°
11. 12.5 cm
12. (i) 8.2 m (ii) 39°
13. (i) 4.2 cm (ii) 25°
14. (i) $\frac{1}{2}$ (ii) $\frac{1}{3}$ (iii) $\frac{3}{4}$
15. proofs
16. $h = 40 \sin 60$; Area $= 400\sqrt{3}$; $20\sqrt{3}$

Exercise 22.5

1. 3.5 m 2. 21 m 3. 56°
4. (i) 124 km (ii) 26°
5. 20 m 6. 4° 7. 47 m
8. (i) 5 m (ii) 8.3 m (iii) 10.1 m
9. 12 m
10. (i) 17 m (ii) 65° (iii) 25°
11. 61°
12. (i) 13.1 m (ii) 9.9 m; 3.2 m
13. No; diagonal of desk $= 2.8$ m, 2.8 m > 2.75 m
14. (i) 14.2 cm (ii) 53.1 cm
15. (i) 50.4 m (ii) 47.0 m; 101.0 m
16. (i) 17.4 m (ii) 68° (iii) 24°
17. (i) 2 rolls (ii) €116
18. (i) 4.0 m (ii) 12.7 m (iii) 0.625

Test Yourself 22

1. $x = 12$; (i) $\frac{5}{12}$ (ii) $\frac{5}{13}$ (iii) $\frac{12}{13}$; 23°
2. 17.8 cm
3. (i) 13 cm^2 (ii) 33 cm^2 (iii) 26 cm^2
4. (i) 8 cm (ii) 22°
5. 15°
6. (i) 4.2 cm (ii) 25°
7. $\frac{3}{2}$
8. (i) 100 cm (ii) 27°
9. 15.8 cm
10. (i) 7 cm (ii) 4 cm (iii) 5 cm
11. 6°
12. (i) 72°, 18° (ii) 0.32

Answers

13. (i) 150 m² (ii) 12 m
14. (i) Radius of base of spire can be obtained from it.
    (ii) 125 m
15. (i) 101.6 cm (ii) 50 cm, 88 cm
    (iii) The 2nd t.v. (542 cm² bigger)
16. $a = 2\sqrt{2}, b = \sqrt{6}$

Chapter 23: Graphing Functions

Exercise 23.1
1. $(-1, -5), (0, -3), (1, -1), (2, 1), (3, 3), (4, 5)$
3. $(-1, -7), (0, -4), (3, 5)$
6. (i) 4 (ii) 1 (iii) -3 (iv) -3 (v) 5
7. (i) (3, 4)
   (ii) The point of intersection of the two lines
   (iii) $x = 3$ (x-value)
   (iv) Simultaneous equations (v) $k = 3$
8. (3, 2) 9. (2, 0), (0, 4)
10. (2, 0), (0, 3) 11. (2, 0)
12. (i) All intersect at (0, 2)
    (ii) All have the same constant number
    (iii) All have different slopes
    (iv) Coefficients of x are different
13. $(-2, 2), (-3, 0), (-4, -2)$
14.

t	0	1	2	3	4	5	6
T	-1	-1.5	-2	-2.5	-3	-3.5	-4

(iv) -3.75°C   (v) -3.75°C

15. (i)

t (mins)	0	1	2	3	4	5
d (metres)	0	40	80	120	160	200

t (mins)	6	7	8	9	10
d (metres)	240	280	320	360	400

(ii)

t (mins)	0	1	2	3	4	5
d (metres)	0	0	0	50	100	150

t (mins)	6	7	8	9	10
d (metres)	200	250	300	350	400

(v) 10 mins; 400 m

Exercise 23.2
1. $(-3, 5), (-2, 0), (-1, -3), (0, -4), (1, -3), (2, 0), (3, 5)$
6. $(-\frac{1}{2}, 0), (3, 0), (0, -3)$
8. $(-1, 0), (3, 0)$
9. $(-1, 0), (1\frac{1}{2}, 0)$
10. (i) $(\frac{1}{2}, 0), (3, 0)$ (ii) $(0, -3)$

11. ; $x = 4$

12.

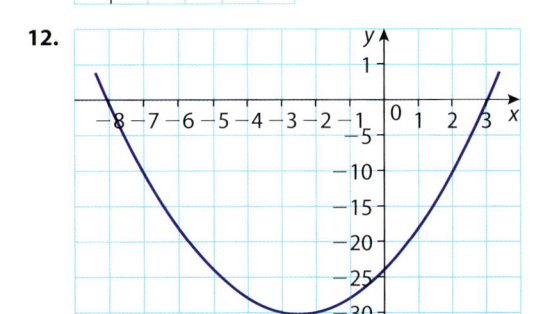

$f(x) = x^2 + 5x - 24 = 0$;
both values make the function $= 0$;
$x = 3$, you cannot have a negative measurement for length or width.

Exercise 23.3
1. (i) (1, 0), (3, 0)   (ii) -1
   (iii) $-1, 5$ (iv) $(2, -1)$
2. (i) 3   (ii) 3   (iii) $(0, -1)$
   (iv) $-1, 1$ (v) $-2, 2$
3. (i) $-1, 4$ (ii) $-2, 5$ (iii) 0, 3 (iv) -6
   (v) $-5\frac{1}{4}$ (vi) $(1\frac{1}{2}, -6\frac{1}{4})$ (vii) $-6\frac{1}{4}$
4. (i) 10, -6 (ii) $-1.4, 3.4$
   (iii) $-2.5, 4.5$ (iv) $(1, -6)$
   (v) -6 (vi) $-1.4 < x < 3.4$
5. (i) $x = -1, 3$ (ii) 0, 2
   (iii) $1\frac{3}{4}$ (iv) 4
   (v) (1, 4)   (vi) $-2 < x < 1$
   (vii) $-1 < x < 3$ (viii) $x = 1$
6. (i) $-1, \frac{3}{2}$ (ii) $-1.9, 2.4$
   (iii) $(0.25, -3.1)$ (iv) $-1 < x < 1\frac{1}{2}$
7. (i) $(-1, 1), (3, 9)$
   (ii) $x = -1, 3$
   (iii) x-values the same
   (iv) The points where the curve and line intersect

613

8. (i) $f(-2) = -4$, $g(3) = 6$
(ii) $x = -3, 2$ (iii) $-3.7, 2.7$ (iv) $x = -1, 3$
(v) $-1 \leq x \leq 3$ (vi) $-3 \leq x \leq 2$
9. (i) $x = 0, 3$ (ii) $x = -1, 4$
(iii) $x = -0.8, 3.8$ (iv) $x = -0.6, 3.6$
10. (i) $x = -1.3, 1.3$
(ii) $x = -2.9, 2.9$; $-2.9 < x < 2.9$
11. (i) $x = 0, 2$ (ii) $x = -1, 3$
(iii) $x = 0.4, 2.6$ (iv) $0 < x < 2$
(v) $x < 0.4$ and $x > 2.6$;
$x^2 - 2x - 2 = 0 \Rightarrow x^2 - 2x = 2$;
Draw the line $y = 2$ and find the x-values of the points of intersection of this line and the curve
12. (i) $x = -3.8, 0.8$
(ii) $x = -3.3, 0.3$
(iii) $-2.4, 0.4$
(iv) -5.25; The curve is below the line; $-2.4 < x < 0.4$
13. (i) $x = -2$ (ii) One value
(iii) Graph touches the x-axis at one point only.
14. (i) Ⓐ corresponds to $g(x) = x^2 - 3x + 3$
Ⓑ corresponds to $f(x) = x^2 - 6x + 9$
(ii) $x = 2$
(iii) Curve touches the x-axis at one point only (tangent)

Exercise 23.4

1. (i) 15 (ii) $x = 0, 4$
(iii) $x = 2$ (iv) 15
(v) 11.12 a.m. and 4.48 p.m.
(vi) 10 hours
2. (i) (0, 0), (1, 16), (2, 24), (3, 24), (4, 16), (5, 0)
(iii) (a) 25 m; 2.5 sec (b) 0.7 sec, 4.3 sec
(c) 3 sec
3. $(-5, -6), (-4, 0), (-3, 4), (-2, 6), (-1, 6), (0, 4), (1, 0), (2, -6)$;
(i) 5.25°C
(ii) 1 p.m.
(iii) 9.24 a.m. and 4.36 p.m.
(iv) 10 hours
4. (i) 13.75 m² (ii) 16 m²; $x = 4$
(iii) $x = 2, 6$
5. (i) 45 m (ii) 34 m
(iii) After 0.4 sec and 5.6 sec (iv) 3 sec
6. (i) (0, 0), (1, 3), (2, 12), (3, 27)
(ii) 18.7 m²
(iii) 1.8 m
(iv) Accurate versions are 19.6 m² and 1.78 cm

7. (i) $A = 20x - x^2$
(iii) 2.25 and 17.75
(iv) $6.8 < x < 13.2$
(v) 100 m²; 10 m by 10 m

Exercise 23.5

1. (i) 1 (ii) 2 (iii) 2.8 (iv) 8 (v) 2.3
2. $(-2, \frac{1}{9}), (-1, \frac{1}{3}), (0, 1), (1, 3), (2, 9), (3, 27)$;
(i) 5.2 (ii) 1.3
3. (i) 3 (ii) 12 (iii) $x = -1.6$
4.

x	−2	−1	0	1	2
2^x	$\frac{1}{4}$	$\frac{1}{2}$	1	2	4
4.2^x	1	2	4	8	16

; 5.7

5. Ⓐ: $f(x) = 3.3^x$; Ⓑ: $f(x) = 3^x$; Ⓒ: $f(x) = 2^x$
6. (i) (0, 1)
7. (i) $k = 5$ (ii) $f(x) = 5.2^x$
8. 2.5

Test Yourself 23

1. (i) 5 (ii) 7 (iii) 3
(iv) −1 (v) 0
2. (i) −1.75 (ii) $x = 1, 3$
(iii) −4 (iv) $x = 2$
3. Ⓐ and $y = k - x$, Ⓑ and $y = x^2 - k$,
Ⓒ and $y = k - x^2$
4. (i) −5.5 (ii) $1\frac{1}{2}$
5. (i) $a = (-3, 0), b = (1, 0), c = (0, -3)$
(ii) $-3 \leq x \leq 1$
(iii) $k = 0, -2$
6. $(-3, \frac{1}{8}), (-2, \frac{1}{4}), (-1, \frac{1}{2}), (0, 1), (1, 2), (2, 4), (3, 8), (4, 16), (5, 32)$; (ii) $x = 2.6$
7. (i) $x = -1\frac{1}{2}, 2$ (ii) −6.1
(iii) 4 (iv) $-1.5 < x < 2$
8. $3x + 2y = 9$; $2x - y = 13$; $x = 5, y = -3$
9. (i) $x = 0, 2$
(ii) $x = -1, 3$; $x = 1$
10. A: $y = x^2 - 2$, B: $y = 2 - x^2$, C: $y = 2x$
11. (i) 36 m² (ii) 2.2 m, 6.8 m
(iii) 4.5 m by 9 m (iv) 40.5 m²
12. (i) $10t - c + 20 = 0$ (ii) €160
13.

x	0	0.5	1	1.5	2	2.5	3
f(x)	1	1.4	2	2.8	4	5.7	8
g(x)	−1	2.75	5	5.75	5	2.75	−1

(i) 0.3, 2.2 (ii) 2.6

Answers

Chapter 24: Geometry 3: Transformations – Constructions

Exercise 24.1
1. (i) 5 units to the right
   (ii) 4 units to the right
   (iii) 1 unit up and 4 units right
   (iv) 1 unit right and 3 units up
   (v) 2 units right and 3 units up
   (vi) 1 unit left and 4 units up
2. (i) 5 units right and 3 units up
   (ii) 11 units right and 1 unit down
   (iii) 4 units right and 5 units up
   (iv) 7 units right and 6 units down
   (v) 4 units left and 5 units down
6. (i) B (ii) [DC] (iii) O (iv) [AB]
7. (i) B (ii) [BC] (iii) △BCE (iv) [BE]
8. (i) [EC] (ii) E (iii) △BEC
   (iv) D (v) [AD] (vi) △BEC
9. (i) A(2, 4), B(3, −2), C(−2, −3), D(−5, 1)
   (ii) A′(7, 6), B′(8, 0), C′(3, −1), D′(0, 3)

Exercise 24.2
3. (i) the point F (ii) [EF] (iii) [DF]
   (iv) △DCF (v) △EFD (vi) [CF]
4. (i) and (iii)
5. M, O, D, A, Y
7. (i) B (ii) A (iii) [DA] (iv) △COD
   (v) [CO] (vi) △CBD (vii) [OA] (viii) CDAB
8. C
9. (i) D (ii) A
10. (i) Axial symmetry in y-axis
    (ii) Axial symmetry in x-axis
    (iii) Central symmetry in origin
11. Central symmetry in C and axial symmetry in AB
12. D
13. (i) A′(4, 5), B′(1, 4), C′(5, 2)
    (ii) A″(−4, −5), B″(−1, −4), C″(−5, −2)
14. (i) 2 (ii) 2 (iii) 5 (iv) 0
15. (i), (ii), (iv)
16. (i) A.S. (ii) Tr. (iii) A.S. (iv) A.S. (v) C.S.
17. (i) A.S. in y-axis
    (ii) Tr.; 3 units right and 3 units down
    (iii) A.S. in line $x + y = 0$
19. (i) △COB (ii) △COD (iii) △AOD
    (iv) △COF (v) [EF]

Exercise 24.3
1. (0, 3), (−2, 3), (−2, 0)
2. (i) clockwise 90° (ii) clockwise 180°
   (iii) anti-clockwise 90°
4. anti-clockwise 85°
7. Yes, 90° clockwise
9. (i) (5, 1) → (−1, 5) (ii) (5, −3) → (3, 5)
   (iii) (−5, 0) → (0, −5) (iv) (−5, −2) → (2, −5)
10. (i) (3, 2) → (−3, −2) (ii) (3, −3) → (−3, 3)
    (iii) (−3, 1) → (3, −1) (iv) (−3, −2) → (3, 2)
11. (i) (2, 2) → (2, −2) (ii) (2, −3) → (−3, −2)
    (iii) (−2, 0) → (0, 2) (iv) (−2, −4) → (−4, 2)
12. (i) anti-clockwise 120° (ii) clockwise 120°
13. Diagonals of a parallelogram bisect one another

Exercise 24.4
Constructions

Exercise 24.5
1. Construction
2. Construction
3. Construction
4. |AC| = 4.6 cm, |DE| = 3.1 cm, |XZ| = 7.7 cm
5. (i) |AC| = 3.1 cm (ii) |AB| = 5.4 cm
6. |AC| = 5.9 cm, |DF| = 5.2 cm, |XZ| = 9.2 cm
7. Construction
8. Construction
9. |AC| = 10.8 cm
10. Construction
11. 8.3 cm
12. Construction
13. Construction
14. Construction

Test Yourself 24
1. (i) 1 (ii) 1 (iii) 1 (iv) 1
2. Construction
3. (i) A.S. in y-axis
   (ii) A.S. in line $y = 2$
   (iii) Tr.; 3 units down
   (iv) A.S. in the line $x = 3$
   (v) C.S. in the point (1.5, 0.5)
   (vi) Tr.; 3 units to the right and 7 units down
4. Construction
5. (i) 3 (ii) 1 (iii) 2
6. (i) A′(−1, 4), B′(−3, 4), C′(−3, 1), D′(−1, 3)
   (ii) A′ = (−4, 1), B′ = (−4, 3), C′ = (−1, 3), D′ = (−3, 1)

615

7. Construction
8. (i) [grid image]
   (ii) [grid image]
   (iii) [grid image]

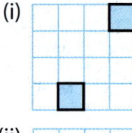

9. (i) C (ii) [CB] (iii) △COD
   (iv) [AB] (v) No (vi) △AOD
10. Construction
11. (i) Tr. (ii) C.S. (iii) A.S.
12. (a) (i) $A' = (-8, 3)$, $B' = (-1, 2)$,
           $C' = (-3, 5)$
       (ii) $A' = (-3, -8)$, $B' = (-2, -1)$,
            $C' = (-5, -3)$
    (b) $A' = (-3, -8)$, $B' = (-2, -1)$,
        $C' = (-5, -3)$
13. $D' = (-3, -2)$, $E' = (-8, -2)$,
    $F' = (-5, -5)$, $G' = (0, -5)$